FOX & BOWEN
ON
THE LAW OF PRIVATE COMPANIES

AUSTRALIA
The Law Book Company
Brisbane * Sydney * Melbourne * Perth

CANADA
Carswell
Ottawa * Toronto * Calgary * Montreal * Vancouver

AGENTS:
Steimatzky's Agency Ltd., Tel Aviv;
N.M. Tripathi (Private) Ltd., Bombay;
Eastern Law House (Private) Ltd., Calcutta;
M.P.P. House, Bangalore;
Universal Book Traders, Delhi;
Aditya Books, Delhi;
MacMillan Shuppan KK, Tokyo;
Pakistan Law House, Karachi, Lahore.

FOX & BOWEN
ON
THE LAW OF PRIVATE COMPANIES

SECOND EDITION

by

MICHAEL BOWEN M.A. (Cantab.)
Principal Lecturer in Law, University of Teesside

With chapters on Taxation, Disclosure and Audit by

J.V.W. USHER M.A. (St. Andrews), F.C.A.
Senior Lecturer in Accountancy, University of Teesside

LONDON
SWEET & MAXWELL
1995

First Edition (1991) By Denis Fox and Michael Bowen
Second Edition (1995) By Michael Bowen

Published in 1995 by
Sweet & Maxwell Limited of
South Quay Plaza, 183 Marsh Wall,
London E14 9FT.
Computerset by P.B. Computer Typesetting
Pickering, N. Yorks.
Printed in Great Britain by
Butler & Tanner, Frome and London.

No natural forests were destroyed to make this product:
only farmed timber was used and re-planted

A CIP catalogue record for this book is available from the British Library

ISBN 0 421 50940 6

FOREWORD

It is sad to record the death of Denis Fox in 1992, barely six months after the first edition of this work was published. We had lost a much respected former colleague, a measure of this respect being the award of a Posthumous Fellowship of the University of Teesside. The name of D.W. Fox will also be more widely remembered by readers of legal journals, in which he had been a regular and highly regarded commentator over a number of years.

This book originated from Denis's idea and each of us felt privileged to accept his invitation to share its authorship and to make a specialist contribution, respectively. The second edition still bears Denis's stamp and we can only hope that we have, in the revisions, remained true to his high standards.

Michael Bowen
Jonathan Usher

PREFACE

In the preface to the first edition of this work, the late Denis Fox and I described modern company law as a subject of burgeoning content and horrendous complexity. Nearly four years later, I would merely add an observation on the unrelenting pace of the process of reform. Apart from the legislative changes since the first edition was published, the Department of Trade and Industry is, at the time of going to press, reviewing several aspects of the law. Not least, the intention appears to be to maintain the momentum of deregulation by further reducing the statutory burdens on small companies.

Some might argue, even more strongly than hitherto, that the time has come for a separate statute to cover private companies, despite the fact that some of its provisions would apply only to small private companies, and most would duplicate those applying to public companies. For the foreseeable future, however, it is submitted that there will still be the need for a work which selects and focuses upon those areas of company law which are of exclusive or particular relevance to private companies. That, quite simply, remains the purpose of this book which is directed primarily towards business lawyers, accountants and company secretaries with the hope that it will also be of interest to directors of, and shareholders in, private companies. Students, too, may find the book useful, at least as a reference work.

The trend has continued of legislating by amending and inserting sections in the Companies Act 1985, and, recently, in the Insolvency Act 1986. The statutory reforms which have occurred since 1991 and which have required attention in this edition include provisions introduced by: The Companies (Single Member Private Limited Companies) Regulations 1992, the Companies Act 1985 (Accounts of Small and Medium-Sized Enterprises and Publication of Accounts in ECUs) Regulations 1992, the Insolvency Act 1994 (though referred to only briefly), the Insolvency (No. 2) Act 1994, and the Companies Act 1985 (Audit Exemption) Regulations 1994. In particular, Chapter 11 has been substantially recast and retitled "Single Member Companies" and a new chapter on Audit has been inserted, to which I shall return below. Current proposals for reform are briefly considered where appropriate.

PREFACE

Recent case law has, inevitably, had an impact on most areas covered by this work and, especially, on just about every aspect of corporate insolvency, necessitating a significant expansion of the chapter "Private Companies in Financial Difficulties". Also, an important decision of the House of Lords has required a new section to be added to Chapter 6, examining the efficacy of voting arrangements in shareholders' agreements. Amongst other issues in which the principles have needed to be reappraised in the light of the courts' decisions include: directors' duties of care and skill, disclosure of directors' interests in contracts, the liability of constructive trustees, theft of company property by controllers, the veil of incorporation, and the extent to which the availability of the statutory minority remedies is uninhibited by alternative provisions in the articles.

In the preparation of this edition, I have benefited greatly from the continued assistance of my colleague, Jonathan Usher, who has, once again, contributed three chapters. His ability to write from the point of view of a chartered accountant has been invaluable in his chapters on Taxation, Disclosure and Audit. The new chapter on Audit was planned, at Jonathan's suggestion, in anticipation of the enactment of provisions exempting a class of small companies from the audit requirement. What neither he nor I could have anticipated was the shortness of time he would have, following the provisions coming into force in the late summer of 1994, to assimilate and analyse the reforms and still meet the publishers' deadline. I am indebted to him. With the Business Expansion Scheme having run its course, Jonathan's chapter bearing that title in the first edition has had to be discarded, though an outline of BES's successor, the Enterprise Investment Scheme, is included in his chapter on Taxation.

I am extremely grateful to Jo Butler who word processed Jonathan's chapters and to my wife Margaret who typed all the remaining chapters, including revisions, on to a new disk, and whose immense support and encouragement throughout the project were worth more to me than I can ever properly express. Finally, my thanks are due to Sweet & Maxwell's helpful, supportive and expert editorial staff.

I have endeavoured to state the law, as I understand it to be, as at September 1, 1994.

University of Teesside
January 1995 **Michael Bowen**

TABLE OF CONTENTS

	Page
Preface	vii
Table of Cases	xv
Table of Statutes	xxxii
Table of Statutory Instruments	xliii
Table of European Materials	xlv

1 HISTORY AND DEVELOPMENT OF THE PRIVATE COMPANY

A. The pre-statutory private company	1
B. The Companies Act 1907	1
C. Post-war developments	4
D. The contemporary status of private companies	6

2 PRIVATE COMPANIES AS BUSINESS VEHICLES

A. The role and status of private companies	11
B. Abuses of the private company system	15

3 SOME ADVANTAGES AND DISADVANTAGES OF PRIVATE COMPANIES TO THE BUSINESS COMMUNITY

A. Introduction	20
B. The veil of incorporation	20
C. The minutiae of company law	28

4 PROMOTION, FORMATION AND REGISTRATION OF PRIVATE COMPANIES

A. Promotion of private companies	30
B. Pre-incorporation contracts	37
C. Formation, registration and commencement of business	42

5 MEMORANDUM OF ASSOCIATION

A. Form and legal requirements of the memorandum 45
B. Name clause 46
C. Registered office clause 51
D. Objects clause 52
E. Liability clause 62
F. Capital clause 63

6 ARTICLES OF ASSOCIATION

A. Purpose and requirements of the Articles of Association 64
B. Control and structure of privare companies by means of the Articles of Association 66
C. Control of private companies by means of weighted voting 72
D. Shareholders' agreements outside the Articles 74
E. Resolving disputes by arbitration 75

7 MEETINGS AND RESOLUTIONS OF PRIVATE COMPANIES

A. Introduction 77
B. General meetings 77
C. One-member "meetings" 80
D. Alternative procedures (1): written resolutions 82
E. Alternative procedures (2): the "elective regime" 87

8 THE COMPANY, ITS CONTROLLERS AND DIRECTORS

A. Introduction 91
B. The directors and third parties 91
C. The relationship between directors and the general meeting 97
D. The duties of directors 113
E. Financial arrangements between company and directors 135

9 SHARE CAPITAL

A. Introduction 142
B. Position of public and private companies under European Community law 142

9 SHARE CAPITAL—*cont.*

C. Restrictions on public offers and advertisements of securities 143
D. Allotment of shares 144
E. Share transactions 146
F. Dividends 152

10 REDEMPTION AND PURCHASE OF SHARES AND FINANCIAL ASSISTANCE

A. Introduction 156
B. Companies redeeming and purchasing their own shares 156
C. Companies providing financial assistance for acquisitions of their own shares 163

11 SINGLE MEMBER COMPANIES

A. The Companies (Single Member Private Limited Companies) Regulations 1992 176
B. Criminal offences by one-person controllers against the company 180
C. Diverting company cheques 185

12 CORPORATE QUASI-PARTNERSHIPS

A. The quasi-partnership concept 187
B. Practical applications of the quasi-partnership concept 189
C. Dealings between quasi-partners 197

13 FAMILY COMPANIES

A. Introduction: meaning of "family company" 206
B. Disputes in family companies 207
C. Entrenched directorships in family companies 212
D. "Negative control" of family companies 216
E. Directors' veto rights in family companies 218
F. Family companies and matrimonial disputes 221
G. Unfairly prejudicial conduct in family companies 223
H. The Matrimonial Causes Act 1973 (as amended) 226

14 VALUING SHARES IN PRIVATE COMPANIES

A. Preliminary considerations 227
B. The mechanism for evaluation 229
C. The valuation date of shares 238

15 TRANSFERS, TAKEOVERS AND DEALINGS IN PRIVATE COMPANY INTERESTS

A. Introduction 240
B. Minorities' immunity from improper eviction 241
C. Sale of shares in private companies by personal representatives 244
D. Directors' duties in private company takeover bids 246
E. Directors' veto clauses and company takeovers 249
F. Private companies and the City Code 250

16 THE TAXATION OF PRIVATE COMPANIES

A. Introduction 251
B. The taxation of private companies: Part I 252
C. The taxation of private companies: Part II 259
D. Taxation incentives for investors in private companies: Part III 264

17 THE DISCLOSURE REQUIREMENTS OF PRIVATE COMPANIES

A. Duty to prepare annual accounts and reports 269
B. Publication of disclosures 274
C. Exemptions in respect of statutory accounts 276
D. Exemptions in respect of the filing of annual accounts 282

18 THE AUDIT OF PRIVATE COMPANIES

A. Introduction 286
B. Audit requirements applying to companies not covered by new section 249A of the Companies Act 1985 287
C. Exemptions from audit: small companies covered by new section 249A of the Companies Act 1985 290

19 COMPANIES LIMITED BY GUARANTEE

A. Introduction 294
B. Liability for guarantee companies 294
C. Purpose and form of guarantee companies 296

20 PRIVATE COMPANIES IN FINANCIAL DIFFICULTIES

A. Introduction 300
B. Company rescue 300
C. Liabilities of directors of insolvent companies 311
D. Avoidance of transactions entered into prior to liquidation or administration 324

21 WINDING-UP OF PRIVATE COMPANIES

A. Introduction 330
B. Voluntary winding-up 330
C. Compulsory winding-up 332
D. Special provisions relating to contributories 335

22 EUROPEAN ECONOMIC INTEREST GROUPINGS

A. Introduction 337
B. Formalities for establishing EEIGs 339
C. Purposes of, liability for, and winding-up of EEIGs 342

APPENDIX 1

THE COMPANIES (TABLES A TO F) REGULATIONS 1985 347

APPENDIX 2

EUROPEAN ECONOMIC INTEREST GROUPING REGULATIONS 1989 380

Index 411

TABLE OF CASES

A. & B.C. Chewing Gum Ltd., Re; Topps Chewing Gum Inc. v. Coakley [1975] 1 W.L.R. 579; (1974) 119 S.J. 233; [1975] 1 All E.R. 1017 195
A. & C. Group Services Ltd., Re [1993] BCLC 1297 316
A.R.V. Aviation Ltd., Re (1988) 4 BCC 708 308
Abbey Leisure Ltd., Re [1990] BCC 60; [1990] BCLC 342; *The Times*, December 19, 1989, C.A.; reversing (1989) 5 BCC 183; [1989] BCLC 619 .... 198, 199, 200, 201, 231, 235, 344, 335
Aberdeen Railway Co. v. Blaikie Bros. (1854) 1 Macq. 461, H.L. (Sc.) ... 128
Adams v. Cape Industries plc [1990] Ch. 433; [1990] 2 W.L.R. 657; [1991] 1 All E.R. 929; [1990] BCLC 479; [1990] BCC 786, C.A. 16, 23, 24
Aerators Ltd. v. Tollit [1902] 2 Ch. 319 48
Agip (Africa) Ltd. v. Jackson [1991] Ch. 547 [1991] 3 W.L.R. 116; [1992] 4 All E.R. 451; (1991) 135 S.J. 117; *The Times*, January 9, 1991; *Financial Times*, January 18, 1991, C.A.; affirming [1990] Ch. 265; [1989] 3 W.L.R. 1367; [1992] 4 All E.R. 385; (1990) 134 S.J. 198; [1989] L.S.Gaz. January 17, 34 124
Air Ecosse Ltd. v. Civil Aviation Authority (1987) 3 BCC 492, Ct. of Session 307
Aldermanbury Trust plc, Re [1993] BCC 598 317
Allen v. Gold Reefs of West Africa Ltd. [1900] 1 Ch. 656, C.A. 108, 109
—— v. Hyatt (1914) 30 T.L.R. 444 132
Arab Bank plc v. Mercantile Holdings Ltd. [1994] 2 W.L.R. 307; [1993] BCC 816; [1993] EGCS 164; [1993] NPC 130; *The Times*, October 19, 1993 163
Ashbury Railway Carriage and Iron Co. v. Riche (1875) L.R. 7 H.L. 653 53
Atkin & Co. v. Wardle (1889) 5 T.L.R. 734 25
Atlantic Computer Systems plc, Re [1992] Ch. 505; [1992] 2 W.L.R. 367; [1992] 1 All E.R. 476; [1990] BCC 859; [1991] BCLC 606; *Financial Times*, August 1, 1990, C.A.; reversing [1990] BCC 454; [1990] BCLC 729; *Financial Times*, June 13, 1990 307
Att.-Gen. v. Great Eastern Railway (1850) 5 App.Cas. 473 55
Att.-Gen.'s Reference (No. 2 of 1982) [1984] Q.B. 624; [1984] 2 W.L.R. 447; (1984) 128 S.J. 221; [1984] 2 All E.R. 216; (1984) 78 Cr.App.R. 131; [1985] Crim.L.R. 241; (1984) 81 L.S.Gaz. 279, C.A. 181, 183
Atwool v. Merryweather (1867) L.R. 5 Eq. 464n 33, 121, 126
Austinsuite Furniture Ltd., Re [1992] BCLC 1047 314
Automatic Self-Cleansing Filter Syndicate Co. Ltd. v. Cunninghame [1906] 2 Ch. 34, C.A. 102
Aveling Barford Ltd. v. Perion Ltd. (1989) 5 BCC 677; [1989] BCLC 626; 1989 PCC 370; *Financial Times*, April 28, 1989 126

Baden Delvaux and Lecuit v. Société General S.A. [1983] BCLC 325 ...... 124, 125
Badgerhill Properties Ltd. v. Cottrell [1991] BCC 463; 54 B.L.R. 23; [1991] BCLC 805; *The Independent*, June 12, 1991, C.A. 38
Bailey, Hay and Co. Ltd., Re [1971] 1 W.L.R. 1357; 115 S.J. 639; [1971] 3 All E.R. 693 79
Bamford v. Bamford [1970] Ch. 212; [1969] 2 W.L.R. 1107; 113 S.J. 123; [1969] 1 All E.R. 969, C.A.; affirming [1968] 3 W.L.R. 317; 112 S.J. 416; [1968] 2 All E.R. 655 .... 121, 128
Bangor and North Wales Mutual Marine Protection Association, Baird's Case, Re [1899] 2 Ch. 593 296
Barber & Nicholls Ltd. v. R & G Associates (London) Ltd. (1982) 132 N.L.J. 1076 26
Barclays Bank Ltd. v. TOSG Trust Fund Ltd. [1984] A.C. 626; [1984] 2 W.L.R. 650; (1984) 128 S.J. 261; [1984] 1 All E.R. 1060; [1984] BCLC 1; (1984) 81 L.S.Gaz. 1360; (1984) 134 New L.J. 656; H.L.; affirming [1984] 2 W.L.R. 49; (1983) 127 S.J. 730; [1984] 1 All E.R. 628, C.A. 94
Barrett v. Duckett, July 27, 1994, C.A. 223
Barron v. Potter [1914] 1 Ch. 895 .... 98, 106
Barry Artist Ltd., Re [1985] 1 W.L.R. 1305; 1985 PCC 364; (1986) 83 L.S.Gaz. 436; (1985) 129 S.J. 853 79
Bath Glass Ltd., Re (1988) 4 BCC 130; [1988] BCLC 329 ...... 311, 314, 317
Beacon Leisure Ltd., Re [1991] BCC 213 .... 326, 327
Beattie v. Beattie (E. & F.) Ltd. [1938] Ch. 708 .... 75, 76
Beauforte (Jon) (London) Ltd., Re Applications of Grainger Smith & Co. (Builders), John Wright & Son (Veneers) and Lowell Baldwin [1953] Ch. 131; [1953] 2 W.L.R. 465; 97 S.J. 152; [1953] 1 All E.R. 634 55
Bede Steam Shipping Co. Ltd., Re [1917] 1 Ch. 123, C.A. 67
Bell Houses Ltd. v. City Wall Properties Ltd. [1966] 2 Q.B. 656; [1966] 2 W.L.R. 1323; 110 S.J. 268; [1966] 2 All E.R. 674; [1965] C.L.Y. 482, C.A.; reversing [1966] 1 Q.B. 207; [1965] 3 W.L.R. 1065; 109 S.J. 898; [1965] 3 All E.R. 427; [1966] C.L.Y. 1425 57
Belmont Finance Corporation v. Williams Furniture Ltd. [1979] 1 Ch. 250; [1978] 3 W.L.R. 712; (1977) 122 S.J. 743; [1979] 1 All E.R. 118, C.A. 123, 124
Belmont Finance Corporation Ltd. v. Williams Furniture Ltd. (No. 2) [1980] 1 All E.R. 392, C.A. 123, 124, 174
Bentley-Stevens v. Jones [1974] 1 W.L.R. 638; 118 S.J. 345; [1974] 2 All E.R. 653 .... 112, 195
Berg Sons & Co. Ltd. v. Adams [1992] BCC 661; [1993] BCLC 1045; *Financial Times*, July 10. 1992 115
Berry and Stewart v. Tottenham Hotspur Football Company Ltd. [1935] Ch. 718 67
Bersel Manufacturing Co. Ltd. v. Berry [1968] 2 All E.R. 552, H.L. 71
Bird Precision Bellows Ltd., Re [1984] 1 Ch. 419; [1984] 2 W.L.R. 869; (1984) 128 S.J. 348; [1984] 3 All E.R. 444; (1984) 81 L.S.Gaz. 187 .... 188, 232, 233, 234
Bishopsgate Investment Management Trust (in liquidation) Ltd. *v.* Maxwell (No. 2) [1994] 1 All E.R. 261; [1993] BCLC 1282; *The Times*, February 16, 1993, C.A.; affirming [1993] BCLC 814; [1993] BCC 120; *The Times*, January 12, 1993 .... 113, 120
Black v. Smallwood [1966] A.L.R. 744; (1966) 39 A.L.J.R. 405 .... 39, 40

Blisset v. Daniel (1853) 10 Hare 493 195
Blum v. O.C.P. Repartition S.A. [1988] BCLC 170; [1988] FLR 229; (1988) 4 BCC 771, C.A. 26
Bondina Ltd. v. Rollaway Shower Blinds Ltd. [1986] 1 W.L.R. 517; (1985) 130 S.J. 264; [1986] 1 All E.R. 564; [1986] FLR 266; [1986] E.C.C. 260; 1986 PCC 325; (1986) 136 New L.J. 116; (1986) 83 L.S.Gaz. 36, C.A. 28
Bonus Breaks Ltd., Re [1991] BCC 546 19
Boswell & Co. (Steels) Ltd., Re (1989) 5 BCC 145 200
Boulting v. Association of Cinematograph, Television and Allied Technicians [1963] 2 Q.B. 606; [1963] 2 W.L.R. 529; 107 S.J. 133; [1963] 1 All E.R. 716, C.A.; affirming *The Times*, March 23, 1962; *The Guardian*, March 23, 1962; [1962] C.L.Y. 3060 130
Bovey Hotel Ventures Ltd., Re, 1981 unreported 225
Bowling & Welby's Contract [1895] 1 Ch. 663 13
Bradford Banking Co. v. Henry Briggs Son & Co. (1886) 12 App.Cas. 29 152
Brady v. Brady [1988] 2 W.L.R. 1308; (1988) 132 S.J. 820; [1988] 2 All E.R. 617; (1988) 4 BCC 390; 1988 PCC 316; [1988] 2 FTLR 181; [1988] BCLC 579, H.L.; reversing [1988] BCLC 20; 1977 PCC 434; (1987) 3 BCC 535; [1987] 2 FTLR 414; (1987) 137 New L.J. 898, C.A. 115, 116, 118, 171, 173, 174, 187, 210
Bratton Seymour Services Co. Ltd. v. Oxborough [1992] BCC 471; [1992] BCLC 693; [1992] EGCS 28; *The Times*, March 2, 1992, C.A. 69
Breckland Group Holdings Ltd. v. London and Suffolk Properties Ltd. (1988) 4 BCC 542; [1989] BCLC 100; 1989 PCC 328 101
Bristol Airport plc v. Powdrill [1990] Ch. 744; [1990] 2 W.L.R. 1362; [1990] 2 All E.R. 493; [1990] BCC 130; [1990] BCLC 585; [1990] L.S.Gaz. May 9, 29, C.A. 307
British Airways Board v. Parish (1979) 123 S.J. 319; [1979] 2 Lloyd's Rep. 361, C.A. 26
British Seamless Paper Box Co., Re (1881) 17 Ch.D. 467 1
British Vacuum Cleaner Co. Ltd. v. New Vacuum Cleaner Co. Ltd. [1907] 2 Ch. 312 48
Broderip v. Salomon [1895] 2 Ch. 323 1
Browne v. La Trinidade (1887) 37 Ch.D. 1, C.A. 98
Buckingham v. Francis, Douglas and Thompson [1986] 2 All E.R. 738; 1986 PCC 347 .... 236, 237, 238
Bugle Press Ltd., Re [1961] Ch. 270; [1960] 3 W.L.R. 956; 104 S.J. 1057; [1960] 3 All E.R. 791, C.A.; affirming [1961] Ch. 270; [1960] 2 W.L.R. 658; 104 S.J. 289; [1960] 1 All E.R. 768 .... 16, 241, 242, 243
Burnham Marketing Services Ltd., Re; Secretary of State for Trade and Industry v. Harper [1993] BCC 518 316
Bushell v. Faith [1970] A.C. 1099; [1970] 2 W.L.R. 272; 114 S.J. 54; [1970] 1 All E.R. 53, H.L.; affirming [1969] 2 Ch. 438; [1969] 2 W.L.R. 1067; 113 S.J. 262; [1969] 1 All E.R. 1002, C.A. 72, 73, 214, 216
Business Properties Ltd., Re (1988) 4 BCC 684, D.C. 305

Cane v. Jones [1980] 1 W.L.R. 1451; (1979) 124 S.J. 542; [1981] 1 All E.R. 533 79

Cape Breton Co., Re (1895) 29 Ch.D. 795, C.A. 34
Carecraft Construction Co. Ltd., Re [1994] 1 W.L.R. 172; [1993] 4 All E.R. 499; [1993] BCC 336; [1993] BCLC 1259 317
Cargo Agency Ltd., Re [1992] BCC 388; [1992] BCLC 686 317
Carr v. British International Helicopters Ltd. [1993] BCC 855 307
Castiglione's Will Trusts, Re, Hunter v. Mackenzie [1958] Ch. 549; [1958] 2 W.L.R. 400; 102 S.J. 176; [1958] 1 All E.R. 480 149
Castleburn Ltd., Re (1989) 5 BCC 652; 1989 PCC 386; [1991] BCLC 89, D.C. 200, 228, 231, 235, 236
Cedac Ltd., Re, Secretary of State for Trade and Industry v. Langridge. *See* Secretary of State for Trade and Industry v. Langridge; Cedac Ltd., Re.
Centrebind Ltd., Re, Centrebind v. I.R.C. [1967] 1 W.L.R. 377; [1966] C.L.Y. 1468; 110 S.J. 905; *sub nom.* Centrebind Ltd., Re [1966] 3 All E.R. 889 331
Champagne Perrier-Jouet S.A. v. Finch (H.H.) Ltd. [1982] 1 W.L.R. 1359; (1982) 126 S.J. 689; [1982] 3 All E.R. 713; (1983) 80 L.S.Gaz. 93 152
Chapman v. Smethurst [1909] 1 K.B. 927 28
Charnley Davies Ltd., Re [1990] BCC 605; [1990] BCLC 760; *Financial Times*, June 15, 1990 309
Charterbridge Corporation Ltd. v. Lloyd's Bank Ltd. [1970] Ch. 62; [1969] 3 W.L.R. 122; (1968) 113 S.J. 465; [1969] 2 All E.R. 1185; *sub nom.* Charterbridge Corporation Ltd. v. Lloyd's Bank and Pomeroy Developments (Castleford) [1969] 2 Lloyd's Rep. 24 .... 55, 56
Chez Nico (Restaurants) Ltd., Re [1991] BCC 736; [1992] BCLC 192 .... 133, 243, 250
City Equitable Fire Assurance Co. Ltd., Re [1925] Ch. 107 .... 118, 120
City Investment Centres Ltd., Re [1992] BCLC 956 314
Cladrose Ltd., Re [1990] BCC 11; [1990] BCLC 204 316
Clemens v. Clemens Bros. Ltd. [1976] 2 All E.R. 268 .... 111, 112, 217
Coalport China Co., Re [1895] 2 Ch. 404, C.A. 67
Coleman v. Myers [1977] 2 N.Z.L.R. 225, N.Z. Sup. Ct. 133, 237
Colman v. Eastern Counties Railway Co. (1846) 10 Beav. 1 54
Columbian Fireproofing Co. Ltd., Re [1910] 2 Ch. 120 329
Company, A (No. 007623 of 1984), Re [1986] BCLC 382 .... 240, 247, 250
—— (No. 002567 of 1982), Re [1983] 1 W.L.R. 927; (1983) 127 S.J. 508; [1983] 2 All E.R. 854; (1983) 80 L.S.Gaz. 2133 .... 196, 198, 238
—— (No. 004475 of 1982), Re [1983] Ch. 178; [1983] 2 W.L.R. 381; (1983) 127 S.J. 153; [1983] 2 All E.R. 36 .... 224, 225
—— (No. 007623 of 1984), Re (1986) 2 BCC 99; [1986] BCLC 362 .... 199, 235, 236
—— (No. 008699 of 1985), Re [1986] BCLC 382; 1986 PCC 296 225
—— (No. 003160 of 1986), Re [1986] BCLC 391 201
—— (No. 003843 of 1986), Re (1987) 3 BCC 624; [1987] BCLC 562 ... 198
—— (No. 00477 of 1986), Re (1986) 2 BCC 99; 1986 PCC 372 202
—— (No. 00596 of 1986), Re (1986) 2 BCC 99 204
—— (No. 005134 of 1986), Re, ex p. Harries [1989] BCLC 365 234
—— (No. 005136 of 1986), Re [1987] BCLC 32 127
—— (No. 00175 of 1987), Re (1987) 3 BCC 124; [1987] BCLC 467 306

Company, A (No. 00370 of 1987), ex p. Glossop, Re [1988] 1 W.L.R. 1068; [1988] BCLC 570; (1988) 132 S.J. 1388; (1988) 4 BCC 506; 1988 PCC 351; [1988] L.S.Gaz. November 9, 43 ... 154, 155, 334
—— (No. 003096 of 1987), Re (1988) 4 BCC 80 .... 188, 198, 200, 203, 204
—— (No. 005009 of 1987), Re (1988) 4 BCC 424 318
—— (No. 001363 of 1988), Re (1989) 5 BCC 18; [1989] BCLC 579 198
—— (No. 001418 of 1988), Re [1990] BCC 526; [1991] BCLC 197, D.C. 323
—— (No. 001992 of 1988), Re (1988) 4 BCC 451; [1989] BCLC 9, D.C. 306
—— (No. 006834 of 1988), Re, ex p. Kremer [1989] BCLC 365 .... 200, 235
—— (No. 001448 of 1989), Re (1989) 5 BCC 706; [1989] BCLC 715 ... 306
—— (No. 00314 of 1989), Re [1990] BCC 221; [1991] BCLC 154 203
—— (No. 00330 of 1992), Re, ex p. Holden [1991] BCC 241 .... 200, 231, 235, 239
Constitution Insurance Co. of Canada v. Kosmopoulos (1987) 34 D.L.R. (4th) 208 178
Consumer and Industrial Press Ltd, (No. 2), Re (1988) 4 BCC 72; [1988] BCLC 177 .... 305, 309
Cook v. Deeks [1910] 1 A.C. 554 .... 121, 126, 127
Cooper (Cuthbert) & Sons Ltd., Re [1937] Ch. 392 .... 208, 209, 219, 220
Cooper (Gerald) Chemicals Ltd., Re [1978] Ch. 262; [1978] 2 W.L.R. 866; (1977) 121 S.J. 848; [1978] 2 All E.R. 49 322
Copecrest Ltd., Re [1993] BCC 844, C.A. 312
Cotman v. Brougham [1918] A.C. 514 57
Cotronic (UK) Ltd. v. Dezonie (t/a Wendaland Builders Ltd.) [1991] BCC 200; [1991] BCLC 721; *The Times*, March 8, 1991, C.A. 38, 40
Coulson Sanderson and Ward Ltd. v. Ward, *Financial Times*, October 18, 1985, C.A. 195
Cowan de Groot Properties Ltd. v. Eagle Trust plc [1991] BCLC 1045 .... 125, 129, 131
Cranley Mansions Ltd., Re [1994] 1 W.L.R. 1610 303
Craven-Ellis v. Canons Ltd. [1936] 2 K.B. 403 136
Creasey v. Breachwood Motors Ltd. [1992] BCC 638; [1993] BCLC 480; *The Times*, July 29, 1992 .... 16, 24
Croftbell Ltd., Re [1990] BCC 781; [1990] BCLC 844 310
Crown Bank, Re (1890) 44 Ch.D. 634 58

DHN Food Distributors v. Tower Hamlets London Borough Council; Bronze Investments v. Same; DHN Food Transport v. Same [1976] 1 W.L.R. 852; 120 S.J. 215; [1976] J.P.L. 363; 74 L.G.R. 506; *sub nom.* D.H.N. Food Distributors v. London Borough of Tower Hamlets [1976] 3 All E.R. 462; *sub nom.* DHN Food Distributors (in liquidation) v. Tower Hamlets London Borough Council; Bronze Investments (in liquidation) v. Same; DHN Food Transport (in liquidation) v. Same (1976) 32 P. & C.R. 240, C.A.; reversing *sub nom.* D.H.N. Food Distributors, Bronze Investments and D.H.N. Food Transport v. London Borough of Tower Hamlets (Ref. Nos. 36, 37 and 38/1974) (1975) 30 P. & C.R. 251, L.T. 16, 21, 24
DKG Contractors Ltd., Re [1990] BCC 903 321
D.R. Chemicals Ltd., Re (1989) 5 BCC 39 234

Dafen Tinplate Co. Ltd. v. Lanelly Steel Co. (1907) Ltd. [1920] 2 Ch. 124 .... 109, 110
Daimler Co. Ltd. v. Continental Tyre and Rubber Co. [1916] 2 A.C. 307 16
Daniels v. Daniels [1978] Ch. 406; [1978] 2 W.L.R. 73; [1978] 2 All E.R. 89; (1977) 121 S.J. 605 .... 34, 121
Davis and Collett Ltd., Re [1935] Ch. 693 .... 191, 333
Davis Investments (East Ham) Ltd., Re [1961] 1 W.L.R. 1396; [1961] 3 All E.R. 926; *sub nom.* Davies Investments (East Ham), Re, 105 S.J. 966, C.A. 188, 191
Dean v. Prince [1954] Ch. 409; [1954] 2 W.L.R. 538; 98 S.J. 215; [1954] 1 All E.R. 749; 47 R. & I.T. 494, C.A.; reversing [1953] Ch. 590; [1953] 3 W.L.R. 271; 97 S.J. 490; [1953] 2 All E.R. 636; [1953] C.L.Y. 525 .... 228, 230, 231
Debtor, A (No. 222 of 1990), Re, ex p. The Bank of Ireland [1992] BCLC 137; *The Times*, June 27, 1991 303
Dicetrade Ltd., Re [1994] BCC 371 312
Diplock, Re. *See* Ministry of Health v. Simpson.
DPP v. Gomez; *sub nom.* R. v. Gomez [1993] A.C. 442; [1992] 3 W.L.R. 1067; [1993] 1 All E.R. 1; (1993) 96 Cr.App.R. 359; (1993) 137 S.J. (LB) 36; (1993) 157 J.P. 1; [1993] Crim.L.R. 304; (1993) 157 J.P.N. 15, H.L. 183
D'Jan of London Ltd., Re [1993] BCC 646 .... 119, 120, 121, 122, 134, 321, 324
Dorchester Finance Co. Ltd. v. Stebbing [1989] BCLC 498 120
Douglas Construction Services Ltd., Re (1988) 4 BCC 558; [1988] BCLC 397 316
Dovey v. Cory [1901] A.C. 477 119
Duomatic Ltd., Re [1969] 2 Ch. 365; [1969] 2 W.L.R. 114; (1968) 112 S.J. 922; [1969] 1 All E.R. 79
Durham Fancy Goods Ltd. v. Jackson (Michael) (Fancy Goods) Ltd. [1968] 2 Q.B. 839; [1968] 3 W.L.R. 225; 112 S.J. 582; [1968] 2 All E.R. 987; *sub nom.* Durham Fancy Goods v. Jackson (Michael) (Fancy Goods) and Jackson [1968] 2 Lloyd's Rep. 98 26

EBM Co. Ltd. v. Dominion Bank [1973] 3 All E.R. 555 79
EDM (Europe) Electronics Ltd., Re [1991] BCC 268 314
ESC. Publishing Ltd., Re [1990] BCC 335 .... 237, 239
Eagle Trust plc v. SBC Securities Ltd. [1993] 1 W.L.R. 484; [1992] 4 All E.R. 388; [1991] BCLC 438; *Financial Times*, February 5, 1991; *The Times*, February 14, 1991 .... 124, 125, 186
East v. Bennett Bros. Ltd. [1911] 1 Ch. 163 81
Ebrahimi v. Westbourne Galleries Ltd. [1973] A.C. 360; [1972] 2 W.L.R. 1289; 116 S.J. 412; [1972] 2 All E.R. 492, H.L.; reversing *sub nom.* Westbourne Galleries, Re [1971] Ch. 799; [1971] 2 W.L.R. 618; (1970) 115 S.J. 74; [1971] 1 All E.R. 56, C.A.; reversing [1970] 1 W.L.R. 1378; 114 S.J. 785; [1970] 3 All E.R. 374 .... 62, 68, 111, 112, 187, 188, 189, 193, 194, 195, 196, 197, 198, 201, 203, 209, 220, 221, 250, 332, 333, 334
Eddystone Marine Insurance Co., Re [1893] 3 Ch. 9 148

Egyptian Delta Land and Investment Co., Re [1907] W.N. 16 61
El Ajou v. Dollar Land Holdings plc [1993] 3 All E.R. 717; [1993] BCLC 735; [1993] BCC 698 125
El Sombrero Ltd., Re [1958] Ch. 900; [1958] 3 W.L.R. 349; 102 S.J. 601; [1958] 3 All E.R. 1 .... 81, 105
Eley v. Positive Life Assurance Co. Ltd. (1876) 1 Ex.D. 88, C.A. 64, 136, 213
Elgindata Ltd., Re [1991] BCLC 959 .... 120, 234, 239
Elliott v. Wheeldon [1992] BCC 489; [1993] BCLC 53; *The Times*, March 12, 1992, C.A. 117
Ellis (Matthew) Ltd., Re [1933] Ch. 458 329
English and Colonial Produce Co. Ltd., Re [1906] 2 Ch. 435, C.A. 40
Equiticorp International plc, Re [1989] 1 W.L.R. 1010; (1989) 133 S.J. 1405; (1989) 5 BCC 599; [1989] BCLC 597; [1989] L.S.Gaz. November 15, 36 306
Erlanger v. New Sombrero Phosphate Co. (1878) 3 App.Cas. 1218, P.C. 32, 33
Estmanco (Kilner House) Ltd. v. Greater London Council [1982] 1 All E.R. 437 .... 112, 113
Etlin (H.B.) & Co. Ltd. v. Asseltyne (1962) 34 D.L.R. (2d) 189; affirming (1962) 32 D.L.R. (2d) 489 28
Evans v. Brunner, Mond & Co. Ltd. [1921] 1 Ch. 359 56
Ewing v. Buttercup Margarine Co. Ltd. [1917] 2 Ch. 1, C.A. 48
Exchange Banking Co., Flitcroft's Case, Re (1882) 21 Ch.D. 519 155
Exchange Travel Agency Ltd. v. Triton Property Trust plc [1991] BCC 341; [1991] BCLC 396 307
Expanded Plugs Ltd., Re [1966] 1 W.L.R. 514; 110 S.J. 246; [1966] 1 All E.R. 877 187
Express Engineering Works, Re [1920] 1 Ch. 466, C.A. 79, 121, 130

F.G. Films Ltd., Re [1953] 1 W.L.R. 483; 97 S.J. 171; [1953] 1 All E.R. 615 .... 16, 23
Fairway Magazines Ltd., Re [1992] BCC 924; [1993] BCLC 643 ... 326, 327, 329
Featherstone v. Cooke (1873) L.R. 16 Eq. 298 205
Fildes Bros. Ltd., Re [1970] 1 W.L.R. 592; [1970] 1 All E.R. 923; 114 S.J. 301 .... 187, 193
Ford and Carter Ltd. v. Midland Bank (1979) 129 N.L.J. 543 21
Forte (Charles) Investments Ltd. v. Amanda [1964] Ch. 240; [1963] 3 W.L.R. 662; 107 S.J. 494; [1963] 2 All E.R. 940, C.A.; reversing (1963) 107 S.J. 494; 234 L.T. 330 221
Foss v. Harbottle (1843) 2 Hare 461 .... 33, 112, 113
Foster v. Foster [1916] 1 Ch. 532 .... 106, 131
Fulham Football Club Ltd. v. Cabra Estates plc (1992) 65 P. & C.R. 284; [1993] 1 PLR 29; [1992] BCC 863; (1992) 136 S.J. (L.B.) 267; *The Times*, September 11, 1992; *The Independent*, September 17, 1992, C.A.; reversing [1992] NPC 115; *The Times*, July 1, 1992 .... 113, 114

GSAR Realisations Ltd., Re [1993] BCLC 409 317
Gaiman v. National Association for Mental Health [1971] Ch. 317; [1970] 3 W.L.R. 42; 114 S.J. 416; [1970] 2 All E.R. 362 295
Gallidoro Trawlers Ltd., Re [1991] BCC 691; [1991] BCLC 411 306
Gardner v. Iredale [1912] 1 Ch. 700 147
German Date Coffee Co. Ltd., Re (1882) 20 Ch.D. 169, C.A. 57, 334
Ghyll Beck Driving Range Ltd., Re [1993] BCLC 1126 202
Gilford Motor Co. Ltd. v. Horne [1933] Ch. 935, C.A. 16, 23
Gluckstein v. Barnes [1900] A.C. 240 33
Godwin Warren Control Systems plc, Re [1992] BCC 557; [1993] BCLC 80 311
Grant v. United Knigdom Switchback Railways (1888) 40 Ch.D. 135 108
Great Wheal Polgooth Co. Ltd. (1883) 53 L.J.Ch. 42 31
Greenhalgh v. Arderne Cinemas Ltd. [1951] Ch. 286; 94 S.J. 855; [1950] 2 All E.R. 1120, C.A. 109, 110, 112, 114
Greenwell v. Porter [1902] 1 Ch. 530 74
Greymouth-Point Elizabeth Railway and Coal Co. Ltd. [1904] 1 Ch. 32 98
Guinness plc v. Saunders [1990] 2 A.C. 663; [1990] 2 W.L.R. 324; (1990) 134 S.J. 457; [1990] 1 All E.R. 652; [1990] BCC 205; [1990] BCLC 402; [1990] L.S.Gaz. March 7, 42, H.L.; affirming Guinness plc v. Saunders *sub nom.* Guinness v. Ward [1988] 1 W.L.R. 863; (1988) 132 S.J. 820; (1988) 4 BCC 377; [1988] 2 All E.R. 940; 1988 PCC 270; (1988) 138 New L.J. 142; [1988] BCLC 607, C.A.; affirming [1988] BCLC 43 .... 99, 101, 123, 129

Halt Garage (1964) Ltd., Re [1982] 3 All E.R. 1016 .... 92, 126, 135, 136, 137, 154
Harman v. BML Group Ltd. [1994] 1 W.L.R. 893, C.A. 72, 81, 106, 216
Harmer (H.R.) Ltd., Re [1959] 1 W.L.R. 62; 103 S.J. 73; [1958] 3 All E.R. 689, C.A. 207, 208, 224
Harris Simons Construction Ltd., Re [1989] 1 W.L.R. 368; (1989) 133 S.J. 122; 1989 PCC 229; [1989] BCLC 202; (1989) 5 BCC 11; [1989] L.S.Gaz. February 22, 43 305
Hatrick v. IRC; Public Trustee v. IRC [1963] N.Z.L.R. 641 237
Hawkes Bay Milk Corporation Ltd. v. Watson [1974] 1 N.Z.L.R. 236 40
Heald v. O'Connor [1971] 1 W.L.R. 497; (1970) 115 S.J. 244; [1971] 2 All E.R. 1105 174
Hely-Hutchinson v. Brayhead Ltd. [1968] 1 Q.B. 549; [1967] 3 W.L.R. 1408; 111 S.J. 830; [1967] 3 All E.R. 98, C.A.; affirming [1968] 1 Q.B. 549; [1967] 2 W.L.R. 1312; 111 S.J. 329; [1967] 2 All E.R. 14 .... 129, 130
Hendon v. Adelman (1973) 117 S.J. 631; *The Times*, June 16, 1973 26
Hickman v. Kent or Romney Marsh Sheep-Breeders Association [1915] 1 Ch. 881 .... 75, 136
Hoare & Co. Ltd., Re (1933) 150 L.T. 374 243
Hogg v. Cramphorn [1967] Ch. 254; [1966] 3 W.L.R. 995; 110 S.J. 887; [1966] 3 All E.R. 420; [1963] C.L.Y. 397 .... 121, 128, 240
Holmes v. Keyes [1959] Ch. 199; [1958] 2 W.L.R. 772; 102 S.J. 329; [1958] 2 All E.R. 129, C.A.; reversing [1958] Ch. 670; [1958] 2 W.L.R. 540; 102 S.J. 231; [1958] 1 All E.R. 721 69
Holt v. Holt [1990] 1 W.L.R. 1250; (1990) 134 S.J. 1076; [1990] BCC 682; [1990] L.S.Gaz. October 3, 36, P.C. 237

Home Treat Ltd., Re [1991] BCC 165; [1991] BCLC 705 .... 61, 62, 79
Hong Kong and China Gas Co. Ltd. v. Glen [1914] 1 Ch. 527 148
Horsley and Weight Ltd., Re [1982] Ch. 442; [1982] 3 W.L.R. 431; [1982] 3 All E.R. 1045; (1982) 79 L.S.Gaz. 919, C.A. 55, 60, 114, 121, 122
Howard v. Patent Ivory Manufacturing Co. (1888) 38 Ch.D. 156 41
Howe v. Earl of Dartmouth (1802) 7 Ves. 137 246
Howie v. Crawford [1990] BCC 331; [1990] BCLC 686 233
Hydrodan (Corby) Ltd., Re [1994] BCC 161 .... 17, 312, 318

Imperial Motors Ltd., Re (1985) 5 BCC 214 305
International Sales and Agencies Ltd. v. Marcus [1982] 3 All E.R. 551; [1982] 2 C.M.L.R. 46 .... 92, 93, 123, 124, 126
Introductions Ltd. v. National Provincial Bank Ltd. [1970] Ch. 199; [1969] 2 W.L.R. 791; 113 S.J. 122; [1969] 1 Lloyd's Rep. 229; *sub nom.* Introductions, Re, Introductions v. National Provincial Bank [1969] 1 All E.R. 887, C.A.; affirming [1968] 2 All E.R. 1221 .... 55, 58, 59
Irish Club Ltd., Re [1906] W.N. 127 295
Irvine v. Union Bank of Australia (1877) 2 App. Cas. 366 108

J.E. Cade & Son Ltd., Re [1991] BCC 373; [1992] BCLC 213 197
Jaber v. Science and Information Technology Ltd. [1992] BCLC 764 .... 205, 297
Jacob (Walter L.) & Co. Ltd., Re, Official Receiver v. Jacob [1993] BCC 512 313
Jacobus Marler Estates Ltd. v. Marler (1913) 85 L.J.P.C. 167 34
Jarvis Motors (Harrow) Ltd. v. Carabott [1964] 1 W.L.R. 1101; 108 S.J. 542; [1964] 3 All E.R. 89 .... 82, 177
Jaymar Management Ltd., Re [1990] BCC 303; [1990] BCLC 617 313
Jenice Ltd. v. Dan [1993] BCLC 1349 27
Jermyn Street Turkish Baths Ltd., Re [1970] 1 W.L.R. 1194; 114 S.J. 583; [1970] 3 All E.R. 57 239
Jesner v. Jarrad Properties Ltd. [1992] BCC 807 .... 187, 206, 225
Jones v. Lipman [1962] 1 W.L.R. 832; 106 S.J. 531; [1962] 1 All E.R. 442 .... 16, 23
Jubilee Cotton Mills v. Lewis [1924] A.C. 958 44

K/9 Meat Suppliers (Guildford) Ltd., Re [1966] 1 W.L.R. 1112; 110 S.J. 348; [1966] 3 All E.R. 320 .... 187, 192
Kelner v. Baxter (1886) L.R. 2 C.P. 174 .... 38, 39, 40
Kenyon Swansea Ltd., Re (1987) 3 BCC 259 .... 188, 203
Kinsela v. Russell Kinsela Pty Ltd. (in liquidation) [1986] 4 N.S.W.L.R. 722 114
Kirby v. Wilkins [1929] 2 Ch. 444 149

Ladywell Mining Co. v. Brookes (1887) 35 Ch.D. 400, C.A. 34
Land & Property Trust Co. plc (No. 2), Re [1993] BCC 462; [1993] EGCS 19; [1993] NPC 24; *The Times*, February 16, 1993, C.A.; reversing [1991] BCLC 849 306

Landes v. Marcus (1909) 25 T.L.R. 478 27
Langunas Nitrate Co. v. Lagunas Syndicate [1899] 2 Ch. 392, C.A. 32, 33
Lawrence v. Metropolitan Police Commissioner [1971] 2 All E.R. 1253, H.L.; affirming *sub nom.* R. v. Lawrence (Alan) [1971] 1 Q.B. 373; [1970] 3 W.L.R. 1103; *sub nom.* R. v. Lawrence, 114 S.J. 864; [1970] 3 All E.R. 933; 55 Cr.App.R. 73, C.A. 182, 183
Leadbitter v. Farrow (1816) 5 M. & S. 345 27
Lee v. Lee's Air Farming Ltd. [1961] A.C. 12; [1960] 3 W.L.R. 758; 104 S.J. 869; [1960] 3 All E.R. 420, P.C. 16, 21, 178, 210
Lee, Behrens & Co., Re [1932] 2 Ch. 46 56
Lee Panavision Ltd. v. Lee Lighting Ltd. [1991] BCC 621; [1992] BCLC 22; *The Times*, June 25, 1991; *The Independent*, August 23, 1991, C.A.; affirming [1991] BCLC 575 .... 99, 129
Leeds and Hanley Theatres of Varieties Ltd., Re [1902] 2 Ch. 809, C.A. 33, 34
Leitch (William C.) Bros. Ltd., Re [1932] 2 Ch. 71 323
Lindholst & Co. A/S v. Fowler [1988] BCLC 166; (1988) 4 BCC 776, C.A. 26
Linvale Ltd., Re [1993] BCC 654; [1993] BCLC 654 315
Lipkin Gorman v. Karpnale Ltd. [1987] 1 W.L.R. 987; (1987) 131 S.J. 940; [1987] BCLC 159; [1986] FLR 271; (1986) 136 New L.J. 659 125
Lloyds Bank v. Duker [1987] 1 W.L.R. 1324; (1987) 131 S.J. 1358; [1987] 3 All E.R. 193; (1987) 84 L.S.Gaz. 3254 .... 206, 240, 244, 245, 246
Loch v. Blackwood (John) Ltd. [1924] A.C. 783 .... 191, 193, 206, 211, 333
Lo-Line Electric Motors Ltd., Re; Companies Act 1985, Re [1988] Ch. 477; [1988] 3 W.L.R. 26; (1988) 132 S.J. 851; [1988] 2 All E.R. 692; 1988 PCC 236; [1988] 3 FTLR 107; (1988) 4 BCC 415; [1988] BCLC 698; (1988) 138 New L.J. 119 .... 311, 314, 317
London Flats Ltd., Re [1969] W.L.R. 711; 113 S.J. 304; [1969] 2 All E.R. 744 81
London School of Electronics, Re [1986] Ch. 211; [1985] 3 W.L.R. 474; (1985) 129 S.J. 573; 1985 PCC 248 .... 232, 238
Lundie Brothers Ltd., Re [1965] 1 W.L.R. 1051; 109 S.J. 470; [1965] 2 All E.R. 692 .... 191, 333
Lyle and Scott Ltd. v. Scott's Trustees; Same v. British Investment Trust [1959] A.C. 763; [1959] 3 W.L.R. 133; 103 S.J. 507; [1959] 2 All E.R. 661; 1959 S.C. (H.L.) 64; 1959 S.L.T. 198, H.L.; reversing 1958 S.C. 230; 1958 S.L.T. 169; [1958] C.L.Y. 445 68

M.C. Bacon Ltd., Re [1991] Ch. 127; [1990] BCC 78; [1990] BCLC 324 327
Macaura v. Northern Assurance Co. Ltd. [1925] A.C. 619, H.L. 16, 21, 22, 178
MacDougall v. Gardiner (1875) 1 Ch.D. 13 105
Mace Builders (Glasgow) Ltd. v. Lunn (1986) 2 BCC 99 328
McGuinness v. Bremner plc [1988] BCLC 673 104
McNulty's Interchange Ltd., Re (1988) 4 BCC 533; [1989] BCLC 709 ... 316
Manlon Trading Ltd., Re *The Times*, August 15, 1994 312
Marshall, Re [1914] 1 Ch. 192 245
Marshall's Valve Gear Co. v. Manning, Wardle & Co. Ltd. [1909] 1 Ch. 267 101

Matthews (F.P. and C.H.) Ltd., Re [1982] Ch. 257; [1982] 2 W.L.R. 495; [1982] 1 All E.R. 338, C.A. 328
Meesan Investments Ltd., Re (1988) 4 BCC 788; *sub nom.* Royal Trust Bank v. Buchler [1989] BCLC 130, D.C. 307
Melcast (Wolverhampton) Ltd., Re [1991] BCLC 288 317
Menier v. Hooper's Telegraph Works (1874) 9 Ch.App 350 .... 121, 126
Ministry of Health v. Simpson [1951] A.C. 251; 66 T.L.R. (Pt. 2) 1015; [1950] 2 All E.R. 1137; *sub nom. Re* Diplock, Minister of Health *v.* Simpson, 94 S.J. 777, H.L.; affirming *sub nom.* Re Diplock, Diplock v. Whintle [1948] Ch. 465; [1948] L.J.R. 1670; 92 S.J. 484; *sub nom.* Re, Diplock's Estate; Diplock v. Wintle [1948] 2 All E.R. 318; C.A.; reversing [1947] Ch. 716; [1947] L.J.R. 1158; 177 L.T. 40; 91 S.J. 248; [1947] 1 All E.R. 522 124
Montagu's Settlement Trusts, Re [1987] Ch. 264; [1987] 2 W.L.R. 1192; (1987) 131 S.J. 411; (1987) 84 L.S.Gaz. 1057 125
Mountforest Ltd., Re [1993] BCC 565 205
Movitex Ltd. v. Bulfield (1986) 2 BCC 99; [1988] BCLC 104 .... 122, 129, 131
Moxham v. Grant [1900] 1 Q.B. 88 155
Multinational Gas and Petroleum Co. v. Multinational Gas and Petroleum Services Ltd. [1983] Ch. 258; [1983] 3 W.L.R. 492; (1983) 127 S.J. 562; [1983] 2 All E.R. 563, C.A. 21, 115, 121, 122
Murray's Judicial Factor, Petitioner [1992] BCC 596 197

N.F.U. Development Trust Ltd. *See* National Farmers' Union Development Trust, Re.
NL Electrical Ltd., Re, Ghosh v. 3i plc [1994] 1 BCLC 22 .... 166, 167
Natal Land Co. Ltd. v. Pauline Colliery Syndicate Ltd. [1904] A.C. 120, P.C. 40
National Farmers' Union Development Trust, Re [1972] 1 W.L.R. 1548; 116 S.J. 679; *sub nom.* NFU Development Trust, Re [1973] 1 All E.R. 135 73
National Motor Mail Coach Co., Clinton's Claim, Re [1908] 2 Ch. 515, C.A. 36
New British Iron Co., ex p. Beckwith, Re [1898] 1 Ch. 324 .... 136, 213
New Cedos Engineering Co. Ltd., Re [1994] 1 BCLC 797 79
New Finance and Mortgage Co. Ltd. (in liquidation), Re [1975] Ch. 420; [1975] 2 W.L.R. 443; (1974) 118 S.J. 714; [1975] 1 All E.R. 684 58
New Generation Engineers Ltd., Re [1993] BCLC 435 .... 315, 316
Newborne v. Sensolid [1954] 1 Q.B. 45; [1953] 2 W.L.R. 596; 97 S.J. 209; [1953] 1 All E.R. 708, C.A.; affirming [1952] W.N. 491; [1952] 2 T.L.R. 763; 96 S.J. 765; [1952] C.L.Y. 456 .... 38, 39, 40
Newstead (Inspector of Taxes) v. Frost [1980] 1 W.L.R. 135; (1980) 124 S.J. 116; [1980] 1 All E.R. 363; [1980] S.T.C. 123; [1980] T.R. 1, H.L.; affirming [1978] 1 W.L.R. 1141; (1978) 122 S.J. 813; [1979] 2 All E.R. 129; [1979] S.T.C. 45; (1978) T.R. 221, C.A.; affirming [1978] 1 W.L.R. 511; (1978) 122 S.J. 33; [1978] 2 All E.R. 241; [1977] T.R. 301; [1978] S.T.C. 239 58
Nicholson v. Permankraft (NZ) Ltd. [1985] N.Z.L.R. 242 114
Nisbet v. Shepherd [1994] BCC 91; *The Times*, July 1, 1993, C.A. ... 13, 179

Noble (R.A.) & Sons (Clothing) Ltd., Re [1983] BCLC 273 .... 195, 203, 225
Noble Trees Ltd., Re [1993] BCC 318; [1993] BCLC 1185 312
Norman v. Theodore Goddard [1991] BCLC 1028; [1992] BCC 14 .... 119, 120
North-West Transportation Co. v. Beatty (1887) 12 App.Cas. 589 .... 108, 121, 131
Northern Counties Securities Ltd. v. Jackson & Steeple Ltd. [1974] 1 W.L.R. 1133; 118 S.J. 498; [1974] 2 All E.R. 625 .... 107, 108
Nothumberland Avenue Hotel Co., Re (1886) 33 Ch.D. 16 41
Nurcombe v. Nurcombe [1985] 1 W.L.R. 370; (1984) 128 S.J. 766; [1985] 1 All E.R. 65; (1984) 81 L.S.Gaz. 2929, C.A. 221, 222

O.C. (Transport) Services Ltd., Re (1984) 1 BCC 99; (1984) 81 L.S.Gaz. 1044 238
Ocean Coal Co. Ltd. v. Powell Duffryn Steam Co. Ltd. [1932] 1 Ch. 654 229
Olympia & York Canary Wharf Ltd., Re; Amercian Express Europe Ltd. v. Adamson [1993] BCC 154; [1993] BCLC 453 307
Omnium Electric Palaces Ltd. v. Baines [1914] 1 Ch. 332 32
Opera Photographics Ltd., Re [1989] 1 W.L.R. 634; (1989) 133 S.J. 848; (1989) 5 BCC 601; 1989 PCC 337; [1989] BCLC 763 ..... 81, 105
Orleans Motor Co. Ltd., Re [1911] 2 Ch. 41 329
Oshkosh B'Gosh Inc. v. Dan Marbel Inc. (1988) 4 BCC 795; [1989] BCLC 507; 1989 PCC 320; [1989] 1 C.M.L.R. 94, C.A.; reversing [1988] 3 C.M.L.R. 214, D.C. 38
Oxted Motor Co. Ltd., Re [1921] 3 K.B. 32 79

Pamstock Ltd., Re [1994] BCC 264 312
Paramount Airways Ltd. (No. 3), Re [1994] BCC 172 310
Parke v. Daily News Ltd. [1962] Ch. 927; [1962] 3 W.L.R. 566; 106 S.J. 704; [1962] 2 All E.R. 929 .... 114, 117
Parker and Cooper v. Reading [1926] Ch. 975 79
Parsons v. Parsons (Albert J.) & Sons Ltd. [1979] I.C.R. 271; [1979] F.S.R. 254; *sub nom.* Parsons (Albert J.) v. Parsons [1979] I.R.L.R. 117, C.A.; affirming [1978] I.C.R. 456; (1977) 121 S.J. 812, E.A.T. 136, 209, 213
Patrick and Lyon, Re [1933] Ch. 786 323
Paul (H.R.) & Son Ltd., Re (1974) 118 S.J. 166; *The Times*, November 17, 1973 81
Pavlides v. Jensen [1956] Ch. 565; [1956] 3 W.L.R. 224; 100 S.J. 452; [1956] 2 All E.R. 518 .... 34, 121
Payne (David) Ltd., Re [1904] 2 Ch. 608 55
Pearce, Duff and Co. Ltd., Re [1960] 1 W.L.R. 1014; [1960] 3 All E.R. 222 80
Pedley v. Inland Waterways Association Ltd. [1977] 1 All E.R. 209 105
Pennel v. Venida Investments Ltd. 1974 Ch.D. unreported 112
Penrose v. Martyr (1858) 120 E.R. 595 .... 25, 26
Percival v. Wright [1902] 2 Ch. 421 .... 114, 132, 133
Phonogram Ltd. v. Lane [1982] Q.B. 938; [1981] 3 W.L.R. 736; (1981) 125 S.J. 527; [1981] 3 All E.R. 182; [1982] C.M.L.R. 615; [1981] Com.L.R. 228, C.A. 38, 39, 41
Plaut v. Steiner (1989) 5 BCC 352 .... 171, 173, 174

Polly Peck International plc v. Nadir (No. 2) [1992] 4 All E.R. 769; [1993] BCLC 187, C.A. 124, 186
Polly Peck International plc, Re, Secretary of State for Trade and Industry v. Ellis [1993] BCC 886 ..... 311, 314
Postgate and Denby (Agencies) Ltd., Re (1986) 2 BCC 99; [1987] BCLC 8; 1987 PCC 1 202
Premier Underwriting Association Ltd. (No. 1), Re [1913] 2 Ch. 29 296
Press Caps Ltd., Re [1949] Ch. 434; [1949] L.J.R. 1460; [1949] 1 All E.R. 1013, C.A. 243
Primlaks (UK) Ltd., Re [1989] BCLC 734 305
Probe Data Systems Ltd. (No. 3), Re, Secretary of State for Trade and Industry v. Desai [1992] BCC 110; [1992] BCLC 405; C.A.; affirming [1991] BCC 428; [1991] BCLC 586 312
Produce Marketing Consortium Ltd. (No. 2), Re [1989] 1 W.L.R. 745; (1989) 133 S.J. 945; [1989] 3 All E.R. 1; 1989 PCC 290, 457; (1989) 5 BCC 569; [1989] BCLC 513 ..... 120, 320, 321
Puddephat v. Leith [1916] 1 Ch. 200 74
Purpoint Ltd., Re [1991] BCC 121; [1991] BCLC 491 321

Quickdome Ltd., Re [1988] BCLC 370; 1989 406, D.C. 43
Quin & Axtens Ltd. v. Salmon [1909] A.C. 442 ..... 101, 107

R. v. Appleyard (1985) 81 Cr.App.R. 319; [1985] Crim.L.R. 723, C.A. 184
—— v. Brockley [1994] BCC 131 36
—— v. Davies [1955] 1 Q.B. 71; [1954] 3 W.L.R. 664; 119 J.P. 15; 98 S.J. 789; [1954] 3 All E.R. 335; 38 Cr.App.R. 143, C.C.A. 181
—— v. Denton [1981] 1 W.L.R. 1446; [1982] 1 All E.R. 65; (1982) 74 Cr.App.R. 81; [1982] Crim.L.R. 107 184
—— v. Gomez. *See* DPP v. Gomez.
—— v. Goodman [1993] 2 All E.R. 789; [1992] BCC 625; (1993) 97 Cr.App.R. 210; (1993) 14 Cr.App.R.(S.) 147; [1992] Crim.L.R. 676, C.A. 35
—— v. Grantham [1984] Q.B. 675; [1984] 2 W.L.R. 815; (1984) 128 S.J. 331; [1984] 3 All E.R. 166; (1984) 79 Cr.App.R. 86; [1984] Crim.L.R. 492; (1984) 81 L.S.Gaz. 1437, C.A. 323
—— v. McDonnell [1966] 1 Q.B. 233; [1965] 3 W.L.R. 1138; 109 S.J. 919; [1966] 1 All E.R. 193; 50 Cr.App.R. 5 ..... 16, 182
—— v. McHugh and Tringham (1988) 88 Cr.App.R. 385, C.A. 184
—— v. Morris; Anderton v. Burnside [1984] A.C. 320; [1983] 3 W.L.R. 697; (1984) 148 J.P. 1; (1983) 127 S.J. 713; [1983] 3 All E.R. 288; (1984) 77 Cr.App.R. 309; [1983] Crim.L.R. 813, H.L.; affirming [1983] Q.B. 587; [1983] 2 W.L.R. 768; (1983) 127 S.J. 205; [1983] 2 All E.R. 448; (1983) 77 Cr.App.R. 164; [1983] Crim.L.R. 559, C.A. 182, 183
—— v. Philippou (1989) 89 Cr.App.R. 290; [1989] Crim.L.R. 585, C.A. 183
—— v. Roffel [1985] V.R. 511 183
—— v. Smith (David) [1974] Q.B. 354; [1974] 2 W.L.R. 20; (1973) 117 S.J. 938; *sub nom.* R. v. Smith (David Raymond) [1974] 1 All E.R. 632; (1973) 58 Cr.App.R. 320; [1974] Crim.L.R. 101, C.A. 184

Radford v. Samuel [1993] BCC 870 .... 16, 178
Rafsanjan Pistachio Producers Co-operative v. Reiss [1990] BCLC 352; [1990] BCC 730 26
Rayfield v. Hands [1960] Ch. 1; [1958] 2 W.L.R. 851; 102 S.J. 348; [1958] 2 All E.R. 194 68
Regal (Hastings) Ltd. v. Gulliver [1967] 2 A.C. 134n; [1942] 1 All E.R. 378 121
Richmond Gate Property Co. Ltd., Re [1965] 1 W.L.R. 335; [1964] 3 All E.R. 936 136
Rita Joan Dairies v. Thompson [1974] N.Z.L.R. 285 40
Roith (W. & M.) Ltd., Re [1967] W.L.R. 432; 110 S.J. 963; [1967] 1 All E.R. 427; [1966] C.L.Y. 1495 56
Rolled Steel Products (Holdings) Ltd. v. British Steel Corporation [1986] Ch. 246; [1985] 2 W.L.R. 908; (1984) 128 S.J. 629; [1985] 3 All E.R. 1; (1984) 81 L.S.Gaz. 2357, C.A.; affirming [1982] Ch. 478; [1982] 3 W.L.R. 715; [1982] 3 All E.R. 1057; [1982] 79 L.S.Gaz. 1291 .... 55, 56, 123, 128, 131
Rolus Properties Ltd., Re (1988) 4 BCC 446 316
Royal British Bank v. Turquand (1856) 6 E.B. 327 .... 95, 96, 131
Runciman v. Walter Runciman plc [1992] BCLC 1084; [1993] BCC 223 .... 99, 129
Russell v. Northern Bank Development Corporation Ltd. [1992] 1 W.L.R. 588; [1992] 3 All E.R. 161; (1992) 136 S.J. (LB) 182; [1992] BCLC 1016; [1992] BCC 578; [1992] *Gazette*, 15 July, 33; *Financial Times*, June 18, 1992; *The Times*, June 19, 1992 H.L.; reversing [1991] BCC 517; [1992] BCLC 431, N.I.C.A. 73, 74
Russell v. Wakefield Waterworks Co. (1875) L.R. 20 Eq. 474 123

SCL Building Services Ltd., Re (1989) 5 BCC 746; [1990] BCLC 98 .... 305, 306
S.H. & Co. (Realisations) 1990 Ltd., Re; Ellis v. Nyckelin Finance Co. Ltd. [1993] BCC 60; [1993] BCLC 1309 166
Safeguard Industrial Investments Ltd. v. Westminster Bank Ltd. [1982] 1 W.L.R. 589; (1982) 126 S.J. 205; [1982] 1 All E.R. 449, C.A.; affirming [1981] 1 W.L.R. 286; (1980) 125 S.J. 184; [1980] 3 All E.R. 849 68
St. Ives Windings Ltd., Re (1987) 3 BCC 634 305
Salomon v. Salomon & Co. Ltd. [1897] A.C. 22 .... 1, 15, 16, 20, 21, 22, 24, 32, 34, 79, 177, 206
Sandeman's Will Trusts, Re [1937] 1 All E.R. 368 245
Sanitary Carbon Co., Re [1877] W.N. 223 81
Sarflax, Re [1979] Ch. 592; [1979] 2 W.L.R. 202; (1978) 123 S.J. 97; [1979] 1 All E.R. 529 .... 21, 323
Scott v. Scott [1943] 1 All E.R. 582 102
Scottish Co-operative Wholesale Society v. Meyer [1959] A.C. 324; [1958] 3 W.L.R. 404; 102 S.J. 617; [1958] 3 All E.R. 66; *sub nom.* Meyer v. Scottish Co-operative Wholesale Scoeity, 1958 S.C.(H.L.) 40, H.L. 239
Secretary of State for Trade and Industry v. Langridge; Cedac, Re [1991] Ch. 402; [1991] 2 W.L.R. 1343; [1991] 3 All E.R. 591; [1991] BCC 148; [1991] BCLC 543; *The Times*, March 4, 1991, C.A.; reversing [1990] BCC 555 .... 313, 314
—— v. Palmer [1993] BCC 650 313

Selangor United Rubber Estates Ltd. v. Craddock (No. 3) [1968] 1 W.L.R. 1555; 112 S.J. 744; [1968] 2 All E.R. 1073; [1968] 2 Lloyd's Rep. 289 123
Sevenoaks Stationers (Retail) Ltd., Re [1991] Ch. 164; [1990] 3 W.L.R. 1165; [1991] 3 All E.R. 578; [1991] BCLC 325; [1990] BCC 765; (1990) 134 S.J. 1367, C.A. 314, 315, 316
Sharp v. Dawes (1876) 2 Q.B.D. 26, C.A. 81
Shaw (John) & Sons (Salford) Ltd. v. Shaw [1935] 2 K.B. 113 102
Shepherd's Trustees v. Shepherd 1950 S.C. 60, H.L. 219
Sheridan Securities Ltd., Re (1988) 4 BCC 200 305
Shoe Lace Ltd., Re, Power v. Sharp Investments Ltd. [1993] BCC 609, C.A. 328, 329
Short v. Treasury Commissioners [1948] A.C. 534; [1949] L.J.R. 143; 64 T.L.R. 400; 92 S.J. 573; [1948] 2 All E.R. 509, H.L. 230, 231
Shuttleworth v. Cox Bros. & Co. (Maidenhead) Ltd. 2 K.B. 9 109
Sidebottom v. Kershaw Leese & Co. Ltd. [1920] 1 Ch. 154 109
Simmonds v. Heffer [1983] BCLC 298; *The Times*, May 25, 1983 56
Simpson v. Westminster Palace Hotel Co. (1860) 8 H.L. Cas. 712 54
Smallman Construction Ltd., Re (1988) 4 BCC 784; [1989] BCLC 420; 1989 PCC 433, D.C. 309
Smith v. Croft (No. 2) [1988] Ch. 114; [1987] 3 W.L.R. 405; (1987) 131 S.J. 1038; [1987] 3 All E.R. 909; [1987] BCLC 355; [1987] 1 F.T.L.R. 319; 1986 PCC 209; (1987) 84 L.S.Gaz. 2449 127
Smith and Fawcett Ltd., Re [1942] Ch. 304 .... 67, 113, 220
Smith, Stone & Knight Ltd. v. Birmingham Corporation [1939] 4 All E.R. 116 .... 16, 21
Southward & Co. Ltd., Re [1979] 1 W.L.R. 1799; (1979) 123 S.J. 718; [1979] 3 All E.R. 556, C.A. 21
Southbourne Sheet Metal Co. Ltd., Re [1993] 1 W.L.R. 244; [1992] BCC 797; [1993] BCLC 135; *The Times*, August 6, 1992, C.A. 312
Southern Foundaries (1926) Ltd. v. Shirlaw [1940] A.C. 701 73
Stanton (F. & E.) Ltd., Re [1929] 1 Ch. 180 329
Steen v. Law [1964] A.C. 287; [1963] 3 W.L.R. 802; [1963] 3 All E.R. 770, P.C. 164
Stephens v. Pittas (T.) Ltd. [1983] S.T.C. 576; 56 T.C. 722, D.C. 263
Steward (Williams) (Holdings) Ltd., Re [1994] BCC 284 220
Sticky Fingers Restaurant Ltd., Re [1991] BCC 754; [1992] BCLC 84 106
Sussex Brick Co. Ltd., Re [1961] Ch. 289n; [1960] 2 W.L.R. 665n; 104 S.J. 329; [1960] 1 All E.R. 772n 243
Sutherland v. British Dominions Land Settlement Corp. [1926] Ch. 746 67
Swaledale Cleaners Ltd., Re [1968] 1 W.L.R. 1710; 112 S.J. 781; [1968] 3 All E.R. 619; 85 L.Q.R. 16, C.A. 66, 68, 209
Swift 736 Ltd., Re, Secretary of State for Trade and Industry v. Ettinger [1993] BCC 312; [1993] BCLC 896; *The Times*, February 18, 1993, C.A.; reversing in part [1992] BCC 93; [1993] BCLC ... 315, 317
Swindon Town Football Co. Ltd., Re [1990] BCLC 467 108
Symington v. Symington Quarries Ltd. (1905) 8 F. 121 187

TCB Ltd. v. Gray [1986] Ch. 621; [1986] 2 W.L.R. 517; (1986) 130 S.J. 224; [1986] 1 All E.R. 587; [1986] 3 C.M.L.R. 439; (1986) 83 L.S.Gaz. 520 99
Tansoft Ltd., Re [1991] BCLC 339 316

Tasbian Ltd., Re [1990] BCC 318; [1991] BCLC 54 C.A.; affirming [1989] BCLC 720; *The Daily Telegraph*, May 15, 1989 ... 313
—— (No.3), Re [1992] BCC 358; [1993] BCLC 297, C.A., affirming [1991] BCC 435; [1991] BCLC 729 ... 312
Taylor v. National Union of Mineworkers (Derbyshire Area) [1985] BCLC 237; [1985] I.R.L.R. 99; [1985] I.R.L.R. 65; [1984] I.R.L.R. 440 ... 127
Tett v. Phoenix Property and Investment Co. Ltd. (1986) 2 BCC 19; 1986 PCC 210; (1985) 129 S.J. 869; (1986) 83 L.S.Gaz. 116, C.A. ... 69, 219, 229
Theakston v. London Trust plc [1984] BCLC 390 ... 68
Thorby v. Goldberg (1964) 112 C.L.R. 597 ... 113
Thorne v. Silverleaf [1994] BCC 109 ... 19
Time Utilising Business Systems Ltd., Re (1989) 5 BCC 851; [1990] BCLC 568 ... 328
Tintin Exploration Syndicate Ltd. v. Sandys (1947) 177 L.T. 412; 91 S.J. 599 ... 148
Towers v. African Tug Co. [1904] 1 Ch. 558 ... 155, 222
Trade Auxiliary Company v. Vickers (1873) L.R. 16 Eq. 298 ... 205
Travel Mondial Ltd., Re [1991] BCC 224; [1991] BCLC 120 ... 315
Trevor v. Whitworth (1887) 12 App.Cas. 409, H.L. ... 156
Twycross v. Grant (1877) 2 C.P.D. 469, C.A. ... 31

Underwood Ltd. v. Bank of Liverpool & Martins Ltd. [1924] 1 K.B. 775 ... 16, 95, 185, 186

Verderame v. Commercial Union Assurance Co. plc [1992] BCLC 793; *The Times*, April 2, 1992, C.A. ... 16, 22, 178

Walker v. Wimborne (1976) 50 A.L.J.R. 446 ... 114
Ward (Alexander) & Co. Ltd. v. Samyang Navigation Ltd. [1975] 1 W.L.R. 673; 119 S.J. 319; [1975] 2 All E.R. 424; [1975] 2 Lloyd's Rep. 1, H.L. ... 106
Weiner, Re, Wyner v. Braithwaite [1956] 1 W.L.R. 579; 100 S.J. 400; *sub nom.* Weiner's Will Trusts, Re, Wyner v. Braithwaite [1956] 2 All E.R. 482 ... 245
Welfab Engineers Ltd., Re [1990] BCC 600; [1990] BCLC 833 ... 324
Weller (Sam) and Sons Ltd., Re (1989) 5 BCC 810 ... 155
West Mercia Safetywear Ltd. (Liquidator of) v. Dodd (1988) 4 BCC 30 ... 115
Westminster Fire Office v. Glasgow Provident Investment Society (1888) 13 App.Cas. 699 ... 22
Whaley Bridge Calico Printing Co. v. Green (1880) 5 Q.B.D. 109 ... 31
Whitchurch Insurance Consultants Ltd., Re [1993] BCLC 1359 ... 106
Wilkes (John) (Footwear) Ltd. v. Lee International (Footwear) Ltd. (1985) 1 BCC 99; *The Times*, July 20, 1985, C.A. ... 26
Willcocks (W.R.) & Co. Ltd., Re [1974] Ch. 163; [1973] 3 W.L.R. 669; 117 S.J. 792; [1973] 2 All E.R. 93 ... 192
Willingdale v. Islington Green Investment Co. [1972] 1 W.L.R. 1533; 116 S.J. 885; [1972] 3 All E.R. 849, 48 T.C. 547, C.A.; affirming 115 S.J. 812; [1972] 1 All E.R. 199; [1971] T.R. 271 ... 261

Windward Island Enterprises (UK), Re [1983] BCLC 293 104
Winkworth v. Baron (Edward) Development Co. Ltd. [1986] 1 W.L.R. 1512; [1987] 1 All E.R. 114; [1987] BCLC 193; [1987] 1 F.T.L.R. 176; (1987) 53 P. & C.R. 378; [1987] 1 FLR 525; (1987) 17 Fam.Law. 166; (1986) 130 S.J. 954; (1987) 84 L.S.Gaz. 340, H.L. 114
Woolfson v. Strathclyde Regional Council (1978) 38 P. & C.R. 521; [1979] J.P.L. 169; (1978) 248 E.G. 777; 1978 S.L.T. 159; [1978] S.C. 90, H.L. 16, 23, 24
Worcester Corsetry Ltd. v. Witting [1936] Ch. 640 103
Wragg Ltd., Re [1897] 1 Ch. 796 148

XYZ Ltd., Re (1986) 2 BCC 99; *sub nom.* A Company (No. 004377 of 1986), Re [1987] 1 W.L.R. 102; 1987 PCC 92 .... 199, 235, 236

Yenidje Tobacco Co. Ltd., Re [1916] 2 Ch. 426 ...... 188, 189, 190, 191, 193, 333
Young v. Naval and Military Society [1905] 1 K.B. 687 135

Zemco Ltd. v. Jerrom-Pugh [1993] BCC 275, C.A. 123
Zinotty Properties Ltd., Re [1984] 1 W.L.R. 1249; (1984) 128 S.J. 783; [1984] 3 All E.R. 754; 1985 PCC 285; (1984) 81 L.S.Gaz. 3589 .... 188, 334

TABLE OF STATUTES

1856 Joint Stock Banks Act (19 & 20 Vict., c. 100)—
s. 31 25
1862 Companies Act (25 & 26 Vict., c. 89) 1, 177, 294
1882 Bills of Exchange Act (45 & 46 Vict., c. 61)—
s. 26(1) 27, 28
s. 73 27
1889 Commissioners for Oaths Act (52 & 53 Vict., c. 10)—
s. 6 381
1890 Partnership Act (53 & 54 Vict., c. 39)
s. 33(1) 192
1900 Companies Act (63 & 64 Vict., c. 48) 1
1907 Limited Partnerships Act (7 Edw. 7, c. 24) 3, 4
s. 15 4
Companies Act (7 Edw. 7, c. 50) 1, 2, 3, 9, 14
s. 1(5) 3
s. 21 3
s. 34(4) 2
s. 37 .... 2, 3, 6
1908 Companies (Consolidation) Act (8 Edw. 7, c. 69) 189
s. 26(3) 3
s. 121 2
s. 129 190
1916 Larceny Act (6 & 7 Geo. 5, c. 50)—
s. 20(1)(ii) 181
1929 Companies Act (19 & 20 Geo. 5, c. 23) 4
s. 26 .... 2, 4
s. 110(3) 3
1947 Companies Act (10 & 11 Geo. 6, c. 47)—
s. 35 5
1947 Companies Act—*cont.*
s. 54 4
1948 Companies Act (11 & 12 Geo. 6, c. 38) .. 4, 379
s. 19 298
s. 28 .... 2, 218
s. 30 2
s. 58 156
s. 127 5
s. 129 4
s. 161 5
s. 184 .... 194, 210, 215
s. 190 5
s. 206 301
s. 209 .... 243, 243
s. 210 ... 193, 194, 201, 202, 208, 224
s. 222(*f*) 194
s. 287 224
s. 332 322
s. 454(2) 348
Sched. 1 .... 37, 82, 101, 105
Pt. II, Table A 86, 218
Sched. 7 4
1960 Mental Health (Scotland) Act (8 & 9 Eliz. 2, c. 61) 363
1961 Trustee Investments Act (9 & 10 Eliz. 2, c. 62) 246
1964 Trading Stamps Act (c. 71) 6
1967 Misrepresentation Act (c. 7)—
s. 2(1) 34
Companies Act (c. 81) .. 5
s. 2 5
s. 26(1) 210
s. 43 5
s. 47 5
1968 Theft Act (c. 60)—
s. 1(1) 182
s. 2(1)(*a*) 182
(*b*) 182
s. 3(1) 182
1971 Criminal Damage Act (c. 48)—
s. 1(1) 184

1971 Criminal Damage Act—*cont.*
s. 5(2)(*a*) 184, 185
1972 Land Charges Act (c. 61)—
s. 3(7) 94
European Communities Act (c. 68)—
s. 2(2) 380, 408
s. 9(1) 93, 126
(2) 37, 39
Sched. 2, para. 1(1)(*d*) 389
1973 Matrimonial Causes Act (c. 18) 226
s. 23 226
s. 24 226
s. 24A 226
(1) 226
(2) 226
(*a*) 226
(*b*) 226
1976 Companies Act (c. 69)—
Sched. 3 5
1977 Unfair Contract Terms Act (c. 50)—
s. 6(3) 50
s. 1978 Employment Protection (Consolidation) Act (c. 44)—
s. 54(1) 210
1979 Sale of Goods Act (c. 54)—
s. 14 50
1980 Companies Act (c. 22) ... 2, 6, 7, 8, 11, 12, 14, 105, 142, 152, 156, 216, 218, 219, 227
s. 1 .... 2, 6, 7
(1) 11, 297
(2) 297
s. 2(1) 3
(2) 7
s. 4 8
s. 5 294
s. 6 8
s. 15 8
s. 47 213
s. 63 17
s. 75 ..... 199, 208, 224, 225, 232, 238
s. 78(3) 7
s. 79 9
1980 Companies Act—*cont.*
s. 82 3
s. 85 8
Sched. 4 82
1981 Matrimonial Homes and Property Act (c. 24) 226
Supreme Court Act (c. 54)—
s. 37 204
Companies Act (c. 62) .. 6, 142, 156, 157, 163
ss. 46–47 224
1983 Mental Health Act (c. 20) 363
1984 County Courts Act (c. 28)—
Pt. VI 36
1985 Companies Act (c. 6) ... 9, 51, 80, 81, 82, 83, 85, 90, 100, 102, 143, 146, 152, 178, 271, 284, 285, 286, 292, 340, 349, 379, 380, 384
Pt. V, Chap. VII 335
Pt. XII 407
Pt. XIIIA 242
Pt. XVIII 407
s. 1 176
(1) 3, 43, 178
(3) ... 7, 11, 45, 78, 297
(3A) ... 3, 9, 12, 46, 178
(4) 46, 297
s. 2 .... 45, 46
(1)(*b*) 51
(4) 294, 296
(5)(*a*) 298
s. 3 .... 347, 348, 349, 379
(1) 46, 53
s. 3A 59, 60, 61
s. 4 .... 61, 150
(2) 61
s. 5 61
s. 6(4) 61
s. 7 295
(1) 64, 65
(2) 64
s. 8 .... 347, 348, 349, 379
(2) 65, 348
(4) 65
s. 10 43
(6) 51
s. 12(1) 44
(2) 44

1985 Companies Act—*cont.*
s. 12(3) 43
s. 13 44
s. 14 ..... 54, 68, 128, 136
(1) 64, 75, 76
s. 15 297
(1) 297
(2) 297
s. 24 .. 12, 13, 22, 176, 177, 178, 179
s. 25(1) 7
(2) 46
s. 26 ..... 47, 385
(1) 47
(*a*) 45
(*c*)–(*e*) 407
(*c*) 385
(2) 407
(3) 407
s. 27 7
(4) 47
s. 28 48
(2)–(5) 407
(2) 385
(6) 38, 48
(7) 48, 407
s. 29(1)(*a*) 407
s. 30 ..... 45, 47, 298, 299
(2) 45
(3) 299
(4) 298
(5) 298
(7) 298
s. 31 299
s. 32 48
(5) 48
(6) 48
s. 33 47
s. 34 47
s. 35 ..... 53, 92, 93, 97, 99
(1) 53, 54, 56
(2) 54, 55, 127
(*a*) 92
(3) .. 56, 108, 121, 122, 125, 126, 127
s. 35A 91, 92, 95, 97, 126, 131, 186
(1) 92, 95
(2)(*b*) 92
(*c*) 92
(3) 93
(4) 54, 127, 128
(5) 125
s. 35B 94

1985 Companies Act—*cont.*
s. 36(4) 37
s. 36C(1) 37, 38, 39, 40, 41
(2) 37
s. 37 27
s. 42(1) 52
ss. 49–50 5
s. 49 336
s. 51 ..... 63, 336
s. 52 63
ss. 53–55 5
s. 54 150
(3)–(10) 168
s. 67(3) 30, 31
s. 80 ..... 89, 146
(1) 144
(4) 145
(5) 145
s. 80A 88, 89, 145
(3) 89
(4) 89
s. 81 8
s. 88 148
ss. 89–90 227
ss. 89–96 ..... 216, 240
s. 89 145
s. 90 146
s. 91 ..... 146, 216, 227, 240
s. 92 217
s. 94 ..... 216, 227
s. 95 ..... 85, 146
s. 96(3) 146
s. 99 147
s. 100 147
s. 101 ..... 8, 63, 143
s. 102 147
s. 103 147
ss. 104–110 30
s. 104 147
s. 106 147
ss. 117–118 ..... 8, 63
s. 117 143
s. 118 143
s. 121 75
s. 125(6)(*a*) 81
ss. 135–136 151
ss. 135–138 160
s. 135 150
s. 137 164
s. 142 143
s. 143(1) 149, 157
(3) 149
(*a*) 149

1985 Companies Act—*cont.*
s. 143(3)—*cont.*
(*b*) 150
(*c*) 150
(*d*) 150
s. 144(1) 151
(2) 151
(3) 134, 151
(4) 134
s. 145(1) 151
(2)(*a*) 151
s. 146 151
(1) 149
(*a*) 150
(2) 149, 150
(*b*) 151
(3) 149, 150
(4) 149, 150
s. 147 151
s. 148 151
s. 149 151
s. 150 152
(4) 152
ss. 151–154 174
ss. 151–158 163
s. 151 .... 163, 173
(1) 164, 171
(2) 164, 171
(3) 164, 167
s. 152(1)(*a*) 164
(2) 166
s. 153 .... 115, 173
(1) 164, 172, 173
(*b*) 174
(2) 164, 172, 173
(*a*) 117
(*b*) ... 115, 116, 117, 174
(3) 164
(4) 164
(*b*) 165
(*c*) 169
(5) 165
s. 154 165
(2) 166
ss. 155–158 .... 117, 165, 168, 172
s. 155 85
(1) 166
(2) 166
(3) 166
(4) 167
(5) 167
(6) 166

1985 Companies Act—*cont.*
s. 156(1) 166
(2) 167
(4) 167, 293
(5) 167
(6) 167
(7) 167, 170
s. 157 168
s. 158 168
ss. 159–181 .... 149, 157
s. 159 .... 70, 157
s. 159A 70, 157, 158
s. 160(2) 160
(4) 159
s. 162 .... 70, 158
(2) 158, 159, 160
s. 163(1)(*a*) 158
s. 164 .... 85, 158
(4) 158
s. 165 85
s. 169 159
(2) 159
(5) 159
s. 170(1) 160
(2) 160
s. 171 159
(1) 161
(3)–(5) 293
(3) 160, 335
(4) 161
(5) 161
(6) 161
s. 172 160
s. 173 .... 85, 161
(2) 161
(5) 293
s. 174 161
s. 175 162
(6) 162
s. 176 162
s. 177 163
s. 183(3) 219
(5) 67, 219
(6) 219
s. 221 ... 270, 289, 290, 291, 292
s. 222 270
s. 223(1) 269
s. 226 270
(1) 269
(3) 291
s. 231 291
s. 232 .... 138, 291
s. 233 282

1985 Companies Act—*cont.*
s. 234 272
(*a*) 281
(1)(*b*) 282
ss. 235–237 273
s. 235(2) 289
(3) 289
s. 236 289
(4) 273
s. 237 .... 288, 289
(2) 290
s. 238 .... 285, 287, 289
(1) 90, 274
s. 239 285
s. 240 274
s. 241 274
s. 242 289
s. 242A 274
(2) 275
s. 244(1) 275
(2) 275
s. 245 276
(3)–(5) 286
s. 245A 276
s. 246 .... 6, 284, 290, 291
(1A) 282
(1B) 282
s. 247 6
(3) 269, 276
(5) 291
s. 249A–E 10, 290
s. 249A 273, 284, 290
(1) 290, 292
(2) 291, 292, 293
(3) 290
(4) 291
(6) 291
(7) 291
s. 249B(1) 290, 292
(2) 292
(3) 292
(4) 292
s. 249C 291
(1) 291
s. 249D 291
(3) 291
s. 249E 293
s. 250 .... 284, 286
s. 252 .... 88, 90, 287
s. 253 90
(2) 90
(3)–(5) 90
s. 254 6
s. 263(1) 153

1985 Companies Act—*cont.*
s. 263(2) 152
(3) 153
(5) 153
s. 264 153
s. 275(1) 153
(2) 153
(3) 153
(4) 153
s. 277(1) 155
s. 282 97
(1) 13
s. 283 9
(2) 13
s. 286 9
s. 287(3) 51
(4) 51, 52
(5) 51
s. 289(2) 382
s. 292 102
(3) 13
s. 300 .... 314, 315
ss. 303–304 210
s. 303 .... 71, 72, 103, 194, 213, 214, 215, 249, 334
(1) 213
(2) 87
(5) 103, 214
s. 304 .... 104, 214
s. 309 .... 114, 117
(2) 118
s. 310 .... 131, 134
(3) 18, 135
s. 317 .... 99, 128, 129, 130, 135
(2) 129
(7) 129
(8) 129
(9) 129
s. 318 .... 210, 214
s. 319 .... 85, 100, 213
(2) 213
(4) 213, 214
s. 320 100
s. 322A 97, 125
(1) 96
(2) 96
(3) 96
(4) 96
(5) 96
(6) 96
(7) 97
(8) 97
s. 322B 179

1985 Companies Act—*cont.*
s. 323 133
s. 324 133
s. 325 134
s. 326 134
s. 328 133
ss. 330–346 137
s. 330 .... 141, 170
(2) 137
(3) 171
(*a*) 138
(*b*) 139
(*c*) 139
(4) 139
s. 331(3) 138
(6) 171
(7) 138
s. 332 140
s. 332A 96
s. 333 140
s. 334 138
s. 335 140
s. 336 138
s. 337 .... 85, 139, 140
(4) 139
s. 338(1)–(3) 139
(1)–(4) 140
(6) 138
s. 339 138
(4) 138
s. 341(1) 140
(2) 141
(4) 141
(5) 141
s. 342 141
s. 346 .... 96, 129, 139
s. 348 .... 48, 103, 299
s. 349 .... 49, 299
(1) 25
(4) 25, 27, 49
s. 351 .... 51, 299
(1)(*d*) 299
s. 352A 179
s. 359 .... 220, 221, 249
s. 364 .... 61, 90, 297
ss. 366–383 77
s. 366A 88, 89
s. 367 81
(2) 81
s. 368(4) 103
(8) 104
s. 369(1) 80
(2) 80
(3) 80

1985 Companies Act—*cont.*
s. 369(4) 80, 88, 89, 241
s. 370 80
(1) 80, 105
(3) 104, 105
(4) 80
(6) 70
s. 370A 80, 180
s. 371 .... 72, 81, 105, 106
s. 372(1) 78
(2) 78
(*a*) 78
(*b*) 78
(*c*) 78
s. 376 .... 104, 105
s. 378 .... 99, 241
(3) 80, 88, 89
s. 379 .... 71, 87, 104
s. 379A 10, 28, 88, 90, 145, 287
(1) 88, 89
(2) 88
(3) 88
(4) 88
(5) 88
s. 380 .... 63, 89
(4)(*bb*) 89
s. 381A–C 10
s. 381A 82, 83, 84, 86, 87, 88, 146, 158, 162, 167, 288
(1) 83
(2) 83
(3) 83
(4) 83
(6) 83, 88
s. 381B 84, 86, 288
(1) 83
(2) 84
(3) 84
(4) 84
s. 381C(1) 84, 86
(2) 86
s. 382A 10
(1) 84
(2) 84
(3) 84
s. 383B 180
s. 384 286
s. 384A(2) 287
s. 385 .... 287, 288
s. 385A 287, 288
(5) 287
s. 386 .... 88, 287, 288

1985 Companies Act—*cont.*
s. 388A ... 290
s. 389A(1) ... 288
(2) ... 288
s. 390 ... 84
(1) ... 288
(2) ... 288
s. 390A(3) ... 284
s. 391 ... 289
s. 391A ... 289
(1) ... 87
s. 392 ... 289
s. 392A ... 289
s. 393 ... 287
s. 425 ... 164, 301, 305
ss. 428–430F ... 242
s. 428(1) ... 242
s. 429 ... 242
(2) ... 242
(8) ... 242
s. 430A–C ... 242
s. 430A(1) ... 242
(2) ... 242
s. 430C ... 242
s. 430D ... 242
s. 430E ... 242
s. 432 ... 407
(1) ... 407
(2) ... 407
s. 434 ... 407
ss. 437–439 ... 407
s. 441 ... 407
ss. 447–451 ... 408
s. 447 ... 407
ss. 448–452 ... 407
s. 458 ... 17, 323, 407
ss. 459–461 ... 104, 150, 199, 204, 208, 221, 223, 224, 228, 232, 309, 335
s. 459 ... 43, 103, 105, 106, 112, 120, 128, 154, 155, 193, 196, 199, 200, 202, 203, 204, 205, 225, 226, 231, 233, 234, 235, 236, 239, 247, 248, 250, 297
(1) ... 199
(2) ... 199, 209, 219
s. 461 ... 221, 232, 234, 249
(1) ... 199
(2)(*d*) ... 232, 238
s. 483 ... 332
s. 558(2) ... 331
s. 631 ... 324
s. 680(1A) ... 180

1985 Companies Act—*cont.*
s. 694 ... 407
s. 697(2) ... 408
s. 704(5) ... 408
s. 705(2) ... 408
s. 706 ... 43, 408
s. 707 ... 408
s. 710(1)–(3) ... 408
(5) ... 408
s. 710B ... 51
s. 711 ... 51
s. 711A ... 94
(2) ... 94, 95
s. 714 ... 47
(1) ... 408
s. 717 ... 3
s. 718(2) ... 408
s. 719 ... 117
s. 723A ... 159
s. 725 ... 408
(1) ... 52
s. 727 ... 120, 134, 135, 321
s. 730 ... 408
s. 731 ... 408
s. 732 ... 408
s. 733 ... 408
s. 736 ... 165
s. 736A ... 165
s. 736B ... 165
s. 741 ... 17
(2) ... 213
(3) ... 179
s. 743 ... 165
s. 744 ... 381
Sched. 1 ... 43
Sched. 4 ... 269, 270, 271, 291
Pt. III ... 283
para. 27(3) ... 281
para. 36 ... 283
para. 38 ... 283
para. 39 ... 283
para. 40 ... 279
para. 41 ... 279
para. 42 ... 283
para. 44 ... 279
para. 47 ... 280
para. 48(1) ... 283
(2) ... 280
(4)(*a*) ... 283
(*b*) ... 280
para. 51(2) ... 280
(3) ... 280
para. 53(2) ... 280

1985 Companies Act—*cont.*
Pt. III—*cont.*
para. 53(3) ... 280
para. 54 ... 280
para. 55 ... 281
para. 56 ... 281
para. 58(1) ... 283
(2) ... 283
para. 88 ... 153
para. 89 ... 153, 154
Sched. 5
paras. 7–0A ... 291
para. 13(1) ... 291
(3)–(4) ... 291
Sched. 6 ... 138, 291
Pt. I ... 284
para. 1(3) ... 281
paras. 2–5 ... 281
para. 7 ... 281
Sched. 7 ... 272
Pts. I–V ... 273
para. 1(1) ... 282
(2) ... 282
para. 5A ... 135, 282
para. 6 ... 282
para. 10 ... 282
Sched. 8 ... 285
Pt. I ... 277
s. A ... 277, 279
Pt. II ... 277, 281
Pt. III ... 6
s. A
para. 17 ... 277, 283
para. 18 ... 283
para. 19 ... 283
para. 20 ... 283
s. C
para. 24 ... 284
Sched. 15A ... 84
Pt. I ... 87
Pt. II ... 85, 146, 167, 168
para. 2(2) ... 85
para. 5 ... 159, 162
para. 8 ... 139
Sched. 15B ... 85
Sched. 24 ... 408
Business Names Act (c. 7) ... 49, 339, 388
s. 1 ... 49
s. 2 ... 49
s. 4 ... 49
s. 5 ... 50
s. 7 ... 49

1985 Company Securities (Insider Dealing) Act (c. 8) ... 131
Companies Consolidation (Consequential Provisions) Act (c. 9) ... 294
s. 10 ... 297
s. 14 ... 72, 213, 214
Insolvency Act (c. 65) ... 300, 311, 318
Bankruptcy (Scotland) Act (c. 66) ... 383
1986 Insolvency Act (c. 45) .. 9, 31, 51, 178, 300, 301, 305, 324, 381
Pt. III ... 344, 389
Pt. V ... 344, 383, 389, 408
Pt. XIII ... 331
ss. 1–7 ... 164, 301
s. 1 ... 302
s. 2 ... 302
s. 3(1) ... 302
(2) ... 302
s. 4 ... 303
s. 5 ... 303
s. 6 ... 304
s. 7 ... 304
ss. 8–27 ... 14, 304
s. 8 ... 305
(3) ... 305
(*a*) ... 305
(*b*) ... 305
(*d*) ... 305
s. 9 ... 306
(4) ... 313
s. 10 ... 306
(1)(*b*) ... 307
(*c*) ... 307
s. 11 ... 306, 307
(3)(*c*) ... 307
(*d*) ... 307
s. 14 ... 308
s. 15 ... 308
s. 17 ... 307
s. 19(4) ... 310
(5) ... 310
(6) ... 310
(7)–(10) ... 310
s. 22 ... 31, 35
s. 23 ... 308
s. 24 ... 308
s. 25 ... 308
s. 27 ... 309

1986 Insolvency Act—*cont.*
s. 47 ..... 31, 35
s. 74 ..... 62, 296
(2)(*a*) 336
(*c*) 336
(3) 295
s. 76 335
s. 77(2) 336
(3) 336
(4) 336
s. 78 336
s. 95 ..... 331, 332
s. 96 ..... 331, 332
s. 98 331
(1) 331
s. 99 331
s. 100 332
s. 101 332
s. 102 332
s. 110 164
s. 114 330
(4) 331
s. 116(7) 331
s. 120 389
s. 122 ..... 103, 330
(1) 333
(*e*) 176
(*f*) 332
(*g*) 62, 155, 180, 190, 194, 196, 198, 203, 221, 235, 330, 332
s. 123 ..... 305, 325, 327, 332
s. 124(2) 335
(3) 335
s. 125(2) 198, 334
s. 131 ..... 31, 35
s. 166 331
s. 212 ..... 17, 31, 34, 122, 170, 323, 324, 331
s. 213 ..... 17, 22, 322, 323
s. 214 ..... 17, 18, 22, 120, 318, 320, 321
(1) 318
(2) 17
(*a*) 319
(*b*) 17, 319
(3) 17, 319, 320
(4) 18, 119, 319, 320
ss. 216–217 ..... 22, 36
s. 216 ..... 19, 31
(4) 19
s. 217 19
(1)(*b*) 19

1986 Insolvency Act—*cont.*
s. 221(1) 383
s. 235 35
s. 238 ..... 126, 306, 324
s. 239 ..... 126, 326, 327
s. 240 ..... 306, 325, 326
(3)(*a*) 325, 326
s. 241 ..... 325, 326
(2) 326
(2A) 326
(3) 326
(3A) 326
(3B) 326
(3C) 326
s. 245 ..... 306, 328
(2) 328
(6) 328
s. 248 307
s. 249 325
s. 251 ..... 17, 318
s. 423 313
s. 435 325
Sched. 1 308
Sched. II
para. 1 310
Company Directors Disqualification Act (c. 46) . 18, 19, 35, 344, 389
s. 1 ..... 311, 389
(1) 35
s. 2) 19, 35, 389
(3) 35
s. 3 ..... 19, 35
(2) 35
ss. 4–11 389
s. 4 ..... 19, 36
s. 5 ..... 19, 35
s. 6 ..... 19, 36, 313, 314
(1) 311
(2) 313
(3) 311
s. 7 312
(2) 312, 313
s. 8 ..... 19, 36, 317
s. 9 309
s. 10 ... 18, 19, 36, 309, 323
s. 11 36
s. 12 36
(2) 389
s. 13 ..... 19, 315
s. 14 19
ss. 15–17 389
s. 15 ..... 19, 22
(3) 19

1986 Company Director Disqualification Act —*cont.*
s. 16(1) 313
s. 20 389
s. 22 389
(2)(*b*) 389
(4) 311
(5) 312
Sched. 1 389
Pt. I 313, 314
Pt. II 313, 314
Financial Services Act (c. 60) 30, 144, 290
Pt. I
Chap. III 144
Chap. V 144
s. 57 144
s. 143 143
(3) 2, 8
s. 150(6) 30
ss. 170–171 8
s. 170 .... 2, 8
(1) 143
(2) 144
(3) 144
(4) 144
s. 171(1) 144
(2) 144
(3) 144
(6) 144
s. 172 242
s. 196(2) 165
Sched. 12 242
Sched. 16
para. 17 158
Sched. 17
Pt. I 8
1987 Finance (No. 2) Act (c. 51) 252
1988 Income and Corporation Taxes Act (c. 1)—
Pt. XI
Chap. III 263
s. 13 251
s. 13A 264
s. 145 262
ss. 154–165 262
ss. 209–211 256
s. 210(1) 256
(2) 257
(3) 257
s. 219 .... 257, 258
1988 Income and Corporation Taxes Act —*cont.*
s. 220 258
s. 221 258
s. 225 258
s. 226 258
ss. 238–312 264
s. 239(3) 255
s. 240 255
s. 241 254
s. 245(4) 255
s. 254(1) 256
ss. 289–312 268
s. 289(2) 265
(6) 265
(7) 265
s. 289A(1) 266
(2) 266
(5) 266
(6)–(8) 267
s. 290(2) 266
s. 291 265
(1) 266
s. 291A 265
(3) 266
(4) 266
(5) 266
s. 291B 265
s. 293(1) 265
(2) 265
ss. 294–298 265
s. 299 268
(A) 265
s. 306(1) 266
(6) 266
ss. 414–430 251
s. 414 259
(5) 260
s. 415 .... 259, 260
s. 416(2) 260
s. 417(1) 260
(3) 261
(5) 261
(7) 261
s. 418 262
s. 419 263
(2) 262
s. 420 263
s. 574 268
s. 704(D) 257
1989 Finance Act (c. 26) 263
s. 103 263
s. 105 263

1989 Companies Act (c. 40) ... 6, 10, 25, 52, 53, 59, 61, 77, 80, 82, 83, 90, 91, 93, 104, 125
Pt. II ... 5
s. 6 ... 138
s. 16 ... 88, 90
s. 17 ... 6
s. 27 ... 291
s. 100(2) ... 61
s. 108 ... 53, 56, 108, 121, 186
(1) ... 92, 94
s. 109 ... 96
s. 110 ... 59
s. 111 ... 62, 97
ss. 113–114 ... 168
ss. 113–117 ... 10
s. 113 ... 82, 88, 146, 162
s. 114 ... 84, 139, 146, 159, 162, 213
(1) ... 85
(2) ... 85
s. 115 ... 145
(1) ... 89
(3) ... 89, 241
s. 116 ... 87
(3) ... 89
s. 117 ... 90
(1) ... 90
(4) ... 90
(5) ... 90
s. 119 ... 88
s. 120 ... 84
s. 128 ... 189
s. 130 ... 37
s. 132 ... 165
s. 133 ... 70, 157, 158
(4) ... 158
s. 136 ... 51, 52
s. 137 ... 18, 135
s. 138 ... 138, 140
s. 139 ... 61, 90
s. 142 ... 94
s. 143(1) ... 159
(2) ... 159
(3) ... 162
s. 144 ... 165
s. 199 ... 144

1989 Companies Act—*cont.*
s. 212 ... 210
Sched. 10
Pt. I
para. 10 ... 140
Sched. 18
para. 33(3) ... 165
Sched. 19
para. 9 ... 104
para. 11 ... 155
Sched. 24 ... 210
1992 Tax on Capital Gains Act ... 252
s. 150 ... 264, 268
s. 150A ... 264, 268
(1) ... 268
(2) ... 267
(3) ... 267
s. 231 ... 268
Trade Union and Labour Relations (Consolidation) Act (c. 52)—
s. 117(1) ... 290
s. 122 ... 290
1993 Charities Act (c. 10)—
s. 64(1) ... 62
(2) ... 62
s. 65 ... 97
(1) ... 97
(2) ... 97
(3) ... 97
(4) ... 97
s. 68 ... 25
Criminal Justice Act (c. 36)—
Pt. V ... 131
Welsh Language Act (c. 38)—
s. 30(6) ... 51
1994 Insolvency Act (c. 7) ... 310
Finance Act (c. 9) ... 252, 253
s. 86(1) ... 252, 253
(2) ... 252
(3) ... 253
s. 137 ... 264
Sched. 15 ... 264
Insolvency (No. 2) Act (c. 12) ... 326

TABLE OF STATUTORY INSTRUMENTS

1981 Company and Business Names Regulations (S.I. 1981 No. 1685) ... 47, 49
1982 Company and Business Names (Amendments) Regulations (S.I. 1982 No. 1653) ... 47, 49
1984 Companies (Alteration of Table A, etc.) Regulations (S.I. 1984 No. 1717) . 65, 378
Table A
reg. 33 ... 379
reg. 65 ... 379
reg. 87 ... 379
reg. 90 ... 379
1985 Companies (Tables A–F) Regulations (S.I. 1985 No. 805) ... 37, 46, 65, 69, 347, 348
reg. 1 ... 348
reg. 2 ... 348
reg. 30 ... 13
reg. 64 ... 13
reg. 80 ... 37
Tables A–F ... 347, 348, 379
Table A ... 65, 82, 101, 130, 348, **349**
Pt. I ... 65
Pt. II ... 65, 66
reg. 1 ... 373
regs. 2–35 ... 372
reg. 2 ... 69, 72
reg. 3 ... 377
reg. 8 ... 152
reg. 24 ... 66
reg. 25 ... 67
reg. 32 ... 377
reg. 34 ... 377
reg. 35 ... 70, 158, 161, 377
reg. 37 ... 103, 104, 105
reg. 38 ... 373, 377
reg. 40 ... 81
reg. 46(d) ... 373
1985 Table A—*cont.*
reg. 49 ... 105
reg. 53 .. 79, 85, 86, 87, 241
reg. 54 ... 81, 82, 372
reg. 55 ... 372
reg. 57 ... 372
reg. 59 ... 372
reg. 70 ... 101, 102
reg. 72 ... 101
reg. 73 ... 71, 102
reg. 74 ... 71
reg. 78 ... 102
reg. 79 ... 102, 103
reg. 80 ... 101, 102
reg. 82 ... 135
reg. 83 ... 135, 374
reg. 84 ... 102, 136
reg. 85 ... 130
reg. 88 ... 98
reg. 89 ... 98
reg. 90 ... 98
reg. 93 ... 99
reg. 94 ... 130, 135
reg. 94(c) ... 374
reg. 95 ... 130, 135
reg. 100 ... 374
regs. 102–108 ... 372
reg. 110 ... 372
reg. 111 ... 379
reg. 112 ... 374, 379
reg. 113 ... 374
reg. 114 ... 372
reg. 116 ... 372, 379
reg. 117 ... 372
Table B ... 46, 52, 57, **371**
Table C ... 46, 65, 295, **372**
reg. 1 ... 379
reg. 10 ... 379
reg. 12 ... 379
Table D ... 65
Pt. I ... **374**
Pt. II ... 46, 375
Pt. III ... **376**
Table E ... 46, 65, **376**
Table F ... 53, **378**
S.I. 1985 No. 1052 ... 348, 349, 350, 370

1986 Insolvency Rules (S.I. 1986 No. 1925)—
r. 1.17(3) ... 303
(6) ... 303
(7) ... 303
r. 2.2 ... 310
r. 2.7(1) ... 306
r. 5.17(6) ... 303
r. 12.9 ... 306
Insolvent Partnerships Order (S.I. 1986 No. 2142)—
art. 13(1) ... 383
Companies (Northern Ireland) Order (S.I. 1986 No. 1032)—
art. 131 ... 75
1989 County Court (Amendment) Rules (S.I. 1989 No. 236) ... 52
European Economic Interest Grouping Regulations (S.I. 1989 No. 638) ... 338, **380**
reg. 3 ... 340
reg. 5(1) ... 341
reg. 5(2) ... 341
reg. 8 ... 344
reg. 8(2) ... 344
reg. 9(1) ... 380
reg. 9(5) ... 381
reg. 9(7) ... 340
reg. 9(8) ... 339
reg. 9(10) ... 339
reg. 10 ... 339
reg. 11 ... 340, 381
reg. 12 ... 342
(1) ... 380
reg. 13 ... 340, 342
reg. 13(1) ... 382
reg. 15(1) ... 382
reg. 16 ... 340
reg. 17 ... 339
reg. 18 ... 340
reg. 19 ... 344
reg. 20 ... 344
Sched. 1 ... 380, **390**
Sched. 2 ... 381, 406
Sched. 3 ... 385, **406**
Sched. 4 ... 340, **407**
reg. 18 ... 385, 386, 407
1990 (S.I. 1990 No. 1393) ... 100, 140
1991 (S.I. 1991 No. 1206) ... 43
Companies (Inspection and Copying of Registers, Indices and Documents) Regulations (S.I. 1991 No. 1998) ... 159
1992 Company and Business Names (Amendment) Regulations (S.I. 1992 No. 1196) ... 47, 49
Companies (Single Member Private Limited Companies) Regulations (S.I. 1992 No. 1699) ... 3, 9, 12, 13, 46, 80, 176 *et seq.*, 330
reg. 2(1) ... 12, 176, 178
reg. 3 ... 13
Companies Act 1985 (Accounts of Small and Medium-Sized Enterprises and Publication of Accounts in ECUs) Regulations (S.I. 1992 No. 2452) .. 6, 269, 277, 279, 281, 285
1994 Companies (Welsh Language Forms and Documents) Regulations (S.I. 1994 No. 117) ... 51
Companies (Welsh Language Forms and Documents) (Amendment) Regulations (S.I. 1994 No. 727) ... 51
Companies Act 1985 (Audit Exemption) Regulations (S.I. 1994 No. 1935) ... 10, 286, 290, 293

TABLE OF EUROPEAN MATERIALS

EEC Treaty

1957 Rome Treaty Establishing the European Economic Community ("The EEC Treaty") March 25; 298 U.N.T.S. 11—
Art. 58 .... 393, 396
Art. 169 405
Art. 170 405
Art. 235 390

E.C. Regulations

Reg. 1985/2137 ([1985] O.J. L199) 338, 380
Arts. 1–38 381
Art. 1 .... 380, 408
(2) 340, 404
(3) 340, 381
Art. 2 .... 382, 397
(1) 340
Art. 3 403
(1) 338
(2) 338
Art. 4(1) 402
(2) 403
(4) 405
Art. 5 .... 339, 384, 386, 395
(c) 400
Art. 6 .... 339, 341, 342, 392, 394, 396, 397, 399, 401, 404, 405
Art. 7 .... 339, 340, 342, 387, 397, 402, 403, 404, 405
(b)–(j) 388, 395
(b) 342
(d) 341, 399
Art. 8 .... 397, 400, 401, 402, 403, 404, 405
(a) 388
(b) 388
(c) 405
Art. 9(1) 397, 398, 400, 401
Art. 10 .... 342, 386, 401, 404, 405
Art. 11 .... 388, 405
Art. 12 .... 339, 403
Art. 14 382

Reg. 1985/2137 ([1985] O.J. L199)—*cont.*
Art. 14(1) 385, 395
(4) 382, 385
Art. 15 .... 395, 401
Art. 16(1) 340
(2) 341
Art. 17(1) 341
(2) 341
(3) 341
(4) 341
Art. 19(1) 341
(2) 341, 382
(3) 341
Art. 20 342
(1) 342
(2) 342
Art. 21(1) 343
(2) 343
Art. 22(1) 344, 395, 402, 403
(2) 344
Art. 23 339
Art. 24 .... 343, 401, 403
(1) 343
(2) 343
Art. 25 .... 340, 388, 405
(d) 342
Art. 26(1) 343
(2) 343, 395
Art. 27(1) 344
(2) 344
Art. 28(1) 282
(2) 402
Art. 31 .... 344, 395, 401, 409

E.C. Regulations—*cont.*

Reg. 1985/2137 ([1985] O.J. L199)—*cont.*
Art. 31(3) 403
Art. 32 .... 344, 395, 401, 409
(1) 383
(3) 383
Art. 33 344
Art. 34 343
Art. 35 .... 383, 395, 398, 408
(1) 344
(2) 344, 395

Reg. 1985/2137 ([1985] O.J. L199)—*cont.*
Art. 36 .... 383, 401, 408
Art. 37(1) 343, 403
(2) 343
Art. 38 383
Art. 39 .... 384, 395
(1) 394, 396
Art. 39 406
Art. 41 406
Art. 42 406
Art. 40 344

E.C. Directives

Council Directive 68/151 40
Art. 3(5) 396
Art. 3(7) 396
Art. 7 38

Council Directive 77/91 [1977] O.J. L26/1 .... 7, 142
Art. 23 .... 174, 175
Directive 89/667 [1989] O.J. L395 .... 9, 176

Chapter 1

HISTORY AND DEVELOPMENT OF THE PRIVATE COMPANY

A. The pre-statutory private company

Although the modern concept of the private company is purely statutory, having its origin in the Companies Act 1907, below, the term "private company" was in frequent use for some considerable time prior to that Act. Examples of such pre-1907 usages can be seen in the judgments of Cotton L.J. in *Re British Seamless Paper Box Co.*[1] and of Vaughan Williams J. in *Broderip v. Salomon.*[2]

However, when the term "private company" was used prior to 1907 it was merely as a convenient expression to describe a company which raised its capital privately and eschewed any invitation to the public to invest in its shares or debentures, any such abstention from calling for public investment being purely voluntary. No statutory dichotomy between public and private companies existed before 1907 so that *all* companies registered with limited liability under the earlier company legislation[3] were subject to the same rights and obligations, including the right to invite the public to invest in the company, and the obligations to have at least seven members and, from 1900, to produce audited accounts.[4]

B. The Companies Act 1907

1. *The statutory genesis of the private company*

The English and Welsh private company, as a statutory concept, emanates from the Companies Act 1907.[5] The

---

[1] (1881) 17 Ch.D. 467 at 479; see also Jessel M.R., *ibid.* at 473.

[2] [1895] 2 Ch. 323 at 329. See also Lord Macnaghten in *Salomon v. Salomon & Co. Ltd.* [1897] A.C. 22 at 52: see Chap. 3, p. 21, *post*.

[3] The Companies Acts 1862–1900

[4] For subsequent developments in these matters, see this chapter, *post.*

[5] Royal Assent on August 28, 1907. The introduction of the statutory concept of the private company followed the recommendations of the Loreburn Commission Report 1906. For the influence of Sir Francis Palmer in establishing this concept of the private company see Preface to *Palmer's Company Law* (Sweet & Maxwell, 24th ed., 1987) "A Biographical Note".

definition of a private company was set out in section 37 of the 1907 Act.[6] This provision states that:

> (1) "For the purposes of this Act the expression 'private company' means a company which by its articles—
>
> (a) restricts the right to transfer its shares; and
> (b) limits the number of its members (exclusive of persons who are in the employment of the company) to fifty: and
> (c) prohibits any invitation to the public to subscribe for any shares or debentures of the company.
>
> (2) ...
> (3) Where two or more persons hold one or more shares in a company jointly they shall, for the purposes of this section, be treated as a single member."

With certain modifications[7] this definition remained applicable until 1980.[8]

2. *Concessions to the private company*

As well as defining the expression "private company"[9] the Companies Act 1907 made certain important concessions concerning the operation of private companies. Thus, section 34(4) of the 1907 Act provided that the minimum number of members needed to form a private company should be two as against a minimum of seven members in the case of a public

---

[6] This legislation was repeated in s. 121 of the Companies (Consolidation) Act 1908.

[7] See s. 26 C.A. 1929 and s. 28 C.A. 1948.

[8] See s. 1 C.A. 1980, p. 7, *post.*

[9] Compliance with the statutory definition of private companies prior to the C.A. 1980 (see p. 7, *post.*) considerably limited the growth potential of these companies. However, such companies automatically became public companies and so free from these self-imposed statutory shackles if they altered their articles so that they fell outside the definition. In this event, however, certain statutory obligations arose (see, *e.g.* s. 30 C.A. 1948, concerning statements in lieu of prospectus) which are now obsolete. A private company must, generally, still not invite the public to invest in it: see s. 170 of the Financial Services Act 1986. See also s. 143(3) F.S.A. 1986, banning applications for listing by private companies. See Chap. 9, *post.* For current position regarding restrictions on transfers see Chaps. 6 and 13, *post.*

company.[10] Further, by section 1(5) of the Companies Act 1907, private companies were relieved of the obligation, to which public companies were subject, of filing a statement in lieu of prospectus where, broadly, on a first allotment of shares or debentures, on formation, a prospectus was not issued.[11]

However, without doubt the most significant concession made to the private company[12] was the dispensation granted by section 21 of the Companies Act 1907[13] from the statutory requirement then imposed on other registered companies, to file an annual balance sheet with the Registrar of Companies. Thus private companies were permitted to keep their financial affairs secret in the same way as sole traders and partnerships. No doubt these relaxations were warmly welcomed by the business community of the day and must certainly have given added impetus to the use of private companies by the proprietors of small and medium-sized businesses.

3. *Unexpected potential of the private company concept*

In a somewhat unobtrusive manner, as has been described above, the private company made its statutory appearance. Indeed, although the legislature certainly intended the private company to be a vehicle for the operation of small and medium-sized businesses, it does seem highly unlikely that when it passed the Companies Act 1907[14] it realised the full potential of its new creation. At any rate this view appears to be strongly reinforced by the fact that in 1907 the Limited Partnerships Act was also introduced.[15]

---

[10] Under s. 2(1) C.A. 1980 the number of members needed to form a public company was also reduced to two. This remains the position for a public company, but the number of members needed to form a private company limited by shares or by guarantee has been reduced to one: s. 1(1), (3A) C.A. 1985, the latter subsection having been inserted by the Companies (Single Member Private Limited Companies) Regulations 1992 (S.I. 1992 No. 1699). See p. 9 and Chap. 11, *post*.

[11] The requirement for statements in lieu of prospectus in respect of public companies was abolished by s. 82 C.A. 1980.

[12] A concession which, subject to some important changes, continued until 1967, see p. 5, *post*.

[13] See also s. 26(3) of the Companies (Consolidation) Act 1908 and s. 110(3) C.A. 1929.

[14] August 28, 1907: see p. 1, *ante*. Most provisions of the 1907 Act including s. 37, p. 2, *ante*, became operative from July 1, 1908.

[15] The Limited Partnerships Act was introduced on August 28, 1907. It became operative on January 1, 1908 and remains in force substantially in its original form; see also s. 717 C.A. 1985.

The Limited Partnerships Act provides for the registration[16] of a species of partnership in which partners can limit their liability to the capital they contribute, provided they do not participate in the management of the firm and provided also there is at least one "general partner" with unlimited liability. Such limited partnerships were clearly also intended by the legislature to be vehicles for conducting small business enterprises. However, in view of the advantages which the private limited company affords to businessmen and which are not provided by the partnership concept,[17] it is hardly surprising that the limited partnership has never achieved a high level of popularity in the business world.[18]

C. Post-war developments

1. *Exempt private companies*

Although the Companies Act 1929 made certain minor modifications to the definition of a private company[19] and also provided that all companies, *other than private companies,* must have at least two directors, the next major development[20] concerning private companies was the introduction of the concept of the "exempt private company" by section 54 of the Companies Act 1947. This was replaced as from July 1, 1948, by the Companies Act 1948.[21]

In effect, the purpose of the introduction of the exempt private company was to narrow the range of private companies which were exempted from filing their annual balance sheets with the Registrar of Companies.

Broadly speaking, to be so "exempt" none of a private company's shares or debentures could be held by a public company.[22]

---

[16] With the Registrar of Companies: see s. 15 of the Limited Partnerships Act 1907.
[17] See Chap. 3, *post.*
[18] 1,737 limited partnerships were registered as at March 31, 1993: *Companies in 1992–93* (HMSO).
[19] See s. 26
[20] Albeit of a limited duration; see p. 5, *post.*
[21] See s. 129 and Sched. 7 C.A. 1948.
[22] This is a simplification of the situation but in general terms an exempt private company was a private company *simpliciter* whereas a non-exempt private company was a subsidiary or associate of a public company.

Another concession made to exempt private companies was that the auditors of such bodies did not need to hold the professional accountancy qualifications referred to in section 161 of the 1948 Act for the auditors of other companies.[23] Another feature of the exempt private company was its right to make loans to its directors, under section 190 of the Companies Act 1948, replacing section 35 of the Companies Act 1947.[24]

2. *Demise of the exempt private company*

Despite vehement protests from the business community the concept of the exempt private company was extinguished by the Companies Act 1967.[25] The legislature did, however, accept that the facility of maintaining financial confidentiality could be retained by those companies which regarded this as being of paramount importance to their business interests, provided such facility was not enjoyed under the umbrella of limited liability. Accordingly, by section 43 of the Companies Act 1967, limited companies were allowed to reregister as *unlimited* provided certain prescribed conditions were met, including the obtaining of the unanimous assent of the members to such reregistration and the making of a statutory declaration by the directors that such unanimous assent had been obtained.[26]

By section 47 of the Companies Act 1967 the unlimited company was excused from the requirement of all other registered companies of filing its annual accounts, directors' reports and auditors' reports with its annual return,[27] provided that such unlimited company was not, during the appropriate accounting reference period, a subsidiary, holding or other

---

[23] This concession ended on the abolition of the exempt private company by the C.A. 1967. The position now is that all registered companies which are subject to statutory audit must have auditors who are statutorily qualified or, if appropriate, authorised: see now, in particular, Pt. II C.A. 1989. For those companies exempt from audit requirements see Chap. 18, *post*.

[24] For the current position concerning loans by a private company to its directors, see Chap. 8, *post*.

[25] See s. 2.

[26] For the current position as to a *private* limited company reregistering as unlimited see ss. 49–50 C.A. 1985, Chap. 5, *post*. A public company cannot, since 1980, be directly registered as unlimited; it would first have to reregister as private: ss. 53–55 C.A. 1985. On March 31, 1993 there were some 3,800 unlimited companies on the Register: *Companies in 1992–93* (HMSO).

[27] Sched. 3 C.A. 1976, by repealing s. 127 C.A. 1948, permitted accounts and reports to be submitted separately from the annual return. However, it will still usually be more convenient for limited companies to register all the documents together.

specified connected company of a limited company and provided also that during this period it had not been in business as promoter of a trading stamp scheme for the purposes of the Trading Stamps Act 1964.[28]

Thus, in abolishing the status of exempt private company (and the introduction of that status had itself amounted to a substantial diminution of the concessions previously enjoyed by private companies as a class: see *ante*), the legislature was insisting that those who wished to avail themselves of the privilege of trading with limited liability must be prepared, as *quid pro quo*, to make available the financial affairs of their corporate trading vehicles for public scrutiny. This broadly remains the current position although certain modest concessions have subsequently been made in this regard, in that "small" and "medium" sized private companies may file "modified" accounts.[29]

D. The contemporary status of private companies

1. *Reclassification of companies*

Prior to the Companies Act 1980 the dichotomy between public and private companies rested on a somewhat illogical foundation, *i.e.* upon registration *all* companies became public companies unless certain provisions were contained in the documents submitted for registration.[30] Clearly, since the vast majority of registered companies are intended by their promoters to be private companies and, in any event, since most public companies start their lives as private companies, it would seem eminently appropriate for all newly registered companies to be *private* unless and until further steps are taken to render them public companies. This, indeed, was the rationale of section 1 of the Companies Act 1980, which required a public company to proclaim itself as such in its memorandum of

---

[28] See now s. 254 C.A. 1985 inserted by s. 17 C.A. 1989.

[29] A concession introduced by the C.A. 1981 and subsequently amended by the C.A. 1989, the relevant provisions now being ss. 246 and 247 C.A. 1985 as amended, and Sched. 8, Pt. III C.A. 1985 as inserted, by the Companies Act 1985 (Accounts of Small and Medium-Sized Enterprises and Publication of Accounts in ECUs) Regulations 1992 (S.I. 1992 No. 2452): see Chap. 17, *post*.

[30] The original definition of a private company, in s. 37 C.A. 1907, p. 2, *ante*, was perpetuated with only slight change until the 1980 Act.

association and which also called for a public company to fulfil certain other requirements.[31] Section 1 of the 1980 Act provided a very simple definition of a private company:

> " 'private company', unless the context otherwise requires, means a company that is not a public company".[32]

2. *The "Ltd."/"plc" dichotomy: a visible indicator*

As a very useful innovation, section 2(2) of the Companies Act 1980[33] prescribed that public companies must add after their names the words "public limited company" or the abbreviated alternative, "plc": section 78(3) of the 1980 Act, now section 27 of the Companies Act 1985. Thus, whereas before 1980 all registered limited companies had to include the word "limited," or abbreviations thereof, as the last word of their names, now this single word (or its abbreviation) can only be used by private limited companies.[34] Accordingly, by a glance at a company letterhead or other documentation a person dealing with a company will now know whether he is dealing with a public or private company. Of course a private company may, nevertheless, be a subsidiary of a public company.

3. *Lifting the membership ceiling*

Whereas before 1980 private companies were statutorily required to limit to 50 their membership number (excluding employees or ex-employees who were members), and to set out this limitation in their articles, no such ceiling was imposed by the new régime for private companies introduced by the Companies Act 1980. This policy of unrestricted membership has been continued by the subsequent legislation. However, private companies must still not invite the public to subscribe for their shares or debentures. Nevertheless, although this prohibition on inviting public investment in private companies effectively continues the policy of the previous legislation, it

---

[31] It was in particular required to register or reregister as a public company.

[32] See now s. 1(3) C.A. 1985 and Chap. 2, *post*. This change in the basis of definition was made in order to comply with the 2nd E.C. Directive 77/91 on Company Law: [1977] O.J. L 26/1.

[33] See now s. 25(1) C.A. 1985.

[34] Since 1980 the Welsh equivalents of the terms have been permitted.

does so in a somewhat different manner. Before the Companies Act 1980 a private company, as an essential requirement to holding that status, had, by its articles, to preclude itself from inviting the public to subscribe for its shares or debentures. The change brought about by section 15 of the Companies Act 1980[35] was that it was now made a criminal offence for a private company (other than a company limited by guarantee and not having a share capital) to offer, allot or agree to allot any of its shares or debentures for public sale purposes.

The position is now covered by section 143(3) and sections 170–171 of the Financial Services Act 1986, as amended.[36] By section 170 of the Financial Services Act 1986 the Secretary of State may, by order, permit private companies to advertise their securities on prescribed conditions, in particular, where such advertisements are of a "private character".

4. *No minimum capital requirement for private companies*

It is appropriate to note at this point that by sections 4, 6 and 85 of the Companies Act 1980 the legislature for the first time required[37] a minimum, albeit somewhat modest, share capital in respect of *public companies*. Thus, section 4 of the 1980 Act declared that a company registered as a public company on its original incorporation must not participate in business or exercice any borrowing powers unless either it reregisters as private or unless the Registrar of Companies certifies, on receipt of a statutory declaration in the prescribed form and signed by a director or secretary of the company, that, *inter alia*, the nominal value of the company's allotted share capital is not less than the "authorised minimum", *i.e.* "£50,000, or such other sum as the Secretary of State may by order made by statutory instrument specify instead".[38]

Clearly, for public companies this mimimum capital requirement is unlikely to give rise to any appreciable problem. Had this provision been extended to private companies, it would

---

[35] Re-enacted by s. 81 C.A. 1985 which itself has now been repealed by the Financial Services Act 1986, Sched. 17, Pt. I.

[36] See Chap. 9, *post.*

[37] This was in compliance with the E.C.'s company law harmonisation programme.

[38] s. 85 C.A. 1980. See now ss. 117–118 C.A. 1985. Further, by what is now s. 101 C.A. 1985, *public companies* must not allot shares except in so far as they are paid up as to at least one-quarter of their nominal value and as to the whole of any premium. See Chap. 9, *post.*

probably have precluded their use as business vehicles for a great many small entrepreneurs. In the event, however, no such statutory mimimum capital requirement has been prescribed for private companies.[39]

5. *Secretaries of private companies*

A further distinction between private companies and public companies was introduced by section 79 of the Companies Act 1980. By this provision, prescribed qualifications were laid down in respect of the office of company secretary of *public* companies.[40] No particular qualifications were prescribed for secretaries of private companies.[41] This is not to say, of course, that the directors of a private company when appointing the secretary can afford to do so without giving a great deal of thought as to the suitability of the person appointed. Clearly, in view of the onerous statutory and other duties imposed on the secretaries of all registered companies, great care should be taken in making such an appointment.

6. *Single-member companies*

As has been seen, the mimimum number of members needed to form a private company was set at two by the Companies Act 1907. This remained the position until 1992 when The Companies (Single Member Private Limited Companies) Regulations[42] came into force,[43] enabling a private company limited by shares or by guarantee to be formed by one person[44] and to have one member. The Regulations and the further amendments which they effect to the Companies Act 1985 and the Insolvency Act 1986 are considered in more detail in Chapter 11, *post*, and, as appropriate, throughout the text.

---

[39] Of course, sufficient capital should be raised to ensure the company's viability, but share capital may be supplemented by loan capital.

[40] See now s. 286 C.A. 1985. A fair amount of discretion is still, however, given to directors to appoint persons not possessing one of the professional qualifications specifically mentioned but they must be satisfied of the appointee's capability to do the job.

[41] Every registered company must have a secretary; in addition, a sole director must not also be the secretary: see s. 283 C.A. 1985.

[42] (S.I. 1992 No. 1699) in compliance with the 12th E.C. Directive 89/667 on Single-member Companies: [1989] O.J. L395.

[43] On July 15, 1992.

[44] s. 1(3A) C.A. 1985 inserted by S.I. 1992 No. 1699.

7. *Moves towards deregulation*

Although, as will be discussed in this work, certain legislative concessions have been granted to private companies, much of the burgeoning companies legislation applies equally to private as to public companies. An increasing recognition in recent years of the need to free private companies of some of their statutory burdens led to the first steps towards deregulation in the Companies Act 1989. The Act introduced important provisions enabling voting members of a private company, by unanimous agreement, to pass written resolutions without the need for a general meeting[45] and to elect to dispense with certain requirements to which the company would otherwise be subject.[46] Also, the Companies Act 1985 (Audit Exemption) Regulations 1994[47] exempt from the audit requirement certain small private companies.

The Department of Trade and Industry, as part of its rolling programme of review of, and consultation on, certain aspects of company law,[48] has constituted a working group to consider the possibility of reducing further the regulatory burdens imposed on private companies. It is likely that any proposals for reform will need to address the nature of, and perhaps define, the typical small private company in respect of which deregulation might be most appropriate, and also weigh in the balance minority shareholders' and creditors' interests which, though different from those of their counterparts in public companies, will nonetheless need continued protection.

[45] Or class meeting, with the unanimous agreement of the voting members of the class.

[46] The provisions, inserted by ss. 113–117 C.A. 1989 as ss. 379A, 381A–C, and 382A C.A. 1985, are further considered in Chap. 7, *post.* Aspects of the written resolution procedure have caused particular uncertaintity and are subject to DTI review.

[47] (S.I. 1994 No. 1935). See new ss. 249A–E C.A. 1985 inserted by the Regulations, and for fuller discussion see Chap. 18, *post.*

[48] Announced in November 1992 and set in motion in June 1993.

Chapter 2

PRIVATE COMPANIES AS BUSINESS VEHICLES

A. The role and status of private companies

1. *Defining the modern private company*

As described in Chapter 1, *ante*, section 1(3) of the Companies Act 1985, replacing section 1(1) of the Companies Act 1980, defines a private company somewhat enigmatically by providing that it is a company that is not a public company. As also explained in Chapter 1, all companies registered with the Register of Companies[1] since the commencement of the Companies Act 1980[2] will automatically become, and remain, private companies unless and until requisite steps are taken to render them public companies. In fact, although it is statutorily possible for a company to attain public status immediately on creation, it seems that comparatively few companies are so initially registered. Thus, even when promoters have the early intention to create a public company they will usually,[3] in the first instance, choose to register a private company and then leave it to the directors to reregister it as public if and when the developing business situation requires this; in particular when it becomes necessary to approach the public for investment.

The current answer, then, to the question, "What is a private company?" is that a private company is any company duly registered at the Companies Registration Office, in regard to which the additional steps have not been taken, either on

---

[1] For the steps currently necessary to register a private company see Chap. 4, *post*.
[2] December 22, 1980. Certain provisions came into operation before this date.
[3] This has apparently been the position in the past. Now, however, where all the conditions for a public company are initially met (in particular where there is adequate issued share capital: see Chap. 1, *ante*) and the prime intention is to create a public company, the promoters may perhaps be more ready to apply for "plc" status from the company's inception.

application for registration or subsequently, to make the company a public company.[4]

2. *Minimum requirements for a private company*

As described in Chapter 1, from the statutory inception of private companies in 1907 until 1992, a minimum membership of two sufficed to form a private company.[5] Yet, since there was nothing to prevent a member holding just one share as nominee or trustee for another member holding the remainder of the shares, that other would be the sole effective member of the company, provided both were entered on the register of members. The Companies (Single Member Private Limited Companies) Regulations 1992[6] removed the need for this façade. The Regulations inserted a new subsection 3A in section 1 of the Companies Act 1985 which permits a private company limited by shares or by guarantee to be formed by one person, and the Regulations also provide that such a company may have just one member.[7] Two members are still necessary, therefore, to form an unlimited company.

The new membership concession necessitated a recasting of section 24 of the Companies Act 1985 which had always carried a danger for private companies with small memberships. Section 24 as amended[8] now provides, in effect, that where a company *other than a private company limited by shares or by guarantee* carries on business with less than two members for more than six months, the remaining member, if he knows that it is carrying on business with only one member after the six-month period will be liable jointly and severally with the company for the debts contracted (but not other liabilities incurred) by the company after the six-month period while he remains the sole member.

---

[4] Public companies in existence prior to the 1980 Act, *i.e.* "old public companies", were, by the 1980 Act, required to reregister as public or choose to become private within the period prescribed.

[5] Since the 1980 Act this membership number is also legally (though not, of course, as a matter of practical reality) sufficient for a public company; prior to the 1980 Act the minimum membership for a public company was seven. There is now no ceiling on membership for any company (see Chap. 1, *ante*); nor *need* a private company's articles contain any restriction on rights of members to transfer shares, although they will often do so: see, *e.g.* Chaps. 6, 12 and 13, *post.*

[6] (S.I. 1992 No. 1699).

[7] Reg. 2(1), *ibid.* There was nothing, however, in previous companies legislation forbidding a company *existing* with one registered member only: see Chap. 11, *post.*

[8] By S.I. 1992 No. 1699.

Thus, a sole member of a private company limited by shares or by guarantee will only now be caught if he has fallen foul of the provision prior to July 15, 1992, the date on which the Companies (Single Member Private Limited Companies) Regulations came into force.[9] Though this would be unusual, it remains, at least for the near future, far from fanciful.

In *Nisbet v. Shepherd*,[10] a case heard at first instance shortly before the Regulations came into force,[11] S and M had been the only members of a private company until April 22, 1983, when M transferred of all his shares to S. The Court of Appeal, dismissing S's argument that the transfer had been a nullity and affirming the order made at first instance at the suit of the liquidator of the company, held that S, as sole member, was by virtue of section 24 of the Companies Act 1985, jointly and severally liable with the company for the company's unsatisfied debts contracted after October 22, 1983. Hoffmann L.J. expressed considerable sympathy with S who had "fallen into a trap created by an ancient and obsolete rule",[12] and it is now clear that a person who has become a sole member of a private company limited by shares or by guarantee in such circumstances, or on the death of the only other member,[13] without having taken the simple remedial action of transferring one share to another person, will only incur unlimited liability for company debts contracted in a relevant period ending in July 1992.

With regard to the requisite number of directors of a private company, section 292(3) of the Companies Act 1985 provides that every private company must have at least one director.[14] Under section 283(2) a sole director cannot also be the secretary of the company.

---

[9] Reg. 3, *ibid.*

[10] [1994] BCC 91.

[11] March 1992.

[12] [1994] BCC 91 at 95.

[13] A deceased member does not remain a "member" for the purposes of s. 24 C.A. 1985 and his personal representative does not become a member unless and until entered on the register of members: *Re Bowling & Welby's Contract* [1895] 1 Ch. 663. Such entry must be permitted by the articles, but this will usually be the case: see, *e.g.* reg. 30 of Table A in Appendix 1, *post.* Presumably the winding-up of a company which is a member of another company is equivalent to the death of an individual member of that other company.

[14] As against a mimimum of two directors which has been necessary for a public company registered on or after November 1, 1929: see now s. 282(1) C.A. 1985. Note, however, reg. 64 of Table A which, when adopted by either a private or a public company, requires, subject to an ordinary resolution to the contrary, a minimum of two directors: see Appendix 1, *post.*

As observed in Chapter 1, unlike public companies since the Companies Act 1980, there is no prescribed minimum capital for private companies.

3. *Popularity and economic significance of private companies*

Since the statutory concept of the private company was introduced by the Companies Act 1907[15] the number of such companies has grown in a quite remarkable way. Thus, in his well-known book, *The Principles of Company Law*[16] the late Judge Charlesworth recorded, at page 211, that the number of registered private companies, according to the then latest Board of Trade return, stood at 134,882. By the end of January 1994, this figure had reached 1,036,365.[17]

Clearly, the number of private companies on the register will continuously fluctuate in view of new registrations, and of company liquidations, compulsory and voluntary, and of the striking-off of defunct companies. Thus, the most helpful figures which give the effective number of private companies on the register at the end of each financial year are those issued by the Department of Trade and Industry.[18] These figures reveal the apparently inexorable upward trend in private company incorporations reversed, almost certainly temporarily, in the recent years of recesession.[19] Nor, in years of record insolvencies, did the administration procedure provided by sections 8 to 27 of the Insolvency Act 1986, play any significant role in rescuing companies from liquidation.[20] Whilst a considerable number of private companies do not long survive their creation, often because of under-capitilisation, it is remarkable, given the number of companies incorporated with a small amount of share capital,[21] how many not only survive, but flourish.

Although the number of private companies on the register includes a significant number of private companies which are

---

[15] As discussed in Chap. 1, *ante*.

[16] (5th ed., 1950), 2nd impression.

[17] Figure supplied by Companies House, Crown Way, Maindy, Cardiff.

[18] As at March 31, 1993, there were some 948,900 private companies on the register: *Companies in 1992–1993* (HMSO).

[19] From a peak of some 131,900 in 1988/89, new private company incorporations had fallen back to some 107,600 in 1992/93: *ibid.*

[20] For further discussion see Chap. 20, *post.*

[21] In 1992/93, some 91,800 (out of a total of some 102,700 incorporated with a share capital) had an issued share capital of £100 or less: *Companies in 1992–93* (HMSO). What a company lacks in share capital can of course be supplemented by loan capital.

subsidiaries of public companies,[22] there is clearly a very large number of companies which, for want of a more precise description, may be termed "purely private companies". It cannot, therefore, be doubted that the combined economic importance of such purely private companies is immense. Certainly the encouragement of new businesses is an important aspect of current governmental economic policy and the purely private company will, as discussed in Chapter 3, *post*, often provide the most advantageous machinery for operating a small or medium-sized business.

B. Abuses of the private company system

1. *The "phoenix syndrome"*

A very severe criticism which has often been levelled at private companies as a class, is based on the alleged propensity of some such companies to emulate the mythical phoenix.[23]

By trading through the medium of companies limited by shares[24] entrepreneurs are, of course, at least *vis-à-vis* unsecured trade creditors,[25] confining their risk to the amount of capital they have invested in the company and not putting the whole of their personal fortunes in jeopardy. This concept of separate legal personality and liability, fully accepted by the House of Lords in the leading authority of *Salomon v. Salomon & Co. Ltd.*,[26] undoubtedly added impetus to the tremendous growth in business activity which characterised the latter part of the nineteenth century.

Although the situation in *Salomon v. Salomon & Co. Ltd.* itself does not disclose an example of the "phoenix syndrome" in operation, the principle of the "veil of incorporation", established in this case by the highest judicial authority, has directly and logically enabled the "phoenix syndrome" to

---

[22] There is no statistical breakdown available separating subsidiaries of public companies from purely private companies. Private companies which are subsidiairies of public companies are also dealt with in this work, as appropriate.

[23] Although, no doubt, in theory public companies could also be operated in this way, in practice the problem is unlikely to extend beyond private companies.

[24] Contrast in particular the position concerning unlimited companies.

[25] In practice the directors and major shareholders of small private companies will often be required to grant personal guarantees to banks, etc., to support bank loans and overdraft facilities provided to their companies.

[26] [1897] A.C. 22.

evolve. In effect, the House of Lords in *Salomon v. Salomon & Co. Ltd.* firmly established that once a company is properly registered it becomes a separate, albeit artificial, legal person so far as the law is concerned.[27] The company is not simply the alias or agent of those who own its shares, even if, as was the situation in *Salomon*, one such owner is overwhelmingly the largest shareholder or is, indeed, the *sole* shareholder.[28] From time to time businessmen, finding their companies in financial difficulties, have succumbed to the temptation offered by the principle in *Salomon*, of defeating unsecured creditors while remaining within the parameters of the law. As a result, numerous private companies have gone into insolvent liquidation leaving the proprietors financially unscathed[29] and free to register new companies. Accordingly, in this situation, a replacement company rises, like the phoenix, from the ashes of the old.

Complementary to this practice it is not unknown for the proprietors of insolvent private companies to purchase assets of the business from the liquidator at knock-down prices,[30] for use by the replacement company.

2. *Combating the "phoenix syndrome"*

The legal facility provided to entrepreneurs of replacing a liquidated company with a newly registered company in order

---

[27] *i.e.* a corporation.

[28] See further Chap. 11, *post.* The doctrine in *Salomon v, Salomon & Co. Ltd.*, (described by Sir Otto Kahn-Freund in (1944) 7 M.L.R. 54 as a "calamitous decision") has been closely and logically followed in many cases since 1897, *e.g. Macaura v. Northern Assurance Co. Ltd.* [1925] A.C. 619 (H.L.); *Underwood Ltd. v. Bank of Liverpool & Martins Ltd.* [1924] 1 K.B. 775; *Lee v. Lee's Air Farming Ltd.* [1961] A.C. 12 (P.C.); for recent examples see *Verderame & ors. v. Commercial Union Assurance Co. plc and anor* [1992] B.C.L.C. 793, and *Radford v. Samuel & anor* [1993] BCC 870. Sometimes, however, *Salomon* has been distinguished in situations in which strict logic appears to demand it should have been applied, *e.g. Jones v. Lipman* [1962] 1 W.L.R. 832; *Gilford Motor Co. Ltd. v. Horne* [1933] Ch. 935 (C.A.); *Creasey v. Breachwood Motors Ltd.* [1992] BCC 638; *Smith, Stone & Knight Ltd. v. Birmingham Corporation* [1939] 4 All E.R. 116; *D.H.N. Food Distributors Ltd. v. London Borough of Tower Hamlets* [1976] 3 All E.R. 462 (C.A.); *Daimler Co. Ltd. v. Continental Tyre Co.* [1916] 2 A.C. 307; *Re F G Films Ltd.* [1953] 1 W.L.R. 483; *R. v. McDonnell* [1966] 1 Q.B. 233; *Re Bugle Press Ltd.* [1961] Ch. 270. For the more restrictive attitude taken by the courts in recent years towards lifting the corporate veil see *Woolfson v. Strathclyde Regional Council* [1978] S.C. 90 (H.L.) and particularly *Adams v. Cape Industries plc* [1990] Ch. 433. For further discussion, see Chap. 3, *post.*

[29] At least from the claims of unsecured trade creditors.

[30] Depending on what the assets are, however, there may be very little interest in purchasing them shown by anyone else.

to operate what is substantially the same business as that previously operated by the liquidated company,[31] has caused considerable public disquiet in recent years. Accordingly, the legislature has found it necessary to intervene in order to curtail the excesses of this practice.

The key weapon enabling the courts to combat the "phoenix syndrome" is the civil remedy for wrongful trading provided by section 214 of the Insolvency Act 1986.[32]

In brief, a director (including a *de facto* director) or shadow director[33] of a company may, on application of the liquidator, be declared liable for wrongful trading if, under section 214(2) of the Insolvency Act 1986:

> "(a) The company has gone into insolvent liquidation.
> (b) at some time before the commencement of the winding up of the company, that person [being a director or shadow director at that time] knew or ought to have concluded that there was no reasonable prospect that the company would avoid going into insolvent liquidation...."

A declaration as above will not be made if, by section 214(3), the court is satisfied that at "the moment of truth" alluded to in section 214(2)(b) above, the defendant director or shadow director, "took every step with a view to minimising the potential loss to the company's creditors as (assuming him to

---

[31] But free from the unsecured trade creditors. On the other hand, the company's borrowing from its bank will usually be secured by charges against its assets and/or personal guarantees from its directors: see n.25, *ante*.

[32] In fact, the long-established concept of fradulent trading, both as a crime and as a civil remedy (s. 458 C.A. 1985 and s. 213 I.A. 1986 respectively) continues to operate in parallel and unlike wrongful trading is not limited in its applicability to directors or shadow directors. However, wrongful trading is likely to prove far more effective than fraudulent trading as a civil remedy. For further discussion concerning both wrongful trading and fraudulent trading, see Chap. 20, *post*. Note also the possibility of misfeasance proceedings against the delinquent officers and others under s. 212 of the I.A. 1986.

[33] s. 251 I.A. 1986 provides, for the purposes, *inter alia,* of s. 214, that " 'director' includes any person occupying the position of director, by whatever name called", and that " 'shadow director' in relation to a company, means a person in accordance with whose directions or instructions the directors of the company are accustomed to act (but so that a person is not deemed a shadow director by reason only that the directors act on advice given by him in a professional capacity)". See also s. 741 C.A. 1985. The term "shadow director" first appeared in s. 63 C.A. 1980. The concept, however, appears in earlier legislation. For the distinction between *de facto* and shadow directors see *Re Hydrodan (Corby) Ltd.* [1994] BCC 161 (Millet J.) and for further discussion, Chap. 20, *post*.

have known that there was no reasonable prospect that the company would avoid going into insolvent liquidation) he ought to have taken." Where an application under section 214 is successful the court may order the defendant to make such personal contribution (if any) to the company's assets as it considers appropriate. The defendant may also be disqualified as a director and in other capacities.[34] The test which the court must apply in deciding whether the director or shadow director ought to have realised the company's plight and whether he took adequate steps in the cirumstances is primarily objective, but with subjective overtones, *i.e.* it depends on the general knowledge, skill and experience which a person in the defendant's shoes *ought* to have had; but, if the defendant had greater than average general knowledge, skill and experience, then, in effect, he should have acted in accordance with that level of knowledge, skill and experience.[35]

It must, however, be stressed that although the above wrongful trading provisions apply to all registered companies the greatest significance of these provisions will almost invariably be in regard private companies.[36]

3. *Further curbs on abuse*

Certain additional restrictions on possible misuse by businessmen of the private company as a business vehicle[37] are contained in recent legislation. Provisions requiring the court to make disqualification orders against "unfit" directors and shadow directors, *i.e.* precluding them, *inter alia*, from being directors or otherwise participating in company management, where the persons concerned were directors or shadow directors of companies which have become insolvent whilst they held such positions, or subsequently, and where the conduct of such directors or shadow directors has, in the view of the court, rendered them unfit for company management, are now contained in the Company Directors Disqualification Act

---

[34] s. 10 of the Company Directors Disqualification Act 1986.

[35] See s. 214(4) of the I.A. 1986. Presumably companies are now, by virtue of s. 310(3) C.A. 1985 as amended by s. 137 C.A. 1989, at liberty to insure their officers against liability under s. 214 I.A. 1986. See Chap. 8, p. 135, *post*.

[36] In particular those private companies which are not subsidiaries of public companies.

[37] Although, again, not specifically limited to private companies the provisions discussed in this section are obviously of far more relevance to private companies than they are to public companies.

1986.[38] The Company Directors Disqualification Act then, by section 15, goes on to provide that, *inter alia*, a person who acts in contravention of a disqualification order shall be jointly and severally liable with the company (and with anyone else so liable) for the company's "relevant debts"[39] incurred while he was acting contrary to a disqualification order.[40]

To counteract a further aspect of the "phoenix syndrome", section 216 of the Insolvency Act 1986 prohibits a director or shadow director of a company which has gone into insolvent liquidation on or after December 29, 1986[41] and if he was a director or shadow director of that company at any time within the 12-month period ending with the day before it went into liquidation, from promoting, forming, acting as a director of or otherwise participating in the management of a company or other business which has the same or similar name to that of the liquidated company. This embargo lasts for five years beginning with the day on which the company went into liquidation, unless the leave of the court for use of the name is obtained.[42] For breach of this provision the director or shadow director is responsible for the company's "relevant debts", jointly and severally with the company and with any other person where appropriate.[43] He is also subject to criminal liability, under section 216(4) of the Insolvency Act 1986.[44]

---

[38] s. 6 C.D.D.A. 1986. See also ss. 8 and 10 C.D.D.A. 1986 for discretionary disqualifications after company investigations and after participation in wrongful trading or fraudulent trading, respectively. For further discussion see Chap. 20, *post*. See also ss. 2, 3, 4 and 5 C.D.D.A. 1986.

[39] As defined in s. 15(3) C.D.D.A. 1986. For liability of a member of a company's management who, without the leave of the court, acts, or is willing to act, on instructions of a person he knows to be subject to a disqualification order (or to be an undischarged bankrupt), see also s. 15 C.D.D.A. 1986.

[40] Criminal sanctions can also be imposed: see ss. 13 and 14 C.D.D.A. 1986.

[41] The appointed date.

[42] For a case where leave was granted, subject to an undertaking designed to ensure that the new company's capital base was maintained, see *Re Bonus Breaks Ltd.* [1991] BCC 546.

[43] Scc s. 217 I.A. 1986; and notc in particular, responsibility under s. 217(1)(b) I.A. 1986.

[44] For a discussion of aiding and abetting this offence see *Thorne v. Silverleaf* [1994] BCC 109, where the Court of Appeal held that an aider and abettor is not necessarily prevented from recovering, as a creditor of the company, from the director personally in accordance with s. 217 provided the former is not pleading or relying on any illegality in his action for recovery.

CHAPTER 3

SOME ADVANTAGES AND DISADVANTAGES OF PRIVATE COMPANIES TO THE BUSINESS COMMUNITY

A. Introduction

The purpose of this chapter is to consider some of the advantages and disadvantages of using private companies as business vehicles. Problems which creditors and customers may encounter will also be discussed, as will some of the difficulties which a private company's officers may have to face. Although, in theory, certain of the points considered below will apply to all registered companies, in practice they will mainly be of relevance to private companies.[1]

B. The veil of incorporation

1. *The principle in* Salomon v. Salomon & Co.

The concept, recognised by the House of Lords in *Salomon v. Salomon & Co. Ltd.*,[2] of the registered company as a legal entity quite separate from its members, has been discussed in Chapter 2, *ante*.

A prime advantage to the entrepreneur of trading through the medium of a registered company[3] is that by so doing he can,

---

[1] The position with regard to particular types of private company, *i.e.* single-member and effective "one person" companies, family companies and quasi-partnerships will be discussed separately in subsequent chapters. Certain problems which directors and creditors of private companies may face have already been alluded to in Chap. 2, *ante* and will not, therefore, be further discussed here: see pp. 17 *et seq*. and pp. 15 *et seq*., *ante*.

[2] [1897] A.C. 22. See also, Chap. 11, *post*.

[3] Particularly a controlling shareholder. A *minority* shareholder in a private company may find himself "locked in" either because the directors, under powers in the articles of association, will not permit him to transfer his shares or because he cannot find a buyer.

except in certain situations,[4] limit his liability to the amount of his capital investment. Thus, as Lord Macnaghten observed in *Salomon v. Salomon & Co. Ltd.*[5]:

> "Among the principal reasons which induce persons to form private companies ... are the desire to avoid the risk of bankruptcy,[6] and the increased facility afforded for borrowing money.[7] By means of a private company ... a trade can be carried on with limited liability, and without exposing the persons interested in it in the event of failure to the harsh provisions of the bankruptcy law."[8]

Generally, therefore, the concept of the separate legal personality of the duly registered company,[9] *i.e.* the creation of a juristic person which in the eyes of the law is quite distinct from the persons which constitute the membership of such a company, will operate for the benefit of the entrepreneur.[10]

Yet this will not always be the case. In *Macaura v. Northern Assurance Association Ltd. & Others*[11] the plaintiff, the owner of a timber estate in Ireland, having transferred the timber to a company which he had formed to conduct his timber business, and in which he and his nominee held all the shares, insured that timber against fire but took out the policy in his own name without joining the company in the policy. When, on the destruction of a large quantity of timber by fire, the plaintiff claimed on the policy, his claim was rejected by the insurers on

---

[4] See in particular, Chap. 2, *ante*.

[5] [1897] A.C. 22 at 52.

[6] No doubt avoidance of personal financial disaster is the most cogent single reason.

[7] Meaning, presumably, the ability which registered companies possess to grant floating charges to creditors, a facility for augmenting their credit-raising capacity which trading organisations other than registered companies do not enjoy.

[8] Assuredly, however, these provisions are somewhat less harsh under the current insolvency legislation than they were under the law prevailing in 1897.

[9] For the steps necessary to register a company see Chap. 4, *post*.

[10] A well-known example of this is *Lee v. Lee's Air Farming Ltd.* [1961] A.C. 12. Note also in this context a parent company is not, *per se*, liable for the debts of its subsidiary: see *Re Southard & Co. Ltd.* [1979] 1 W.L.R. 1799; *Re Sarflax* [1979] Ch. 592; *Ford and Carter Ltd. v. Midland Bank* (1979) 129 N.L.J. 543; *Multinational Gas and Petroleum Co. v. Multinational Gas and Petroleum Services Ltd.* [1983] Ch. 258. Alternatively, if the subsidiary is found to be a trustee or an agent of its parent company, see, respectively, *DHN Food Distribution Ltd. v. Tower Hamlets London Borough Council* [1976] 1 W.L.R. 852 and *Smith, Stone & Knight Ltd. v. Birmingham Corporation* [1939] 4 All E.R. 116, although these two cases did not involve liability for debt. See also C. M. Schmitthoff [1978] J.B.L. 218 and [1984] J.B.L. 9–10.

[11] [1925] A.C. 619.

the ground that he had no insurable interest in the timber since it was not his property but that of the company. The plaintiff's claims both as shareholder and creditor[12] of the company were rejected by the Northern Ireland courts. This ruling was unanimously upheld on appeal to the House of Lords.

In *Verderame and others v. Commercial Union Assurance Co. plc and another*[13] the Court of Appeal provided a logical extension to the principle in the *Macaura* case. V and his wife were the sole directors and shareholders of a company. Insurance brokers advised V that the business should be insured by the defendant, but the brokers effected the insurance in the name of V rather than that of the company. When stock was stolen, the defendant insurers refused to pay because V had no insurable interest in the stock. It was held that V had no claim against the brokers in negligence.[14] The proposition that the brokers owed a duty of care to V and his wife was, according to Nourse L.J.,[15]

> "... not only novel but ... startling. If it was sustained it would have very wide ranging consequences not only in relation to insurance brokers, but also to others who provide services to small private companies, for example, solicitors, accountants, estate agents and so forth. Not only would it pierce the corporate veil on a vast scale, it would lead to quite unjustifiable procedural impracticabilities and rights or potential rights of double recovery."

2. *Flexible veil of incorporation*

As described above, a rigid application of the *Salomon* principle may result either in advantages or disadvantages to entrepreneurs who operate their business through registered companies. However, in certain circumstances, the courts are prepared to lift the corporate veil,[16] and it is now well

---

[12] But contrast the position regarding a secured debenture holder: *Westminster Fire Office v. Glasgow Provident Investment Society* (1888) 13 App.Cas. 699.

[13] [1992] BCLC 793.

[14] Though *ibid.* at 802, *per* Balcombe L.J., since it was the company which had lost the right to indemnity, *it* might have a claim against the brokers.

[15] *ibid.* at 804.

[16] Which may, in certain circumstances, be of disadvantage to company officers: see pp. 25 *et seq.*, *post.* For other statutory examples of "lifting the veil", consider also, in particular, s. 24 C.A. 1985, ss. 213, 214 and 216–217 I.A. 1986 and s. 15 C.D.D.A. 1986; see Chap. 2, *ante*.

established that they will do so where the corporate form is no more than a "mere façade concealing the true facts".[17]

In *Gilford Motor Co. Ltd. v. Horne*[18] the defendant, on taking up an appointment as joint managing director of the plaintiff company, undertook, *inter alia*, that for five years from the termination of his employment with the company he would not engage in any business similar to that of the plaintiff company[19] anywhere within three miles of its business premises. Yet when the defendant's employment terminated, he effected the formation of a private company which engaged in just such a business. Though all the issued shares in the company were divided equally between his wife and an employee, it was the defendant, the evidence showed, who was regarded as the "boss" or "guv'nor". The Court of Appeal, unanimously upholding the first instance ruling on this point,[20] would not allow the new company, which it regarded as "a cloak or sham" to be used to avoid a contractual undertaking. As Lord Hanworth M.R. observed[21]:

> "... this company was formed as a device, a strategem, in order to mask the effective carrying on of a business of ... [the defendant]".

Similarly in *Jones v. Lipman*[22] where the first defendant, who had contracted to sell his house to the plaintiff, changed his mind and transferred the house to a company[23] (the second defendant) which he had formed, Russell J. did not hesitate to issue a decree of specific performance against both defendants. The company was:

> "... a device and a sham, a mask which [the first defendant] holds before his face in an attempt to avoid recognition by the eye of equity".[24]

---

[17] The words used by the House of Lords in *Woolfson v. Strathclyde Regional Council* [1978] S.C. 90 (H.L.) and accepted, without detailed definition, by the Court of Appeal in *Adams v. Cape Industries plc* [1990] Ch. 433.

[18] [1933] Ch. 935.

[19] Assembling vehicles and selling spare parts.

[20] Other important points in issue, concerning restraint of trade, are not relevant to the present discussion.

[21] [1933] Ch. 935 at 956.

[22] [1962] 1 All E.R. 442. See also *Re F G (Films) Ltd.* [1953] 1 All E.R. 615.

[23] The only shareholders and directors of this company were the defendant and a clerk of the defendant's solicitor.

[24] [1962] 1 All E.R. 442 at 445.

The Court of Appeal in *Adams v. Cape Industries plc*[25] whilst assuming that the veil could be pierced where a defendant by the device of a corporate structure attempted to evade either limitations imposed on his conduct by law or rights of relief against him possessed by third parties, rejected a submission that the veil could be pierced where the attempt was to evade such rights of relief as third parties might acquire in the future. This did not prevent the court in *Creasey v. Breachwood Motors Ltd.*,[26] a decision which appears to go further than the "façade" cases considered above, from lifting the veil where not to have done so would have enabled a group of companies to evade contingent liability to the plaintiff for breach of his contract of employment. In that case, C, before being summarily dismissed, had been employed by company W, against whom he issued a writ for wrongful dismissal. F and S, the directors and controlling shareholders of W, caused W to cease trading and to transfer all of its assets to M, another company owned and controlled by them. To maintain trading goodwill, M paid off all the creditors of W, except that it made no provision for C's claim should it succeed. C obtained judgment against W shortly before it was struck off the register as defunct. Richard Southwell Q.C.[27] affirmed an order obtained by C substituting M as defendant, though he struck out the judgment in order to give M a chance to defend the action.

Apart from there being evidence of an increasing reluctance on the part of the courts to depart from the *Salomon* principle,[28] there remains considerable uncertainty surrounding the issue of lifting the corporate veil.[29] Such uncertainty must

---

[25] [1990] Ch. 433.

[26] [1992] BCC 638.

[27] Sitting as Deputy High Court Judge.

[28] Compare the pragmatic approach of the Court of Appeal in *DHN Food Distributors Ltd. v. London Borough of Tower Hamlets* [1976] 3 All E.R. 462 (group of companies treated as one economic unit for purpose of recovering compensation under statutory compulsory purchase provisions) with the criticism of this decision by the House of Lords in *Woolfson v. Strathclyde Regional Council* [1978] S.C. 90 (H.L.), referred to by the Court of Appeal in *Adams v. Cape Industries plc* [1990] Ch. 433. For a fuller list of cases in which the courts have lifted the veil, see Chap. 2, n.28, *ante*.

[29] To what extent, for example, can the court lift the veil in the interests of justice? In *Adams v. Cape Industries plc*, the Court of Appeal limited this principle to cases turning on the wording of particular statutes or contracts, but in *Creasey v. Breachwood Motors Ltd.* [1992] BCC 638 at 646–647, Richard Southwell Q.C. (sitting as Deputy High Court Judge) recognised that the court's power to lift the veil was "a strong power which can be exercised to achieve justice where its exercise is necessary for that purpose, but, which misused, would be likely to cause not inconsiderable injustice."

itself rank as a disadvantage so far as entrepreneurs who choose to undertake their business through the medium of registered companies are concerned.

3. *Veil of incorporation and company officers*

Section 349(4) of the Companies Act 1985 provides:

> "If an officer of a company or a person on its behalf signs or authorises to be signed on behalf of the company any bill of exchange, promissory note, endorsement, cheque or order for money or goods in which the company's name is not mentioned as required by subsection (1),[30] he is liable to a fine; and he is further personally liable to the holder of the bill of exchange, promissory note, cheque or order for money or goods for the amount of it (unless it is duly paid by the company)."[31]

The personal liability of company officers resulting from the removal of the veil of incorporation in the circumstances indicated in the above subsection is clearly far more likely to materialise in the case of a private company than in the case of a public company.[32] In any event the danger, from an officer's point of view, of incurring personal liability under this provision has been considerably enhanced by the interpretation placed upon it (and predecessor provisions), by the court.

In *Penrose v. Martyr*[33] a company secretary signed a bill of exchange on behalf of a company from the name of which the term "limited", or abbreviation thereof, had been omitted. The secretary was held to be personally liable when the bill was subsequently dishonoured by the company.[34] If this decision appears, at first glance, somewhat draconian, it can probably be supported on the ground that the word "limited" or "Ltd."[35] is

---

[30] See s. 349(1): "... in legible characters".

[31] This provision originally made its statutory appearance as s. 31 of the Joint Stock Act 1856. For charitable companies see s. 68 Charities Act 1993, a provision introduced by C.A. 1989.

[32] The criminal sanction in respect of this provision also applies to officers of both public and private companies.

[33] (1858) 120 E.R. 595.

[34] See also *Atkin & Co. v. Wardle & Others* (1889) 5 T.L.R. 734.

[35] Now "plc", of course, in the case of a public company.

an extremely meaningful part of a company's name so that its ommission may be misleading to a payee.[36]

Not only, however, will the omission of the key-word, "limited"[37] bring personal liability upon the signatory if the company defaults on the instrument; any other error in the stating of the company name, however insignificant that error may appear to be, will also carry the same consequences.

In *Hendon v. Adelman and Another*[38] a cheque drawn on a company's account signed by the defendants as directors and in regard to which the company subsequently refused payment, incorrectly stated the company's name as "L.R. Agencies Ltd.", instead of "L. & R. Agencies Ltd.," Despite the apparently trivial nature of the error the defendant directors were held liable to the payee.[39] Where, however, the plaintiff himself has prepared the instrument for signature he will be estopped from relying on any error in the company's name in any action to enforce personal liability against the defendant officer signatory.

Accordingly, in *Durham Fancy Goods Ltd. v. Michael Jackson (Fancy Goods) Ltd.*[40] the name of the drawee company on a bill was incorrectly stated as "M. Jackson (Fancy Good) Ltd.", instead of "Michael Jackson (Fancy Goods) Ltd". On the company's default the plaintiff's action against the signatory directors was dismissed because the plaintiffs had themselves drawn up the bill and this worked an estoppel against them.[41]

---

[36] For more modern examples, decided by the Court of Appeal, see *British Airways Board v. Parish* [1979] 2 Lloyds Rep. 361 and *Blum v. O.C.P. Repartition S.A.* [1988] BCLC 170.

[37] Or "Ltd.", or indeed in the case of a public company, the words, "public limited company" or "plc". In *Blum v. O.C.P. Repartition S.A.* and in *Rafsanjan Pistachio Producers Co-operative v. Reiss* [1990] BCLC 352 (where the cheques in question did not mention the company's name, only its account number), it was held that the court could not order rectification of the document in favour of the defendant.

[38] (1973) 117 S.J. 631.

[39] See also *Barber & Nicholls Ltd. v. R & G Associates (London) Ltd.* (1982) 132 N.L.J. 1076, where the word "London" was omitted from the company's name. See also *John Wilkes (Footwear) Ltd. v. Lee International (Footwear) Ltd.* (1985) 1 BCC 99, 452 (C.A.).

[40] [1968] 2 Q.B. 839. But note *Lindholst & Co. A/S v. Fowler* [1988] BCLC 166, where Sir John Donaldson M.R. (as he then was), referred to his earlier decision in *Durham Fancy Goods*, and pointed out that estoppel operated in that case because *the form of words* of the bill had been prescribed by the plaintiffs. In *Lindholst*, although the plaintiffs had put forward the bills of exchange and, in so doing, had omitted the word "Ltd." from the company's name, this did not work an estoppel against them, since they had not prescribed the form of words for acceptance.

[41] In fact, in *Penrose v. Martyr*, *ante*, the plaintiff had also prepared the instrument on which the company's name was incorrectly stated. However, in that case the plaintiff had been unaware that the company concerned was a limited liability company.

Even so, in giving judgment for the defendant directors, Donaldson J. felt constrained to observe that:

> "[t]his is a cautionary tale which should, perhaps, be required reading for all directors of companies".[42]

In *Jenice Ltd. and Others v. Dan*,[43] the court, distinguishing the earlier cases as turning on missing words, refused to declare personally liable a director who had signed cheques on which the company name, "Primekeen Ltd." was misspelt "Primkeen Ltd." R Titheridge Q.C. (sitting as deputy High Court Judge), whilst accepting that binding authority required a strict construction of section 349(4), refused to reach a conclusion which he regarded as nonsensical. Moreover, he stated that he:

> "should find it extremely difficult to say that somebody responsible for an understandable and simple and common spelling error, were guilty of a criminal offence on the basis that, because of the spelling error, the court could be satisfied so that it was sure, that the company name was not mentioned in the document."[44]

Whether this focus on the penal nature of section 349(4) will herald a more sensitive approach to company officers than hitherto shown by the courts remains to be seen.

Certainly, a less rigid stance has been adopted by the courts with regard to the application of section 26(1) of the Bills of Exchange Act 1882. This subsection provides, in effect, that where a company officer signs a bill of exchange,[45] as drawer, indorser or acceptor and adds words to indicate that he signs as agent or in a representative capacity, he will not be subject to personal liability on that bill, but that simply adding words to his signature describing him as agent or representative[46] will be insufficient to relieve the officer of personal liability on the bill.[47]

---

[42] [1968] 1 Q.B. 839 at 844.
[43] [1993] BCLC 1349.
[44] *ibid.* at 1355.
[45] Which includes a cheque: see s. 73 of the Bills of Exchange Act 1882. See also s. 37 C.A. 1985.
[46] Such as "director" or "company secretary".
[47] See *Landes v. Marcus & Another* (1909) 25 T.L.R. 478; see also *Leadbitter v. Farrow* (1816) 5 M. & S. 345.

In *Bondina Ltd. v. Rollaway Shower Blinds Ltd. & Others*[48] it was held that, for the purposes of determining personal liability under section 26(1), the bill must be considered in its entirety. Thus, in that case, even though the signatories had not added words to show that they signed in a representative capacity,[49] the Court of Appeal took the view[50] that the printed cheque-form which stated the company's name and which contained the company's account number made it sufficiently clear that the directors had not signed in their personal capacities.[51]

C. The minutiae of company law

All registered companies, and their appropriate officers, must, in the course of corporate operations, comply with a plethora of statutory requirements, and although a number of important concessions are made to private companies,[52] in general such requirements are imposed on all registered companies. It is not proposed in this work to attempt to provide a comprehensive list of points of company secretarial practice emanating from the companies legislation; reference should be made to any of the specialist works on company secretarial practice.

Some examples can, however, conveniently be stated: keeping of accounting records including the requirements as to form and contents of accounts and the directors' duty to lay accounts and reports before general meetings[53] and to file accounts and reports with the Registrar of Companies[54]; the annual return; requirement to notify the Registrar of Companies of change of address of the company's registered office; requirement to keep a register of directors and secretaries; requirement to notify the Registrar of Companies of any change in the personnel of the company's directors or secretary and in the particulars of such

---

[48] [1986] 1 All E.R. 564.

[49] Absence of "Relevant words", *per* Dillon L.J.

[50] As Dillon L.J. pointed out the *Bondina* case raised "... in a procedural context a point of law of some importance on which there is no recent English authority".

[51] See also *Chapman v. Smethurst* [1909] 1 K.B. 927; *H.B. Etlin & Co. Ltd. v. Asseltyne* 34 D.L.R. (2d) 189.

[52] Particularly the concessions relating to written and elective resolutions: see Chap. 7, *post*.

[53] Unless dispensed with by elective resolution under s. 379A C.A. 1985: see Chap. 7, *post*.

[54] For accounting disclosure requirements in respect of private companies see Chap. 17, *post*.

personnel; requirement to cause minutes of general meetings and meetings of directors and managers to be taken and kept; requirements to file copies of certain resolutions with the Registrar of Companies.

Compliance with the detailed rules of company law is, in effect, the price which entrepreneurs must pay for being allowed to enjoy the privilege of incorporation in respect of their businesses and to shelter behind the "veil of incorporation". For small private companies in particular such compliance will often be found to be extremely irksome and the Department of Trade and Industry is at present considering freeing small companies from some of their statutory burdens.[55] Nevertheless, the growth in the number of private companies on the register in recent times indicates that the disadvantages of compliance with the minutiae of company law[56] are heavily outweighed by the advantages conferred by incorporation.

[55] See Chap. 1, *ante*.

[56] By comparison with sole traders, partnerships or other unincorporated associations, which are, of course, free from the companies legislation.

CHAPTER 4

PROMOTION, FORMATION AND REGISTRATION OF PRIVATE COMPANIES

A. Promotion of private companies

1. *Meaning of "promoter"*

The common law relating to promoters was developed by the courts in the late nineteenth century at a time when the possibilities of abuse by "professional" company promoters were great. The dangers of individuals forming a company and causing it to issue shares against grossly overvalued assets have been eradicated in the case of public companies by statutory controls in sections 104 to 110 of the Companies Act 1985 on the valuation of non-cash consideration for shares whilst the Financial Services Act 1986 and Stock Exchange regulations ensure disclosure to investors in listing particulars and prospectuses. It is arguable that much of the common law relating to promoters is now largely relevant only to private companies.

Nowhere in companies legislation is the term "promoter" defined. The term is used, without elaboration, in section 150(6) of the Financial Services Act 1986, a section that deals with compensation for false or misleading statements by persons responsible for any listing particulars in relation to the securities of public companies. Prior to 1986, the term "promoter" had been given a partially circular definition by section 67(3) of the Companies Act 1985 for the purposes of liability for misleading statements in prospectuses. Section 67(3), now repealed by the Financial Services Act 1986, provided as follows:

> " 'promoter' means a promoter who was party to the preparation of the prospectus ... but does not include any person by reason of his acting in a professional capacity for persons engaged in procuring the formation of the company".

The distinction drawn in section 67(3) of the Companies Act 1985 between businessmen "engaged in procuring the formation of the company" and professionals acting on their behalf, the former alone being promoters, merely restated the common law since it has been held that solicitors employed to prepare the necessary documents or draft contracts will not be promoters[1] and there is no doubt that this will also apply to other professionals such as accountants, bankers, or business consultants whose services are engaged in company formation. Some sections of the Insolvency Act 1986 refer to persons who have "taken part in the company's formation"[2] whilst elsewhere this Act distinguishes between promotion and formation.[3] Thus it seems that whilst a promoter is undoubtedly one who is engaged in company formation, one who is enagaged in company formation is not necessarily a promoter.

What features, then, distinguish and characterise the promoter? The courts, keen to ensure that those making an improper profit from company formation should be made liable, were understandably reluctant to make too precise a limitation on the concept of promotion. According to Bowen L.J., "the term 'promoter' is a term not of law but of business, usefully summing up in a single word a number of business operations familiar to the commercial world by which a company is generally brought into existence".[4] One of the most helpful definitions is that given by Cockburn C.J. in *Twycross v. Grant*[5] where a promoter is described as "one who undertakes to form a company with reference to a given project and to set it going, and who takes the necessary steps to accomplish that purpose". It is these elements of *animus* and *factum* in combination, it has been suggested, that crucially characterise the promoter.[6]

2. *Duties and liabilities of promoters*

Promoters are not, strictly speaking, either trustees or agents for the company, but they nevertheless stand in an analogous

---

1 *Re Great Wheal Polgooth Co. Ltd.* (1883) 53 L.J.Ch. 42.
2 ss. 22, 47, 131 Insolvency Act 1986.
3 ss. 212, 216 I.A. 1986.
4 *Whaley Bridge Calico Printing Co. v. Green* (1880) 5 Q.B.D. 109.
5 (1877) 2 C.P.D. 469 at 541 (C.A.).
6 J.H. Gross, "Who is a Company Promoter?" in (1970) 86 L.Q.R. 493.

fiduciary position.[7] Promoters may not therefore make a secret profit from the formation at the expense of the company. Any profit made from the sale of the promoter's property to the company must be disclosed either to an independent board of directors,[8] or, more likely in the case of a private company, to the existing and intended shareholders,[9] *e.g.* by a declaration in the articles of association.

In *Salomon v. Salomon and Co. Ltd.*,[10] the House of Lords held that it was sufficient for the promoter's profit to be disclosed to the other subscribers to the memorandum. In that case Salomon sold his business to the company for £39,000, the company issuing 20,001 fully paid £1 shares to Salomon and one share each to the six members of Salomon's immediate family. Part of the balance of the purchase price was satisfied by the issue of debentures to the value of £10,000 by the company to Salomon. Since Salomon's family knew of the profit and acquiesced therein, there had been no breach of fiduciary duty by Salomon. There seems no doubt, however, that if Salomon's intention has been that others should subscribe for shares in the newly formed company, full disclosure would have had to be made to them either by a statement in the articles or by some other method.

The essence of the fiduciary duty, therefore, is not that no profit is to be made by a promoter, but simply that any profit must be disclosed. Further, it seems clear that the courts will not assume that property, acquired after the promotion has commenced but intended for transfer to the company, is held by the promoter on trust for the company. As stated by Sargant J. in *Omnium Electric Palaces Ltd. v. Baines*,[11] the intended relationship of the promoter to the company in respect of the acquired property will depend on the facts:

> "Whether promoters are in fact acquiring any assets as trustees for a company must, in my judgment, be a question of fact; and whereas here the whole scheme has throughout been that they are to sell to the intended company at a profit the assets which they are acquiring, the

---

[7] *Erlanger v. New Sombrero Phosphate Co.* (1878) 3 App.Cas. 1218 (P.C.), *per* Lord Cairns.
[8] *ibid.*
[9] *Langunas Nitrate Co. v. Lagunas Syndicate* [1899] 2 Ch. 392 (C.A.).
[10] [1897] A.C. 22.
[11] [1914] 1 Ch. 332.

natural inference of fact is that, *qua* those assets, they are not intending to be trustees for the company, but are intending to occupy the relationship to the company of vendors."[12]

Cases of fraud by promoters of private companies, in the sense that they intentionally make a secret profit at the expense of the company (as against simply forgetting to make disclosure), will be rare in practice. Such cases are, however, conceivable. Suppose A, who is promoting a company together with B and C, sells property to the company for cash without disclosing to B and C that he is making a profit. A, B and C subsequently become directors and the only shareholders of the newly formed company. A will have breached his fiduciary duty, which is owed to the company.

By virtue of the rule in *Foss v. Harbottle*, it is the company which is the proper plaintiff in any action against A, and so B and C, on discovering the non-disclosed profit, should be able, as directors, to cause the company to sue A even if A is the majority shareholder.[13] If, however, A had been the sole director as well as being the majority shareholder, B and C, as minority shareholders, should be able to bring a derivative action against A since his effective expropriation of corporate assets is a fraud on the minority which is an exception to the rule in *Foss v. Harbottle*.

In *Atwool v. Merryweather*,[14] the plaintiff, a minority shareholder, successfully brought a derivative action against the defendant who had sold mines at a concealed profit to the company he was promoting.

The company has a choice of actions against a promoter for breach of fiduciary duty. First, it may seek to rescind the contract,[15] and on general equitable principles, this right will be lost if the parties cannot be substantially restored to their original positions[16] or if third parties have acquired rights for value, *e.g.* the property has been mortgaged.[17] Alternatively, the company may sue the promoter to account for the profit he has made,[18] but not, it appears, if the defendant had acquired the

---

[12] *ibid.* at 347.
[13] (1843) 2 Hare 461. But A could dismiss B and C as directors.
[14] (1867) L.R. 5 Eq. 464n.
[15] *Erlanger v. New Sombrero Phosphate Co.* (1878) 3 App.Cas. 1218 (P.C.).
[16] *Lagunas Nitrate Co. v. Lagunas Syndicate* [1899] 2 Ch. 392.
[17] *Re Leeds and Hanley Theatres of Varieties Ltd.* [1902] 2 Ch. 809 (C.A.).
[18] *Gluckstein v. Barnes* [1900] A.C. 240.

property before he became a promoter.[19] Thirdly, it has been held that the company may sue the promoter for damages for breach of fiduciary duty[20] even though the award of damages for breach of an equitable obligation appears to be contrary to principle. Finally, if the promoter has intentionally or recklessly made a misrepresentation to the company he may be liable to damages in the tort of deceit.

Where a promoter is forming a company to purchase his business, fraud will be most unlikely. More conceivable, however, might be the case where such a promoter negligently overvalues his business by arriving at a valuation figure which in the words of Lord Macnaghten in *Salomon's* case, represents "the sanguine expectations of a fond owner rather than anything which can be called a businesslike or reasonable estimate of value".[21]

It has been held that a promoter might be liable in damages for negligently allowing a company to purchase his property at above market value.[22] Damages for negligent misrepresentation may also be recovered under section 2(1) of the Misrepresentation Act 1967. A promoter's duties to take care and to refrain for misrepresentation are, like the fiduciary duty of disclosure, owed to the company. Since it is probable that the promoter will become the majority shareholder in the company, the enforcement of these duties is unlikely in practice. In the event that there is an independent minority shareholder, such a shareholder would, it is submitted, by analogy with the cases involving directors,[23] have to allege, not merely negligence on the promoter's part, but negligence which benefited the promoter, in order to be permitted to bring a derivative suit. It might in particular be possible to show such benefit in the unusual case where the promoter has received cash or perhaps debentures from the company at least in part payment for the negligently overvalued property.

Where a company is being wound up, any person who has been, *inter alia*, a promoter of a company may, by virtue of section 212 of the Insolvency Act 1986, be liable for

---

[19] *Re Cape Breton Co.* (1895) 29 Ch.D. 795 (C.A.); *Ladywell Mining Co. v. Brookes* (1887) 35 Ch.D. 400 (C.A.); *Jacobus Marler Estates Ltd. v. Marler* (1913) 85 L.J.P.C. 167n.

[20] *Re Leeds and Hanley Theatres of Varieties* [1920] 2 Ch. 809 (C.A.).

[21] [1897] A.C. 22 at 49.

[22] *Jacobus Marler Estates Ltd. v. Marler* (1913) 85 L.J.P.C. 167n.

[23] *Pavlides v. Jensen* [1956] Ch. 565 and *Daniels v. Daniels* [1978] Ch. 406.

misapplying, retaining or becoming accountable for any money or other property of the company or in respect of any misfeasance or breach of fiduciary or other duty towards the company. This includes liability for negligence. Further, any persons who have been concerned in a company's formation within one year of any insolvency office holder taking office are under a duty to co-operate with the office holder.[24] If so required, a former promoter must supply a statement of the company affairs to an administrator,[25] or administrative receiver,[26] or official receiver.[27]

3. *Disqualification of promoters and directors*

Several provisions of the Company Directors Disqualification Act 1986 apply equally to promoters as they do to directors. A disqualification order debars a person from being, without the leave of the court, a director, liquidator, administrator, receiver or manager of a company, or from being directly or indirectly concerned in the promotion, formation or management of a company.[28] A person who has been in persistent default[29] of obligations imposed by the companies legislation in relation to the filing or delivery of any return, account or other document with, or the giving of any notice to, the Registrar may be disqualified for up to five years.[30]

The Company Directors Disqualification Act 1986 also provides that disqualification orders of up to 15 years may be made in the following cases: conviction on indictment of an indictable offence[31] in connection with the promotion, formation, management, liquidation or receivership of a company[32];

---

[24] s. 235 I.A. 1986.
[25] s. 22 I.A. 1986.
[26] s. 47 I.A. 1986.
[27] s. 131 I.A. 1986.
[28] s. 1(1) Company Directors Disqualification Act 1986.
[29] It is conclusive proof of persistent default that a person has been guilty of three defaults in the previous five years. Guilt in this context means that the person has been convicted (either on indictment or summarily) of an offence, or had a default order made against him, in respect of the appropriate provisions of the companies legislation: s. 3(2) C.D.D.A. 1986.
[30] s. 3 C.D.D.A. 1986; see also s. 5 C.D.D.A. 1986 (disqualification on summary conviction), for a similarly cumulative provision.
[31] Where a person is summarily convicted of an indictable offence the maximum period of disqualification is five years: s. 2(3) C.D.D.A. 1986.
[32] s. 2 C.D.D.A. 1986. Even if the offence is one peculiar to a public company, such as insider dealing, the disqualification order must apply no less to private than to public companies: *R. v. Goodman* [1993] 2 All E.R. 789.

fraudulent trading or any other fraud by an officer, liquidator, or receiver or manager in the course of a winding-up[33]; cases where, following a Department of Trade and Industry investigation of the company, it appears expedient in the public interest that a disqualification order should be made against a present or former director or shadow director[34]; cases where the court has declared a director or shadow director in the case of wrongful trading, or a knowing party in the case of fraudulent trading, liable to contribute to the assets of the company.[35] Failure to pay under an administration order made by virtue of Part VI of the County Courts Act 1984 may lead to a disqualification of up to two years.[36] Under section 6 of the Company Directors Disqualification Act 1986 the court *must* make a disqualification order of not less than two years or more than 15 years in cases where directors of insolvent companies have been shown to be unfit.[37] It is an offence for an undischarged bankrupt to act as a director or to be directly or indirectly concerned in the promotion, formation or management of a company, except with the leave of the court.[38]

The five-year embargo on a former director or shadow director of a company in insolvent liquidation from being a director, or from being involved in the management of a company or business of the same of similar name without the leave of the court, applies equally to involvement in the promotion of such a company.[39]

4. *Payment of promoters*

In the absence of a contract between the promoter and the company, the promoter is not entitled to be paid for his services in promoting the company, nor even to be reimbursed his promotion expenses.[40] Since the company lacks any contractual capacity prior to incorporation, any contract for the remuneration of promoters would have to be made on the company's

[33] s. 4 C.D.D.A. 1986.
[34] s. 8 C.D.D.A. 1986.
[35] s. 10 C.D.D.A. 1986.
[36] s. 12 C.D.D.A. 1986.
[37] For fuller discussion see Chap. 20, *post*.
[38] s. 11 C.D.D.A. 1986. It has been held by the Court of Appeal that this is an offence of strict liability: *R. v. Brockley* [1994] BCC 131.
[39] ss. 216–217 of the Insolvency Act 1986, Chap. 2, p. 19, *ante*.
[40] *Re National Motor Mail Coach Co., Clinton's Claim* [1908] 2 Ch. 515 (C.A.).

incorporation and would need to be under seal in order to avoid the difficulties of past consideration. In practice, however, promotion expenditure may well be recoverable. Since the promoters of private companies are usually the first directors, reimbursement of expenditure will normally be made in accordance with a provision inserted in the articles such as that contained in the former Table A, regulation 80[41] which, though not constituting a contract, provides: "The business of the company shall be managed by the directors, who may pay all expenses incurred in promoting and registering the company".[42]

B. Pre-incorporation contracts

1. *The legal status of pre-incorporation contracts*

A pre-incorporation contract is a contract entered into by a promoter, prior to the company's incorporation and thus before the company has attained legal personality, the intention being that the company, when formed, shall benefit from and be liable on the contract.

The legal position relating to pre-incorporation contracts is regulated both by statute and the common law. The statutory provision is section 36C[43] of the Companies Act 1985, subsection (1) of which states:

> "A contract which purports to be made by or on behalf of a company at a time when the company has not been formed has effect, subject to any agreement to the contrary, as one made with the person purporting to act for the company or as agent for it, and he is personally liable on the contract accordingly."

Section 36C(2) extends subsection (1) to the making of a deed. Subject to this addition, section 36C(1) is in susbtance the same as its predecessor, section 36(4) of the Companies Act 1985. Section 36(4) was itself a re-enactment of section 9(2) of the European Communities Act 1972, which had been passed to

---

[41] Sched. 1 C.A. 1948.

[42] The present Table A in the Companies Tables (A-F) Regulations 1985 (see Appendix 1, *post*) does not contain a parallel article to the former reg. 80.

[43] Inserted by s. 130 C.A. 1989.

implement Article 7 of the First E.C. Council Directive.[44] Although Article 7 provides for liability on the part of persons, unless otherwise agreed, acting in the name of a company "*en formation*", it has been held that what is now section 36C(1) of the Companies Act 1985 does not require any steps to have been taken, at the time of the contract, to form the company,[45] but a contract cannot be said to be purportedly made by a company which no-one had at that time thought of forming.[46] Conversely, a company, such as a shelf company, awaiting a new certificate of incorporation on a change of name[47] is not a company that "has not been formed" for the purposes of section 36C(1)[48] nor is a company whose name has been misdescribed on a contract.[49]

2. *Liability under pre-incorporation contracts*

Section 36C(1) of the Companies Act 1985, in imposing personal liability on those who purport to commit a company to a contract, or to contract on its behalf, prior to the company's formation, goes some way towards clarifying the position that had existed at common law. The courts would look to the intention of the parties and in some cases relied on the mode of signature on the contracts. Thus in *Kelner v. Baxter*,[50] where three promoters signed a contract in their own names "on behalf of the Gravesend Royal Alexandra Hotel Company Limited" when the company had not yet been formed, it was held that the three men were personally liable to pay for the quantity of wine which had been ordered. On the other hand in *Newborne v. Sensolid*,[51] the Court perceived a different intent. In that case the plaintiff was promoter, later becoming a director, of Leopold Newborne (London) Ltd. He made a contract with the defendant before the company had been registered. The Contract was signed "Leopold Newborne

---

[44] 68/151: [1968] J.O. L65/8; [1968] O.J. Sp. Ed., 41.
[45] *Phonogram Ltd. v. Lane* [1982] Q.B. 938.
[46] *Cotronic (UK) Ltd. v. Dezonie (t/a Wendaland Builders Ltd.) & Ors.* [1991] BCC 200, where D had thought he was contracting on behalf of a company which, unknown to D, had been struck off the register, a new company of the same name being incorporated some three years later.
[47] This is required by s. 28(6) C.A. 1985.
[48] *Oshkosh B'Gosh Inc. v. Dan Marbel Inc. & Another* (1988) 4 BCC 795.
[49] *Badgerhill Properties Ltd. v. Cottrell* [1991] BCC 463.
[50] (1866) L.R. 2 C.P. 174.
[51] [1954] 1 Q.B. 45.

(London) Ltd.", with the plaintiff's name signed underneath for the purposes of authentication. When the plaintiff sought to enforce the contract, he was unsuccessful; the court distinguished *Kelner v. Baxter* on the way the contract had been signed and held that in the instant case the contract was purportedly made with the "company", which did not exist, and not with the plaintiff. The contract was therefore a nullity. It appears that the promoter in this case would similarly not have been liable on the contract.[52]

That section 36C(1) has rendered irrelevant any such fine distinctions based on the form of the contract is clear from the Court of Appeal's judgement in *Phonogram Ltd. v. Lane.*[53] In this case Lane intended to form a company "Fragile Management Ltd." to promote a pop group and, to help finance the venture, borrowed £6,000 from Phonogram Ltd., being the first instalment of an agreed loan of £12,000. In a letter coutersigned by Lane "for and on behalf of Fragile Management Ltd.", an undertaking was given to repay the £6,000 in the event of the deal never being completed. The venture failed, the company was never formed and Phonogram sued to recover the money from Lane. It was held by the Court of Appeal that Lane was liable by virtue of what was then section 9(2) of the European Communities Act 1972. He was clearly purporting to act as agent for a company at a time when it had not been formed within the meaning of the subsection and it did not matter that both parties to the contract knew that the company was not yet in existence. Even if distinctions based on the mode of signature were valid at common law, these distinctions had been swept away by section 9(2).

It seems clear that if circumstances such as those in *Newborne v. Sensolid* were to recur, the promoter would be liable. In that case, however, the promoter was trying to enforce the contract, a situation for which section 36C(1) makes no provision. Most commentators believe that, in accordance with the normal principle of contractual mutuality, the subsection must at least by implication contemplate a right to sue on the part of the promoter. This was the view of the judge at first

---

[52] There has been no decision on whether a promoter in such cases might be liable for breach of warranty of authority; dicta at first instance in *Newborne v. Sensolid* [1954] 1 Q.B. 45 at 47 suggest not, but *cf.* dicta to the contrary by the High Court of Australia in *Black v. Smallwood* [1966] A.L.R. 744.

[53] [1982] Q.B. 938.

instance in *Cotronic (UK) v. Dezonie (t/a Wendaland Builders Ltd.)*.[54] In the Court of Appeal Dillon L.J. disagreed with this approach but only, it seems, because he did not regard section 36C(1) as having any application to the case.[55] Though on a strict intepretation of section 36C(1) the promoter would not be entitled to sue,[56] it may well be that the courts will hold that the statement in the subsection that "*A contract ... has effect ... as one made with the person purporting to act for the company ...*" (italics added) comprehends a right of enforcement by the promoter.

Section 36C(1) leaves unchanged most of the common law relating to pre-incorporation contracts, so the remaining principles are to be found in the cases. A pre-incorporation contract does not bind the company,[57] cannot be enforced by a company,[58] nor can it be ratified by a company[59] after its incorporation. The Jenkins Committee Report on Company Law Reform (1962) recommended that a company should be able unilaterally to adopt a premilinary agreement, and there is no reason why the law should not adopt such a recommendation, as was proposed in the abortive Companies Bill 1973. Several Commonwealth countries have enacted provisions to this effect. It is possible for a promoter to assign the benefit of the contract to the company on its incorporation, but since the burden of the contract cannot be assigned, the promoter would continue to be liable. There seems no reason in principle why a promoter should not be able to enter into a contract as trustee for the company that is being formed, but such an approach was rejected by the court in *Rita Joan Dairies Ltd. v. Thompson*.[60]

---

[54] His Honour Judge Wootton, Birmingham County Court, November 8, 1989, who based his opinion on a passage in *Gore-Browne on Companies* (44th ed., 1986), Vol. 1, para. 8.3: see [1991] BCC 200 at 204.

[55] *ibid.*

[56] Such an interpretation would, arguably, be consistent with the spirit of the First E.C. Directive 68/151 [1968] J.O. L65/8; [1968] O.J. Sp. Ed., 41, the original source of the statutory provision, which concerned the rights of persons dealing with companies. On the other hand, the common law on pre-incorporation contracts shows no particular leaning towards outsider protection. Lord Goddard C.J. in *Newborne v. Sensolid* [1954] 1 Q.B. 45 at 51 regarded it as "unfortunate" that the promoter could not enforce the contract, whilst in *Black v. Smallwood* [1966] A.L.R. 744 and *Hawkes Bay Milk Corporation Ltd. v. Watson* [1974] 1 N.Z.L.R. 236 the respective promoters were held not liable to the other parties.

[57] *Re English and Colonial Produce Co. Ltd.* [1906] 2 Ch. 435 (C.A.).

[58] *Natal Land Co. Ltd. v. Pauline Colliery Syndicate Ltd.* [1904] A.C. 120 (P.C.).

[59] *Kelner v. Baxter* (1886) L.R. 2 C.P. 174 (Court of Common Pleas).

[60] [1974] N.Z.L.R. 285.

The only sure method of the newly formed company "adopting" a pre-incorporation contract is through a process of novation by which the company enters into a new contract with the third party on the same terms as the original contract. Novation may be implied by the conduct of the parties, but it appears that the courts will require the directors of the newly formed company to direct their minds to the issue, and the fact that the contract as acted upon by the company contains a variation in terms from the pre-incorporation contract will be sufficient for the courts to infer that a novation has taken place.[61] In the absence of evidence such as a change in terms, it may be difficult to persuade the court that the parties have done anything other than to act in the erroneous belief that the pre-incorporation contract is binding, and it has been held that such conduct is insufficient.[62]

While the promoter will be concerned to have a binding agreement with the third party, he will also wish to take steps to exclude his personal liability imposed by section 36C(1). The subsection provides for such an exclusion by stating that the promoter incurs personal liability "subject to any agreement to the contrary". It had been suggested that merely for the promoter to sign the contract "as agent" might arguably be sufficient, by implication, to negate personal liability,[63] but this argument was rejected by all three judges in the Court of Appeal in *Phonogram Ltd. v. Lane.*[64] Indeed, such an approach would run contrary to the precise wording of section 36C(1), *i.e.* that "A contract ... has effect as one made with the person purporting to act for the company *or as agent for it* ..." (italics added). The Court of Appeal was unanimous that a clear exclusion of personal liability was required and Lord Denning M.R. added that such an exclusion should be express. The safest course for a promoter is therefore to make it clear to the other contracting party, preferably by a term in the contract, that he is not to be personally liable on the contract. The ideal form of clause from the promoter's point of view would appear to be one which provides that the promoter's liability shall cease if and when the company is incorporated and enters into an identical agreement with the vendor and which further allows

---

[61] *Howard v. Patent Ivory Mfg. Co.* (1888) 38 Ch.D. 156.
[62] *Re Northumberland Avenue Hotel Co.* (1886) 33 Ch.D. 16.
[63] *Cheshire and Fifoot's Law of Contract* (9th ed., 1976), p. 462.
[64] [1982] Q.B. 938.

the promoter to rescind if the company has not entered into the contract by a specified date.[65] The rider relating to rescission is essential to ensure that the promoter's personal liability is absolutely excluded. Such a provision may or may not be acceptable to a vendor depending on the nature of the property and the state of the market. Alternatively, it has been suggested that in contracts for the purchase or the lease or hire of property, promoters might protect themselves by taking an option to purchase or to take a lease or hire of the property, and assigning the option to the company on incorporation.[66]

If it is not essential for the promoter to have a binding agreement immediately (and this will obviously be the case where the contract is for the sale of the promoter's business to the company which is being formed for that purpose) an agreement will be prepared in draft and, in accordance with a provision in the memorandum, will be executed on the company's incorporation.

C. Formation, registration and commencement of business

When forming a company, the promoter has a choice. On the one hand, a solicitor may be instructed to draw up the necessary documents. This has the advantage of precision since the promoter will be able to give specific instructions as to his requirements for inclusion in the memorandum of association[67] and articles of association.[68] The disadvantages will be expense and inevitably a certain delay between the idea to establish the company and its eventual incorporation. Alternatively, in most situations, the promoter may purchase a so-called "shelf" company from one of the many agencies that specialise in company formations and which advertise in the legal, financial and business press. These agencies will already have formed a large number of companies by the process of registration described below, the purpose of the companies merely being to lie dormant and await sale. The original directors and members will be employees of the agency and the agency will have chosen a company name. On purchase, the directors resign in favour of the promoters (or their nominees) and the shares that have been

---

[65] See *Charlesworth's Company Law* (13th ed., 1987), p. 125.
[66] *Pennington's Company Law* (6th ed., 1990), p. 91.
[67] Chap. 5, *post*.
[68] Chap. 6, *post*.

issued are transferred to the new members.[69] Yet even from the stock of companies available in the chosen agency, the promoter may sometimes not find a company which fits his exact requirements. In this event, either the agency, or the new company controllers after purchase, can secure the passing of special resolutions in order to effect the desired alterations to the memorandum or articles. It is quite likely that a change of name, at least, will be required.

In order to obtain registration of a company, the following documents must be delivered to the Registrar of Companies at Companies House in Cardiff:

(i) the memorandum of association;
(ii) articles of association are usually delivered though as will be seen,[70] for a company limited by shares, their delivery is not essential;
(iii) a statement, signed by or on behalf of the subscribers to the memorandum, which must contain the names and requisite particulars of the first director or directors and secretary together with their signed consent to act as such and which must also specify the intended situation of the company's registered office[71];
(iv) a statutory declaration of compliance with the statutory requirements relating to registration signed by a solicitor engaged in the company's formation or by one of the proposed first directors or secretary.[72]

The above documents, and indeed all documents, must be in legible form, satisfy any requirements prescribed by regulations and conform with any specifications made by the Registrar to facilitate copying.[73] A registration fee is payable.[74]

When the Registrar is satisfied that the statutory requirements have been complied with and that the company is being formed for a lawful purpose,[75] he will register the memorandum and

---

[69] For a problem which may confront an *intended* transferee of subscribers' shares from the point of view of *locus standi* to petition for winding up or to seek relief under s. 459 C.A. 1985 see *Re Quickdome Ltd.* [1988] BCLC 370.
[70] Chap. 6, *post*.
[71] s. 10 and Sched. 1 C.A. 1985.
[72] s. 12(3) C.A. 1985.
[73] s. 706 C.A. 1985.
[74] Currently £50 (S.I. 1991 No. 1206).
[75] s. 1(1) C.A. 1985.

articles (if any).[76] On registration the Registrar issues a certificate of incorporation which confers corporate personality on the company and which is conclusive evidence that the statutory registration requirements have been complied with.[77] It has been held that the certificate of incorporation is also conclusive evidence as to the date on which the company was incorporated.[78]

Unlike a public company, a private company does not need a further certificate from the Registrar to enable it to begin trading and may thus commence business and exercise borrowing powers on the issue of the certificate of incorporation.

---

[76] s. 12(1), (2) C.A. 1985.
[77] s. 13 C.A. 1985.
[78] *Jubilee Cotton Mills v. Lewis* [1924] A.C. 958.

Chapter 5

MEMORANDUM OF ASSOCIATION

A. Form and legal requirements of the memorandum

1. *Purpose*

The memorandum of association is the document in the company's constitution which provides essential information to persons dealing with the company and which sets limits for the dealings between the company and those persons. It is essential, for example, that persons contracting with a company know that they are in fact dealing with a company rather than an individual trader or partnership, and further, that they know whether the company is registered with limited liability, whether its registered office is in England and Wales on the one hand or Scotland on the other, and what businesses it is authorised to undertake.

In addition, there are two aspects of a private company's memorandum which distinguish it from a public company. First, the last word in the name of a private company limited by shares (with only a few exceptions)[1] will be "Limited" or "Ltd.",[2] and secondly there will be no statement that the company is a public company, a compulsory addition in the memorandum of a public company.[3]

2. *Essential information to be included*

Whatever other clauses the memorandum might contain section 2 of the Companies Act 1985 provides that it *must*

---

[1] See s. 30(2) Companies Act 1985. For a more detailed consideration of s. 30 in relation to Guarantee Companies, see Chap. 19, *post*.

[2] In contrast, unlimited companies, which must be private by virtue of s. 1(3) C.A. 1985, are not compelled to use the word "unlimited" (though if they do, it must be the last word in the name: s. 26(1)(a) C.A. 1985), and are forbidden from ending their names with "limited".

[3] s. 1(3) C.A. 1985.

include the following five: name, registered office, objects, liability and capital; and the forms of memoranda, depending on the particular class of private company, must be "as specified respectively for such companies by regulations made by the Secretary of State or as near to that form as circumstances admit."[4]

It will be seen below that this statutory requirement of similarity is given a flexible interpretation in the matter of objects clauses, the short forms provided by the regulations having proved inadequate in practice for the requirements of corporate business.[5] The regulations relating to the forms of memoranda applicable to the various classes of private companies are contained in the Companies (A–F) Regulations 1985[6]: Table B for a private company limited by shares, Table C for a company limited by guarantee not having a share capital, Table D Part II for a private company limited by guarantee and having a share capital,[7] and Table E for an unlimited company having a share capital. Section 2 goes on to provide that each subscriber to the memorandum (and there need now only be one in the case of a private company limited by shares or guarantee[8]) must sign the memorandum in the presence of at least one witness who must attest the signature, and in the case of a company limited by shares, the number of shares taken by each subscriber (and each subscriber must take at least one) must be stated.

B. Name clause

1. *"Limited"*

A private company limited by shares or guarantee must have the word "limited" as its last word, or "cyfyngedig" if its registered office is situated in Wales[9] and the abbreviated forms

---

[4] s. 3(1) C.A. 1985.

[5] See pp. 52 *et seq.*, *post*, and note the new statutory short form objects clause which is permitted.

[6] (S.I. 1985 No. 805): see Appendix 1, *post.*

[7] Since no new incorporations in this form have been permitted since December 22, 1980 (s. 1(4) C.A. 1985) such companies will become increasingly rare. On guarantee companies generally, see Chap. 19, *post.*

[8] s. 1(3A) C.A. 1985 inserted by the Companies (Single Member Private Limited Companies) Regulations 1992 (S.I. 1992 No. 1699). On single-member companies see Chap. 11, *post.*

[9] s. 25(2) C.A. 1985.

"Ltd." and "cyf." are permissible.[10] Guarantee companies may, however, in the circumstances specified in section 30 of the Companies Act 1985 be exempted from the requirement to have "limited" as the last word of their names.[11] Private companies will not be registered if they include the words "limited" or "unlimited" or their Welsh equivalents otherwise than at the end of their names,[12] and sole traders, partnerships and unlimited companies, etc., commit an offence if their names end with the words "limited" or "cyfyngegid" or abbreviations thereof.[13]

2. *Index of company names*

The Registrar must keep an index of company names[14] and section 26 of the Companies Act 1985 provides that the Registrar will refuse registration with a name which is the same as a name already appearing on the index, discounting, *inter alia*, the word "the", the various words denoting liability, the type of letters used and punctuation. Section 26 further provides that a company shall not be registered with a name which would, in the opinion of the Secretary of State, constitute a criminal offence or which would be otherwise offensive, and registration will only be permitted with the approval of the Secretary of State if the name suggests a connection with central or local government or includes any word or expression specified in the Company and Business Names Regulations 1981 as amended by the Company and Business Names (Amendment) Regulations 1982 and 1992.[15]

3. *Change of company name*

The company may, of its own volition, change its name by special resolution and the Secretary of State may direct a change of name within 12 months if the name is too similar to a name already appearing on the Registrar's index, and within five years if misleading information was given for the purposes of

---

[10] s. 27(4) C.A. 1985.
[11] See Chap. 19, *post*.
[12] s. 26(1) C.A. 1985.
[13] s. 34 C.A. 1985. A similar prohibition, which also extends to private limited companies, is imposed in relation to unauthorised use of the term "public limited company" or its Welsh equivalent: s. 33 C.A. 1985.
[14] s. 714 C.A. 1985.
[15] (S.I. 1981 No. 1685); (S.I. 1982 No. 1653); (S.I. 1992 No. 1196).

registration with a particular name or there are unfulfilled undertakings or assurances which were given in connection with that registration.[16] Furthermore, the Secretary of State may direct a change of name at any time if he is of the opinion that the name gives so misleading an indication of the nature of the company's activities as to be likely to cause harm to the public, in which case the company must change its name within six weeks, or such longer period as the Secretary of State may allow, subject to the right to apply to the court within three weeks for the direction to be cancelled.[17] A change of name under the foregoing provisions takes effect on the issue by the Registrar of an altered certificate of incorporation and does not affect the rights and obligations of the company and does not render defective any suit by or against it, and actions against the company that might have been continued or commenced by its old name can proceed against it by its new name.[18]

A company may also effectively be required to change its name as a result of a successful passing-off action brought against it. Under the tort of passing off, the court may grant an injunction preventing the carrying on of a business under a name that is likely to deceive the public into believing that it is dealing with another previously established business. Thus, an injunction was granted against using the name "Buttercup Margarine Co. Ltd." at the suit of a plaintiff who carried on business under the name of "Buttercup Dairy Co."[19] A company has no monopoly, however, of nouns in common use describing specific things such as "vacuum cleaner"[20] and "areator".[21]

4. *Display and use of the company name*

A company must display its name conspicuously and legibly outside every office or place of business[22] and must also state its name on all letters, notices, bills of exchange, promissory notes, indorsements, cheques, orders for money or goods,

---

[16] s. 28 C.A. 1985.
[17] s. 32 C.A. 1985.
[18] s. 28(6), (7); s. 32(5), (6) C.A. 1985.
[19] *Ewing v. Buttercup Margarine Co. Ltd.* [1917] 2 Ch. 1 (C.A.).
[20] *British Vacuum Cleaner Co. Ltd. v. New Vacuum Cleaner Co. Ltd.* [1907] 2 Ch. 312.
[21] *Aerators Ltd. v. Tollit* [1902] 2 Ch. 319.
[22] s. 348 C.A. 1985.

invoices and receipts.[23] Failure to comply with these publication requirements renders the company and every officer in default liable to a fine and section 349(4) of the Companies Act 1985 provides that if an officer signs on the company's behalf any bill of exchange, promissory note, indorsement, cheque or order for money or goods on which the name of the company is not properly stated, he is also liable personally in the event of default by the company.[24]

5. *Business names*

The rules relating to business names are contained in the Business Names Act 1985. Generally, a company may trade under a business name of its choice except that the approval of the Secretary of State is required for a name giving the impression of a connection with central or local government or which includes an expression specified in the Company and Business Names Regulations 1981 as amended by Company and Business Names (Amendment) Regulations 1982 and 1992. This provision does not apply, however, to companies continuing to use a name which was a lawful business name prior to February 26, 1982, nor does it apply, for an initial 12-month period, to a transferee of a business with a name that was a lawful business name immediately before the transfer.[25]

Where a company undertakes business under a business name, *i.e.* a name which does not consist of its corporate name without addition,[26] its corporate name and address of its registered office must be stated on all letters, orders, receipts and demands for payment, must be displayed prominently in business premises to which customers and suppliers have access, and must also be disclosed in writing to any person doing business with the company who requests such information.[27] Breach of these provisions renders the company liable to a fine together with any officer, purported officer, or member (where the affairs of the company are managed by its members) who has consented to, connived at, or shown neglect in relation to, the default.[28]

---

[23] s. 349 C.A. 1985.
[24] This provision is examined in more detail in Chap. 3, pp. 25 *et seq.*, *ante*.
[25] s. 2 of the Business Names Act 1985.
[26] s. 1 B.N.A. 1985.
[27] s. 4 B.N.A. 1985.
[28] s. 7 B.N.A. 1985.

Default in the disclosure requirements may also have civil law consequences. Section 5 of the Business Names Act 1985 provides that if a company is bringing an action on a contract which was made at a time when the company was in breach of the disclosure provisions, the action will be dismissed by the court if the defendant can show either that he had a claim against the company which he was unable to pursue because of the company's default, or that he has suffered some financial loss in connection with the contract by reason of the default. The court will, however, allow the action to continue if satisfied that it is just and equitable to do so. Further, the provisions of section 5 are without prejudice to any rights that the company may have in an action brought by the other party.

An example of the operation of section 5 of the Business Names Act 1985 might be where A Ltd. which operates under a business name, but which has not disclosed its corporate name as required, supplies goods to B Ltd., which the latter claims are defective. Suppose A Ltd. is suing B Ltd. for the price, but B Ltd. claims that it has been unable to bring an action against A Ltd. for breach of the implied conditions of fitness and/or merchantable quality in section 14 of the Sale of Goods Act 1979 because A Ltd. had not disclosed its corporate name and address as required. The court might in such circumstances dismiss A Ltd.'s action. Suppose, however, that A Ltd. had purported to exclude its liability for the implied conditions by means of a term in the contract. Since this is a sale between businesses, such an exclusion is valid provided that it satisfies the test of reasonableness.[29] If the court is satisfied as to the reasonableness of the exclusion clause it might conclude that it is just and equitable for A Ltd.'s action on the price to continue.

If a defendant did not have a possible claim against the plaintiff, which he was unable to pursue, we have seen above that section 5 of the Business Name Act 1985 provides that he might alternatively be able to show that he had suffered some financial loss "in connection with the contract." These words seem broad enough to cover financial loss that goes beyond the substance of the contract, and it has been suggested that it ought to be sufficient for the defendant to show that he had incurred expense in trying to ascertain the corporate name.[30]

---

[29] s. 6(3) Unfair Contract Terms Act 1977.
[30] *Smith and Keenan's Company Law for Students* (9th ed., 1993) p. 58.

C. Registered office clause

1. *Domicile of the company*

This clause in the memorandum states whether the registered office is to be situated in England (the practice is to state "England and Wales"), Wales or Scotland.[31] The domicile of the company, *i.e.* England (or Wales) on the one hand or Scotland on the other, will determine whether the company is registered at the Companies Registration Office in Cardiff or Edinburgh respectively. If the memorandum states that the registered office is to be situated in Wales, any document delivered to the Registrar under the Companies Act 1985 or the Insolvency Act 1986 may be in Welsh and, apart from certain prescribed documents, must be accompanied by a certified translation into English.[32] Although the situation of the registered office may be freely altered as between England and Wales, the domicile, once chosen, is unalterable as between England or Wales and Scotland, other than by reregistration.

2. *Address of the company*

The address of the registered office is not stated in the memorandum but is included in the separate statement which is sent to the Registrar with the other documents for registration.[33] This address is alterable by the company giving notice to the Registrar and the change takes effect on the notice being registered by the Registrar, though the company can act on the change at any time within 14 days of giving the notice.[34] The Registrar must also publish notice of the change in the *Gazette.*[35] The address of the registered office, together with place of registration and registered number must also be mentioned on all business letters and order forms.[36] Apart from

[31] s. 2(1)(b) C.A. 1985.

[32] s. 710B C.A. 1985 inserted by s. 30(6) of the Welsh Language Act 1993. Documents which do not require an accompanying translation into English and which apply to companies other than public companies whose shares or debentures (or any class thereof) are listed, include, *inter alia*, copies of the annual accounts, directors' report and auditors' report: The Companies (Welsh Language Forms and Documents) Regulations 1994 (S.I. 1994 No. 117) as amended by The Companies (Welsh Language Forms and Documents)(Amendment) Regulations 1994 (S.I. 1994 No. 727).

[33] s. 10(6) C.A. 1985.

[34] s. 287(3), (4), (5) C.A. 1985 substituted by s. 136 C.A. 1989.

[35] s. 711 C.A. 1985.

[36] s. 351 C.A. 1985.

being the place where certain company registers and documents must be kept, the registered office is also the place of service for most legal documents, service being effected by leaving the document at the registered office or sending it by post.[37] Following a change of registered office, service of a document by another party to the old address will be valid if:

(i) service takes place within 14 days of the registration of the change[38]; or

(ii) the change of address was not Gazetted by the Registrar and the other party cannot be shown to have known of the change or if the document was served to the previous address within 15 days of official notification by the Registrar to the *Gazette* and it is shown that the other party was unavoidably prevented from knowing of the event at that time.[39]

D. Objects clause

1. *Origin*

The original purpose of the objects clause in the memorandum of association, as contemplated by successive Companies Acts, was to provide a concise statement of a company's business whilst allowing for incidental activities. Yet in practice objects clauses have become lengthy lists of objects and powers as those in business have attempted to counteract the *ultra vires* rule. Even though, as will be seen, the Companies Act 1989 introduced important reforms, abolishing the external effects of the *ultra vires* rule and permitting a new short form comprehensive objects clause, it is likely that draftsmen may still choose the longer form which has become traditional.

2. *Traditional objects clauses*

Table B of the Companies (Tables A–F) Regulations 1985[40] contains a concise single paragraph objects clause for a private

---

[37] s. 725(1) C.A. 1985. The County Court (Amendment) Rules 1989 (S.I. 1989 No. 236) permit a plaintiff to serve a summons on a company registered in England and Wales at a place of business other than its registered office.

[38] s. 287(4) C.A. 1985, substituted by s. 136 C.A. 1989.

[39] s. 42(1) C.A. 1985.

[40] (S.I. 1985 No. 805): see Appendix 1, *post*.

company limited by shares which provides specifically for a well-defined activity and which concludes with words enabling the company to do "all such other things as are incidental or conductive to the attainment of that object". A similar short model clause is provided for a public company by Table F of the Regulations. Yet despite the statutory requirement that the memoranda of association of companies must be as specified in the Regulations "or as near to that form as circumstances admit,"[41] the modern practice for private companies, no matter how small,[42] is to have long objects clauses containing a comprehensive list of potential activities supplemented by a list of ancillary powers, enabling the company to embark upon a very wide range of activity if it so chooses.

(a) *The ultra vires rule*

The reason for the width of objects clauses has been the desire by corporate business to counteract the application by the courts of the *ultra vires* rule to corporate capacity. If a company performed activities which fell outside the scope of its objects clause, such activities were *ultra vires*, void and incapable of ratification even by a unanimous vote of the company's members.[43] The courts applied the *ultra vires* principle to companies in order to defend the objects clause as a protection to both shareholders, who could learn from it the purposes for which they had invested their money, and creditors, who could feel assured that the company's capital was not at risk of being wasted on unauthorised purposes.

The Companies Act 1989, following the recommendations of the Prentice Report,[44] abolished the *ultra vires* rule in respect of the company and outside contracting parties. The position of outsiders is further considered elsewhere in this work.[45] We are here concerned with how far the recent reforms will affect the drafting of objects clauses.

(b) *The Companies Act 1985, section 35*

Section 108 of the Companies Act 1989 inserted a new section 35 into the Companies Act 1985. Section 35(1) provides:

---

[41] s. 3(1) C.A. 1985.
[42] *A fortiori* for public companies.
[43] *Ashbury Railway Carriage Co. v. Riche* (1875) L.R. 7 H.L. 653.
[44] Dr D. D. Prentice, "Reform of Ultra Vires," (1986 D.T.I.)
[45] Chap. 8, *post*.

> "The validity of an act done by a company shall not be called into question on the ground of lack of capacity by reason of anything in the company's memorandum."

Yet whilst the external effects of *ultra vires* have thus been abolished, the internal aspects of the rule remain. Section 35(2) preserves the right of a member to bring proceedings to restrain the doing of an act "which but for subsection (1) would be beyond the company's capacity" except that no proceedings can be brought to restrain an act to be done in fulfilment of a legal obligation arising from a previous act of the company.[46] The member's right is based on the contract created by section 14 of the Companies Act 1985 which provides that the memorandum and articles bind the company and its members as though they had been signed and sealed by each member and contained covenants on the part of each member to observe all their provisions. Apart from this contractual right, members have always had a more general personal right to restrain proposed *ultra vires* activity.[47] According to the Prentice Report[48] the instances where a shareholder will have the necessary forewarning to prevent a company acting outside its objects (if, indeed, the shareholder is acquainted with the objects) will be rare. Whilst this is certainly true of a public company, the opportunity afforded to a shareholder is likely to be greater in the case of a small private company. It should be mentioned that section 35A(4) preserves "any right of a member" to restrain acts beyond the powers of the directors, again prior to the creation of a legal obligation, but, as discussed in a later chapter, the scope of a member's right in this respect is uncertain.[49]

Where a member does seek an injunction to prevent a company acting outside its capacity it will remain the task of the court to determine, on a true construction of the objects clause, whether the proposed activity would be *ultra vires* and there will therefore continue to be a corresponding desire by company directors to ensure that objects clauses are drafted so as to afford them the greatest possible latitude. Even though the courts have been prepared to imply powers on the part of

---

[46] Thus a member cannot prevent the completion of an executory contract.

[47] *Colman v. Eastern Counties Ry. Co.* (1846) 10 Beav. 1; *Simpson v. Westminster Palace Hotel Co.* (1860) 8 H.L. Cas. 712.

[48] Prentice, *op. cit. ante*, pp. 15 and 61.

[49] Chap. 8, *post*.

companies to undertake activities incidental to or consequential upon their stated objects[50] the practice has been for objects clauses to include a comprehensive list of express powers which purport to be indistinguishable from objects. In *Re Horsley and Weight Ltd.*,[51] Buckley L.J. stated that the exercise of an implied power, or a power which was, on a proper construction, ancillary to the dominant object of the company, was *ultra vires* unless undertaken for a purpose ancillary or incidental to the pursuit of the dominant object. In *Rolled Steel Products (Holdings) Ltd. v. British Steel Corporation*,[52] however, the Court of Appeal, narrowing considerably the scope of the *ultra vires* rule, held that directors who exercised powers, express or implied, for purposes other than proper corporate purposes as set out in the objects clause were acting in abuse of their powers, and thus in breach of duty, rather than committing the company to acts falling outside its capacity. *Ultra vires* was confined to acts which were incapable of falling within the authorization of the objects clause. Cases previously regarded as having been decided on the basis of *ultra vires* were interpreted by the Court of Appeal as being cases of abuse of directors' powers. Examples of such breaches of duty by directors would include the following: causing company A to guarantee and secure the liability of company B without intending to benefit company A[53]; exercising a company's power to borrow money for purposes outside the company's objects[54]; purchasing goods for purposes not falling within the objects clause.[55]

Companies normally include in their objects clauses powers enabling the payment of gratuities, annuities and pensions and the making of donations to any charitable or public object. In the absence of such express powers the courts may hold that any proposed payment would be beyond the capacity of the company, and thus challengeable by a member under section 35(2) of the Companies Act 1985, unless it would be reasonably incidental to the carrying on of the company's business, would

---

[50] *A.-G. v. Great Eastern Railway* (1850) 5 App.Cas. 473.

[51] [1982] Ch. 442.

[52] [1986] Ch. 246.

[53] *Rolled Steel Products (Holdings) Ltd. v. British Steel Corporation*, *ibid.*; *per* Pennycuick J. in *Charterbridge Corpn. Ltd. v. Lloyds Bank Ltd.* [1970] Ch. 62. Objects clauses now usually include a power to guarantee third-party liability.

[54] *Re David Payne Ltd.* [1904] 2 Ch. 608; *Introductions Ltd. v. National Provincial Bank Ltd.* [1970] Ch. 199.

[55] *cf. Re Jon Beauforte (London) Ltd.* [1953] Ch. 131, a case not referred to in the judgments in *Rolled Steel*, *ante*.

be a bona fide transaction and would benefit and promote the prosperity of the company. These tests, originally propounded by Eve J. in *Re Lee Behrens & Co.*[56] as requirements for holding the exercise of an express power *intra vires*, were held by Pennycuick J. in *Charterbridge Corpn. Ltd. v. Lloyds Bank Ltd.*[57] to be relevant to implied powers, the bona fides test being principally relevant to directors' duties.[58] Proposed payments by way of gratuity or annuity to relatives and dependants of directors or employees which are not expressly authorised by a power in the objects clause may therefore be vulnerable[59] as might proposed political or other donations.[60] *Rolled Steel*[61] is an authority on the *exercise* of corporate powers by directors: it does not decide that the courts will in all cases recognise the *existence* of an implied power.

The effect of section 35(1) of the Companies Act[62] is, as has been seen, that once a company has performed an act, even one patently unauthorised by the objects clause, that act cannot be challenged on the ground of lack of corporate capacity by either the company or a third party. Furthermore, section 35(3) provides that such acts are now ratifiable for the first time, but only by special resolution. That subsection also provides that directors remain liable to observe limitations on their powers flowing from the memorandum and any liability incurred may only be relieved by a special resolution separate from any special resolution which ratifies the unauthorised act.

(c) *Specific clauses*

In addition to drafting long lists of objects and powers, it has become usual for companies to include specific clauses designed to increase the flexibility of action of company directors.

---

[56] [1932] 2 Ch. 46.

[57] [1970] Ch. 62.

[58] In *Rolled Steel Products (Holdings) Ltd. v. British Steel Corporation* [1986] Ch. 246 at 288, Slade J. was of the opinion that all three of Eve J.'s tests were now useful only in helping to determine whether directors had acted in breach of duty. It is difficult, however, to see how a court would be prepared to recognise an implied power which was not reasonably incidental to the company's business.

[59] The facts of *Re Lee Behrens and Co. Ltd.* [1932] 2 Ch. 46 and *Re W. & M. Roith Ltd.* [1967] 1 W.L.R. 432 may serve as examples. Since in both cases, however, the payments were made under express powers, the issue would now be seen as breach of directors' duties rather than lack of corporate capacity.

[60] *Simmonds v. Heffer* [1983] BCLC 298, but compare *Evans v. Brunner, Mond & Co. Ltd.* [1921] 1 Ch. 359.

[61] [1986] Ch. 246.

[62] Inserted by s. 108 C.A. 1989.

First, an "independent objects clause" or *Cotman v. Brougham*[63] clause traditionally appears at the end of the objects clause and provides that the listed activities are to be regarded as independent objects and are not, except where the context expressly so requires, to be in any way limited or restricted by reference to or inference from the terms of any other sub-clause, or by the name of the company. Such a clause effectively excludes the possibility of the courts discerning any main object or objects and construing other paragraphs as being merely ancillary. It also renders less likely, though not out of the question, the possibility of a shareholder successfully petitioning for a just and equitable winding-up of the company on the basis that the substratum of the company has disappeared.[64]

Secondly, a "subjective ancillary clause" is usually included, the validity of such a clause having been accepted by the court in *Bell Houses Ltd. v. City Wall Properties Ltd.*[65] where the relevant clause enabled the company "to carry on any other trade or business whatsoever which can, in the opinion of the board of directors, be advantageously carried on by the company in connection with or as ancillary to ... the general business of the company". In addition a clause may be included enabling the company to undertake any activity which the company considers to be in any way incidental or conducive to any of the objects, or otherwise likely to be advantageous to the company.

These formulations differ in an important respect from the wording in the model objects clause contained in Table B of the Companies (Tables A–F) Regulations. The latter, enabling a company to do "all such other things as *are* incidental or conducive" to the attainment of the given objects would allow the court, in the case of any challenge to the company's capacity to undertake a particular activity, to apply an objective test and require the activity in question to be reasonably incidental or conducive. It is clear, on the other hand, that the standard clauses quoted above, in making the issue one for the opinion of the directors or the company, are purely subjective and do not contain any requirement of reasonableness provided that the

---

[63] [1918] A.C. 514, the case in which the use of such a clause was first approved by the court.

[64] As occurred in *Re German Date Coffee Co. Ltd.* (1882) 20 Ch.D. 169 (C.A.).

[65] [1966] 2 Q.B. 656 (C.A.).

directors have, or the company has, acted bona fide.[66] It also appears that where the decision is stated to be one for the directors, no board meeting need have been held, provided consensus and commitment can be inferred from the directors' actions.[67] The issue of whether it is the opinion of the directors or the opinion of the company which is required will be irrelevant to many private companies whose directors will hold the controlling shares.

It is important, however, to appreciate the limitations of a subjective ancillary clause. It would not, for example, allow the directors completely to abandon the existing business of the company and embark upon a new activity otherwise unprovided for in the objects clause.[68]

3. *The new short form objects clause*

(a) *Construction of objects clauses*

The courts have, in recent years, tended towards a liberal construction of the wording of objects clauses rather than following a strict *ejusdem generis* approach. In *Re New Finance and Mortgage Co. Ltd. (in liquidation)*[69] the term "and merchants generally," following a specific list of commercial and financial functions, was held to include the operation of a petrol station. Viscount Dilhorne went further in *Newstead (Inspector of Taxes) v. Frost.*[70] Unable to discern a *genus* in the paragraph at issue he concluded that the words "or other operations" were intended to encompass activity not covered by the preceding words. He added: "It is true that if they are given an unlimited meaning it is hard to see the purpose of the other words ... for a statement that the objects of the company were to carry on and execute all kinds of operations would cover all the other stated objects."[71]

Yet, in *Re Crown Bank* North J. stated that a provision in the objects clause that a company might carry on any business whatever, which the company might think profitable to the shareholders, would not be a sufficient statement of objects.[72]

---

[66] *ibid.*
[67] *ibid.*
[68] *Introductions Ltd. v. National Provincial Bank Ltd.* [1970] Ch. 199 (C.A.).
[69] [1975] Ch. 420.
[70] [1980] 1 W.L.R. 135.
[71] *ibid.* at 141.
[72] (1890) 44 Ch.D. 634 at 644.

Further, in *Introductions Ltd. v. National Provincial Bank Ltd.* Harman J. declared that "you cannot have an object to do every mortal thing you want"[73] and this statement appears to continue to represent the law notwithstanding the new comprehensive short clause introduced by the Companies Act 1989.

(b) *Companies Act 1985, section 3A*

Section 110 of the Companies Act 1989 inserted a new section 3A in the Companies Act 1985 which provides:

> "Where the company's memorandum states that the object of the company is to carry on business as a general commercial company—
>
> (a) the object of the company is to carry on any trade or business whatsoever, and
> (b) the company has power to do all such things as are incidental or conducive to the carrying on of any trade or business by it."

(c) *Limitations of the new short form objects clause*

Whereas the great majority of trading private companies will be able to adopt the new clause if they so choose, corporate charities and many typical guarantee companies are excluded by the term "general commercial company". It has been suggested that whilst it may not necessarily be easy to persuade shareholders of the advantage of the new clause where shareholding and management is split, the clause will prove useful in companies where the shareholders are themselves managers.[74] With respect, however, there may be many private companies such as those set up to undertake a single venture or companies which are essentially quasi-partnerships where a stricter delineation of objects will be required by promoters.

Moreover, it is by no means certain that the new clause will, of itself, meet all the requirements of managers of private companies. The abandonment of an existing business in favour

[73] [1970] Ch. 199 at 209.
[74] Nigel Furey, *The Companies Act 1989: A Practitioner's Guide* (1990), p. 54.

of a completely new business is certainly comprehended, but it has been suggested that the sale or other disposal of a company's entire undertaking may not be covered.[75]

Further, it has already been seen that the courts may be reluctant to imply a power to pay certain gratuities or make donations and it must be at least doubtful that the courts would rule that such dispositions, or proposed dipositions, are, or would be, "incidental or conducive to the carrying on of any trade or business". In *Re Horsley and Weight Ltd.*[76] Buckley L.J. in holding that a pension granted to a director just before his retirement was expressly authorised by the company's objects clause stated:

> "The objects of a company *do not need to be commercial*; they can be charitable or philanthropic ...".[77]

As Sealey has argued, "there is no reason why a 'one-man' company should not have as its objects *both* the carrying on of the founder's business *and* the support of his family—especially after his death—and any other objects of his benevolence",[78] but the new provision appears to be of little help in achieving the second of these objectives.

It is also questionable whether the giving of third-party guarantees would be covered, though in such cases, since the court would probably imply a general power to make guarantees, the issue would be one of abuse of power and breach of duty by directors rather than corporate capacity.

In the light of the foregoing, it is perhaps unsurprising that the new short form clause has been received cautiously by company draftsmen. If the clause is adopted at all, it tends to be used in combination at least with many of the powers which it has become traditional to express. Indeed, research has revealed that it is common also to include additional objects,[79] even though the wording of section 3A does not appear to

---

[75] *ibid.*

[76] [1982] Ch. 442.

[77] *ibid.* at 450 (Italics added.)

[78] L. S. Sealy, *Cases and Materials in Company Law* (5th ed., 1992), pp. 157–158.

[79] A survey of a sample of 20 firms of company registration agents showed that 60 per cent used the short clause together with the additional objects from their long form objects clause (25 per cent of these offered the long form as an alternative), 15 per cent used the short clause together with the additional powers from their long form objects clause and 25 per cent did not use the short clause: Sarah de Gay, "Problems surrounding use of the new single objects clause" (1993) 137 S.J. 146–147.

contemplate this.[80] There seems to be no objection to the inclusion of additional powers, though it has been suggested that the precaution is taken of either expressly deeming such powers to be incidental or conducive to the carrying on of any business or stating that they are capable of being exercised whether or not they are so incidental or conducive.[81]

The Companies Act 1989 did not go as far as the Prentice Report's recommendation that private companies should have the option of not filing objects clauses,[82] but, doubtless in anticipation of the widespread use of the short form objects clause, the Report's recommendation that a company should include a statement of its principal business activities in its annual return was adopted.[83]

4. *Alteration of objects*

Section 4 of the Companies Act 1985[84] enables a company to alter its objects by special resolution.[85] Confirmation of the court is only required when the alteration is challenged under section 5 of the Companies Act 1985.[86] Section 5 provides that members who did not vote for the alteration and who hold at least 15 per cent of the issued shares or any class thereof (or 15 per cent of the members where the company does not have a share capital) may object to the alteration within 21 days. A similar right of objection is given to a very limited class of debenture holders. The court may reject the alteration, confirm it wholly or in part and on such conditions as it thinks fit (*e.g.* that the company change its name[87]) and may order that the company buy out the dissentients.

Section 6(4) of the Companies Act 1985 provides that the validity of an alteration to the objects cannot be questioned "on the ground that it was not authorised by section 4" except in proceedings taken under section 5 or otherwise within 21 days

---

80 Only if the memorandum states that "*the object* of the company is to carry on business as a general commercial company" (italics added) is the full benefit of s. 3A acquired.

81 Furey, *op. cit. ante*, n. 74, pp. 54–55.

82 Prentice, *op. cit.*, *ante*, n. 44, Chap. V.

83 s. 364 C.A. 1985 substituted by s. 139 C.A. 1989.

84 Substituted by s. 100(2) C.A. 1989.

85 Previously, the alteration was restricted by a list of seven purposes (contained in old s. 4 C.A. 1985) none of which covered a complete change of business: *Re Home Treat Ltd.* [1991] BCC 165.

86 s. 4(2) C.A. 1985.

87 *Re Egyptian Delta Land and Investment Co.* [1907] W.N. 16.

of the date of the resolution.[88] This would not prevent a member in a quasi-partnership type company from petitioning, in appropriate circumstances, for a just and equitable winding-up under section 122(1)(g) of the Insolvency Act 1986 on the grounds that an alteration to the objects constitutes a denial of a legitimate expectation of the member and evidences a breakdown in mutual trust and confidence.[89] Also, whether or not the company is a quasi-partnership, a member might petition on the ground that the alteration or proposed alteration is, or would be, unfairly prejudicial conduct by the majority.

A charitable company may alter its objects but an alteration which causes the company to cease to be a charity will not affect the application of previously donated property.[90] Any alteration of objects needs the prior written consent of the Charity Commissioners.[91]

E. Liability clause

In the case of companies limited by shares or by guarantee, the fact that the liability of members is limited must be stated by a clause in the memorandum. In companies limited by shares, members' liability is limited to such amount, if any, unpaid on their shares and in companies limited by guarantee, to the sum they have each agreed to contribute in the event of the company being wound up while they are still members or within a year of their ceasing to be so.[92]

A private limited company may re-register as unlimited provided that it has not previously re-registered as limited. An application for such a re-registration, signed by a director or the secretary, must be lodged with the Registrar and must set out such alterations to the memorandum and articles as are appropriate. Printed copies of the memorandum and articles as altered must be lodged with the application together with a prescribed form of assent to the company being registered as unlimited subscribed by or on behalf of all the members of the company, and verified by a statutory declaration by the

[88] See *Re Home Treat Ltd.*, *ante*, n. 85.

[89] On the principles established in *Ebrahimi v. Westbourne Galleries Ltd.* [1973] A.C. 360, see Chaps. 12 and 21, *post*.

[90] s. 64(1) Charities Act 1993.

[91] s. 64(2) Charities Act 1993. This provision was introduced by s. 111 C.A. 1989.

[92] s. 74 Insolvency Act 1986.

directors. On re-registration the Registrar issues to the company a new certificate of incorporation which is conclusive evidence of compliance with the statutory requirements.[93]

Conversely, an unlimited company, except one that has become unlimited by the process of re-registration described above, may re-register as limited. The company must confirm its desire to re-register by passing a special resolution[94] which must state whether the company is to be limited by shares or by guarantee, the amount of the share capital if appropriate, and the requisite alterations to the company's memorandum and articles. An application to re-register, signed by a director or the secretary, must be lodged with the Registrar, following receipt by the latter of a copy of the special resolution, and the application must be accompanied by printed copies of the memorandum and articles as altered. Once again, the new certificate of incorporation issued by the Registrar is conclusive evidence that all the statutory requirements have been complied with.[95]

F. Capital clause

This clause must state the amount of the company's share capital and its division into shares of a fixed amount. This is the company's nominal or authorised share capital and represents the amount of capital which the company is authorised to issue. As noted earlier, whilst a public company must have an "authorised minimum" capital of at least £50,000, a private company's authorised capital can be of any amount.[96] The nominal or par value of each share is a matter to be decided by the promoters, and though marketability is obviously not the vital consideration it is in public companies, £1 is usually found to be a convenient figure. There are of course cases where the shares of private companies are bought and sold, and the market value of each share will to a large extent depend on the company's asset value, business prospects and dividend record.[97]

[93] ss. 49, 50 C.A. 1985.
[94] A copy must be sent to the Registrar within 15 days: s. 380 C.A. 1985.
[95] ss. 51 and 52 C.A. 1985.
[96] Chap. 1, *ante*. Note ss. 117–118 C.A. 1985; also s. 101 C.A. 1985.
[97] For the issues surrounding the valuation of shares in private companies, see Chap. 14, *post*.

Chapter 6

ARTICLES OF ASSOCIATION

A. Purpose and requirements of the Articles of Association

1. *Effect of articles on members*

The Articles of Association of a company constitute its internal regulations, governing such matters as the powers, appointment and disqualification of directors, shares, alteration of capital and meetings procedure. As noted in Chapter 5, *ante*, section 14(1) of the Companies Act 1985 provides that the memorandum and articles when registered bind the company and its members as though they had been signed and sealed by each member and contained covenants by each member to observe their provisions. Though it has been held that a company is only bound to a member in his capacity as member,[1] certain decisions by the courts are difficult to reconcile with this principle. These decisions and the effect of section 14(1) are considered where appropriate in the text as they relate to specific issues.

2. *Formalities*

Companies limited by guarantee and unlimited companies must register articles[2] and if an unlimited company has a share capital, the amount of that share capital must be stated in the articles.[3] The appropriate forms of articles for the aforementioned types of companies are contained in the Companies

---

[1] *Eley v. Positive Life Assurance Co. Ltd.* (1876) 1 Ex.D. 88 (C.A.).
[2] s. 7(1) C.A. 1985.
[3] s. 7(2) C.A. 1985.

(Tables A–F) Regulations 1985[4]: Table C for a company limited by guarantee and not having a share capital, Table D for a company limited by guarantee and having a share capital, and Table E for an unlimited company having a share capital, the statutory requirement being that the articles accord with the prescribed form or are as near thereto as the circumstances admit.[5]

A company limited by shares need not register articles[6] but if no articles are registered Table A of the Regulations as above will apply and even if articles are registered, Table A will apply in so far as it is not expressly modified or excluded.[7] Prior to 1980 the prescribed form of articles for a private company limited by shares was found in Table A Part II which contained a restriction on the transfer of shares, limited the number of members to 50, and prohibited an invitation to the public to subscribe for the company's securities, in order to comply with the former statutory definition of a private company.[8] With the repeal of the statutory requirements (except that forbidding a private company from making a public invitation for its securities[9]) and of Table A Part II, Table A Part I, as it then was, became the model form of articles for a private as well as for a public company. Even though Table A was substantially amended and streamlined by statutory instrument in 1984[10] into the form in which it now appears in the 1985 Regulations, and certain amendments (*e.g.* the omission of the former restriction on the borrowing powers of directors) were appropriate to private companies, many of the provisions are particularly relevant to public companies, and it is therefore important for private companies to register their own articles, amending Table A according to their needs. The ideal form of articles will provide a balance between the interests of controllers and of the minority. The sections which immediately follow examine how the articles may provide for the genuine ambitions and aspirations of management and also consider the extent to which the law will intervene to prevent the articles from becoming an instrument of oppression.

---

4 See Appendix 1, *post.*
5 s. 8(4) C.A. 1985.
6 s. 7(1) C.A. 1985.
7 s. 8(2) C.A. 1985.
8 Chap. 1, *ante.*
9 Chap. 9, *post.*
10 The Companies (Alteration of Table A, etc.) Regulations 1984, revoked by the Companies (Tables A–F) Regulations 1985.

B. Control and structure of private companies by means of the Articles of Association

1. *Providing for a close membership: restricting the right to transfer shares*

The controllers of private companies will often wish to provide, so far as possible, that the company's shares remain within a family or amongst a particular group of business associates. In order to achieve this end, the articles of private companies usually restrict the right to transfer shares by giving the directors power to refuse registration of a proposed transferee of shares and providing for pre-emption rights on share transfer. The attitude of the court to share transfers is nicely summed up by Harman L.J. in *Re Swaledale Cleaners Ltd.* where he stated:

> "A shareholder prima facie has a transferable right of property in his shares and that can only be taken away from him by an express prohibition in the articles of association."[11]

(a) *Directors' powers to refuse registration: "directors' veto clauses"*

Table A regulation 24 provides in effect that directors may refuse to register a transfer of a partly-paid share to a person of whom they do not approve, a transfer of a share on which the company has a lien,[12] a transfer which has not been properly lodged or which lacks such proof of the transferor's title as the directors may reasonably require, a transfer of shares other than of a single class, and a transfer in favour of more than four transferees. These restrictions will, of themselves, be too narrow to satisfy the needs of many private companies which will in practice also include an article of the type that was contained in the repealed Table A Part II which provided:

> "The directors may in their absolute discretion and without assigning any reason therefor decline to register any

---

[11] [1968] 1 W.L.R. 1710 at 1715.

[12] For liens on shares see Chap. 9, p. 152, *post*.

transfer of any share whether or not it is a fully paid share."

This was the most common form of clause adopted by private companies registered before 1980 which had to comply with the statutory requirement that the articles contain some restriction on the right to transfer shares. Even though a share transfer restriction has not been mandatory since 1980, most private companies will almost certainly still wish to include such a provision, which may conveniently be called a directors' veto clause, in their articles. Directors' veto clauses are discussed further in relation to family companies in Chapter 13, *post*.

The restriction looks watertight. By providing that the directors need furnish no reasons for refusing to register a transfer, it is intended to avoid the courts placing any qualifications on the directors' discretion. It has been held, for example, that where refusal is restricted to certain grounds, the directors must disclose the ground chosen[13] unless the articles provide otherwise,[14] though even where the ground needs to be disclosed, the reason for choosing it need not be.[15] Where the directors' power to refuse registration has to be exercised for a reason stated in the articles, the exercise of the directors' discretion can be questioned by the courts.[16]

Despite the "absolute discretion" given to the directors by such a provision, the power to refuse is construed as a fiduciary one and the court will at least expect the directors to have exercised the discretion in good faith. Yet provided the directors, in refusing, have acted bona fide for the benefit of the company, the exercise of their discretion will not be questioned further.[17] The discretion to refuse must, however, be positively exercised by the board (or by the director, if only one) and within a reasonable time. Table A regulation 25 states that a proposed transferee must be notified of a refusal within two months, but even if this article is omitted, it is probable that the courts will regard two months, at least prima facie, as the longest reasonable delay since this is the time period for notifying refusal specified in section 183(5) of the Companies Act 1985 (the parallel provision to Table A regulation 25), and

---

[13] *Sutherland v. British Dominions Land Settlement Corp.* [1926] Ch. 746.
[14] *Berry and Stewart v. Tottenham Hotspur Football Company Ltd.* [1935] Ch. 718.
[15] *Re Coalport China Co.* [1895] 2 Ch. 404 (C.A.).
[16] *Re Bede Steam Shipping Co. Ltd.* [1917] 1 Ch. 123 (C.A.).
[17] *Re Smith and Fawcett Ltd.* [1942] Ch. 304.

will hold that the directors' power to refuse registration is lost thereafter.[18]

The court may also, on the priniples established by the House of Lords in *Ebrahimi v. Westbourne Galleries Ltd.*,[19] apply equitable considerations to any purported reliance by directors on a veto clause. This issue and the remedies of an aggrieved transferee are considered further in a later chapter.[20]

(b) *Pre-emption rights*

The articles normally provide that in the event of a member wishing to transfer his shares, existing members have a right of pre-emption, the usual provision being that no transfer to a non-member is permitted so long as existing members are willing to buy the shares at a fair price to be determined by the auditors.[21] Such clauses are, by virtue of the contract established by section 14 of the Companies Act 1985, enforceable by the company against individual members,[22] and by one member against another where the other is placed under an obligation by the clause.[23]

A pre-emption clause in the articles cannot be evaded by an intended transferor agreeing to transfer his shares on the basis that the transferee whilst receiving general proxies will not seek registration[24] but an executor who has been placed on the register of members and who *remains* registered at the request of the beneficiaries is not a "proposing transferor" for the purpose of setting in motion a pre-emption procedure provided by the articles.[25] It has been held that a pre-emption provision was complied with where one member sold to another member even though the purchase price was paid by an outsider and the transferee was to vote at the outsider's direction.[26]

---

[18] *Re Swaledale Cleaners Ltd.* [1968] 1 W.L.R. 1710, where the delay had been four months.

[19] [1973] A.C. 360 (H.L.).

[20] See Chap. 13, *post.*

[21] On valuation of shares see Chap. 14, *post.*

[22] *Lyle and Scott Ltd. v. Scott's Trustees* [1959] A.C. 763, H.L.(Sc.).

[23] *Rayfield v. Hands* [1960] Ch. 1 where the articles contained an obligation on directors to purchase shares in the event of a member wishing to transfer them. Even though the obligation was placed on the directors, the fact that the defendant directors were members was sufficient for the plaintiff member to rely on the s. 14 contract.

[24] *Lyle and Scott Ltd. v. Scott's Trustees, ante*, n. 22.

[25] *Safeguard Industrial Investments Ltd. v. National Westminster Bank Ltd.* [1982] 1 All E.R. 449 (C.A.).

[26] *Theakston v. London Trust plc* [1984] BCLC 390.

If the articles contain a pre-emption provision, they normally contain, in addition, a procedure for informing the existing members of any proposed transfer of shares. Typically, the company secretary is made the proposed transferor's agent in the matter of giving the necessary notice to the other members. Even in the absence of such a provision, it has been held by the Court of Appeal in *Tett v. Phoenix Property and Investment Co. Ltd.*[27] that a term will be implied requiring the transferor to take reasonable measures to ensure that the other members are given an opportunity to purchase the shares. Such an implied term was necessary, according to the Court of Appeal, in order to give business efficacy[28] to the intention to restrict share transfer revealed in the pre-emption clause. The term would require a member who intended to transfer his shares to a non-member to give reasonable notice of that fact to the other members and would afford them the opportunity of offering to purchase the shares at a fair value, to be determined by the auditors in default of agreement. In the opinion of Robert Goff L.J. the procedure to be implied should be the communication of the transferor's intention to the company secretary, who would give notice to the members, and a reasonable period for members to offer to purchase the shares might be between 14 days and one month.[29]

2. *Maintaining control whilst raising share capital*

Whilst the issues relating to a private company's share capital are dealt with in Chapter 9, *post*, it is worth noting in the present context that class rights attaching to shares are normally provided for in the articles. Moreover, Table A regulation 2[30] provides that subject to the provisions of the Companies Act, and without prejudice to any rights attached to any existing shares, any share may be issued with such rights or restrictions as the company may determine by ordinary resolution. A company may, therefore, raise capital through an issue of shares whilst ensuring that the existing majority does not lose voting

---

[27] (1986) 2 BCC 19,140.

[28] The courts will, as far as possible, construe the articles so as to give them reasonable business efficacy: *Holmes v. Keyes* [1959] Ch. 199 at 215 (C.A.), *per* Jenkins L.J., but will not, for this purpose, imply into the articles a term from extrinsic evidence of surrounding circumstances, unless apparent from the wording of the memorandum or articles: *Bratton Seymour Services Co. Ltd. v. Oxborough* [1992] BCC 471.

[29] (1986) 2 BCC 99, 140 at 99, 153.

[30] Companies (Tables A–F) Regulations 1985; see Appendix 1, *post*.

control. In particular, the company may issue the following types of shares:

(a) *Non-voting ordinary shares*

Whilst such shares are discouraged by the Stock Exchange in the case of listed companies and, if issued, must be clearly designated as such in order to avoid misleading investors, they can prove particularly useful to private companies. An investor might not be deterred by the lack of a vote provided he can be convinced that the company's profitability is such that he can feel confident of receiving a good dividend.

(b) *Preference shares*

Such shares have, prima facie, the same voting rights as ordinary shares,[31] so it is therefore essential to a majority that wishes to retain control, that the articles provides otherwise. The most common provision in the articles in this respect is that preference shares shall have no voting rights unless the preferential dividend is in arrears or there is a proposal to vary the rights attaching to the shares.

(c) *Redeemable shares of any class*

These may be issued, if authorisation is contained in the articles, and on terms of redemption in accordance with provisions in the articles, provided that, at the time of issue, not all the company's shares are redeemable. The shares must be fully paid at the time of redemption.[32] Redemption of shares, and purchase by a company of its own shares, which is considered in outline below, are covered in more detail in Chapter 10, *post*.

Though not relating to the raising of new share capital, a company's power to purchase its own shares, including redeemable shares pursuant to section 162 of the Companies Act 1985, is worth noting. A company must be permitted by its articles to take advantage of this statutory power, the standard provision being contained in Table A regulation 35 which provides:

---

[31] s. 370(6) C.A. 1985.

[32] ss. 159, 159A C.A. 1985, s. 159A having been inserted by s. 133 C.A. 1989.

> "Subject to the provisions of the Act, the company may purchase its own shares (including redeemable shares) and, if it is a private company, make a payment in respect of the redemption or purchase of its own shares otherwise than out of distributable profits of the company or the proceeds of a fresh issue of shares."

This facility for own share purchase can be crucial to a company wishing to maintain family or other close control.

3. *Entrenching the position and powers of management*

Although Table A regulations 73 and 74 provide for the directors to retire by rotation (all to retire at the first annual general meeting and one-third to retire at each A.G.M. thereafter), these provisions may well be excluded from the articles. Further, the statutory rule that directors must retire and cannot be reappointed after reaching the age of 70 does not apply to private companies unless they are subsidiaries of public companies; even in the case of public companies and their subsidiaries the rule can be excluded by the articles or avoided by ordinary resolution of the company of which special notice[33] has been given stating the age of the director. The articles of private companies may therefore create permanent life directors with special powers to remove other directors. In *Bersel Manufacturing Co. Ltd. v. Berry*[34] the House of Lords held that on a true construction of an article empowering a husband and wife, as permanent life directors, to remove any ordinary directors by notice in writing, the power continued to be exercisable by the husband after the death of his wife.

An article providing that an individual is to be a permanent life director does not insulate such an individual from the possibility of removal by the company by ordinary resolution under section 303 of the Companies Act 1985. Removal of a director under section 303 cannot, however, be satisfied by the private company's new power to pass a written resolution, introduced by the Companies Act 1989, which is considered in Chapter 7, *post*. Section 303 applies "notwithstanding anything

---

[33] 28 days' notice of the intention to move the resolution to the company and not less than 21 days' notice of the resolution by the company to members when it gives them notice of the meeting: s. 379 C.A. 1985.

[34] [1968] 2 All E.R. 552.

in [the company's] articles," except in the rare case of an individual holding the office of life director in a private company on July 18, 1945, in respect of whom section 303 has no application.[35] The defence against the possible application of section 303 is for the directors to weight their votes by a provision in the articles. The validity of such a provision was accepted by the House of Lords in *Bushell v. Faith*.[36] The facts of this case and its significance in protecting the position of directors is considered in greater detail in Chapter 13, *post*. The following section considers *Bushell v. Faith* in the context of weighted voting rights generally.

C. Control of private companies by means of weighted voting

Table A Regulation 2, permitting a company to issue shares with such rights and restrictions as the company may determine by ordinary resolution, enables the company to issue shares with special voting rights. In *Bushell v. Faith* Lord Upjohn, having given the example of preference shares commonly being excluded from the right to vote unless the class rights of the shareholders are affected, went on:

> "It is equally commonplace that particular shares may be issued with specially loaded voting rights which ensure that in all resolutions put before the shareholders in general meeting the holder of these particular shares can always be sure of carrying the day ...".[37]

Yet the decision in *Bushell v. Faith* goes further than merely to accept the validity of provisions in companies' articles which effect a general weighting of certain shareholders' votes in respect of all resolutions. The House of Lords by a four to one majority held that a weighted voting provision in the articles

---

[35] s. 14 Companies Consolidation (Consequential Provisions) Act 1985.

[36] [1970] A.C. 1099. An equally effective defence against possible removal is for a director to be the sole holder of a class of shares which carry the right that no meeting shall be quorate without the attendance of the holder of such shares or his proxy. The director can then protect his position (and that of any ally on the board) by refusing to attend any meeting at which a resolution for removal is to be put, since the court will not use its power to call a meeting under s. 371 C.A. 1985 so as to override such a class right: *Harman & Another v. BML Group Ltd.* [1994] 1 W.L.R. 893 (C.A.).

[37] [1970] A.C. 1099 at 1109.

was valid even though it was not intended to apply generally but only purported to secure a director's position in the face of any resolution to remove him.[38]

Suppose a weighted voting provision in the articles is expressed to apply to resolutions to alter the company's articles or memorandum. In *Southern Foundries (1926) Ltd. v. Shirlaw* Lord Porter stated that it was "common ground and indeed long established law that a company cannot forgo its right to alter its articles",[39] and it was accepted by Lord Jauncey of Tullichettle in *Russell v. Northern Bank Development Corporation Ltd.*[40] that the same principle applied to the memorandum.

To what extent, then, will a weighted voting provision be viewed by the courts as a derogation from the company's right in this respect? In *Bushell v. Faith* in the Court of Appeal, Russell L.J. distinguished, *obiter*, between a provision that a special resolution to alter the articles could not be passed without the consent of a particular individual or group, which would be invalid, and a provision as to weighted voting which had the effect of making the special resolution incapable of being passed if a particular shareholder or group exercised his or its votes against a proposed alteration, which would be acceptable irrespective of the fact that the result would be the same.[41] Given further judicial dicta[42] the principle now seems well established that a weighted voting provision will not be seen as a fetter on a company's statutory powers to alter its articles or memorandum.[43] On the other hand in *Russell v.*

---

[38] It appears that even Lord Morris in his dissenting judgment would have accepted that a general weighting of votes would have had this effect.

[39] [1940] A.C. 701 at 739.

[40] [1992] 1 W.L.R. 588 at 592, agreeing with the views expressed by Murray J. at first instance and MacDermott L.J. in the Court of Appeal of Northern Ireland [1991] BCC 517.

[41] [1969] 2 Ch. 438 at 447–448.

[42] In *Bushell v. Faith* [1970] A.C. 1099 at 1105–1106 and 1108 respectively, Lord Reid, albeit reluctantly, and Lord Upjohn accepted the validity of general weighted voting provisions in the articles whilst Kelly L.J. in the Court of Appeal of Northern Ireland in *Russell v. Northern Bank Development Corporation Ltd.* [1991] BCC 517 at 535 asserted that it is "trite law" that the memorandum or articles can vary voting rights as is seen fit.

[43] For a contrary argument see *Palmer's Company Law* (25th ed., 1992), Vol. 1, p. 8031, para. 8.033 where the opinion is expressed that if an article such as that in *Re N.F.U. Development Trust Ltd.* [1972] 1 W.L.R. 1548 providing for weighted voting rights, *inter alia*, on any resolution to alter the memorandum or articles was contained in the articles of a private company limited by shares (the company was in fact limited by guarantee and the validity of the article was not at issue) it would not be upheld by the courts since it would contravene the fundamental right of a company to alter its articles (or, presumably, memorandum).

Northern Bank Development Corporation Ltd., Lord Jauncey, having referred to the distinction made in Russell L.J.'s dictum, did not doubt that had a requirement for the written consent of all the present shareholders in a company before a resolution could be passed increasing the company's share capital been contained in the articles, it would have been invalid since it would have bound future shareholders.[44] The House of Lords held, however, that such an arrangement contained in a shareholders' agreement was acceptable. This decision is further considered below.

D. Shareholders' Agreements outside the Articles

It has long been established that shareholders may agree *inter se* to exercise their votes in a particular way and that such an agreement may be enforced by injunction[45] including mandatory injunction.[46]

An unanswered question until recently was to what extent an agreement between shareholders that their unanimous consent is necessary to secure the passage of a statutory resolution would be struck down as an illegal restraint on the company. The answer was provided by the House of Lords in *Russell v. Northern Bank Development Corporation Ltd.*[47] In that case, an agreement, to which all the shareholders of a company and the company itself were expressed to be parties, provided *inter alia* that no new capital could be issued without the written consent of all the parties. The House of Lords, reversing the majority decision of the Court of Appeal of Northern Ireland,[48] held that the agreement was only offensive inasmuch as it purported to make the company a party and, since the company's undertaking could be severed, the remainder of the agreement was valid. Lord Jauncey of Tullichettle saw no reason why the shareholders' undertaking should not be enforceable *inter se* as a personal agreement which in no way fettered the company in the exercise of its statutory power to

---

[44] [1992] 1 W.L.R. 588 at 594.
[45] *Greenwell v. Porter* [1902] 1 Ch. 530.
[46] *Puddephat v. Leith* [1916] 1 Ch. 200.
[47] [1992] 1 W.L.R. 588.
[48] [1991] BCC 517, Lord Hutton C.J. and Kelly L.J. in the majority, MacDermott L.J. dissenting.

increase capital[49] and thus to alter its memorandum. Though the decision is of great practical significance in further establishing the efficacy of shareholders' agreements, it is certainly arguable that for as long as the parties to the agreement remained the only members of the company, the power of the company[50] to pass the appropriate resolution had, at least *pro tem*, effectively been fettered.

E. Resolving disputes by arbitration

It is in the interests both of the controllers and of the minority that disputes between the company and its members are settled without resort to litigation. The promoters of the company may therefore wish to include an arbitration clause in the articles. It has been held that section 14(1) of the Companies Act 1985 makes such a clause enforceable by a member, in the capacity of a member, against the company and by the company against a member.

In *Hickman v. Kent or Romney Marsh Sheep-Breeders Association*[51] the plaintiff member, who was in dispute with the Association and under threat of expulsion, brought an action in respect of alleged irregularities in the conduct of the Assoca-tion's affairs. The defendants successfully applied to have the action stayed on the basis that the plaintiff was bound as a member by a provision in the Association's articles that disputes between the Associa-tion and its members had to be referred to arbitration.

A member cannot claim, however, that a company is bound to him by an arbitration clause if his dispute with the company relates to his position other than as a member, *e.g.* as a director. In *Beattie v. E. & F. Beattie Ltd.*[52] the plaintiff brought a representative action alleging, *inter alia*, improper payments by the company to a director. The director, relying on an arbitration clause in the articles, argued that disputes between the company and its members should be referred to arbitration

[49] The power of the general meeting to increase capital was contained in art. 131 Companies (Northern Ireland) Order 1986 which is in the same terms as the power conferred by s. 121 C.A. 1985.

[50] It is difficult to see how "the company" in this context should mean anything other than the company's voting shareholders at any particular time.

[51] [1915] 1 Ch. 881.

[52] [1938] Ch. 708.

and sought to have the proceedings stayed. The Court of Appeal held that what is now section 14(1) of the Companies Act 1985 gave the arbitration clause binding force as a contract only between the company and members in their capacity as such. The appellant could not rely on the arbitration clause in a dispute that involved him as a director, even though he was also a member.

The arbitration clause in *Beattie v. E. & F. Beattie Ltd.* referred, *inter alia*, to disputes relating to "any act or default of the directors, or any of them." Whether such a clause will bind the company to its *members* by virtue of section 14(1) is uncertain. On the one hand Greene M.R. stated in *Beattie's* case that "the contractual force given to the articles of association by the section is limited to such provisions of the articles as apply to the relationship of the members in their capacity as members."[53] Yet in the same judgment Greene M.R. also accepted that a member (other than the director in dispute) might claim that the company was bound to that member to refer the dispute with the director to arbitration. His Lordship added, however, that the right "is one which a member might find very great difficulty in enforcing in the Courts because it concerns a matter relating to the internal management of the company, with which the courts will not, in general, interfere."[54]

[53] *ibid.* at 721.
[54] *ibid.* at 722.

Chapter 7

MEETINGS AND RESOLUTIONS OF PRIVATE COMPANIES

A. Introduction

In Chapter 3, *ante*, some of the advantages and disadvantages of the private company to the entrepreneur are discussed. One considerable disadvantage (compared to trading without incorporation) was seen to be the administrative burden under the companies legislation which the use of registered companies as business vehicles imposes.[1]

As briefly alluded to in Chapter 3, *ante*, a number of important concessions in this context have been made in favour of private companies. These concessions, mainly, but not exclusively, concerned with company meetings and resolutions, some of which derive from statute and some from judicial precedent, will be considered in this chapter, including the concessions introduced by the Companies Act 1989.

B. General meetings

1. *Companies Act 1985, sections 366 to 383*

The provisions relating to meetings and resolutions of companies are contained in sections 366 to 383 of the Companies Act 1985 and apply for the most part equally to private and public companies. Certain matters need to be highlighted, however, as applying distinctly to private companies or as having especial relevance thereto. The relationship between the board of directors and the general meeting, and the

---

[1] Under the section heading, "The minutiae of company law".

rights of members to requisition meetings, will be discussed, *inter alia*, in Chapter 8, *post*.

2. *Proxies*

A member of a private company entitled to attend and vote at a general meeting has a right to appoint a proxy (whether or not a member of the company), not only to attend and vote in his place,[2] but also to speak for him at the meeting.[3] The consideration of possible delay in the proceedings, which influenced the denial of the right to proxies to speak at meetings of public companies, will not generally apply in the context of the smaller membership of private companies. Moreover, the right of a proxy to speak for a member may be essential where the number of members is small. Subject to enabling provisions in the articles, a member of a private company is not entitled to appoint more than one proxy to attend on the same occasion[4] and, in common with public companies, a proxy is not entitled to vote except on a poll.[5]

It should be noted, however, that the right to appoint a proxy will not apply to all private companies, since the right is denied to companies not having a share capital.[6] Such companies must, by statutory definition, be private[7] and will include all companies limited by guarantee formed on or after December 22, 1980. This restriction can, however, be overcome by an appropriate provision in the company's articles.[8]

3. *Dispensing with formalities*

The courts have taken the view that the statutory rules exist to provide a basic framework for the conduct of meetings and the procedure relating to resolutions, and that in certain cases, therefore, a requisite degree of consensus amonst the membership may reveal that the spirit, even if not the letter, of the companies legislation has been complied with. Such consensus can only realistically be discerned in private companies.

---

[2] The right to attend and vote *simpliciter* by proxy applies equally to public companies.
[3] See s. 372(1) C.A. 1985.
[4] s. 372(2)(b) C.A. 1985.
[5] s. 372(2)(c) C.A. 1985. Again, subject to the articles.
[6] s. 372(2)(a) C.A. 1985.
[7] s. 1(3) C.A. 1985.
[8] s. 372(2) C.A. 1985.

(a) *Obtaining the consent of all the members*

In *Salomon v. Salomon and Co. Ltd.* Lord Davey stated[9] that the "company is bound in a matter *intra vires* by the unanimous consent of its members" and this principle has been widened by the courts in subsequent cases. Thus it was held that the consent of all the members could authorise a transaction in breach of the directors' fiduciary duties even though the meeting was not properly constituted,[10] and that such unanimous consent could also waive the normal length of notice for a meeting.[11] The position now seems to be that provided there is agreement among all the voting members of a company, such agreement obtained informally by means of individual consents will be equivalent to a resolution passed at general meeting,[12] even to special resolutions to alter the articles[13] or the objects clause,[14] and will also suffice to ratify an act beyond the powers of the directors.[15] Whilst it is necessary to obtain the agreement of all members, even of shareholders holding minute proportions of the overall share capital,[16] consent, in the case of members with the requisite knowledge, may be inferred from acquiescence by conduct[17] including abstention at an improperly convened meeting.[18] It should also be noted that Table A, regulation 53[19] provides that a resolution in writing executed by or on behalf of each member who would have been entitled to vote upon it if it had been proposed at a general meeting at which he was present shall take effect as a resolution passed at a duly convened general meeting.[20]

---

[9] [1897] A.C. 22 at 57.
[10] *Re Express Engineering Works* [1920] 1 Ch. 466 (C.A.).
[11] *Re Oxted Motor Co. Ltd.* [1921] 3 K.B. 32.
[12] *Re Duomatic Ltd.* [1969] 1 All E.R. 161. But this principle will not apply to a "meeting" at which there is only one registered shareholder who is not the only corporator: *Re New Cedos Engineering Co. Ltd.* [1994] 1 BCLC 797 (judgment delivered in 1975).
[13] *Cane v. Jones* [1980] 1 W.L.R. 1451.
[14] *Re Home Treat Ltd.* [1991] BCC 165. But compare *Re Barry Artist Ltd.* [1985] 1 W.L.R. 1305 where Nourse J., whilst reluctantly confirming a reduction of capital sanctioned by a resolution signed by all the members of the company, held that such an informal arrangement was not generally appropriate in procedures which required the court's confirmation. This would now be allowed, however, under the statutory written resolution procedure: see pp. 82 *et seq.*, *post.*
[15] *Parker and Cooper v. Reading* [1926] Ch. 975.
[16] *EBM Co. Ltd. v. Dominion Bank* [1973] 3 All E.R. 555.
[17] *Re Home Treat Ltd. ante*, n. 14.
[18] *Re Bailey Hay and Co. Ltd.* [1971] 1 W.L.R. 1357.
[19] See Appendix 1, *post.*
[20] See pp. 85, *et seq.*, *post.*

(b) *Varying the notice periods for meetings*

The Companies Act 1985, re-enacting previous legislation, has also relaxed the normal rules relating to the required length of notice for meetings, *i.e.* written notice of at least 21 days for an annual general meeting and an extraordinary general meeting at which a special resolution is to be proposed, and for any other E.G.M. 14 days in the case of a limited company and seven days for an unlimited company, or such longer period in each case as may be prescribed by the articles.[21] Subsections (3) and (4) of section 369 provide that a meeting may be called by shorter notice provided that, if it is an A.G.M. all the members entitled to attend and vote must have agreed and, in the case of any other meeting, the agreement of a majority in number of members being holders of not less than 95 per cent of the relevant voting share capital or, where a company does not have a share capital, of not less than 95 per cent of the total voting rights must have been obtained. In order for the company to take advantage of this concession, every member present at the meeting so called must understand that it has been called at short notice.[22]

Further, section 378(3) of the Companies Act 1985 provides that, with the agreement of the above proportion of members, a resolution may be proposed and passed as a special resolution at a meeting of which less than 21 days' notice has been given. As will be seen below a private company is permitted by reforms introduced by the Companies Act 1989 to reduce, by elective resolution, these percentages from 95 per cent to a minimum of 90 per cent.

C. One-member "meetings"

Section 370A[23] of the Companies Act 1985 provides that in respect of single-member private companies limited by shares or by guarantee, despite anything to the contrary in the articles, one member present in person or by proxy will constitute a quorum at a general meeting. Otherwise, section 370[24] provides

---

[21] s. 369, subss. (1) and (2) C.A. 1985.

[22] *Re Pearce Duff and Co. Ltd.* [1960] 1 W.L.R. 1014.

[23] Inserted by the Companies (Single Member Private Limited Companies) Regulations (S.I. 1992 No. 1699).

[24] See subss. (1) and (4).

that, subject to the articles, a quorum at a general meeting is satisfied by two members present in person. Table A regulation 40[25] also sets the minimum number for a quorum at two, but this number may be made up of, or include, members' proxies or representatives of corporations.

Apart from the case of a single-member company, the Companies Act 1985 recognises two other situations in which one member may be sufficient to constitute a meeting.

First, by virtue of section 367, where a company is in default of the requirements regarding the holding of an A.G.M., the Secretary of State may, on the application of a member, call a meeting or direct that one be called and make such consequential directions as he deems expedient, including a direction that one member present in person or by proxy will be sufficient to constitute a meeting.[26]

Secondly, under section 371, the court is empowered to direct that one member attending in person or by proxy is sufficient when, either of its own motion or on the application of a director or voting member, it directs that a meeting be called in circumstances where it has been impracticable for the meeting to be called or conducted in the usual way. Section 371 is particularly useful to a majority shareholder whose efforts to call an effective meeting are being denied by minority shareholders whose refusal to attend causes the would-be meetings to be inquorate,[27] and the utility of the provision when what is sought is the removal of a minority shareholding director is considered further in the next chapter.[28] It has been held, however, that if there are rights attaching to a class of shares which provide that a meeting will be inquorate without the attendance of the holder of shares of that class, section 371 cannot be used to override these class rights.[29]

Apart from the statutory exceptions, the courts have normally required more than one member to constitute a quorum.[30] As regards adjourned meetings, the *former* Table A regulation

---

[25] See Appendix 1, *post*.

[26] See s. 367(2).

[27] *Re El Sombero Ltd.* [1958] Ch. 900; see also *Re Opera Photographics Ltd.* [1989] 1 W.L.R. 634 and *Re H. R. Paul & Son Ltd.* (1974) 118 S.J. 166.

[28] See Chap. 8, pp. 105–106, *post*.

[29] *Harman & Another v. BML Group Ltd.* [1994] 1 W.L.R. 893 (C.A.).

[30] *Sharp v. Dawes* (1876) 2 Q.B.D. 26 (C.A.); *Re Sanitary Carbon Co.* [1877] W.N. 223; *Re London Flats Ltd.* [1969] 1 W.L.R. 711. Compare, however, *East v. Bennett Bros. Ltd.* [1911] 1 Ch. 163, where it was held that a single shareholder constituted a class meeting. See also s. 125(6)(a) C.A. 1985, concerning adjourned class meetings.

54,[31] provided, *inter alia*, that if a quorum was not present within half an hour then the "members present" should constitute the quorum[32] and in *Jarvis Motors (Harrow) Ltd. v. Carabott*[33] it appears that Ungoed-Thomas J. was sympathetic to the arguments that "members" in this context might be satisfied by a single member. The present Table A makes no provision in this respect.

D. Alternative procedures (1): written resolutions

1. *De-regulation of private companies: Companies Act 1989*

In addition to the concessions described in the foregoing parts of this chapter,[34] the Companies Act 1989 introduced important, though in some respects controversial, provisions for the purpose of further simplifying the operation of private companies. The provisions, grouped in the 1989 Act under the heading "De-regulation of private companies" and inserted by that Act into the Companies Act 1985, grant to private companies the right, subject to prescribed conditions, to curtail certain formalities and procedures otherwise required by statute. The remainder of this chapter will be devoted to a discussion of this "de-regulation of private companies".

2. *Written resolutions as alternatives to meetings*

Section 381A of the Companies Act 1985[35] permits private companies to dispense with the holding of general meetings and class meetings on condition that every person who is entitled to attend such meetings consents, in the prescribed manner, to their being so dispensed with.

---

[31] Sched. 1 C.A. 1948, which, of course, will probably still apply to many companies.
[32] This provision was repealed by Sched. 4 C.A. 1980.
[33] [1964] 1 W.L.R. 1101.
[34] Concessions of which, in practice, as previously mentioned, only private companies are likely to be in a position to take advantage.
[35] Inserted by s. 113 C.A. 1989. For a review of written and elective resolutions at the Companies Bill 1989 stage, see Fox in (1989) 133 S.J. 932–934, and subsequent correspondence thereon.

(a) *Procedure*

Section 381A(1) of the Companies Act 1985 provides:

> "Anything which in the case of a private company may be done—
>
> (a) by resolution of the company in general meeting, or
> (b) by resolution of a meeting of any class of members of the company,
>
> may be done, without a meeting and without any previous notice being required, by resolution in writing signed by or on behalf of all the members of the company who at the date of the resolution would be entitled to attend and vote at such meeting."

Section 381A(2) then states that the signatures, as above, need not be on a single document provided each signature is on a document which sets out accurately the terms of the resolution.

Provision is also made[36] for fixing the date of a resolution as above, *i.e.* it is the date when "... the resolution is signed by or on behalf of the last member to sign."

(b) *Effect*

By virtue of section 381A(4), a resolution agreed to in accordance with section 381A shall have effect as if passed by the company in general meeting or, in the case of a class meeting, by a meeting of the relevant class of members of the company. Section 381A(6) points out that the machinery of the written resolution extends to the passing of special, extraordinary and elective[37] resolutions.

(c) *Requirements*

In accordance with section 381B(1), a copy of any written resolution proposed to be agreed to in accordance with section

---

[36] See s. 318A(3) C.A. 1985. Note that section numbers followed by capital letters in this chapter are sections of the C.A. 1985, as inserted therein by the C.A. 1989.
[37] See pp. 87 *et seq.*, *post.*

381A must be sent to the company's auditors. Section 381B(2) states that if the resolution concerns the auditors as auditors they may notify the company within seven days from the day on which they receive the copy, that in their view the resolution should be considered at an actual general meeting or, where appropriate, a class meeting. Section 381B(3) provides that a written resolution shall not have effect unless: the auditors notify the company that the resolution does not concern them as auditors; or that it does so concern them but need not be considered at a general or class meeting, as the case may be; or the notice period in section 381B(2), above, expires without any such notice having been given.[38] In any event a resolution under section 381A cannot be used to remove an auditor before the expiration of his term of office. Similarly, by this provision a director cannot be removed before the expiration of his term of office by a section 381A resolution.[39]

In order to ensure that the machinery of the written resolution will be available for all private companies, section 381C(1) provides:

> "Sections 381A and 381B have effect notwithstanding any provision of the company's memorandum or articles."

Section 382A(1) provides that where a written resolution is agreed to, under section 381A, as if agreed to in a general meeting, the company must cause a record of such resolution and the necessary signatures to be entered in a book, in the same way as minutes of a general meeting. The provision then goes on to state[40] that where such a record purports to be signed by a director or by the company secretary it shall be evidence of the proceedings in agreeing to the resolution, and where a record is made pursuant to this section then the requirements of the Act in respect of such proceedings shall, until the contrary be proved, be deemed to have been met.

Section 382A(3) covers penalties for default in this context and also provides for inspection of minute books containing these records.

---

[38] s. 381B(4) provides that a written resolution previously agreed to in accordance with s. 381A shall not have effect until notification, as above, is given, or, as the case may be, the above period expires. In regard to auditors' rights in this context see also s. 390 C.A. 1985: s. 120 C.A. 1989.

[39] See Sched. 15A C.A. 1985 as inserted by s. 114 C.A. 1989.

[40] s. 382A(2).

3. *Adaptation of procedural requirements*

Part II of Schedule 15A to the Companies Act 1985[41] sets out, under the above heading, the necessary adaptations in respect of certain specified provisions, where written resolutions are used. Paragraph 2(2) of Part II of the schedule states that: "a written resolution is not effective if any of the requirements of this Part of this Schedule is not complied with".

In general, it appears that the adaptations are those which naturally follow where the transaction in question is conducted by means of the written resolution procedure rather than by meeting.[42]

The following matters are listed[43]

s. 95—disapplication of pre-emption rights[44]
s. 155—financial assistance for purchase of company's own shares or those of its holding company[45]
ss. 164, 165—authority for off-market purchase or contingent purchase contract of company's own shares[46]
s. 173—approval for payment out of capital[47]
s. 319—approval of director's service contract[48]
s. 337—funding of director's expenditure in performing his duties[49]

4. *Written resolutions in context*

Although written resolutions now constitute an important feature of the Companies Act 1985, the concept is not altogether innovatory.

Thus, regulation 53 of Table A[50] states:

---

[41] New Sched. 15A is inserted in the C.A. 1985 by s. 114(1) C.A. 1989; *per* s. 114(2) C.A. 1989 the former Sched. 15A becomes Sched. 15B.
[42] For detailed requirements see the relevant paragraphs of Pt. II of Sched. 15A.
[43] All sections listed are those of the C.A. 1985.
[44] See Chap. 9, p. 146, *post.*
[45] See Chap. 10, pp. 167–168, *post.*
[46] See Chap. 10, pp. 158–159, *post.*
[47] See Chap. 10, pp. 161–162, *post.*
[48] See Chap. 13, p. 213, *post.*
[49] See Chap. 8, pp. 139, 140, *post.*
[50] See Appendix 1, *post.* For judicial acceptance of informal unanimous assent by members without an actual meeting see p. 79, *ante.*

> "A resolution in writing executed by or on behalf of each member who would have been entitled to vote upon it if it had been proposed at a general meeting at which he was present shall be as effectual as if it had been passed at a general meeting duly convened and held and may consist of several instruments in the like form each executed by or on behalf of one or more members."

This regulation, in theory applicable to all companies, public as well as private,[51] which avail themselves of it, is in one sense narrower than the statutory written resolution procedure. Regulation 53 does not cover class meetings. Yet in other senses the regulation is wider than the statutory procedure, in particular in not requiring the involvement of a private company's auditors.

Indeed, the relationship between an article like regulation 53 and the statutory regime is somewhat obscure and has become an issue of controversy. In the case of private companies, does the facility provided by such an article remain an alternative to, or has it been superseded by, the statutory procedure? Whereas, as noted above, section 381C(1) provides that sections 381A and 381B have effect "notwithstanding any provision of the company's memorandum or articles", section 381C(2) goes on to state that nothing in sections 381A and 381B:

> "affects any enactment or rule of law as to—
>
> (a) things done otherwise than by passing a resolution, or
> (b) cases in which a resolution is treated as having been passed, or a person is precluded from alleging that a resolution has not been duly passed".

Though the DTI is apparently of the opinion that the two written resolution procedures co-exist as alternatives, a significant body of legal opinion is more cautious and there have been calls for the law to be clarified.[52]

---

[51] In practice, of course, only companies with small memberships are in a position to take advantage of this regulation—thus, in effect, ruling out public companies. A regulation similar to reg. 53, *ante*, appeared in the 1948 C.A. Table A, Pt. II, thus relevant to private companies exclusively.

[52] See the Memorandum of the Company Law Committee of the Law Society, "Written Resolutions of Private Companies", in response to the DTI's consultative document of August 5, 1993. See also Howard Kleiman in (1993) 137 S.J. 995.

Even if private companies can still avail themselves of regulation 53 or a similar article, a further uncertainty remains. The regulation does not specifically exclude resolutions for the premature dismissal of directors or auditors. Could, therefore, the two exceptions to section 381A set out in Part 1 of Schedule 15A, concerning dismissal of directors and auditors, nevertheless be effected by written resolutions under a regulation 53 type article? It is submitted that they could not, since in both cases[53] "special notice" to the company involved must be given, *i.e.* 28 days' notice before a meeting at which the resolution for premature removal is to be proposed.[54] If an actual meeting is not going to be held, clearly the "special notice" condition cannot be met.

5. *Proposals for reform*

It is ironical that statutory provisions aimed at simplifying procedures for private companies should impose an additional burden in the form of the requirement to involve auditors in the written resolution procedure. The Department of Trade and Industry responded to criticism of the law by issuing a consultation letter on the August 5, 1993. The Department sought views on two options for reform: either (1) to dispense entirely with the requirement to consult auditors or (2) to make it clear that private companies without auditors may still rely on the statutory written resolution procedure. Since the consultation on this issue forms part of a wider review of company law by the Department, with particular emphasis on small companies, it is to be hoped that whichever option is preferred, it will form part of a comprehensive and coherent, rather than piecemeal, reform process.

E. Alternative procedures (2): the "elective regime"

1. *The elective resolution: procedure and requirements*

Section 116 of the Companies Act 1989, by inserting section 379 into the Companies Act 1985, made available to private

---

[53] See ss. 303(2) and 391A(1) C.A. 1985 covering removal of directors and auditors respectively.

[54] See s. 379 C.A. 1985.

companies the machinery of the elective resolution for certain specified purposes.

Section 379A(1) provides that:

> "An election by a private company for the purposes of—
>
> (a) s. 80A (election as to duration of authority to allot shares),
> (b) s. 252 (election to dispense with laying of accounts and reports before general meeting),[55]
> (c) s. 366A (election to dispense with holding of annual general meeting),
> (d) s. 369(4) or s. 378(3) (election as to majority required to authorise short notice of meeting), or
> (e) s. 386 (election to dispense with appointment of auditors annually),[56]
>
> shall be made by resolution of the company in general meeting in accordance with this section."[57]

Section 379A(2) points out that an elective resolution is not effective unless at least 21 days' written notice is given of the meeting, stating the intention to propose an elective resolution and setting out its terms. Further, the resolution must be agreed at the meeting, in person or by proxy, by all members entitled to attend and vote.[58] Section 379A(3) provides that the company can revoke an elective resolution by passing an ordinary resolution to that effect.

Moreover, since elective resolutions apply only to private companies any elective resolution passed by such a company will cease to have effect if that company reregisters as a public company.[59] In addition, s. 379A(5) provides that an elective resolution may be passed or revoked in accordance with s. 379A, and the provisions listed in s. 379A(1)[60] shall have effect irrespective of any contrary provision in the company's articles.

---

[55] Inserted by s. 16 C.A. 1989.

[56] Inserted by s. 119 C.A. 1989.

[57] s. 379A(1) then goes on to state that such a resolution is called an "elective resolution".

[58] Note that *per* s. 381A(6) C.A. 1985 (s. 113 of the C.A. 1989), an elective resolution can, *inter alia*, be effected by means of a written resolution under s. 381A.

[59] s. 379A(4).

[60] See *ante*.

In addition, an elective resolution or a resolution revoking such a resolution must be registered in accordance with section 380 of the Companies Act 1985.[61]

2. *The elective resolution: some further points*

Section 379A(1) sets out those matters which may currently be made subject to elective resolutions: see above. Some brief observations on certain of these matters may be useful. With regard to the duration of authority to allot shares under section 80 of the Companies Act 1985, a private company can now, by elective resolution, authorise the directors to allot shares for an indefinite period or for a fixed period, which may be renewed by elective resolution, with a specified expiry date.[62] Any such authority can, however, be revoked or varied by the company in general meeting.[63] The authority must, however, state the maximum amount of relevant securities that may be allotted pursuant to it.

Under section 366A of the Companies Act 1985[64] a private company may dispense with annual general meetings by passing an elective resolution to this effect. However, the section also provides that any member of the company can by notice given not later than three months before the end of the year in question, require a meeting for that year.

Also, with regard to company meetings, section 369(4) and section 378(3) of the Companies Act 1985[65] enable private companies, by elective resolution, to lessen the percentage of the voting shares required to permit reduced notice of certain meetings[66] from 95 per cent to a chosen lesser percentage, so long as this is not less than 90 per cent. The chosen percentage will then either be specified in the resolution or at a subsequent general meeting.

---

[61] *i.e.* with the Registrar of Companies within 15 days of being passed or made: see s. 380(4)(bb) C.A. 1985 inserted by s. 116(3) C.A. 1989.

[62] s. 80A C.A. 1985 inserted by s. 115(1) C.A. 1989. Apart from this, the period for which directors can, *per* s. 80, be authorised, either by the articles or in general meeting, to issue shares without further reference to the members is up to five years, renewable, from the relevant date, as specified in the provision. See Chap. 9, pp. 144–145, *post*.

[63] See s. 80A(3). Also an authority given for a fixed period may be renewed or further renewed by the company in general meeting: s. 80A(4).

[64] Inserted by s. 115(2) C.A. 1989.

[65] As amended by s. 115(3) C.A. 1989.

[66] See p. 80, *ante*.

Further, by section 252 of the Companies Act 1985,[67] a private company may, by elective resolution, dispense with the laying of accounts and reports before the members in general meeting. Section 253 then goes on to require that where an elective resolution, as above, is in operation, the copies of the accounts and reports sent out under section 238(1) of the Companies Act 1985 shall be sent not less than 28 days before the end of the period allowed for laying and delivering accounts and reports[68] and, in the case of members of the company, shall be sent with a notice informing every member of his right to have the accounts and reports laid before a general meeting. Under section 253(2), before the end of the 28-day period, beginning with the day on which the accounts and reports were sent out, any member or auditor of the company may, by written notice left at the company's registered office, require a general meeting so that the accounts and reports may be laid before the company. Subsections 253(3)–(5) state what can be done if the directors do not within 21 days of the date of deposit of such notice, proceed to convene the meeting as required.[69]

3. *Potential future changes*

Although the machinery of the elective resolution is only at present available for those purposes mentioned in section 379A, above, the Companies Act 1989 certainly contemplates further development in this regard. Accordingly, section 117 of the 1989 Act empowers the Secretary of State to make regulations[70] enabling private companies to elect, by elective resolution in accordance with section 379A, to dispense with such requirements of the Companies Act 1985[71] as may be specified in such regulations.

Clearly, the power thus vested in the Secretary of State is of very great potential significance, so far as those who operate private companies are concerned. Developments in this field are, therefore, awaited with considerable interest.

---

[67] Inserted by s. 16 C.A. 1989.

[68] See Chap. 17, *post*.

[69] *per* s. 364 C.A. 1985, as substituted by s. 139 C.A. 1989, a company which elects to dispense with laying accounts and reports before a general meeting, or with A.G.M.s, (see *ante*), is required to include a statement to this effect in its annual return.

[70] Draft statutory instruments must be approved by resolution of both Houses of Parliament: see s. 117(4), (5) C.A. 1989.

[71] Being requirements which, in the view of the Secretary of State, relate primarily to the internal administration and procedure of companies: see s. 117(1) C.A. 1989.

CHAPTER 8

THE COMPANY, ITS CONTROLLERS AND DIRECTORS

A. Introduction

This chapter examines the relationship between a private company and its directors and, where relevant, the implications that this relationship has for third parties. Since, in the typical private company, the directors will possess or control the majority voting power at general meeting, the duality of roles of director and controller is crucial.

Directors are, of course, the agents through which a company transacts its business, but it is not proposed to undertake a detailed analysis of the actual and apparent authority of a company's agents to bind the company in a transaction with a third party. These principles apply with no greater force to private companies than they do to public companies. This chapter begins, however, with an analysis of the reforms relating to third party protection contained in the Companies Act 1989.

B. The directors and third parties

1. *Outside persons dealing with the company: Companies Act 1985, section 35A*

It has been seen that a company now has full capacity in relation to its dealings with third parties.[1] The issue for third-party protection is the authority of the directors to bind the

---

[1] Chap. 5, pp. 53–54, *ante*.

company if the act is beyond the company's memorandum or is otherwise irregular under the company's constitution.

The position of outsiders dealing with companies is covered by section 35A of the Companies Act 1985.[2] Section 35A(1) provides:

> "In favour of a person dealing with a company in good faith, the power of the board of directors to bind the company, or authorise others to do so, shall be deemed to be free of any limitation under the company's constitution."

This provision represents a more comprehensive piece of third party protection than was effected by the old section 35 of the Companies Act 1985, now repealed. Gone is the former requirement for a transaction "decided on by the directors".

Moreover, section 35(2)(a) extends the notion of dealing by a third party with a company to cover not only a transaction but any "other act", thus covering the donee of a gratuitous disposition.[3] Further, the same paragraph makes it clear that a person need only be a party to any such transaction or other act to which the company is a party. A recipient of improperly paid company cheques would now, therefore, be dealing with the company and not merely with the defaulting director.[4]

2. *Third parties must deal "in good faith"*

It remains a pre-requisite that the third party deals in good faith though, as previously, good faith is presumed unless the contrary is proved.[5] Section 35A(2)(b) provides that a person shall not be regarded as acting in bad faith by reason only of his knowing that an act is beyond the powers of the directors under the company's constitution. Parliament appears to have followed the recommendation in the Prentice Report[6] that not only actual knowledge but also understanding of lack of

---

[2] Inserted by s. 108(1) C.A. 1989.

[3] Dispelling the doubts raised by Oliver J. in *Re Halt Garage (1964) Ltd.* [1982] 3 All E.R. 1016, where he stated, *obiter*, that such a person would not be "dealing" for the purposes of old s. 35.

[4] As had been asserted, *obiter*, by Lawson J. in *International Sales and Agencies Ltd. v. Marcus* [1982] 3 All E.R. 551.

[5] s. 35A(2)(c) C.A. 1985.

[6] D. D. Prentice, *Reform of Ultra Vires* (D.T.I., 1986), p. 33.

authority on the part of the directors must be proved against the third party.

Whether or not an appreciation that a transaction is unauthorised should in all cases deprive a third party of protection depends on how the courts interpret the requirement of good faith. Can it be said, for example, that a bank acts in bad faith if it makes a commercially sound loan to a small, fully solvent, private company in the knowledge either that the loan is to be used for a purpose falling outside the company's objects or that the directors have exceeded their borrowing limits, if, in either case, the bank has been assured that the transaction will be ratified? The argument in favour of good faith on the bank's part becomes even stronger if it is dealing with a single-member, or effective one-person, company. It is arguable that, in order to be in bad faith, the third party must reveal some lack of probity in the form of an appreciation that the directors are acting in bad faith and that actual knowledge by the third party should include situations where he has wilfully shut his eyes or has wilfully and recklessly failed to make such enquiries as an honest and reasonable man would make.[7]

3. *Third party knowledge of the company's constitution*

In favour, then, of a person dealing with a company in good faith, the authority of the board is deemed to be unfettered by the company's constitution. Limitations on directors' powers in the constitution include limitations deriving from a resolution of the general meeting or a class meeting or from an agreement of members or any class of shareholders.[8] Though not specifically stated, it is clear that the main elements of a company's constitution are taken as understood by the statutory provisions to be the memorandum and articles and it is in these documents that limitations on the directors' powers are most commonly found.

Prior to the Companies Act 1989 a person was, except in so far as old section 35 applied, fixed with constructive notice of the memorandum, articles and a company's other registered

---

[7] See Prentice, *op. cit.*, p. 32 and *cf.* Lawson J. in *International Sales and Agencies Ltd. v. Marcus* [1982] 3 All E.R. 551 at 559, who stated that a person who "could not in view of all the circumstances have been unaware" of the *ultra vires* nature of a transaction would be lacking good faith for the purposes of s. 9(1) European Communities Act 1972, the predecessor of the old s. 35 C.A. 1985.

[8] s. 35A(3) C.A. 1985.

documents and was therefore deemed to know if a company was acting beyond its capacity or whether the directors were exceeding their authority. Section 711A of the Companies Act 1985[9] provides that a person is no longer taken to have notice of any matter merely because it is disclosed in any document kept by the registrar or made available by the company for inspection except for matters disclosed on the companies charges register and of certain registered land charges under section 3(7) of the Land Charges Act 1972. Constructive notice of the memorandum, articles and special resolutions has therefore disappeared.

Furthermore, section 35B of the Com-panies Act 1985[10] provides that a party to a transaction with a company is not bound to enquire as to whether it is permitted by the company's memorandum or as to any limitation on the powers of the board of directors. A provision which might be difficult to reconcile with this is section 711A(2) which provides that the abolition of constructive notice does not affect the question of whether or not a person is affected by notice of any matter by reason of a failure to make such enquiries as ought reasonably to be made. New section 35B applies, however, only to "transactions". Is it therefore the case that a donee of a gratuitous corporate disposition is under a duty to make reasonable enquiries including inspection of the public documents? Does mere receipt of the donation, on a literal interpretation of new section 35B without resort to new section 711A(2), put the donee under a duty to enquire? Even the former interpretation seems too harsh.

A yet more difficult question is how far other persons, though not bound, prima facie, to make such enquiries, ought reasonably to do so. It is submitted that a third party, including a gratuitous donee, should reasonably make only such enquiries (which might encompass an inspection of the public documents) as an honest person would make. There should be a want of probity. Mere negligence should not suffice. This would accord with the interpretation of good faith suggested above.[11] So, for example, actual suspicion by a third party of impropriety in a

---

[9] Inserted by s. 142 C.A. 1989.

[10] Inserted by s. 108(1) C.A. 1989.

[11] See also Nourse L.J. in *Barclays Bank Ltd. v. TOSG Trust Fund Ltd.* [1984] BCLC 1 at 18: "But I emphatically refute the suggestion, if such it is, that reasonableness is a necessary ingredient of good faith."

director's conduct should make further enquiry reasonable: the mere existence of suspicious circumstances should not.[12] It may be that a constructive trustee is covered by section 711A(2), but to what extent a test akin to negligence is applicable to recipients of misapplied corporate assets for the purposes of the law of constructive trusts is uncertain.[13]

4. *Effect on agency and the rule in Turquand's case*

The statutory provisions do not go as far as the Prentice Report recommendation that companies should be bound by the acts of individual directors.[14] The rules of agency continue to apply. Since section 35A(1) now provides, however, that the power of the board to bind the company "or authorise others to do so" is unfettered by limitations in the company constitution, the doctrine of apparent authority through holding-out appears to have been considerably extended. A company may, in future, find itself bound by the acts of individual directors, other officers or employees.

How significant, now, is the rule in *Royal British Bank v. Turquand*[15] which protects outsiders in good faith from any irregularity in internal company management? The abolition of constructive notice in relation to the memorandum, articles and special resolutions (albeit subject to the uncertain proviso regarding reasonable enquiries) and the extended definition of a company's constitution to include all shareholder resolutions and agreements, have certainly diminished the need for outsiders to rely on the *Turquand* rule. The rule, however, will continue to give protection to third parties, in addition to that provided by section 35A of the Companies Act 1985, in cases such as inquorate boards, defectively appointed directors or non-disclosure by directors of their interests in contracts. The procedures covering these matters will normally be found in the articles, and thus in the company's "constitution" and it would seem to be open to the court to treat them as limitations on the power of the board to bind the company for the purposes of protecting persons dealing with the company. If not, the third

---

[12] Compare *A. L. Underwood Ltd. v. Bank of Liverpool and Martins* [1924] 1 K.B. 775 which is further discussed, in Chap. 11, *post.*

[13] See pp. 123–125, *post.*

[14] Prentice, *op. cit., ante*, n. 6, p. 30.

[15] (1850) 6 E.B. 327.

party in good faith should certainly be able to rely on the *Turquand* rule.

5. *Directors, etc., parties to transactions*

Section 332A of the Companies Act 1985[16] deals with the position where at least one of the parties to a transaction with a company is a director or connected person. It provides that where a company enters into a transaction to which the parties include a director of the company or of its holding company or a person connected with such a director or a company with whom such a director is associated, and the board has exceeded any of its powers under the company's constitution, the transaction is voidable at the instance of the company, and that party together with any director who authorised the transaction is liable to account to the company for any direct or indirect gain and to indemnify the company in respect of any resultant loss or damage.[17] This is without prejudice to any other ground on which the legality of the transaction may be questioned or any liability to the company may arise.[18] The transaction ceases to be voidable if:

(a) restitution is no longer possible; or
(b) the company is indemnified for any loss or damage resulting from the transaction; or
(c) rights acquired bona fide and for value by a third party without actual notice of the directors' exceeding their powers would be affected; or
(d) the transaction is ratified by the company in general meeting by ordinary or special resolution or otherwise as the case may require.[19]

A person other than a director is not liable if he can show that at the time the transaction was entered into he did not know that the directors were exceeding their powers.[20] It is submitted that a party should "know" for these purposes where he has wilfully shut his eyes or wilfully and recklessly failed to make honest and reasonable enquiries. Any party in good faith

---

[16] Inserted by s. 109 C.A. 1989. For "connected person" see s. 346 C.A. 1985.
[17] s. 322A(1), (2), (3) C.A. 1985.
[18] s. 322A(4) C.A. 1985.
[19] s. 332A(5) C.A. 1985.
[20] s. 322A(6) C.A. 1985.

who is not either a director or connected person is prima facie protected by section 35A but where the contract is both voidable at the instance of the company and valid in favour of such a party the court may, on the application of that person or the company, make such order affirming, severing or setting aside the transaction as appears just.[21] It is further provided, to be consistent with section 35A, that "transaction" includes any act.[22]

6. *Liability of charities*

Section 65 of the Charities Act 1993,[23] provides that the conferral of full corporate capacity under section 35 and the powers of the directors to bind the company under section 35A of the Companies Act 1985 do not apply to acts of charitable companies except in favour of a person who has given full consideration in money or money's worth and who did not know that the act was beyond the company's memorandum or the powers of the directors or, alternatively, did not know at the time of the act that the company was a charity, the burden of proving such knowledge lying on the person making the allegation.[24] The title to any property or interest in property acquired by a person who gives full consideration without actual notice of any such circumstances affecting the validity of the company's act is protected.[25] Ratification of an act under either section 35 or section 322A of the Companies Act 1985 requires the prior written consent of the Charity Commissioners.[26]

C. The relationship between directors and the general meeting

1. *The board of directors*

The term "board" of directors will not, of course, be relevant in all private companies since the statutory minimum number of directors is one.[27]

---

[21] s. 332A(7) C.A. 1985.
[22] s. 322A(8) C.A. 1985.
[23] The provision was introduced by s. 111 C.A. 1989.
[24] s. 65(1), (3) Charities Act 1993.
[25] s. 65(2) Charities Act 1993.
[26] s. 65(4) Charities Act 1993.
[27] s. 282 C.A. 1985.

(a) *The quorum*

Where the company has more than one director the articles will usually provide that the necessary quorum at directors' meetings is to be fixed by the directors, and Table A regulation 89[28] provides that unless fixed at any other number, the quorum is two. The articles usually provide, as does Table A regulation 88, that the directors may regulate their proceedings as they see fit; that a meeting may be called by a director or by the secretary at the request of a director; and that a majority vote suffices.

It is especially important in the case of companies with a small number of directors to provide in the articles that a remaining director or the remaining directors may continue to act on behalf of the company notwithstanding that the number has fallen below that required for a quorum.[29] Directors who are excluded from voting on any matter under discussion cannot be counted towards a quorum.[30]

(b) *Notice of meetings*

Directors are entitled to reasonable notice of meetings, otherwise the proceedings will be invalidated, but what constitutes reasonable notice will depend on the circumstances and a few minutes, if effective, may suffice in emergencies. Any complaint relating to shortness of notice will not be upheld by the court unless made by a director without delay.[31] Though, as a matter of practice, directors of private companies may in some cases be accustomed to meet informally, a casual encounter will not be regarded by the court as being equivalent to a board meeting if a director objects, at least if the objector has received no notice of the meeting.[32]

(c) *Formal meeting not required*

Despite what is said above, it is clear that in certain circumstances no "meeting" of directors is required at all.

---

[28] See Appendix 1, *post*.
[29] Table A reg. 90 restricts continuing directors' authority in such cases to filling vacancies and calling a general meeting.
[30] *Re Greymouth-Point Elizabeth Ry. and Coal Co. Ltd.* [1904] 1 Ch. 32.
[31] *Browne v. La Trinidade* (1887) 37 Ch.D. 1 (C.A.).
[32] *Barron v. Potter* [1914] 1 Ch. 895.

Obviously this is the case where the company has the statutory minimum of one director, but even where there is more than one director, an article such as Table A regulation 93 may provide that a written resolution signed by all the directors entitled to receive notice of meetings will be as valid as if passed at a directors' meeting.

Yet it appears, at least for some purposes, that even this formality is not required if there is evidence that the directors have individually and informally agreed to a course of conduct. In *TCB Ltd. v. Gray*, at first instance,[33] it was held that a debenture issued with the knowledge and consent of directors individually was a transac-tion "decided upon by the directors" for the purposes of the old section 35 of the Companies Act 1985.

Also, in *Runciman v. Walter Runciman plc*[34] it was held that unanimous informal agreement by the directors was effective to vary a director's service contract. Where, however, there is a statutory requirement that a particular course of action is undertaken at a board meeting, *e.g.* disclosure of a director's interest in a contract under section 317 of the Companies Act 1985, it appears that the court will normally require literal compliance and that the knowledge of directors individually will not suffice.[35]

2. *The relationship between the board and the general meeting*

In most private companies (other than private companies which are subsidiaries of public companies), the company's directors are also the majority shareholders. Such directors can obviously control the voting at general meetings and if they hold 75 per cent. of the voting power they will be able to secure, under section 378 of the Companies Act 1985, the passing of any special resolution that might be required. It may therefore be thought to be irrelevant to consider the relationship between the board and the general meeting in such private companies. Yet it is important for directors to appreciate that certain decisions can only legally be taken by them exercising

---

[33] [1986] 2 W.L.R. 517.

[34] [1992] BCLC 1084.

[35] *Guinness plc v. Saunders* in the Court of Appeal [1988] 2 All E.R. 940, *per* Fox L.J. at 944, unless the non-disclosure is a technicality: *Runciman v. Walter Runciman plc*, *ante* and *per* Dillon L.J. in *Lee Panavision Ltd. v. Lee Lighting Ltd.* [1991] BCC 621 at 637. For a fuller discussion of s. 317 C.A. 1985 see pp. 128 *et seq.*, *post.*

their votes as shareholders, along with the minority, at a general meeting.

(a) *Decisions requiring a formal resolution of the general meeting*

The Companies Act 1985 specifies several courses of action which can only be taken by resolution of the general meeting, often a special resolution. Matters such as alternations to the memorandum and articles of association, alterations to the company's capital, and voluntary winding-up are decisions for the shareholders generally and not merely for the directors.

Also, the general meeting is given certain supervisory powers over the directors by the Companies Act 1985. For example, the general meeting must approve directors' service agreements with the company where the agreement is for more than five years[36] and also substantial property transactions between the company and a director,[37] however toothless these controls may prove to be in practice.[38]

If it is important for directors/controllers to appreciate that in certain cases they will have to exercise their votes as shareholders rather than as directors, it is equally important that they recognise the substantive as well as formal differences between the respective roles since, as will be seen later in this chapter, the duties which they owe in exercising their votes are different in the two cases.

Apart from the matters reserved by statute to the general meeting, it must also be considered to what extent the shareholders in general meeting can remedy a breach of duty or action in excess of powers by directors or intervene in cases where the board is unable or unwilling to act. All these issues are examined in the following sections of this chapter.

(b) *Division of powers of management and control between the board and the general meeting*

Subject to the foregoing, the general meeting in practice has little part to play in management. The division of powers between board and general meeting is a matter for the articles

---

[36] s. 319 C.A. 1985. Includes shadow directors.
[37] s. 320 C.A. 1985; and see S.I. 1990 No. 1393. Includes shadow directors.
[38] There is nothing to prevent the directors voting as shareholders on such matters. See pp. 107 *et seq., post.*

to determine, but it is usual for the management function to be delegated to the directors. Table A regulation 70 provides:

> "Subject to the provisions of the Act, the memorandum and the articles and to any directions given by special resolution, the business of the company shall be managed by the directors who may exercise all the powers of the company...".[39]

By making it clear that the directors' powers of management may be disturbed only by a special resolution of shareholders in general meeting, Table A regulation 70 has clarified a doubt which had existed in connection with its predecessor, Table A regulation 80,[40] which includes the provision that the directors' powers are subject "to such regulations ... as may be prescribed by the company in general meeting." The words "in general meeting" suggest that an ordinary resolution will suffice, but in *Quin & Axtens Ltd. v. Salmon*[41] Lord Loreburn L.C. interpreted "regulations" as equating with "articles," the clear implication being that a special resolution would be required.

Yet in *Marshall's Valve Gear Co. v. Manning, Wardle & Co. Ltd.*[42] Neville J., construing a substantially similar article, had concluded that "... the majority of the shareholders in the company at a general meeting have a right to control the actions of the directors, so long as they do not affect to control it in a direction contrary to any of the provisions of the articles which bind the company".[43]

In *Breckland Group Holdings Ltd. v. London and Suffolk Properties Ltd.*[44] Harman J. held that *Marshall's* case was inconsistent with a weight of authority to the contrary. Indeed, the predominant view of the courts in modern cases is that the general meeting cannot normally intervene in matters concerning the company's management which have been vested in the directors by the articles. Thus it has been held that the general

---

[39] Such a provision may be fortified by an article, such as Table A reg. 72 enabling the board to delegate any powers to a committee of directors or of one director. In *Guinness plc v. Saunders and Another* [1990] 2 A.C. 663, the House of Lords held, on a construction of the articles, that the board could not delegate to a committee the power to pay a special remuneration to a director.

[40] Sched. 1 C.A. 1948. This version of Table A, often with modifications, will still, of course, continue to be used by many companies.

[41] [1909] A.C. 442.

[42] [1909] 1 Ch. 267.

[43] *ibid.* at 274.

[44] (1988) 4 BCC 542.

meeting cannot by ordinary resolution disturb the directors' powers either to declare an interim dividend[45] or to sue in the company's name,[46] nor can the general meeting compel directors to sell company property where the powers of sale are vested by the articles in the directors.[47]

It now seems to be the case, therefore, that whether an article such as regulation 80 of the former Table A is employed, or, alternatively, regulation 70 of the current Table A is included, the shareholders may only control the directors' powers by passing a special resolution or by exercising their powers in relation to the appointment and removal of directors.

3. *Appointment and removal of directors*

The Companies Act 1985 lays down no rules regarding the appointment of directors but rather leaves the matter to the articles. If Table A regulation 73 is employed, all directors must retire at the first annual general meeting of the company and one-third of their number (with the exceptions mentioned in regulation 84) must retire by rotation at each subsequent A.G.M., submitting themselves for re-election by the shareholders. If the company does not fill a vacancy, then in the absence of a resolution to the contrary, a retiring director is deemed to have been re-appointed. Section 292 of the Companies Act 1985 provides that in the case of a public company two or more directors cannot be appointed by a single resolution (unless a previous resolution authorising this has been passed without dissent) and any attempt to appoint more than one director by a single resolution will be void. Since section 292 does not specifically make private companies subject to such a prohibition, it has always been accepted, by way of inference, that the general meeting in private companies may appoint more than one director by a single resolution.

Table A regulations 78 and 79 give concurrent powers to the general meeting and to the board, respectively, to appoint additional directors and to fill casual vacancies, although, under regulation 79, a person appointed by the directors must seek re-appointment at the next annual general meeting of the company. It appears that the company in general meeting has

[45] *Scott v. Scott* [1943] 1 All E.R. 582.
[46] *John Shaw & Sons (Salford) Ltd. v. Shaw* [1935] 2 K.B. 113.
[47] *Automatic Self-Cleansing Filter Syndicate Co. Ltd. v. Cunninghame* [1906] 2 Ch. 34 (C.A.).

inherent power to fill vacancies on the board unless the articles makc it plain that this right is exclusive to the directors, but the inclusion of an article such as regulation 79 does not deprive the company of this inherent right.[48]

The power to remove directors by ordinary resolution under section 303 of the Companies Act 1985, though theoretically a potent weapon in the hands of shareholders, may in practice be difficult to use. Though the right cannot be excluded or modified (*e.g.* by a requirement that a special resolution is needed for removal) by a provision in the articles, it has been seen how weighted voting rights can effectively achieve the same end and entrench the position of a director.[49] Even in the absence of weighted voting rights in the articles, it may be difficult to remove a director for financial reasons since section 303(5) gives a removed director a right to compensation from the company in respect of any separate contract which is broken as a result of the termination of his directorship. In companies which are, in particular, quasi-partnerships, however, the power to remove a director may sometimes be, as several cases have shown, all too easy to use and inequitable use of the power conferred by section 303 may lead to a successful petition by the victim to have the company wound up by the court under section 122 of the Insolvency Act 1986 or to a petition alleging unfair prejudice under section 459 of the Companies Act 1985.[50]

4. *Members' rights to requisition general meetings*

The articles normally provide, as does Table A regulation 37, that directors may call extraordinary general meetings. Under section 368 of the Companies Act 1985, however, members holding at least one-tenth of the paid-up voting share capital, or, where the company has no share capital, members holding at least one-tenth of the total voting rights, may requisition the directors to convene an E.G.M. by depositing at the registered office a requisition signed by the requisitionists stating the purposes of the meeting. The mustering of the required percentage of members to make such a requisition will pose few problems in most private companies. Section 368(4) provides an effective time limit for directors to convene to E.G.M. by

---

[48] *Worcester Corsetry Ltd. v. Witting* [1936] Ch. 640.

[49] Chap. 6, *ante*. For more detailed discussion, see Chap. 13, *post*.

[50] Chap. 12, *post*.

allowing the requisitionists, or the holders of more than half of their voting rights, to convene the meeting to be held within three months of the requisition if the directors have not done so within 21 days, and to recover reasonable expenses in so doing.

Prior to the Companies Act 1989 there was no time limit for the *holding* of the meeting convened by the directors and once the directors had convened the meeting, the requisitionists could not themselves do so.[51] It was held however in the Scottish case *McGuinness v. Bremner plc*,[52] that where directors had convened a meeting to be held seven months in the future, the delay was, in the circumstances of the case, sufficient to constitute unfairly prejudicial conduct for the purpose of granting relief to the petitioners under sections 459 to 461 of the Companies Act 1985. The position is now settled by section 368(8) of the Companies Act 1985, subsection 8 having been inserted by Schedule 19, paragraph 9 of the Companies Act 1989. This provides that the directors are deemed not to have duly convened the meeting if they convene it for a date more than 28 days after the convening notice. Table A regulation 37 which provides that on a shareholder's requisition, the directors must proceed to convene the meeting forthwith for a date not more than eight weeks after receipt of the requisition has presumably been superseded in this regard. If the petitioners intend to move, at the meeting, a resolution to remove a director, they must give the company special notice of the resolution, *i.e.* 28 days before the meeting,[53] and since they are bound to meet one of the minimum number requirements of section 376 of the Companies Act 1985[54] they can compel the company to circulate to members entitled to notice of the meeting, a statement of not more than 1,000 words with respect to this (or any other) resolution at that meeting. The director who is the target of the resolution is also entitled to require the company to circulate to members his own written representations, of reasonable length, and has a right to be heard at the meeting.[55]

Section 370(3) of the Companies Act 1985 gives a further right to members to call a meeting. This provides that a meeting

---

[51] *Re Windward Island Enterprises (UK)* [1983] BCLC 293.

[52] [1988] BCLC 673.

[53] s. 379 C.A. 1985.

[54] *i.e.* they will hold at least one-twentieth of the total voting rights in respect of that meeting; the alternative requirement of 100 members, each having paid up an average of £100 on his shares is unlikely to be of relevance to most private companies.

[55] s. 304 C.A. 1985.

may be called by two or more members holding not less than one-tenth of the issued capital or by at least five per cent in number of the members where the company does not have a share capital. Section 370(1) provides, however, that this rule only has effect "in so far as the articles of the company do not make other provision in that behalf". Table A regulation 37 provides that any member or director may call a general meeting if there are insufficient directors in the United Kingdom to do so.[56] Whether this constitutes "other provision in that behalf" so as to exclude the statutory right conferred on members by section 370(3) is uncertain. It is arguable that it would be open to the court to hold that the power conferred on members by regulation 37 (and by its predecessor article, regulation 49 of the former Table A) adds to, rather than excludes, the members' rights under section 370(3).

A minority which falls short of the appropriate statutory minimum will not generally be able to compel the directors to call a meeting[57] unless perhaps in the circumstances it can be argued that the refusal constitutes unfair prejudice for the purposes of section 459. Furthermore, a minority wishing to move a resolution for the removal of a director at an A.G.M. will be frustrated unless the members can muster the minimum support required by section 376 to compel the company to circulate notice of the resolution to all the members. The mere giving of special notice to the company by a smaller proportion of members will be insufficient. If notice of the resolution is not circulated, the resolution cannot be discussed at the meeting.[58]

It may be the case that a majority shareholder is attempting to hold a meeting in order to remove a minority shareholding director who is frustrating the attempt by refusing to attend, thus rendering the meeting inquorate. In such circumstances, the court may, on the majority shareholder's application, exercise its powers under section 371 of the Companies Act 1985[59] and order that the meeting be called.[60] The existence of a section 459 petition alleging unfairly prejudicial conduct towards the

---

[56] The former Table A reg. 49 (Sched. 1 C.A. 1948) required two members. The change was not only appropriate to accommodate the needs of private companies, but also became necessary for public companies when their minimum membership was reduced from seven to two by the Companies Act 1980.

[57] *MacDougall v. Gardiner* (1875) 1 Ch.D. 13.

[58] *Pedley v. Inland Waterways Association Ltd.* [1977] 1 All E.R. 209.

[59] See Chap. 7, p. 81, *ante*.

[60] *Re El Sombrero Ltd.* [1958] Ch. 900; *Re Opera Photographic Ltd.* (1989) 5 BCC 601.

minority shareholder will not be a bar to the court ordering that a meeting is called for the purpose of removing the minority shareholder as a director, but it will be a factor for the court's consideration in deciding whether to exercise its discretion under section 371.[61]

5. *Residual powers of the general meeting*

Even though the articles normally vest firmly in the directors the usual powers of management, there are certain circumstances in which powers will revert to the general meeting.

Thus, if the board is deadlocked and therefore unable to operate effectively, the general meeting is the only organ (assuming it is not likewise deadlocked) which can resolve that deadlock, the directors exercising their votes as shareholders in the process. In *Barron v. Potter*[62] where communication had broken down between the only two directors of a company, the court held that the power resided in the general meeting to resolve the conflict by appointing additional directors.

This decision was followed in *Foster v. Foster*[63] where the board was in dispute over the issue as to who should be managing director. The board purported to remove the plaintiff as managing director, replacing him with the defendant, but the resolution was invalid since the defendant's votes, which were crucial, should not have been counted due to an article preventing directors from voting in respect of contracts in which they had an interest. The court held, however, that the general meeting, at which the defendant was able to exercise her votes as shareholder, could pass the necessary resolution.

More recently, the House of Lords has expressed the opinion that the same principles apply to a case where the company has no directors.[64]

---

[61] *Harman & Another v. BML Group Ltd.* [1994] 1 W.L.R. 893 (C.A.) where Dillon L.J., *obiter*, expressed approval of the decision of Harman J. in *Re Whitchurch Insurance Consultants Ltd.* [1993] BCLC 1359. Harman J. in that case had disagreed with the decision of Mervyn Davies J. in *Re Sticky Fingers Restaurant Ltd.* [1991] BCC 754 that the existence of a s. 459 petition was a bar in such circumstances. Note, however, that the Court of Appeal held in *Harman & Another v. BML Group Ltd.* that s. 371 cannot be used to override a quorum requirement which is attached as a class right of shares, see Chap. 7, p. 81, *ante*, and Chap. 6, p. 72, n. 36, *ante*.

[62] [1914] 1 Ch. 895.

[63] [1916] 1 Ch. 532.

[64] *per* Lord Hailsham in *Alexander Ward & Co. Ltd. v. Samyang Navigation Ltd.* [1975] 1 W.L.R. 673 at 679, where the House of Lords held that the general meeting or (as on the particular facts) the liquidator may authorise or ratify proceedings brought in the company's name.

In order for the residual authority of the general meeting to come into effect, it seems that the board's deadlock must be complete, the incapacity or unwillingness of the directors to act preventing effective management of the company. The fact that a director refuses consent to a particular transaction under a power of veto in the articles does not entitle the general meeting to pass a resolution authorising the transaction.[65]

6. *Directors voting as shareholders*

Whilst directors owe in all circumstances a duty to act bona fide for the benefit of the company as a whole, it is clear that when directors vote as shareholders, they are not under the same fiduciary duties[66] to which they are subject when acting as directors and may therefore take account of their personal interests when voting.

The position has been well expressed by Walton J. in *Northern Counties Securities Ltd. v. Jackson & Steeple Ltd.*:

> "... when a director votes as a director for or against any particular resolution in a directors' meeting, he is voting as a person under a fiduciary duty to the company for the proposition that the company should take a certain course of action. When a shareholder is voting for or against a particular resolution he is voting as a person owing no fiduciary duty to the company and who is exercising his own right of property, to vote as he thinks fit. The fact that the result of the voting at the meeting (or at a subsequent poll) will bind the company cannot affect the position that, in voting, he is voting simply in exercise of his own property rights.
>
> Perhaps another (and simpler) way of putting the matter is that a director is an agent, who casts his vote to decide in what manner his principal shall act through the collective agency of the board of directors; a shareholder who casts his vote in general meeting is not casting it as an agent of the company in any shape or form. His act, therefore, in voting as he pleases cannot in any way be regarded as an act of the company...
>
> ... I think that a director who has fulfilled his duty as a director of the company ... is nevertheless free, as an

---

[65] *Quin & Axtens Ltd. v. Salmon* [1909] A.C. 442.

[66] See pp. 113 *et seq., post.*

individual shareholder, to enjoy the same unfettered and unrestricted right of voting at general meetings of the members of the company as he would have if he were not also a director...".[67]

Director controllers of private companies can, by changing hats, use their majority voting power at general meetings to ratify, in certain instances, their own irregular conduct. It has been held that the general meeting may ratify by ordinary resolution a borrowing[68] or other contract[69] which is in excess of the directors' authority as set out in the articles. The general meeting may now, by special resolution, ratify directors' conduct which causes the company to act in a way which would previously have been regarded as being beyond its capacity, but this does not affect any liability incurred by the directors.[70] Ratification and relief from duty is considered in more detail below.[71]

(a) *Duty of directors who are controlling shareholders to act bona fide*

In many private companies, directors will hold the majority of shares and so it is important, therefore, to consider the duties to which controlling shareholders are subject when exercising their votes at general meeting. Despite the words of Walton J. in *Northern Counties Securities Ltd. v. Jackson & Steeple Ltd.*, *ante*, it is clear that shareholders do not in all circumstances enjoy an "unfettered and unrestricted right of voting at general meeting." It appears that the courts will intervene to prevent an abuse of voting power by the majority. It is difficult, however, to discern a coherent principle in the cases.

In cases involving an alteration of the company's articles majority shareholders must act bona fide for the benefit of the company as a whole.[72] The cases appear to show that the

---

[67] [1974] 1 W.L.R. 1133 at 1144. See also *North-West Transportation Co. v. Beatty* (1887) 12 App. Cas. 589; also *Re Swindon Town Football Co. Ltd.* [1990] BCLC 467.

[68] *Irvine v. Union Bank of Australia* (1877) 2 App.Cas. 366.

[69] *Grant v. United Kingdom Switchback Railways* (1888) 40 Ch.D. 135.

[70] s. 35(3) C.A. 1985 inserted by s. 108 C.A. 1989.

[71] See pp. 120 *et seq.*, *post*.

[72] The test was first applied in *Allen v. Gold Reefs of West Africa Ltd.* [1900] 1 Ch. 656 (C.A.).

majority must be guided by what they honestly believe to be for the benefit of the company.[73] Bona fides may be negatived by any evidence of malice or improper motive on the part of the majority,[74] and, moreover, an alteration of the articles "may be so oppressive as to cast suspicion on the honesty of the persons responsible for it, or so extravagant that no reasonable man could really consider it for the benefit of the company".[75]

Subject to these qualifications, however, a measure voted on by the majority will be valid provided that there is subjective good faith, even though the measure discriminates against a minority. Thus, in *Sidebottom v. Kershaw Leese & Co. Ltd.*[76] the directors of a private company who held the majority of the voting shares effected an alteration to the articles enabling the directors to buy out at fair value, any member who competed with the company. The court held that the alteration was valid, Lord Sterndale M.R. stating: "I cannot have any doubt that in a small private company like this the exclusion of members who are carrying on competing businesses may very well be of great benefit to the company."[77]

Further, it has been held that alterations to articles have been valid which have the effect of enabling a company to remove a life director who had allegedly committed several accounting irregularities,[78] permitting a majority shareholder to transfer his holding to an outsider thus depriving the minority shareholders of their pre-emptive rights,[79] and giving a company a lien over a deceased shareholder's fully-paid shares in respect of debts owed to the company by that shareholder.[80]

In cases, however, where the majority purport to alter the articles to enable an expropriation of members' shares, even for fair value, then unless as in *Sidebottom v. Kershaw Leese & Co. Ltd.* the measure is of apparent benefit to the company, it is likely that the courts will rule it invalid, thus applying objective criteria of benefit to the company.[81]

---

[73] *Shuttleworth v. Cox Bros. & Co. (Maidenhead) Ltd.* [1927] 2 K.B. 9; *Greenhalgh v. Arderne Cinemas Ltd.* [1951] Ch. 286.

[74] *per* Sterndale M.R. in *Sidebottom v. Kershaw Leese & Co. Ltd.* [1920] 1 Ch. 154 at 168 and, *per* Scrutton L.J. in *Shuttleworth v. Cox Bros & Co. (Maidenhead) Ltd.* [1927] 2 K.B. 9 at 21.

[75] *per* Banks L.J. [1927] 2 K.B. 9 at 18.

[76] [1920] 1 Ch. 154.

[77] *ibid.* at 165.

[78] *Shuttleworth v. Cox Bros & Co. (Maidenhead) Ltd., ante*, n. 73.

[79] *Greenhalgh v. Arderne Cinemas Ltd. ante*, n. 73.

[80] *Allen v. Gold Reefs of West Africa Ltd.* [1909] 1 Ch. 656 (C.A.).

[81] As in *Dafen Tinplate Co. Ltd. v. Lanelly Steel Co. (1907) Ltd.* [1920] 2 Ch. 124.

(b) *Meaning of "bona fide for the benefit of the company"*

What does it mean to say that the majority must act bona fide "for the benefit of the company as a whole"? Evershed M.R. in *Greenhalgh v. Arderne Cinemas Ltd.* defined the test as follows:

> "... the phrase, 'the company as a whole,' does not (at any rate in such a case as the present) mean the company as a commercial entity, distinct from the corporators: it means the corporators as a general body. That is to say, the case may be taken of an individual hypothetical member and it may be asked whether what is proposed is, in the honest opinion of those who voted in its favour, for that person's benefit."[82]

The phrase "corporators as a general body" begs an obvious question, the answer to which may be difficult in the case of private companies. In *Dafen Tinplate Co. Ltd. v. Llanelly Steel Co. (1907) Ltd.*,[83] Peterson J., in holding that an alteration of articles to permit compulsory purchase of the minority's shares by the majority was invalid, stated the problem thus:

> "To say that such an unrestricted and unlimited power of expropriation is for the benefit of the company appears to me to be confusing the interests of the majority with the benefit of the company as a whole."[84]

Yet the confusion referred to by Peterson J., may be unavoidable in the case of a private company. In *Greenhalgh v. Arderne Cinemas Ltd.*[85] M, the managing director, together with other members of his family, held a controlling interest in a private company, the articles of which contained the usual pre-emption provision in favour of other shareholders. The majority, wishing to transfer their shares to a non-member, secured the passing of a special resolution which altered the articles to provide for such a transfer. G, a minority shareholder, challenged the alteration claiming fraud on the minority but, despite the discriminatory nature of the alteration,

---

[82] [1951] Ch. 286 at 291.
[83] [1920] 2 Ch. 124.
[84] *ibid.* at 141.
[85] [1951] Ch. 286.

the court held that the majority had exercised their votes bona fide for the benefit of the company as a whole.

(c) *The principle in* Ebrahimi v. Westbourne Galleries Ltd.

It may be too easy for the majority to mask an abuse of voting power against the minority by claiming that the measure taken was bona fide for the company's benefit and it is arguable that the test provides little protection for minorities in private companies. In cases which have not involved alterations of articles, a different judicial approach has been evident. In *Ebrahimi v. Westbourne Galleries Ltd.*,[86] where the House of Lords held that a petition to wind up a three-member private company should succeed due to the inequitable use of voting power by the majority to remove a director, Lord Wilberforce rejected a defence based on bona fides in the interests of the company. Whilst there might be many cases where the courts would have to assume that decisions taken by majorities or directors were bona fide in the interests of the company, his Lordship warned against the formula becoming "little more than an alibi for a refusal to consider the merits of the case" and concluded that in the context of small private companies, "it seems to have little meaning other than 'in the interests of the majority'".[87]

In *Clemens v. Clemens Bros. Ltd.*,[88] Foster J. applied the *Westbourne Galleries* principle to a case which did not involve the just and equitable winding-up of a company and held that the decision of a majority could be subjected to equitable considerations. In this case, the plaintiff's aunt, who was majority shareholder in the company, carried resolutions to increase the company's share capital and effect a new share issue. Though the aunt claimed that the object of the increase in capital was to give other directors and also employees a stake in the company, Foster J. held that since the effects of the new arrangements were to deprive the plaintiff of her ability to block special and extraordinary resolutions and thus of her "negative control" and also to deny her the opportunity of eventually becoming controlling shareholder,[89] the aunt had exercised her votes unfairly and the resolutions were set aside.

---

[86] [1973] A.C. 360; see Chap. 12, *post.*
[87] *ibid.* at 381.
[88] [1976] 2 All E.R. 268. For fuller discussion see Chap. 13, *post.*
[89] The articles contained the usual pre-emption provision.

Foster J. was surely right to reject the "bona fide for the benefit of the company" test as being unhelpful in the particular circumstances. More difficult, however, was the application by the judge, in favour of the niece, of the "hypothetical member" test suggested by Evershed M.R. in *Greenhalgh v. Arderne Cinemas Ltd.*[90] Sealy has cogently argued that "the plaintiff was no more a 'hypothetical' shareholder than Miss Clemens [the aunt] herself; and if the test had been understood in this sense in *Greenhalgh's* case itself, the decision must surely have gone in Greenhalgh's favour." Sealy concludes that the hypothetical shareholder test is unhelpful in the context of small companies.[91]

The decision in *Clemens v. Clemens Bros. Ltd.*, though controversial,[92] represents an attractive approach to the protection of minority interests and also, on its facts, had the effect of maintaining the status quo in a family company.[93] Yet the line, beyond which the majority's valid exercise of a legal right becomes unjust, necessitating the application of equitable principles, will not be easy to draw[94] and the most satisfactory solution appears to be for an aggrieved minority shareholder to petition the court for an order under section 459 of the Companies Act 1985 on the grounds of unfair prejudice.

(d) *Abuse of voting power as a fraud on the minority*

An alternative approach is for the courts to interpret fraud on the minority as including an abuse of voting power, thus enabling an exception to be made to the rule in *Foss v. Harbottle*[95] and permitting a minority shareholder to bring an action. In *Estmanco (Kilner House) Ltd. v. Greater London*

---

[90] [1951] Ch. 286 at 291.

[91] L. S. Sealy, *Cases and Materials in Company Law* (5th ed., 1992), p. 179.

[92] The court had extended the *Westbourne Galleries* principle to a non-winding-up situation in one previous case, *Pennel v. Venida Investments Ltd.* (1974, Ch.D., unreported) Templeman J., discussed by Burridge in "Wrongful Rights Issues" (1981) 44 M.L.R. 40. Yet the decision in *Clemens v. Clemens Bros. Ltd.* is at variance with *Bentley-Stevens v. Jones* [1974] 1 W.L.R. 638, where the court held that the *Westbourne Galleries* principle could not be invoked to prevent the majority from exercising their legal right to remove a director by ordinary resolution; the principle only came into play on any subsequent winding-up petition which might result.

[93] See Chap. 13, *post*.

[94] Even the decision in *Clemens v. Clemens Bros. Ltd.* might be regarded as marginal on its facts since it is clear that Foster J. did not regard the aunt's conduct as being an obvious example of oppression.

[95] (1843) 2 Hare 461.

Council[96] Megarry V.-C., holding that a resolution by the only voting shareholder in a company to alter the terms of a contract and thereby deprive the minority of their rights constituted a fraud on the minority, stated:

> "Plainly there must be some limit to the power of the majority to pass resolutions which they believe to be in the best interests of the company and yet remain immune from interference by the courts. It may be in the best interests of the company to deprive the minority of some of their rights or some of their property, yet I do not think that this gives the majority an unrestricted right to do this, however unjust it may be, and however much it may harm shareholders whose rights as a class differ from those of the majority. If a case falls within one of the exceptions from *Foss v. Harbottle*, I cannot see why the right of the minority to sue under that exception should be taken away from them merely because the majority of the company reasonably believe it to be in the best interests of the company that this should be done. This is particularly so if the exception from the rule falls under the rubric of 'fraud on the minority.'"[97]

D. The duties of directors

1. *Fiduciary duties*

Directors are under a duty to exercise their powers bona fide in what they believe, and not what the court believes, is for the benefit of the company and not for any collateral purpose.[98] Furthermore, directors are under a duty not to place themselves in a position in which their duties and personal interests are

[96] [1982] 1 All E.R. 437.
[97] *ibid.* at 444.
[98] *per* Lord Greene M.R. in *Re Smith and Fawcett Ltd.* [1942] Ch. 304 at 306 (C.A.). See also *Bishopsgate Investment Management Ltd. v. Maxwell* [1993] BCC 120. It is an accepted principle that directors, as fiduciaries, may not fetter their future discretion, but their duty to act bona fide for the benefit of the company as a whole does not preclude them from binding themselves as to the future exercise of their powers by a contract which they believe is for the benefit of the company, nor is it an implied term of such a contract that they will not thereby be required to do anything inconsistent with their fiduciary duties to the company: *Fulham Football Club Ltd. v. Cabra Estates plc* [1992] BCC 863 (C.A.), following the Australian case *Thorby v. Goldberg* (1964) C.L.R. 597.

likely to be in conflict; they may not make a secret profit deriving from their position as directors and in particular they must not be secretly interested in any contract involving the company. Specific examples of these fiduciary duties of particular relevance to private companies, and the implications arising from their breach, are considered later in this chapter.

Directors' duties are, in general, owed to the company and not to individual shareholders.[99] What, then, does "company" mean in this context? In *Fulham Football Club v. Cabra Estates plc*,[1] Neill L.J. stated: "The duties owed by the directors are to the company and the company is more than just the sum total of its members. Creditors, both present and potential, are interested, while section 309 of the Companies Act 1985 imposes a specific duty on directors to have regard to the interests of the company's employees in general."[2]

As will be seen below, however, the extent to which the notion "company" comprehends creditors is still being worked out by the courts, whilst the effectiveness of the statutory duty owed to employees is questionable.

(a) *Duty owed to creditors (as well as to shareholders)*

Until recently, it had been held that the duty to act for the benefit of the company was to be equated with the duty to act in the best interests of the general body of shareholders,[3] with the weight of judicial dicta being balanced against the need for directors to consider the interests of creditors.[4]

Commonwealth decisions, however, have held that the interests of creditors are relevant where a company is insolvent, or near insolvent.[5] The Court of Appeal has now held in

---

[99] *Percival v. Wright* [1902] 2 Ch. 421, but see pp. 132–133, *post*.

[1] [1992] BCC 863.

[2] *ibid.* at 876.

[3] *Parke v. Daily News Ltd.* [1962] Ch. 927, where Plowman J. applied to directors Evershed M.R.'s test for controlling shareholders' duties set out in *Greenhalgh v. Arderne Cinemas Ltd.* [1951] Ch. 286.

[4] *e.g.* in *Re Horsley and Weight Ltd.* [1982] Ch. 442 at 453–454 Buckley L.J. stated:

> "It is a misapprehension to suppose that the directors of a company owe a duty to the company's creditors to keep the contributed capital of the company intact."

For a contrary view see Lord Templeman in *Winkworth v. Edward Baron Development Co. Ltd.* [1986] 1 W.L.R. 1512 at 1516.

[5] *Walker v. Wimborne* (1976) 50 A.L.J.R. 446; *Nicholson v. Permankraft (NZ) Ltd.* [1985] N.Z.L.R. 242. For a discussion of these cases see *Farrar's Company Law* (3rd ed., 1991), pp. 386–387. See also *Kinsela v. Russell Kinsela Pty Ltd. (in Liquidation)* [1986] 4 N.S.W.L.R. 722.

Liquidator of West Mercia Safetywear Ltd. v. Dodd and Another[6] that where a company is insolvent a director's duty to act in the best interests of the company includes a duty to protect the interests of creditors. Dillon L.J. explained his statement in an earlier case, *Multinational Gas and Petrochemical Co. v. Multinational Gas and Petrochemical Services Ltd.* that directors "owe fiduciary duties to the company though not to the creditors, present or future"[7] on the basis that in that case the company had been solvent.

In *Berg Sons & Co. Ltd. v. Adams*,[8] however, Hobhouse J. interpreted the *West Mercia* case as turning on the fact that the director, against whom misfeasance proceedings had been brought by the liquidator, had caused the company to give a fraudulent preference (as the law then stood) in order to reduce his own guarantee liability. The director had thus acted contrary to the principles governing insolvency and it was "only in this sense that it can be said that once a company is insolvent the interests of the company becomes those of its creditors".[9]

Most problems are likely to occur in the context of a group of a private companies, often controlled by the same individual, where one company, risking its own solvency, makes a transfer of assets to another company which is in financial difficulties. The interests of creditors may also be prejudiced where, on a corporate re-structure, it is proposed to transfer a substantial proportion of assets from one company to another. On such facts, and on the issue whether the directors of a company had acted "in good faith in the interests of the company" for the purposes of determining whether the company had satisfied the conditions in section 153(2)(b) of the Companies Act 1985 to render lawful the giving of financial assistance for the purchase of its shares, Nourse L.J. made the following observations in the Court of Appeal in *Brady v. Brady*[10]:

> "The interests of a company, an artificial person, cannot be distinguished from the interests of the persons who are interested in it. Who are those persons? Where a company

---

[6] (1988) 4 BCC 30.

[7] [1983] 2 All E.R. 563 at 585.

[8] [1992] BCC 661.

[9] *ibid.*, *per* Hobhouse J. at 679.

[10] (1987) 3 BCC 535 at 552. Section 153 C.A. 1985 does not in terms place the duty to act in good faith on the directors but rather its effect is to place the duty on those in a position to procure the company's act in giving the financial assistance. In practice, as in *Brady v. Brady*, this will be the directors.

is both going and solvent, first and foremost come the shareholders, present and no doubt future as well. How material are the interests of creditors in such a case? Admittedly existing creditors are interested in the assets of the company as the only source for the satisfaction of their debts. But in a case where the assets are enormous and the debts minimal it is reasonable to suppose that the interests of the creditors ought not to count for very much. Conversely where the company is insolvent or even doubtfully solvent, the interests of the company are, in reality, the interests of the existing creditors alone."

In the judgment of Nourse L.J., the directors of a solvent company making a large disposition of assets, on the facts of the case one-half, were bound to ask themselves whether the remaining half of the assets would, in all eventualities, be sufficient to discharge all existing debts. The House of Lords in *Brady v. Brady*[11] proceeded on a different factual base. Whereas the Court of Appeal, and apparently the judge at first instance, had made their decisions on the assumption that the disposition had taken place, it was clear on the evidence before the House of Lords that the agreement remained executory. Given this fact it is unsurprising that Lord Oliver was of the opinion that it was not necessarily fatal to the agreement "that the individual parties to it may not at the date of the agreement, when everybody knew that the companies were solvent, have had in mind specifically the interests of future creditors".[12] Whereas it would be appropriate, when the disposition came to be made, for the directors to consider the interests of creditors, in order to satisfy the requirement in section 153(2)(b) that financial assistance be given "in the interests of the company",[13] it appears that such "consideration" is satisfied by a passive test. Whereas Nourse L.J. believed that directors causing such a large disposition of corporate assets were under a duty positively to turn their minds to the possible effect on creditors, Lord Oliver was of the opinion that it was sufficient that the directors knew the state of the audited accounts and that "there was no reason to suppose that the position of any present

---

[11] [1988] 2 W.L.R. 1308. Also, see Chap. 10, *post*.

[12] *ibid.* at 1326.

[13] It is interesting, however, that when considering whether the directors had committed a misfeasance or breach of fiduciary duty, Lord Oliver separated the interests of creditors from the interests of the company: [1988] 2 W.L.R. 1308 at 1324.

creditor was in the least affected".[14] The statements by Lord Oliver, which are *obiter*,[15] make it clear that whilst he did not expressly dissent from the principle set out by Nourse L.J., which is quoted above, he was not prepared to go as far as Nourse L.J. in its application to solvent companies.[16]

(b) *Duty owed to employees*

How far do the interests of the company encompass the interests of employees? In *Parke v. Daily News Ltd.*,[17] where the directors of a company proposed, on the sale of the company's undertaking, that the purchase price should be distributed among the former employees, Plowman J. was clear that employee interests could not be equated with the interests of the company:

> "... the directors of the defendant company are proposing that a very large part of its funds should be given to its former employees in order to benefit those employees *rather than the company* [italics added] and that is an application of the company's funds which the law, as I understand it, will not allow."[18]

The effect of the decision in *Parke v. Daily News Ltd.* has been reversed by section 719 of the Companies Act 1985 which empowers a company to make provision for employees or former employees on the cessation or transfer of the company's undertaking. More generally, section 309 of the Companies Act 1985 provides that the matters to which company directors and shadow directors must have regard in the performance of their functions "include the interests of the company's employees in general as well as the interests of its members", though the

---

[14] *ibid.* at 1326. There had been no misfeasance or breach of duty.

[15] On the issue of financial assistance the House of Lords held that even if s. 153(2)(b) was capable of being satisfied, the assistance would still have been unlawful as failing to satisfy the purpose test in s. 153(2)(a), but that the disposition would be saved by complying with ss. 155–158: see Chap. 10, *post*.

[16] But see *Elliott v. Wheeldon* [1992] BCC 489 where Nourse L.J. at 492, responding to counsel's argument that a director whilst owing a fiduciary duty to a company owed no duty to strangers with whom the company is dealing nor to creditors and *a fortiori* not to a contingent creditor such as a guarantor, stated: "As a general proposition all of that may well be true." The statement is *obiter*, as the ratio of the case is that a director of a joint-venture company owes a duty to his fellow joint venturer who is guarantor of the company's liabilities.

[17] [1962] Ch. 927.

[18] *ibid.* at 963.

section contains no guidance as to how the directors are to balance these respective interests when making decisions.

Moreover, it is probable that directors will always have claimed to have had regard for the interests of employees and one commentator, analysing the almost identically worded provision in the Companies Bill 1978, described the provision as being "no more than a managerial platitude elevated into a legal principle."[19]

Yet the provision does enable the courts, on any issue as to whether the directors have acted in the interests of the company, to consider whether the interests of employees have been regarded.[20] The duty to employees is, under section 309(2), owed to the company alone and is enforceable in the same way as any other fiduciary duty owed by the directors to the company. It is thus for the company, at least prima facie, to bring an action in respect of any alleged breach. There seems to be no way in which an employee, acting as an employee, can have *locus standi.* The most that can be argued is that a derivative action might lie at the suit of an employee shareholder (or, indeed, any other shareholder) but even this presupposes that the breach of duty cannot be ratified by the majority, an issue which is by means no means clear.

(c) *Balance of interests*

Whereas it clearly appears inappropriate for directors to give overriding consideration to the interests of the company as a separate legal entity as against the interests of persons closely associated with it, the corporate commercial interests are, it seems, factors which directors should weigh in the balance.[21]

2. *Duties of care and skill*

In *Re City Equitable Fire Assurance Co. Ltd.*[22] Romer J., having reviewed the few existing authorities on directors' duties of care, made the three following general propositions:

(1) a director need exhibit only the degree of skill to be expected of a person of his knowledge and experience;

---

[19] Ralph Instone, "Duties of Directors" [1979] J.B.L. 221 at 230.
[20] See Lord Oliver in *Brady v. Brady* [1988] 2 W.L.R. 1308 at 1324 and 1325.
[21] *per* Lord Oliver, *ibid.* at 1325.
[22] [1925] Ch. 107.

(2) a director need not give continuous attention to the company's affairs, but should discharge his duties at periodical board meetings, attending when he is reasonably able to do so;
(3) subject to the nature of the business and the requirements in the company's articles, a director may delegate his functions to another official within the company in the absence of any grounds for doubting that official's honesty.

These somewhat lax criteria were consistent with the court's attitude, earlier exemplified by the observation of Lord Macnaghten in *Dovey v. Cory*[23] that he did "not think it desirable for any tribunal to do that which Parliament has abstained from doing—that is to formulate precise rules for the guidance or embarrassment of business men in the conduct of business affairs...".

As has already been seen,[24] Parliament has now intervened to impose liability on negligent directors for wrongful trading preceding an insolvent liquidation. Hoffmann J., in *Norman v. Theodore Goddard*,[25] was "willing to assume", and in *Re D'Jan of London Ltd.*[26] to hold, that a director's common law duty of care was as stated in section 214(4) of the Insolvency Act 1986 which establishes the model for determining whether a director has committed wrongful trading as being "a reasonably diligent person having both (a) the general knowledge, skill and experience that may reasonably be expected of a person carrying out the same functions as are carried out by that director in relation to the company, and (b) the general knowledge, skill and experience that that director has." In both cases his Lordship referred to the subjective as well as the objective element in determining a director's liability for breach of duty of care and skill. It has been seen, however, that the test in section 214(4) is essentially objective, with the subjective elements providing an extra penalty for especially skilled and experienced directors.[27] This has the potential to be a much sterner test for liability than that adopted by the common law

---

[23] [1901] A.C. 477 at 488.
[24] Chap. 2, *ante*.
[25] [1991] BCLC 1028.
[26] [1993] BCC 646. Hoffmann L.J. as he had then become, but sitting as an additional Judge of the Chancery Division.
[27] Chap. 2, pp. 17–18, *ante*, and for fuller discussion see Chap. 20, pp. 318 *et seq.*, *post*.

hitherto. Indeed, Hoffmann J.'s conclusion in *Norman v. Theodore Goddard* that "[a] director who undertakes the management of the company's properties is expected to have reasonable skill in property management, but not in offshore tax avoidance"[28] goes beyond Romer J.'s first proposition, set out above, since, presumably, in such a case, any allegation of negligence in respect of property management could not be met by claims of lack of experience or knowledge on the part of the director.

Whatever the nature of the test to be applied, it is clear that some allowance should be made for the fact that a company is a small private company,[29] and in *Re D'Jan of London Ltd.*, *ante* this factor was important in the court's determination that the director could be partially excused for his negligence by section 727 of the Companies Act 1985.[30]

Though the line between mismanagement and a breach of duty of care and skill may not always be an easy one to draw,[31] there is now ample authority that a director should be especially careful, and not be too trusting of others, in signing any document or form, whether it be a blank cheque,[32] an insurance proposal form,[33] or an authorisation for the transfer of a company's assets.[34]

3. *Ratification and assent*

Shareholders may, by ordinary resolution, validate an act by a director in breach of duty. This is particularly important in

---

[28] [1991] BCLC 1028 at 1030. The quotation effectively encapsulates the decision in the case and thus the director was found not to be in breach of his duties of care and skill to the company.

[29] In *Re City Equitable Fire Insurance Co. Ltd.* [1925] Ch. 407 at 426, Romer J. stated that the "position of a director of a company carrying on a small retail business is very different from that of a director of a railway company," whilst in *Re Produce Marketing Consortium Ltd. (No. 2)* (1989) 5 BCC 569, Knox J. made a similar concession in regard to accountancy procedures in small companies when applying s. 214 I.A. 1986 in a case of wrongful trading.

[30] This aspect of the case is discussed at p. 134, *post*.

[31] It is important that the line is crossed in order to make an allegation of unfair prejudice for the purposes of s. 459 C.A. 1985: *Re Elgindata Ltd.* [1991] BCLC 959.

[32] *Dorchester Finance Co. Ltd. v. Stebbing* [1989] BCLC 498 (non-executive directors negligent in signing blank cheques presented to them by sole executive director).

[33] *Re D'Jan of London Ltd.* [1993] BCC 646: see p. 134, *post*.

[34] *Bishopsgate Investment Management Ltd. v. Maxwell* [1993] Ch. 1 where the Court of Appeal did not deal with the issue as one of negligent signature, but rather as a misuse of power by a director and a consequent breach of fiduciary duty in disposing of corporate assets.

private companies where the directors will typically hold the majority of the shares, since the directors are able to vote as shareholders on the resolution.[35]

Among the alleged breaches of duty which have been held to be ratifiable are the following: non disclosure of interests in contracts with the company[36]; obtaining a secret profit by virtue of being a director[37]; share issues for an improper purpose[38]; and negligent dispositions of corporate property,[39] provided that the negligence has not benefited the directors[40] and provided, probably, that the negligent disposition does not constitute a misfeasance against creditors.[41]

Breaches of duty by directors may not be ratified, at least with the help of the directors' own votes, if the directors have not acted bona fide or if their conduct has constituted a fraud on the minority, such as an expropriation of corporate assets or opportunities.[42] No ratification is possible if a director's conduct has caused an infringement of the personal rights of shareholders. Whereas *ultra vires* activity was previously unratifiable, section 35(3) of the Companies Act 1985[43] provides that action by the directors which would previously have been regarded as being beyond a company's capacity may now be ratified, but only by special resolution.

As opposed to subsequent ratification, the shareholders may have given prior assent to directors' conduct. Such prior assent, as with ratification, need not be made by ordinary resolution at general meeting but is satisfied by the informal *unanimous* agreement of the voting members,[44] a condition which can only practicably be met in the case of small private companies.

Prior authorisation protects a director not because it operates to release or absolve him from the consequences of a breach of

---

[35] *North-West Transportation Co. Ltd. v. Beatty* (1887) 12 App. Cas. 589.

[36] *ibid.* and see p. 131, *post.*

[37] *Regal (Hastings) Ltd. v. Gulliver* [1967] 2 A.C. 134n (H.L.).

[38] *Hogg v. Cramphorn* [1967] Ch. 254; *Bamford v. Bamford* [1970] Ch. 212.

[39] *Pavlides v. Jensen* [1956] Ch. 565.

[40] *Daniels v. Daniels* [1978] Ch. 406 (alleged sale at undervalue).

[41] See pp. 122–123, *post.*

[42] *Cook v. Deeks* [1910] 1 A.C. 554; *Atwool v. Merryweather* (1867) L.R. 5 Eq. 464n; *Menier v. Hooper's Telegraph Works* (1874) 9 Ch.App. 350.

[43] Inserted by s. 108 C.A. 1989.

[44] *Re Express Engineering Works Ltd.* [1920] 1 Ch. 466 (C.A.); *Re Horsely and Weight Ltd.* [1982] Ch. 442 (C.A.); *Multinational Gas & Petrochemical Services Ltd.* [1983] Ch. 258 (C.A.). But informal ratification or assent cannot be claimed if the shareholders have given no thought to the director's conduct in question: *Re D'Jan of London Ltd.* [1993] BCC 646.

duty, but because it prevents the breach of duty from ever arising.[45] In the case of ratification, the breach of duty will have occurred and it is uncertain whether the effect of the ratification is to relieve the director from liability for the breach or merely to cure the irregularity in the transaction.[46] Section 35(3) of the Companies Act 1985 provides that any special resolution ratifying an act which would previously have been regarded as being beyond a company's capacity does not relieve the directors (or any other person) of liability incurred by virtue of the directors exceeding their powers. It is arguable that such a distinction should be recognised generally by the courts. Section 35(3) is further considered in the following section of this chapter.

Whilst it is probably the case that no misfeasance which prejudices creditors can be made the subject of prior assent or ratification, the position regarding directors' negligence is uncertain.

In *Re Horsley and Weight Ltd.*,[47] Templeman L.J., *obiter*, was not satisfied that directors holding all the company's shares could excuse themselves just because they had "as shareholders ratified their own gross negligence as directors which inflicted loss on creditors." Cumming-Bruce L.J., also *obiter*, expressed similar doubts, though he referred to purported ratification of *negligence*.

These doubts were not shared, however, by Lawton L.J. in *Multinational Gas and Petrochemical Co. Ltd. v. Multinational Gas and Petrochemical Services Ltd.*,[48] where he interpreted the references of Templeman and Cumming-Bruce L.JJ. as being to misfeasance going beyond mere negligence.

Moreover, in *Re D'Jan of London Ltd.*,[49] Hoffmann L.J.,[50] on a liquidator's summons under section 212 of the Insolvency Act 1986, assumed that a 99 per cent. shareholding director's negligent conduct might have been informally ratified or

---

[45] *per* Vinelott J. in *Movitex Ltd. v. Bulfield & Ors.* (1986) 2 BCC 99, 403.

[46] In his dissenting judgment in *Multinational Gas and Petrochemical Co. Ltd. v. Multinational Gas and Petrochemical Services Ltd.* [1983] Ch. 258, May L.J., taking the latter view, was of the opinion that shareholder approval, even prior approval, did not deprive the company of its right to sue the directors in breach of duty in respect of their alleged negligence. This right might be exercised by the liquidator or by the company following a change in management.

[47] [1982] Ch. 442 and 456.

[48] [1983] Ch. 258.

[49] [1993] BCC 646.

[50] Sitting as an additional Judge of the Chancery Division.

mandated by himself and his wife, the only other shareholder, had they given any thought to the matter.

4. *Improper disposition of corporate assets*

Whilst problems relating to improper disposal of, or dealing with, corporate assets by directors are not unique to private companies, the possibilities of abuse are obviously greater in those companies in which the directors are the effective controllers.

(a) *Directors and others as constructive trustees*

Directors owe a fiduciary duty to the company to apply its assets only for proper corporate purposes, their duty in this respect being akin to that of trustees.[51] The position of directors and third parties to whom a company's assets might be transferred was thus explained by Sir George Jessel M.R. in *Russell v. Wakefield Waterworks Co.*:

> "In this Court the money of the company is a trust fund, because it is applicable only to the special proposes of the company in the hands of the agents of the company, and it is in that sense a trust fund applicable by them to those special purposes; and a person taking it from them with notice that it is being applied to other purposes cannot in this Court say that he is not a constructive trustee."[52]

Whilst directors themselves will become accountable as constructive trustees if they receive misapplied corporate assets,[53] companies have more often sought a remedy on this ground from third parties.[54] Personal liability as a constructive trustee is additional to the proprietary remedy of tracing which is available against identifiable trust property in the hands of a third party unless the third party is a bona fide purchaser for value without actual, constructive or imputed notice of the

---

[51] *Selangor United Rubber Estates Ltd. v. Craddock (No. 3)* [1968] 1 W.L.R. 1555.

[52] (1875) L.R. 20 Eq. 474 at 479.

[53] See *Guinness plc v. Saunders and Another* [1990] 2 A.C. 663 (H.L.); *Zemco Ltd. v. Jerrom-Pugh* [1993] BCC 275 (C.A.).

[54] *e.g. Belmont Finance Corpn. v. Williams Furniture Ltd.* [1979] 1 Ch. 250; *Belmont Finance Corpn. v. Williams Furniture Ltd. (No. 2)* [1980] 1 All E.R. 392; *International Sales and Agencies Ltd. v. Marcus* [1982] 3 All E.R. 551; *Rolled Steel Products (Holdings) Ltd. v. British Steel Corporation* [1986] Ch. 246.

breach of trust.[55] There are two types of constructive trustee falling, according to the courts' classification, into either a "knowing assistance" category or a "knowing receipt or dealing" category. In *Baden Delvaux and Lecuit v. Societé General S.A.*[56] Peter Gibson J. listed five states of mind which might be relevant to establishing liability as a constructive trustee:

(i) actual knowledge;
(ii) wilfully shutting one's eyes to the obvious;
(iii) wilfully and recklessly failing to make such enquiries as an honest and reasonable man would make;
(iv) knowledge of circumstances which would indicate the facts to an honest and reasonable man;
(v) knowledge of circumstances which would put an honest and reasonable man on enquiry.

His Lordship agreed with counsel that no distinction should be drawn in this respect between "knowing assistance" and "knowing receipt." The tests can be put into two categories; whilst (i)–(iii) require knowledge, actual or inferred, (iv) and (v) require only constructive knowledge or notice, a difference between want of probity on the one hand, and "negligence" on the other.

It had previously been held, in the two *Belmont Finance Corpn. v. Williams Furniture Ltd.* cases[57] that whilst an assister (*e.g.* a bank acting as a channel through which misapplied corporate funds pass) required knowledge in the sense described above, constructive knowledge sufficed for a recipient, *i.e.* he would be liable if he ought to have known of the breach of trust. It has been said now to be "settled law" that a want of probity is required for liability in the knowing assistance category.[58] The state of mind necessary to establish liability under the head of knowing receipt has, however, proved to be

[55] *Re Diplock* [1948] Ch. 465.
[56] [1983] BCLC 325.
[57] [1979] 1 Ch. 250; [1980] 1 All E.R. 392. Followed by Lawson J. in *International Sales and Agencies Ltd. v. Marcus* [1982] 3 All E.R. 551.
[58] *per* Vinelott J. in *Eagle Trust plc v. SBC Securities Ltd.* [1992] 4 All E.R. 388 at 499, approved by Scott L.J. in *Polly Peck International plc v. Nadir (No. 2)* [1992] 4 All E.R. 769 at 777. This is despite the view of Fox L.J. in *Agip (Africa) Ltd. v. Jackson* [1991] Ch. 547 that the *Baden* tests (i)–(v) were relevant in cases of knowing assistance.

more controversial, though, on the present state of the authorities, the following principles appear to have emerged: whilst knowledge in the *Baden* (i)–(iii) sense, *i.e.* a want of probity, is probably not a pre-condition for liability as a knowing recipient,[59] such knowledge is normally required in the context of commercial transactions,[60] and, in any case, a recipient will not be expected to be unduly suspicious.[61]

Thus, a person who, in good faith, purchases corporate assets at an undervalue, or receives misapplied corporate funds in discharge of a liability should not be liable as a constructive trustee, but the possibility remains that a bona fide gratuitous donee of corporate assets will be so liable on the basis of constructive knowledge or notice.

(b) *Statutory liability for misapplication of corporate property*

What effect do the new statutory provisions introduced by the Companies Act 1989 relating to dealings between the company and others have on misapplications of corporate property and particularly on the constructive trustee?

It has been seen that where the company's own directors (or persons connected with them) are parties in transactions or other acts with the company in which the board has exceeded its powers, then, apart from the transaction being voidable, the director is liable to the company to account for any personal gain and indemnify any loss or damage. This is without prejudice to any other liability the director may have incurred.[62] The directors are under a duty to observe their powers whether contained in the memorandum[63] or elsewhere in the company's constitution and in unauthorised dealings with third parties "any liability incurred by the directors or any other person" is preserved.[64] In cases where the directors have exceeded

---

[59] Contrary to the view of Megarry V.-C. in *Re Montagu's Settlement Trusts* [1987] Ch. 264, followed by Alliot J. at first instance in *Lipkin Gorman v. Karpnale Ltd.* [1987] 1 W.L.R. 987 (neither the Court of Appeal nor House of Lords in this case, for whose judgment see [1991] 2 A.C. 548, dealt with this issue).

[60] *Eagle Trust plc v. SBC Securities Ltd.* [1992] 4 All E.R. 488 (receipt of company moneys in discharge of a liability); *Cowan de Groot Properties Ltd. v. Eagle Trust plc* [1991] BCLC 1045 (purchase of company assets at an undervalue).

[61] *El Ajou v. Dollar Land Holdings plc* [1993] BCC 698, at first instance, *per* Millett J. at 718 (the Court of Appeal, [1994] BCC 143, did not deal with this issue).

[62] s. 322A C.A. 1985, p. 96, *ante*.

[63] s. 35(3) C.A. 1985.

[64] s. 35(3) C.A. 1985; s. 35A(5) C.A. 1985.

limitations on their powers flowing from the memorandum so that the company has acted in a way which would previously have been regarded as being beyond its capacity, this liability survives ratification of the act itself by special resolution.[65] Where directors have otherwise exceeded their powers, the common law rules relating to ratification and relief should apply.

Leaving aside for the moment the curative powers of the general meeting, Parliament, in preserving the liability of "any other person" has, whether intentionally or not, used words apt to cover a constructive trustee. Thus a person in good faith who is a gratuitous donee of corporate assets and who is, prima facie, protected by section 35A of the Companies Act 1985,[66] may retain liability as a constructive trustee on the basis of "knowing receipt".[67]

(c) *Ratification of misapplications of corporate property*

As noted above, transactions or other acts which would previously have been regarded as being beyond a company's capacity can now, under section 35(3) of the Companies Act 1985, be ratified by special resolution. Dispositions of corporate property which are generally illegal as being, for example, unauthorised reductions of capital or distributions[68] or transactions at an undervalue or preference[69] are not ratifiable. One must question, moreover, how far expropriations of corporate assets are ratifiable at all. It is probable that Parliament in conferring this new power of ratification intended to make it clear that *ultra vires* activity is now in principle ratifiable by special majority and not to render ratifiable acts traditionally seen as frauds on the minority.[70] Certainly ratification with the aid of the wrongdoing directors' votes should not be

---

[65] s. 35(3) C.A. 1985.

[66] See pp. 91 *et seq.*, *ante.*

[67] This would accord with the previous legal position: in *International Sales and Agencies Ltd. v. Marcus* [1982] 3 All E.R. 551, Lawson J. held that s. 9(1) of the European Communities Act 1972 (a predecessor provision of s. 35A) had no application to constructive trusts. Note that a person who has received corporate assets in good faith in the course of commercial dealing, is unlikely to incur liability as a constructive trustee, see p. 125, *ante.*

[68] *Re Halt Garage (1964) Ltd.* [1982] 3 All E.R. 1016; *Aveling Barford Ltd. v. Perion Ltd.* (1989) 5 BCC 677.

[69] ss. 238 and 239 Insolvency Act 1986.

[70] See, *e.g. Cook v. Deeks* [1916] 1 A.C. 554; *Atwool v. Merryweather* [1967] L.R. 5 Eq. 464n; *Menier v. Hooper's Telegraph Works* (1874) 9 Ch.App. 350.

acceptable.[71] This applies equally to the common law power to ratify other acts in excess of directors' powers.

Section 35(3) further provides that ratification of an act by special resolution does not affect the liability of the directors or any other person. It is arguable that this distinction should now apply, by analogy, to breaches of duty arising from other excesses of directors' powers. Where the wrongdoing directors are in control, their duties to the company can be enforced by a member suing in a derivative capacity who may also seek to enforce a remedy against the third party constructive trustee. In order to succeed, it appears that the member must have the backing of the majority of the independent shareholders.[72]

Section 35(3) goes on to provide that the liability itself may be relieved by separate special resolution. An ordinary resolution will suffice, on general principles, where the capacity of the company is not in issue. Such a resolution should probably be passed bone fide in the interests of the company[73] and, once again, for the wrongdoing directors to secure a majority using their own votes as members should constitute a fraud on the minority and provide no bar to a derivative suit.

(d) *Pre-emptive right of members to prevent misapplication*

A member with the necessary foreknowledge may, under section 35(2) of the Companies Act 1985 sue for an injunction to prevent a disposal of corporate assets which would previously have been beyond a company's capacity provided that the company has not yet placed itself under a legal obligation to the third party. As has been seen,[74] a member's right to prevent *ultra vires* acts is well established. Though section 35A(4) also recognises "any right of a member" to restrain proposed acts, which are beyond the powers of the directors, the authority for the existence of any such right is slender.

In *Re a Company (No. 005136 of 1986)*[75] Hoffmann J. held that a member might restrain a proposed share issue in abuse of the directors' powers. The basis of the member's right was the contract in the memorandum and articles. Could this be applied

---

[71] *Cook v. Deeks, supra.*
[72] *Smith v. Croft (No. 2)* [1988] Ch. 114.
[73] *cf. Taylor v. National Union of Mineworkers (Derbyshire Area)* [1985] BCLC 237.
[74] Chap. 5, p. 54, *ante.*
[75] [1987] BCLC 32.

to unauthorised dispositions of corporate property as occurred in *Rolled Steel Products (Holdings) Ltd. v. British Steel Corporation*[76] where the Court of Appeal held that causing a company to give a guarantee and grant security in respect of the debts of another company, though within the capacity of the company on an interpretation of the memoran-dum, was an abuse of directors' powers? Certainly Hoffmann J. expressed himself in terms broad enough to cover other abuses of directors' powers. The problem is that a shareholder's contractual rights under section 14 of the Companies Act 1985 should not in principle be defeasible by ratification, but similar abuses of powers relating to share issues have been held to be ratifiable so as to stay a shareholder's action whether essentially personal[77] or derivative[78] in character.

It may be, therefore, that a member's attempt to seek an injunction in reliance on section 35A(4) can be prevented by prior authorisation of the general meeting, albeit, perhaps, by an independent majority. A member's petition under section 459 of the Companies Act 1985 might succeed on the basis of proposed conduct which is unfairly prejudicial to part of the members or to members generally and this remedy might also be useful in the cases considered above where the disposal of assets has taken place.

5. *Directors' interests in company contracts*

An aspect of a director's fiduciary duty is the equitable rule that he must not put himself in a position in which his duties and his personal interests conflict. Thus a director must not be interested in a contract involving his company.[79] Such contracts are voidable at the company's option and any profit made by the director is recoverable by the company.

(a) *Disclosure of directors' interests*

Section 317 of the Companies Act 1985, imposes a duty on directors to disclose any interests in contracts. Disclosure must be made to the other directors either at the board meeting which first considers the contract or the first board meeting

---

[76] [1986] Ch. 246.
[77] *Hogg v. Cramphorn Ltd.* [1967] Ch. 254.
[78] *Bamford v. Bamford* [1970] Ch. 212.
[79] *Aberdeen Ry Co. v. Blaikie Bros* (1854) 1 Macq. 461 (H.L.Sc.).

after the director acquires his interest in the contract.[80] Disclosure to a committee of the board is not sufficient,[81] but, in many private companies, the duty to disclose, even to a full board, hardly imposes a realistic restraint on directors.

Section 317 provides that the nature of the director's interest must be disclosed and it has been said that the duty is to disclose full information on the nature of the relevant transaction so that the other directors can see what the interest is and its extent.[82]

The section does provide, however, that it is a sufficient declaration of interest for a director to give a general notice that he is a member of a company or firm or that he is connected[83] with a person with which, or with whom, his company may contract.

Section 317 also applies to shadow directors, who must declare their interests, not in a board meeting, but by a specific or general notice in writing to the directors.[84] Though section 317 applies to a director's interest in his service contract, any non-disclosure of such an interest at a board meeting which varies that contract is a pure technicality,[85] as, it seems, is non-disclosure by directors of interests held by, and known to, them all.[86]

Breach of section 317 renders the director in default liable to a fine under section 317(7), but does not, on the present weight of judicial authority, result in the contract becoming voidable at the instance of the company.[87]

(b) *Effect of waiver clauses*

Section 317(9) makes it clear that the section is without prejudice to the general equitable rule forbidding directors from having an interest in contracts with the company. Thus,

---

[80] s. 317(2) C.A. 1985.
[81] *Guinness plc v. Saunders & Another* (1988) 4 BCC 377 (C.A.).
[82] *per* Vinelott J. in *Movitex Ltd. v. Bulfield & Ors.* (1986) 2 BCC 99, 403.
[83] s. 346 C.A. 1985, p. 139, n. 24, *post.*
[84] s. 317(8) C.A. 1985.
[85] *Runciman v. Walter Runciman plc* [1992] BCLC 1084.
[86] *per* Dillon L.J. in *Lee Panavision Ltd. v. Lee Lighting Ltd.* [1991] BCC 629 at 637.
[87] *per* Lord Pearson in *Hely-Hutchinson v. Brayhead Ltd.* [1968] 1 Q.B. 549 at 594, followed by Lord Goff in *Guinness plc v. Saunders* [1990] 2 A.C. 663 at 697; also *per* Harman J. at first instance in *Lee Panavision Ltd. v. Lee Lighting Ltd.* [1991] BCC 620 at 626–627 (Dillon L.J. in the Court of Appeal, declined to express an opinion on the matter), and *per* Knox J. in *Cowan de Groot Properties Ltd. v. Eagle Trust plc* [1991] BCLC 1045 at 1113.

compliance with section 317 does not prevent a contract from becoming voidable at the instance of the company nor does it save a director from liability to account to the company for any profit made from the contract. These consequences can be only be prevented, otherwise than by disclosure to, and the consent of, the general meeting, by a waiver clause in the articles. Table A regulation 85 provides that a director who has disclosed, in accordance with section 317, the nature and extent of any material interest in a contract, is permitted to be so interested.

Furthermore, regulation 85 provides that such contracts are not to be avoided by the company and directors not to be made accountable for any profits. The combined effects of regulations 94 and 95 of Table A prevent a director from voting on any board resolution concerning a contract in which he is interested, subject to certain listed exceptions, and also to prevent such a director from counting towards a quorum at the board meeting in respect of the resolution.

Private companies, however, may find such restrictive provisions inconvenient, especially where there is a small number of directors. In *Re Express Engineering Works Ltd.*,[88] a company's articles provided that no director should vote on a contract in which he was interested. The five directors, who were also the only members of the company, purported to pass a resolution at a board meeting authorising the purchase by the company of property from a syndicate of which they were members. It was fortunate, however, that the directors were the only members, the court holding that their unanimous consent to the transaction was equivalent to an authorising resolution passed at general meeting. In practice, therefore, it is not unusual for private companies to modify the Table A provisions and to include more permissive waiver clauses since "articles may validly permit directors to be present at board meetings and even to vote when proposed contracts in which they are interested are being discussed."[89]

Failure to make disclosure as required by the relevant articles will, in accordance with the general equitable duty, render the contract voidable at the option of the company, provided the parties can be restored to their original positions,[90] and the

---

[88] [1920] 1 Ch. 466.

[89] *per* Upjohn J. in *Boulting & Another v. Association of Cinematograph Television and Allied Technicians* [1963] 2 Q.B. 606 at 636.

[90] *Hely-Hutchinson v. Brayhead Ltd.* [1968] 1 Q.B. 549, where, on the facts, such restoration of the parties was impossible.

director liable to account. Non-disclosure or failure to observe any voting or quorum restrictions in the articles (thus rendering invalid a board resolution purporting to authorise the contract) will be internal irregularities and an outsider in good faith, whilst arguably protected by section 35A of the Companies Act 1985, is certainly protected by the rule in *Royal British Bank v. Turquand.*[91]

If there is no waiver clause in the articles, a transaction in which a director has an interest can be ratified, following full disclosure, by the general meeting and the interested director may vote as a shareholder on the resolution.[92] The director's votes are, of course, likely to be crucial, if not in themselves decisive, in ratification. Similarly ratifiable is an irregularity caused by an interested director voting at a board meeting in respect of the transaction in defiance of a restrictive provision in the articles.[93]

(c) *Validity of waiver clauses*

There has been some controversy as to whether or not waiver clauses in the articles are at odds with section 310 of the Companies Act 1985 which renders void, *inter alia*, any provision in the articles purporting to exempt an officer from any liability for negligence, default, breach of duty or breach of trust.

In a recent judicial pronouncement on the question, Vinelott J. in *Movitex Ltd. v. Bulfield & Others,*[94] asserted the validity of waiver clauses. The general equitable principle establishing the duty on directors could be excluded or modified by a company's shareholders in their formulation of the articles, but this was not to exempt a director from the consequences of a breach of duty owed to the company.

6. *Directors' dealings and interests in their company's shares*

The offence of insider dealing, now provided by Part V of the Criminal Justice Act 1993,[95] applies only to acquisitions or

---

[91] (1856) 6 E. & B. 327. *Rolled Steel Products (Holdings) Ltd. v. British Steel Corporation* [1986] Ch. 246; *Cowan de Groot Properties Ltd. v. Eagle Trust plc* [1991] BCLC 1045.

[92] *North-West Transportation Co. Ltd. v. Beatty* (1887) 12 App.Cas. 589.

[93] *Foster v. Foster* [1916] 1 Ch. 532.

[94] (1986) 2 BCC 99, 403.

[95] Replacing and repealing the Company Securities (Insider Dealing) Act 1985.

disposals on a regulated market or where the dealer relies on a professional intermediary or is himself acting as a professional intermediary. In private companies, therefore, in circumstances such as those occurring in *Percival v. Wright*,[96] the law remains unchanged.

(a) *The rule in* Percival v. Wright

In this case, the company involved was one which would now be categorised as private in that its shares, which were held in few hands, had no market price and were not quoted on the Stock Exchange. The plaintiff members approached the defendant directors and offered to sell them their shares. The defendants accepted the offer, not disclosing to the plaintiffs that the board had been negotiating with an outsider for the sale of the company's shares at a much higher price. The negotiations proved abortive and the plaintiffs sued to have the sale set aside for non-disclosure. The court, dismissing the action, held that the directors owed no fiduciary duties to the individual shareholders.

It is now clear that it would be too sweeping to regard *Percival v. Wright* as authority for the proposition that in no circumstances can directors owe fiduciary duties to the company's individual shareholders. Indeed, Swinfen Eady J. in that case laid great stress on the particular circumstances surrounding the transaction:

> "There is no question of unfair dealing in this case. The directors did not approach the shareholders with the view of obtaining their shares. The shareholders approached the directors, and named the price at which they were desirous of selling."[97]

In *Allen v. Hyatt*[98] the court distinguished *Percival v. Wright*. In *Allen v. Hyatt*, directors approached shareholders to request options to purchase their shares, the directors representing that this would strengthen the board's hand in negotiations for an amalgamation with another company. In fact the directors made a profit when they exercised the options. The court held that

---

[96] [1902] 2 Ch. 421.
[97] *ibid.* at 426–427.
[98] (1914) 30 T.L.R. 444.

the directors owed a fiduciary duty to the shareholders concerned, having held themselves out as the latter's agents in the negotiations.

In *Re Chez Nico (Restaurants) Ltd.*[99] Browne-Wilkinson V.-C., agreeing with the interpretation of *Percival v. Wright* by the New Zealand Court of Appeal in *Coleman v. Myers*,[1] considered the law to be that:

> "... in general directors do not owe fiduciary duties to shareholders but owe them to the company: however, in certain special circumstances fiduciary duties, carrying with them a duty of disclosure, can arise which place directors in a fiduciary capacity vis à vis the shareholders."[2]

The decision in *Coleman v. Myers* is of particular significance to private companies. The facts involved the acquisition at an alleged undervalue by a director of other shareholders' shares with a view to obtaining complete control of a family company. The New Zealand Court of Appeal held that whilst *Percival v. Wright* was correctly decided on its facts, a fiduciary duty was nevertheless owed by the directors to the shareholders in the circumstances of the present case. Particularly influential in the court's decision were the facts that the company was a closely held family company, that a relationship of confidence existed, particularly in the matter of business advice, between the shareholders and the directors, and that the particular transaction had a special significance for the parties.

(b) *Disclosure of directors' interests in the company's securities*

Directors of private companies are not subject to the prohibitions on dealing in options on shares or debentures of the company contained in section 323 of the Companies Act 1985 since the prohibitions are expressed to apply only to listed securities. However, in common with his counterpart in a public company, a director (or shadow director) of a private company is under a duty to notify the company of his, his spouse's and infant children's interests in any of the company's securities.[3] In

---

[99] [1991] BCC 736.
[1] [1977] 2 N.Z.L.R. 225.
[2] [1991] BCC 736 at 750.
[3] ss. 324, 328 C.A. 1985.

default the director (or shadow director) is liable to imprisonment or a fine or both. Furthermore, every company must keep a register of directors' interests so notified or of any right to subscribe for its shares or debentures granted by the company to a director.[4] In contravention, the company and every officer in default are liable to fines.[5]

7. *Relief from breach of duty by court and indemnity insurance*

Section 727 of the Companies Act 1985 gives the court power to grant relief to an officer or auditor of the company if in any proceedings against such a person for negligence, default, breach of duty or breach of trust, it appears that the officer or auditor is or may be liable but has acted honestly and reasonably and ought fairly in the circumstances to be excused. The court may relieve him from liability in whole or in part on such terms as it thinks fit. The court has the same power if an officer or auditor seeks relief in anticipation of a claim being brought against him.

Strange as it may seem, as observed by Hoffmann L.J.[6] in *Re D'Jan of London Ltd.*,[7] section 727 contemplates that a court may excuse, as reasonable, conduct which is negligent. In that case D, a director, holding 99 of a company's 100 issued shares, signed on behalf of the company a fire insurance proposal form without realising that a wrong answer had been given to one of the questions. As a result, following a fire, the insurance company repudiated liability. Hoffmann L.J. held that D's conduct had been negligent, but not grossly so, and a factor for consideration was, at a time when the company was prosperous, the only interests foreseeably put at risk were those of D and his wife, the holder of the other share. In these circumstances, D was partially excused from liability by virtue of section 727.

Section 310 of the Companies Act 1985 provides, *inter alia*, that a company cannot by virtue of any provision in the articles or any contract indemnify an officer or auditor in respect of any liability for negligence, default, breach of duty or breach of trust, though it may indemnify him against any liability incurred in successfully defending any proceedings against him or in making an application under section 144(3) or (4) (relief from

---

[4] s. 325 C.A. 1985.
[5] s. 326 C.A. 1985.
[6] Sitting as an additional Judge of the Chancery Division.
[7] [1993] BCC 646.

liability for sums due from nominee holder of partly paid shares) or section 727 in which relief is granted by the court.

Further, by virtue of section 310(3) of the Companies Act 1985[8] a company may also purchase and maintain for the officer or auditor an insurance policy against liability, and, if it does so, this fact must be stated in the Directors' Report.[9] It has been pointed out[10] that in order to take advantage of this facility, the company should have appropriate enabling provisions in its memorandum and articles. In particular, at any board meeting seeking to approve such an insurance policy the directors' interests will be declarable under section 317 of the Companies Act 1985.[11] Thus, a company with articles containing regulations 94 and 95 of Table A may find it difficult, in the absence of appropriate amendment, to achieve the necessary quorum at the board meeting.

E. Financial arrangements between company and directors

1. *Remuneration of directors*

Since directors as such are not servants of the company, they have no entitlement to remuneration for their services unless the articles include an appropriate provision. Table A regulation 82 provides that the directors are entitled to such remuneration as is decided by the general meeting and that, subject to the terms of the resolution, the remuneration is deemed to accrue from day to day. A director who receives remuneration is not entitled to recover expenses connected with travel to, and the attendance of, board meetings[12] unless this is provided for by one of the articles such as regulation 83 of Table A.

In family companies, it is not uncommon for relatives, especially spouses, to be accorded the title "director" even though no active participation in management is expected from such individuals. In *Re Halt Garage (1964) Ltd.*[13] Oliver J. asserted the validity of an article providing the company power

---

[8] As amended by s. 137 C.A. 1989.

[9] Sched. 7, para. 5A C.A. 1985.

[10] See Steven Turnbull and Vanessa Edwards, "Companies Act 1989: directors' and officers' liability insurance" (1990) 134 S.J. 768.

[11] See pp. 128 *et seq.*, *ante*.

[12] *Young v. Naval and Military Society* [1905] 1 K.B. 687.

[13] [1982] 3 All E.R. 1016.

to determine and pay remuneration for the mere assumption of the post of director since the "mere holding of office involves responsibility even in the absence of any substantial activity" and there was nothing to prevent the shareholders, in accordance with such an article "from paying a reward attributable to the mere holding of the office of director, for being, as it were, a name on the notepaper and attending such meetings or signing such documents as are from time to time required."[14]

Apart from provisions in the articles, a director may have an express service agreement with the company providing for remuneration. If such a contract proves to be invalid, for example because a managing director has failed to take up the necessary qualification shares, the director can claim in quasi-contract on a *quantum meruit* in respect of services actually rendered to the company.[15] Even in the absence of an express contact, a contract may be inferred from the conduct of the parties incorporating an article providing for remuneration where it can be shown that the director has accepted office on the basis of its terms.[16] Despite the general rule that the articles do not constitute a contract for the purposes of section 14 of the Companies Act 1985 between the company and another except in that other's capacity as a member of the company,[17] it was held by Plowman J. in *Re Richmond Gate Property Co. Ltd.*[18] that an article providing for a managing director to receive such remuneration as was determined by the directors, similar to Table A regulation 84, coupled with the fact that the managing director was also a member, constituted a contract between the managing director and the company. Since the directors had not determined that any remuneration should be paid, the managing director was entitled to none and a claim on a *quantum meruit* was also excluded because of the existence of an express contract.

It is common, as Oliver J. observed in *Re Halt Garage (1964) Ltd.* for private family companies to apply distributable profits to the payment of directors' remuneration rather than making a

---

[14] *ibid.* at 1042. For the position when an employee-director of a family company cannot show he has received a service contract, see *Parsons v. Albert J. Parsons & Sons Ltd.* [1979] I.C.R. 271, Chap. 13, *post.*

[15] *Craven Ellis v. Canons Ltd.* [1936] 2 K.B. 403.

[16] *Re New British Iron Co., ex p. Beckwith* [1898] 1 Ch. 324.

[17] See, *e.g. Eley v. Positive Life Assurance Co. Ltd.* (1876) 1 Ex.D. 88; *Hickman v. Kent or Romney Marsh Sheep-breeders Association* [1915] 1 Ch. 881.

[18] [1965] 1 W.L.R. 335.

distribution by way of dividend.[19] Yet Oliver J.'s judgment makes it clear that the funds available to pay directors' remuneration are not restricted to distributable profits:

> "In the absence of fraud on the creditors or on minority shareholders, the quantum of such remuneration is a matter for the company. There is no implication or requirement that it must come out of profits only and, indeed, any requirement that it must be so restricted would, in many cases, bring business to a halt and prevent a business which had fallen on hard times from being brought around."[20]

Provided the shareholders have honestly determined the amount of remuneration to be paid, the court will not subject that remuneration to an objective test of bona fides for the benefit of the company. The sums paid must, however, constitute genuine remuneration and there comes a point where the court will hold, as it did in *Re Halt Garage* in respect of certain payments to an inactive director, that the payments are so out of proportion to the value of holding office as a director as to constitute disguised dividends out of capital.

2. *Loans to directors*

The rules relating to loans to directors (applying equally to shadow directors) are contained in sections 330 to 346 of the Companies Act 1985. The Act provides a more permissive code for private than for public companies, though if the private company is part of a group containing a public company, it is subject to the stricter rules applicable to public companies.

The basic prohibition, applying to all companies, is set out in section 330(2) which provides that a company may not make a loan to a director of the company or its holding company or enter into a guarantee or provide security in relation to a loan made by another to such a director. There are, however, a number of exceptions and the following transactions, in particular, may be entered into by *all* companies:

(a) a loan to a director of the company or of its holding company where the aggregate of the relevant amounts

---

[19] [1982] 3 All E.R. 1016 at 1033. But for a check on directors' refusal to pay reasonable dividends in such companies see Chap. 9, pp. 154–155, *post*.

[20] *ibid.* at 1023.

does not exceed £5,000 (section 334, as amended by section 138 C.A. 1989);

(b) a loan or quasi-loan[21] to, or a credit transaction[22] for, its holding company, or providing any guarantee or security in respect of a loan or quasi-loan to, or credit transaction for, its holding company made by another (section 336);

(c) if a money-lending company, a loan to a director of the company or of its holding company to help purchase or improve a dwelling-house which is the director's only or main residence, or in substitution for a loan made by another person for one of these purposes, provided the company ordinarily makes such loans to employees on terms no less favourable and the aggregate of the relevant amounts[23] does not exceed £100,000 (section 338(6) as amended by section 138 C.A. 1989).

Apart from the transactions listed above, several other permitted transactions are recognised in regard to private companies but their nature or scope is determined by whether the private company is or is not part of a group of companies containing a public company.

(1) *Where the private company is not part of a group containing a public company*, it may enter into the following transactions:

(a) a quasi-loan to a director of the company or of its holding company (*cf.* section 330(3)(a));

---

[21] A quasi-loan is a transaction by which the creditor agrees to pay, or pays otherwise than pursuant to an agreement, a sum for the borrower or agrees to reimburse, or reimburses otherwise than pursuant to an agreement, expenditure incurred by another party for the borrower (a) on terms that the borrower, or a person on his behalf, will reimburse the creditor, or (b) in circumstances giving rise to a liability on the borrower to reimburse the creditor: s. 331(3) C.A. 1985. Information specified in Sched. 6 C.A. 1985, as amended, concerning loans and quasi-loans, *inter alia*, must be disclosed in notes to the accounts: s. 232 C.A. 1985, substituted by s. 6 C.A. 1989.

[22] A credit transaction is defined as a transaction under which the creditor (a) supplies goods or sells land under a hire-purchase or conditional sale agreement, or (b) leases or hires land or goods for periodical payments, or (c) otherwise disposes of land or supplies goods or services on the understanding that payment is to be deferred: s. 331(7) C.A. 1985.

[23] See s. 339 C.A. 1985. For special provision relating to banking companies in respect of housing loans, see s. 339(4).

(b) a loan or quasi-loan to a person connected with a director[24] (*cf.* section 330(3)(b));

(c) the giving of a guarantee or provision of security in connection with a loan or quasi-loan made by any other person to a director or a person connected with a director (*cf.* section 330(3)(c));

(d) a credit transaction with a director or a person connected with a director, or a guarantee or security in connection with a credit transaction made by another for a director or a person so connected (*cf.* section 330(4));

(e) the provision of funds to a director to cover expenditure, past or future incurred or to be incurred for the purposes of the company or for the purpose of fulfilling his duties as an officer of the company, or the doing of anything to avoid the director incurring such expenditure provided either the prior approval of the general meeting has been obtained following the necessary disclosure[25] or the disposition contains a condition that if no approval is obtained at or before the next A.G.M., the loan is to be repaid or liability discharged within six months of that meeting (section 337);

(f) if a money-lending company, a loan or quasi-loan to a director or a guarantee in respect of any other loan or quasi-loan to a director, provided the company is acting in the ordinary course of its business and the terms are not more favourable than the company would have offered to a person of the same financial standing but unconnected with the company (section 338(1)–(3)).

(2) *Where the private company is part of a group containing a public company*, it may enter into the following transactions:

(a) a quasi-loan to one of its directors or to a director of its holding company provided the terms cover reimbursement within two months and that the amount does not

---

[24] Persons connected with a director include, *inter alia*, a director's spouse, child or step-child, a body corporate with which the director is associated, a trustee of a trust whose beneficiaries include the director, his spouse, children or step-children, or the director's business partner: s. 346 C.A. 1985.

[25] The matters to be disclosed are the purpose of the expenditure, the amount of the funds to be provided by the company and the extent of the company's liability: s. 337(4) C.A. 1985. Where the company adopts the written resolution procedure (see Chap. 7, *ante*) the matters must be disclosed to each relevant member at or before the time at which the resolution is supplied to him for signature: Sched. 15A, para. 8 C.A. 1985 inserted by s. 114 C.A. 1989.

exceed £5,000 (section 332, as amended by section 138 C.A. 1989);

(b) a loan or quasi-loan to another company in the same group, or a guarantee or security in connection with a loan or quasi-loan made to such a company by another (section 333);

(c) a credit transaction with a director or a person connected with a director, or a guarantee or security in connection with a credit transaction made by another for a director or a person so connected, but only if:
   (i) the aggregate of the relevant amounts does not exceed £10,000; or
   (ii) the transaction is entered into in the ordinary course of the company's business and the value is not greater, and the terms no more favourable, than the company would reasonably have offered to a person of the same financial standing but unconnected with the company (section 335, as amended by S.I. 1990 No. 1393);

(d) thc provision of funds to cover a director's expenditure on company duties, on the terms set out in (1)(e) above, but with the additional requirement that the aggregate of the relevant amounts does not exceed £20,000 (section 337, as amended by S.I. 1990 No. 1393);

(e) if a money-lending company, a loan or quasi-loan to a director or a guarantee in respect of any other loan or quasi-loan to a director set out in (1)(f) above, but with the additional requirement that the company may not, unless it is a banking company, enter into such a transaction if the aggregate of the relevant amounts exceeds £100,000 (section 338(1)–(4) as amended by section 138 and Schedule 10, Part 1, paragraph 10 C.A. 1989).

If the foregoing prohibitions are contravened, the transaction is voidable at the instance of the company unless restitution has become impossible or the company has been indemnified by the director or any rights acquired by a bona fide purchaser for value without actual notice of the contravention would be affected by its avoidance.[26]

[26] s. 341(1) C.A. 1985.

Furthermore, a director or person connected with a director for whom the arrangement or transaction in question was made, or a director who has authorised the transaction, is liable, whether or not the transaction has been avoided, to account to the company for any direct or indirect gain, and is also jointly and severally liable to indemnify the company for any loss or damage.[27] Where the transaction or arrangement is for the benefit of a person connected with a director, it is a defence for that director to show that he took all reasonable steps to ensure that the company complied with the provisions in section 330,[28] and it is a defence for a person so connected or another director who authorised the transaction to show that he did not know of the relevant circumstances constituting the contravention.[29]

There are, in addition, criminal penalties, but these apply only to a private company which is in the same group as a public company.[30] A director of such a company who authorises or permits, or any other person who procures, the transaction or arrangement, knowing or having reasonable cause to believe that the company was in contravention of the provisions is guilty of an offence. The company, too, commits an offence unless it can show that it was not, at the time, aware of the relevant circumstances.[31]

---

[27] s. 341(2) C.A. 1985.
[28] s. 341(4) C.A. 1985.
[29] s. 341(5) C.A. 1985.
[30] And to a public company, *a fortiori*.
[31] s. 342 C.A. 1985.

Chapter 9

SHARE CAPITAL

A. Introduction

This chapter considers the position of private companies in relation to the raising of share capital (including for convenience the restrictions on public offers and advertisements of securities) and the maintenance of share capital. As will be seen below, private companies are exempted from the more rigorous statutory capital requirements prescribed for public companies in accordance with the European Communities Second Directive on Company Law.[1] In some areas however, such as pre-emption rights and dividends, statute has gone further than was required by the Second Directive by creating rules to cover private companies. Yet, as will also be seen, even in these cases private companies are treated differently from public companies.

Since the provisions, first introduced in the Companies Act 1981, governing companies purchasing their own shares and providing financial assistance for others to do so have a wider importance than their, albeit crucial, relationship to capital maintenance, they are treated separately in the next chapter.

B. Position of public and private companies under European Community Law

The Second E.C. Directive on Company Law was substantially concerned with the raising and maintenance of share capital. The directive was expressed to apply only to public companies in the United Kingdom and the effect of its implementation by the Companies Act 1980 was to bring public companies into line with their continental counterparts and at the same time to create sharp distinctions between public and private companies. The result is that private companies are

---

[1] 77/91: [1977] O.J. L26/1.

subject to a less rigorous capital regime than applies to public companies, the statutory rules, now consolidated in the Companies Act 1985, usually being expressed to apply only to public companies. In contrast with public companies there is no requirement that the nominal value of a private company's allotted share capital must reach any authorised minimum value before it may commence business,[2] nor any requirement that at least a quarter (or any proportion) of the nominal value of each share is paid up on allotment.[3]

Furthermore, there is no statutory obligation placed on the directors of private companies, as is the case with directors of public companies, to call an extraordinary general meeting where the company's net assets have fallen to half or less of its called up share capital.[4] The position of public companies will be further contrasted, as appropriate, in this chapter.

C. Restrictions on public offers and advertisements of securities

A private company must not, under section 143 of the Financial Services Act 1986, apply for its securities to be listed on the Stock Exchange nor can it issue an advertisement offering its securities[5] except if permitted to do so by an order of the Secretary of State on the grounds that the advertisement appears to be private in character either because of a connection between the issuer of the advertisement and the addressee, or for some other reason, or the advertisement appears to deal only incidentally with investments, or the advertisement is issued to those who appear to him to be sufficiently expert to be able to understand any risks, or the advertisement falls into some other class which the Secretary of State deems should be excepted.

The foregoing types of advertisement may only be permitted if issued in such circumstances as the Secretary of State's order may specify, but the Secretary of State may also permit an advertisement, issued in any circumstances, relating to securities which appear to him to be of a kind that can be expected

---

[2] £50,000 is the minimum amount currently required by a public company: ss. 117, 118 C.A. 1985.

[3] *cf.* s. 101 C.A. 1985.

[4] *cf.* s. 142 C.A. 1985.

[5] s. 170(1) F.S.A. 1986.

normally to be bought or dealt with only by persons sufficiently expert to understand any risks involved.[6] The Secretary of State's order may require the issuer of the advertisement to comply with such requirements as the order specifies.[7]

The Financial Services Act 1986 further provides as follows for contravention of the advertisement restrictions. Any authorised person[8] who issues on behalf of the company, an advertisement in contravention of the general prohibition against private companies advertising securities or in contravention of any requirement in an order of the Secretary of State will be deemed to have broken the rules governing the conduct of his investment business, *i.e.* rules by the Secretary of State under Chapter V, Part 1 of the Financial Services Act 1986, or rules made by the individual's self-regulating organisation, or rules made by his professional body, whichever are appropriate.[9] An advertisement issued in contravention of the prohibition will render the company liable to a criminal offence and will have the further civil consequence that, unless the court is satisfied that the other party was not materially influenced or misled by the advertisement, the company may not enforce any agreement or obligation arising from its issue and will be liable to restore any money or property transferred by the other party and to pay compensation.[10] A person, other than an authorised person, will be criminally liable for the issue of an advertisement in contravention of the statutory provisions or of a requirement in an order by the Secretary of State. An action for breach of statutory duty will lie at the suit of a person who has suffered loss as a result of any contravention.[11]

D. Allotment of shares

1. *Authority for allotment*

Section 80(1) of the Companies Act 1985 provides that the directors of a company shall not exercise any power of the

---

[6] s. 170(2), (3) F.S.A. 1986 substituted by s. 199 C.A. 1989.
[7] s. 170(4) F.S.A. 1986 substituted by s. 199 C.A. 1989.
[8] This is a person authorised to conduct an investment business as defined in Pt. 1, Chap. III F.S.A. 1986.
[9] s. 171(1) F.S.A. 1986.
[10] ss. 171(2) and 57 F.S.A. 1986.
[11] s. 171(3), (6) F.S.A. 1986.

company to allot relevant securities unless authorised to do so by the general meeting or the articles. Under section 80(4) the authority must state the maximum amount of relevant securities (as defined) to which it relates and its expiry date which must not exceed five years from either the passing of the resolution in general meeting or from the company's incorporation (where the authority was contained in the company's articles at the time of incorporation). The authority may, under section 80(5), be renewed or further renewed by the company in general meeting for a further period not exceeding five years, the resolutions stating or restating the amount of relevant securities which may be allotted or which remain to be allotted under the authority and specifying the expiry date of the renewed authority.

Section 115 of the Companies Act 1989 inserted section 80A into the Companies Act 1985 which provides that a private company may elect (by elective resolution in accordance with section 379A of the Companies Act 1985: see Chapter 7, *ante*) to dispense with the requirements contained in section 80(4) and (5) and instead confer authority for an indefinite period or any chosen fixed period provided the authority states the maximum amount of relevant securities to which it relates. An authority given for a fixed period may be renewed or further renewed by the company in general meeting, the resolution stating or restating the amount of relevant securities which may be allotted or the amount remaining to be allotted and also whether the authority is renewed for an indefinite or fixed period, in the latter case stating the expiry date. An authority including an authority contained in the articles, may be revoked or varied by the company in general meeting. If the elective resolution ceases to have effect (because it is revoked by ordinary resolution or the company is re-registered as public), any authority which was given for an indefinite period or for a fixed period of more than five years expires forthwith if given five years or more before the election ceases to have effect and otherwise has effect as if conferred for a five-year period.

2. *Pre-emption rights on allotment*

Section 89 of the Companies Act 1985 provides that a company proposing to allot equity securities (other than shares held or to be held under an employee share scheme) wholly for cash must first offer them to persons holding equity shares or employee shares in proportion to their existing holding and on terms at least as favourable as those proposed. The offer must be in writing and the offerees must be given at least 21 days to accept.[12] The statutory right of pre-emption may be excluded in the case of private companies by an express provision to that effect in the memorandum or articles or by a provision therein which is inconsistent with the statutory right.[13] If such an inconsistent provision was imposed on a private company otherwise than in the memorandum or articles, prior to June 22, 1982, it has effect as if it were contained in one of those documents.[14]

In private companies, as in public companies, where the directors are generally authorised by the articles or by ordinary resolution of the company to allot securities, pursuant to section 80 of the Companies Act 1985, they may be further authorised by the articles or by special resolution of the company to make allotments of shares inconsistent with the statutory pre-emption right. If the directors have a general or specific authorisation to allot securities, the company can by special resolution exclude or modify the pre-emption right in respect of a specified allotment, provided that such special resolution has been recommended by the directors and the recommendation is supported by their written statement to members which is circulated with the notice of the meeting.[15]

As has been seen, in Chapter 7, *ante*, a private company may, within section 381A of the Companies Act 1985 (inserted by section 113 of the Companies Act 1989), act on a written resolution of members who would have been entitled to attend and vote at the relevant meeting. If a written resolution is used in the above circumstances, it is provided by Schedule 15A, Part II of the Companies Act 1985 (inserted by section 114 of the Companies Act 1989) that the written statement by the directors must be supplied to each member at or before the time the resolution is supplied to him for signature.

E. Share transactions

1. *Payment for shares*

The strict statutory rules contained in the Companies Act 1985 relating to the value required to be received by a company

---

[12] s. 90 C.A. 1985.
[13] s. 91 C.A. 1985.
[14] s. 96(3) C.A. 1985.
[15] s. 95 C.A. 1985.

for its allotted shares apply only to public companies. Thus a private company may, prima facie, allot shares on the basis of the allottee's undertaking to transfer property to the company, with no time limit within which the undertaking is to be performed,[16] and also accept as payment for its shares, including any premium thereon, non-cash consideration which has not been the subject of independent expert valuation.[17] Subscribers to the memorandum of a private company need not pay up their shares, and any premium thereon, in cash,[18] and also there is no prima facie restriction on the amount of consideration, which may include an issue of shares, that the company may agree to pay to a subscriber to the memorandum in respect of a transfer of non-cash assets by the subscriber to the company in any initial period following the company's commencement of business.[19]

Even though there is no statutory restriction on private companies accepting payment for their shares in the form of an allottee's undertaking to do work or perform services for the company,[20] it is doubtful whether such an arrangement, of itself, would be approved by the courts. In *Gardner v. Iredale*[21] Parker J. stated *obiter* that a company could not allot shares in consideration of an undertaking to perform work for the company as this would be to replace the statutory liability of the allottee to pay for the shares with an action by the company for damages for breach of contract. On the other hand, in the opinion of Parker J., a company might, having agreed a contract price for future work, satisfy the debt by an issue of fully paid shares, and it was this interpretation that the judge placed on the agreement on the facts of the case.

Private companies are, at least in theory, subject to the same prohibition contained in section 100 of the Companies Act 1985 as applies to public companies on the issue of shares at a discount, yet the continued application to private companies of

[16] *cf.* s. 102 C.A. 1985. This section imposes a time limited of five years, in such circumstances, for a public company.
[17] *cf.* s. 103 C.A. 1985.
[18] *cf.* s. 106 C.A. 1985.
[19] *cf.* s. 104 C.A. 1985. This section limits, in this situation, in respect of public companies formed as such, the permitted consideration to less than one-tenth of the company's nominal issued share capital if the transfer is to take place within two years of the issue of the "trading certificate," unless the consideration has been subject to independent valuation and report and the agreement has been approved by the general meeting following prior publicity to members.
[20] *cf.* s. 99 C.A. 1985.
[21] [1912] 1 Ch. 700 at 716.

the common law principles relating to the receipt of non-cash consideration for shares means that the prohibition can in practice be circumvented. It has been held that a company may pay for property or services in shares at any price it thinks proper,[22] provided the company does so "honestly and not colourably and provided that it has not been so imposed upon as to be entitled to be relieved from its bargain".[23]

Thus, provided the directors have made an honest assessment of the value of the consideration, the courts, following normal contractual principles, will not enquire into the adequacy of the consideration. If, however, no such assessment has been made by the directors, the allotted shares will not be regarded as having been paid up.[24] Where shares are allotted for non-cash consideration, the company must, within one month, with its return of allotments, deliver to the registrar a written contract constituting the title of the allottee together with any contract of sale or for services or any other consideration, and a return stating the number and nominal value of the allotted shares, the extent to which they are treated as paid up and the consideration received by the company. Where the contract is not in writing, the prescribed particulars of it must be delivered to the registrar.[25] Where the contract reveals on its face in money terms that the consideration is inadequate, shares will only be regarded as being paid up to the true value of such consideration.[26] An agreement to pay for property in part by allotting shares up to an uncertain value in the future, such as a proportion of any future increase in capital, clearly shows that the consideration is illusory,[27] whilst to allot shares in consideration of the past services of the allottees to the company is, on general contractual principles, to allot the shares for no consideration at all.[28]

2. *Acquisitions by companies of their own shares*

Just as in the case of raising capital, a private company is subject to less stringent legal control than applies to a public

---

[22] *Re Wragg Ltd.* [1897] 1 Ch. 796.
[23] *ibid., per* Lindley L.J. at 830.
[24] *Tintin Exploration Syndicate Ltd. v. Sandys* (1947) 177 L.T. 412.
[25] s.88 C.A. 1985. This section applies to companies limited by shares and to guarantee companies having a share capital.
[26] *per* Smith L.J. in *Re Wragg* [1897] 1 Ch. 796 at 836.
[27] *Hong Kong and China Gas Co. Ltd. v. Glen* [1914] 1 Ch. 527.
[28] *Re Eddystone Marine Insurance Co,* [1893] 3 Ch. 9.

company in the matter of capital maintenance. The general rule contained in section 143(1) of the Companies Act 1985 is that a company limited by shares or limited by guarantee and having a share capital is prohibited from acquiring its own shares by purchase, subscription or any other means. To this rule there are the following exceptions:

(a) acquisition of its own fully paid shares by a company limited by shares "otherwise than for valuable consideration": section 143(3) of the Companies Act 1985. The common law provides that fully paid shares may be held by a nominee on a company's behalf either following a gift during the shareholder's lifetime[29] or a bequest in a will.[30] Section 143(3) makes it unnecessary for such fully paid shares to be held by a nominee on trust for the company, thus the company may hold such shares beneficially. There is no limit on the length of time for which the shares may be held by a private company.[31] As regards the right to vote on the shares, Romer J. held in *Kirby v. Wilkins,* in respect of a gift of shares by shareholders to one of their number to hold on trust for the company, that "the transaction was not made invalid by reason of the transfer having been made to a nominee on trusts which involved an obligation on the trustee to vote in respect of the shares as the company might from time to time direct".[32] This principle, which was followed by Danckwerts J in *Re Castiglione's Will Trusts,*[33] remains unaffected by statute in relation to private companies,[34] so where shares are held beneficially by the company, the company itself may exercise the votes. This necessarily enhances the voting power of the controllers. The position is different where the private company converts to a public company following the acquisition, and this is dealt with below.
(b) redemption and purchase of fully-paid shares under sections 159 to 181 of the Companies Act 1985[35]: section 143(3)(a);

---

[29] *Kirby v. Wilkins* [1929] 2 Ch. 444.
[30] *Re Castiglione's Will Trusts* [1958] Ch. 549.
[31] *cf.* s. 146(1), (2), (3) C.A. 1985 for the position in respect to public companies.
[32] [1929] 2 Ch. 444 at 453–454.
[33] [1958] Ch. 549
[34] *cf.* s. 146(4) C.A. 1985 for the position of public companies.
[35] This important exception is considered in Chap. 10, *post.*

(c) acquisition in a reduction of capital under section 135 of the Companies Act 1985: section 143(3)(b);
(d) purchase of shares following a court order under sections 4, 54 or 459 to 461 of the Companies Act 1985: section 143(3)(c);
(e) forfeiture of shares or surrender in lieu: section 143(3)(d). Where a private company, in accordance with the necessary authorisation in its articles, forfeits the shares of a member for non-payment of a call or instalment or accepts a surrender of shares from a member in lieu of such forfeiture, the shares may be sold or reissued by the company with no statutory restriction on the duration for which the shares may be held by the company in the interim.[36] Furthermore, there is no statutory restriction on the company voting with the shares during the period for which they are held.[37] The position where a private company converts into a public company is dealt with in the following paragraph.

Where shares in a private company have been acquired:

(1) by the company by way of gift; or
(2) by the company through forfeiture or surrender; or
(3) by a nominee of the company from a third person with no financial assistance by the company, the company having a beneficial interest in the shares; or
(4) by a person with financial assistance from the company, the company having a beneficial interest in the shares, and the company re–registers as public, the following rules apply.

Where the shares have been acquired by one of the methods specified in (1)–(3), the company must dispose of the shares within three years of the date of re-registration or else cancel the shares and reduce its share capital accordingly.

Where the shares have been acquired by method (4) the period for disposal or cancellation is one year. From the date of

---

[36] *cf.* s. 146(1)(a), (2), (3) C.A. 1985 for the position in respect to a public company.
[37] *cf.* s. 146(4) C.A. 1985 for the position in respect to a public company.

re-registration, and pending disposal or cancellation, neither the company, nominee, nor shareholder, as appropriate, may exercise any votes in respect of the shares, and any attempt to exercise such votes is void.[38]

Where the shares are cancelled the company need not comply with the procedure set out in sections 135 to 136 of the Companies Act 1985 in order to reduce capital. A resolution of the board of directors suffices, a copy of such resolution having to be filed with the registrar within 15 days.[39]

Where the cancellation brings the nominal value of the allotted share capital below £50,000 the company must apply to be re-registered as private.[40] Failure to cancel shares as required renders the company and any officer in default liable to fines, and failure by a public company in appropriate circumstances to apply for re-registration as private causes the company to be treated as private with regard to a restriction on public offers of its securities, but to be treated as public for other purposes.[41]

Where a company's nominee acquires partly-paid shares in the company (other than shares in which the company has no beneficial interest[42]) either through issue or by transfer from a third person, the shares are regarded as held by the nominee on his own account, any beneficial interest of the company being disregarded.[43] This appears to be the case in private companies even where the nominee has acquired the shares with financial assistance from the company and the company has a beneficial interest in the shares.[44] The nominee is thus liable, jointly and severally with other subscribers where the shares have been acquired by subscription to the memorandum, or with the company's directors at the relevant time in the case of other issues or acquisitions, to pay any sums due on the shares.[45] The court may relieve a subscriber or director from liability in whole or in part if it appears that he acted honestly and reasonably and that in all the circumstances he ought fairly to be excused.[46]

---

38 ss. 148, 146 C.A. 1985.
39 s. 147 C.A. 1985.
40 s. 146(2)(b) C.A. 1985.
41 s. 149 C.A. 1985.
42 s. 145(2)(a) C.A. 1985.
43 s. 144(1) C.A. 1985.
44 This contrasts with the position of nominees acquiring shares, other than subscribers' shares, in such circumstances, in a public company: s. 145(1) C.A. 1985.
45 s. 144(2) C.A. 1985.
46 s. 144(3) C.A. 1985.

3. *Lien on shares*

A private company is not subject to the restriction specified in section 150 of the Companies Act 1985[47] in respect to liens and charges on its shares. Thus a private company's articles may be more permissive than Table A regulation 8[48] and enable a company to have a lien on any of its shares, fully as well as partly paid, and in respect not only of sums owing on its shares but also for any other debts owed by a shareholder to the company. A lien or charge taken by a private company and in existence immediately prior to application for re-registration as a public company continues to be effective after that time.[49] Articles giving companies "first and paramount" liens on shares in respect of debts owed by shareholders take priority over subsequent equitable mortgagees,[50] but not over mortgages created and notified to the company before the lien arises.[51]

F. Dividends

Before the Companies Act 1980 came into operation, the rules relating to payment of dividends had been governed by the common law though the courts had, by and large, been prepared to leave control to the accountancy profession. The statutory rules, now contained in the Companies Act 1985, whilst representing a significant tightening on the *laissez-faire* approach of the common law in respect of the calculation of profits from which dividends may be paid, include a significant exemption for private companies from the doctrine of capital maintenance. Most of the rules governing private companies are, however, applicable to all companies.

Private companies, like public companies, may make a "distribution", *e.g.* pay a cash dividend,[52] out of profits

[47] This provides that a public company (other than a money-lending or credit or hire purchase company in the ordinary course of its business) may only take a lien or charge in respect of sums payable on partly-paid shares.

[48] See Appendix 1, *post.*

[49] s. 150(4) C.A. 1985.

[50] *Champagne Perrier-Jouet S.A. v. H.H. Finch Ltd.* [1982] 3 All E.R. 713.

[51] *Bradford Banking Co. v. Henry Briggs Son & Co.* (1886) 12 App.Cas. 29.

[52] "Distribution" is defined to include distributions to members in kind as well as cash, other than a fully or partly paid bonus issue or redemption or purchase of shares out of capital or out of unrealized profits as specified in the provision, or a reduction of capital as indicated in the provision or a distribution of assets to members on a winding-up: s. 263(2) C.A. 1985.

available for distribution,[53] *i.e.* accumulated realised profits so far as not previously utilised by distribution or capitalisation less accumulated realised losses so far as not previously writtten off in a reduction or reorganisation of capital duly made.[54] Where directors after making all reasonable enquiries, cannot determine whether a profit or loss made before December 22, 1980, is realised or unrealised, they may treat the profit as realised and the loss unrealised.[55]

Generally, provisions relating to depreciation or diminution in value of assets or to liability or loss likely to be incurred, or certain to be incurred but uncertain as to amount or to the date on which it will arise, are treated as a realised loss. Excepted from this rule however is a provision relating to a diminution in value of a fixed asset appearing on a revaluation[56] of all the fixed assets, or of all the fixed assets other than goodwill.[57]

Furthermore, if following an upward revaluation of a fixed asset subject to a depreciation provision, more is needed to be set aside by the company, the excess over the amount which would otherwise have to have been set aside is treated as realised profit.[58] Where there is no record of the original cost of an asset or obtaining such a record would cause unreasonable expense or delay, its cost is deemed to be its value stated in the earliest available record made by the company.[59]

The important respect in which private companies differ from public companies in the calculation of profit available for distribution is that private companies, unlike public companies, need not take account of unrealised losses. This results from a further requirement over and above the realised profits test being placed on public, but not private, companies before a distribution can be made.

Section 264 of the Companies Act 1985 provides that a public company may only make a distribution when its net assets are, before the distribution, and will be after the distribution, not less than the aggregate of its called up share capital and its undistributable reserves. The company's net

---

[53] s. 263(1) C.A. 1985.
[54] s. 263(3) C.A. 1985.
[55] s. 263(5) C.A. 1985.
[56] Expert revaluation is not required, but merely a consideration of value by the directors, provided they are satisfied that the aggregate value is not less than that stated in the accounts: see s. 275(4) C.A. 1985.
[57] s. 275(1) and Sched. 4, paras. 88 and 89 C.A. 1985.
[58] s. 275(2) C.A. 1985.
[59] s. 275(3) C.A. 1985.

assets are the aggregate of its assets less the aggregate of its liabilities, such liabilities including any provision for liabilities or charges.[60] The undistributable reserves are the share premium account, the capital redemption reserve, the balance of the company's accumulated unrealised profits (so far as not previously utilised by capitalisation[61]) over its accumu-lated unrealised losses (so far as not previously written off in a reduction or reorganisation of capital duly made), and any other reserve which the company is prevented from distributing either by law or by its memorandum or articles.

It may be more appropriate, of course, for private companies to plough back their profits or utilise them for directors' remuneration rather than distribute them by way of dividend. As Oliver J. observed in *Re Halt Garage (1964) Ltd.*:

> "It is commonplace in private family companies, where there are substantial profits available for distribution by way of dividend, for the shareholder directors to distribute those profits by way of directors' remuneration rather than by way of dividend, because the latter course has certain fiscal disadvantages."[62]

The fiscal disadvantages to the payment of dividends referred to be Oliver J. are now less obvious following significant reductions in the level of taxation.[63] Moreover, a refusal by majority-shareholding directors in private companies to recommend reasonable dividends in frustration of the reasonable expectations of the minority may be grounds for action by the minority. Controller/directors deny themselves, as shareholders, the benefit of realistic dividends as much as they deny this benefit to the minority. The directors will, however, receive an income from the company; the retention of the bulk of the profits to enhance capital growth does not of itself immediately benefit the minority. There was judicial disagreement as to whether denial of reasonable dividends was capable of amounting to unfairly prejudicial conduct to *some part* of the members for the purposes of the previously worded section 459

[60] Defined in Sched. 4, para. 89.

[61] Such capitalisation not to include a transfer of profits of the company to its capital redemption reserve on or after December 22, 1980.

[62] [1982] 3 All E.R. 1016 at 1033.

[63] See Harman J. in *Re a Company (No. 00370 of 1987) ex p. Glossop* [1988] BCLC 570.

of the Companies Act 1985.[64] The issue was resolved by the amendment of section 459[65] to include conduct unfairly prejudicial to members *generally*. Such conduct also provides grounds for a minority petition to wind up a company on the just and equitable ground under section 122(1)(g) of the Insolvency Act 1986.[66]

At common law, directors who pay a dividend to shareholders out of capital are jointly and severally liable to repay to the company the sums improperly distributed, and any such payment is incapable of ratification, as being *ultra vires*.[67] If directors are liable to make restitution to the company, they may recover against each shareholder, to the extend of the sum received by each, provided the shareholder knew of the irregularity.[68] Any member can sue for an injunction to restrain a company from paying a dividend out of capital, but a member who has knowingly received such a payment cannot bring a derivative action against the directors on behalf of the company unless that member repays to the company the money received.[69] In addition, section 277(1) of the Companies Act 1985 provides that any shareholder who receives a distribution which he knows or has reasonable grounds to believe has been made in contravention of the statutory rules, is liable to repay the money or, in the case of a distribution in kind, the value.

---

[64] Peter Gibson J. in *Re Sam Weller and Sons Ltd.* (1989) 5 BCC 810 held such conduct might be unfairly prejudicial but *contra* Harman J. in *Re a Company, ex p. Glossop, supra*. Peter Gibson J. took the view that although members may have the same *rights* their *interests* may be different.

[65] Sched. 19, para. 11 C.A. 1989.

[66] *Re a Company, ex p. Glossop, ante*, n. 63.

[67] *Re Exchange Banking Co., Flitcroft's Case* (1882) 21 Ch. D. 519.

[68] *Moxham v. Grant* [1900] 1 Q.B. 88.

[69] *Towers v. African Tug Co.* [1904] 1 Ch. 558.

Chapter 10

REDEMPTION AND PURCHASE OF SHARES AND FINANCIAL ASSISTANCE

A. Introduction

If a company is permitted to acquire its own shares for valuable consideration the major danger is that of a reduction of capital. A similar problem arises when a company provides financial assistance, whether directly or indirectly, to aid a purchase of its own shares by another.[1] When Parliament came to formulate rules on share redemption and purchase, and reformulate rules on financial assistance, in the Companies Act 1981, it recognised that many of the tight controls appropriate to public companies should be relaxed in favour of private companies.

B. Companies redeeming and purchasing their own shares

1. *Statutory provisions*

The case *Trevor v. Whitworth*[2] established that a company was not permitted to purchase its own shares since this involved a reduction of capital to the prejudice of creditors. It took until the Companies Act 1980 for this rule to be given statutory force, yet ironically it was clear at that time that the principle would soon be qualified by subsequent legislation.

In 1979 the Wilson Committee's Interim Report on the Financing of Small Firms[3] had recommended that small companies should be permitted to issue redeemable equity shares,[4] and in 1980 the Government issued a consultative

---

[1] In the case of a public company there is also the problem of the creation of a false market for its shares in this way.

[2] [1887] 12 App.Cas. 409 (H.L.).

[3] Cmnd. 7503.

[4] At this time only preference shares were redeemable: s. 58 C.A. 1948, now repealed.

document entitled "The Purchase by a Company of its Own Shares".[5] In this document Professor Gower identified several advantages to a private company of permitting it to purchase its own shares. For example, in cases where the existing members did not have sufficient funds to effect the necessary share purchase it would enable the company to buy out a retiring controller, thus facilitating the retention of family or other close control. Also, it would provide a means whereby a shareholder or the estate of a deceased shareholder in an unlisted company could find a buyer. Furthermore, it would be particularly useful in relation to employee share schemes in enabling the shares of employees to be repurchased on their leaving the company's employment.

The Companies Act 1981 permitted companies to issue redeemable shares of any class and to purchase their own shares, including redeemable shares, subject to certain safeguards. Special provision was made for private companies in this regard.

The rules are now contained in sections 159 to 181 of the Companies Act 1985. The Act, whilst repeating the general prohibition on limited companies acquiring their own shares,[6] provides by way of exception in section 159 that any company, private or public, having a share capital may issue redeemable shares to be redeemed at the option of the company or the shareholder provided the articles permit, they are not issued at a time when there are no issued shares which are not redeemable, and the shares are fully paid on redemption. Section 159A of the Companies Act 1985[7] provides the following rules as to the terms and manner of redemption. The date on or by which, or the dates between which, the shares are to be or may be redeemed must be specified in the articles or, in accordance with the articles, fixed by the directors in which case the date or dates must be fixed before the shares are issued. The amount payable on redemption must be specified in, or determined in accordance with, the articles, but the articles must not provide that the amount may be determined by reference to any person's discretion or opinion. Any other circumstances in which the shares are to be or may be redeemed and any other terms and conditions of redemption must be specified in the articles.

---

[5] Cmnd. 7944.

[6] s. 143(1) C.A. 1985. Unlimited companies are not included in this prohibition. Such companies can redeem (or purchase) their shares without restriction provided they are so authorised by their articles.

[7] Inserted by s. 133 C.A. 1989.

Section 162 of the Companies Act 1985 provides that any limited company may purchase its own shares including redeemable shares. Again, such purchase must be authorised by the articles,[8] but section 159A does not apply as to the terms and manner of the purchase[9] since the Act contains other procedures in this regard and these are dealt with in the next section below. The purchase must not result in there being no member left holding shares other than redeemable shares.

2. *Procedure for purchase*

A private company must follow the procedure appropriate to an "off-market" purchase, *i.e.* a purchase otherwise than on a recognised investment exchange,[10] which is set out in section 164. The contract of purchase must, subject to what is said below, be authorised by a special resolution of the company and the authority may be varied, revoked or renewed by special resolution. There is no time limit for which the authority is to remain valid.[11] The special resolution will be invalid if a member votes shares to which the resolution relates and those votes have been crucial to the passing of the resolution. The resolution will only be effective if a copy of the contract (if in writing) or a written memorandum of its terms has been available for inspection by members for not less than 15 days prior to the date of the meeting at which the resolution is passed and is also available at the meeting itself. A contract may be varied if authorised by a special resolution; the publicity requirements regarding inspection by members, as set out above, apply not only to the variation but also to the original contract (or memorandum) and variations previously made.

As has been seen, a private company is now generally permitted to do by written resolution, signed by or on behalf of all the members who at the date of the resolution would be entitled to attend and vote at a general meeting, anything which can be done by resolution at general meeting.[12] If a company takes advantage of this concession rather than following the procedure set out in section 164, the copy contract or written

[8] See Table A reg. 35, Chap. 6, pp. 70–71, *ante*; also Appendix 1, *post*.

[9] s. 162(2) C.A. having been substituted by s. 133(4) C.A. 1989.

[10] s. 163(1)(a) C.A. 1985, as amended by Sched. 16, para. 17 F.S.A. 1986.

[11] *cf.* s. 164(4) C.A. 1985 which provides that in the case of a public company the authority or any renewal of authority must be stated to expire not later than 18 months from the date of the resolution.

[12] s. 381A C.A. 1985, inserted by s.133 C.A. 1989. See Chap. 7, *ante*.

memorandum (together with proposed variation if relevant) must be supplied to each relevant member at or before the time the resolution is supplied to him for signature and a member who holds shares to which the resolution relates is not treated as a member who is entitled to attend and vote at the relevant meeting.[13]

Section 169 of the Companies Act 1985 provides for disclosure requirements following the purchase. Within 28 days of the purchased shares being delivered to the company it must deliver to the Registrar a return stating the number and nominal value of each class of shares purchased and the date of acquisition. The return need not state the aggregate amount paid by the company for the shares nor the maximum and minimum prices paid in respect of shares of each class.[14] A copy of the contract of purchase or a memorandum of its terms (including a copy of any variation) must be kept at the company's registered office for a period of 10 years from the conclusion of the contract and must be available for inspection by members, without charge.[15] If default is made either in relation to delivery of the return, or keeping the contract for inspection, or allowing a member to inspect, the company and every officer in default are liable to fines and, where the contravention has related to a member's right to inspect, the court may compel immediate inspection.

3. *Reduction of capital*

Whilst public companies may only use distributable profits or the proceeds of a fresh share issue to fund a redemption or purchase of their own shares, it is provided by section 171 of the Companies Act 1985 that a private limited company, if authorised by its articles, may use capital for these purposes. Since shares redeemed or purchased must be cancelled immediately on such redemption or purchase,[16] the concession enables a private company to undertake a reduction of capital which is less formal and expensive than the procedure in

---

[13] Sched. 15A, Pt. 11, para. 5 C.A. 1985, inserted by s. 114 C.A. 1989.

[14] *cf.* s. 169(2) C.A. 1985 which requires such information to be included in a return delivered by a public company.

[15] s. 169(5) C.A. 1985 as amended by s. 143(2) C.A. 1989. For provisions relating to inspection of this document (and other registers, indices or documents kept by companies) see the Companies (Inspection and Copying of Registers, Indices and Documents) Regulations (S.I. 1991 No. 1998) made pursuant to s. 723A C.A. 1985 inserted by s. 143(1) C.A. 1989.

[16] ss. 160(4), 162(2) C.A. 1985.

sections 135 to 138. The extent to which a private company may utilise its capital is restricted to the "permissible capital payment," which is the balance required to make up the purchase price after aggregating the company's available profits[17] and, if any, the proceeds of a fresh issue of shares made for the purpose of helping the redemption or purchase.[18]

If therefore a private company has sufficient distributable profits to cover the whole of the purchase price, those profits must be utilised in order to maintain capital. The company must transfer to a capital redemption reserve an amount equivalent to the nominal value of the redeemed or purchased shares.[19]

Where a private company does not have sufficient distributable profits to effect the redemption or purchase and does not wish to reduce its capital, it may finance the balance required from the proceeds of a fresh share issue. Yet any premium payable must come from distributable profits unless the shares which are being redeemed or purchased were issued at a premium in which case a certain proportion of the premium now payable may be paid out of the proceeds of a fresh issue, that proportion being the lesser of either (1) the aggregate of the premiums that the company received when it issued the shares it is purchasing, or (2) the current amount of the company's share premium account after crediting the premium, if any, on the fresh share issue it has made for the purpose of the redemption or purchase.[20] In order to maintain capital, any sum by which the nominal value of the shares redeemed or purchased exceeds the aggregate proceeds of the new issue must be transferred to the capital redemption reserve.[21]

Commonly, private companies will not have the necessary distributable profits to effect the redemption or purchase since such profits may have been ploughed back into the business or used as directors' remuneration. The statutory concession enabling private companies to utilise capital in the redemption or purchase is a recognition of this fact. In practice, therefore, a private company may use capital to fund the redemption or purchase to the extent that its distributable profits are

---

[17] These are distributable profits determined by reference to accounts prepared within three months before the necessary statutory declaration by directors: see s. 172 C.A. 1985.

[18] s. 171(3) C.A. 1985.

[19] s. 170(1) C.A. 1985.

[20] ss. 160(2), 162(2) C.A. 1985.

[21] s. 170(2) C.A. 1985.

insufficient. There is no compulsion to make a fresh share issue to aid the redemption or purchase. Indeed, if the company has no distributable profits there is nothing in the statutory provisions to prevent the whole of the required sum being drawn from capital. The company must have authorisation in its articles[22] to utilise capital.[23] If the payment out of capital (plus the proceeds of a new issue, if any) is less than the nominal value of the shares redeemed or purchased, the difference must be transferred to the company's capital redemption reserve.[24] This is to ensure that the reduction of capital is confined to the permissible capital payment. Conversely, where the payment out of capital (plus the proceeds of a new issue, if any) exceeds the nominal value of the shares redeemed or purchased, the excess may be used to reduce one or more of the following: the capital redemption reserve, the share premium account, the fully paid up share capital, and any unrealised profit in the statutory revaluation reserve.[25]

4. *Procedure for redemption or purchase out of capital*

The directors of the company must, in accordance with section 173 of the Companies Act 1985, make a statutory declaration, annexed to which must be a supporting auditors' report, specifying the permissible capital payment and stating that in their opinion, after full enquiry, the company will be solvent immediately after the payment and will be able to continue its business and pay its debts as they fall due throughout the year following the payment. A director who has no reasonable grounds for the opinion expressed in the declaration is liable to imprisonment or a fine or both.

The payment out of capital must, under section 173(2) of the Companies Act 1985, be approved by a special resolution the procedure for which is set out in section 174. The resolution must be passed within one week of the statutory declaration and the payment out of capital must be made no earlier than five weeks nor more than seven weeks after the date of the resolution. The resolution is invalid if a member exercises votes in respect of shares which are the subject of the resolution and those votes have been crucial to the passing of the resolution.

---

[22] See Table A, reg. 35 at Appendix 1, *post.*
[23] s. 171(1) C.A. 1985.
[24] s. 171(4), (6) C.A. 1985.
[25] s. 171(5), (6) C.A. 1985.

The resolution is also ineffective unless the statutory declaration by directors and the auditors' report are available to members for inspection at the meeting at which the resolution is passed. If the company adopts the procedure of a written resolution, signed by, or on behalf of, all relevant members,[26] the documents referred to above must be supplied to such members at or before the time the resolution is supplied to them for signature and a member holding shares to which the resolution relates is not treated as relevant for these purposes.[27]

Section 175 of the Companies Act 1985 prescribes publicity requirements regarding the payment out of capital. Within the week following the date of the special resolution, the company must publish in the Gazette a notice stating that the company has approved a payment out of capital to purchase and/or redeem its shares, the amount of the permissible capital payment, the availability for inspection at the registered office of the directors' statutory declaration and auditors' report, and the rights of creditors to object to the payment (see *infra*).

Within the same time limit, the company must also publish such a notice in a national newspaper or give notice in writing to each of its creditors. Not later than the date of the first publication of the notice, the company must deliver to the registrar a copy of the directors' statutory declaration and auditors' report, and the originals must be available at the registered office for inspection[28] without charge by members or creditors for a period beginning on the date on which the notice outlined above is first published and ending five weeks after the passing of the special resolution. If inspection is refused, the company and every officer in default are liable to fines, and the court may compel an immediate inspection.

5. *Rights to object to payment out of capital*

Any member, other than one who consented to or voted for the special resolution, and any creditor, has, under section 176 of the Companies Act 1985, five weeks from the passing of the special resolution to apply to the court for its cancellation. Members or creditors entitled to object may appoint in writing one or more of their number as their representatives in making

[26] s. 381A C.A. 1985 inserted by s. 113 C.A. 1989. See Chap. 7, *ante*.
[27] Sched. 15A, Pt. II, para. 5, C.A. 1985, inserted by s. 114 C.A. 1989.
[28] s. 175(6) C.A. 1985 as amended by s. 143(3) C.A. 1989. For the provisions relating to inspection of documents generally see *ante*, n. 15.

the application. The company must immediately give notice of such an application to the registrar, the company and officers being liable to fines in default.

Section 177 of the Companies Act 1985 provides that the court may, on hearing the application, adjourn the proceedings for arrangements to be made to the court's satisfaction to buy out the dissentient members or to protect dissentient creditors and may cancel or confirm the resolution on such terms and conditions as it thinks fit and in particular may alter any time periods specified in the resolution or in the Act in relation to the redemption or purchase. The court's order may provide for the purchase by the company of any of its members' shares and for the resulting reduction in capital, and if in consequence the court orders alterations to the memorandum or articles, it may also require the company not to make any (or any specified) further alterations without its leave.

6. *Liability of past directors and shareholders*

The liability of former directors and shareholders of a private company which is wound up within one year of redeeming or purchasing its shares out of capital is considered in Chapter 21, *post*.

C. Companies providing financial assistance for acquisitions of their own shares

1. *General exceptions to the inability of a company to give financial assistance for acquiring its own shares*

The rules on the provision of financial assistance by a company, which were reformed in the Companies Act 1981, granting special exemptions to private companies, are now contained in sections 151 to 158 of the Companies Act 1985.

The basic prohibition applying to all companies is contained in section 151, which makes it unlawful for a company or any of its subsidiaries[29] to give financial assistance, directly or

[29] But it was held by Millett J. in *Arab Bank plc v. Merchantile Holdings Ltd. and Another* [1994] 2 W.L.R. 307 that the words "any of its subsidiaries" in s. 151, though amenable on a literal reading to a contrary interpretation, did not prohibit a foreign subsidiary giving financial assistance for the purpose of an acquisition of shares in its English registered parent. Millett J. also held that the mere giving of assistance by such a subsidiary did not *ipso facto* necessarily constitute the unlawful giving of financial assistance by the parent.

indirectly, to a person acquiring or proposing to acquire the company's shares, before or at the time of, and for the purpose of, such acquisition,[30] or to give such assistance directly or indirectly to a person following an acquisition, for the purpose of reducing or discharging any liability incurred by that, or any other, person in making the acquisition.[31] In contravention of this prohibition, the company is liable to a fine and every officer in default to imprisonment or a fine or both.[32] Financial assistance is defined to include gifts, loans, credit arrangements, any guarantee, security, indemnity, release or waiver, or any other financial assistance by the company the net assets of which are thereby materially reduced or which has no net assets.[33]

There are, however, certain permitted transactions which apply to private as well as public companies. Section 153(3) of the Companies Act 1985 includes the following cases where the giving of financial assistance is lawful; distributions of lawful dividends; the allotment of bonus shares; a reduction of capital confirmed by court order under section 137 of the Companies Act 1985; a redemption or purchase of shares made in accordance with the Act; anything done in pursuance of a court order sanctioning a compromise or arrangement under section 425 of the Companies Act 1985 or under a voluntary arrangement with creditors under sections 1 to 7 of the Insolvency Act 1986, or under an arrangement whereby the liquidator of company A, which is either in, or which is proposed to be put into, voluntary liquidation, receives shares in company B in consideration of a transfer of assets from company A to company B under section 110 of the Insolvency Act 1986.

Furthermore, section 153(4) of the Companies Act 1985 provides for the following specific permitted transactions (for the "purpose" exemptions under section 153(1) and (2) of the Companies Act 1985, see *infra*):

(1) A money-lending company may lend money in the ordinary course of its business.[34]

---

[30] s. 151(1) C.A. 1985.
[31] s. 151(2) C.A. 1985.
[32] s. 151(3) C.A. 1985.
[33] s. 152(1)(a) C.A. 1985.
[34] A loan for the direct purpose of financing an acquisition of the company's shares will not be a loan in the ordinary course of its business: *Steen v. Law* [1964] A.C. 287.

(2) A company may provide, in good faith in the interests of the company, financial assistance for the purposes of an employees' share scheme.[35]

(3) A company or any of its subsidiaries may provide financial assistance in connection with anything done by the company or by a company in the same group[36] to enable or facilitate transfers of shares between bona fide employees or former employees of the company or of another company in the same group, or the spouses, widows, widowers, children or step-children (under the age of eighteen) of such employees or former employees.[37]

(4) A company may make loans to persons employed in good faith, other than directors, to enable such employees to acquire beneficially fully-paid shares in the company or its holding company.

Whereas the four exceptions listed above apply also to public companies, there is no requirement in the case of a private company, as there is for a public company, that the company has net assets which are not reduced by the giving of the assistance or to the extent that they are reduced, the assistance is provided out of distributable profits.[38]

2. *Special exception for private companies*

Where the purpose of the assistance is not covered by the permitted transactions set out above, a private company may rely on the provisions contained in sections 155 to 158 of the Companies Act 1985 which enable a private company, subject to following a certain procedure, to provide financial assistance for the acquisition of its shares. The permission extends to the giving of financial assistance for the acquisition of shares in a private company's holding company provided the holding

[35] s. 153(4)(b) C.A. 1985 as amended by s. 132 C.A. 1989. An employees' share scheme is defined in s. 743 C.A. 1985.

[36] A company is in the same group as another company if it is a holding company or subsidiary of that company, or a subsidiary of a holding company of that company: subs. (5) of s. 153 C.A. 1985 substituted by Sched. 18, para. 33(3) C.A. 1989. For the definition of "subsidiary" and "holding company" see ss. 736, 736A, 736B C.A. 1985 inserted by s. 144 C.A. 1989.

[37] s. 153(4)(b), inserted by s. 196(2) F.S.A. 1986, and covering the same persons as are covered by an employees' share scheme.

[38] *cf.* s. 154 C.A. 1985.

company is also private and does not have another subsidiary which is public and which is also a holding company of the company giving the assistance.[39] In order to give the assistance, the company must have net assets which are not thereby reduced, or in so far as they are reduced the assistance must be provided out of distributable profits.[40]

(a) *Company must be declared solvent*

A statutory declaration of solvency is required to be given by the directors of the company proposing to give the assistance and also, if the assistance is in respect of an acquisition of shares in its holding company, by the directors of that holding company and of any intervening holding company.[41] The statutory declaration must contain prescribed particulars of the financial assistance, the company's business and the identity of the person to whom the assistance is to be given.[42] It is clear from recent decisions that technical omissions or inaccuracies will not necessarily invalidate the statutory declaration. Thus, it was held to be sufficient where the statutory declaration referred only to a "group debenture" and omitted to mention the identity of the property charged, the kind of charge granted and an accompanying guarantee by the company.[43] Also, the directors comply with the statutory obligation where the particulars are *in* the prescribed form[44] even though the information is contained *on* an inappropriate form.[45]

The statutory declaration must state that in the directors' opinion the company will be able to pay its debts immediately after the date on which the assistance is to be given and will remain solvent during the year following that date. If it is

[39] s. 155(1), (3) C.A. 1985.

[40] s. 155(2) C.A. 1985, which makes "net assets" subject to the book-value test contained in s. 154(2). Compare s. 152(2).

[41] s. 155(6) C.A. 1985. For an argument that where a subsidiary is providing assistance for the acquisition of shares in its holding company, the statutory provisions are ambiguous as to whether the directors of the holding company must make the declaration as to the solvency of the subsidiary or the holding company, see Sujata Sharma, "Whose solvency is it anyway?" in (1993) 137 S.J. 318.

[42] s. 156(1) C.A. 1985.

[43] *Re S. H. & Co. (Realisations) 1990 Ltd.*; *Ellis & Anor. v. Nyckeln Finance Co. Ltd.* [1993] BCC 60, though Mummery J. advised solicitors in future to err on the side of caution and include a fuller form of particulars.

[44] As required by s. 155(6) C.A. 1985.

[45] *Re NL Electrical Ltd., Ghosh and another v. 3 i plc* [1994] 1 BCLC 22, where the statutory declaration had been made on a form which was not then, but which had been, the prescribed form.

proposed that the company be wound up within 12 months of the date of the assistance, the directors must state their opinion that the company will be able to discharge its debts in full within 12 months of the commencement of the winding up.[46] A director who has no reasonable grounds for the opinion expressed in the declaration is liable to imprisonment or a fine or both.[47] Annexed to the statutory declaration must be an auditors' report stating that, following enquiry, the auditors are not aware of anything to render unreasonable the directors' opinion as to the company's solvency.[48] The statutory declaration and auditors' report must be delivered to the Registrar of Companies within 15 days of the making of the declaration, or, where a special resolution of the company is required (see below), within 15 days of the passing of that resolution together with a copy thereof.[49] Failure to comply renders the company and every officer in default liable to fines,[50] but late delivery does not result in the financial assistance having been improperly provided so as to constitute an offence under section 151(3) of the Companies Act 1985 nor does it render void a collateral debenture.[51]

(b) *Shareholders' special resolution is required*

Except where the company proposing to give the financial assistance is a wholly owned subsidiary, the financial assistance must be approved by a special resolution of shareholders and where the acquisition relates to shares in its holding company, then that company and any intervening holding company must also pass special resolutions.[52] The resolution must be passed on the date of the making of the directors' statutory declaration or in the week following that date. The statutory declaration and auditors' report must be available for inspection by members at the meeting at which the special resolution is passed. If a company adopts, within the provisions of section 381A of the Companies Act 1985, a written resolution as an alternative to the special resolution then Part II of Schedule 15A

---

[46] s. 156(2) C.A. 1985.
[47] s. 156(7) C.A. 1985.
[48] s. 156(4) C.A. 1985.
[49] s. 156(5) C.A. 1985.
[50] s. 156(6) C.A. 1985.
[51] *Re NL Electrical Ltd., ante*, n. 45.
[52] s. 155(4), (5) C.A. 1985.

to the Companies Act 1985 provides that the statutory declaration and auditors' report must be supplied to each relevant member at or before the time the resolution is supplied to him for signature.[53] The holders of at least 10 per cent of the nominal value of the company's issued share capital, or any class thereof, or, if the company is not limited by shares, 10 per cent of the company members who did not consent to, or vote for the resolution, may apply to the court within 28 days of the passing of the resolution for the resolution to be cancelled. The court may make an order cancelling or confirming the resolution on such terms and conditions as it thinks fit and in particular may adjourn the proceedings for the dissentients to be bought out. The order may provide for the purchase of the dissentient members' shares by the company and for the consequent reduction of capital and any alteration to the memorandum and articles that may be required. The court's order may require the company not to make any, or any specified, alteration to its memorandum or articles, in which case any future alteration by the company can only be undertaken with the court's leave. Where an application by dissentients is made, the company must give the Registrar notice forthwith and after the court order is made the company must send an office copy to the Registrar within 15 days or such longer time as the court may direct.[54]

Where a special resolution is required, the financial assistance must not be given before the end of four weeks of the date of the resolution or, if more than one resolution has been passed, four weeks of the date of the last one to be passed. This time limit does not apply however if the resolution (or, if more than one, each of them) was passed unanimously by every member entitled to vote at general meetings. If an application to the court is made to cancel the special resolution, the assistance cannot, unless the court otherwise orders, be given before the court decides the application. The financial assistance must not be given after the end of the eight weeks from the date of the directors' statutory declaration, or from the date of the first such declaration where more than one is needed, unless the court otherwise orders on an application by dissentients.[55]

Two important advantages of the sections 155 to 158 procedure (hereinafter referred to as the "special procedure")

[53] These provisions are inserted by ss. 113–114 C.A. 1989.
[54] ss. 157, 54(3)–(10) C.A. 1985.
[55] s. 158 C.A. 1985.

are that it enables private companies to provide financial assistance in the context of management buy-outs and corporate restructures.

3. *Management buy-outs*

The issues surrounding management buy-outs are by no means straightforward.[56] Certainly, where director/controllers of a private company are selling their shares to managers who are not themselves directors, the company can, on following the necessary steps under the special procedure, charge its assets as security for a loan obtained by the managers to undertake the purchase. A direct loan might be made by the company to non-director/managers to enable the share purchase without the need to resort to the special procedure since under section 153(4)(c) of the Companies Act 1985 the company can make a loan to persons employed in good faith to enable those persons to buy shares to be held by them beneficially. It has been argued, however, that the cases of management buy-outs where reliance is placed on section 153(4)(c) are likely to be few since, *inter alia*, the managers will not be directors immediately following the purchase and also they may prefer to protect their personal liability by undertaking the transaction through the medium of a company set up for that purpose.[57]

These factors would seem equally to apply to those cases where the company, under the special procedure, gives security to a third party lender to the managers. Indeed, as explained below, it may be crucial to the carrying out of the special procedure that the managers are appointed as directors.

(a) *Disadvantages for directors involved in assisting buy-outs*

In the case of a profitable private company in which the retiring proprietor is keen to ensure continuity through a sale of his shares to non-director managers or employees, the proprietor, as director, will probably make, or participate in making, the necessary statutory declaration to facilitate the giving of financial assistance. Even so, the procedure has its dangers for directors and there may be certain cases in which

---

[56] See C. G. M. Lumsden, "Financial Assistance Problems in Management Buy-Outs" in [1987] J.B.L. 111.

[57] Lumsden, *op. cit. supra*, who also argues that the loan might become repayable on the manager being appointed as a director.

existing directors are reluctant to become involved in the financial assistance arrangements.

Section 156(7) of the Companies Act 1985 in imposing criminal liability on directors who make a statutory declaration of solvency "without having reasonable grounds for the opinion expressed in it" appears to make the offence one of negligence. Such negligence may also make the directors liable to compensate the company for any loss in summary proceedings under section 212 of the Insolvency Act 1986 in a liquidation.

Thus, in cases of management buy-outs in groups of private companies, for example where a holding company is selling a loss-making subsidiary to its managers, it may well be that the holding company will not wish its nominee directors on the board of the company giving the assistance to participate in the statutory declaration. These directors will therefore have to resign in favour of the managers who, now being directors, will then make the necessary statutory declaration.[58] Such reluctance to become involved in the financial assistance may also make the special resolution impossible to pass unless a share transfer to the managers, or more usually a company formed by them to undertake the share purchase, is registered before the giving of the assistance.[59]

(b) *Formation of a company to undertake the buy-out*

The formation by the managers of a company to undertake the share purchase and to receive financial assistance for that purpose is essential where the managers are directors, whether appointed especially to ensure compliance with the special procedure, or of longer standing. This is due to the prohibition on loans to the directors.[60]

Section 330 of the Companies Act 1985 renders illegal any direct loan or the provision of any security for a loan by a company in favour of its directors. This difficulty is overcome, however, by the formation of a company by the manager/directors since any giving of a loan, or provision of any security for a loan, by the company whose shares are being

---

[58] It might be a wise precaution for the directors immediately to declare their interest at a board meeting and possibly also a general meeting (see Chap. 8, pp. 128 *et seq.*, *ante*) to avoid any possible future charge by a liquidator of breach of fiduciary duty through conflict of duty and interest.

[59] For a fuller discussion of all these issues see Lumsden, *op. cit. ante*, n. 56.

[60] Chap. 8, pp. 137 *et seq.*, *ante*.

purchased to the newly formed company will be made in favour of a "connected person" to the directors of the company, and this is permitted in the case of a private company[61] provided it is not part of a group containing a public company.[62]

4. *Corporate restructure within a group of private companies*

The special procedure may prove useful in facilitating a corporate restructure within a group of private companies, particularly in cases where, because of management disputes or deadlock, it is desired to split a business between corporators.

In *Brady v. Brady*,[63] two brothers carried on business through B Ltd. and a number of subsidiaries. The two main activities were road haulage run by one brother and soft drinks run by the other. Following a dispute, and in order to avoid the possible liquidation of B Ltd., a complex scheme was devised to divide the business equally between the two brothers. The scheme involved the proposed transfer of half of B Ltd.'s assets which constituted financial assistance within section 151(2) of the Companies Act 1985 in that it would reduce the liability incurred by the purchaser of its shares. The House of Lords, however, held that the financial assistance could lawfully be given by complying with the special procedure. Since B Ltd. was a wholly owned subsidiary of a company created as part of the scheme, no special resolution of B Ltd. was required, but the brothers would, as directors, have to make the necessary statutory declarations in respect of B Ltd. and a subsidiary. Even if the arrangement involved a reduction in B Ltd.'s net assets, the company had sufficient distributable profits to cover the value of the transferred assets.

In *Plaut v. Steiner*,[64] two families were equal shareholders in four commercially integrated companies. The facts again involved a division of the business between the families in order to resolve management deadlock. Morritt J. held that the arrangement involved financial assistance contrary to section 151(1) of the Companies Act 1985, but refused to accept the argument that the assistance could lawfully have been given by compliance with the special procedure. The net asset reduction of one of the companies proposing to give the financial

---

[61] *cf.* s. 330(3) C.A. 1985.
[62] s. 331(6) C.A. 1985.
[63] [1988] 2 W.L.R. 1308.
[64] (1989) 5 B.C.C. 352.

assistance for the purchase of its own shares could not have been limited to its available distributable profits. Indeed, the arrangement would have made the company insolvent and thus the directors could not properly have sworn the statutory declaration of solvency nor could the auditors have produced the necessary report.

5. *The "purpose" exemptions*

Where a private company is unable to rely on the special procedure provided by sections 155 to 158 of the Companies Act 1985, then, assuming the assistance does not fall within one of the permitted categories already considered, the only way the company can lawfully provide financial assistance for the acquisition of its own shares is under a broader exemption available to all companies.

(a) *Incidental purpose of giving assistance*

Subsections (1) and (2) of section 153 of the Companies Act 1985 provide that a company may give financial assistance to aid an acquisition of its shares or to reduce or discharge the liability of a person incurred by the acquisition if either the company's principal purpose is not to give the assistance for the purpose of such an acquisition or for the reduction or discharge of such liability, as appropriate, or the giving of the assistance, in either case, is but an incidental part of some larger purpose of the company. The assistance must be given in good faith in the interests of the company.

In *Brady v. Brady*,[65] the plaintiff's argument as to the lawfulness of the proposed financial assistance based on the special procedure was first made before the House of Lords. The plaintiff had previously argued that the transaction was covered by the purpose exemptions in that although the proposed transfer of B Ltd.'s assets was intended to reduce or discharge the liability of the acquirer of B Ltd.'s shares, the larger purpose was to enable B Ltd. to exist independently, free of management deadlock and so avoid the threat of liquidation. These arguments were accepted by the trial judge and by the Court of Appeal, though with some reluctance on the part of

---

[65] [1988] 2 W.L.R. 1308. For facts see p. 171, *ante*.

Nourse L.J. On this issue, the House of Lords overturned the Court of Appeal. In the opinion of Lord Oliver, "larger" was not the same as "more important" and "purpose" was not the same as "reason." No matter how beneficial the intended results of the arrangement, its sole purpose was to reduce or discharge the liability of the acquirer of the shares.

Brady v. Brady involved an interpretation of section 153(2) which covers post-acquisition assistance, but that the same interpretation applies to section 153(1), which deals with assistance given for the purpose of the acquisition itself, is clear from the judgment of Morritt J. in *Plaut v. Steiner.*[66] Though Morritt J., on similar facts, follows *Brady v. Brady*, the decision does not rely on the distinction between "purpose" and "reason" that was made by Lord Oliver. Assuming that a company has two purposes, purpose A being the division of its business and purpose B being an acquisition of its shares (in respect of which the company has allegedly provided financial assistance) then the principles which emerge from Morritt J.'s judgment in *Plaut v. Steiner* appear to be:

(1) if A can be achieved quite independently of the financial assistance, then A cannot be the principal purpose of the giving of that assistance;
(2) if A cannot, on the facts, exist without B, A is no more a larger purpose than B is merely incidental; both purposes are equally "large".

Though it is clear from the above that the courts have been keen to give section 153 a meaning which, in the words of Lord Oliver, "does not in effect provide a blank cheque for avoiding the effective application of section 151 in every case",[67] it appears, as a result of their decisions, that the instances where a company can rely on the purpose exemptions at all are now likely to be few. Indeed, it seems that unless a principal or larger purpose can be discerned in the transaction itself, the exemptions will not apply. By anology with the cases involving a proposed division of a company's business, management buy-outs are almost certainly excluded. It would, however, be open to a company to argue, for example, that its principal purpose was the purchase of an asset which it genuinely needed even

[66] (1989) 5 BCC 352. For facts see pp. 171–172, *ante*.
[67] *Brady v. Brady* [1988] 2 W.L.R. 1308 at 1327.

though it knew that the vendor would thereby be put in funds to make a purchase of its shares.[68]

(b) *Position of Banks*

Given the uncertainties surrounding the purpose exemptions, there may be some doubt as to whether a bank would wish to become involved in an arrangement involving financial assistance especially since the effect of any illegality is that a security or guarantee from the company in respect of the loan is void.[69] There is also the possibility that a bank may, depending on its knowledge, even incur liability as a constructive trustee for assisting in the design.[70]

(c) *Financial assistance must be given in good faith*

Even if a company is able to satisfy the "principal" or "larger" purpose tests, it must also show that the financial assistance was given in good faith in the interests of the company.[71] The duty is effectively placed on those who are in a position to procure the act of the company, *i.e.* in practice, the directors in these circumstances. Lord Oliver's opinion in *Brady v. Brady* that the test is what the directors genuinely believe to be in the interests of the company accords with the principle that applies generally to directors' duties.[72] In *Plaut v. Steiner*, above, however, there appears to be a suggestion by Morritt J. that the yardstick is what a reasonable board could have concluded.

6. *Proposals for reform*

As part of its review of selected areas of company law, announced in November 1992, the Department of Trade and Industry issued, in October 1993, a Consultative Document on financial assistance. Amongst the proposals are that sections 151 to 154 of the Companies Act 1985 be replaced by a new two-tier structure, the first tier implementing Article 23 of the

---

[68] *cf. Belmont Finance Corporation Ltd. v. Williams Furniture Ltd. (No. 2)* [1980] 1 All E.R. 392, and see Lord Oliver in *Brady v. Brady* [1988] 2 W.L.R. 1308 at 1326.
[69] *Heald v. O'Connor* [1971] 1 W.L.R. 497.
[70] See Chap. 8, pp. 123, *et seq.*, *ante*. See also Chap. 11, p. 186, *post*.
[71] s. 153(1)(b), (2)(b), C.A. 1985.
[72] Chap. 8, pp. 113 *et seq.*, *ante*.

Second E.C. Company Law Directive,[73] that the present purpose exemptions be recast, and that the special procedure for private companies be simplified.

[73] 77/91: [1977] O.J. L26/1.

CHAPTER 11

SINGLE MEMBER COMPANIES

A. The Companies (Single Member Private Limited Companies) Regulations 1992

The Companies (Single Member Private Limited Companies) Regulations,[1] implementing the European Community's 12th Company Law Directive on single member companies,[2] came into force on July 15, 1992. Regulation 2(1) provides that notwithstanding any enactment or rule of law to thc contrary, a private company limited by shares or by guarantee within the meaning of section 1 of the Companies 1985 may be formed by one person, in so far as permitted by section 1 as amended by the Regulations, and may have one member.

1. *The Regulations in context*

Though the provision enabling the *formation* by one person of a private company limited by shares or by guarantee was an important reform[3] nothing in previous companies legislation had prevented the *existence* of a private company with just one member. Indeed, that the precusor provisions of section 24 of the Companies Act 1985, providing for personal liability on the part of a remaining member following a reduction in the statutory minimum membership for more than six months, and section 122(1)(e) of the Insolvency Act 1986, allowing for the compulsory winding up of a company whose membership had

---

[1] (S.I. 1992 No. 1699).
[2] 89/667: [1989] O.J. L395.
[3] For the history of the minimum membership requirement for private companies see Chap. 1, *ante*.

been reduced below two,[4] contemplated the existence of a single member company,[5] received judicial recognition by Ungoed-Thomas J. in *Jarvis Motors (Harrow) Ltd. v. Carabott.*[6]

If single member companies had existed *de jure* prior to 1992, the validity of the *de facto* "one-person company", in which one person is the legal holder of the vast majority of the shares and is beneficial holder of all, was established beyond doubt in *Salomon v. Salomon & Co. Ltd.* where Lord Macnaghten stated:

> "It has become the fashion to call companies of this class 'one-man companies'. That is a taking nickname, but it does not help one much in the way of argument. If it is intended to convey the meaning that a company which is under the absolute control of one person is not a company legally incorporated, although the requirements of the Act of 1862 may have been complied with, it is inaccurate and misleading: if it merely means that there is a predominant partner possessing an overwhelming influence and entitled practically to the whole of the profits, there is nothing in that that I can see contrary to the true intention of the Act of 1862, or against public policy, or detrimental to the interests of creditors."[7]

In a sense, therefore, the Regulations have merely recognised business reality, obviating the need in the case of private companies limited by shares or by guarantee for the legal device of the registration of a nominee shareholder.

The concept of the veil of incorporation has been discussed earlier in this work,[8] and the cases establishing that the corporate veil separates a company from its sole beneficial shareholder apply with no less force to a single member. Thus, such a member need not, in the absence of misfeasance or breach of duty, indemnify the company against the claims of its creditors,[9] has no insurable interest in the property of the

---

[4] Both provisions are necessarily amended by the Regulations, see *post*, and for an earlier discussion of s. 24 C.A. 1985 see Chap. 2, *ante*.

[5] Albeit, in effect, as an unlimited company after the six-month period in the case of s. 24 C.A. 1985.

[6] [1964] 1 W.L.R. 1101 at 1103.

[7] [1897] A.C. 22 at 53. See also Lord Herschell at 44.

[8] Chap. 3, *ante*.

[9] *Salomon v. Salomon & Co. Ltd.* [1897] A.C. 22.

company,[10] may be regarded as an employee of the company,[11] and may not appear on behalf of a company in litigation in lieu of the required legal representation.[12] On the other hand, for a discussion of those cases where the court is prepared to lift the corporate veil see Chapter 3, *ante*.

2. *The effect of the Regulations*

Regulation 2(1) provides that any enactment or rule of law applying to a private company limited by shares or by guarantee is to apply, in the absence of any express provision to the contrary, with such modification as may be necessary to accommodate such a company formed by one person or having only one person as a member. Without prejudice to the generality of this provision, the Regulations have, however, made several amendments to the Companies Act 1985 and one to the Insolvency Act 1986. The changes are set out below.

(i) *Formation by one person*

A new subsection (3A) is inserted in section 1 of the Companies Act 1985 which provides that notwithstanding subsection (1), which requires two members to form a company, one person may form a private company limited by shares or by guarantee by subscribing his name to the memorandum and otherwise complying with the registration requirements. Thus, two persons are still required to form an unlimited company.[13]

(ii) *Sole remaining member excepted from personal liability*

Section 24 of the Companies Act 1985 has been amended to provide that if a company, other than a private company limited by shares or by guarantee, carries on business for more than six months without having at least two members, any person who is a member for the whole or any part of the period after the six months and who knows that the company is carrying on

---

[10] *Macaura v. Northern Assurance Co. Ltd.* [1925] A.C. 619; *Verderame and others v. Commercial Union Assurance Co. plc and another* [1992] BCLC 793 (for fuller discussion of both cases see Chap. 3, pp. 21–22, *ante*). But for the Canadian view on this topic where there is only one shareholder see *Constitution Insurance Co. of Canada v. Kosmopoulos* (1987) 34 D.L.R. (4th) 208.

[11] *Lee v. Lee's Air Farming Ltd.* [1961] A.C. 12.

[12] *Radford v. Samuel & Anor* [1993] BCC 870.

[13] And, of course, a public company.

business with only one member, is jointly and severally liable for the company's debts contracted during the period or the relevant part of it. As observed in a previous chapter,[14] sole members of private companies limited by shares or by guarantee need now only be concerned with section 24 if they have fallen foul of its terms in a relevant period prior to July 15, 1992.[15] Otherwise the provision, albeit more in theory than in reality, applies only to public companies.

(iii) *Contracts with sole members who are directors*

By virtue of new section 322B of the Companies Act 1985, inserted by the Regulations, where a private company limited by shares or by guarantee enters into a contract, other than a contract in the ordinary course of the company's business, with its sole member who is also a director or shadow director, the company must, unless the contract is in writing, ensure that the contract's terms are either set out in a written memorandum or are recorded in the minutes of the first meeting of the directors following the making of the contract. Fines in default are placed on the company and its officers. Section 741(3) of the Companies Act 1985 is also amended to provide that for the purposes of section 322B, a company is not to be treated as the shadow director of any of its subsidiaries by reason only that the directors of the subsidiary are accustomed to act in accordance with its directions or instructions.

(iv) *Statement that company has only one member*

New section 352A, added to the Companies Act 1985 by the Regulations, provides that if the membership of a private company limited by shares or by guarantee falls to one, a statement that the company has only one member must immediately be entered on the company's register of members together with the name and address of the sole member and the date on which the event occurred. Conversely, if the membership of such a company increases from one to two or more, a statement to that effect, the date of the event and the name and address of the former sole member must immediately be entered in the register of members. The company and officers are liable to fines in default.

---

[14] Chap. 2, pp. 12–13, *ante*, where s. 24 is covered in more detail, and see particularly the discussion of *Nisbet v. Shepherd* [1994] BCC 91.

[15] The date on which the Regulations came into force.

(v) *Quorum at meetings*

The Regulations insert a new section 370A of the Companies Act 1985 to provide that, notwithstanding anything to the contrary in the articles of a private company limited by shares or by guarantee having only one member, one member present in person or by proxy is sufficient to constitute a quorum at a meeting of the company.

(vi) *Recording decisions of sole member*

By virtue of new section 382B of the Companies Act 1985, inserted by the Regulations, where the sole member of a private company limited by shares or by guarantee takes any decision which can be taken by the company in general meeting and which has effect as if so agreed, the member must, unless the decision is taken by written resolution,[16] provide the company with a written record of the decision. Failure to comply renders the sole member liable to a fine but does not affect the validity of the decision.

(vii) *Registration of company not formed under Companies Legislation*

Such a company, being a private company limited by shares or by guarantee, is not prevented from registering under the Companies Act 1985 solely because it has only one member: new subsection 680(1A) inserted by the Regulations.

(viii) *Exception from winding up by the court*

Section 122(1)(g) of the Insolvency Act 1986 is amended so as to provide that a private company limited by shares or by guarantee is not subject to winding up by the court if its membership is reduced below two.

B. Criminal offences by one-person controllers against the company

Difficult issues have arisen on the question whether a person in total control of a private company can commit criminal

---

[16] See Chap. 7, *ante*.

offences against the company's property, though, as will be seen below, the law has, to a large extent, been clarified. The vulnerability of the property of private companies was stressed by Lord Goddard in *R. v. Davies*,[17] a case in which the House of Lords held that section 20(1)(ii) of the Larceny Act 1916[18] applied to directors of private companies as it did to directors of public companies. Lord Goddard stated:

> "Private companies require just the same protection as any other sort of trading company, for directors of private companies sometimes fail to distinguish between their own property and the property of the company. They may have turned their business into a company for many reasons—sometimes because they want to avoid the risk of bankruptcy. Therefore, anybody who obtains credit, if credit can be obtained, is well advised to get it from the company; and it is thus important that a company should not be deprived of its assets, because it is the company which will have to pay and which can be sued."[19]

1. *Theft of the company's property*

As the law now stands, the sole controller of a company is capable of stealing the property of the company. In *A.-G.'s Reference (No. 2 of 1982)*[20] the question for the Court of Appeal was whether a man in total control of a limited liability company, by reason of his shareholding and directorship, was capable of stealing the property of the company, and (to accommodate the facts of the case which gave rise to the reference)[21] whether two men in such control were capable of jointly stealing in these circumstances. The facts alleged were that the two defendants who were the only shareholders and directors of several companies had used the companies' money to finance their personal needs. They were acquitted of theft at first instance.

---

[17] [1955] 1 Q.B. 71.

[18] This subsection provided that it was an offence for a director, member or officer fraudulently to use for that person's benefit, or otherwise to misapply, the property of any "body corporate or public company".

[19] [1955] 1 Q.B. 71 at 76.

[20] [1984] Q.B. 624.

[21] Case heard at Winchester Crown Court.

In the Court of Appeal it was common ground that the defendants had appropriated property belonging to another (the companies) with the intention of permanently depriving the other of it for the purposes of section 1(1) of the Theft Act 1968. The argument thus turned on dishonesty. Section 2(1)(b) of the Theft Act 1968 provides that a person is not to be regarded as dishonest if he appropriates another's property in the belief that he would have the other's consent if the other knew of the appropriation and the circumstances of it. The Court of Appeal held that section 2(1)(b) required a belief in genuine consent, honestly obtained, and due to the defendants' identification with the various companies by virtue both of their shareholdings and directorships, the companies could not sensibly be regarded as "the other" for the purposes of giving the necessary consent.[22] Though on the alleged facts of this case the Court of Appeal thought it possible that a jury would have concluded that the defendants had acted disho-nestly, it might be possible in similar cases for defendants to rely on section 2(1)(a) of the Theft Act 1968 to show they were not dishonest because they believed they had in law the right to deprive the company of the property.

Establishing an appropriation in order to satisfy the *actus reus* of theft for the purposes of section 1(1) of the Theft Act 1968 in cases of alleged theft of company property by "one-person controllers" of that company has proved to be a controversial issue. Two questions in particular had, until recently, been the subject of conflicting judicial decisions:

(1) did an appropriation require some act unauthorised by the owner of the property as stated by Lord Roskill in *R. v. Morris, Anderton v. Burnside*,[23] in contradiction to the earlier House of Lords decision in *Lawrence v. Metropolitan Police Commissioner*?[24]; if so,

---

[22] Compare *R. v. McDonnell* [1966] 1 Q.B. 233 where it was held that a sole responsible director could not be guilty of conspiring with the company since the crime of conspiracy required the agreement of two independent minds.

[23] [1983] 3 All E.R. 288 at 293 where Lord Roskill stated that in order to satisfy s. 3(1) Theft Act 1968 which defines an appropriation as an assumption of the rights of an owner, there had to be "not an act expressly or impliedly authorised by the owner but an act by way of adverse interference with or usurpation of those rights".

[24] [1971] 2 All E.R. 1253 where the House of Lords held that s. 1(1) Theft Act 1968 was not to be construed as though it contained the words "without having the consent of the owner".

(2) did not companies, in such circumstances, authorise dispositions of their property to the defendants through the will of the defendants themselves as controllers and directors?[25]

In *A.-G.'s Reference (No. 2 of 1982)*, *ante*, counsel conceded that an appropriation had occurred and so the issue was not discussed. The questions were addressed, however, in *R. v. Philippou*[26] where the Court of Appeal, though favouring the decision in *Lawrence v. Metropolitan Police Commissioner* and endeavouring to reconcile Lord Roskill's statement in *R. v. Morris, Anderton v. Burnside*, held, in any case, that a company no more "authorises" *dishonest* transactions by its sole directors and shareholders than it "consents" to them. Even though it might be said, on the facts of the case, that the company consented to the transfer of money from its bank account to Spain (since the instruction to the bank by the two sole shareholders was the company's instruction) it did not consent to the use of the money by the defendants to buy themselves a block of flats. Putting the two components of the transaction together, the drawing of the money from the bank was an adverse interference with the rights of the company and there was an appropriation.

This approach is now supported by dicta of the House of Lords in *R. v. Gomez.*[27] The decision of the majority in that case,[28] answering question (1) above in the negative and re-establishing the authority of *Lawrence v. Metropolitan Police Commissioner*, is sufficient to settle the issue. Company property is appropriated by company controllers irrespective of any authorisation by the company. According to Lords Browne-Wilkinson[29] and Lowry,[30] however, there is no authorisation in such circumstances. Lord Browne-Wilkinson stated:

---

[25] This was held to be the case by the majority of the Supreme Court of Victoria in *R. v. Roffel* [1985] V.R. 511 and referred to with approval by the Court of Appeal in *R. v. McHugh and Tringham* (1988) 88 Cr.App.R. 385, a case which did not require a decision on the issue.

[26] (1989) 89 Cr.App.R. 290.

[27] [1993] 1 All E.R. 1.

[28] Which was not a case concerning appropriation of company property.

[29] [1993] 1 All E.R. 1 at 40 where Lord Browne-Wilkinson expressed approval of the concession made by counsel in *A.-G.'s Reference (No. 2 of 1982)* [1984] Q.B. 624 and of the decision of *R. v. Philippou* (1989) Cr.App.R. 290, and disapproval of the decision in *R. v. Roffel* [1985] V.R. 511 and the statements of principle in *R. v. McHugh and Tringham* (1988) 88 Cr.App.R. 385.

[30] *ibid.* at 35–38. Lord Lowry dissented from the actual decision in the case.

> "The pillaging of companies by those who control them is now all too common. It would offend both common sense and justice to hold that the very control which enables such people to extract the company's assets constitutes a defence to a charge of theft from the company. The question in each case must be whether the extraction of the property from the company was dishonest, not whether the alleged thief has consented to his own wrongdoing."[31]

2. *Damage to the company's property*

Can the controller of a one-person company commit criminal damage against the company's property? Section 1(1) of the Criminal Damage Act 1971 provides that property destroyed or damaged must belong to another.

In *R. v. Appleyard*[32] the court held that a managing director had been rightly convicted of damaging his company's premises. In principle, the position should be the same where the defendant is the sole shareholder and, *a fortiori*, the sole beneficial shareholder in the company.

Where, however, such a controller mistakenly believes, even unreasonably, that the company's property belongs to him, he does not commit the offence of criminal damage in respect of that property since he is not, for the purposes of section 1(1) of the Criminal Damage Act 1971, intentional or reckless as to whether "any property belonging to another is destroyed or damaged."[33] This should be the case whatever the defendant's motive in destroying or damaging the property since a fraudulent motive does not convert conduct which would otherwise be lawful into criminal damage.[34]

It appears too that an employee acting on the controller's instructions would have a defence to a charge of criminal damage of the company's property by virtue of section 5(2)(a)

---

[31] *ibid.* at 40. See also Lord Lowry at 36:

> "... it is absurd to suppose that a company consents to the theft of its own property, merely because the thief is for most purposes of the company its directing mind. The act of the directing mind is here unilateral and not consensual and bilateral."

[32] (1985) 81 Cr.App.R. 319.

[33] *R. v. Smith* [1974] Q.B. 354, and see the discussion of *R. v. Appleyard*, *ante.* in Smith and Hogan, *Criminal Law* (7th ed., 1992), p. 690.

[34] *R. v. Denton* [1982] 1 All E.R. 65.

of the Criminal Damage Act 1971 if he genuinely believed that the sole controller was entitled to consent to the damage.[35]

C. Diverting company cheques

1. *Conversion by third parties*

Third parties dealing with a one-person company may find themselves civilly liable by virtue of the fraud of that person. Banks, especially, need to be vigilant in respect of cheques intended for companies being diverted into personal accounts. This problem arose in *A. L. Underwood Ltd. v. Bank of Liverpool and Martins.*[36] In this case U, a sole trader, had kept his account with the defendant bank for a number of years. He formed a limited company to take over his business, U holding all the issued shares except one, which was held by his wife. U retained his personal account with the defendant bank, but the company's account was, unknown to the defendant, with another bank. U paid a number of cheques drawn in favour of the company, and indorsed by U, into his personal account. An action for conversion was brought against the defendant by the company on behalf of a debenture holder.[37] The defendant argued that it should be able to rely on the apparent authority of the director. The articles of the company provided that the company's business was to be managed by the directors and also that U was to be the sole director. The Court of Appeal held, however, that the defendant could not rely on U's apparent authority. The circumstances in this case were so unusual as to put the defendant bank on inquiry and not to have made such inquiry was negligent. The defendant was therefore liable for conversion. It appears, however, that the bank had acted in accordance with the normal banking practice then current. In his judgment, Scrutton L.J. made reference to the evidence given by the London manager of the defendant bank before the judge at first instance:

> "He admitted that in all ordinary cases where an official of a company was paying cheques made payable to the

---

[35] *ibid.*
[36] [1924] 1 K.B. 775.
[37] The debenture holder was another bank which had a floating charge over the assets of the company.

> company into his private account, the bank would make inquiries and consult the employer, but he said that where the official was a sole director of a one-man company, and himself the one-man, it would not be necessary, partly, I think, because he treated such a director as the same as his company, partly because he thought that inquiry of such an employer would give no good result, for it would be answered by the official whose conduct was inquired into."[38]

Scutton L.J. rejecting this argument, stated that the bank could not have been certain that there were no independent shareholders and, indeed, there was a debenture holder whose interests were affected. Moreover, inquiries in this case might have been effective. He concluded: "If banks for fear of offending their customers will not make inquiries into unusual circumstances, they must take with the benefit of not annoying their customer the risk of liability because they do not inquire."[39]

2. *Protection of bank acting in good faith*

The good faith of the bank was accepted in *Underwood's* case. It is arguable that a bank in such a position may now be protected by section 35A of the Companies Act 1985,[40] as being a person dealing with a company in good faith in whose favour the power of a sole director to bind the company should be deemed free of any limitation deriving from what is expressed in, or presumably to be implied from, the company's constitution. If the argument advanced earlier in this work is correct, then, in order to be in bad faith, the bank would need to have actual suspicions and wilfully and recklessly fail to make honest and reasonable inquiries.[41] Since such a state of mind also appears to be the normal threshold for liability as a constructive trustee through knowing assistance, a bank in good faith should not be liable under this head either.[42]

---

[38] [1924] 1 K.B. 775 at 793.

[39] *ibid.*

[40] Inserted by s. 108 C.A. 1989. See Chap. 8, pp. 91, *et seq.*, *ante.*

[41] Chap. 8, pp. 92–93, *ante.*

[42] In *Eagle Trust plc v. SBC Securities Ltd.* [1992] 4 All E.R. 488 at 499, Vinelott J. took it as "settled law" that want of probity was necessary to establish liability as a constructive trustee on the basis of knowing assistance. This opinion was accepted by Scott L.J. in *Polly Peck International plc v. Nadir (No. 2)* [1992] 4 All E.R. 769 at 777. For a fuller discussion of the standard of knowledge required for liability as a constructive trustee, with particular reference to receipt of misapplied corporate assets, see Chap. 8, pp. 123–125, *ante.*

Chapter 12

CORPORATE QUASI-PARTNERSHIPS

A. The quasi-partnership concept

1. *Origins and meaning of "quasi-partnership"*

Although the terms "quasi-partner" and "quasi-partnership" seem to have come into general use in the 1960's and early 1970's,[1] the concept of the quasi-partnership is as old as the private company itself and, indeed, predates the statutory private company.[2]

Difficult though it is to give an all-embracing definition of the term "quasi-partnership," which in any event has no precise legal meaning, it is clear that this convenient expression connotes that type of private company[3] which, while operating under the trappings of corporate status, having been registered under the prevailing companies legislation, is, by its true and substantial nature, a partnership.[4]

2. *Types of quasi-partnerships*

The most clear-cut example of a corporate quasi-partnership will be apparent when two or more businessmen who had

---

[1] See, *e.g. Re K/9 Meat Supplies (Guildford) Ltd.* [1966] 1 W.L.R. 1112, *Re Expanded Plugs Ltd.* [1966] 1 All E.R. 877 and *Re Fildes Bros Ltd.* [1970] 1 W.L.R. 592; also *Ebrahimi v. Westbourne Galleries Ltd. & Others* [1973] A.C. 360, but note, p. 194, *post*, the admonition by Lord Wilberforce in this case concerning the use of this term.

[2] An early example is the Scottish case of *Symington v. Symington Quarries Ltd.* (1905) 8 F.121, cited by Lord Wilberforce in *Ebrahimi v. Westbourne Galleries Ltd., supra.*

[3] A quasi-partnership type of company can at the same time also be a family company. See, *e.g. Brady v. Brady* [1988] 2 W.L.R. 1308, Chap. 13, *post* and Chap. 10, *ante*; *Jesner v. Jarrad Properties Ltd.* [1992] BCC 807, Chap. 13, *post.*

[4] An "in substance partnership"; see, *e.g.* Lord Wilberforce in *Ebrahimi v. Westbourne Galleries Ltd.* [1973] A.C. 360 at 379 but note the significance of the corporate form, even to a quasi-partnership: see p. 194, *post.*

previously traded as partners incorporate their business and retain, through the voting power of their shares and through their seats on the company's board, the same position *vis-à-vis* each other as they held when they were actual partners.[5]

Sometimes a quasi-partnership comes into being from the merger into corporate status of two (or more) separate pre-existing businesses.[6] But it must not be thought that the categories of quasi-partnerships are limited to those mentioned above. Two or more entrepreneurs may establish and immediately incorporate a business enterprise which from the start is a quasi-partnership[7]; or a "one-person" company, may, in due course, develop into a quasi-partnership as, for example, where the original owner of the company takes on a quasi-co-partner.[8]

Again, although quasi-partners often enjoy equality of shareholding and voting rights and, consequently, of management rights, such equality is by no means an essential requisite of a quasi-partnership, any more than equality of control is essential for an actual partnership.[9] What is required is a relationship between parties operating a business together on the basis of mutual trust and confidence.

It must be stressed, however, as was pointed out by Peter Gibson J. in *Re a Company (No. 003096 of 1987)*,[10] that the mere fact that parties join together to form a small company is not, in itself, sufficient to constitute the company a quasi-partnership in the eyes of the court. As his Lordship also stated in the above case, at 84, "there must be averments that something equivalent to partnership obligations were created".

In particular, although a pre-existing actual partnership is by no means a *sine qua non* to a corporate quasi-partnership,

---

[5] This was the immediate post-incorporation position in *Ebrahimi v. Westbourne Galleries Ltd.*, *ante*, n. 1.

[6] See, *e.g. Re Yenidje Tobacco Co. Ltd.* [1916] 2 Ch. 426; p. 189, *post*.

[7] An example can be seen in *Re Davis Investments (East Ham) Ltd.* [1961] 1 W.L.R. 1396.

[8] See, *e.g. Re Kenyon Swansea Ltd.* (1987) 3 BCC 259, *post*.

[9] See *Re Zinotty Properties Ltd.* [1984] 1 W.L.R. 1249: shareholding divided between two sides on a 25 per cent: 75 per cent basis. Note also, Nourse J. in *Re Bird Precision Bellows Ltd.* [1984] 1 Ch. 419 at 433:

> "The proposition ... that there can only be a quasi-partnership in a case where all the shareholders make similar contributions to the company is supportable neither on authority nor in principle."

[10] (1988) 4 BCC 80.

where there has been such a pre-existing partnership the obligations arising therefrom "might be taken to continue."[11]

3. *Partnership companies under the Companies Act 1989*

Section 128 of the Companies Act 1989 paves the way for a new kind of statutory "partnership company," *i.e.* a company limited by shares, the shares of which are intended to be held to a substantial extent by or on behalf of employees. The Secretary of State may by statutory instrument prescribe what will be known as Table G articles, appropriate for such companies, which they may adopt in whole or in part. It will be interesting to see how these partnership companies compare with the corporate quasi-partnerships discussed in this chapter.

B. Practical applications of the quasi-partnership concept

1. *The Yenidje principle*

A classic example of a quasi-partnership is the company on which the dispute was centred in *Re Yenidje Tobacco Co. Ltd.*[12] In this case two entrepreneurs, W. & R., who hitherto had operated independent businesses, merged these businesses and registered a company[13] as the vehicle for their future joint enterprise. W. and R. were the only members, having equal shareholding and equal management rights. Some 15 months after the company's formation the partners found themselves in a state of complete management deadlock regarding the company's operation, this coming to a head, in particular, on a difference of opinion concerning the employment of a works manager.[14]

[11] *ibid.*, *per* Peter Gibson J. at 84.

[12] [1916] 2 Ch. 426.

[13] Under the Companies (Consolidation) Act 1908.

[14] In fact, an arbitration provision contained in the articles was found to be ineffective in this situation because one of the parties refused to abide by a ruling given under it. But although the deadlock in management was the "catalyst" for the petition, the real reason for the winding-up order was, as pointed out by Lord Cross of Chelsea in *Ebrahimi v. Westbourne Galleries Ltd.*, see *post*, the fact that the parties had lost confidence in each other.

In view of the managerial impasse into which the company had thus fallen, and despite the fact that it continued to make considerable profits, one of the parties applied to the court to have the company wound up on the ground that winding up was "just and equitable" in the circumstances.[15] This application was opposed by the other quasi-partner.[16] The winding-up petition was, in the circumstances, granted by Astbury J. and, on appeal, upheld by the Court of Appeal. In essence the conclusion reached by the Court of Appeal was that since the company was substantially a partnership it should be treated in exactly the same way as a real partnership would be treated if the partners had lost confidence in each other, *i.e.* it would be dissolved on application by either of the interested parties. Thus, as Lord Cozens-Hardy M.R. observed, at 432:

> "I think that in a case like this we are bound to say that circumstances which would justify the winding up of a partnership between these two by action are circumstances which would induce the Court to exercise its jurisdiction under the just and equitable clause and to wind up the company."

Likewise, Warrington L.J. declared, at 435:

> "I am prepared to say that in a case like the present, where there are only two persons interested, where there are no shareholders other than those two, where there are no means of overruling by the action of a general meeting of shareholders the trouble which is occasioned by the quarrels of the two directors and shareholders, the company ought to be wound up if there exists such a ground as would be sufficient for the dissolution of a private partnership at the suit of one of the partners against the other."

It can, therefore, be seen from the foregoing that the "*Yenidje* principle" states, in effect, that a company which is in substance a partnership, though not technically one, can be dissolved on the statutory "just and equitable"[17] ground, on application by

---

[15] The petition was presented under s. 129 of the Companies (Consolidation) Act 1908: see now s. 122(1)(g) of the Insolvency Act 1986.
[16] The term "quasi-partner" was not, however, used in the judgment.
[17] See now s. 122(1)(g) I.A. 1986.

one of two quasi-partners, in such circumstances as an actual two-person partnership can be dissolved on the "just and equitable" ground.

The correctness of this principle was confirmed by the Judicial Committee of the Privy Council in *Loch v. John Blackwood Ltd.*[18] The same principle can be seen in operation in the decision of Crossman J. in *Re Davis and Collett Ltd.*[19] in which the judgment, at 701, includes the following passage:

> "The same circumstances which entitle a partner to require the dissolution of a partnership entitle a person who is equally interested with one other person in a company to have that company wound up on the ground that the circumstances render it just and equitable."

In fact, the issue in *Re Davis and Collett Ltd.* was quite different from that in *Yenidje*, since in *Davis and Collett Ltd.* the problem giving rise to an application for dissolution was not a managerial deadlock but an allegation by one of two equal shareholders that he had been improperly excluded from the management of the company by the other shareholder. Nevertheless, Crossman J. found it to be necessary to apply the *Yenidje* principle and, accordingly, ordered the dissolution of the company on the "just and equitable" ground.

2. *Delimiting the Yenidje principle*

Having thus established the *Yenidje* principle the courts in due course found it necessary to prescribe certain limits to the operation of that principle. In *Re Davis Investments (East Ham) Ltd.*[20] the Court of Appeal (Donovan and Danckwerts L.JJ.) upheld the judgment at first instance by Plowman J. that the mere statement by one equal shareholder[21] that he had lost confidence in his co-shareholders, was in itself insufficient to justify a winding-up order. *Evidence* of the legal rights of the parties was required—for example, the company's articles. Thus, as Donovan L.J. observed, at 1399:

---

18 [1924] A.C. 783.

19 [1935] Ch. 693; see also *Re Lundie Brothers Ltd.* [1965] 1 W.L.R. 1051, *per* Plowman J.

20 [1961] 1 W.L.R. 1396.

21 In the company in question two members each held 50 out of the 100 issued shares and were directors of the company.

> "[Counsel for the petitioner's] argument goes to this length: that in a case of a two-man company, if the shareholders, being equal in their shareholding, fall out, one of them alleging that further co-operation is impossible, then the court, in the absence of a reply from the other shareholder, must at once treat them as though they were partners and order a winding up, as it would, in a partnership case, order a dissolution. *I do not think that this is the law.*" [emphasis added]

This passage was cited and followed by Plowman J. in *Re W. R. Willcocks & Co. Ltd.*[22] In this case the only two directors and equal shareholders became antagonistic towards each other. One of the director/shareholders presented a winding-up petition to the court on the "just and equitable" ground, asserting that "irreconcilable differences" had arisen between her and the other shareholder/director, making it impossible to conduct the company's business. In the event, however, the affidavit supporting the petition did nothing more than verify the contents of the petition and gave no particulars of the allegations made. In these circumstances, Plowman J. felt unable to allow the petition.

Another interesting case which also sets parameters to the *Yenidje* principle, albeit in a somewhat different direction from the cases discussed above, is *Re K/9 Meat Supplies (Guildford) Ltd.*[23] The point at issue in this case was whether the personal bankruptcy of one of the three quasi-partners would, by analogy with section 33(1) of the Partnership Act 1890,[24] and, as argued by the bankrupt quasi-partner's trustee in bankruptcy, constitute grounds for winding up the company. In rejecting that contention Pennycuick J. was in no doubt that although the business organisation under consideration was, indeed, a quasi partnership it "... must be treated as having been constituted on the terms of the company's articles".[25] Accordingly, it was

---

22 [1974] Ch. 163, at 167.

23 [1966] 1 W.L.R. 1112. Another distinction between this and the cases previously discussed was that, as indicated, there were more than two quasi-partners in this case.

24 s. 33(1) of the Partnership Act 1890 provides as follows:

> "Subject to any agreement between the partners, every partnership is dissolved as regards all the partners by the death or bankruptcy of any partner."

25 [1966] 1 W.L.R. 1112 at 1118.

necessary to turn to the company's articles since they clearly set out what was to happen in the event of any members being adjudicated bankrupt.[26]

In another case, a winding-up order on the just and equitable ground was refused when the applicant quasi-partner was, in effect, a semi-sleeping partner, *i.e.* a shareholder and director who had not previously participated in the management of the company.[27]

3. *The* Westbourne Galleries *case*

The *Yenidje* princple was, as described earlier in this chapter, established by the Court of Appeal in 1916. Although it was, indeed, approved by the Judicial Committee in 1924 in *Loch v. John Blackwood*[28] it was not until 1972 that the House of Lords made full use of an opportunity to further develop the principle in *Ebrahimi v. Westbourne Galleries Ltd. & Others.*[29] The facts of this leading case can be summarised as follows. E and N had been equal partners in a business originally founded by N which dealt in Persian and other carpets. In due course E and N formed a private company to take over the partnership business, E and N each originally holding 500 of the 1,000 shares issued. Both were directors and had equal say in the company management. Some time later N's son was appointed to the board and at that point N and E transferred 100 of their shares to him. The company was commercially successful, profits being distributed by way of directors' remuneration rather than dividend on shares.

Differences arose between E on the one side and N and his son on the other. This management friction culminated in the proposal of a resolution for the dismissal of E from his seat on the board and, inevitably, because of the voting weight carried by N and his son, the resolution was passed. Aggrieved by the treatment thus meted out to him, E, claiming that he had been the victim of oppressive conducted, petitioned the court under section 210 of the Companies Act 1948[30] asking the court to

[26] In point of fact, the articles provided that on a member's bankruptcy his shares were to vest in his trustee in bankruptcy. This clearly, therefore, rules out any question of winding up.

[27] See *Re Fildes Brothers Ltd.* [1970] 1 W.L.R. 592.

[28] [1924] A.C. 783 at 791.

[29] [1973] A.C. 360.

[30] Now replaced by the "unfairly prejudicial conduct" provisions of s. 459 C.A. 1985.

order N and his son to purchase E's shares at a fair value; in the alternative E also petitioned under section 222(f) of the Companies Act 1948[31] that the company be wound up. Hearing the case at first instance, Plowman J. dismissed the section 210 petition, finding that insufficient grounds had been shown. His Lordship did, however, allow the section 222(f) petition and ordered the company to be wound up pursuant to that provision. Although this winding-up order was set aside on appeal to the Court of Appeal, Plowman J.'s order was reinstated on further appeal to the House of Lords.

The speech delivered by Lord Wilberforce in the *Westbourne Galleries* case is particularly illuminating. His Lordship indicated that the use in many cases of the terms "quasi-partnership" and "in substance partnership" may be convenient but also confusing. As he said, at 379:

> "It may be convenient because it is the law of partnership which has developed the conceptions of probity, good faith and mutual confidence, and the remedies, where these are absent...; the words 'just and equitable' sum these up in the law of partnership itself."

But as his Lordship continued at 380, these expressions may also be confusing,

> "... if they obscure, or deny, the fact that the parties (possibly former partners) are now co-members in a company, who have accepted, in law, new obligations. A company, however small, however domestic, is *a company not a partnership or even a quasi-partnership* [emphasis added] and it is through the just and equitable clause that obligations, common to partnership relations, may come in."

Accordingly as Lord Wilberforce went on to explain, a director may be deprived of his seat on the board as a consequence of the exercise by the company of lawful powers whether granted by statute or contained in the articles[32] and unless such director can prove that the power was exercised in

[31] The "just and equitable" ground; see now s. 122(1)(g) I.A. 1986.

[32] *i.e.* by being dismissed under s. 184 C.A. 1948, now s. 303 C.A. 1985, or under special provisions contained in the articles, or, where, *per* the articles, directors must retire by rotation, they are not re-elected.

bad faith there is nothing which can be done to preserve his directorship. However, if such a dismissed director is, by his true status, a quasi-partner, he is at liberty to call upon the court to dissolve the company on the "just and equitable" ground, if, as Lord Wilberforce stated at 380,

> "... he can point to, and prove, some special underlying obligations of his fellow member(s) in good faith, or confidence, that so long as the business continues he shall be entitled to management participation...".

This is in accordance with the principle established for actual partnerships in, for example, *Blisset v. Daniel*[33] whereby, in appropriate circumstances, a partner who has been excluded from management can obtain the dissolution of the partnership even when his exclusion has, strictly speaking, been in accordance with the articles of partnership.[34]

However, as Lord Wilberforce indicated, at 379: "the superimposition of equitable considerations" requires something more than a purely commercial association. What is required:

> "... typically may include one, or probably more, of the following elements: (i) an association formed or continued on the basis of a personal relationship, involving mutual confidence—this element will often be found where a pre-existing partnership has been converted into a limited company; (ii) an agreement, or understanding, that all, or some (for there may be "sleeping" members), of the shareholders shall participate in the conduct of the business; (iii) restriction upon the transfer of the members' interest in the company—so that if confidence is lost or one

---

[33] (1853) 10 Hare 493. In *Blisset v. Daniel* the court, in the event, ordered that an unfairly expelled partner be reinstated, despite the fact that his expulsion had been strictly in accordance with the partnership articles.

[34] For another example of the application of the principle in *Westbourne Galleries* see *Re A & BC Chewing Gum Ltd.* [1975] 1 W.L.R. 579, *per* Plowman J. Note also how Plowman J. reconciled the principle in *Westbourne Galleries* with a refusal to grant an injunction to restrain a company from removing a quasi-partner from his seat on the board, in *Bentley-Stevens v. Jones & Others* [1974] 1 W.L.R. 638. Note also *Coulson Sanderson and Ward Ltd. v. Ward*, *Financial Times*, October 18, 1985, in which the Court of Appeal refused to restrain a quasi-partner from petitioning for the winding-up of a company where there were allegations that the "special underlying obligation" between quasi-partners mentioned by Lord Wilberforce in *Ebrahimi v. Westbourne Galleries Ltd.*, *ante*, n. 29, had been breached; see also *Re R. A. Noble & Sons (Clothing) Ltd.* [1983] BCLC 273.

> member is removed from management, he cannot take out his stake and go elsewhere."

4. *The* Westbourne Galleries *principle: judicial explanation*

It must not be thought that the principle established in the *Westbourne Galleries* case is simply that if, where a private company is in essence a partnership despite its corporate form, a quasi-partner applies for the company's dissolution he has exactly the same right in this regard as he would have if he were a member of an actual partnership. It has been seen above that Lord Wilberforce pointed out that a company is "not a partnership or even a quasi-partnership"[35] and, as observed by Vinelott J. in *Re a Company (No. 002567 of 1982)*,[36] the dissolution of a registered company is likely to have a more damaging effect on shareholders than the appointment of a receiver and sale of a partnership business will have on partners. His Lordship stated at 935:

> "... when partners transfer their business to a company, they accept a new legal structure with different rights and liabilities, albeit that equitable principles will govern the way in which those rights are exercised".

Nevertheless, the *Westbourne Galleries* principle has had far reaching effects. Not only has it become the guiding principle in cases involving petitions for a just and equitable winding-up under section 122(1)(g) of the Insolvency Act 1986, but it has also been applied, by analogy, to petitions alleging unfair prejudice under section 459 of the Companies Act 1985. A useful summary of the development of the principle was given in the Scottish case *Murray's Judicial Factor, Petitioner*[37] where Lord Justice-Clerk Ross stated at 606:

> "It is now well recognised that the court will have regard to what is just and equitable in order to regulate the exercise of legal powers in a company where the company can properly be described as a quasi-partnership. That arises where the company has been formed and continued

---

[35] See p. 194, *ante*.
[36] [1983] 1 W.L.R. 927.
[37] [1992] BCC 596.

> upon the basis of personal relationship including mutual confidence; there may then be inferred an agreement or an understanding between members of the company which gives rise to legitimate expectations on the part of the members that certain legal rights will not be insisted on or will not be exercised in a particular manner. It is clear from the reported cases that the basis must be informal agreements or understandings of the members *inter se.*"

The extent to which equitable principles will be taken to override legal rights and obligations arising from the company's constitution is still being worked out by the courts. How far, for example, should the shares of a departing quasi-partner, on the break up of a quasi-partnership, be dealt with in accordance with a share transfer and valuation provision in the company's articles? This issue, which has been explored in several judicial decisions, is considered in the next section in this chapter.

The following limits to the *Westbourne Galleries* principle should be noted. Even where equitable considerations arise from agreements and understandings between shareholders outside the constitution of the company, the court is not free to superimpose on any rights, expectations and obligations springing from such agreements any further rights and obligations arising from its own concept of fairness.[38] Also, any legitimate expectations held by a quasi-partner, resulting from agreements with the other members on the formation of a company, are not transmissible on the death of the quasi-partner to his executors or heirs.[39]

C. Dealings between quasi-partners

1. *Obligatory share transfer provisions*

The articles of a corporate quasi-partnership will often contain provisions for the obligatory sale[40] of the shares of the quasi-partner to his co-shareholder(s) in the event of his leaving

---

38 *Re J. E. Cade & Son Ltd.* [1991] BCC 373.
39 *Murray's Judicial Factor, Petitioner* [1992] BCC 596.
40 The articles will usually provide that the share transfer will be at fair valuation, often as calculated by the auditors. For the position generally concerning valuation of shares in quasi-partnerships: see Chap. 14, *post*.

the company, whether such departure be by choice or by compulsion. Certainly, in cases where mutual trust and confidence has been lost, a quasi-partner may petition for a just and equitable winding-up under section 122(1)(g) of the Insolvency Act 1986 on the principle established in the *Westbourne Galleries* case as explained in subsequent decisions,[41] but to what extent will such a petitioner's refusal to abide by a share transfer and valuation provision in the company's articles defeat his petition? Section 125(2) of the Insolvency Act 1986 provides that the court must not make a winding-up order if it is of the opinion "both that some other remedy is available to the petitioners and that they are acting unreasonably in seeking to have the company wound up".

A number of cases in the Chancery Division had held that it was unreasonable to pursue a winding-up petition rather than accept a reasonable offer by other members to purchase the petitioner's shares[42] before the matter came before the Court of Appeal in *Re Abbey Leisure Ltd.*[43] In this case V, a minority shareholder, petitioned, *inter alia*, to have the company wound up on the just and equitable ground contending that there was an understanding between the members that the company's only purpose was to buy, refurbish and then sell a nightclub, and once this had been achieved, to distribute the proceeds of the sale and dissolve the company. On this premise, the Court of Appeal agreed with Hoffmann J. at first instance that V would have a good prima facie case for winding up the company, but held, reversing Hoffmann J.'s decision, that V was not unreasonble in rejecting an offer by the other two members to purchase his shares in accordance with a pre-emption provision in the company's articles. It was not unreasonable of V to want to avoid the risk of a valuer applying a discount on his shares as constituting a minority holding.

Instead of applying for the winding up of a company, or in addition to such an application, a quasi-partner who wishes to

---

[41] See pp. 193 *et seq.*, *ante*, n. 1.

[42] *Re a Company (No. 002567 of 1982)* [1983] 1 W.L.R. 927; *Re a Company (No. 00384 of 1986)* (1987) 3 BCC 624; *Re a Company (No. 003096 of 1987)* (1988) 4 BCC 80. But for a quasi-partnership case in which a winding up petition was not struck out see *Re a Company (No. 001363 of 1988)* (1989) 5 BCC 18, where Warner J. held that it was not unreasonable for the petitioner to reject an offer to buy the one share registered in his name when he claimed a beneficial interest in half of the 6,500 issued shares of the company.

[43] [1990] BCC 60.

resist being bought out, despite the articles, may apply to the court under sections 459 to 461 of the Companies Act 1985. Section 459(1) provides:

> "A member of a company may apply to the court by petition for an order under this Part on the ground that the company's affairs are being or have been conducted in a manner which is unfairly prejudicial to the interests of its members generally or of some part of its members (including at least himself) or that any actual or proposed act or omission of the company (including an act or omission on its behalf) is or would be so prejudicial."

The provision also applies, by virtue of section 459(2), to persons who are not members but to whom shares have been transferred or transmitted by operation of law.

Section 461(1) then goes on to state:

> "If the court is satisfied that a petition under this Part is well founded, it may make such order as it thinks fit for giving relief in respect of the matters complained of."

In his first instance decision in *Re Abbey Leisure Ltd.*, Hoffmann J. had relied on his decision in *Re a Company (No. 007623 of 1984)*,[44] in which, in relation to a petition brought under the predecessor provision of section 459 of the Companies Act 1985,[45] he stated at 99,195–196:

> "In general it seems to me that if a petitioner is complaining of conduct which would be unfairly prejudicial only if accompanied by a refusal on the part of the majority to buy his shares at a fair price, and the articles provide a mechanism for determining such a price, he should not be entitled to petition under [s. 459] until he has invoked or offered to invoke that mechanism and the majority have refused to buy at the price so determined."

Hoffmann J. continued this theme in *Re XYZ Ltd.*[46] in which he again dismissed a section 459 petition:

---

[44] (1986) 2 BCC 99,191.
[45] s. 75 C.A. 1980.
[46] (1896) 2 BCC 99,520, *sub nom Re A Company (No. 004377 of 1986)* [1987] 1 W.L.R. 102.

> "I am satisfied that, having regard to the articles, the petitioner could have had no legitimate expectation that in the event of a breakdown of relations ... they would not be relied on to require him to sell his shares at fair value. To hold to the contrary would not be to 'superimpose equitable considerations' on his rights under the articles but to relieve him from the bargain he made."[47]

The Court of Appeal, in reversing Hoffmann J's first instance judgment in *Re Abbey Leisure Ltd.* expressed no view on the section 459 cases, Balcombe L.J. preferring to leave it to some future case at which the point was clearly in issue. The opportunity was soon to arise. In *Re a Company (No. 00330 of 1992) ex p. Holden*,[48] Harman J., granting a section 459 petitioner an injunction restraining the directors from activating a compulsory share transfer provision in the articles, interpreted *Re Abbey Leisure Ltd.* to hold that it would not be unreasonable for a petitioner to refuse to accept not only the risk of a valuer applying a discount to his shares,[49] but any risk which might depreciate the valuation. Moreover, Harman J. saw *Re Abbey Leisure Ltd.* as effecting an important shift in judicial opinion. He stated at 247:

> "That decision [*Re Abbey Leisure Ltd.*] in my judgment has altered the balance against the view that shareholders who enter into a company with articles allowing for compulsory transfer are bound to go through compulsory transfer provisions rather than exercising their statutory rights and are unreasonable if they do not accept the transfer provision. ... There must be questions of fact. In some cases a petitioner may be held to be unreasonable to refuse to follow the contractual term. ... But the broad brush approach that it is always reasonable to insist upon the articles and it is always unreasonable to refuse to do so

---

[47] *ibid.* at 99, 528. See also decisions to the same effect in *Re a Company (No. 003096 of 1987)* (1988) 4 BCC 80, *Re a Company (No. 00683 of 1988) ex p. Kremer* [1989] BCLC 365, and *Re Castleburn Ltd.* (1989) 5 BCC 652. It would be otherwise if there had been bad faith or impropriety on the part of the respondents or the articles provided for some arbitrary or artificial method of valuation (*per* Hoffmann J. (1986) 2 BCC 99,520 at 99,527) or the valuer could not be seen to be independent (*Re Boswell & Co. (Steels) Ltd.* (1989) 5 BCC 145).

[48] [1991] BCC 241.

[49] The application of such a discount was in fact precluded by the company's articles.

is no longer, as I understand *Abbey Leisure*, the law as it must be applied."

2. *Legitimate expectations of quasi-partners*

However a quasi-partnership has come into being[50] it is quite likely that the quasi-partners will assume that the business arrangements which they have initially negotiated or which subsequently develop will continue indefinitely and not be subject to peremptory termination. From time to time, therefore, a quasi-partner in dispute with other quasi-partners in the business, will claim that he had been denied the legitimate expectations which emanate from his position. This section will examine the extent to which the courts will protect those legitimate expectations to which a quasi-partner is entitled as a quasi-partner and also the nature of such legitimate expectations.

(a) *Continuing rights of management*

That quasi-partners as such are, prima facie, entitled to continuing rights of management in regard to the relevant business was clearly recognised in *Ebrahimi v. Westbourne Galleries Ltd. & Others.*[51] In this case the remedy afforded to the petitioning quasi-partner who had been expelled from the company's board was an order for the winding-up of the company. This would, therefore, allow the petitioner, who would otherwise have been a "locked-in" minority shareholder,[52] to retrieve his capital from an organisation which had deprived him of the management rights to which, in the court's finding, he was entitled.

In the *Westbourne Galleries* case, therefore, the outcome of the company's failure to uphold what the House of Lords accepted as being the quasi-partner's legitimate expectation of management rights, was, as stated above, the judicial dissolution of the company. The petition under section 210 of the

---

[50] See pp. 187–189, *ante*.

[51] [1973] A.C. 360: see pp. 193–196, *ante*. In *Re a Company (No. 003160 of 1986)* [1986] BCLC 391 Hoffmann J. expressed the view that if such had been the understanding between the parties concerned, a member's spouse would enjoy the right to participate in the management of the company and receive salary therefor.

[52] Clearly, the position of such a "locked-in" minority shareholder would have been considerably weaker if he had not been a quasi-partner.

Companies Act 1948 in that case, in respect of alleged oppressive conduct, was rejected at first instance and was not pursued further. It is now well established, however that an allegation of management exclusion may found a petition for unfair prejudice under section 459 of the Companies Act 1985, the provision which replaced section 210. The position was clearly stated by Hoffmann J. in *Re Postgate and Denby (Agencies) Ltd.*[53]:

> "... the concept of unfair prejudice which forms the basis of the jurisdiction under sec. 459 enables the court to take into account not only the rights of members under the company's constitution but also their legitimate expectations arising from the agreements or understandings of the members *inter se*. ...The common case of such expectations being superimposed upon a member's rights under the articles is the corporate quasi-partnership in which members frequently have expectations of participating in the management and profits of the company, which arise from the understandings upon which the company was formed and which it may be unfair for the other members to ignore."

An important case is *Re a Company (No. 00477 of 1986).*[54] The section 459 petitioners, S and his wife, had originally been the only members of A Co., a small private company. Both were directors, S being managing director. In due course, arrangements were made with O plc, an unquoted public company, whereby O plc would acquire the shares of A Co. held by S and his wife in exchange for shares in O plc. Under the arrangement, S remained managing director of A Co. and his wife remained a director, and, further, S was appointed to the board of O plc. In addition, it was agreed that O plc would invest substantial funds in A Co.

The petitioners' grievances consisted of the following allegations: that they had been induced to transfer their shares in A Co. by a false representation that O plc would make substantial investment in A Co., and that S had been wrongfully dismissed as managing director of A Co. and had been required to leave

[53] (1986) 2 BCC 99,352 at 99,357–99, 358.

[54] (1986) 2 BCC 99,171. For a recent case in which a quasi-partner successfully petitioned under s. 459 on the grounds of management exclusion see *Re Ghyll Beck Driving Range Ltd.* [1993] BCLC 1126.

the board of O plc. The relief which the petitioners sought in this case was that their shares in O plc, which they claimed were worthless, should be purchased by O plc or by those who were in control of O plc, at a price which was equal to the value of the petitioners' shares in A Co. at the time these shares were transferred to O plc. Hoffmann J., rejecting an application by the respondents to have the petition struck out,[55] held that those who risk their capital in a private company may have legitimate expectations qua members that they will not be deprived of their directorships or management rights in that company, or that where they are so deprived they shall be fully compensated. Although in this particular case a public company was involved, a "partnership" element was also present in that the petitioners claimed that the relationship between them and the individual respondent was, in essence, one of partnership.

The mere fact that a small private company has been formed by certain individuals does not automatically make the company a quasi-partnership or give all these individuals continuing management right in the company,[56] but, whilst a just and equitable winding-up petition under section 122(1)(g) of the Insolvency Act 1986 may thus be dismissed, an allegation of management exclusion, or proposed management exclusion, may still form one of the bases of a section 459 petition.[57] On the other hand, in a quasi-partnership, whilst management exclusion may not be unfairly prejudicial for the purposes of section 459, it may indicate that mutual trust and confidence has been destroyed so as to justify a winding-up.[58]

(b) *Expectations of control*

Another "disappointed expectation" case is *Re Kenyon Swansea Ltd.*[59] In this case, a minority shareholder who, in effect, had been the "junior partner" of the founder of the business and majority shareholder, claimed, *inter alia*, that in

---

[55] In substance the petitioners' case was founded on allegations of breach of contract and fraud, matters more appropriate to common law proceedings than to proceedings under s. 459 C.A. 1985. However, Hoffmann J. did, with some hesitation, accept that the petition could be regarded as falling within the letter of s. 459 if not within its spirit. He thus declined to dismiss the petition.

[56] *Re a Company (No. 003096 of 1987)* (1988) 4 BCC 80 in which Peter Gibson J. followed Lord Wilberforce in the *Westbourne Galleries* case, *ante*.

[57] *Re a Company (No. 00314 of 1989)* [1990] BCC 221.

[58] *Re R. A. Noble & Sons (Clothing) Ltd.* [1983] BCLC 273.

[59] (1987) 3 BCC 259.

view of his lengthy association with the company and agreement reached with the majority shareholder, it had become reasonable for him to expect that the majority shareholder, on his retirement, would allow his shares to be dealt with in such a way as to enable the petitioner, in effect, to acquire control of the company. On these alleged facts, Vinelott J. refused to strike out a petition presented under section 459 of the Companies Act 1985.

3. *Holding the ring between quasi-partners*

Sometimes, where quasi-partners are in dispute, the court may, pending the outcome of an application under section 459 of the Companies Act 1985 and as a short-term measure, appoint a receiver pursuant to section 37 of the Supreme Court Act 1981. This occurred in *Re a Company (No. 00596 of 1986)*.[60]

In this case the quasi-partners in question were, on the one hand, the petitioner, Mrs J who held 50 out of 100 issued shares in the relevant company and, on the other hand, the individual respondents, Mr and Mrs S, who between them held the remaining 50 of the issued shares. All three were directors and so the respondents enjoyed a 2:1 advantage on the board, with Mr S, as chairman of the company, having, by virtue of the articles, a casting vote at general meetings.[61] The position was further complicated by the fact that Mrs J had also become a secured creditor of the company.

As a result of serious disagreements, Mrs J petitioned under sections 459 to 461 of the Companies Act 1985 for a purchase order to be made in her favour in respect of the shares of Mr and Mrs S or, alternatively, for the winding-up of the company on the just and equitable ground. The individual respondents in turn cross-petitioned for a purchase of the petitioner's shares. As an interim measure, the petitioner moved for the appointment of a receiver.

Harman J., ordering the appointment of a receiver, found a helpful, if imperfect, analogy with the position of partners. Accordingly, since in the early stage of an action between actual partners it would normally be appropriate to appoint a receiver

---

[60] (1986) 2 BCC 99, 063.

[61] Contract the position in this case, where the chairmanship was held permanently by one member, with the position in *Re a Company (No. 003096 of 1987)*, *ante*, in which the chairmanship rotated.

to "hold the ring", pending the sorting out of the partners' positions and without in any way prejudging these positions, the same would apply to a quasi-partnership in the instant case. However, Harman J. noted the limitations to appointing a receiver. In citing the rulings of Malins V.-C. in *Featherstone v. Cooke*[62] and *Trade Auxiliary Company v. Vickers*,[63] he pointed out that these cases:

> "... illustrate that the court will not interfere with the ordinary day to day management of the company and yet they hold that a receiver can be appointed, although for a limited time, when there are serious dissentions and a high degree of difficulty in managing the company properly while the dissentions are sorted out".[64]

Recent cases have revealed a reluctance by the courts to appoint a receiver in the context of disputes in private companies generally.

In *Jaber & Ors. v. Science and Information Technology Ltd. & Ors.*,[65] Ferris J., dealing with a section 459 application[66] which concerned a company limited by guarantee which Ferris J. appears to have regarded as analogous to a quasi-partnership, concluded that a receiver should not be appointed because he thought it "inevitable that it would be difficult for those in the outside world to distinguish between receivers appointed on the grounds of insolvency and receivers appointed on the basis that would be applicable in this case. ... This would be likely to have a most adverse effect on [the company's] business."[67] Moreover, a receivership would be highly expensive. This reasoning was followed by Harman J. himself in *Re Mountforest Ltd.*[68] where the Judge did not appoint a receiver because of the slur which receivership would cast on the assets of the business, the fact that competent directors, who had conducted the business very well as far as trading was concerned, would thereby be ousted, and the expense.

---

62 (1873) L.R. 16 Eq. 298.
63 (1873) L.R. 16 Eq. 298.
64 (1986) 2 BCC 99,063 at 99,067.
65 [1992] BCLC 764.
66 The dispute concerned the removal of a director and the extent of voting rights in the company.
67 [1992] BCLC 764 at 789.
68 [1993] BCC 565.

Chapter 13

FAMILY COMPANIES

A. Introduction: meaning of "family company"

For the purposes of this chapter the term "family company" will be taken to mean that type of private company which is controlled, entirely or predominantly, by members of the same family. Strictly speaking, of course, many effective "one-person" companies, can be described as "family companies", *i.e.* where the "one person" has given nominal holdings to his or her spouse and/or other members of his family.[1] Companies of this nature are, however, discussed separately in Chapter 11, *ante*.

The type of private company which will be considered in this chapter is that in which every corporator (family member) has a substantial holding, rather than a nominal holding.[2] This position may date from the company's registration, as where members of a family[3] form a company as a vehicle for conducting an existing or newly created business; or may have come about because the shares, though originally concentrated in the hands of one person, have on his death, been spread among his family as a result of his will or intestacy.[4] There are also other situations in which family companies falling within the parameters of this chapter, will be brought into being.[5]

---

[1] See, for example, *Salomon v. Salomon & Co. Ltd.* [1897] A.C. 22.

[2] The actual number of shares held by each member of the family need not, of course, be large for the purpose of this classification, so long as the holding constitutes more than a nominal part of the total number of shares issued.

[3] A family company may also, of course, be a corporate quasi-partnership; see for example, *Jesner v. Jarrad Properties Ltd.* [1992] BCC 807, pp. 225–226, *post*, and for quasi-partnerships generally see Chap. 12, *ante*.

[4] For share distribution problems which, in certain circumstances, can arise on the death of the controller of a "one-person" company, see *Lloyds Bank v. Duker* [1987] 1 W.L.R. 1324.

[5] See, *e.g.* *Loch v. John Blackwood* [1924] A.C. 783. Although the company in this case was registered (in Barbados) as a public company, in effect its attributes were that of a private company: see pp. 211–212, *post*.

B. Disputes in family companies

1. *The effect of family disputes on family companies*

Where relatives are directors and/or shareholders of a family company, any domestic quarrels are very likely to spread to, and have damaging effect on, the management of the company. Conversely disputes which arise between the shareholders and/or directors of family companies purely on issues of business may very well sour the domestic relationships of the parties concerned, making rational solutions to the underlying business differences considerably more difficult to attain than if the parties involved were only bound by business ties. A selection of leading cases involving family company disputes will now be considered.[6] Obviously, the situations in which such disputes can arise are without limit so that any attempt to describe all the reported cases involving disputes in family companies would be a task approaching sisyphean proportions.

2. *Types of disputes within family companies*

(a) *Reluctance to relinquish control*

The first case which will be considered under this heading, a case which was concerned with what appears to have been a mixture of business and domestic dissension, is *Re H.R. Harmer Ltd.*[7] In this case H had, by dint of hard work and enterprise, built up a thriving philatelic business and, in due course, had incorporated a private company to which he transferred this business. Although H had been the founder and for many years the sole proprietor of the business, following the registration of the company, and as a consequence of both selling and giving shares to his sons, he found himself to be a minority shareholder only. However, since he had arranged that the shares which he and his wife retained were heavily weighted with voting rights, he was able to keep control of the company. H and his sons were life directors in the company.

Serious dissension now developed between H[8] and his sons because, despite his voting power, H was unwilling to adhere to

---

[6] Ensuing sections of this chapter will then consider a number of further examples of such disputes in family companies.

[7] [1958] 3 All E.R. 689.

[8] He was, by that time, in his late eighties.

proper company procedures and continued to behave as if he were still the sole proprietor of the business. Thus, he did not hesitate to intervene in the management of the company and, for example, without board authorisation established a new branch in Australia; he also, on his own initiative, dismissed a key employee.

In these circumstances, no doubt as a last resort, his sons were constrained to apply to the court for relief under section 210 of the Companies Act 1948.[9] In the event, Roxburgh J. concluded that the appropriate remedy was that H should be made honorary president for life, that he should be appointed consultant to the company but that he be ordered to desist from interfering in the management of the company. H's appeal against this ruling was unanimously dismissed by the Court of Appeal. This ruling effectively disposed of this issue from a business point of view; it is to be hoped that any personal rift between the father and his sons was also quickly healed.[10]

(b) *Sibling dissension*

By contrast to the somewhat unusual circumstances which gave rise to the dispute in *Re H.R. Harmer Ltd.*, above, the underlying problem in cases like *Re Cuthbert Cooper & Sons Ltd.*[11] is a far more common phenomenon, *i.e.* animosity between relatives who inherit the shares of a major shareholder, in particular those of the founder of the company.

In *Re Cuthbert Cooper & Sons Ltd.*, a father was managing director and majority shareholder of a family company in which his two eldest sons were also directors and minority shareholders. The father also had two other sons who, although they did not hold shares in and were not directors of the company, were employed by it. On the death of the father his shares passed by his will to his two younger sons who were also appointed his executors. In due course the younger sons applied

---

[9] This was, in fact, one of the few successful reported applications for relief under s. 210 C.A. 1948; the "oppressive conduct" provision, s. 210, was replaced by s. 75 C.A. 1980, now ss. 459–461 C.A. 1985 (as amended), covering allegations of "unfairly prejudicial" conduct.

[10] Happily H obeyed the injunction. Had he not done so, however, his sons would clearly have been in a very unenviable position since they would have had the choice of either applying to have their father, at 88, committed to prison or of allowing the company to continue to be subjected to his individualistic business behaviour.

[11] [1937] Ch. 392. For further discussion of this case, particularly the "directors' veto" aspects, see pp. 219–221, *post*.

to be entered on to the company's register in respect of the shares which had so devolved to them but this application was rejected by their elder brothers acting in accordance with powers granted by the articles to refuse to register transfers. The directors also dismissed the younger brothers from their employment with the company. In these circumstances the younger brothers applied to the court to have the company wound up on the just and equitable ground.

This application was, however, dismissed by Simonds J. on the grounds that in refusing to allow the younger brothers to be entered on the register of members the applicants' siblings were acting entirely within the powers granted to the directors by the company's articles. This conclusion was, however, criticised by *Ebrahimi v. Westbourne Galleries Ltd.*[12]

Although the judgment of Simonds J. in *Re Cuthbert Cooper Ltd.* has thus been subject to a great deal of criticism,[13] in rejecting the winding-up application sought by the younger brothers the judge did, at least, preserve the continuity of the company. Since there is now, at least, a possibility that in circumstances as in *Re Cuthbert Cooper Ltd.* a winding-up order would, indeed, be granted,[14] a potential weakness of this type of family company as a business vehicle, may, perhaps, thus be revealed.

The next case to be considered in the present context, also involving dissensions between brothers,[15] is *Parsons v. Albert J. Parsons & Sons Ltd.*[16] In this case three brothers were shareholders and directors of a group of family companies which had been founded by their father. Following discord as to the running of the companies one of the brothers was dismissed from his position as a working director. He had, in fact, been

---

[12] [1973] A.C. 360. Thus in the *Westbourne Galleries* case, Lord Wilberforce referring to Simonds J.'s judgment in *Re Cuthbert Cooper Ltd.*, stated, at 377, that he was "unable to agree as to the undue emphasis [Simonds J.] puts on the contractual rights arising from the articles, over the equitable principles which might be derived from partnership law, for in the result the latter seem to have been entirely excluded in the former's favour". For further comment see pp. 219–221, *post*.

[13] See also the view of Danckwerts L.J. in *Re Swaledale Cleaners Ltd.* [1968] 1 W.L.R. 1720.

[14] It would, however, appear that for a similar situation now, an alternative application, for a remedy less drastic than winding-up, could be made to the court, on the grounds of unfairly prejudicial conduct, *per* s. 459(2) C.A. 1985. The court might then order that one side must buy out the other at fair valuation.

[15] This case is, however, very different from the other cases discussed in this chapter, from the point of view of the remedy sought.

[16] [1979] I.C.R. 271.

appointed director for life. He thereupon applied to an industrial tribunal for compensation for alleged unfair dismissal.[17] This application was, however, dismissed on the ground that "there was no express contract of service and insufficient evidence from which to infer a contract of service". Although the industrial tribunal's ruling was reversed, on a point of law, by the Employment Appeal Tribunal, it was reinstated by the Court of Appeal: Lord Denning M.R., Stephenson and Shaw L.JJ.

In this case the specific reason for the failure of the applicant's claim for unfair dismissal was that he was unable to establish that he had a contract of employment with the companies involved. The absence in the companies' files of a copy of a service contract in respect of the dismissed director, or of a memorandum of such a contract,[18] was regarded as being of particular significance.

Further, although the brothers worked full time for the companies, they were paid not by way of salary but by fees or emoluments, as shown in the accounts. On the other hand, Lord Denning M.R. did point out that the applicant's failure to establish unfair dismissal was without prejudice to any claim he might have under section 184 of the Companies Act 1948[19] for dismissal from his seat on the board.

Another noteworthy aspect of this case is the judicial observations which it elicited, concerning the nature of a family company of this type. The industrial tribunal regarded the companies involved as amounting, *de facto* to a "family partnership with corporate status". In the Court of Appeal Shaw L.J. developed this view further in observing, at 277–278, that "the members of the family were utilising the companies concerned as agencies to carry on [the] business rather than the other way round".[20]

To complete a trilogy of cases involving disputes between corporator-brothers it is appropriate at this point to make brief reference to the House of Lords' decision in *Brady v. Brady.*[21]

---

[17] The application was made under s. 54(1) of the Employment Protection (Consolidation) Act 1978.

[18] As required by s. 26(1) C.A. 1967; see now s. 318 C.A. 1985, as amended, and s. 212 and Sched. 24 C.A. 1989.

[19] See now ss. 303–304 C.A. 1985.

[20] *cf.* the view taken by the Judicial Committee in *Lee v. Lee's Air Farming Ltd.* [1961] A.C. 12.

[21] [1988] 2 W.L.R. 1308.

The dispute in this case, which is discussed in more detail in Chapter 10, *ante*, arose from a scheme for the restructuring of a group of family companies, this scheme having become necessary because of the enmity which had arisen between two brothers[22] and which, because of the resultant management deadlock, was threatening the future commercial viability of what otherwise was a thriving family business organisation.

(c) *Disputes between successors of major shareholders/controllers*

To conclude this selection of family dispute cases[23] it is instructive to consider *Loch v. John Blackwood Ltd.*,[24] a case which originated in Barbados, went on appeal to the West Indian Court of Appeal and which in due course came before the Judicial Committee. In this case the owner of an established engineering business[25] had, by his will, left this business to his trustees on trust for his sister as to one-half of the business and, for his niece and nephew, one-quarter each. As a means of enabling the beneficiaries under the owner's will to enjoy their beneficial interests a company was registered and the business transferred to that company.

In the company so-created, the testator's sister held half the shares and the other half was divided between the testator's niece and nephew, except that three shares were detached from the niece and nephew's block and transferred to M or M's nominees. M, who for several years had been in charge of the testator's business, and was the husband of the testator's sister, became managing director of the company. He was also one of the trustees of the testator's will. There can be no doubt that M operated the business extremely efficiently but, perhaps because of the hard work he put into the business, he appeared to treat it as if it belonged to him. He was, mainly because of his wife's holdings (she was also a director), in a position to command a preponderance of voting power.

---

22 They had equal shareholding and management rights in respect of the companies involved.

23 As already indicated, no attempt is being made here to produce a comprehensive list of cases involving family companies.

24 [1924] A.C. 783. Although technically the company involved in this case was a public company it is treated, for the purpose of this discussion, as being a private family company.

25 A sole trader.

On the footing of a number of grievances against M concerning his handling of the affairs of the company,[26] adding up to the fact that the applicant had lost confidence in the management of the company, an application for the winding-up of the company, on the "just and equitable" ground, was now made by the niece. This application, though successful at first instance in Barbados, was reversed by the West Indies Court of Appeal. It was, however, reinstated by the Judicial Committee of the Privy Council on the footing that, in all the circumstances, the applicant's loss of confidence in the management of the company was fully justified.

This then illustrates once more the possible inherent dangers of attempts to accommodate diverse family interests within the framework of a private company.

C. Entrenched directorships in family companies[27]

1. *Purpose of creating entrenched directorships*

As alluded to earlier in this chapter, the danger of family quarrels spilling over to the boardrooms of family companies appears to be not inconsiderable with regard to this type of business organisation. If a method can be found of isolating[28] family directorships from family quarrels, and thereby protecting boardrooms from the destabilising effects of such quarrels, this will[29] add to the efficacy of family companies as business vehicles. One method by which this desirable end result[30] can, perhaps to some extent, be achieved will now be discussed in this section.

2. *Steps towards establishing entrenched directorships*

The obvious first step towards giving a director an entrenched position will be for the company to appoint him, by a contract

[26] The allegations made included claims that general meetings of the company were not held, that accounts were not submitted in the prescribed manner, that dividends were not recommended. Also it was alleged that an attempt was made to buy out the niece and nephew at what appeared to be a low value.

[27] Of course, family companies are not the only type of company in which entrenched directorships are found.

[28] Or, at least, providing some measure of protection.

[29] Certainly in theory but, hopefully, in practice also.

[30] Desirable from the point of view of the cohesion of the company.

outside the articles,[31] life director or director for a fixed lengthy period. However, as an essential requisite to making such an appointment, it will first be necessary for the company to comply with section 319 of the Companies Act 1985.[32] Section 319 attacks any director's contract of employment with his company which is for more than five years' duration (*i.e.* where it cannot be terminated by the company within such period at all or in specified circumstances), unless a resolution has been passed by the company in general meeting approving such a contractual term, of which a written memorandum has been made available for inspection by the members as prescribed. Unless so authorised such employment can be terminated by the company at any time by reasonable notice. These rules also apply to the directors of holding companies and to shadow directors.[33] Further, section 319(2) aims, in the manner therein specified, to prevent avoidance of these rules by the renewal of periodic contracts.

Assuming, therefore, compliance with section 319,[34] extended service contracts can be awarded by a family company, *inter alia*, to its directors, or, indeed, they may be appointed life directors.[35] However, whatever the period of a director's service contract may be, and even though section 319 of the Companies Act 1985 has been complied with, the matter still remains subject to section 303 of the Companies Act 1985. Section 303(1) provides:

> "A company may by ordinary resolution remove a director before the expiration of his period of office, notwithstanding anything in its articles or in any agreement between it and him."

---

[31] See *Eley v. Positive Life Assurance Co.* (1876) 1 Ex.D. 88. Articles purported to appoint plaintiff solicitor to company; *cf. Re New British Iron Co., ex p. Beckwith* [1898] 1 Ch. 324.

[32] This provision was originally introduced in s. 47 C.A. 1980. The provision clearly aims to prevent directors exploiting their position by granting themselves long and lucrative contracts without reference to the members. The position of a life director of a private company in office on July 18, 1945 is entrenched by s. 14 of the Companies Consolidation (Consequential Provisions) Act 1985.

[33] Defined as: "a person in accordance with whose directions or instructions the directors of the company are accustomed to act. However, a person is not deemed a shadow director by reason only that the directors act on advice given by him in a professional capacity": see s. 741(2) C.A. 1985. For the position of wholly-owned subsidiaries see. s. 319(4). For the "written resolution" procedure in respect of s. 319, as introduced by s. 114 of the C.A. 1989, see Chap. 7, *ante*.

[34] Where at the inception of a family company it is intended to give family directors extended service contracts, s. 319 will not, of course, present any undue difficulty.

[35] See, *e.g. Parsons v. Albert J. Parsons & Sons Ltd.* [1979] I.C.R. 271.

Certain statutory requisites for such removal are contained in sections 303 and 304 but, provided these are met, the clear policy of the legislature is that a company[36] may rid itself, whenever it pleases and for whatever reason, of a director who, whether by his own fault or not, has fallen out of favour with the majority in voting power of the company. The particular constraint imposed on a company in these circumstances is of an economic nature, *viz.* the company may find it necessary to pay damages to a director dismissed in breach of contract,[37] and section 303(5) declares that section 303 shall not be construed as depriving a director who is dismissed from his directorship under this provision, of any rights to compensation he may have against the company as a result of such dismissal.

Effectively, therefore, the constraint to which a company is subjected when it wishes to dismiss a director under section 303 is of a financial nature; the company must estimate the likely costs to itself of the dismissal[38] and then decide whether ridding itself of the director justifies that cost. The availability for inspection at the company's registered office of a copy of the director's contract, or a memorandum thereof, as required by section 318 of the Companies Act 1985,[39] will enable the members to have at least some indication of the expenditure they will incur by passing a resolution under section 303.

Nothing so far discussed, therefore, has pointed to any completely effective method of entrenching a director's position in a family company.[40] However, that it is perfectly possible to create fully entrenched directorships has been shown by the House of Lords in the leading case of *Bushell v. Faith*.[41]

3. *The principle in* Bushell v. Faith

In this case the shares of a private company incorporated some years earlier by the plaintiff and her mother for the

---

[36] In effect, the majority in voting power of the company's members.

[37] There is no question of a director applying for an injunction to prevent a threatened rescission of his service contract. But for the position where a dismissed director is a quasi-partner in a corporate quasi-partnership, see Chap. 12, *ante*.

[38] The normal rule of mitigation of damages in respect of a breach of contract will, of course, apply in this context. Further, there may be circumstances which justify dismissal of a director *without* compensation, *e.g.* if he has been guilty of dishonesty or even negligence in performing his duties; or in circumstances covered by the articles.

[39] See n. 18, *ante*.

[40] Or, indeed, in any other type of company, but for a "wholly-owned subsidiary" see s. 319(4) of the C.A. 1985; also Companies Consolidation Act 1985, n. 32, *ante*.

[41] [1970] A.C. 1099.

purpose of leasing and managing a block of flats were now held as follows: 100 shares by the plaintiff; 100 shares by the plaintiff's brother (defendant); 100 shares by the plaintiff's sister. Both the plaintiff and the defendant were directors of the company.

The plaintiff, having fallen out with her brother, since she took the view that he was not adequately performing his duties, now determined to have him dismissed from the board. To this end she enlisted the aid of her sister, the other shareholder, who was not a director.

A general meeting was, accordingly, called at which a resolution for the dismissal of the defendant director was proposed. Although on a show of hands the voting was two to one in favour of this resolution, the brother thereupon demanded a poll and claimed that he was entitled to cast 300 votes against the resolution, thus out-voting his sisters. The brother based this claim on the articles since, although voting was normally on the footing of one vote per share, regulation 9 of the articles read as follows:

> "In the event of a resolution being proposed at any general meeting of the company for the removal from office of any director, any shares held by that director shall on a poll in respect of such resolution carry the right to three votes per share."

The plaintiff accordingly applied to the court for a declaration that the above regulation contained in the articles was invalid as being contrary to section 184 of the Companies Act 1948.[42] At first instance the plaintiff was, indeed, successful since Ungoed-Thomas J. took the view that to permit the above provision of the articles to operate would "make a mockery" of the law. This view, was, however, rejected by the Court of Appeal and the Court of Appeal's ruling was upheld by a majority of four to one in the House of Lords. Although, as Lord Donovan made plain, section 184 of the 1948 Act clearly overrides any article which requires a special or an extraordinary resolution for the dismissal of a director, Parliament has never prohibited the granting of weighted voting rights in respect of shares. This in fact was all that the article presently

[42] Now s. 303 C.A. 1985, see *ante*.

under consideration wished to do. How a director-shareholder used the votes granted to him in these particular circumstances was entirely a matter for him.[43]

It is clear, therefore, that the "weighted vote" method in *Bushell v. Faith* is a legitimate means whereby companies can, if they so wish, provide entrenched positions for their directors. As Lord Donovan pointed out in his speech in *Bushell v. Faith* at 1110–1111, in justification of this policy:

> "There are many small companies which are conducted in practice as though they were little more than partnerships, particularly family companies running a family business; and it is, unfortunately, sometimes necessary to provide some safeguard against family quarrels having their repercussions in the boardroom."

The decision of the majority in *Bushell v. Faith* may thus be supported on the grounds that, where the articles contain an appropriate provision, this allows a director in a family company (or a corporate quasi-partnership or, indeed, other private company) to defend and maintain his position.[44]

D. "Negative control" of family companies

The provisions of sections 89 to 96 of the Companies Act 1985[45] concerning pre-emption rights of existing shareholders when equity securities[46] are allotted by companies, and the powers granted to private companies to exclude, by the memorandum or articles, such pre-emption rights[47] have already been discussed in Chapter 9, *ante*.

---

[43] For a dissenting view on this issue, supporting Ungoed-Thomas J. at first instance, see the speech of Lord Morris of Borth-y-Gest.

[44] Thus as Russell L.J. observed, see [1969] 2 Ch. 438 at 448, "... it may be highly desirable that 'partners' should be safeguarded in directorships by special voting rights". For an analysis of the extent to which management may more generally entrench its powers by weighted voting rights in the articles, see Chap. 6, *ante*. Also, for another effective defence against removal for directors, see *Harman & Another v. BML Group Ltd.* [1994] 1 W.L.R. 893, Chap. 6, p. 72, n. 36, *ante*.

[45] Provisions originally introduced by the C.A. 1980.

[46] As defined in s. 94 C.A. 1985.

[47] See s. 91 C.A. 1985.

A new issue of equities in a private company may present two basic problems to a minority shareholder. First, the company may have excluded pre-emption rights, under section 92 of the Companies Act 1985, so that if such minority shareholder is not given the opportunity to subscribe in the new issue his position within the company will be further diminished; secondly, even if pre-emption rights have not been excluded and if the minority shareholder is given the opportunity to participate in the new issue, he may be unable to afford to subscribe for his entitlement. In either of these situations, therefore, a shareholder in a private company is likely to consider that his position within the company has been eroded. The difficulties which such a development may cause in a family company can be clearly seen in the interesting decision in *Clemens v. Clemens Bros. Ltd. & Another.*[48]

The company at the centre of this case had been incorporated by two brothers in 1913, as a vehicle for conducting the business of building contractors and shop-fitters. The case arose from what the trial judge, Foster J., described as the "unhappy difference" between an aunt (the second defendant) and her niece (the plaintiff). In fact, the aunt, who held 55 per cent of the issued shares was the daughter and the niece, who held 45 per cent of the issued shares, was the granddaughter, of one of the founding brothers. At one point both aunt and niece had been directors but, after a disagreement, the niece resigned from the board. The aunt continued to take an active part in the company's management, with four other directors, none of these other four being shareholders. In time the aunt formed the view that the company's issued share capital[49] should be increased by 1,650 £1 shares and that 200 of these should be allocated to each of the directors other than herself and that the balance of 850 shares should be placed in a trust fund for the benefit of the company's employees. In order to effect this scheme an extraordinary general meeting was called, at which three ordinary resolutions were proposed: to increase the company's share capital; to make the allotment to the directors; to establish the trust fund. The niece attended the E.G.M. by proxy, voting against these resolutions but, on being out-voted by her aunt, applied to the court to have the resolutions set aside.

---

48 [1976] 2 All E.R. 268. This case pre-dates the statutory pre-emption provisions.
49 Then standing at a total of £2,000, consisting of preference and ordinary shares.

The plaintiff claimed that the resolutions were oppressive toward her since, if implemented, their effect would be to reduce her voting power to less than 26 per cent, so taking away her "negative control" of the company, *i.e.* her right to veto special and extraordinary resolutions.[50] Further, a regulation contained in the company's articles gave existing members first refusal, on a fair valuation, of another member's shares before such shares could be transferred to outsiders.[51] This, in effect, meant that if the niece's position in the company was not "watered down", and if she survived her aunt,[52] she would have an opportunity to acquire complete control of the company. The potential benefit to the niece of this regulation would clearly be considerably diminished if the aunt's proposal for widening the shareholding in the company were put into operation.

In granting the order sought by the niece to have the aunt's resolutions set aside Foster J. took the view that a court of equity was entitled to prevent a shareholder using his or her voting rights in a manner which would be unjust towards another member. His Lordship did, however, state, at 282, that he had "... come to the conclusion that it would be unwise to try to produce a principle, since the circumstances of each case are infinitely varied."[53]

E. Directors' veto rights in family companies

Prior to the Companies Act 1980 one of the essential features of a private company was that it was required, by its articles, to place a restriction on the transferability of its shares.[54] This statutory obligation for a private company could be satisfied in whatever manner the company chose but it was very frequently satisfied by the inclusion within the articles of what might conveniently be called a "directors' veto" clause. As an example see, in particular, the regulation contained in Table A, Part II of the First Schedule of the Companies Act 1948 which allowed

---

[50] These require a majority of at least 75 per cent of the votes cast by members attending (in person or by proxy) and voting.

[51] A provision quite commonly found in the articles of private companies.

[52] The aunt was some 18 years older than the niece.

[53] For a criticism of this decision see L. S. Sealy, *Cases and Materials in Company Law* (5th ed., 1992), p. 179. See also Chap. 8, *ante*.

[54] *per* s. 28 C.A. 1948 and predecessor legislation. See Chap. 1, *ante*.

directors, at their absolute discretion and without giving any reason, to refuse to register share transfers.[55]

Although since the Companies Act 1980 a provision in the articles[56] to restrict freedom of transfer of shares is no longer a *sine qua non* to a private company, many, probably most, private companies will, nevertheless, include such a provision in their articles. This will be particularly attractive to the founders of a family company who, not unnaturally, are likely to wish to keep the company within the family.

A case discussed earlier in this chapter, which arose from the use of a directors' veto provision in the articles of a family company, is *Re Cuthbert Cooper & Sons Ltd.*[57] The article in question read as follows:

> "The directors in their absolute uncontrollable discretion may refuse to register any transfer of shares including fully-paid shares without assigning any reason therefor."

As outlined earlier, the elder brothers, who were directors, invoked this provision and refused to register the transfer into the names of the younger brothers who were not directors, of shares which the younger brothers had been left in their father's will, and which would have given them control of the company.

In rejecting the younger brothers' application to have the company wound up[58] Simonds J. held that, in the absence of proof of improper conduct on the part of the directors, there was nothing in their conduct, falling as it did within the terms of the company's articles, which justified the making of a winding-up order. His Lordship did, however, reserve his

---

[55] See also, Chap. 6, *ante*. Giving directors power to decline to *register* transfers is, perhaps, for many practical purposes, tantamount to making transfers subject to directors' approval, although technically it is not the same thing. However, in a situation where a share transfer has taken place but registration of such transfer is refused by the directors the transferor will hold the legal title in the shares concerned on trust for the transferee; unless, presumably, the articles also preclude a transfer of the beneficial ownership without the directors' consent. Note also the possibility of an application under s. 459(2) C.A. 1985 in this context. Note that in any event directors would have no authority to register a transfer which, to their knowledge, was contrary to the articles: see, *e.g. Tett v. Phoenix Property Co. Ltd.* (1986) 2 BCC 99, 140. The transfer must, of course, be properly stamped. Note also s. 183(3).

[56] Or anywhere else, of course. For the strict attitude the court will take towards the enforcement of a restriction on transfer provision see the Scottish case of *Shepherd's Trustees v. Shepherd* 1950 S.C. 60, H.L. Note that, *per* s. 183(5) C.A. 1985, if a company declines to register the transfer of a share (or a debenture) it must notify the transferee within two months: see also s. 183(6) for fines.

[57] [1937] Ch. 392; see pp. 208–209, *ante*.

[58] On the just and equitable ground.

judgment as to what would have been the position if there had been proof that the directors had exercised their veto for an improper purpose.[59]

Another case in which the exercise of a directors' veto provision found powerful judicial support is *Re Smith and Fawcett Ltd.*[60] In this case an application to the court was made for rectification of the share register[61] when the applicant's request to register the transfer of the shares he had inherited from his father was rejected by the sole remaining director in exercise of veto rights contained in the articles. The applicant's motion for rectification was rejected by Simonds J. and the applicant's appeal was also dismissed by the Court of Appeal. In considering this matter Lord Greene M.R. observed, at 306, that when directors are granted a discretion to decline to register transfers:

> "They must exercise their discretion bona fide in what they consider, not what a court may consider, is in the interests of the company, and not for any collateral purpose."

In *Re Smith and Fawcett Ltd.* nothing was shown to suggest that the director had vetoed the transfer out of any improper motive.

As explained earlier,[62] the decision in *Re Cuthbert Cooper & Sons Ltd.* must now be considered in the light of the criticism expressed by the House of Lords in *Ebrahimi v. Westbourne Galleries Ltd.*[63] The gist of this criticism is that the judge in *Re Cuthbert Cooper & Sons Ltd.* placed excessive emphasis on the contractual rights arising under the articles to the detriment of the equitable principles arising from the relationship of the parties towards each other. Following the views expressed in the

---

[59] Presumably, an improper purpose in this context would have been to pressurise the younger brothers into selling their shares to the directors at an undervalue.

[60] [1942] 1 Ch. 304, C.A. This case did not involve a family company, as such, but, rather, a quasi-partnership in which the son of a deceased quasi-partner was in dispute with the surviving quasi-partner.

[61] See now s. 359 C.A. 1985. For a case in which the Court of Appeal, overturning the decision at first instance, held that on a true construction of the articles in the particular case, the directors could not refuse to register a transfer of a deceased shareholder's shares by his executors to his widow, and thus ordered rectification of the register, replacing the name of the deceased with that of his widow, see *Re Williams Steward (Holdings) Ltd.* [1994] BCC 284.

[62] See p. 209, *ante*.

[63] [1973] A.C. 360. It is arguable that, strictly speaking these views are *obiter*. No reference was made by the House of Lords in *Ebrahimi v. Westbourne Galleries Ltd.* to the conclusions reached in *Re Smith and Fawcett Ltd.*

Westbourne Galleries case the position appears to be that directors who invoke veto clauses in family (and other) companies must now, when so required, justify such actions to the court on equitable principles and should not rely solely on the words of the articles.[64] In the absence of justification, rectification of the register may be ordered under section 359 of the Companies Act 1985 or relief under section 461; or, of course, if appropriate, the company may possibly even be wound up on the just and equitable ground under section 122(1)(g) of the Insolvency Act 1986. It was held, however, by the Court of Appeal in *Charles Forte Investments Ltd. v. Amanda*[65] that a member who was aggrieved because directors had invoked a directors' veto clause should be restrained by injunction from presenting a winding-up petition since this would have been an inappropriate remedy in respect of the claim being made in that particular case.

F. Family companies and matrimonial disputes

Matrimonial problems which lead to divorce and separation are likely to have drastic repercussions on any company in which the spouses share substantial business interests. Business disputes which have been caused, or exacerbated, by matrimonial disputes may be capable of being dealt with by the court by treating the parties as quasi-partners.[66] Therefore the remedy may, on application, be the winding-up of the company or other appropriate remedy under sections 459 to 461 of the Companies Act 1985. The two reported cases in which particular problems have arisen have, however, both involved derivative actions.

Nurcombe v. Nurcombe and Another[67] concerned overlapping issues of family law and company law. In this case the only two shareholders of a company had been married to each other, the husband holding 66 per cent of the issued shares and the wife holding 34 per cent.[68] In the course of earlier proceedings

---

[64] For further discussions on the topic see D. W. Fox, "Disputes in Family Companies" (1984) 128 S.J. 555 at 575.
[65] [1964] Ch. 240 (C.A.).
[66] See Chap. 12, *ante*.
[67] [1985] 1 All E.R. 65.
[68] At the time of the action now under discussion the parties were no longer husband and wife. For the sake of convenience they will, nevertheless, be so described in the following paragraphs.

in the Family Division, in which a divorce decree had been granted, the wife had been informed by her legal advisers that the husband, the sole director of the company mentioned above, had allegedly diverted a lucrative contract from that company to another company in which he had a controlling interest. Despite this knowledge the wife continued with the matrimonial proceedings, claiming maintenance plus a lump sum payment. The present proceedings concerned the viability of a derivative action which the wife wished to bring against the husband, as the company's director, to make good to the company the loss he had allegedly caused it to incur.

The wife's action was dismissed at first instance by Vinelott J., whose ruling was unanimously upheld by the Court of Appeal.[69] In assessing the husband's means in the matrimonial proceedings and awarding a lump sum to the wife, the judge, Rees J., had expressly taken into consideration the profit which the husband was likely to make from the property transaction which, it was claimed, he had wrongfully diverted to his other company. It would be inequitable, in these circumstances, to allow a minority action for misfeasance against the director since a judgement in such an action in favour of the wife would have meant that having, with knowledge of the material facts, chosen one course of action, she had subsequently been allowed a different course of action on the ground that this seemed more beneficial from her point of view. Their Lordships found it appropriate to cite in this context *Towers v. African Tug Co.*[70]

In a situation such as in *Nurcombe v. Nurcombe* the necessity of making a binding election[71] will only arise if the minority shareholder/spouse is aware of all the material facts. But where the necessity for election does arise it is incumbent on the party concerned to choose with extreme care. Sir Denys Buckley pointed out in *Nurcombe v. Nurcombe* that if, prior to the judgment in the matrimonial proceedings, the wife had launched a minority shareholder's action, alleging misfeasance against the

[69] Lawton and Browne-Wilkinson L.JJ. and Sir Denys Buckley.

[70] [1904] 1 Ch. 558. It was held in this case that shareholders who, with knowledge, received unlawful dividends could not afterwards sue the directors for repayment to the company of the money which had been used for those dividends.

[71] *N.B.* Browne-Wilkinson L.J. pointed out that strictly this was not a case of election since the obligation to elect only arises *where the same person* finds himself with alternative rights. This was not the case here since two different persons were involved: the wife and the company. However, as his Lordship also made clear, such a technical objection could not be allowed to cause injustice, which would have been the case if a derivative action had been permitted in these circumstances.

husband, this would have probably delayed the outcome of the matrimonial proceedings and, if it had succeeded, have caused the loss or reduction of the lump sum provision in those proceedings. On the other hand, a successful derivative action may possibly have resulted in heavy damages being awarded to the company which would, in turn, have caused the shares to rise in value.

A divorce which led to soured relationships in the wider family posed a difficulty in *Barrett v. Duckett and Others.*[72] In that case, the plaintiff, B, was a 50 per cent shareholder in T Ltd., her shares having passed to her on the death of her husband. D, the other 50 per cent shareholder was divorced from B's daughter, C, a former director of T Ltd., and was now married to J. The proceedings involved motions to strike out a derivative action being brought by B on behalf of T Ltd., in circumstances described by Peter Gibson L.J. in the Court of Appeal as "a bitter matrimonial dispute" between C and D, against, *inter alia*, D, J and C Ltd., a company owned and controlled by D and J. Amongst the allegations was a diversion of moneys belonging to T Ltd. The Court of Appeal, allowing the defendants' appeal,[73] struck out the derivative action on two grounds: first, a winding-up of the company, which was being offered by D, would be a more appropriate alternative remedy; secondly, B was being impelled by personal rather than financial motives, her partiality[74] precluding her from pursuing the action bona fide for the benefit of the company.

G. Unfairly prejudicial conduct in family companies

This section considers the extent to which the courts have made use of the powers conferred on them by sections 459 to 461 of the Companies Act 1985 on applications in respect of allegedly unfairly prejudicial conduct in family companies.

---

[72] July 27, 1994, Court of Appeal (Lexis).

[73] From the first instance decision of Sir Mervyn Davies, sitting as a Judge of the High Court, [1993] BCC 778. The Court of Appeal did, however, reach the same conclusion as the Judge as to the entitlement of a 50 per cent shareholder to bring a derivative action in these circumstances since B was, in her disability to procure the suit of the company, in the same position as a minority shareholder.

[74] Revealed particularly by B's admitted reluctance to sue her daughter, C, an alleged beneficiary of some of the diverted moneys. Though B had joined C as a defendant in the action, this was, in the opinion of Peter Gibson L.J., "a token gesture" since the pleadings had not been amended to include claims against C nor had proceedings been served on her.

It is, first, interesting to note that one of the few reported cases in which an application under section 210 of the Companies Act 1948 succeeded did, indeed, involve a dispute in a family company, albeit a dispute of a somewhat unusual nature, *i.e. H.R. Harmer Ltd.*[75]

Then, shortly after section 75 of the Companies Act 1980[76] had replaced section 210, an opportunity for testing the breadth of the new provision arose in the context of a family company, *i.e. in Re A Company (No. 004475 of 1982).*[77] In this case the issued shares of a private company had been held by three sisters and two brothers in the following proportions: one sister, the chairman, held 46 per cent; the other sisters and brothers held 13.5 per cent each. On the death of one of the brothers his 13.5 per cent holding passed to his two children, aged 11 and 15. Since the executors of the deceased brother's will wished to sell this holding in order to raise funds to provide for the children's education and benefit, they offered to sell the shares to the existing members. However, none of the existing members was willing to increase his/her holding in the company.

Although the articles did, indeed, contain a "directors' veto" clause[78] the company was, nevertheless, willing to permit a sale of the shares held by the executors to an outsider so long as such sale was not to a competitor of the company. A sale to an outsider would, however, have been, in the view of the executors, unsatisfactory in that, since it would constitute the sale of a minority holding in a private company, this could probably only have been effected at a discount. In these circumstances, the executors asked the company either to formulate a scheme of reconstruction for the purposes of section 287 of the Companies Act 1948 or to purchase the block of shares pursuant to sections 46 to 47 of the Companies Act 1981.[79] In the event, the company declined to comply with either of these proposals[80] since, although there would have been sufficient liquid reserves for these purposes, the directors

---

[75] [1958] 3 All E.R. 689; see pp. 207–208, *ante*.

[76] See now ss. 459–461 C.A. 1985.

[77] [1983] Ch. 178.

[78] For discussion of such clauses, see pp. 218–221, *ante*.

[79] For discussion of problems of valuing minority holdings in private companies see Chap. 14, *post*.

[80] Although the auditors did suggest a price at which the shares might be bought by the company this was rejected as insufficient by the executors.

had other business plans in mind for which the reserves were required. In these circumstances the executors claimed relief under section 75 of the Companies Act 1980, alleging that the company's refusal to fulfil these requirements amounted to unfairly prejudicial conduct on the part of the majority shareholders against a minority.

This argument did not find favour with Lord Grantchester Q.C., sitting as a deputy High Court Judge in the Chancery Division, who, on the company's application, dismissed the executors' petition. His Lordship was unable to accept that the company's refusal to co-operate in the implementation of the schemes proposed had in any way affected the plaintiffs in their capacity as members. Similarly, his Lordship was unable to accept that it would amount to unfairly prejudicial conduct for the directors to consider the use of the company's liquid funds in order to expand into new fields of business.

In *Re A Company (No. 008699 of 1985)*[81] Hoffmann J. commented that in *Re A Company (No. 004475 of 1982)*, above, the directors' failure to fall in line with the minority holders' wishes, though prejudicial to that minority, could not be said to be *unfairly* prejudicial. A similar conclusion was reached by the Court of Session (Inner House) in the Scottish case *Jesner v. Jarrad Properties Ltd.*,[82] in which the court, in considering a section 459 petition in the context of a family company, was prepared to take account of the interests of the family as a whole.

The allegations of unfair prejudice in this case included certain loan and security transactions between two companies which were essentially run as a single family business. The court accepted that since the inception of the two companies, the directors had acted with complete disregard to Companies Act formalities, and that any gratuitous or favourable arrangements made by one company for the benefit of the other would prejudice the members of the former. Lord Morrison commented, however, that in judging whether a "reasonable bystander"[83] would regard the transactions as being unfair as well as prejudicial,

[81] [1986] BCLC 382.

[82] [1992] BCC 807.

[83] His Lordship was here using the test adopted by Nourse J. in *Re R. A. Noble & Sons (Clothing) Ltd.* [1983] BCLC 273 at 292, following Slade J. in *Re Bovey Hotel Ventures Ltd.* (1981; unreported).

> "... it would be absurd to ignore the fact that the two companies had been run as a single family business since ... 1963. ... Equally in my view it would be wrong to ignore the fact that in making the arrangements complained of the directors ... were acting bona fide in what they considered to be the interests of the family as a whole."[84]

Though the facts of the case did not justify a section 459 petition, the court held, however, that since the company involved was a quasi-partnership in which mutual trust and confidence had been lost, it would be just and equitable to wind-up the company.

H. The Matrimonial Causes Act 1973 (as amended)

An added provision in the Matrimonial Causes Act 1973, *viz.*, section 24A,[85] is of particular significance in regard to family companies. Section 24A(1) provides that where, in matrimonial proceedings, the court makes a secured periodical payments order, a lump sum payment order or a property adjustment order,[86] "on making that order, or at any time thereafter, the court may make a further order for the sale of such property as may be specified in the order, being property in which or in the proceeds of sale of which either or both of the parties to the marriage has or have a beneficial interest, either in possession or reversion".

Section 24A(2) then goes on to provide that an order under section 24A(1), above, may contain any consequential or supplementary provisions which the court thinks fit, including provision requiring the making of a payment out of the proceeds of sale of the relevant property[87] and also including a "provision requiring any such property to be offered for sale to a person, or class of persons, specified in the order".[88]

In particular, therefore, where a husband and wife hold shares in a family company, in respect of any matrimonial proceedings between them in which the court orders the sale of either or both of their interests in that company, it may also provide (if it considers this appropriate) for the sale to be limited to family members or to be otherwise restricted.

---

[84] [1992] BCC 807 at 815.
[85] Inserted by s. 7 of the Matrimonial Homes and Property Act 1981.
[86] Under ss. 23 and 24 of the Matrimonial Causes Act 1973.
[87] See s. 24A(2)(a) M.C.A. 1973.
[88] See s. 24A(2)(b) M.C.A. 1973.

CHAPTER 14

VALUING SHARES IN PRIVATE COMPANIES

A. Preliminary considerations

1. *The problems in outline*

This chapter considers the problems of valuing shares in private companies not in situations in which such shares are transferred by the free consent of the transferor and the transferee but by court order or by obligatory transfer in accordance with the articles or by transmission on death.[1] Clearly, when shares in private companies are transferred pursuant to an agreement freely entered into between the parties concerned it is for those parties to make whatever bargain for the transfer they think fit. Thus, provided such parties are *sui juris*, in the absence of fraud, misrepresentation or operative mistake, the court will not concern itself with the basis on which the parties have valued the shares covered by the transaction. But this assumes a willing buyer and a willing seller in a situation in which either there are no restrictions[2] on transfer contained in the articles or any such restrictions are not being enforced by those with power to enforce them. It is then incumbent on parties of full age and capacity to make their own bargains and to fulfil the bargains they so make.

---

[1] Or, indeed, the shareholder's bankruptcy, although transmission of shares on bankruptcy does not appear to have given rise to reported share valuation disputes. But presumably, the same principles apply as for transmission on death.

[2] Although since the Companies Act 1980, a provision restricting the members' rights to transfer their shares is no longer a *sine qua non* to a private company, in practice such a provision, not infrequently in the form of a pre-emption clause and/or of a directors' veto clause, will very often appear in a private company's articles. Pre-emption provisions, as above, should not, however, be confused with the pre-emption provisions covered by ss. 89–90 C.A. 1985, with regard to the issue of new equity "securities" (defined in s. 94) and from which, *per* s. 91, *private companies*, by appropriate provisions in their memoranda or articles, may opt out. See Chap. 9, *ante*.

Somewhat different considerations will apply, however, when there is an element of compulsion in dealings in shares in private companies. As will be considered below, that element of compulsion may arise out of provisions in the articles, out of purchase orders made by the court in exercise of powers granted by sections 459 to 461 of the Companies Act 1985 or on the death of a shareholder. Valuation problems will frequently arise in connection with the transmission of a deceased member's shares to his legatee or next-of-kin since, as pointed out by Wynn-Parry J. in *Dean v. Prince*,[3] in the absence of a free market in such shares,[4] "certain assumptions having no basis in reality" will have to be made.[5]

Further, as will also be discussed in this chapter, the circumstances which have necessitated a sale of shares in a private company and/or the fact that the shares in question constitute a majority or a minority holding may greatly influence the appropriate method of valuation of those shares. An additional matter for discussion is the precise time at which such a valuation should be effected.

2. *Alternative criteria for valuation*

As will become apparent from the cases discussed in the ensuing parts of this chapter, there are two broad criteria for the valuation of private company shares where such shares are subject to some form of compulsory transfer:

(i) valuation on a pro rata basis, so that each share of the same denomination and class is valued at the same unit price;

(ii) valuation at a premium or discount on the pro rata share value, such premium or discount reflecting the commercial situation when what is being transferred is respectively a majority holding which will usually give control over the company, or a minority holding which will not usually give the holder a voice in the company management or policy-making, or not a dominant voice.

---

[3] [1954] Ch. 409 at 430. But for a case in which the observations of Wynn-Parry J. were distinguished see *Re Castleburn Ltd.* (1989) 5 BCC 652, p. 231, *post.*

[4] Particularly since the articles of a private company will usually contain restrictions on transfer: see n. 2, *ante.*

[5] A deceased member's personal representatives will, presumably, be anxious to have the shares valued at the lowest figure acceptable to the Inland Revenue.

When a pro rata valuation is found to be appropriate it will first, of course, be essential for the person making the valuation to ascertain the total "worth" of the company. This preliminary task may itself, however, be fraught with difficulties. It will therefore be necessary to decide whether a continuing company should in all circumstances be treated as a going-concern with regard to its assets or whether there are circumstances in which the assets of even a continuing company should be given the value they would have if the company were being broken up. Furthermore, in respect of a continuing company, in order to decide what the business is worth, and then to divide that "worth" pro rata between the shares, it is arguable that the company's earning capacity including earnings record and estimated future prospects must also be considered by the valuer.

However, if it is decided that private company shares are to be valued not on the footing of a uniform unit price but at a premium or discount to take into account that they constitute a majority or minority holding, then the additional problem which requires to be resolved is how the rate of such premium or discount should be set. How some of these questions have been answered by the courts will be examined below.

B. The mechanism for evaluation

1. *Pre-emption provisions in the articles*

Frequently, as discussed in Chapter 6, *ante*, articles will contain provisions conferring on members pre-emption rights in respect of other members' shares, *i.e.* granting to continuing members first refusal[6] in regard to those shares in the company which, for various reasons, are put up for sale. Where such pre-emption rights are granted by the articles, the articles will, very likely, go on to state that if any shares are so offered to existing members they must be offered at a fair value. Frequently such fair value will, also, pursuant to the terms of the articles, fall to

[6] See, *e.g. Tett v. Phoenix Property and Investments Co. Ltd.* (1986) 2 BCC 99, 140 (C.A.). Note that with regard to a pre-emption provision the existing members must be prepared to take all the shares on offer, otherwise the selling member can offer to outsiders: *The Ocean Coal Co. Ltd. v. The Powell Duffryn Steam Co. Ltd.* [1932] 1 Ch. 654.

be calculated by the company's auditors or by other specified experts. A leading case on share valuation in circumstances as above is the decision of the Court of Appeal in *Dean v. Prince*.[7]

In this case the relevant company was, in effect, a corporate quasi-partnership, having three directors, X, Y and Z, who were the company's only shareholders. Of the 200 issued shares in the company X held 140 and Y and Z held 30 each. The company's articles provided that on the death of a director/shareholder his shares were to be sold to the remaining directors at a fair price, as ascertained by the company's auditor. In the event, X was the first director to die, so, following the articles, his holding of 140 shares (which thus constituted a majority holding in the company) had to be valued and made available for purchase by Y and Z. The auditor decided that the purchase price of these shares should be calculated simply on a pro rata basis on the aggregate value of the company's assets taken at their break-up value. On this footing the fact that the block of shares involved constituted a controlling interest in the company made no difference to the unit price at which they were to be made available for purchase by the remaining directors.

The basis of valuation arrived at by the auditor was challenged by X's widow who argued, in effect, that a premium factor should have been built into the valuation to take account of the fact that X's 140 shares had constituted the controlling share block. At first instance Harman J. accepted this contention but it was unanimously rejected by the Court of Appeal: Evershed M.R., Denning L.J. and Wynn-Parry J.

Although the Court of Appeal was in no doubt in *Dean v. Prince* that the auditor's pro rata valuation had to be upheld even though the block of shares in question carried control of the company, it seems clear that this conclusion was reached on the particular facts of the case and that no general principle requiring share valuation to be on a pro-rata footing on a compulsory sale can be deduced from this decision.[8] Wynn-Parry J. pointed out that in this case, although the 140 shares had given their owner control of the company, neither of the two surviving directors would automatically gain control of the company[9] since they would acquire equal rights to purchase the

---

[7] [1954] Ch. 409.

[8] For an incisive commentary on this case see L. S. Sealy, *Cases and Materials in Company Law* (5th ed., 1992), pp. 450–451.

[9] Compare the position in *Short v. Treasury Commissioners* [1948] A.C. 534.

deceased director's holding. Also, Denning L.J., whilst observing that the auditor was justified in taking the break-up value of the assets since the company was a losing concern,[10] pointed out that the position would have been different if the company had been making a profit at the time of the valuation.[11]

Dean v. Prince was, moreover, distinguished by Judge Paul Baker Q.C.[12] in *Re Castleburn Ltd.*[13] Though the basis for the decision in this case may perhaps, at least in part, be questionable[14] in the light of *Re Abbey Leisure Ltd.*[15] as interpreted in *Re a Company (No. 00330 of 1991) ex p. Holden*,[16] the judgment reveals the importance of the wording of the articles as forming a proper basis for valuation. Whereas in *Dean v. Prince* the articles had provided that the fair value should be the auditor's valuation of the current worth of the *company's shares (i.e.* requiring a valuation of the *whole* of the company's shares), in *Re Castleburn Ltd.* a close reading of the articles persuaded the judge that in this case, it was the *parcel* of shares of the departing member which required valuation.[17] Also, the warning of Wynn-Parry J. in *Dean v. Prince* against making more artificial assumptions than are necessary in share valuation, particularly regarding a sale between a notional willing buyer and a notional willing seller, was distinguished on the basis that the articles in *Re Castleburn Ltd.* expressly incorporated such an assumption. The company's auditors had therefore been justified in applying a discount to the value of the minority holding of the petitioner.

2. *Valuation of shares in corporate quasi-partnerships*[18]

Following a successful application under section 459 of the Companies Act 1985 the court has power, *inter alia*, to:

---

[10] Accordingly, Denning L.J. mentioned the element of "negative goodwill" which must be taken into account in valuing a losing business, since a sale in these circumstances can only be effected on a "piecemeal basis".

[11] For share valuation when the company concerned is a going concern with the prospect of profits but no appreciable assets see pp. 236–237, *post*.

[12] Sitting as a High Court Judge.

[13] (1989) 5 BCC 652.

[14] Insofar as the Judge, in striking out a petition brought under s. 459 C.A. 1985, held that the petitioner should abide by the compulsory share purchase and valuation provisions in the articles.

[15] [1990] BCC 60.

[16] [1991] BCC 241. For fuller discussion see Chap. 12, *ante*, and p. 235, *post*.

[17] Following *Short v. Treasury Commissioners* [1948] A.C. 534.

[18] See Chap. 12, *ante* for corporate quasi-partnerships generally.

> "provide for the purchase of the shares of any members of the company by other members or by the company itself and, in the case of a purchase by the company itself, the reduction of the company's capital accordingly."[19]

It is now necessary to consider how shares in a corporate quasi-partnership, which are the subject-matter of a purchase order made under section 461(2)(d) of the Companies Act 1985 should be valued. The leading authority on this topic is the judgment of Nourse J. in *Re Bird Precision Bellows Ltd.*,[20] as confirmed by the Court of Appeal: Oliver and Purchas L.JJ. The problems in *Re Bird Precision Bellows Ltd.* arose out of a management dispute in a quasi-partnership type company from which two directors, who were also minority shareholders, had been dismissed from their directorships. The dismissed directors thereupon applied to the court under section 75 of the Companies Act 1980,[21] claiming that the affairs of the company had been conducted in a manner unfairly prejudicial to themselves, as members, and, in particular, that they had been wrongfully excluded from the management of the company. The relief sought by the applicants was that the respondents be required to purchase the applicants' shares "at the fair value thereof".

The case originally came before Vinelott J., at which point the parties consented, without any admission of unfairly prejudicial conduct on the part of the respondents, to the petitioners' shares being purchased by the respondents, "at such price as the court shall hereafter determine". The matter was, pursuant to the consent order, than remitted to Nourse J. to determine the purchase price of the shares.

Nourse J., while accepting that there is no universal rule for the valuation of shares in a private company, did nevertheless point out that, as a general rule, shares in a quasi-partnership[22] which were the subject of a purchase order under what is now section 461 should be valued on a pro rata footing rather than at their commercial value which would include such discount or premium to reflect the minority or majority nature of the

---

[19] See s. 461(2)(d) C.A. 1985.

[20] See [1984] Ch. 419 for judgment at first instance and [1986] 2 W.L.R. 158 for judgment of the Court of Appeal. See also D.W. Fox, "Valuing Minority Holdings in Private Companies" in (1985) 129 S.J. 456 and (1986) 130 S.J. 467.

[21] Predecessor provision to ss. 459–461 C.A. 1985.

[22] This point was again stressed by Nourse J. in *Re London School of Electronics* [1985] 3 W.L.R. 474.

holding. The appropriate method of valuation (*i.e.* the company's worth which had to be divided equally among the issued shares), was to take account of both the earnings of the company and its "net tangible assets value".[23]

The pro rata valuation was upheld by the Court of Appeal. Nourse J. had pointed out however that the same principle should apply not only on a finding of unfairly prejudicial conduct, but also (as on the facts of the case) where a consent order for valuation had been made, or even where there had been no unfairly prejudicial conduct. This was the one aspect of the judgment that was criticised by Oliver L.J. in the Court of Appeal. Nourse J. had in fact found that there had been unfairly prejudicial conduct by the respondents but he had regarded his enquiry into the respondents' conduct as being a matter which affected only the valuation of the petitioner's shares. Oliver L.J., on the other hand, stated that it was this finding which had established that the section 459 petition was well founded and which had thus given Nourse J. the jurisdiction to make the purchase order.

The principle established by *Re Bird Precision Bellows Ltd.* is, therefore, that a pro rata valuation of shares is a quasi-partnership is usually appropriate on a successful section 459 petition, and not that such a valuation is necessarily appropriate in quasi-partnerships generally.

Thus, in *Howie & Others v. Crawford*,[24] Vinelott J., on an appeal against an arbitrator's valuation, held that the arbitrator had been wrong to follow *Re Bird Precision Bellows* in his valuation of shares in a company which he had regarded as possessing some if not all the elements of a quasi-partnership. In that case, where a shareholders' agreement contained a pre-emption provision which referred to valuation at "fair market price", Vinelott J. held that a discount should have been applied to the minority holding.[25]

---

[23] The company's dividend record will also be a factor in valuation; see n. 25, *post.*

[24] [1990] BCC 331.

[25] *ibid.*, *per* Vinelott J. at 332;

> "The market price of an asset is the price which that asset will fetch in the open market between a willing vendor and a willing purchaser. If the asset is a holding of shares in a private company the market price will normally if not invariably depend on the proportion of the shares of the company comprised in the holding and on any special rights or restrictions contained in the articles of association of the company as well as on the value of the net assets of the company and its profit and dividend record."

Also, in *Re Bird Precision Bellows Ltd.* Nourse J. had accepted that there may be situations, even in the context of a purchase order under section 461, where a pro rata valuation of a holding in a quasi-partnership would be inappropriate.[26] Nourse J. gave two examples, neither of which applied on the facts before him. First, the valuation might be in respect of the shares of an expelled quasi-partner who deserved to be expelled. Secondly, the minority member, even though subjected to unfairly prejudicial conduct, might have acquired his interest in a quasi-partnership by purchase at a discount from an original quasi-partner, perhaps purely for investment purposes; Nourse J. took as *a fortiori* the case where such an investment is made in a company which has never been a quasi-partnership and this was held to be so in *Re Elgindata Ltd.*[27]

Also, it was held in *Re D.R. Chemicals Ltd.*[28] that where a company had ceased to be a quasi-partnership, it was appropriate that the shares of a section 459 petitioner should be purchased at a discount to reflect the fact that they constituted a minority holding.

3. *Whether available machinery needs to be utilized*

As has already been indicated,[29] the articles of a private company will often, as an adjunt to pre-emption or compulsory purchase provisions, contain a procedure for valuing that

---

[26] Nourse J. observed, *obiter*, that where, as a matter of law, the judge rules that shares should be valued at a discount, the amount of that discount is a matter for the professional judgment of an appropriate expert. No doubt the same position will obtain, *mutatis mutandis*, when a judge finds that the shares should be transferred at a premium.

[27] [1991] BCLC 959, where Warner J., at 1007, held that where shares had been acquired as an investment in a private company which was not a quasi-partnership, it was appropriate to apply a discount to the valuation of the shares of a successful section 459 petitioner. However, since a valuation expert had concluded that a discount was inappropriate because the majority shareholders had given an undertaking not to part with their controlling interest without a special resolution (which the petitioners, holding 33 per cent of the shares could block), Warner J.'s order contained a proviso that if this could be agreed between the valuation experts, or was held to be so by the court after hearing the evidence, the valuation would be on a pro rata basis.

[28] (1989) 5 BCC 39, (*sub nom. Re a Company (No. 005134 of 1986) ex p. Harries* [1989] BCLC 365) where Peter Gibson J. observed, at 54, that the petitioner might have sought relief earlier on the basis that the company was a quasi-partnership but he "elected not to do so and instead chose to sit it out as an ordinary minority shareholder."

[29] See pp. 229–231, *ante*.

company's shares. It has been seen in Chapter 12, *ante*, that the line of cases which held that such available machinery should normally be utilized before the court would be prepared to undertake a valuation on a petition for unfair prejudice under section 459 of the Companies Act 1985[30] must now be reviewed in the light of *Re Abbey Leisure Ltd.*[31] as interpreted in *Re a Company (No. 00330 of 1991) ex p. Holden.*[32] In some of the earlier cases, Hoffmann J., in particular, had asserted the efficacy of following valuation provisions in the articles. The parties were contractually bound to these terms. Moreover, even though a valuer was unlikely to give reasons for the valuation (*i.e.* to give a "speaking" valuation) and thus make it difficult for a petitioner to challenge, such a valuation, albeit having a rough and ready aspect to it, was far quicker and cheaper than a valuation by the court.[33]

The position now seems to be that the courts will not necessarily expect a section 459 petitioner to abide by the articles in such cases. A change of emphasis was evident in *ex p. Holden*, above, where Harman J. asserted that a "non-speaking" valuation increased the vulnerability of the petitioner who was not unreasonable in refusing to accept the risk of a detriment in the valuation. There was, on the facts of the case, no risk of a discount being applied since the articles expressly provided that there should be no discount or enhancement, but stated, rather, that the fair value of each share should be taken as being "a rateable proportion of the total of all the issued shares of the company". Harman J. held that a valuation of the share capital, in circumstances where the company owned property but had large liabilities on it, was likely to be very speculative.

Where the courts hold that it is reasonable to expect a section 459 petitioner to pursue the valuation procedure in the articles, a party who believes that his shares have been incorrectly

---

[30] See, *e.g. Re a Company (No. 007623 of 1984)* (1986) 2 BCC 99, 191; *Re XYZ Ltd.* (1986) 2 BCC 99, 520 *sub nom. Re A Company (No. 004377 of 1986)* [1987] 1 W.L.R. 102; *Re a Company (No. 006834 of 1988) ex p. Kremer* [1989] BCLC 365; *Re Castleburn Ltd.* (1989) 5 BCC 652.

[31] [1990] BCC 60, a decision relating to a just and equitable winding-up petition under s. 122(1)(g) I.A. 1986.

[32] [1991] BCC 241.

[33] See *Re a Company (No. 006834 of 1988) ex p. Kremer* [1989] BCLC 365 at 369–370 and *Re a Company (No. 007623 of 1984)* (1986) 2 BCC 99, 191 at 99, 195–196.

valued can bring proceedings in negligence or to have the valuation set aside,[34] but any such alleged shortcomings in the auditors cannot amount to conduct of the company's affairs for the purposes of section 459.[35]

4. *Valuation based on projected profits*

There may well be a situation in which a private company has very few assets but, nevertheless, considerable earning potential. This was indeed the position in *Buckingham v. Francis and Others.*[36] In this case the Judge, Staughton J., was asked, pursuant to a consent order, to value the shares of a minority member[37] who, in fact held two fifths of the issued share capital of the company. The valuation was to be made, as agreed by the parties, on the footing that no distinction should be made in the value per share between majority and minority holdings[38] and that the company had to be valued as a going-concern, with break-up value only being used as a "long-stop". In addition to these points of common ground the judge found, on the available evidence, that the break-up value of the company "was very small or nothing at all".

In *Buckingham v. Francis* the Judge came to the conclusion that "[t]he value of the company was the capitalised sum representing future profits".[39] But this, as Staughton J. pointed out, at 741, involved two unknown factors, *viz.* the future profits and "what price/earnings ratio would commend itself to a purchaser as appropriate for capitalisation". Future profits were to be calculated on a "best realistic guess" basis, on the footing of the judge's evaluation of the company's prospects. The price/earnings ratio[40] is the number of years a purchaser would be willing to wait before pre-tax profits would bring reimbursement of his expenditure. This, again, would be for the judge to ascertain.

---

[34] *Re a Company (No. 007623 of 1984)*, n. 30, *ante*; *Re XYZ Ltd.*, n. 30, *ante*; *Re Castleburn Ltd.*, n. 3, *ante.*

[35] *Re Castleburn Ltd.*, n. 3, *ante.*

[36] [1986] 2 All E.R. 738. The company involved in this case was also a quasi-partnership.

[37] A quasi-partner.

[38] Thus there was no question in this case as to valuation at a premium or a discount.

[39] [1986] 2 All E.R. 738 at 741.

[40] In other words, the "multiplier".

Clearly, no exact formula is available to enable a judge to calculate either of the above figures with precision and, therefore, as Staughton J. stated in *Buckingham v. Francis*, at 741, "it is possible to make an allowance for risks in calculating either figure",[41] or such allowance may be split between the two figures. However, as the same Judge also pointed out, "allowance for risks" must not be duplicated by subjecting both these figures to the same allowance.

Where, therefore, the appropriate valuation method in respect of any given company is one based on the company's potential future profits the judge will, on evidence available to him,[42] work out, as best he can, a sum which represents the company's likely future maintainable annual profit and also a figure which is the number of years a hypothetical purchaser of the company would be willing to wait, before, by receipt of pre-tax profits, he would recoup the purchase price. The first of these figures, multiplied by the second figure, gives the company's "worth".[43] Assuming, therefore, a "potential profits" basis for valuation and where it is appropriate that the company's shares should be valued on a pro rata footing, the value of each individual share will be that "worth" divided by the total number of shares issued.[44]

---

[41] [1986] 2 All E.R. 738 at 741.

[42] Including, in particular, evidence provided by experts such as accountants; but only such evidence as would have been available at the valuation date, except that as his Lordship pointed out (at 470), "... regard may be had to later events for the purpose only of deciding what forecasts for the future could reasonably have been made [on the valuation date]." Staughton J. also stated (at 742): "I resolutely exclude after events save for the purpose of checking what was a proper estimate for that [*i.e.* valuation] date." Note also the position in *Re E.S.C. Publishing Ltd.* [1990] BCC 335: see p. 239, *post*.

[43] Note, however, the following observations of Staughton J., in *Buckingham v. Francis* [1986] 2 All E.R. 738 at 743:

> "Frankly I doubt whether businessmen are ruled by accountants when deciding how much to pay for a private company ... I wonder whether ... business acumen or hunch does not play a far larger part than the calculations of accountants."

[44] Sometimes, however, the court will find it necessary to rule that the shares contained in a particular block must be valued at a discount or premium from their pro rata value; see *ante*. Note, however, the more recent New Zealand case of *Holt v. Holt* [1990] 1 W.L.R. 1250, involving a dispute between divorced spouses, shareholders in a private company, about the value of one particular share which carried the voting control of the company. The Judicial Committee of the Privy Council accepted the ruling of the New Zealand courts that, for the purpose of the appropriate matrimonial legislation, the valuation test required "... an inquiry as to the value at which a willing but not anxious vendor would sell and a willing but not anxious purchaser would buy". This principle was derived from earlier New Zealand authorities, *viz., Hatrick v. Commissioner of Inland Revenue* [1963] N.Z.L.R. 641 and *Coleman v. Myers* [1977] 2 N.Z.L.R. 225.

C. The valuation date of shares

In *Buckingham v. Francis*, above, the date on which the value of the shares was required to be calculated was stated in the consent order. On many occasions, however, the valuation date itself will be in dispute[45] and so for the judge to ascertain. The approach of the judges in recent cases will now, therefore, be discussed.

In fact the position in this regard can be summarised by citing a passage from the judgment of Nourse J. in *Re London School of Electronics Ltd.*[46] in which, in reply to arguments advanced by counsel that there is a general rule for fixing the valuation date of shares, he made the following observations, at 484:

> "If there were to be such a thing as a general rule, I myself would think that the date of the order or the actual valuation would be more appropriate than the date of the presentation of the petition or the unfair prejudice. Prima facie an interest in a going concern ought to be valued at the date on which it is ordered to be purchased. But whatever the general rule might be it seems very probable that the overriding requirement that the valuation should be fair on the facts of the particular case would, by exceptions, reduce it to no rule at all."

A few years earlier, in *Re a Company (No. 002567 of 1982)*,[47] Vinelott J., having concluded that the petitioner had acted unreasonably in rejecting an offer by the respondent to purchase his shares, refused to back-date the valuation now called for. By contrast, however, the decision of Mervyn Davies J. in *Re O.C. Transport Services Ltd.*[48] is an example of a case in which fairness was found to necessitate a retrospective valuation to the date when unfairly prejudicial conduct began, *i.e.* developments which had taken place before the date of the

---

[45] Particularly where a purchase order is sought under s. 461(2)(d) C.A. 1985: see pp. 231–232, *ante*.
[46] [1985] 3 W.L.R. 474. The appropriate valuation date in this case was found to be the date of presentation of the petition (under s. 75 of the C.A. 1980).
[47] [1983] 1 W.L.R. 927.
[48] (1984) 1 BCC 99, 068.

petition made valuation at the date of the petition wholly inappropriate.[49]

It does, therefore, appear very clear from the cases that the only rule for fixing the share valuation date, when the court is required to value shares in a private company, is that the date chosen must be the one which, in the prevailing circumstances, most closely meets the demands of justice.[50]

Finally, it should be noted that although changes in market value after the valuation date[51] clearly cannot be taken into consideration by the valuer, evidence which goes to show what the shares are worth *as at the valuation date*, is admissable as a factor which the valuer can take into account, even if such evidence is received after the valuation date. Thus, in *Re ESC Publishing Ltd.*,[52] an offer by an outside party, just after the valuation date, to purchase all the shares of a company, was held to be potential evidence for use by an independent valuer in a share purchase/sale transaction between transferee/transferor members on the compromise of section 459 proceedings.

---

[49] For earlier cases in which problems concerning share valuation dates were considered see, *e.g. Scottish Co-operative Wholesale Society v. Meyer* [1959] A.C. 324 and the judgment at first instance (Pennycuick J.) in *Re Jermyn Street Turkish Baths Ltd.* [1970] 1 W.L.R. 1194; the share valuation point remains of interest even though the judgment itself was overruled by the Court of Appeal: see [1971] 1 W.L.R. 1042.

[50] In *Re Elgindata Ltd.* [1991] BCLC 959, Warner J. set the valuation date as the date of the order on a section 459 petition. In *Re a Company (No. 00330 of 1991) ex p. Holden* [1991] BCC 241, Harman J., without it being possible to decide the point, felt that the appropriate valuation date might be the date of the trial of a s. 459 petition, and also took into account certain tax considerations in determining that the valuation date set by the articles might be unfair to the petitioner.

[51] Whatever that date may be found to be in any given case.

[52] [1990] BCC 335, Knox J.

CHAPTER 15

TRANSFERS, TAKEOVERS AND DEALINGS IN PRIVATE COMPANY INTERESTS

A. Introduction

The corporators of a private company may, where there is no disagreement between them, transfer controlling or lesser interests in such a company entirely as they think fit. This chapter is, however, concerned with problems which can arise out of dealings in interests in a private company where there is an element of dissension between the corporators in regard to the transfer of an interest in the company, or in regard to the takeover of the company by outsiders, or where the transaction in question is otherwise a matter of dispute between the membership.[1]

In practice, one important advantage which the boards of private companies usually enjoy, by clear contrast with their counterparts in public companies, is freedom from hostile takeover bids, since private company boards will frequently command majority voting power.[2] Sometimes the boards of private companies, even where they do not control the majority of voting power, will be supported by a "directors' veto" clause[3] in the articles, although how far such a provision can be used by them to ward off a takeover bid will be discussed later in this chapter.

---

[1] No attempt will be made to discuss the taxation issues involved in the type of transaction considered in this chapter.

[2] But note *Lloyds Bank plc v. Duker & Others* [1987] 1 W.L.R. 1324; also *Re a Company* [1986] BCLC 382, *post*. For a case in which the directors of a family company which had "gone public" (but remained unquoted) were held to have acted improperly in issuing new shares for the purpose of forestalling a takeover bid until, as in the event occurred, this was ratified by a general meeting, see *Hogg v. Cramphorn Ltd.* [1967] Ch. 254. See now the pre-emption provisions of ss. 89–96 C.A. 1985, which may, *per* s. 91 C.A. 1985, be excluded for private companies.

[3] Sometimes directors may wish to invoke a directors' veto provision contained in the articles in order to safeguard their directorships: see n. 48, *post*.

B. Minorities' immunity from improper eviction

It is axiomatic that, subject to any provision in the articles to the contrary, majority shareholders in a company must not expropriate the shares of minority shareholders and thus expel them from that company.[4] In the case of a small private company it may sometimes be extremely inconvenient from the point of view of the majority shareholders[5] for there to be an independent, sometimes recalcitrant, minority, even if that minority commands no more than 25 per cent of the voting power of the company.[6] This can particularly be seen with regard to the giving of prescribed notice of general meetings. It is possible that less than the usual statutory minimum notice for an annual general meeting can be given if *all* the members entitled to attend and vote agree; for extraordinary general meetings reduced notice can be given if a majority in number holding a minimum of 90 per cent of the total voting power so agree.[7]

Furthermore, it will be possible, in the case of small private companies where *all* the members so concur, to dispense with *formal* general meetings.[8] In these circumstances, a minority shareholder who insists on his strict legal rights with regard to notices and meetings may become the object of considerable resentment from the other shareholders. The easiest solution to a problem of this nature would clearly be for the majority to buy out the minority shareholders,[9] assuming, of course, that the minority can be induced to sell.

However, where what the majority may regard as a troublesome minority refuses to be bought out, then if that minority does not command more than 10 per cent of the value of the company's shareholding, the majority may be tempted to

---

[4] See, *e.g.* the observation to this effect by Harman L.J. in *Re Bugle Press Ltd.* [1961] Ch. 270 at 287–288.

[5] Who will often, of course, also be the company's directors.

[6] A minority with no more than 25 per cent of a company's voting power would not be in a position to prevent the majority passing special and extraordinary resolutions and so, in this respect, would be devoid of "negative control".

[7] Provided the company has, by elective resolution, reduced the percentage from 95 per cent: s. 369(4) C.A. 1985 as amended by s. 115(3) C.A. 1989. See also s. 378 C.A. 1985, and see, generally, Chap. 7, *ante*.

[8] See Chap. 7, *ante* and, in particular, the "elective regime" and written resolutions, *supra*. Note also reg. 53 of Table A of the Companies (Tables A–F) Regulations 1985: see Appendix 1, *post*.

[9] Such a transaction would probably have to be at a price considerably higher than the open-market value of the minority shares: see Chap. 14, *ante*.

use the machinery of sections 428 to 430F, of the Companies Act 1985[10] to evict the minority. That any such temptation should be resisted is discussed below.

Section 429 of the Companies Act 1985 provides for the "rounding off" of a takeover operation where, pursuant to a "takeover offer"[11] a person has taken over another company and in the process[12] has acquired or contracted to acquire at least 90 per cent in value of the shareholding of the target company.[13] Dissentients may then be compulsorily bought out on the takeover terms,[14] unless the court orders, on application, that such compulsory sale shall not take effect.[15]

At first glance, therefore, it might appear an attractive proposition for the controllers of a company, assuming that they have reached the requisite 90 per cent threshold and that they wish to get rid of the remaining members, to register a new company in which they will hold 100 per cent of the shares and then to arrange for that new company to make an offer for all the shares of the original company. The next stage would be for the majority of the original company to accept the new company's offer and transfer their shares to it. The new company would thereupon invoke the machinery of section 429, above, to buy out compulsorily the minority, should that minority not be prepared willingly to sell their shares to the new company on the terms of the takeover offer. That the courts would, on application by dissentients under what is now section 430C of the Companies Act 1985, very likely refuse to support such a scheme, is clearly indicated by the leading case of *Re Bugle Press Ltd.*[16]

In this case two members of a company, X and Y, who between them held 90 per cent of the issued shares of that company, with the intention of getting rid of Z, who held the

---

[10] Pt. XIIIA C.A. 1985; this Part was substituted for the original provision of the C.A. 1985 by s. 172 of and Sched. 12 to the Financial Services Act 1986. These provisions replaced s. 209 C.A. 1948.

[11] s. 428(1) C.A. 1985; this now includes joint offers: see s. 430(D). Note also position of "associates", s. 430E.

[12] This, in particular, excludes shares already held or contracted for at the date of the offer: see ss. 428–430F.

[13] Or 90 per cent of the shares of a particular class: see s. 429(2). Note also s. 429(8).

[14] Dissentients who find themselves left "high and dry" after a successful takeover bid can also, if they wish and in the prescribed circumstances, compel the majority to buy them out at the takeover price: see s. 430 A-C, C.A. 1985. *N.B.* s. 430A(1) & (2).

[15] See s. 430C C.A. 1985; the court can alternatively by this provision "specify terms of acquisition different from those of the offer".

[16] [1961] Ch. 270.

remaining 10 per cent of the shares, formed a second company of which they, X and Y, held all the shares. The second company then offered to purchase all the shares of the first company at a stated price, an offer which, obviously, was accepted by X and Y but which was rejected by Z. The new company accordingly gave the appropriate notice under section 209 of the Companies Act 1948[17] for the compulsory acquisition of Z's shares.

The Court of Appeal, upholding the ruling at first instance, concluded that this was a situation in which the minority shareholder was entitled to resist being bought out. Even where the statutory threshold of 90 per cent has been reached by the purchaser and the onus imposed on the minority to convince the court that compulsory purchase should be disallowed is very heavy,[18] in a situation as in *Re Bugle Press Ltd.*, where the membership of the acquiring company is exactly the same as the assenting majority of the target company,[19] this onus may be regarded as being discharged. Although in *Re Bugle Press Ltd.* the minority shareholder had, in fact, objected to the price which he had been offered for his shares, it was, as Lord Evershed M.R. indicated, the "broad ground" which was important in this situation rather than details as to what would be the correct price for shares. The onus would then pass to the majority to convince the court that there was some proper reason for, in effect, evicting the minority.[20]

In *Re Hoare & Co. Ltd.*[21] Maughan J. had stated that a scheme which commanded the support of such a large majority of shareholders should prima facie, be regarded by the court as fair. Just as such a presumption was held to be displaced in *Re Bugle Press Ltd.*, it was again held to be inapplicable in *Re Chez Nico (Restaurants) Ltd.*[22] where the bidder was already a

---

[17] This provision has been replaced, as mentioned in n. 10, *ante*.

[18] As Vaisey J. pointed out in *Re Sussex Brick Co. Ltd.* [1961] Ch. 289 at 291, the onus placed on the minority is that of showing "... that he being the only man in the regiment out of step, is the only man whose views ought to prevail". Of course, there will often be more than a single dissentient but the same principle applies.

[19] This fact distinguished *Re Bugle Press Ltd.* form cases such as *Re Hoare & Co. Ltd.* (1933) 150 L.T. 374 and *Re Press Caps Ltd.* [1949] Ch. 434. These latter cases involved public companies.

[20] Such as some misbehaviour on the part of the minority sufficient to merit ejection from the company: no such reason was shown in *Re Bugle Press Ltd.*

[21] (1933) 150 L.T. 374 at 375.

[22] [1991] BCC 736. When the offer was made in this case, the company was a public company which had been formed as such under a business expansion scheme (see now the Enterprise Investment Scheme, Chap. 16, *post*).

director and shareholder of the target company and it was shown that the information made available to the assenting shareholders fell far short of what should have been provided.

C. Sale of shares in private companies by personal representatives

When the controlling shareholder of a private company dies and his shares then devolve, via his personal representatives, to members of his family or to other designated beneficiaries, it is usual for control of the company to remain in the hands of the recipients of those shares unless and until they decide to sell or otherwise dispose of them. This certainly will be the position when a testator specifically bequeaths a given number of shares to beneficiaries unless, of course, the personal representatives need to sell the shares to pay off debts of the estate. However, complications in this regard may arise where a person dies and leaves not a particular number of shares to beneficiaries but, rather, given fractions of his estate, when that estate consists of or contains shares in a private company.

The problem as envisaged above did in fact come before the court in the case of *Lloyd's Bank plc v. Duker and Others.*[23] In this case the owner of 999 out of 1,000 shares in a substantial private company (his wife held the remaining share), died, having, by his will, appointed his wife and a bank to be his executors on trust either to sell or retain his residuary estate and to pay one-half thereof to his wife, the balance to be divided among other beneficiaries as directed by the will. The testator's 999 shares, as above, were included within his residuary estate. In the event, the wife became entitled to 46/80ths of the residuary estate.[24] However, before any distribution of the testator's estate could take place, the wife also died, leaving her entire estate to X who had by now been appointed the managing director of the company.[25] X, accordingly, called upon the wife's executors to transfer to him at least 574 shares in the company, this figure being 46/80ths of the total of 999 shares.[26]

---

[23] [1987] 1 W.L.R. 1324.

[24] Including under a partial intestacy.

[25] The bank which had been one of her late husband's executors was also appointed executor under the wife's will.

[26] In fact one share had been transferred to X as nominee, so that the statutory minimum of two members could be maintained.

On objections being raised to such transfer by other beneficiaries of the original testator the bank applied to the court by way of originating summons for a ruling as to whether it should transfer the shares to X, as he had requested, or sell all 999 shares on the open market, or take some other course of action. The conclusion of the court[27] was that such a sale must be ordered. The Judge was, indeed, prepared to assume,

> "... for the purpose of answering the question that anyone entitled to an aliquot part of such an estate as this is normally entitled to insist on a corresponding part of any easily divisible property being distributed to him as it is, rather than the whole property being sold and the money proceeds distributed."

Thus, in normal circumstances a beneficiary entitled to shares from a deceased's estate[28] can take his entitlement *in specie* even if this breaks up a controlling interest in the hands of the deceased's personal representatives and so reduces the value of other beneficiaries' interests: see *Re Sandeman's Will Trusts*[29] and *Re Weiner, decd.*[30]; see also *Re Marshall*,[31] a decision of the Court of Appeal.

However, in the above three cases there was no question of any difference in value per unit between the shares distributed and those retained. On the other hand, in *Lloyds Bank plc v. Duker* it was clear that the unit value of a share in the majority block of 574 would be higher than the unit value of the remaining minority shares.[32] Thus, if the 574 shares were transferred *as shares* to X the value of what he would receive would be somewhat greater than 46/80ths of the estate to which he was entitled. In order, therefore, to "hold the scales evenly" between the relevant beneficiaries, a sale of the entire block of 999 shares on the open market was necessary. This, therefore, constituted "special circumstances" sufficient to require the normal rule in *Re Marshall*, *Re Sandeman* and *Re Weiner*,

---

[27] Mr John Mowbray Q.C., sitting as deputy High Court Judge: see p. 1326.

[28] Assuming the personal representatives do not require the shares to be sold to pay off debts.

[29] [1937] 1 All E.R. 368; shares in a private company.

[30] [1956] 1 W.L.R. 579: shares in a private company.

[31] [1914] 1 Ch. 192: shares in a public company. See also the general rule set out in *Snell's Equity* (29th ed., 1990), p. 234.

[32] For the problems of valuing majority and minority holdings in private companies see Chap. 14, *ante*.

above, to be departed from. It is also interesting to note that a similar requirement for a sale will arise where the rule in *Howe v. Earl of Dartmouth*[33] operates.

It is apparent that a situation as in *Lloyds Bank plc v. Duker* could lead to the real possibility of the control of the company passing to an "outsider", perhaps to a public company. In this particular case the judge expressly stated that X, the managing director, would be free to become a buyer of the shares on offer to the open market. Whether he could retain control of the company would thus depend on how much he was able or willing to pay for the shares relative to other purchasers; although he would clearly start with an in-built advantage.[34]

D. Directors' duties in private company takeover bids

Frequently, of course, the directors of a private company will also be the controlling shareholders. As such shareholders they will clearly be free to accept or reject any takeover proposal from any source. Sometimes, however, the directors, even though, perhaps, controlling the largest single block of shares in a private company,[35] do not control the majority voting power. In these circumstances bids to buy out the current shareholders may be made from various sources.[36] The duties of directors in

---

[33] (1802) 7 Ves. 137; the rule is, *per Snell's Equity* (29th ed., 1990), p. 226, that:

> "—where there is a residuary bequest of personal estate to be enjoyed by persons in succession, the trustees must, unless the will shows a contrary intention, realise such parts of the estate as are of a wasting character ... or of a reversionary nature ... or are otherwise not investments authorised by the general law or by the will, and invest the proceeds in some authorised security".

Shares in private companies would not be investments "authorised by the general law", *i.e.* authorised by the Trustee Investments Act 1961 for this purpose, but they could be authorised by the will itself. It is quite possible that the will will expressly exclude the rule in *Howe v. Earl of Dartmouth*. Note that the Law Reform Committee has recommended that the rule in *Howe v. Earl of Dartmouth* should be replaced by a statutory obligation to hold a fair balance between beneficiaries, particularly between interests in capital and interests in income.

[34] *i.e.* his entitlement, under the wife's will, to the value of 46/80ths of the original testator's residuary estate plus the fact that if he did lose control of the company and was replaced as managing director he would, depending on any service contract, probably be entitled to substantial compensation.

[35] Sometimes, of course, they will fall short even of that position. In the case of a private company which is the subsidiary of another company (public or private) the directors, or at least some of them, will usually be nominees of that other company.

[36] Including bids from the directors themselves: see this chapter, *post*.

this type of situation will now be discussed, particularly in the light of the judgment of Hoffmann J. in *Re a Company.*[37]

In this case a substantial private company, which had originally been a family company but in regard to which the shareholding had become somewhat dispersed with the passage of time, was the target of a takeover bid by two other companies. The beneficial holding of the directors in the target company amounted to 14 per cent of the total but a further 35 per cent was held by the directors in a trustee capacity. The directors considered that further investment in the company was necessary and were themselves prepared to make such investment. However, prior to doing so and to running the attendant risk, they were desirous of buying out the independent members.[38] Accordingly, as a vehicle to bring about this result the directors formed a new company. The new company (Company A) then made an offer for all the shares of the target company at a price which an independent accountant had expressed to be, in his view, "fair and reasonable".

Shortly after Company A's offer was made, a competing offer was made for the shares of the target company by a public company which operated in the same field of business as the target company. The public company's offer was, in cash terms, higher than that of Company A. Nevertheless, in a circular letter to the shareholders, the chairman, on behalf of the target company, set out a number of reasons why the rival offer from the public company should not be accepted and indicated that it could not succeed. This letter went on to urge, instead, acceptance of Company A's offer and indicated that, failing such acceptance, the shareholders of the target company might find themselves without any offer.

Subsequent to the issue of this circular letter the holders of 29 per cent of the issued capital of the target company petitioned the court for relief under section 459 of the Companies Act 1985. The petitioners alleged that the directors had acted in a manner unfairly prejudicial towards them, claiming that the directors were in breach of their fiduciary duty by not recommending acceptance of the higher offer. The petitioners claimed that the letter was misleading in certain particulars. The

---

[37] [1986] BCLC 382.

[38] As Hoffmann J. pointed out in his judgment, the directors were quite open about this in their communications to the shareholders and no criticism was levelled against the directors on this point.

directors applied by motion to have the section 459 petition struck out but this application was rejected by Hoffmann J.

Although Hoffmann J. accepted that it was not incumbent on the directors to make a positive recommendation for acceptance of the higher price,[39] his Lordship also concluded that it was at least arguable[40] that the chairman's circular letter had the effect of depriving the shareholders of the opportunity of selling their shares to the higher bidder or of reducing their chances of such sale, and that, in so doing, the chairman had acted in a manner which was unfairly prejudicial to the petitioners.

Thus, as his Lordship observed, at 388:

> "Whether or not the board of a company faced with competing bids is under a positive duty to advise the shareholders to accept the higher offer, I think that if the board choose to give advice on the matter, fairness requires that such advice should be factually accurate and given with a view to enabling the shareholders (who, *ex hypothesi*, are being advised to sell) to sell, if they so wish, at the best price."

However, Hoffmann J. also went on to state, at 389, that he did not think that in the instant case, where the directors, as they were perfectly entitled so to do, proposed to accept the lower offer, "... fairness can require more of the directors than to give the shareholders sufficient information and advice to enable them to reach a properly informed decision and to refrain from giving misleading advice or exercising their fiduciary powers in a way which would prevent or inhibit shareholders from choosing to take the better price".

Sometimes, indeed, as Hoffmann J. also pointed out, the directors can, particularly where private companies are concerned, discharge their duties in this regard by saying nothing. This will, presumably, cover the case where the shareholders already have sufficient information on which to make up their minds. However, as indicated, where the directors do proffer advice in this field it must certainly not be in any way misleading.[41]

---

[39] Since mere omission to make such a recommendation would not deprive the shareholders of an opportunity to accept the higher offer.

[40] Thus precluding the striking out of the s. 459 petition.

[41] It is submitted that where directors are aware that shareholders are under a misapprehension regarding a takeover bid, even though they in no way induced this, it would be the directors' duty to correct such misapprehension.

However, before leaving this topic it must also be stressed, as intimated above, that irrespective of a director's duty in the capacity of a director in connection with takeover bids, he is, in the role of a shareholder, entitled to dispose of any personal holding in the company entirely as he pleases in the same way as if he were not a director. This point is also clearly confirmed by the judgment of Hoffmann J.[42]

E. Directors' veto clauses and company takeovers

Directors' veto clauses have already been discussed, in particular with regard to family companies.[43] Where the directors of a private company take steps to block a takeover by invoking a directors' veto clause contained in the articles, they must, on application to the court by the aggrieved party and as appropriate, be prepared to justify this to the court or risk an order under section 461 of the Companies Act 1985 or an order for rectification of the register under section 359. Directors might make use of such a veto clause to stop a takeover going ahead despite the majority's wishes, on the footing that they were doing so in what they honestly believed to be the best long-term interests of the company as a whole. If the court concluded that, on balance, this was the view of the directors[44] or that it could not be demonstrated that they were primarily or substantially motivated by a wish to retain their seats on the board[45] then it would, no doubt, find the exercise of the veto provision to be justified and so would refuse relief to the petitioner.

Conversely, however, if the court were to conclude, on the evidence placed before it, that the directors had made use of such a veto provision in order to maintain their own

---

[42] His Lordship referred (see at 389) to the directors' "undoubted right as shareholders to accept the lower offer in respect of their own shares".

[43] See Chap. 13, *ante*. As previously mentioned, such provisions are by no means confined to the articles of family companies.

[44] The court's own view of the correctness of the directors' judgment would be irrelevant. The onus would be on the applicants to adduce prima facie evidence that the directors were motivated by their own and not the company's interests. If the majority also have a majority voting power (which will not invariably be the case of course), they would be in a position to dismiss the directors under s. 303 C.A. 1985 and appoint other directors who would not invoke the veto clause.

[45] Presumably the fact that the directors would benefit personally by remaining on the board would also be irrelevant if the court was satisfied that this propsect was only incidental as far as the directors were concerned.

directorships, and without proper regard to the interests of the company as a whole, it would clearly not condone the directors' actions, even if they were operating strictly within the letter of the articles.[46]

F. Private companies and the City Code

Although the City Code on Takeovers and Mergers does not usually apply to private companies it does, since June 1, 1983, apply where the private company concerned has, in the 10-year period preceding the particular transaction, had a public dealing. Thus, in particular, a company which is now a private company may have been a public company within this period.[47] But although the City Code does not, except as mentioned above, apply directly to private companies, there are circumstances in which it can have indirect relevance, as is shown in the judgment of Hoffmann J. in *Re a Company*.[48]

Thus, in considering whether the directors in that case had been guilty of unfairly prejudicial conduct for the purpose of section 459 of the Companies Act 1985 in regard to the information and advice they provided to shareholders concerning the competing offers, his Lordship found that the provisions of the City Code[49] were "a helpful guide" as to the City's view on "fairness" in this context. However, Hoffmann J. also found it necessary to point out, at 389, that, "... the detailed provisions of the Code do not necessarily coincide with the requirements of fairness for the purposes of section 459".

[46] Consider *Ebrahimi v. Westbourne Galleries Ltd.* [1973] A.C. 30 and the discussions concerning "equitable principles" as against strict contractual rights, in Chap. 12, *ante*.

[47] *cf. Re Chez Nico (Restaurants) Ltd.* [1991] BCC 736, particularly at 473 where the ruling of the Takeover Panel is cited.

[48] [1986] BCLC 382, see n. 3, *ante*.

[49] In particular general principle no. 4, from which his Lordship, as he stated in his judgment, borrowed the phrase, "sufficient information and advice to enable the shareholders to reach a properly informed decision".

Chapter 16

THE TAXATION OF PRIVATE COMPANIES

A. Introduction

Although there are no taxation provisions which apply solely to private companies, there are certain features of taxation law which apply to *most* private companies and, broadly speaking, give such companies advantages in the field of revenue law not enjoyed by larger, mostly public companies.

The purpose of this chapter is therefore to highlight those aspects of taxation law which will be of considerable significance to most private companies. No attempt will, however, be made to discuss company taxation as a topic in its entirety. It has therefore been necessary to assume, in adopting this approach, that the reader will already possess a basic understanding of taxation in general and company taxation in particular.[1]

The key statutory provisions governing the taxation of the majority of private companies are first, section 13 of the Income and Corporation Taxes Act 1988, covering "small companies",[2] and secondly, sections 414 to 430 of the Income and Corporation Taxes Act 1988, which define "close companies".[3] As intimated above these provisions do not cover all private companies, but certainly a very great number of private companies do come within their parameters.

This chapter will also consider and examine important fiscal measures which affect investors in many private companies. Sources of long-term finance for non-listed companies has been an object of government policy regardless of political ideology. The purpose of the legislation is to make it more attractive to invest in trading companies which do not have a listing and therefore enhance the growth potential of that sector of the economy. For ease of exposition, therefore, this chapter is divided into three main parts.

---

[1] The reader is referred to such standard works as *British Master Tax Guide*, CCH (13th ed., 1994/95); *Tolley's Corporation Tax 1994/95*, Saunders and Dolton (eds.).

[2] See pp. 252 *et seq.*, *post.* For necessity to make a claim see I.R. Practice Statement S.P. 1/91.

[3] See pp. 259 *et seq.*, *post.*

B. The taxation of private companies: Part I

1. *"Small companies" rate*

Since the Finance Act 1987 (No. 2) chargeable gains computed by reference to the provisions of the Tax on Capital Gains Act 1992 (T.C.G.A. 1992) are treated like other forms of income liable to Corporation Tax.

The rate of Corporation Tax applicable to small companies has been fixed at 25 per cent for the financial year ending March 31, 1995.[4] This rate applies to the profits chargeable to Corporation Tax provided the total profits of the accounting period do not exceed the limit of £300,000 imposed by the Finance Act 1994.[5] A simple example will demonstrate the operation of Corporation Tax on companies whose profits do not exceed this threshold.

W.J.B. Ltd. has results as follows for the year to March 31, 1995:

	£
Trading Income	200,000
Chargeable gains	30,000
Rental Income	10,000
Franked Investment Income	40,000

The Corporation Tax computation would be as follows:

Schedule D(1)	200,000
Schedule A	10,000
Chargeable Gains	30,000
Profits chargeable to Corporation Tax	240,000
Franked Investment Income	40,000
Profits for Small Company Rate purposes	280,000

Profits chargeable to corporation tax = £240,000 @ 25 per cent = £60,000

[4] s. 86(1) F.A. 1994.
[5] s. 86(2) F.A. 1994.

The threshold for the operation of the small companies rate was increased from £250,000 to £300,000 by the Finance Act 1994 (see *ante*). It will therefore be necessary to apportion profits which are made up to a date between March 31, 1994, and March 31, 1995, to test whether the Small Company Rate applies.[6]

Where the threshold for the application of the Small Company Rate is exceeded by profits as defined for these purposes the marginal rate of corporation tax is @ 35 per cent on the excess of such profits up to a level of £1,500,000.[7] A company therefore with trading income of say £1,400,000 for the year to March 31, 1995, would be liable to Corporation Tax as follows:

		£
1,400,000 @ 33 per cent =		462,000
− 1/50 (1,500,000 − 1,400,000) =		2,000
		460,000
This is the equivalent of:		
300,000 @ 25 per cent =	75,000	
1,100,000 @ 35 per cent =	385,000	460,000

Following the change in thresholds introduced by the Finance Act 1994, profits computed by reference to a period ending between March 31, 1994 and March 31, 1995, must be apportioned and the appropriate fraction applied to the threshold. A simple example will demonstrate the point. J.B. Ltd. makes up accounts to September 30, 1994, and has results as follows:

	£
Trading Income	280,000
Franked Investment Income	20,000

[6] s. 86(3) F.A. 1994.
[7] s. 86(1) F.A. 1994.

The Corporation Tax computation in respect of these profits would be:

	Financial Year 1993	Financial Year 1994
Schedule D (1)	140,000	140,000
Franked Investment Income	10,000	10,000
	150,000	150,000
Corporation Tax Payable:		
140,000 @ 33 per cent =		46,200
140,000 @ 25 per cent =		35,000
Less 1/50 (625,000 × 150,000) × 14/15 =		8,866
Corporation Tax Payable	37,334	35,000

2. *Advance Corporation Tax and Franked Investment Income*

The rate of Advance Corporation Tax for the financial year 1993 was 22.5/77.5 and for the financial year 1994 is 20/80.

Prior to the implementation of the set-off rules for ACT, section 241 of the Income and Corporation Taxes Act 1988 permits a company to offset or "frank" distributions made by the company against franked investment income received by the company. Franked investment income has already borne Corporation Tax in the hands of the company making the distributions but, as has been shown, it is used to determine the profit levels at which the Small Companies Rate is applied. If F11 exceeds qualifying distributions (Franked Payments) the excess is known as "surplus franked investment income": and may be carried forward for set off against future franked payments indefinitely. Where franked payments give rise to ACT which exceeds the maximum permitted (20/80 of the profits chargeable to corporation tax for the financial year

1994) this unrecovered ACT may be used in the following ways[8]:

(a) Carried back and offset against the Corporation Tax charged on income of accounting periods commencing within six years of the commencement of the year in which the unrecovered ACT arose, subject of course to the usual maximum permitted set off in each of the years used.
(b) Carried forward and set against future corporation tax liabilities. This does not apply when there is major change in the ownership of the company and in the nature or conduct of its business.[9] A change of ownership for these purposes means the acquisition by an individual of more than 50 per cent of the ordinary share capital of the company or by a group of persons each of whom holds more than 5 per cent and whose combined holdings exceed 50 per cent.
(c) Surrendered to a subsidiary.[10] The parent company must own more than 50 per cent of the equity share capital of the subsidiary and in addition own more than 50 per cent of rights to net assets on a winding-up and 50 per cent of the income rights. The recipient must be a subsidiary for the whole of the accounting period for which the ACT was paid. Only current ACT can be surrendered and the subsidiary can only use the ACT in its current accounting period or carry it forward.

It has been noted that ACT is payable only on qualifying distributions and it is therefore essential to take a closer look at distributions falling within this definition and those which fall outside it and which do not therefore give rise to ACT payments.

3. *Distributions*

The law governing distributions can best be seen in the light that every attempt is made to bring into charge to ACT any

---

[8] s. 239(3) I.C.T.A. 1988.
[9] s. 245(4) I.C.T.A. 1988.
[10] s. 240 I.C.T.A. 1988.

transaction which confers upon the recipient a benefit which is similar to that conferred by the payment of a dividend. Distributions accordingly include, *inter alia*[11]:

(a) dividends paid by the company, including capital dividends;
(b) all other distributions from the company's assets in respect of its shares (including non-cash distributions) except where such distributions are a payment of capital or are equivalent to new consideration received by the company;
(c) any redeemable share capital or any redeemable securities issued by the company in respect (a) of its own shares, or (b) securities[12] unless the issue was for new consideration;
(d) any interest or other distribution out of the assets of the company in respect of the securities of the company, where the amount distributed gives more than reasonable commercial return on the securities;
(e) any interest or distribution out of the company's assets in respect of bonus securities where the securities were issued after April 5, 1965, in respect of shareholdings, and issued after April 5, 1972, in respect of a holding of securities;
(f) any interest or distribution out of the company's assets in respect of unquoted convertible securities;
(g) any interest or distribution out of the company's assets in respect of securities giving a return related to the company's results;
(h) any interest or distribution out of the assets of the company in respect of securities connected with the shares of the company such that the holder of the securities has rights over the company's shares which are proportional to the holding of securities.

Section 210(1) I.C.T.A. 1988 deals with the rules governing the making of a bonus issue following a repayment of share capital. If a company repays share capital after April 6, 1965,

---

[11] ss. 209–211 I.C.T.A. 1988.
[12] s. 254(1) I.C.T.A. 1988. "Security" includes securities not creating or evidencing a charge on assets and interest paid by a company on money advanced without the issue of a security for the advance.

and subsequently issues new share capital as paid up without new consideration then the bonus issue will be treated as a distribution.

Section 210(2) relaxes this provision where the original share capital repaid consists of fully-paid preference shares in existence at April 6, 1965 or those issued after that date for new consideration. Where the bonus issue is of non-redeemable capital and takes place after April 5, 1973, and more than 10 years after the original repayment of capital, it will not be treated as a distribution.[13] The benefit conferred by section 210(3) I.C.T.A. 1988, however, does not apply to companies defined by section 704(D), namely, companies under the control of not more than five persons or any other company which is unquoted.

4. *Private company purchasing its own shares*[14]

It is now necessary to consider the situation where an unquoted company purchases its own shares. Section 219 I.C.T.A. states the conditions under which a purchase by a company of its own shares shall not be treated as a qualifying distribution.

First, the company must be unquoted and either be a trading company or the unquoted holding company of a trading company. Secondly, the purchase of the shares must have been made wholly or mainly for the purpose of benefiting a trade carried on by the company or any of its 75 per cent subsidiaries.

If, however, the whole, or a substantial part, of the payment for such shares is to be applied by the recipient shareholder in meeting an Inheritance Tax liability charged on death within two years of the death, the transaction will not be a qualifying distribution. If the purchase of the company's shares forms part of a scheme to permit shareholders to share in company profits without receiving a dividend, then the purchase of its shares by the company will indeed be treated as a distribution and ACT will be payable. The Revenue detailed its interpretation of how a company may satisfy the all-important "benefiting a trade" test in Statement of Practice (S.P. 2/82) which states, *inter alia*:

---

[13] s. 210(3) I.C.T.A. 1988.

[14] For this topic, generally, see Chap. 10, *ante*. The treatment possible in certain situations under the Capital Gains Tax provisions has not been considered.

> "If the problem being resolved by the transaction is a disagreement over the management of the company, the main purpose may nonetheless be to benefit a trade if the disagreement ... can reasonably be expected to have an adverse effect on the running of the trade. It would not be so however if, exceptionally, the disagreement were for example of the question of whether the company should discontinue trading and become an investment company and the shareholder being bought out advocated the continuance of trading. Where a shareholder is only reducing his proportionate interest in shares and profits ... it is less likely that the condition will be satisfied."

As far as the vendor is concerned, he must be resident and ordinarily resident in the United Kingdom in the tax year in which the purchase is made and he must have owned the shares for the whole of a period of at least five years ending with the date of purchase of the shares, under section 220 I.C.T.A. 1988. The benefits conferred by the legislation only apply if there is at least a substantial reduction in the vendor's interest as a shareholder. If the reduction in the vendor's interest is such that his new holding exceeds 75 per cent of his old holding no substantial reduction of interest would occur.[15] A simple example will demonstrate the point:

Jake sells 200 shares of £1 in Tyne Chugging Ltd.; his original shareholding is 900 shares of £1 out of an issued share capital of 1,000 shares of £1. This old holding is 90 per cent of the issued share capital and his new holding is 700 shares and consequently no substantial reduction of his shareholding has occurred.

Where the purchase by an unquoted company of its own shares is not deemed to be a distribution,[16] the payment will not give rise to a liability for ACT in the hands of the purchaser, and the recipient will be liable only to the extent of any chargeable gain which may arise.

Under the advance clearance procedures[17] the company must make an application in writing to the Board of Inland Revenue disclosing all material facts. If the Board requires further particulars it must respond within 30 days of the receipt of the original application or the receipt of any further particulars

---

[15] s. 221 I.C.T.A. 1988.
[16] ss. 219, 220 and 221 I.C.T.A. 1988.
[17] ss. 225 and 226 I.C.T.A. 1988.

required by it. If the company does not furnish the Board with the particulars it has requested within 30 days of the Board's written notice, the Board is under no obligation to proceed further with the application. The Board in turn must give its decision to the company within 30 days of its receipt of the original application or of its receipt of any further particulars required by it.

5. *Summary of Part I*

It may be helpful before considering the tax treatment of close companies to summarise the discussion so far. Private companies will usually pay Corporation Tax at the Small Companies Rate (presently 25 per cent) and this rate will apply to chargeable gains as well as other profits chargeable to Corporation Tax. Advance Corporation Tax is levied on all qualifying distributions and can be offset against the Gross Corporation Tax liability providing that the set off of ACT does not exceed an amount equivalent to 20 per cent of company profits computed for Corporation Tax purposes.

C. The taxation of private companies: Part II

1. *Close companies*

It is appropriate to consider, from the taxation point of view, those companies closely controlled by a small number of persons.

A close company is a United Kingdom resident company controlled by five or fewer participators or by any number of participators who are directors of a company over half of whose assets could be distributed on a notional winding-up among five or fewer participators or among any number of participators who are directors.

Notwithstanding the provisions of section 414 of the I.C.T.A. 1988, a company cannot be a close company if the public holds 35 per cent of the voting power of the ordinary share capital, if the ordinary shares have been listed and quoted on a recognised stock exchange within the previous 12 months and if the shares have been the subject of dealings in the previous 12 months.[18]

[18] s. 415 I.C.T.A. 1988.

There are, in effect, two possible tests of whether a company is a close company[19]:

(1) the control test;
(2) the more than 50 per cent entitlement of net assets test.

2. *Control test*

A person controls a company if he is able to control its policies whether directly or indirectly. If a person has the power to make appointments and dismissals in respect of directors then he is deemed to have control. A person is also deemed to have control if he is entitled to acquire or actually possesses more than 50 per cent of a company's issued share capital or its nominal share capital or its voting power.[20] Thus, a person who has convertible preference shares or debentures would have potential control if more than 50 per cent of the voting power would be vested in him once the conversion rights had been exercised. For example, an existing company's shareholdings are as follows:

	£
Shareholder X	500 shares
Shareholder Y	100 shares
Shareholder Z	200 shares
	800 shares

Debenture holder A has 1,000 debentures of £1 convertible into ordinary shares at one share for each debenture held. Accordingly he has control.[21]

Control must be exercised by participators who number five or fewer or by directors who are also participators without any restriction as to numbers. A participator is defined in section 417(1) of the I.C.T.A. 1988 as a person having an interest or

[19] For companies which are not to be treated as close companies despite otherwise falling within the above definition, see s. 414(5) and s. 415 I.C.T.A. 1988. Private companies which are subsidiaries of public companies will come within this exclusion: see s. 414(5) I.C.T.A.

[20] s. 416(2) I.C.T.A. 1988.

[21] Assume the authorised capital of the company is £1,800.

share in the capital or income of the company and includes a loan creditor. The definition of loan creditor[22] excludes a bank which has loaned funds to the company in the ordinary course of business, but includes creditors for money borrowed and capital assets purchased. It also includes creditors who have a right to receive income from the company, and creditors whose consideration was worth materially less to the company than the debt. Finally, the definition includes any person who has a beneficial interest in a debt in respect of which someone else is a loan creditor as defined by section 417(7) of the I.C.T.A. 1988. A participator will also include a person who has the rights and powers of associates.[23] Associates include the following[24]:

(a) the participator's partner;
(b) the participator's spouse, parent, grandparent or remoter ancestor, child, grandchild or remoter issue, brother or sister. Not included are aunts, uncles, nephews and nieces;
(c) the trustees of any settlement in respect of which the participator or any of his relations as defined in (b) above is or was the settlor.

Additionally, if the participator has an interest either beneficially or as a trustee in any shares or loans of the company which are subject to a trust, such an interest will be aggregated with his own in determining whether the company falls within the definition of a close company.[25] Frequently several participators are associated with each other but they must be linked to form the minimum number of participators; thus a husband and wife form one but if one spouse has a brother who is also a participator the total number remains one.

Section 417(5) of the I.C.T.A. 1988 defines "directors" for close company purposes and once again the definition is drawn with such width as to make it extremely difficult for people to circumvent the essential principles of close company legislation by simply claiming they are not directors. The definition includes anyone occupying the position of a director, any person whose instructions are generally followed by directors, and any person who is a manager of the company; provided they are

---

22 s. 417(7) I.C.T.A. 1988.
23 s. 417(3) I.C.T.A. 1988.
24 s. 417(3) I.C.T.A. 1988.
25 *Willingdale v. Islington Green Investment Co.* [1972] 3 All E.R. 849 (C.A.).

able to control, with associates, 20 per cent or more of the company's ordinary shares.

Even if these stringent conditions are not met a company may nonetheless be a close company if, on a notional winding-up, five or fewer participators or directors who are participators would receive more than 50 per cent of net assets.

3. *Tax implications of close companies*

It is now necessary to turn to the tax implications of a company which meets the criteria set out above. The legislation attempts to catch those transactions the effects of which would confer a benefit which would not be taxed in the hands of the recipient.

Section 418 of the I.C.T.A. 1988 deals with the provision of benefits in kind provided by the company for participators and directors and includes living accommodation, domestic services, entertainment or other benefits of whatever nature. Where such benefits are conferred the company will be deemed to have made a distribution. Relief is, however, provided where the payment would be taxed on the recipient as a benefit in kind which would be the case if he were a higher-paid employee or director.[26]

It is also given where the living accommodation is provided by reason of employment.[27] In the first case, the recipient would be taxed under Schedule E in respect of the benefit provided, but in the second, no benefit arises under Schedule E and therefore it would be inequitable to regard transactions of this type as distributions.

Additionally, relief is given where payments are made in respect of pension provision for the recipient's spouse or other dependants providing he is employed by the company. ACT is charged on distributions covered by section 418 under the quarterly accounting system and may be offset against the gross corporation tax liability in the normal way.

Next we must consider the position where loans are made by the company to participators and directors. This would be an obvious and attractive way of benefiting such people because the loan would not give rise to a tax liability in the hands of the borrower. Money misappropriated by a participator or director does not fall within the definition set out in section 419(2) of

---

[26] ss. 154–165 I.C.T.A. 1988.
[27] s. 145 I.C.T.A. 1988.

the I.C.T.A. 1988 although it could be caught if all shareholders agreed or "ratified" the misappropriation.[28] Section 419 does not apply to loans made in the ordinary course of a moneylending business, nor does it apply to loans made to directors or employees who work full time for the company, and who have no material interest in the company, providing the loan does not exceed £15,000.[29] For these purposes a material interest is defined as having control of more than 5 per cent of the ordinary share capital of the company or an entitlement to more than 5 per cent of net assets on a winding-up. Loans which are caught by the provisions of section 419 give rise to the payment of ACT at the rate appropriate to the year[30] but this is regarded as notional ACT only and therefore cannot be relieved under the provisions governing surplus ACT or offset against franked investment income.

4. *Apportionment of relevant income*

Prior to the Finance Act 1989, one of the most important consequences of close company status was the Revenue's duty to apportion a company's income to its participators. The intention of the legislation was to ensure that adequate levels of distributions were made by close companies and that the owners did not as a consequence accumulate profits in the company which were liable to lower rates of taxation than would be applicable had such profits been distributed to them. The impact of the apportionment provisions fell mainly upon non-trading as opposed to trading companies thanks to the more generous reliefs available to the latter.

The former legislation in effect applied to the fiscal context which prevailed before 1979, characterised as it was by a wide disparity between rates of personal and corporate taxation.

Since 1979 personal and corporate rates of taxation have been brought more into line and the apportionment provisions were seen by the Chancellor as complex legislation which lacked relevance. Section 103 of the Finance Act 1989 abolished all the provisions of Chapter III of Part XI of the Taxes Act 1988 in respect of accounting periods commencing after March 31, 1989. The Finance Act 1989 (section 105) defined a new type of close company known as the "close investment company". A

---

[28] *Stephens v. T. Pittas Ltd.* [1983] S.T.C. 576.
[29] s. 420 I.C.T.A. 1988.
[30] 1994/95, 20/80.

close investment company is basically a close company which is not a trading company.[31] Some private companies will be close investment companies and they will accordingly be unable to claim the small companies rate of corporation tax on their profits.

5. *Summary of Part II*

Many private companies will fall within the parameters of the legislation covering close companies. In terms of the breadth of cover the definitions of "director" and "participator" ensure that the close company provisions will apply to the majority of family owned trading companies. Although benefits provided by close companies for directors will be taxed under the normal Schedule E provisions, the legislation taxes benefits received by participators who are not employees or directors. ACT is payable on such deemed distributions. Notional ACT is also payable on loans to participators unless the relaxing provisions in respect of directors apply.

D. Taxation incentives for investors in private companies: Part III

1. *Enterprise Investment Scheme*[32]

The Enterprise Investment Scheme (E.I.S.) replaced the Business Expansion Scheme (B.E.S.) which finished on December 31, 1993. Effectively E.I.S. amends the old B.E.S. legislation. The amendments contained in Schedule 15 of the Finance Act 1994 must be considered in conjunction with the full B.E.S. provisions contained in sections 238 to 312 I.C.T.A. 1988 and sections 150 and 150A of the Tax on Capital Gains Act 1992.

2. *Definitions and qualifications to the scheme*

QUALIFYING COMPANIES

A qualifying company must be an unquoted trading company which exists for the purpose of conducting a

---

[31] s. 13A I.C.T.A. 1988.
[32] s. 137 and Sched. 15 F.A. 1994.

qualifying activity for at least three years. It need neither be resident nor incorporated in the United Kingdom although at least 50 per cent of its qualifying Business activity must be carried on in the U.K.[33]

QUALIFYING TRADES

The legislation defines certain "non-qualifying trades" which are very similar to those defined in this way for B.E.S. purposes.[34] Property Development and Farming are no longer non-qualifying trades. Where however a company has land and buildings exceeding 50 per cent of its net asset value it will not be a qualifying company unless no more than £50,000 is raised by the company under E.I.S. in any 12-month period.

ELIGIBLE SHARES

Eligible shares are new ordinary shares which carry no preferential rights to dividends or assets in a winding-up within five years of issue.[35] E.I.S. relief will not be available where the shares are issued for purposes other than a bona fide commercial one.[36] In order to prevent companies raising loan finance on favourable terms in consideration for a subscription for E.I.S. shares section 299(A) and S.P. 3/94 set out the circumstances in which the relief will be withheld.

QUALIFYING INDIVIDUAL

The rules governing qualification for an individual wishing to subscribe for eligible shares in a qualifying company are similar to those which prevailed under B.E.S. The individual subscriber cannot own or have entitlement to acquire more than 30 per cent of the issued share capital of the company. A subscriber cannot qualify if he is an employee.[37] In contrast to the B.E.S. provisions, however,

---

[33] s. 289(2), s. 293(1) and (2) I.C.T.A. 1988 and S.P. 2/94.
[34] ss. 294–298 I.C.T.A. 1988.
[35] s. 289(7) I.C.T.A. 1988.
[36] s. 289(6) I.C.T.A. 1988.
[37] ss. 291, 291A and 291B I.C.T.A. 1988.

an investor can be a paid director providing the following apply:

(i) the remuneration including any benefit in kind is a reasonable compensation for his services as a director, and
(ii) the investor has neither been connected with the company before the share issue nor been an employee of a person who carried on the trade now conducted by the company.[38]

The requirement for the subscriber to be resident or ordinarily resident in the United Kingdom has also been relaxed.[39] Under B.E.S. legislation property let by an individual to a qualifying company had the effect of denying relief for any subscription that individual might make. The E.I.S. provisions allow relief in these circumstances providing the rent is reasonable and at a commercial rate.[40]

3. *The relief provisions*

Where a claim for E.I.S. relief is made the taxpayer's claim must be made not later than 12 months after the issue of the E.I.S. certificate in respect of the eligible shares.[41] The relief provisions are as follows:

(a) The minimum subscription for qualifying is £500 and the maximum subscription for 1994/95 and subsequent years is £100,000.[42]
(b) The amount of the income tax relief available to the qualifying investor is the lower of 20 per cent of the amount subscribed (up to a maximum of £100,000 in a tax year) and the taxpayers income tax liability BEFORE deductions for personal reliefs in respect of maintenance payments, interest paid, and medical insurance premiums.[43]
(c) If the eligible shares have been issued within the first six months of a tax year relief can be claimed in respect of

---

[38] s. 291A(4) and (5) I.C.T.A. 1988.
[39] s. 291(1) I.C.T.A. 1988.
[40] s. 291A(3) I.C.T.A. 1988.
[41] s. 306(1), (6) I.C.T.A. 1988.
[42] s. 290(2) I.C.T.A. 1988.
[43] s. 289A (1), (2) and (5) I.C.T.A. 1988.

the previous tax year for up to half the value of the relevant shares up to a maximum of £15,000.

(d) E.I.S. relief will not usually be allowed unless the qualifying company has carried on its qualifying activity for four months. This condition is relaxed where the company is wound-up during this four months period as a result of bona fide business considerations.[44]

(e) Where E.I.S. shares are disposed of after the period of five years has elapsed since issue, two situations can arise in respect of Capital Gains Tax.[45] Any chargeable gain arising on disposal will be fully exempt providing the original investment qualified in full for the 20 per cent relief. An investor therefore who invested £100,000 in 1994/95 claiming £20,000 relief would not be liable to Capital Gains Tax on a sale of these shares for £200,000 in 2001/02. If however the investor was only able to claim say £10,000 by way of income tax reduction in 1994/95, any gain arising on the sale in 2001/02 would be calculated as follows:

	£	£
Disposal proceeds		200,000
Less cost	100,000	
Indexation (assumed) @ 0·30	30,000	130,000
Total gain		70,000
Less E.I.S. exemption @ $\frac{10,000}{20,000} \times 70,000 =$		35,000
Chargeable gain		35,000

(f) Where shares are disposed of within the relevant five-year period for proceeds which exceed the original cost, E.I.S. relief is withdrawn in its entirety. A capital gains tax computation will arise in the normal way.

[44] s. 289A (6)–(8) I.C.T.A. 1988.
[45] s. 150A (2) and (3) T.C.G.A. 1992.

(g) Where shares are sold at a loss, the acquisition cost is reduced by whatever E.I.S. relief has been granted thereby reducing the allowable loss.[46] This applies whether the qualifying shares are sold within the relevant five-year period or beyond it. Allowable losses which arise as a result of the sale of eligible E.I.S. shares may be relieved against the taxpayer's general income in the tax year in which the disposal takes place and/or the preceding tax year.[47]

(h) Qualifying shares in respect of which E.I.S. relief has been claimed are not available as a basis for Capital Gains Tax reinvestment relief.[48]

(i) In the event of a sale of qualifying shares within the five year relevant period E.I.S. relief will be withdrawn at the same rate of tax in respect of which the relief was given in the first instance.[49] A simple example will demonstrate the point: Gill Geddes applied for 20,000 shares in 1994/95 for £30,000 on which E.I.S. relief of £3,000 was claimed. If these shares were sold for £15,000 in the tax year 1996/97 the tax relief given in 1994/95 would be reduced by £1,500.

4. *Summary of Part III*

E.I.S. is an important source of equity finance for private companies. In some respects its provisions are more generous than B.E.S. which it replaces. The position of directors is more favourably treated and may encourage investment by those managing E.I.S. companies. The scope of the E.I.S. Scheme has been modified, reflecting more favourable treatment for property development and farming. It is difficult to judge the impact of E.I.S. upon individuals in comparison with B.E.S. The maximum tax relief under B.E.S. for an individual in any tax year was £16,000; under E.I.S. it is £20,000 but this requires an investment of £100,000 rather than £40,000 under B.E.S.

E.I.S. is a specialist area requiring close attention to the full statutory provisions of sections 289 to 312 I.C.T.A. 1988 and sections 150 and 150A T.C.G.A. 1992: the text has sought only to highlight the important features of E.I.S. as well as distinguishing it from B.E.S., its predecessor.

---

[46] s. 150A (1) T.C.G.A. 1992.
[47] s. 574 I.C.T.A. 1988.
[48] ss. 164 M.A. and 231 T.C.G.A. 1992 (s. 164 M.A. is a section of the T.C.G.A.).
[49] s. 299 I.C.T.A. 1988.

CHAPTER 17

THE DISCLOSURE REQUIREMENTS OF PRIVATE COMPANIES

A. Duty to prepare annual accounts and reports

1. *Annual accounts*

All limited companies are required to prepare and publish their accounts annually.[1] This obligation is part of the price to be paid for the benefit of limited liability. Schedule 4 to the Companies Act 1985 determines not only the content of the profit and loss account and balance sheet but also the form. Additionally, the accounts must also comply with relevant statements of standard accounting practice (SSAPs). The disclosure requirements are not altered by a company's status as a private company although there are differences in the time period in which accounts may be presented to members and lodged with the Registrar and penalties for failure: see *post*.

In the case of small and medium-sized companies, however, the disclosure requirements for statutory accounts are somewhat less onerous and all small and medium-sized companies must also be private companies. Small and medium-sized companies are defined by the Companies Act 1985, section 247(3) as amended by the Companies Act 1985 (Accounts of Small and Medium-Sized Enterprises and Publication of Accounts in ECUs) Regulations 1992.[2] However, since the majority of private companies will conform with the definition of a small company, the focus on exemptions from disclosure in this chapter will be on small, rather than medium-sized companies.

(a) *Basic requirements for all companies*

Although the law requires the signature of only one director on the face of the company's balance sheet,[3] all directers are

---

[1] s. 226(1) C.A. 1985.
[2] (S.I. 1992 No. 2452).
[3] s. 223(1) C.A. 1985.

liable to fines if the annual accounts of the company do not comply with the provisions of the Act: additionally the company and the directors are liable to fines if an unsigned balance sheet is published or circulated or delivered to the Registrar. These provisions do, of course, apply to all companies but their impact may be particularly significant in the case of private companies, where executive control is often exercised by a very small number of directors. In this respect the provisions of Companies Act 1985, sections 221 and 222, are even more important as they define stringent responsibilities for the company in terms of its day-to-day accounting records. Specifically all sums of money paid and received must be recorded and supported by appropriate explanatory material and a record must be kept showing the company's assets and liabilities.

In the case of a company dealing in goods the accounting records must also contain relevant stock records and statements of stock and details of purchases and sales which would enable the identification of these transactions with the appropriate suppliers and customers. For obvious reasons the requirement which attempts to ensure that purchases and sales can be identified with suppliers and customers is relaxed in the case of the retail trade.

In the case of a private company the accounting records which must be kept as defined above must be preserved for three years from the date upon which the transactions were recorded. It should be noted that an officer of the company on conviction is liable to imprisonment and/or fine unless all reasonable steps are taken to comply with these provisions. The provisions of section 221 place a detailed responsibility on directors of companies to keep reliable day to day records and it is the duty of auditors to form an opinion as to whether proper accounting records have been kept. Section 221 insists that the accounting records should enable the financial position of the company to be disclosed at any time and with reasonable accuracy.

The duty to prepare individual company accounts is defined by section 226 of the Companies Act 1985 and requires the directors to prepare for each financial year a balance sheet made up to the last day of the financial year and a profit and loss account for the financial year. The individual accounts must comply with the provisions of the Companies Act 1985, Schedule 4. It should be noted that the provisions of section 226 confer an overriding responsibility for preparing accounts which give a true and fair view of the state of affairs of a company and its profit or loss for the financial year. Compliance with the statutory provisions and appropriate notes must be supplemented by such additional information as may be necessary for the accounts to give a true and fair view.

(b) *Form and content of annual accounts*

It is the responsibility of the directors to prepare accounts which show a true and fair view of the profit or loss for the year and of the company's state of affairs at the end of the relevant accounting period. The signature of a director on the company's balance sheet reflects the discharge of this responsibility.

Schedule 4 sets out two formats for the balance sheet: a horizontal format and a vertical format. Today the vertical format is almost invariably used rather than the alternative. In respect of the profit and loss account, again the information can be presented horizontally or vertically but expenditure may either be analysed operationally or by type of expenditure. Thus there are four possible formats for the profit and loss account. Once a company has decided on an appropriate format for its profit and loss account and balance sheet, it must maintain consistency of presentation in future years. Should the directors decide to change the format of either of the documents they are obliged to state this and the reasons for it by way of a note to the accounts. All items appearing in the profit and loss account and balance sheet are given a reference either of a letter and/or Roman and Arabic numbers. Although these references do not have to be disclosed in the accounts, the Companies Act 1985 gives them to facilitate referencing, *e.g.* the balance sheet item "stocks" would be referenced as follows:

C. Current Assets

- I Stocks
    1. Raw materials and consumables
    2. Work in progress
    3. Finished goods and goods for resale
    4. Payments on account

(c) *Conventions of notation*

An item preceded by a letter or Roman numeral must be shown on the face of the profit and loss account or balance sheet.

Any item preceded by an Arabic number may be amalgamated with another item preceded by an Arabic number provided that the individual items are not material or the amalgamation makes it easier to appraise the state of affairs of the company. Under these circumstances the individual items must be disclosed in the notes to the published accounts.

Any item preceded by an Arabic number may be inserted in the accounts in a different position and its title may be altered should the altered title be more appropriate to the business of the company.

The law prescribes the minimum disclosure requirements and does not inhibit a company from displaying any item, whatever its reference, in greater detail than that required by the format. In the case of the profit and loss account where every item is preceded by an Arabic reference number some items must nonetheless appear on the face of the profit and loss account and cannot be disclosed by way of notes to the profit and loss account. These items are:

1. Profit or loss on ordinary activities before taxation.
2. Transfers to and from reserves.
3. Dividends paid and proposed.

Comparative figures for the previous financial year must be disclosed in the published accounts for every item which is disclosed in the profit and loss account or balance sheet or in the notes to the accounts.

2. *Directors' Report*

In addition to the duty to prepare individual company accounts, section 234 of the Companies Act 1985 imposes a duty on directors to prepare a Directors' Report. The report must contain a fair review of the company's progress over the year and of its position at the end of the year. The report also must state the amount which is recommended as dividend for the year and any transfers to reserve. It is a requirement of section 234 that the Directors' Report states the names of all persons who were directors of the company at any time in the financial year and the principal activities of the company and any material changes in those activities. The Directors' Report must also comply with Schedule 7 to the Companies Act 1985, in respect of disclosure of the following matters:

Part I	Contributions for charitable and political purposes, changes in directors' shareholdings and other matters of a general nature.
Part II	The purchase by a company of its own shares or the making of a charge upon them.
Part III	The employment, training and advancement of disabled persons.[4]
Part IV	The health, safety and welfare at work of employees.
Part V	The involvement of employees in the affairs, policy and performance of the company.[5]

The Directors' Report must be signed on behalf of the board by a director or the secretary of the company and failure to observe this requirement is an offence and renders the company and every defaulting officer liable to a fine.

3. *Auditors' report*

Except in respect of companies covered by new section 249A of the Companies Act 1985 the auditors' report is the final document required by law in support of the individual company accounts and Directors' Report.[6] The auditors must report to the company members on all annual accounts of the company to be presented in general meeting whilst they hold office. The auditors must give an opinion as to whether the annual accounts have been prepared in accordance with the Act and specifically give an opinion as to whether the balance sheet and profit and loss account give a true and fair view respectively of the state of affairs of the company at the end of the financial year and of the profit or loss for the year.

Additionally, the auditors must give an opinion as to whether the information in the Directors' Report is consistent with the annual accounts. The auditors' report must state the names of the auditors and be signed by them. An unsigned copy of the auditors' report which does not give a statement of the auditors' names will render the officers of the company liable to a fine if it is circulated or delivered to the Registrar.[7]

---

[4] This provision only applies to companies where the weekly average number of employees exceeds 250 and therefore would not apply to many private companies.
[5] See n. 4, *supra*.
[6] ss. 235–237 C.A. 1985; see Chap. 18, *post*.
[7] s. 236(4) C.A. 1985.

B. Publication of diclosures

1. *Presentation and distribution*

Once the accounts and reports have been prepared they must be sent to every member of the company, every debenture holder of the company and every person entitled to receive notice of general meetings not less than 21 days before the date of the general meeting at which they are to be presented.[8] The provision requiring 21 days' notice may be waived if all members entitled to attend and vote at the general meeting agree. This waiver may be particularly helpful to private companies with small numbers of shareholders and in effect simply gives legal recognition to what is in many cases custom and practice.

A company may well, under section 240 of the Companies Act 1985, publish non-statutory accounts but it is obliged to state that they are non-statutory accounts and also to state whether audited statutory accounts have been presented to the Registrar and whether such accounts have been qualified by the auditors. An audit report cannot be made and published in respect of non-statutory accounts. The effect of this section is to ensure that members of a company are aware that the publication of non-statutory accounts which may not accord with the provisions of the Act, does not relieve the directors of their obligations in respect of the statutory accounts.

2. *Late submission*

Section 242A of the Companies Act 1985 addresses the issue of late submission of annual accounts and reports to the Registrar and delay in laying such accounts before the company in general meeting. Excessive delay strikes at the root of the responsibilities and rights conferred by incorporation although the period allowed for laying and delivering accounts and reports and indeed the penalties are less onerous for private companies. The provisions of sections 241 and 242A provide a strong incentive to the directors of private companies to act responsibly in relation to their duties to members. It is a defence for a director charged with the offence of late submission that

---

[8] s. 238(1) C.A. 1985.

all reasonable steps were taken in order to secure compliance but the onus of proof lies with the defendant.

The period allowed for presenting and delivering accounts and reports for private companies is 10 months after the end of the relevant accounting reference period unless the accounting reference period spans more than 12 months and is the first one. In these circumstances the accounts and reports must be presented to members and delivered to the Registrar by the later of 10 months after the first anniversary of incorporation or three months after the end of the reference period.[9]

In the case of failure on the part of the directors to lay the accounts and reports of a company before the members in general meeting within the prescribed time limits every person who was a director at the end of the prescribed period is liable to a fine and also to a daily default fine for continued failure to observe this requirement. The directors are also liable to fines and additional daily default fines when they fail to deliver to the Registrar a copy of the relevant accounts and reports within the prescribed time limits. In addition to the liability of directors outlined above the company itself is liable to a civil penalty in the event of failure to lodge the accounts and reports with the Registrar within the relevant time limits as follows:[10]

Length of Period	Private Company £	Public Company £
Not more than 3 months	100	500
More than 3 months but not more than 6 months	250	1,000
More than 6 months but not more than 12 months	500	2,000
More than 12 months	1,000	5,000

A private company, therefore, which submits its accounts and reports to the Registrar more than 22 months after the beginning of its accounting reference period would be liable to a civil penalty of £1,000 in addition to the fines which would be

[9] s. 244(1) and (2) C.A. 1985.
[10] s. 242A(2) C.A. 1985.

imposed on the directors.[11] Where the directors are served with a notice requiring compliance with the obligation to file accounts and reports with the Registrar, they must comply within 14 days failing which the court may make an order requiring compliance on application of the Registrar or any member or creditor; the court may order any costs incurred by the application to be charged to the directors personally.

3. *Revision of defective accounts and reports*

Section 245 of the Companies Act 1985 provides that if it comes to the attention of the directors of a company that defective accounts or Directors' Reports have been prepared, they may revise the accounts or report.

However, where the defective accounts have been presented to the members in general meeting or lodged with the Registrar any revisions are restricted to those required to ensure compliance with the Act and the making of any alterations which become necessary as a consequence.

The Secretary of State has, under section 245A, the power to give notice to the directors of a company where defective accounts appear to have been presented to the members, sent to them or lodged with the Registrar. The notice from the Secretary of State must give a period of at least a month for the directors to provide an appropriate explanation or prepare appropriately revised accounts. In the event of failure on the part of the directors to comply with the Secretary of State's notice, he may make application to the court which may order the directors who were party to the defective accounts to bear the costs of the application and any expenses incurred by the company in connection with the preparation of revised accounts.

C. Exemptions in respect of statutory accounts

The text will focus on the disclosure requirements relating to small companies as defined by section 247(3) of the Companies Act 1985. A great many private companies will be covered by these provisions and, as stated above, it is not intended to set out the provisions applying to all private companies.

---

[11] *ibid.*

The legislation identifies certain respects in which the statutory accounts of small companies differ from other companies and also important ways in which the accounts filed with the Registrar of Companies differ from the statutory accounts.[12] The text will detail first the provisions relating to the statutory accounts.[13]

1. *Small companies*

A small company is a private company to which at least two of the following apply:

1. Annual turnover does not exceed £2.8m
2. Balance sheet total does not exceed £1.4m
3. Average number of employees does not exceed 50

Balance sheet format: small companies

Schedule 8, Part I of the Companies Act 1985, inserted by S.I. 1992 No. 2452, provides two alternative formats for the individual accounts of a small company. Format 1 is as follows:

A Called up share capital not paid

B Fixed assets

- I Intangible Assets
  1. Goodwill
  2. Other intangible assets

- II Tangible assets
  1. Land and buildings
  2. Plant and machinery, etc.

- III Investments
  1. Shares in group undertakings and participating interests
  2. Loans to group undertakings and undertakings in which the company has a participating interest
  3. Other investments other than loans
  4. Others

[12] Sched. 8, Pt. III, section A C.A. 1985.
[13] Sched. 8, Pt. I, section A and Pt. II C.A. 1985, inserted by S.I. 1992 No. 2452.

C Current Assets

I Stocks
1. Stocks
2. Payments on account

II Debtors
1. Trade debtors
2. Amounts owed by group undertakings and undertakings in which the company has a participating interest
3. Others

III Investments
1. Shares in group undertakings
2. Other investments

IV Cash at bank and in hand

D Prepayments and accrued income

E Creditors: amounts falling due within one year

1. Bank loans and overdrafts
2. Trade creditors
3. Amounts owed to group undertakings and undertakings in which the company has a participating interest
4. Other creditors

F Net current assets (liabilities)

G Total assets less current liabilities

H Creditors: amounts falling due after more than one year

1. Bank loans and overdrafts
2. Trade creditors
3. Amounts owed to group undertakings and undertakings in which the company has a participating interest
4. Other creditors

I Provisions for liabilities and charges

J Accruals and deferred income

K Capital and reserves

I Called up share capital
II Share premium account
III Revaluation reserve
IV Other reserves
V Profit and loss account

Where a small company produces a Balance Sheet in accordance with Format 2, the disclosure requirements are similarly amended.

In respect of the Statutory Notes to the Accounts of small companies *exemption from disclosure* is provided by Schedule 8, Part I, section A of the Companies Act 1985, inserted by S.I. 1992 No. 2452 in respect of the following matters in particular:

1.	Sched. 4, para. 40	Details of contingent rights to the allotment of shares covering: (i) number and amount of shares involved (ii) period duting which rights apply (iii) price to be paid
2.	Sched. 4, para. 41	Debentures Where issued in the year, a statement of the reason for issue, type issued, amount issued and consideration. Particulars of any redeemed debenture available for re-issue. Nominal amount and book value of any debentures of the company held by a nominee or trustee of the company.
3.	Sched. 4, para. 44	Land and buildings net book amount to be split between: (i) freehold (ii) long leasehold (iii) short leasehold

4.	Sched. 4, para. 47	Distinguishing between provisions for deferred tax and other taxation provisions
5.	Sched. 4, para. 48(2)	For each balance sheet item under creditors falling due after more than five years, a statement of the terms of payment or repayment, and the rates of any interest payable on the debt
6.	Sched. 4, para. 48(4)(b)	For each item shown under creditors, a note of the nature of security given
7.	Sched. 4, para. 51(2)	Details of any outstanding loans to provide assistance for the acquisition of the company's own shares
8.	Sched. 4, para. 51(3)	Dividends proposed
9.	Sched. 4, para. 53(2)	Interest or similar charges in respect of: (i) bank loans and overdrafts, and other loans made to the company, wholly repayable within five years (ii) all other loans
10.	Sched. 4, para. 53(3)	Amounts set aside for redemption of share capital and redemption of loans
	(4)	Income from listed investments
	(5)	Net rent from land
	(6)	Hire of plant and machinery
11.	Sched. 4, para. 54	Taxation —basis on which charge is computed —special circumstances affecting charge —amount of U.K. corporation tax charge —amount of UK income tax —any double tax relief (if any) —any overseas tax (if any) —tax on extraordinary items to be shown separately

12.	Sched. 4, para. 56	Employee information: (i) average numbers by category of employee; (ii) aggregate remuneration of such employees split between: • wages and salaries • social security costs • other pension costs
13.	Sched. 4, para. 27(3)	Difference between purchase cost and replacement cost of stock
14.	Sched. 4, para. 55	Analysis of turnover and profits except in respect of the percentage of turnover attributable to geographical markets outside the United Kingdom
15.	Sched. 6, para. 1(3)	Separate disclosure of directors' fees and other emoluments
16.	Sched. 6, paras. 2–5	Disclosure of the following where total directors' emoluments (including pension contributions) are £60,000 or more: (i) total emoluments waived and the number of directors concerned (ii) numbers within bands of £5,000 (iii) chairman's emoluments (iv) highest paid directors' emoluments
17.	Sched. 6, para. 7	Disclosure of pensions to former directors or their spouses

Directors Report for small companies

The following items may be excluded from the Directors Report of a small company (see Schedule 8, Part II of the Companies Act 1985, inserted by S.I. 1992 No. 2452):

(i) s. 234(a)	Fair review of the business of the company during the year, and its position at the end of it

(ii)	s. 234(1)(b)	Recommended dividend and proposed transfer to reserves
(iii)	Sched. 7, para. 1(1)	Significant changes in fixed assets
(iv)	Sched. 7, para. 1(2)	Market value of land where it is substantially different from the book value at the year end
(v)	Sched. 7, para. 5A	Purchase or maintenance of insurance provided by the company for officers or auditors of the company
(vi)	Sched. 7, para. 6	Important events occurring since the year end Future developments Research and development Indication of branches outside the United Kingdom
(vii)	Sched. 7, para. 10	Health, safety and welfare at work of company's cmployccs
(viii)	Sched. 7, para. 11	Employee involvement

Balance sheet statement

A company which qualifies as a small company in relation to a financial year is entitled to the exemptions considered above for that year if its balance sheet contains a statement (immediately above the signature required by section 233 of the Companies Act 1985) that advantage has been taken of the exemptions in the preparation of the accounts and/or the Directors' Report, and also a statement of the grounds on which, in the directors' opinion, the company is entitled to those exemptions: section 246(1A), (1B) of the Companies Act 1985.

D. Exemptions in respect of the filing of annual accounts

1. *Balance sheet, profit and loss account and Directors' Report.*

The right to file modified accounts with the Registrar of Companies does not of course relieve the directors of small companies of the burden of preparing accounting information but adds to it! The purpose of the exemptions, which we shall consider, is to allow such companies a measure of protection against competitors and possible predators. The directors must use their judgment in evaluating the extra costs of preparing two sets of accounts against the benefit in terms of protection.

In the case of small companies the "modified" accounts require the submission of a balance sheet showing only items which are referenced in the statutory format by a letter or a Roman numeral: no items referenced by an Arabic numeral need to be disclosed.[14] If a company does decide to lodge an abbreviated balance sheet with the Registrar it must disclose the aggregate amount of debtors due after one year and the total amount of creditors due within one year and after more than one year. A profit and loss account and Directors' Report need not be filed.[15]

2. *Notes to accounts*

Part III of Schedule 4 to the Companies Act 1985, details the disclosure requirements for information to be given by way of notes to the accounts if the information is not included in the accounts. The information required to be disclosed by way of note for small companies is restricted, by Part III, section A (paragraph 19, as amended) of Schedule 8, to the following:

1.	Accounting policies	para. 36, Sched. 4, Pt. III C.A. 1985.
2.	Share Capital	para. 38 "
3.	Particulars of Shares Allotted	para. 39 "
4.	Fixed Assets referenced by a letter or Roman numeral	para. 42 "
5.	Details of debts	para. 48(1) and (4)(a) "
6.	Basis of conversion of foreign currency into sterling	para. 58(1) "
7.	Corresponding amounts for previous financial year	para. 58(2) "

[14] Sched. 8, Pt. III, section A, para. 17 C.A. 1985.
[15] Sched. 8, Pt. III, section A, paras. 18 and 20 C.A. 1985.

In addition to the disclosure exemptions outlined above, information required by Part I of Schedule 6 in respect of directors emoluments need not be given. This information is no longer required in respect of the statutory accounts (see *ante*); also, the information required by section 390A(3) (Auditors remuneration) need not be given. The modified accounts must include a report by the company's auditors stating that in their opinion the directors are entitled to file modified accounts and that they have been properly prepared. The report must also include the auditors' report, except in respect of companies covered by new section 249A of the Companies Act 1985,[16] on the statutory accounts presented to members in general meeting.[17]

3. *Dormant companies*

Before summarising briefly the main provisions of the law in relation to small companies, for the sake of completeness it would perhaps be appropriate to consider the treatment of dormant companies.[18] A company cannot be dormant if it is a public company, and is dormant providing no significant accounting transaction occurs which would require inclusion in the company's records as determined by the provisions of the Companies Act 1985. A subscriber to the memorandum who takes up shares in accordance with the provisions of the memorandum does not involve the company in a significant accounting transaction. The only advantage of dormant status is that a company may make itself by special resolution exempt from those provisions of the law which relate to the audit of accounts. The special resolution must be passed, in the case of a company which has been dormant since incorporation, before the first general meeting at which the annual accounts are presented.

However, in the case of a company which has been dormant since the end of the last financial year, providing, *inter alia*, it is entitled to the exemptions conferred by section 246 on small companies, it may pass a special resolution exempting itself from the audit provisions at the general meeting at which the current accounts are to be presented. Dormant companies

---

[16] See Chap. 18, *post*.
[17] Sched. 8, Pt. III, section C, para. 24 C.A. 1985.
[18] s. 250 C.A. 1985.

therefore need not observe the audit provisions of the Companies Act, sections 238 and 239, but the copy of the balance sheet sent to the Registrar must contain a statement that the company is dormant positioned above the signature of the director who has signed the balance sheet. In the event of a company ceasing to be dormant or failing to qualify as a small company, the audit provisions automatically apply.

4. *Conclusion*

Perhaps it would be appropriate in finishing this chapter to summarise the provisions of the Companies Act 1985, as amended, in relation to the accounts of *small* companies. First, the disclosure requirements in respect of a small company's accounts have been substantially revised following the introduction of Statutory Instrument 1992 No. 2452. The effect of the legislation now incorporated into Schedule 8 of the Companies Act 1985 is to reduce the amount of information which must be disclosed and offer further protection against competitors and predators. The additional benefits to be gained where modified accounts are submitted to the registrar will always have to be considered against the accounting costs of compliance.

Chapter 18

THE AUDIT OF PRIVATE COMPANIES

A. Introduction

The requirement for a company to appoint auditors has long been regarded as an essential protection for the shareholders of limited companies. Company law had not sought to distinquish the audit requirements of substantial listed companies from those of small private companies. However, in the 1980s debate focused on the audit requirement, relating as it did, to all companies.[1] Dormant companies were already allowed to exempt themselves from the audit requirement[2] but no relief was available to small private companies.

It is not the purpose of the text to expound in detail the arguments put forward both for and against the "small company audit": in very general terms abolitionists argued for the removal of an irrelevant cost to small companies whilst protagonists argued in favour of the enhanced credibility of financial statements which had been the subject of an audit. Legislation was finally laid before Parliament on July 21, 1994[3] and the exemption from audit became a reality for certain categories of small company. The provisions of the legislation governing the audit of small companies are authorised by the powers conferred on the Secretary of State by the Companies Act 1985.[4] These provisions govern the audit of certain small companies but do not cover private companies as a class. The text will accordingly examine the audit requirements which apply to companies not covered by the exempting provisions

[1] s. 384 C.A. 1985.
[2] s. 250 C.A. 1985.
[3] (S.I. 1994 No. 1935).
[4] s. 245(3)–(5) C.A. 1985

before considering the criteria for audit exemption and the consequences of such exemption.

B. Audit requirements applying to companies not covered by new section 249A of the Companies Act 1985

1. *Appointment of Auditors*

It is duty of the company to appoint auditors[5] and the appointment must be made at the general meeting at which accounts are laid.[6] The appointment lasts until the conclusion of the next general meeting at which accounts are laid. In respect of a company which has just been formed, the first auditors can be appointed by the directors of the company to hold office until the conclusion of the first general meeting at which accounts are laid.

Although a private company, regardless of size, may, by elective resolution, dispense with the laying of accounts and reports before the company in general meeting, the provision requiring the appointment of auditors remains.[7] Once the company's annual accounts have been sent to members in accordance with the provisions of section 238 of the Companies Act 1985, the company's auditors must be appointed in general meeting within 28 days of the date on which the accounts were sent.[8] The effect of this provision is to ensure that the members are not denied the right to appoint auditors simply because the audited accounts are not laid before them in general meeting. The auditors will hold office until the end of the time for appointing auditors in respect of the next financial year.[9] A private company may, however, elect, by elective resolution,[10] to dispense with the obligation to appoint auditors annually under the provisions of section 386 of the Companies Act 1985. The effect of these provisions is that the auditors are deemed to be reappointed annually unless a resolution under section 393 terminates their appointment. On the passing of such a

---

[5] See n. 1, *ante*.
[6] s. 385 C.A. 1985.
[7] ss. 252, 379A and 385A C.A. 1985. For discussion of elective resolutions see Chap. 7, *ante*.
[8] s. 384A(2) C.A. 1985.
[9] s. 385A(5) C.A. 1985.
[10] See Chap. 7, *ante*.

resolution (or on the election ceasing to be in force) the auditors will cease to hold office at the conclusion of the next general meeting of the company at which accounts are laid or from the end of the time for reappointment in respect of the following financial year.[11]

2. *Rights of auditors*

Auditors have an onerous responsibility to the members of a company; the duties arising from this responsibility are spelt out in the provisions of section 237 of the Companies Act 1985 (see *post*). Clearly the auditors could not discharge this responsibility unless they possessed appropriate rights. In general terms the auditors have an unfettered right to information provided they are of the opinion that it is necessary for the performance of their duties as auditors, and a company officer commits an offence by providing information which is misleading, false or deceptive in a material particular.[12]

Auditors are entitled to attend all general meetings and receive all notices of, and communications relating to, general meetings: additionally they have a right to be heard on any aspect of the business which is of concern to them as auditors.[13] In respect of written resolutions of private companies which fall within the parameters of section 381A of the Companies Act 1985, the auditors are entitled to receive all communications relating to such a resolution that are required to be sent to members and also to give notice, in accordance with section 381B, of their opinion that the resolution concerns them as auditors and should be considered by a general meeting or class meeting as appropriate.[14] The detailed rights of auditors in respect of written resolutions, as set out in section 381B, have already been considered, along with proposals for the reform of the law in this respect, in Chapter 7, *ante*.

The working relationship between auditors and the management of a company is a complex one. The duties of the auditors are in relation to the members of the company but the existence of mutual trust between directors and auditors is an important ingredient; the auditors must form an opinion as to the truth and fairness of the financial statements and, especially in the

---

[11] ss. 385, 385A and 386 C.A. 1985.
[12] s. 389A(1), (2) C.A. 1985.
[13] s. 390(1) C.A. 1985.
[14] s. 390(2) C.A. 1985.

context of small private companies, confidence in the management is important. The company has the right, under section 391 of the Companies Act 1985, to remove an auditor at any time on the passing of an ordinary resolution. An auditor has a parallel right to resign under the provisions of section 392. The members of a company whose auditor has resigned or been removed are protected from management malpractice by provisions which allow the auditors to make full disclosure of the circumstances surrounding their resignation or removal.[15]

3. *Duties of auditors*

Fundamentally it is the responsibility of auditors to form an opinion as to whether the annual accounts have been prepared in accordance with the Companies Act 1985 and whether they express a true and fair view of the business. Specifically, they must form an opinion as to whether the balance sheet gives a true and fair view of the state of affairs of the company at the end of the financial year and whether the profit and loss account gives a true and fair view of the profit or loss for the year.[16] They must also express an opinion as to whether the Director's Report is consistent with the annual accounts to which it relates.[17] The auditors' report gives effect to these requirements and must be signed by the auditors and state their names.[18] This report must also accompany the accounts sent to the Registrar under section 242 of the Companies Act 1985 as well as the accounts required to be sent to members under section 238.

There are no specific investigations required by the Companies Act but the auditors have a duty to carry out whatever investigations they consider necessary.[19] They must satisfy themselves that proper accounting records have been kept as required by section 221,[20] and whether the accounts are in agreement with the underlying records. In the case of many private companies internal control procedures characteristic of large companies are inappropriate and expensive; the directors are, however, in no way relieved of their responsibility under

[15] ss. 392A and 391A C.A. 1985.
[16] s. 235(2) C.A. 1985.
[17] s. 235(3) C.A. 1985.
[18] s. 236 C.A. 1985.
[19] s. 237 C.A. 1985.
[20] See Chap. 17, *ante*.

section 221 and the auditors are required to report to the members if they are unable to form an opinion based on the accounting records which have been maintained.[21]

C. Exemptions from audit: small companies covered by new section 249A of the Companies Act 1985

1. *Introduction*

On August 11, 1994, the Companies Act 1985 (Audit Exemption) Regulations[22] came into force. For the first time, company law has removed the requirement for an audit in relation to certain active, as opposed to dormant, companies. This is effected by the Regulations inserting new sections 249A to E into the Companies Act 1985.[23] The exemptions do not apply to all private companies but to certain small companies. Companies excluded from the exemption provisions are listed in new section 249B(1) which provides that a company cannot be exempt in respect of a financial year if, at any time within that year, the company was: a public company, a banking or insurance company, an enrolled corporate insurance broker, an authorised person or appointed representative under the Financial Services Act 1986, a special register body as defined in section 117(1) of the Trade Union and Labour Relations (Consolidation) Act 1992 or an employers' association as defined in section 122 of that Act, or a parent company or subsidiary undertaking.

2. *Total exemption from audit*

In accordance with new section 249A subsections (1) and (3) of the Companies Act 1985 a private company will, subject to what is said in 4 and 5 below, be totally exempt from the audit requirement in a financial year provided it qualifies in respect of that year as a small company for the purposes of section 246 of the Companies Act 1985 and the following conditions are met:

---

[21] s. 237(2) C.A. 1985.
[22] (S.I. 1994 No. 1935).
[23] The Regulations also amend s. 388A C.A. 1985 so as to add the new category of exempt company to dormant companies as being exempt from the obligation to appoint auditors; the section goes on to provide for appointment if the company ceases to be exempt.

(i) its turnover for the year does not exceed £90,000[24]; and
(ii) its balance sheet total[25] for that year does not exceed £1.4 million.

3. *Exemption from audit subject to report*

The combined effect of subsections (2) and (4) of new section 249A of the Companies Act 1985 is that a private company which qualifies in respect of a financial year as a small company for the purposes of section 246 of the Companies Act 1985, whose balance sheet total[26] does not exceed £1.4 million and whose turnover exceeds £90,000 but is not more than £350,000[27] is, subject to what is said in 4 and 5 below, exempt from audit in that year provided its directors cause a report in respect of the company's individual accounts for the year to be prepared and made to the company's members.

The report must be prepared by a "reporting accountant"[28] eligible under the provisions of new section 249D. The reporting accountant must be a member of a recognised body as defined by new section 249D(3) and either be entitled to engage in public practice or be eligible for appointment as a company auditor. A person is ineligible for appointment as a reporting accountant if the provisions relating to independence are not met.[29] The report must, in accordance with new section 249C, state whether, in the opinion of the reporting accountant:

(i) the accounts of the company for the financial year are in agreement with the accounting records as required by section 221 of the Companies Act 1985[30]; and
(ii) based only on those records, the accounts are consistent with specific provisions of the Companies Act 1985[31]; and

---

[24] Adjusted proportionately if the period of accounts is other than one year: new s. 249A(6) C.A. 1985.
[25] This has the meaning given by s. 247(5) C.A. 1985: new s. 249A(7) C.A. 1985.
[26] See n. 25, *ante*.
[27] See n. 24, *ante*.
[28] New s. 249C(1) C.A. 1985.
[29] See. s. 27 C.A. 1989.
[30] See Chap. 17, *ante*.
[31] s. 226(3) and Sched. 4; s. 231 and Sched. 5, paras. 7–9A and 13(1), (3) and (4); s. 232 and Sched. 6 C.A. 1985, *i.e.* the reporting accountant must be satisfied that the accounts are prepared in accordance with the appropriate formats, that there is disclosure in respect of significant holdings by the company in undertakings other than subsidiaries, and that appropriate details of directors' emoluments are disclosed.

(iii) again based only on those records, the company met the requirements for exemption for the financial year and did not, at any time in that year, fall within one of the categories excluded from exemption in new section 249B(1).

4. *Statement by directors*

Neither of the exemptions considered above is available to a company unless its balance sheet contains, in accordance with new section 249B(4) of the Companies Act 1985, a statement by the directors:

(i) that the company was entitled for the year in question to exemption under subsection (1) or (2) of new section 249A of the Companies Act 1985, as appropriate;
(ii) that no notice requiring an audit has been deposited by members[32]; and
(iii) that the directors acknowledge their responsibilities for ensuring that the company keeps accounting records in accordance with section 221 of the Companies Act 1985 and for preparing accounts which give a true and fair view of the state of affairs of the company as at the end of the financial year and its profit or loss for the year, and which otherwise comply with the requirements of the Companies Act 1985.

5. *Right of members to require audit*

New section 249B(2) provides that any member or members holding at least 10 per cent of the nominal value of the company's issued share capital or any class of it, or, if the company does not have a share capital, 10 per cent of the company's members, may deposit a written notice at the company's registered office not later than one month before the end of a financial year requiring the company to obtain an audit of its accounts for that year. Where such a notice has been deposited, new section 249B(3) provides that the company is not, in respect of the financial year in question, entitled to exemption from audit under new section 249A(1) or (2).

---

[32] See *infra*.

6. *Conclusion*

The effect of the exemptions will, for a large number of small private companies, be a saving of the audit fee. On the other hand, the new provisions underline the responsibility of directors to ensure that the annual accounts and underlying records reflect the good practice required by the law. Indeed, as seen above, a pre-requisite for exemption is that the directors acknowledge, in a balance sheet statement, their responsibilities in this respect including their responsibility to ensure that the company prepares accounts which give a true and fair view.

Onerous as the duties of the reporting accountant are in respect of companies exempt under new section 249A(2) of the Companies Act 1985, and embodying as they do many of the features of the statutory audit, they do not include the need to express an opinion as to whether the accounts give a true and fair view. Gone, too, is the possibility of an auditor, in the context of a qualified report, alerting directors to the risk of the company paying an unlawful dividend, since new section 249E disapplies section 171(3) to (5) which sets out the auditor's duty in this respect.

It is worth noting, finally, that whilst new section 249E provides for certain other deemed amendments to the law in respect of companies exempt from audit,[33] there is no mention either in that section or in the Regulations[34] of sections 156(4) or 173(5) of the Companies Act 1985 each of which requires an auditors' report to substantiate a statutory declaration of solvency by directors when it is proposed that a private company provides financial assistance for the purchase of its own shares or purchases its own shares out of capital, respectively.[35] These provisions are clearly important for creditor protection and it would have been an option to reform the law to provide that such reports should be prepared by a suitably qualified person. As the law now stands, however, it appears to be the case that a private company which is exempt from the audit requirement cannot, whilst it remains so exempt, take advantage of either facility.

---

[33] Where specified, references to the auditors and the auditors' report are taken to be omitted and, where appropriate, subtituted by references to the reporting accountant and his report.

[34] (S.I. 1994 No. 1935).

[35] See Chap. 10, *ante*.

Chapter 19

COMPANIES LIMITED BY GUARANTEE

A. Introduction

For reasons which will be explained below, all companies limited by guarantee and incorporated on or after December 22, 1980, must be private companies. Prior to December 22, 1980, guarantee companies[1] could be either private companies or public companies although, in practice, most guarantee companies would be registered as private companies.

Thus, although no doubt a small number of pre-December 1980 public guarantee companies will have taken steps[2] to remain public companies, it is clear that the vast majority of guarantee companies will be private companies. In continuance, therefore, of this exposition of the law of private companies it is necessary to set out, albeit in outline only, the law of guarantee companies.

Generally speaking, the law relating to private companies limited by shares also extends to private guarantee companies; there are, however, a number of very important points of difference.

B. Liability for guarantee companies

1. *Liability of members of a guarantee company*

The extent of the liability[3] of a member of a company limited by guarantee is indicated by section 2(4) of the Companies Act 1985 which provides:

---

[1] The concept of the company limited by guarantee was introduced by the C.A. 1862, *i.e.* well before the statutory dichotomy of public/private companies appeared.

[2] See s. 5 C.A. 1980; also the Companies Consolidation (Consequential Provisions) Act 1985.

[3] But for possible additional liability, see n. 4, *infra*.

> "The memorandum of a company limited by guarantee must also state that each member undertakes to contribute to the assets of the company if it should be wound up while he is a member, or within one year after he ceases to be a member, for payment of the debts and liabilities of the company contracted before he ceases to be a member, and of the costs, charges and expenses of winding up, and for adjustment of the rights of the contributories among themselves, such amount as may be required, not exceeding a specified amount."

The liability of a member of a guarantee company is limited not by any amount outstanding on shares[4] but by the amount which such member undertakes to contribute, or is deemed so to undertake by virtue of joining the company, should he be called upon to do so on the company's winding up in the circumstances set out in the memorandum. The maximum amount of a member's liability will be whatever sum is stated in the memorandum in this regard. Although this amount can be substantial,[5] in practice and in keeping with the purposes for which probably most guarantee companies are formed,[6] usually it will be quite modest. Thus Table C of the Companies (Tables A–F) Regulations 1985,[7] the model form of memorandum[8] appropriate to a company limited by guarantee and not having a share capital, specifies the sum guaranteed by each member as not exceeding £100. However, for many, perhaps most, guarantee companies the sum specified in the memorandum will be considerably less than £100.[9]

---

[4] However in the case of a guarantee company with a share capital formed before December 22, 1980 a member will have a dual liability, on his shares and on his guarantee: see s. 74(3) Insolvency Act 1986.

[5] Obviously, prudence demands that anyone who contemplates becoming a member of a guarantee company should satisfy himself concerning the extent of his potential liability. But whatever may be the aggregate amount of the guarantee it may not be charged or mortgated by the company while it is a going concern: *Re Irish Club Ltd.* [1906] W.N. 127.

[6] See *post.*

[7] (S.I. (1985) No. 805): see Appendix 1, *post.*

[8] A model form of articles for this type of company is also contained in Table C. See Appendix 1, *post.* Articles must actually be filed, not left to be incorporated by implication as is possible with a company limited by shares: see s. 7 C.A. 1985. Note that in this context "form" does not include "contents", *per* Megarry J. in *Gaiman v. National Association for Mental Health* [1971] Ch. 317.

[9] *e.g.*, the guaranteed sum for each member in respect of the British Institute of Management, a company limited by guarantee, is an amount not exceeding £1.

2. *Liability of past members*

As is clear from section 2(4) of the Companies Act 1985, *supra*, and section 74 of the Insolvency Act 1986, a former member of a guarantee company will not be liable under his guarantee if he ceased to be a member at least one year before the winding up commenced.[10]

Further, even when a person has ceased to be a member less than a year before commencement of winding up, he is only liable on his guarantee in respect of debts contracted while he was still a member and for which, as it appears to the court, existing members are unable to satisfy the contributions required of them.[11]

C. Purpose and form of guarantee companies

1. *The purpose of modern guarantee companies*

A guarantee company can be incorporated for any lawful purpose, in just the same way as any other registered company.[12] In practice, however, the modern guarantee company will often be formed for a non-profit-making activity, *e.g.* for research, educational or other charitable purposes, as a trade or consumers' association or as a professional association.[13] Examples of some well-known organisations which are companies limited by guarantee are: the British Institute of Management; the Institute of Legal Executives; the Business and Technician Education Council; the Consumers' Association; the Advertising Standards Authority; the Open College; and the National Council for Vocational Qualifications.

It is very clear that for important specialist activities of this nature the private guarantee company is an extremely appropriate vehicle and it seems likely that the numbers of such companies on the register will continue to increase.

---

[10] In this context see *Re Bangor and North Wales Mutual Marine Protection Association Baird's Case* [1899] 2 Ch. 593.

[11] See s. 74 of the Insolvency Act 1986. See also *Re Premier Underwriting Association Ltd. (No. 1)* [1913] 2 Ch. 29.

[12] In the past, guarantee companies have been formed for the purpose, *e.g.* of the provision to members of insurance. See *Re Bangor and North Wales Mutual Marine Protection Association* and *Re Premier Underwriting Association Ltd.*, *supra*.

[13] Particularly in the latter case, the body concerned may sometimes, as it grows and becomes more established in its field, decide that a Royal Charter is more appropriate to its needs and make the requisite application therefor.

In *Jaber & ors v. Science and Information Technology Ltd. & ors.*[14] counsel for the defendants argued that the interests of a member for the purposes of an unfair prejudice petition under section 459 of the Companies Act 1985 must be directly or indirectly of a financial nature and thus a member of a guarantee company, the memorandum of which prohibits distribution of its surplus assets among its members, has no sufficient financial interest of this kind. Ferris J. responded, at 783–784:

> "I do not propose to say anything about this submission save that I should hesitate long before limiting the expression 'interests of its members' in this way as a general proposition."

2. *Companies without share capital*

Section 1(4) of the Companies Act 1985 provides as follows:

> "With effect from 22nd December 1980, a company cannot be formed as, or become, a company limited by guarantee with a share capital."[15]

This means that from the above date no *new* public guarantee companies can come into existence since, *per* section 1(3) of the Companies Act 1985,[16] one of the prerequisites of a public company is that it has a share capital.

Two further important points which may also be considered in this context are contained in section 15 of the Companies Act 1985.

First, subsection (1) provides that in the case of a company limited by guarantee and not having a share capital, anything contained in its memorandum or articles and any resolution of that company purporting to permit any person to participate in the company's divisible profits, except as a member, is void.[17]

Secondly, section 15(2), in effect, reinforces the rule that guarantee companies, other than certain pre-December 22,

---

[14] [1992] BCLC 764.

[15] This provision derives from s. 1(2) C.A. 1980. For the contents of the annual return of a company not having a share capital, see s. 364 C.A. 1985.

[16] Originally s. 1(1) C.A. 1980.

[17] Thus, each member of the company will enjoy equal rights in this regard. But note the exception covered by s. 10 of the Companies Consolidation (Consequential Provisions) Act 1985.

1980, guarantee companies,[18] must not have a share capital, by blocking what might possibly otherwise have been a way round that rule. Thus, this subsection indicates that every provision in the memorandum or articles of a guarantee company covered by this section or any resolution of such a company, which purports to divide a company's undertaking into shares or interests, shall be deemed to be a provision for share capital, even though there is no nominal amount or number specified with regard to such shares or interests.

3. *Omission of "Ltd." from company names*

Sometimes private companies, especially private guarantee companies, wish to dispense with the use of the word "limited" or "Ltd."[19] as the last word of their names. Section 30 of the Companies Act 1985, the important provision which in prescribed circumstances grants such dispensation must, therefore, now be examined.

In fact, all private guarantee companies, plus other private companies which on February 25, 1982, had a licence to omit "limited" as the last word of their names, pursuant to section 19 of the Companies Act 1948, can, under section 30 of the 1985 Act, omit "limited"[20] in the prescribed circumstances: the objects of any such company must be "the promotion of commerce, art, science, education, religion, charity or any profession, and anything incidental or conducive to any of those objects".

Further, such a company's memorandum or articles must require any profits or other income to be used for promoting its objects, must prohibit any payment of dividends to its members and must also require that all corporate assets which, on winding up would otherwise be available for members generally shall be transferred to another body with objects similar to its own, or to a charitable body, "whether or not the body is a member of the company."

Section 30(7) of the Companies Act 1985 then goes on to provide that where a company does take advantage of the above dispensation it is also exempt from the statutory requirements

---

[18] In respect of these companies the nominal share capital would have to be stated in the memorandum, *per* s. 2(5)(a) C.A. 1985.

[19] Or the Welsh equivalents. A statutory declaration may be delivered to the Registrar of Companies, *per* s. 30(4), (5) C.A. 1985.

[20] Or abbreviations, or Welsh equivalents, as appropriate.

regarding publication of the company name generally required by companies.[21] Such an exempt company is also, by this subsection, excused from sending lists of its members to the Registrar of Companies.

Nevertheless, section 351(1)(d) of the Companies Act 1985 does require that "in the case of a limited company exempt from the obligation to use the word 'limited' as part of its name, the fact that it is a limited company" must be stated in legible characters in all business letters and order forms of that company. This is in addition to the information which section 351 requires in respect of all companies.

Following from the provisions of section 30 of the Companies Act 1985, certain consequential measures are contained in section 31. Thus, in particular, a company which is permitted to omit "limited" from its name must not alter its memorandum or articles so as to cease to comply with the requirements set out in section 30(3).[22] The section also empowers the Secretary of State to order a company to change its name so that it ends with the word "limited" if it appears to him that the company has operated a business other than of promoting the objects mentioned in section 30(3), or has applied its profits or other income for purposes other than promoting such objects, or has paid a dividend to any of its members.[23]

---

[21] *e.g.* the requirements under ss. 348 and 349 C.A. 1985.
[22] See *ante*.
[23] s. 31 also provides for the imposition of fines against companies and their officers who are in default under this section.

CHAPTER 20

PRIVATE COMPANIES IN FINANCIAL DIFFICULTIES

A. Introduction

This chapter considers the statutory means first introduced by the Insolvency Act 1985 and now contained in the Insolvency Act 1986, by which a private company in financial difficulties may escape insolvent liquidation. Also considered are the legal liabilities of directors of insolvent companies whose conduct has prejudiced creditors, and the consequences of certain dispositions of, and charges created on, corporate assets prior to winding-up or administration.

B. Company rescue

1. *Cork Report*

The Report of the Cork Committee on Insolvency Law and Practice[1] in 1980 recommended two innovatory procedures by which an insolvent or doubtfully solvent company might save itself from liquidation.

First, there was a need for a facility for a company to make a binding moratorium or composition with creditors through a procedure less cumbersome and costly than that required by existing schemes of arrangement.

Secondly, if a receiver appointed by a creditor under a debenture secured by a floating charge might, if possible,

[1] Cmnd. 8558.

continue a company's business until the company had regained financial viability, why should not a similar facility be available for all companies and not merely those whose assets happened to be covered by floating charges giving the debenture holders the right to appoint a receiver? To fulfil both needs, the Insolvency Act 1986, following the Cork Committee's recommendations, made provision for voluntary arrangements which may be entered into by companies in financial difficulties and their creditors, and for a new administration procedure together with the office of administrator.

2. *Voluntary arrangements*

Schemes of arrangement under section 425 of the Companies Act 1985, formerly section 206 of the Companies Act 1948, have never proved particularly successful for insolvent companies. Not only is there the expense involved in obtaining the court's approval, but in the time between the formulation of the scheme and its taking effect on the order of the court, there is, as the Cork Committee observed, no way of enforcing an informal moratorium and therefore nothing to stop any individual creditor from enforcing his rights against the company. Whilst the Cork Committee felt that existing schemes of arrangement should continue to be available particularly to give effect to complicated schemes proposed by large companies, it recommended a new streamlined procedure for voluntary arrangements between companies and creditors, which the Committee felt "will prove of great value to small companies urgently seeking a straightforward composition or moratorium."[2] The numbers of voluntary arrangements have, however, remained comparatively small,[3] especially in years of record insolvencies, and the procedure is now subject to review by the Department of Trade and Industry.[4] The provisions relating to voluntary arrangements, which reduce the role of the court from that of sanctioner of the scheme to that of watchdog, are contained in sections 1 to 7 of the Insolvency Act 1986.

---

[2] Cmnd. 8558 at 103, para. 430.

[3] The numbers of voluntary arrangements in the years 1987–1993 are: 1987, 21; 1988, 47; 1989, 43; 1990, 58; 1991, 137; 1992, 76; 1993, 134: see Insolvency General Annual Reports for the years 1992 and 1993 (HMSO).

[4] A DTI consultation document, also covering administration procedures, was published in November 1993.

(a) *Proposal for a voluntary arrangement*

Section 1 of the Insolvency Act 1986 provides that the directors of a company, other than one which is in the process of being wound up or one in respect of which an administration order is in force, may make a proposal to the company and its creditors to effect a composition with creditors or other scheme of arrangement, to be known as a voluntary arrangement. In the cases of companies being wound up and companies subject to an administration order, the liquidator or administrator respectively may make such a proposal. The proposal must specify a nominee to supervise the implementation of the arrangement. The nominee must be a person who is qualified to act as an insolvency practitioner.

In practice, where a proposal has emanated from a liquidator or administrator, then that liquidator will act as nominee and must call meetings of the company and of its creditors to consider the proposal.[5]

Where, however, the liquidator or administrator wishes another to be nominee, or in any case where the proposal has been made by the directors, the nominee must within 28 days (or such longer period as the court may allow) of receiving notice of the proposal, report to the court on whether in his opinion meetings of the company's members and creditors should be called to consider the proposal and if so, the date, time and place proposed for the meetings. If the nominee fails to submit the required report, the court may, on the application of the proposer of the arrangement, remove the nominee and substitute another qualified insolvency practitioner.[6] It is the nominee's responsibility to summon the meetings.[7]

(b) *Approval and modifications*

The meetings must decide whether to approve the proposed voluntary arrangement, with or without modifications. The modifications may include the replacement of the nominee by another qualified insolvency practitioner. No approval can be given to proposals which affect the right of a secured creditor to

---

[5] s. 3(2) I.A. 1986.
[6] s. 2 I.A. 1986.
[7] s. 3(1) I.A. 1986.

enforce his security or which affect rights of preferential creditors unless the concurrence of such creditors has been obtained. On the conclusion of each meeting, the chairman must forthwith report its results to the court.[8] On approval, the voluntary arrangement takes effect as if made by the company at the creditors' meeting and binds every creditor entitled to vote at the meeting. Where the company is being wound up or is subject to an administration order, the court may give such directions as are necessary for facilitating the voluntary arrangement in the context of the winding-up or administration.

Alternatively, or additionally, the court may stay the winding-up proceedings or discharge the administration order, but not before 28 days have elapsed from the court receiving the reports of the meetings and not at any time when an application (or appeal in respect thereof or within the period for bringing such an appeal) to challenge the voluntary arrangement is pending.[9] Such an application to the court may be made by any person entitled, in accordance with the Insolvency Rules, to vote at either of the meetings,[10] the nominee or his replacement, or, in appropriate circumstances the liquidator or administrator. The grounds for the application must be that the voluntary arrangement unfairly prejudices the interests of any creditor, member or contributory and/or there has been a material irregularity in relation to either of the meetings.[11] The application must be made within 28 days of the court's receipt of the reports of each meeting. If the allegation is one of unfair

---

[8] s. 4 I.A. 1986.

[9] s. 5 I.A. 1986.

[10] *i.e.* all creditors who have received notice of their meeting, and members, according to their usual voting rights. The Insolvency Rules 1986, r. 1.17(3) provides, however, that a creditor is not entitled to vote in respect of a debt for an unliquidated amount or of unascertained value unless the chairman agrees to put an estimated minimum value on the debt. In *Re Cranley Mansions Ltd.* [1994] 1 W.L.R. 1610, Ferris J., exercising the court's jurisdiction under I.R. 1986, r. 1.17(7), held that where a chairman had made, without agreement, a unilateral determination of the value of a creditor's debt, there had been a material irregularity, the creditor should not have been entitled to vote, and thus the creditor was not bound by the voluntary arrangement approved at the meeting.

[11] I.R. 1986, r. 1.17(6) provides that if the chairman of the creditors' meeting is in doubt whether a claim should be admitted or rejected, he should mark it as objected to and allow the creditor to vote, subject to his vote being subsequently declared invalid of the objection is sustained. This is the only proper course for a chairman to follow when a debt is disputed, and to fail to admit creditors' votes in such circumstances is a material irregularity: *cf. Re a debtor (No. 222 of 1990) ex p. The Bank of Ireland & others* [1992] BCLC 137, a decision on the identically worded r. 5.17(6) in respect of individual insolvency.

prejudice, the court may revoke or suspend approvals given at the meetings give directions as to the calling of further meetings to consider any revised proposal, and make such supplemental directions as it thinks fit.

Where the complaint relates to an irregularity in connection with a meeting, the court may revoke or suspend any approvals given at that meeting and may direct that a further meeting be called to reconsider the original proposal, making such supplemental directions as it thinks fit, but unless a challenge is made within the 28 days, such an irregularity cannot subsequently invalidate any approval given at the meeting concerned.[12]

(c) *Appointment of a supervisor*

Once the voluntary arrangement takes effect, the nominee (or his substitute) becomes the supervisor of the scheme. The court may, on the application of the supervisor, give directions on any matter arising in the voluntary arrangement and may also, in appropriate circumstances, appoint another person to act with the supervisor or as substitute for him, or to fill a vacancy. The supervisor may, if appropriate, apply to the court for a winding-up or administration order. Any creditor or any other person dissatisfied with the conduct of the supervisor, may apply to the court which may confirm, reverse or modify the supervisor's decision, give him directions, or make any other order.[13]

3. *Administration orders*

The new administration procedure was designed to be of help, in appropriate circumstances, to all companies and not merely private companies but, perhaps inevitably, however, the vast majority of cases which have already arisen in connection with the administration procedure have involved private companies.

The statutory provisions relating to administration orders are contained in sections 8 to 27 of the Insolvency Act 1986.

---

[12] s. 6 I.A. 1986.
[13] s. 7 I.A. 1986.

(a) *Reasons for making an administration order*

Section 8 of the Insolvency Act 1986 provides that the court may make an administration order in respect of a company (other than an insurance company or a recognised bank) and appoint an administrator to manage its affairs, if the company is, or is likely to become, unable to pay its debts.[14] The court must also be satisfied that the order will be likely to achieve[15] one or more of the following purposes which are set out in section 8(3):

(a) the survival of the company and the whole or part of its undertaking as a going concern;
(b) the approval of a voluntary arrangement under the Insolvency Act 1986;
(c) the sanctioning of a compromise or arrangement under section 425 of the Companies Act 1985;
(d) a more advantageous realisation of the company's assets than would be achieved on a winding-up.

Section 8(3)(a) and 8(3)(d) purposes are often sought in the alternative; indeed they appear to be mutually exclusive.[16] It may be useful to state a section 8(3)(b) purpose for without a voluntary arrangement the administrator will not be able to produce a scheme to effect a distribution to creditors which will bind dissentients[17] and if the purpose is not stated, the administrator may be investigated in any subsequent compulsory winding-up if he puts a proposal for a voluntary arrangement to a creditors' meeting.[18]

It has been held that whilst it is not essential in a section 8(3)(b) case that there is evidence of the attitude of creditors to

---

[14] As defined by s. 123 I.A. 1986, see Chap. 21, p. 332, *post*. Thus, an order may be made if the company is unable (or is likely to become unable) to pay its debts as they fall due even though the company is solvent on a balance sheet test and all creditors could be fully paid on a realisation: *Re Imperial Motors Ltd.* (1985) 5 BCC 214; and even though there might be a surplus for distribution to members, but an administration order would not be the most suitable route if such a distribution was sought: *Re Business Properties Ltd.* (1988) 4 BCC 684.

[15] A "real prospect" of achievement must be shown and this does not require a degree of probability greater than 50 per cent (as had been suggested in *Re Consumer and Industrial Press Ltd.* [1988] BCLC 177): *Re Harris Simons Construction Ltd.* [1989] 1 W.L.R. 368, followed in *Re Primlaks (UK) Ltd.* [1989] BCLC 734 and *Re SCL Building Services Ltd.* (1989) 5 BCC 746.

[16] See Hoffmann J. in *Re Harris Simons Construction Ltd., supra.*

[17] *Re St. Ives Windings Ltd.* (1987) 3 BCC 634.

[18] *Re Sheridan Securities Ltd.* (1988) 4 BCC 200.

a voluntary arrangement, there must nevertheless be some evidence that gives reality to the prospect of a voluntary arrangement being acceptable to them.[19]

(b) *Effect of an administration order*

An application for an administration order is by petition which may be brought by the company, the directors,[20] a creditor or creditors (including any contingent or prospective creditor or creditors) or any combination of the foregoing. Notice of the petition must be given forthwith[21] to any person who has appointed or who is entitled to appoint an administrative receiver, *i.e.* the holder of a floating charge.

Where an administrative receiver has been appointed, the court must dismiss the administration petition unless either the floating charge holder has consented to the making of the administration order or the floating charge constitutes a transaction at an undervalue or a preference under sections 238 to 240 of the Insolvency Act 1986 or is liable to be avoided under section 245 of thc Insolvency Act.[22]

Sections 10 and 11 of the Insolvency Act effect a moratorium on the presentation of the petition and the making of the administration order respectively. In either case, the company cannot thereafter be wound up,[23] but an important difference in that whilst an administrative receiver may be appointed following the presentation of the petition, this is not possible after the making of the order.

---

[19] By Peter Gibson J. in *Re SCL Building Services Ltd.*, *ante*, and followed by Harman J. in *Re Land & Property Trust Co. plc (No. 2)* [1991] BCLC 849.

[20] Once a board resolution has been passed, any director may make the application and it is the duty of all the directors, including dissentients and absentees, to implement the resolution: *Re Equiticorp International plc* (1989) 5 BCC 599.

[21] The Insolvency Rules 1986, r. 2.7(1) provides that service must be effected five clear days before the date of the hearing, though r. 12.9 enables the court to abridge the time for service as occurred in *Re a Company (No. 00175 of 1987)* (1987) 3 BCC 124, where the court, having no power to appoint an interim administrator, appointed an interim manager; and *Re Gallidoro Trawlers Ltd.* [1991] BCC 691, where the court saw no need to appoint an interim manager but ordered that the directors and the company be restrained from charging or dealing with the company's assets except in the ordinary course of business and for full value.

[22] s. 9 I.A. 1986.

[23] But in the period between the presentation of the petition and the making of an administration order, a winding-up petition may be presented, though the court may restrain the advertisement of such a petition (*Re a Company (No. 001992 of 1988)* (1988) 4 BCC 451) and may also do so where there is an undertaking to present an administration petition (*Re a Company (No. 001448 of 1989)* (1989) 5 BCC 706).

Also, in either case,[24] no other steps may be taken to enforce any security[25] over the company's property or to re-possess goods in the company's possession under any hire-purchase agreement, and no other proceedings[26] or execution or other legal process[27] may be commenced or continued and no distress levied against the company or its property without the leave of the court and subject to such terms as the court may impose, following the presentation of the petition, or without the leave of the court or the consent of the administrator, following the making of the order. A secured creditor making an application to enforce his security need not show any grounds for criticising an administrator's conduct and on such an application the court will balance the interests of the secured creditor against the interests of the unsecured creditors.[28]

(c) *Powers and duties of the administrator*

The administrator is under a duty to take custody and control of the property of the company and to manage the company's affairs, business and property.[29] He has the power to do

---

[24] See s. 10(1)(b) and (c) and s. 11(3)(c) and (d) I.A. 1986.

[25] "Security" is defined in s. 248 I.A. 1986 as "any mortgage, charge, lien or other security" and has been held for the purposes of s. 11(3)(c) I.A. 1986 to include the statutory right of an airport to detain an aircraft (*Bristol Airport plc v. Powdrill* [1990] Ch. 744) and a landlord's right of re-entry (*Exchange Travel Agency Ltd. v. Triton Property Trust plc* [1991] BCC 341).

[26] It was held in *Air Ecosse Ltd. v. CAA* (1987) 3 BCC 492 that "other proceedings" in s. 11(3)(d) I.A. 1986 meant other proceedings by the company's creditors, and thus did not include an application to the CAA by a competitor to have the airline's air transport licence revoked. However, in *Carr v. British International Helicopters Ltd.* [1993] BCC 855, the Employment Appeal Tribunal, distinguishing *Air Ecosse* as being concerned with administrative proceedings, held that the appellant's complaint that he had been unfairly selected for redundancy by the company was within s. 11(3)(d): "It seems to us that there is no way of construing s. 11 so as to exclude from its scope claims under the employment protection legislation", *per* Lord Coulsfield at 862.

[27] In *Re Olympia & York Canary Wharf Ltd.; American Express Europe Ltd & Ors. v. Adamson & Ors.* [1993] BCC 154 it was held by Millet J. that "other legal process" in s. 11(3)(d) contemplated the assistance of the court and thus did not extend to the service of a contractual notice, whether or not such service was a precondition to bringing legal proceedings. Millet J. refused to follow what he took to be a dictum of Harman J. in *Exchange Travel Agency Ltd. v. Triton Property Trust plc* [1991] BCC 341 that the exercise of a landlord's right of re-entry amounted to the commencement of "other legal process".

[28] *Re Meesan Investments Ltd.* (1988) 4 BCC 788 (*sub nom. Royal Trust Bank v. Buchler* [1989] BCLC 130) where Peter Gibson J. dismissed the application of a fixed charge holder. For general guidelines on the giving of leave or consent for the purposes of s. 11, see the judgment of the Court of Appeal in *Re Atlantic Computers plc* [1990] BCC 859.

[29] s. 17 I.A. 1986.

anything necessary to facilitate such management; he may remove and appoint directors and call meetings of members and creditors, further powers being detailed in Schedule 1 to the Insolvency Act 1986. In exercising his powers the administrator is deemed to be the company's agent and a person dealing in good faith and for value with the administrator need not enquire as to whether the administrator has exceeded his powers.[30]

Section 15 of the Insolvency Act 1986 is particularly important as it deals with an administrator's powers in respect of charged property. The administrator may, without the consent of the court, dispose of any property subject to a *floating* charge as though the property were not charged, the chargee having the same rights and priority over any property directly or indirectly representing the property disposed of. Property subject to a *fixed* charge or a hire purchase agreement (including agreements for conditional sale, chattel leasing and retention of title) can only be disposed of by the administrator with the court's consent. The court's order must make it a condition that the net proceeds of any disposal, including where necessary a sum to make it up to the amount which would be realised on a sale in the open market by a willing vendor, must be used towards discharging the sums secured by the security or payable under the hire-purchase agreement.[31]

The Insolvency Act sets out the administrator's duties and a timetable for him to follow, with default fines in the absence of reasonable excuse. In particular, he must, within three months of the making of the order, (or longer period if the court so permits), lay his proposals before a creditors' meeting.[32] The proposals may be approved (with modifications if the administrator consents) or rejected by the meeting.[33] Any subsequent substantial revision of the proposals by the administrator must also be approved by a creditors' meeting.[34] The meetings must be called at 14 days' notice. Only in exceptional circumstances will the court authorise a disposal of assets without the need for the administrator to lay his

---

[30] s. 14 I.A. 1986.

[31] In *Re A.R.V. Aviation Ltd.* (1988) 4 BCC 708, Knox J. held that "sums secured by the security" included not only the capital but also any interest and costs. Knox J. was also of the opinion that the amount determined as the market sale figure should not be significantly less than the secured creditor might have realised.

[32] s. 23 I.A. 1986.

[33] s. 24 I.A. 1986.

[34] s. 25 I.A. 1986.

proposals before a creditors' meeting,[35] for example where substantial loss might result from the time taken to comply with the procedure.[36]

(d) *Protection of creditors and members*

Creditors and members are protected by section 27 of the Insolvency Act 1986 which provides a remedy against the administrator similar to the remedy afforded to minority members against controllers by sections 459 to 461 of the Companies Act 1985. At any time during which an administration order is in force, a creditor or member may petition on the ground either: that the administrator's management of the company's affairs, business and property is or has been unfairly prejudicial to the interests of creditors or members generally or of some part of its creditors or members, including at least himself; or that any actual or proposed act or omission of the administrator is or would be unfairly prejudicial. The court may make such order as it thinks fit, but may in particular regulate the administrator's future management of the company's affairs, business and property, require the administrator to do or refrain from doing a particular act, require a meeting of creditors to be summoned, or discharge the administration order.[37]

(e) *Efficacy of administration orders*

Whether administration procedure will ever, at least in its present form, make a significant numerical impact must be doubted[38] and the procedure is now subject to review by the Department of Trade and Industry.[39]

The main problem is the power of veto given by the combined effects of sections 9 and 10 of the Insolvency Act

---

[35] *Re Consumer and Industrial Press Ltd. (No. 2)* (1988) 4 BCC 72.

[36] *Re Smallman Construction Ltd.* (1988) 4 BCC 784.

[37] In *Re Charnley Davies Ltd.* [1990] BCC 605, the first s. 27 petition heard by the courts, Millett J. held that where the allegation was essentially one of professional negligence (held on the facts not to have been made out) a s. 27 petition was misconceived, though he did not rule out altogether the possibility that negligent or inadvertent conduct might be unfairly prejudicial for the purposes of the section.

[38] In 1992, the record year for insolvencies, whilst there were 24,425 insolvent liquidations and 8,324 receiverships, there were 179 administrator appointments. The figures for 1993 were 20,825, 5,362 and 122 respectively: Insolvency General Annual Report for the year 1993 (HMSO).

[39] Along with voluntary arrangement procedure. The DTI published its consultative document in November 1993.

1986 to the holder of a floating charge whose debenture contains a power to appoint an administrative receiver.[40] Such debentures are likely in practice to include the presentation of an administration petition as an event entitling the debenture holder to appoint an administrative receiver.[41] The Cork Committee had expressed the expectation that "the new procedure will be used primarily in cases where the company has not granted a debenture secured by a floating charge" but had not intended to limit the procedure to such cases.[42]

To some extent, therefore, the success of the administration procedure is dependent upon whether floating charge holders such as banks would prefer to appoint administrative receivers rather than consent to the appointment of administrators. Moreover, an administrator's remuneration and expenses are a prior charge on property subject to a *floating* charge but not on property subject to a *fixed* charge.[43]

Also, the issue of cost may prove to be a prohibitive factor for many private companies. The Cork Committee stated that administration procedure was "likely to be beneficial only in cases where there is a business of a sufficient substance to justify the expense of an Administration"[44] and, more recently, it has been argued that "the costs involved mean that the procedure is unsatisfactory for use where smaller companies are involved and accordingly the potential economic and social benefits are greatly reduced."[45]

---

[40] Note, too, the emergence in this context of the so-called "lightweight" floating charge taken by creditors whose primary security is a fixed charge, and see *Re Croftbell Ltd.* [1990] BCC 781.

[41] Floating charges created before December 29, 1986 (the day on which the Insolvency Act 1986 came into force) are deemed to include such a provision: Sched. 11, para. 1 I.A. 1986.

[42] Cmnd. 8558 at 118, para. 503.

[43] s. 19(4) I.A. 1986. Any sums payable under contracts of employment adopted by an administrator on or after March 15, 1994 have priority not only to floating charges but also to the remuneration and expenses of the administrator, but only in respect of liabilities, under such contracts, for services rendered wholly or partly after adoption: s. 19(5) and (6), as amended by, and subs. (7)–(10) as inserted by, the Insolvency Act 1994, reversing the effect of the Court of Appeal decision in *Re Paramount Airways Ltd. (No. 3)* [1994] BCC 172. The I.A. 1994 makes similar provision for contracts of employment adopted by administrative receivers.

[44] Cmnd. 8558 at 103, para. 430.

[45] Andrew Campbell, "Administration orders: white knight or white elephant?" (1993) 137 S.J. 562 at 563. But see Practice Note (Administration order applications: content of independent reports) [1994] BCC 35, where Nicholls V.-C. stated that reports which may be prepared under I.R. 1986, r. 2.2 should not be unduly detailed so as to add unnecessarily to the expense of administration procedure.

C. Liabilities of directors of insolvent companies

1. *Disqualification for unfitness*

As part of the general overhaul of insolvency legislation, the government, following the recommendations of the Cork Committee, was determined to tighten the law relating to the disqualification of unfit directors of insolvent companies. The resulting provisions, which were less stringent than those initially favoured by the government, first came into force as part of the short-lived Insolvency Act 1985 and are now contained in the Company Directors Disqualification Act 1986. The vast majority of disqualification orders involve directors of small private companies.[46]

(a) *Circumstances in which a disqualification order will be made*

Section 6(1) of the Company Directors Disqualification Act 1986 provides that the court must make a disqualification order against a person if it is satisfied that he is or has been a director of a company which has become insolvent, either while he was a director or since, and that his conduct as a director of that company, either taken alone or together with his conduct as a director of any other company or companies,[47] makes him unfit to be concerned in the management of a company.[48] The term "director" includes a *de facto* director[49] and a shadow director,[50] *i.e.* a person in accordance with whose directions or

---

[46] For the effect of a disqualification order see s. 1 C.D.D.A. 1986; Chap. 4, p. 35, *ante*.

[47] The courts have held that there must be some nexus between the director's conduct in relation to the insolvent company and any other companies considered. Thus the court is not entitled to look at conduct in relation to any company whatsoever, for example to find that the director was not unfit, *per* Peter Gibson J. *in Re Bath Glass Ltd.* (1988) 4 BCC 130. On the other hand unsatisfactory conduct in relation to other unconnected companies will not be considered if the director's conduct in respect of the insolvent company is blameless: *Re Godwin Warren Control Systems plc* [1992] BCC 557.

[48] *i.e. any* company, thus it would be no defence for a director of a public company to claim that he would be fit to manage a private company: *Re Polly Peck International plc, Secretary of State for Trade and Industry v. Ellis & Ors.* [1993] BCC 886, *per* Lindsay J. at 897.

[49] *Re Lo-Line Electric Motors Ltd.* [1988] Ch. 477, and *cf.* s. 22(4) C.D.D.A. 1986.

[50] s. 6(3) C.D.D.A. 1986.

instructions the directors are accustomed to act except that a person is not deemed to be a shadow director by reason only that the directors act on advice given by him in a professional capacity.[51] The duration of the disqualification must be a minimum of two and a maximum of 15 years.

Section 7 of the Company Directors Disqualification Act 1986 provides that an application may be made by the Secretary of State (or, at his discretion, the official receiver) if it appears to the Secretary of State expedient in the public interest that a disqualification order should be made.[52] An insolvency office holder is under a duty to report any prima facie evidence of unfitness to the Secretary of State (who may then require further information from the office holder), but it does not appear that the Secretary of State is restricted to acting only on information supplied from this source. Except with the court's leave, an application may not be made after a two-year period beginning on the day the company became insolvent.[53]

---

[51] s. 22(5) C.D.D.A. 1986. In *Re Tasbian Ltd. (No. 3)* [1992] BCC 358, Vinelott J. at first instance, [1991] BCC 435 at 443 had accepted that the dividing line between the position of a "watch-dog" or adviser imposed by an outsider creditor and a *de facto* or shadow director was difficult to draw, and the Court of Appeal held that where an adviser monitored a company's trading and controlled its bank account through the bank mandate, there was an arguable case that the individual was a shadow or *de facto* director. But for the importance of distinguishing between *de facto* and shadow directors see *Re Hydrodan (Corby) Ltd.* [1994] BCC 161 (a wrongful trading case). For a case where a specialist in assisting small and newly formed companies with financial advice and the obtaining of outside finance, accepting, in the process, seats on boards, was disqualified for the minimum period, see *Re Pamstock Ltd.* [1994] BCC 264.

[52] It was held by the Court of Appeal in *Re Southbourne Sheet Metal Co. Ltd.* [1992] BCC 797 that there is no special rule exempting the Secretary of State or official receiver from having costs awarded against them where an application is discontinued or fails after a contested hearing. Beldam L.J. warned, at 805–806, against uncritical acceptance by the Secretary of State of an office holder's report. Also, the general rule is that the Secretary of State should have his costs on a standard basis and only in exceptional circumstances on an indemnity basis: *Re Dicetrade Ltd.* [1994] BCC 371.

[53] s. 7(2) C.D.D.A. 1986. If the Secretary of State does not make an application until towards the end of the two-year period, he must then ensure that all steps are taken to bring the proceedings before the court without delay: *Re Noble Trees Ltd.* [1993] BCC 318, and for the principles relevant to striking out an application for want of prosecution see in *Re Manlon Trading Ltd.*, *The Times*, August 15, 1994. But the two-year period has to be treated as having built into it a contingency allowance for unexpected delays for which the Secretary of State is not responsible, though an extension is not automatic: *Re Copecrest Ltd.* [1993] BCC 844 (C.A.). In deciding an application for leave to bring disqualification proceedings out of time the court should take account of the length of, and reasons for, the delay, the strength of the case against the director and the degree of prejudice caused to the director by the delay, *per* Scott L.J. in *Re Probe Data Systems Ltd. (No. 3), Secretary of State for Trade & Industry v. Desai* [1992] BCC 110 at 118, a test again adopted by the Court of Appeal in *Re Tasbian Ltd. (No. 3)* [1992] BCC 358 and *Re Copecrest Ltd.*, *ante.*

For these purposes, and for the purposes of section 6, *infra*, a company becomes insolvent if it goes into liquidation[54] at a time when its assets are insufficient to meet its debts, other liabilities and the expenses of the winding-up, or an administration order[55] is made or an administrative receiver is appointed.[56] If two of these events occur, the two-year period runs from the first.[57] Section 16(1) of the Company Directors Disqualification Act 1986 provides that not less than 10 days notice of the intention to make an application must be given to the person against whom the disqualification order is sought, but it has been held by a majority decision of the Court of Appeal that this requirement is directory rather than mandatory and thus that its non-observance is a procedural irregularity which does not nullify the application.[58]

(b) *Factors to be considered in determing unfitness*

The matters for the court's consideration in determining a director's or shadow director's unfitness are set out in detail in Parts I and II of Schedule 1 to the Company Directors Disqualification Act 1986. The matters listed in Part I are: any misfeasance or breach of fiduciary or other duty by the director; misapplication of corporate property; any responsibility for company transactions at an undervalue to defraud creditors[59]; any responsibility for default in relation to keeping accounting records and registers, making the annual return, registering charges, or preparing annual accounts.

Part II lists the following: responsibility for the company's insolvency; responsibility for the company's failure to supply

[54] Time runs for the purposes of s. 7(2) C.D.D.A. 1986 from the date of the winding-up order and not the date of the presentation of the petition: *Re Walter L. Jacob & Co. Ltd., Official Receiver v. Jacob* [1993] BCC 512.

[55] But not an interim order under s. 9(4) Insolvency Act 1986: *Secretary of State for Trade and Industry v. Palmer* [1993] BCC 650.

[56] s. 6(2) C.D.D.A. 1986.

[57] *Re Tasbian Ltd.* [1990] BCC 318, the Court of Appeal affirming the decision of Peter Gibson J. at first instance, but, *per* Dillon and Woolf L.JJ., if a company was returned to solvency following the appointment of an administrator or administrative receiver and subsequently became insolvent again, a fresh two-year period should begin.

[58] *Re Cedac Ltd., Secretary of State for Trade and Industry v. Langridge* [1991] BCC 148, the Court of Appeal, by majority, allowing the appeal of the Secretary of State from the first instance decision. It has also been held that the statutory requirement is for 10 clear days notice: *Re Jaymar Management Ltd.* [1990] BCC 303.

[59] Contrary to s. 423 I.A. 1986.

any goods or services which have been paid for; responsibility for the company entering into any transaction or giving any preference liable to be set aside; failure to comply with certain statutory obligations placed on directors in relation to winding-up, administration or administrative receivership. Where the court is considering a director's conduct in relation to an insolvent company, it can have regard to matters listed in Parts I and II: in relation to any other company, Part I only is relevant.

Whilst it is clear that "ordinary commercial misjudgment" will not justify a finding of unfitness,[60] "incompetence or negligence in a very marked degree" will suffice.[61] The court, it has been said, must be satisfied that the director "has been guilty of a serious failure or serious failures, whether deliberately or through incompetence, to perform those duties of directors which are attendant on the privilege of trading through companies with limited liability."[62] The aim of section 6 of the Company Directors Disqualification Act 1986 is to protect the public, in particular the creditors of companies,[63] and this need has to be balanced against the individual liberty of the director. In *Re Cedac Ltd., Secretary of State for Trade and Industry v. Langridge*,[64] Balcombe L.J. stated:

> "While a disqualification order is not in itself penal, it is clearly restrictive of the liberty of the person against whom

---

[60] *per* Browne-Wilkinson V.-C. in *Re Lo-Line Electric Motors Ltd.* [1988] Ch. 477 at 486, where his Lordship continued:

> "In the normal case, the conduct complained of must display a lack of commercial probity, although I have no doubt that in an extreme case of gross negligence or total incompetence disqualification could be appropriate."

This test is still often cited by the courts, see, *e.g. Re EDM (Europe) Electronics Ltd.* [1991] BCC 268; *Re Austinsuite Furniture Ltd.* [1992] BCLC 1047; but, *per* Dillon L.J. in *Re Sevenoaks Stationers (Retail) Ltd.* [1991] Ch. 164, incompetence need not be total. *Re Lo-Line* involved an application under the differently framed statutory predecessor, s. 300 C.A. 1985, as did some other cases cited *infra*, the principles established in which, it is submitted, remain perfectly valid.

[61] *Re Sevenoaks Stationers (Retail) Ltd.* [1991] Ch. 164, *per* Dillon L.J. at 184. See also, *Re City Investment Centres Ltd.* [1992] BCLC 956 at 968 and 969, *per* Morrit J.

[62] *per* Peter Gibson J. in *Re Bath Glass Ltd.* (1988) 4 BCC 130 at 133. In *Re Polly Peck International plc, Secretary of State for Trade & Industry v. Ellis & Ors. (No. 2)* [1993] BCC 890, Lindsay J., at 895, perceived a "clear thread" in the authorities that a director's conduct had to be serious to justify disqualification.

[63] *Re Sevenoaks Stationers (Retail) Ltd.*, n. 61, *ante.*

[64] [1991] BCC 148 at 159.

it is made, and its contravention can have penal consequences under sec. 13."[65]

With a disqualification order of at least two years being mandatory on a finding of unfitness and the maximum period increased to 15 years,[66] it is perhaps inevitable that the longer periods of disqualification will be reserved for those cases where it is perceived that the public requires a significant degree of protection. In *Re Sevenoaks Stationers (Retail) Ltd.*,[67] Dillon L.J. in the Court of Appeal laid down the following broad guidelines: periods of disqualification over 10 years should be reserved for particularly serious cases, which might include cases where a director had been previously disqualified; two to five years was appropriate where the case was relatively[68] not very serious; the intermediate bracket should apply to serious cases which did not merit the top bracket.[69] Browne-Wilkinson V.-C. in *Re Travel Mondial Ltd.*[70] viewed as serious "an attempt to carry on the same business on the same premises, leaving behind the creditors of the old business." This, according to his Lordship, "is exactly the kind of behaviour by directors that is most to be deplored in that it is the use of the fabric of a limited company to deprive creditors of their money and simply to change the cloak in which that is done from one company to the next."[71]

Persistent failure to comply with the statutory duties to keep books, make returns and prepare accounts may itself warrant a significant period of disqualification. In *Re Swift 736 Ltd., Secretary of State for Trade and Industry v. Ettinger*,[72] Nicholls V.-C., seeking to dispel any misconceptions in the business community on this score, stated strongly:

> "It may be that, despite the disqualification provisions having been in operation for some years, there is still a

---

[65] s. 13 C.D.D.A. 1986 imposes criminal penalties for acting in contravention of a disqualification order.

[66] As compared with the predecessor provision, s. 300 C.A. 1985, where disqualification was at the court's discretion and the maximum period was 5 years.

[67] [1991] Ch. 164.

[68] *i.e.* in comparison with other cases: *per* Warner J. in *Re New Generation Engineers Ltd.* [1993] BCLC 435.

[69] In 1993, 292 directors were disqualified for 2 to 5 years; 115 for 6 to 10 years, and 12 for 11 to 15 years: Insolvency General Annual Report for the year 1993 (HMSO).

[70] [1991] BCC 224.

[71] *ibid.* at 226. Followed by Mervyn Davies J. in *Re Linvale Ltd.* [1993] BCC 654.

[72] [1993] BCC 312.

lingering feeling in some quarters that a failure to file annual accounts and so forth is a venial sin. If this is still so, the sooner the attitude is corrected the better it will be."[73]

Leaving matters to be run by another director, or other directors, will not save a director from disqualification.[74] Indeed, in many small companies, it may well be normal to expect that all directors will play an active role in management. This is not necessarily so, however, in a family company, and the following example has been given.[75]

Suppose a father who has built up a successful business hands control to his son, but remains a director because his name is useful to the business. The father receives regular reports from his son and has sight of accounts which appear to show a healthy picture. If this turns out to be false and the company has in fact been trading on creditors' money, then whilst the father might be criticised for being too trusting, it would be harsh to label him as unfit to be concerned in the management of a company.

It is now clear that failure to pay Crown debts is not an automatic ground for disqualification but that taking unfair advantage of the Crown's (or indeed any other creditor's) forbearance in pressing for payment is a ground for declaring unfitness.[76]

Whilst, as has been seen, dishonesty on a director's part is not a prerequisite to the making of a disqualification order against him, lack of dishonesty may in some cases be a mitigating factor

---

[73] *ibid.* at 315. See also *Re Tansoft Ltd.* [1991] BCLC 339, especially at 357. The fact that a director has enlisted professional help, for example from a chartered secretary may be a mitigating factor: *Re Rolus Properties Ltd.* (1988) 4 BCC 446; conversely, a higher standard in this respect is expected of a director who is a chartered accountant: *Re Cladrose Ltd.* [1990] BCC 11.

[74] *Re A & C Group Services Ltd.* [1993] BCLC 1297. It should be noted, however, that mismanagement does not of itself render a director unfit if he has acted in reliance on the advice of people on whom any reasonable person could properly expect to be able to rely: *Re Douglas Construction Services Ltd.* (1988) 4 BCC 558; and to suggest that a director acts improperly in failing to appreciate that professional financial advice is wrong is untenable: *Re McNulty's Interchange Ltd.* (1988) 4 BCC 533.

[75] In *Re Burnham Marketing Services Ltd. & Anor*; *Secretary of State for Trade and Industry v. Harper* [1993] BCC 518, by District Judge Sonnex in Slough County Court.

[76] *Re Sevenoaks Stationers (Retail) Ltd.* [1991] Ch. 164; *Re New Generation Engineers Ltd.* [1993] BCLC 435.

in reducing the duration of the order[77] and may even, when weighed with other factors, preclude a finding of unfitness.[78] Another mitigating factor may be the age of a director.[79]

(c) *Summary procedure*

In *Re Carecraft Construction Co. Ltd.*,[80] Ferris J. held that, on a disqualification application, the court has power to adopt a summary procedure and dispense with a full hearing, thus taking account of agreements and admissions of material facts. Ferris J., however, set out the following safeguards[81]:

(1) there had to be some evidence establishing the director's unfitness; mere unsupported assertions and admissions would not suffice;
(2) if the potential impact of the disputed evidence might be substantial, the court would probably decline to deal with the matter summarily;
(3) if the court was not satisfied of unfitness on the agreed evidence and also considered that the disputed evidence, even if accepted, would not tip the scales in favour of a finding of unfitness, it would no doubt dismiss the application; where the position was less clear, directions should be given for a full hearing;
(4) in case a matter being dealt with summarily was adjourned for a full hearing, parties who might properly wish, not only not to be bound by any admissions or concessions, but also to conceal the fact that they had

---

[77] *Re Lo-Line Electric Motors Ltd.* [1988] Ch. 477. See too *Re Cargo Agency Ltd.* [1992] BCC 388 and *Re GSAR Realisations Ltd.* [1993] BCLC 409 where, in each case, there was no evidence of want of probity and the minimum period of disqualification was set.

[78] *Re Bath Glass Ltd.* (1988) 4 BCC 130. But see Nicholls V.-C. in *Re Swift 736 Ltd., Secretary of State for Trade and Industry v. Ettinger* [1993] BCC 312 at 315, where, referring to persistent lapses in filing documents, he said:

> "Such lapses are serious and cannot be condoned even though, and it is right to have this fairly in mind, they need not involve any dishonest intent."

[79] In *Re Melcast (Wolverhampton) Ltd.* [1991] BCLC 288, Harman J. disqualified a director for seven rather than 10 years taking account of the fact that he was 68.

[80] [1993] BCC 336. Followed by Ferris J. in *Re Aldermanbury Trust plc* [1993] BCC 598, an application under s. 8 C.D.D.A. 1986 (disqualification after investigation of company).

[81] [1993] BCC 336 at 345–346.

been made, would be wise to protect themselves by express words.

2. *Wrongful trading*

It has already been observed that the new civil wrong of wrongful trading was one of the provisions introduced to combat the so-called "phoenix syndrome."[82] So keen was the government that liability for wrongful trading, first recommended by the Cork Committee, should take effect, that it was one of the few provisions of the Insolvency Act 1985 to be brought into force.[83]

(a) *Requirement of an application for wrongful trading*

The present provision for wrongful trading, contained in section 214 of the Insolvency Act 1986, has already been considered in outline.[84]

It will be recalled that if it appears to the court, on the application of a liquidator, that a person who is, or has been, a director or shadow director of the company in liquidation has been responsible for wrongful trading, the court may order that person to make such contribution (if any) to the company's assets as the court thinks proper.[85] In *Re Hydrodan (Corby) Ltd.*,[86] Millet J. stressed the importance of distinguishing between a *de facto* director,[87] who would also be covered by the provision, and a shadow director. Whilst the former claimed or purported to be a director, though not validly appointed as such, the latter lurked behind others who, he claimed, were the only directors of the company. Though the extension of liability to shadow directors was designed to catch individuals who, whilst not themselves directors, nevertheless act through a puppet board, the provision has caused some concern to creditor banks on whose instructions the board has become accustomed to act. In *Re a company (No. 005009 of 1987)*,[88] Knox J. was not prepared to say that the claim that a bank was

---

[82] Chap. 2, pp. 15, *et seq.*, *ante*.
[83] Together with, *inter alia*, the provisions relating to disqualification of unfit directors.
[84] Chap. 2, pp. 17–18, *ante*.
[85] s. 214(1) I.A. 1986.
[86] [1994] BCC 161.
[87] See also s. 251 which includes in the definition of "director" any person occupying the position of director, by whatever name called.
[88] (1988) 4 BCC 424.

a shadow director for the purposes of wrongful trading was "obviously unsustainable".

The company must be in insolvent liquidation,[89] a requirement which is narrower than that proposed by the Cork Committee which recommended that an application should be capable of being brought in the context of any winding-up, receivership, or administration.[90] Confining the power to make an application to the liquidator (including the official receiver where the company is in compulsory liquidation) is also more limited than the Cork Committee's proposal that any creditor or contributory should be competent to make an application.[91]

(b) *Definition of wrongful trading: "moment of truth"*

Wrongful trading is vaguely defined by reference to a point in time, a "moment of truth" prior to the commencement of the winding-up at which the director knew or ought to have concluded that there was no reasonable prospect of the company avoiding insolvent liquidation.[92] It is a defence, under section 214(3) of the Insolvency Act 1986, for the director to satisfy the court that following this "moment of truth" he took every step which he ought to take with a view to minimising the potential loss to creditors. The standard for judging what a director ought to know or conclude or what steps he ought to take, is the reasonably diligent person having both the general knowledge, skill and experience that would reasonably be expected of a person carrying out the director's functions in relation to the company, and the general knowledge, skill and experience that that director has.[93]

The test is, therefore, fundamentally objective, with a subjective element to penalise directors with specialist knowledge if they fail to make use of such knowledge. It seems, therefore, to be the clear intention of the legislature that whilst an inexperienced director who has acted in good faith, but has been unreasonably inadvertent, will have no defence if the company's financial plight would have been apparent to a reasonably diligent person in his position, an experienced

---

[89] s. 214(2)(a) I.A. 1986.

[90] Cmnd. 8558 at 401, para. 1792.

[91] *ibid.* 404, para. 1806, sub-clause (2) of the Proposed Draft Clause relating to wrongful trading.

[92] s. 214(2)(b) I.A. 1986.

[93] s. 214(4) I.A. 1986.

director with, for example, an accountancy qualification, whose specialist knowledge ought to have caused him to anticipate the imminent insolvency, cannot exculpate himself by claiming that an ordinary diligent person could not reasonably have been expected to perceive the danger signals.

Moreover, the defence in section 214(3), based on the taking of reasonable steps to protect creditors, is framed, as it must be, to cover only those who had known that there was no reasonable prospect of the company avoiding insolvent liquidation. The steps which directors might take include making an application for an administration order or a proposal for a voluntary arrangement, undertaking a voluntary winding-up of the company, or advising that a receiver be appointed, as appropriate in the circumstances. The fact that a director, lacking specialist knowledge, has acted in accordance with professional advice should be sufficient to exonerate him.

(c) *Determining liability for wrongful trading*

Whilst liability for wrongful trading applies to directors of all companies, it is inevitable that the great majority of cases will involve private companies. In so far as the Cork Committee saw its proposal as applying to under-capitalised businesses and as going "a long way to meet the criticisms of those who complain of the absence of a statutory minimum paid-up share capital for all trading companies,"[94] it was specifically directed at private companies.

Yet the objective test to determine a director's liability will not always be easy to apply in the context of a private company. Section 214 of the Insolvency Act 1986 postulates a minimum required standard of professional competence in the matters of foreseeing insolvency and taking measures to minimise the loss to creditors. The standard as set out in section 214(4) is that of the reasonably diligent person with the knowledge, skill and experience reasonably to be expected of "a person carrying out the same functions as are carried out by *that* director in relation to *the* company" (emphasis added). This must require the objective test to be tempered by a consideration of the type of company in question. In *Re Produce Marketing Consortium Ltd. (No. 2)*[95] Knox J. conceded that for the purposes of section 214:

---

[94] Cmnd. 8558 at 400, para. 1785.
[95] (1989) 5 BCC 569.

> "... the general knowledge, skill and experience postulated will be much less extensive in a small company in a modest way of business, with simple accounting procedures and equipment, than it will be in a large company with sophisticated procedures."[96]

Knox J. nevertheless held that the minimum accounting requirements of the Companies Act (*e.g.* keeping accounting records, preparing a profit and loss account) must be assumed to have been attained. On the facts of the case the accounts for 1984/85 which should have been prepared by July 1986 were not in the two directors' hands until January 1987. The relevant information was therefore taken as known by the directors at the end of July 1986, at which time they ought to have concluded that the company could not avoid insolvent liquidation. The appropriate level of contribution was, prima facie, the amount by which the company's assets had been depleted by the directors' conduct.[97] Absence of fraudulent intent was not of itself a reason for fixing a nominal or low figure but was not a fact that should be ignored totally.

Though it was held as a matter of law by Knox J. in *Re Produce and Marketing Consortium Ltd. (Halls v. David & Another)*[98] that section 727 of the Companies Act 1985, which requires a court to look at all the circumstances of the case to see whether a director has acted honestly and reasonably and ought fairly to be excused, was not available as a defence to directors in proceedings under section 214 of the Insolvency Act 1986, John Weekes Q.C. was prepared to consider the applicability of section 727 in *Re DKG Contractors Ltd.*,[99] though he held, on the facts, that the directors had acted honestly but not reasonably.

3. *Fraudulent trading*

One of the main reasons for the Cork Committee's recommending the introduction of wrongful trading was the

---

[96] *ibid.* at 594–595.

[97] Followed by Vinelott J. in *Re Purpoint Ltd.* [1991] BCC 121, but compare *Re DKG Contractors Ltd.* [1990] BCC 903 where it was held that the directors should make a contribution equal to the amount of the trade debts incurred by the company after the critical date.

[98] (1989) 5 BCC 399.

[99] [1990] BCC 903; *cf.* the approach of Hoffmann L.J. in *Re D'Jan of London Ltd.* [1993] BCC 646, Chap. 8, p. 134, *ante*.

difficulty in holding a person liable to contribute to a company's assets on the basis of fraudulent trading. Fraudulent trading was then covered by section 332 of the Companies Act 1948 which provided, unusually, both a civil remedy and a criminal penalty. The Cork Committee recommended that whilst fraudulent trading should remain as a criminal offence, it should be replaced as a civil remedy by wrongful trading.[1] Despite this recommendation civil liability for fraudulent trading has remained, though the civil and the criminal liability are dealt with by separate statutory provisions.

(a) *Definition of fraudulent trading*

Section 213 of the Insolvency Act 1986 provides that if in the course of a winding-up it appears to the liquidator that any business of a company has been carried on with intent to defraud creditors of the company or of another person or for any fraudulent purpose, he may make an application to the court. The court may, on such an application, declare that persons who were knowingly parties to such a carrying on of business are liable to make such contribution (if any) to the company's assets as the court thinks proper.

(b) *Differences between fraudulent and wrongful trading*

Fraudulent trading differs from wrongful trading in important respects. Whereas an application for wrongful trading can only be made where a company is in *insolvent* liquidation, the remedy for fraudulent trading is available in the context of *any* winding-up. Moreover, whilst wrongful trading is designed to cover the conduct of directors or shadow directors, "any persons who were knowingly parties" may be liable for fraudulent trading.

Thus, a creditor who accepts payment knowing that the debtor company has fraudulently obtained the money to make the payment is a knowing party to the fraudulent trading.[2] Where the conduct complained of is that of a director, it is likely that liquidators will now rely on wrongful rather than fraudulent trading. This is because fraudulent trading requires an intent to defraud creditors. Dishonesty involving a breach of

---

[1] Cmnd. 8558 at 399, paras. 1778–1779.

[2] *Re Gerald Cooper Chemicals Ltd.* [1978] Ch. 262, involving an allegation of fraudulent trading under s. 332 of the C.A. 1948.

commercial morality is required,[3] and whilst it has long been held that directors are liable where they know that there is no reasonable prospect of the creditors ever being paid,[4] it has been held more recently that it is sufficient if directors realise when the company incurs a debt that there is no good reason for supposing that funds will become available to pay that debt when it falls due or shortly thereafter.[5] To prefer to pay one creditor rather than another at a time when there are insufficient funds to pay all may be voidable as a preference[6] but it does not of itself constitute fraudulent trading.[7]

(c) *Sanctions and penalties for fraudulent trading*

The criminal offence of fraudulent trading is provided for by section 458 of the Companies Act 1985. The persons liable to imprisonment or a fine or both, and the improper conduct, are the same as set out in section 213 of the Insolvency Act 1986, but for the offence to be committed, the company need not have been nor need it be in the process of being, wound up.

Where a person is held liable to contribute to a company's assets on a liquidator's application in respect of either wrongful or fraudulent trading, the court may, of its own motion, make a disqualification order against that person. No minimum period is prescribed, but the maximum is 15 years.[8]

4. *Summary remedy against directors and others*

Under section 212 of the Insolvency Act 1986, if in the course of a winding-up it appears that any present or former officer of the company, any liquidator, administrator or administrative receiver, or any person who has taken part in the promotion, formation or management of the company, has misapplied, retained or become accountable for the company's money or other property, or has been guilty of any misfeasance or breach of fiduciary or other duty to the company, the court may compel him to repay, restore or account for the property, or to contribute such sum to the company's assets by way of

---

[3] *Re Patrick Lyon Ltd.* [1933] Ch. 786.
[4] *Re William C. Leitch Bros. Ltd.* [1932] Ch. 71.
[5] *R. v. Grantham* [1984] Q.B. 675; *Re a Company (No. 001418 of 1988)* [1990] BCC 526.
[6] See pp. 326–328, *post.*
[7] *Re Sarflax Ltd.* [1979] Ch. 592.
[8] s. 10 of the Company Directors Disqualification Act 1986.

compensation that the court thinks just. An application may be brought by the official receiver, liquidator, any creditor, or, with the court's leave, any contributory, it being irrelevant that the contributory does not stand to benefit from any court order. If the complaint relates to the conduct of a liquidator or administrator who has been released, an application can only be made with the leave of the court.

Section 212 is broader than its predecessor, section 631 of the Companies Act 1985, in that it extends to breaches "of any fiduciary *or other duty*" (emphasis added) thus encompassing breaches of duty of care and skill.[9] It has already been seen that a director, at least in the case of an insolvent company, owes a duty to creditors[10] but it has been held that directors who honestly tried to save a business by arranging its sale as a going concern rather than liquidating it were not in breach of fiduciary duty and were thus not liable for misfeasance.[11]

D. Avoidance of transactions entered into prior to liquidation or administration

1. *Abuse of power by controllers to undermine creditors*

There is an obvious danger that controllers of a company which is in financial difficulties will cause the company to make some disposition or create some charge which will improperly advantage certain creditors or other persons including, in some cases, themselves. The Insolvency Act 1986 contains provisions which are designed to counteract such abuses.

2. *Transactions at an undervalue*

Section 238 of the Insolvency Act 1986 provides that where a company is in administration or liquidation and has, at a relevant time, entered into a transaction at an undervalue, the court will, on the application of the administrator or liquidator, make such order as it thinks fit to restore the position to what it would have been had the transaction not been entered into. A transaction at an undervalue is a gift by the company or other

---

[9] For a liquidator's application alleging negligence by a director see *Re D'Jan of London Ltd.* [1993] BCC 646, Chap. 8, pp. 122–123, 134, *ante*.
[10] Chap. 8, pp. 114 *et seq.*, *ante*.
[11] *Re Welfab Engineers Ltd.* [1990] BCC 600.

transaction for no consideration or for consideration significantly less than that given by the company. The court will not make an order if the company entered the transaction in good faith for the purpose of carrying on its business and there were, at the time, reasonable grounds for believing that the transaction would benefit the company.

Section 240 of the Insolvency Act 1986 provides that the time the company entered into the transaction is a relevant time if it was within two years before the successful presentation of a petition for an administration order[12] or the commencement of a winding-up, provided that the company was, at that time, unable to pay its debts (for the purposes of section 123 of the Insolvency Act 1986), or became unable to do so as a result of the transaction. This requirement of insolvency is presumed, unless the contrary is shown, where the other party to the transaction was a person connected with the company.[13] A transaction at an undervalue is also caught if entered into by the company between the presentation of a petition for, and the making of, an administration order irrespective of the company's solvency after the transaction.

The court is given wide additional powers by section 241 of the Insolvency Act 1986, as amended, including *inter alia* requiring any property transferred by the company (or its proceeds in the hands of the recipient) to be vested in the company, releasing or discharging, in whole or in part, any security given by the company, and requiring the other party to pay a sum to the administrator or liquidator representing the benefits received by him. The court order may affect the property of, or impose an obligation on, a third party, but not so as to prejudice the proprietary interest of a person who acquired the interest in good faith and for value from a person other than the company; nor is a person who has received, in good faith and for value, a benefit from the transaction required to pay any sums to the administrator or liquidator unless he was a party to the transaction.

However, a person who acquires such a proprietary interest or benefit at a time when he either has notice that the company entered into the transaction at an undervalue and also of the

---

[12] This time period also applies where the company goes into liquidation immediately on the discharge of an administration order: s. 240(3)(a) I.A. 1986.

[13] A "connected person" is a director, shadow director or associate (including *inter alia* spouse, relative, business partner, employer, employee, company) of such a director or shadow director, or an associate of the company: ss. 249 and 435 I.A. 1986.

relevant insolvency proceedings, or is connected with or is an associate either of the company or the person with whom the company entered the transaction, is presumed, unless the contrary is shown, to have acquired the interest or received the benefit otherwise than in good faith.[14]

3. *Preferences*

Under section 239 of the Insolvency Act 1986 an administrator or liquidator may apply to the court to set aside a preference given by a company to any person within a relevant time period. The company gives a preference when it does anything which would advantage a creditor, surety or guarantor in the event of the company going into insolvent liquidation, but the court will not make an order unless the company was influenced in deciding to give the preference by a desire to produce the advantage. This desire is presumed, unless the contrary is shown, where the preference is given to a person connected with the company[15] provided such a person is not so connected only by reason of being the company's employee. The court can make such order as it thinks fit for restoring the position to what it would have been had the preference not been given, and the court is given the same wide additional powers as apply to orders in respect of transactions at an undervalue, with similar protection for persons who, in good faith and for value, have acquired an interest in property from a person other than the company, or received a benefit from the preference.[16]

Section 240 of the Insolvency Act 1986 provides that the relevant time within which a preference is caught by section 239 is two years before the successful presentation of a petition for an administration order[17] or the commencement or a winding-up where the preference is given to a person connected with the company (otherwise than by reason only of being the company's

---

[14] s. 241(2), (2A), (3), (3A), (3B), (3C) I.A. 1986 as amended and inserted by the Insolvency (No. 2) Act 1994.

[15] See n. 13, *ante*. For cases where the presumption was rebutted see *Re Beacon Leisure Ltd.* [1991] BCC 213 and *Re Fairway Magazines Ltd.* [1992] BCC 924.

[16] s. 241 I.A. 1986 as amended by the Insolvency (No. 2) Act 1994; see discussion of transactions at an undervalue, *ante*, for fuller details. But a person receiving a benefit from a preference in good faith and for value is not protected from having to make payment to the administrator or liquidator if the payment is in respect of a preference given to that person as a creditor: s. 241(2).

[17] This time period also applies where the company goes into liquidation immediately on the discharge of the administration order: s. 240(3)(a) I.A. 1986.

employee), or six months before either of these events where the preference is given to any other person and not at an undervalue, provided in each case the company was unable to pay its debts (for the purposes of section 123 of the Insolvency Act 1986), at the time or became unable to pay its debts as a result of the preference. A preference is also given at a relevant time when it is given to any person between the presentation of a petition for, and the making of, an administration order, irrespective of whether or not the company is solvent after the preference is given.

In *Re Fairway Magazines Ltd.*[18] Mummery J. summarised as follows the principal points to emerge from the earlier cases *Re M. C. Bacon Ltd.*[19] and *Re Beacon Leisure Ltd.*[20] on the interpretation of section 239:

(1) in contrast to the old law of fraudulent preference, it is no longer necessary to prove commercial dishonesty in the form of a dominant intention to prefer; the test is, rather, whether the decision was influenced by a desire to produce the effect of improving the creditor's position in the event of an insolvent liquidation;
(2) a desire to produce that effect is a subjective state of mind which may be inferred from all the relevant circumstances;
(3) a desire to grant a debenture or make a payment does not necessarily equate with a desire to prefer the creditor since the company may be influenced by proper commercial considerations and not by a positive wish to improve the creditor's position in the event of insolvent liquidation, but if the desire to prefer is present, it is sufficient that it influences the decision, without it having to be the sole or decisive influence.

On the facts, Mummery J. held that the company was solely influenced, in granting a debenture, by the desire to raise money from a source other than the bank, which had placed an upper limit on the company's overdraft, in order that the company could continue trading. It is no defence that the company

---

[18] [1992] BCC 924.
[19] [1990] BCC 78, where it was held that granting a debenture to a bank when the company was motivated by the desire to avoid an overdraft being called in and so to be able to continue trading did not constitute a preference.
[20] [1991] BCC 213.

controllers, who cause the company to make the disposition at issue, believe that all the creditors will eventually be paid off in full, but it is otherwise if they believe that debts can be paid as they fall due.[21]

4. *Avoidance of floating charges*

To deter a controller of a company in financial difficulties from attempting to place himself or others in priority to unsecured creditors in a liquidation by causing the company to execute a floating charge in his or their favour, the Insolvency Act 1986 provides that floating charges may, in certain circumstances, be avoided.

Section 245 of the Insolvency Act 1986 provides that a floating charge is, subject to what is said below, invalid if created:

(i) in favour of a person connected with the company[22] within two years of the presentation of a petition for an administration order or the commencement of a winding-up[23]; or
(ii) in favour of a person other than a connected person within 12 months before the presentation of a petition for an administration order or the commencement of a winding-up, provided that the company was unable to pay its debts when the charge was created or became unable to do so as a result of the transaction under which the charge was created; or
(iii) in favour of any person between the presentation of a petition for, and the making of, an administration order.

Floating charges created within the above time will not be invalid, however, to the extent of any consideration[24] given to

---

[21] *Re F. P. and C. H. Matthews Ltd.* [1982] Ch. 257; *Re Time Utilising Business Systems Ltd.* (1989) 5 BCC 851.

[22] See n. 13, *ante*.

[23] s. 245 does not take effect in the case of a compulsory liquidation until the winding up order is made, but on the making of the order, the invalidity of the floating charge relates back to the date of the presentation of the petition: *Re Shoe Lace Ltd., Power v. Sharp Investments Ltd. & Anor.* [1993] BCC 609 (C.A.) applying *Mace Builders (Glasgow) Ltd. v. Lunn* (1986) 2 BCC 99, 532.

[24] Such consideration is the aggregate value of money paid, goods or services supplied (at their reasonable market value at the time they were supplied), and the discharge or reduction of any debt of the company: s. 245(2), (6) I.A. 1986.

the company[25] at the same time as, or after, the creation of the charge[26] together with interest, if any.

[25] If the payment is made in order that the company can reduce its bank overdraft which in turn reduces the payer's guarantee liability then it is not paid "to the company" since the money never becomes available to the company to use as it likes: *Re Fairway Magazines Ltd.* [1992] BCC 924 following *Re Orleans Motor Co. Ltd.* [1911] 2 Ch. 41. But provided the company benefits in some way from the payment, it does not matter that the floating charge holder also benefits: *Re Matthew Ellis Ltd.* [1933] Ch. 458.

[26] In *Re Shoe Lace Ltd.*, n. 23 *ante*, the Court of Appeal, affirming Hoffmann J. at first instance, held that the purpose of the words "at the same time as, or after, the creation of the charge" was to exclude monies paid to the company before the creation of the charge even though paid in consideration of it. The earlier decisions, *Re Columbian Fireproofing Co. Ltd.* [1910] 2 Ch. 120 and *Re F. & E. Stanton Ltd.* [1929] 1 Ch. 180, on a differently worded statutory predecessor were disapproved. Sir Christopher Slade felt that the statutory provision would not be satisfied if the making of the advance preceded the formal execution of the debenture by any time whatsoever "unless the interval between payment and execution is so short that it can be regarded as minimal and payment and execution can be regarded as contemporaneous" (at 620). But see Nolan L.J. at 624, who favoured some degree of latitude in certain circumstances.

CHAPTER 21

WINDING-UP OF PRIVATE COMPANIES

A. Introduction

It is not the purpose of this chapter to consider all aspects of winding-up which may be equally applicable to both private and public companies, but only to focus on issues of particular (or in some cases exclusive) relevance to private companies. With regard to voluntary winding-up, it is only proposed to outline here the provisions introduced by the Insolvency Act 1986, which were designed to strengthen creditor protection in voluntary liquidations. As for compulsory winding-up, the seven grounds on which a company may be wound up by the court are set out in section 122 of the Insolvency Act 1986. It is appropriate in this chapter to highlight only two of these grounds,[1] namely that the company is unable to pay its debts and that it is just and equitable that the company be wound up.

B. Voluntary winding-up

The law had needed reform in order to protect a company's assets between the company's resolution to wind up and the appointment of a liquidator, and also to curb the abuse, particularly prevalent in small companies, of directors or members, in a creditors' voluntary winding-up, appointing a "friendly" liquidator who could dispose of the company's assets to nominees of the directors or members before a meeting of creditors had been summoned.

Section 114 of the Insolvency Act 1986 provides that where a company is in a voluntary winding-up and no liquidator has

[1] A third ground previously, but no longer, applicable to private companies limited by shares or by guarantee is, as has been seen in Chap. 11, *ante*, that the company's membership has fallen below two: s. 122(1)(g) I.A. 1986 as amended by the Companies (Single Member Private Limited Companies) Regulations 1992 (S.I. 1992 No. 1699).

been appointed or nominated by the company, the directors' powers are limited. Prior to the appointment of a liquidator, the directors may not exercise any of their powers, unless the court otherwise orders, except, in the case of a creditors' voluntary winding-up, to call a meeting of creditors[2] and lay before it a statement of affairs,[3] and in the case of any voluntary winding-up, to dispose of any perishable or other goods likely to diminish in value or to do anything necessary to protect the company's assets. Directors in default are liable to fines[4] and will probably also be liable to proceedings in respect of misfeasance or other breach of duty under section 212 of the Insolvency Act 1986.

The above provision is bolstered by section 166 of the Insolvency Act 1986. This provides that where, in a creditors' voluntary winding-up, the company has nominated a liquidator, that liquidator's powers are, save with the court's consent, limited to taking control of the company's assets, disposing of perishable or other rapidly depreciating goods, and doing anything necessary to protect the assets. The liquidator must attend the creditors' meeting, when summoned, and report on the exercise of his powers. In default, the liquidator is liable to a fine[5] and also to the summary remedy under section 212 of the Insolvency Act 1986. Section 166 overrules *Re Centrebind Ltd.*[6] which held that the fact that a creditors' meeting had not been summoned within the required period of the company meeting did not invalidate the liquidator's appointment nor the exercise of any of his powers. The increase of the time period within which the creditors' meeting is to be held, *i.e.* 14 days[7] as opposed to one day[8] of the company meeting, in no way adversely prejudices creditors when the functions of the company's appointee as liquidator are effectively restricted to the protection of the company's assets. Moreover, any liquidator must be a qualified insolvency practitioner.[9]

Other provisions which enhance creditor protection are sections 95 and 96 of the Insolvency Act 1986. Section 95 provides that if, in a members' voluntary winding-up, the

---

[2] As required by s. 98 I.A. 1986.
[3] As required by s. 99 I.A. 1986.
[4] s. 114(4) I.A. 1986.
[5] s. 116(7) I.A. 1986.
[6] [1967] 1 W.L.R. 377.
[7] s. 98(1) I.A. 1986.
[8] s. 588(2) C.A. 1985, now repealed.
[9] See generally Pt.XIII I.A. 1986.

liquidator forms the opinion that the company will not be able to pay its debts in full, with interest, within the period stated in the directors' declaration of solvency, he must summon a meeting of creditors to be held within 28 days of his forming such an opinion. Although the liquidator had a similar duty under the provision replaced by section 95,[10] section 96 now provides that the winding-up is treated as a creditors' voluntary winding-up and thus the creditors' meeting may appoint its nominee as liquidator in accordance with section 100 of the Insolvency Act 1986[11] and also appoint a liquidation committee in accordance with section 101 of the Insolvency Act 1986.[12]

C. Compulsory winding-up

1. *Inability to pay debts: section 122(1)(f) of the Insolvency Act 1986*

Whilst this ground does not, of course, apply exclusively to private companies, it is worthy of mention as being the ground on which most petitions are presented to the court. Section 123 of the Insolvency Act 1986 provides that a company is deemed to be unable to pay its debts if, *inter alia*, the company has failed to pay, secure or compound to the reasonable satisfaction of a creditor, a debt exceeding £750 within three weeks of a written demand, in the prescribed form and manner, by the creditor served at the registered office, or has not fully satisfied an execution or other process issued by the court in favour of a creditor, or it is proved to the satisfaction of the court that the company is unable to pay its debts as they fall due, or that the value of the company's assets is less than its liabilities, taking into account contingent and prospective liabilities.

2. *Court of the opinion that it is just and equitable to wind up company: section 122(1)(g) of the Insolvency Act 1986*

It is clear from the judgment of the House of Lords in *Ebrahimi v. Westbourne Galleries Ltd.*[13] that the words "just

[10] s. 583 C.A. 1985, which provided, in such circumstances that the liquidator had a duty to summon the creditors' meeting "forthwith."
[11] This section provides that the creditors' nominee has precedence over the nominee of the members.
[12] s. 102 I.A. 1986.
[13] [1973] A.C. 360.

and equitable" are not to be construed as including only matters *ejusdem generis* with the other grounds for dissolution by the court contained in section 122(1), nor is the generality of the words to be confined to particular categories or headings of action.[14]

The broad principle to emerge from *Ebrahimi v. Westbourne Galleries Ltd.* is that in certain types of private company, where the rights of the parties cannot be said to be exhaustively laid down in the articles, the court will subject to equitable considerations the conduct of the members, even conduct carried out in strict reliance on a legal right and which is bona fide. Lord Wilberforce, whilst stressing that it would be "impossible and wholly undesirable" to define the circumstances which might give rise to such equitable considerations, nevertheless went on to suggest that a company, subject to a petition, might display one or more of the following characteristics: (i) an association formed or continued on the basis of personal relationship, involving mutual confidence; (ii) an agreement or understanding that shareholders are to participate in the conduct of the business; (iii) a restriction on the transfer of shares.[15]

It appears that many of the earlier cases which involved successful petitions to wind up a company on the just and equitable ground can now be brought under the umbrella of the *Westbourne Galleries* principle. This is certainly true of those cases where mutual confidence of members had been lost in companies which were essentially quasi-partnerships,[16] resulting in management deadlock[17] or arising from management exclusion,[18] or where confidence in management had been lost due to alleged lack of probity in the conduct of the company's affairs.[19]

Mutual confidence may be lost through the controllers' denial of the legitimate expectations of a member. In the *Westbourne Galleries* case, the successful petitioner's understanding was that

---

[14] *ibid.*, *per* Lord Wilberforce at 374.

[15] *ibid.* at 379. For a fuller quotation of the relevant passage see Chap. 12, pp. 195–196, *ante*.

[16] For a discussion of the development of the quasi-partnership concept and of the cases, including the *Westbourne Galleries* case, involving just and equitable winding-up petitions in respect of companies which are in essence quasi-partnerships, see Chap. 12, *ante*.

[17] *Re Yenidje Tobacco Co. Ltd.* [1916] 2 Ch. 426.

[18] *Re Davis and Collett Ltd.* [1935] Ch. 693; *Re Lundie Brothers Ltd.* [1965] 1 W.L.R. 1051.

[19] *Loch v. John Blackwood* [1924] A.C. 783.

he would continue in a management position in the company. His removal as a director, even in accordance with what is now section 303 of the Companies Act 1985, constituted good cause for winding up the company.

Similarly, it has been held that where a petitioner joined a company on the understanding that he would be appointed a director, his non-appointment was one of the factors which justified the making of a winding-up order.[20] Yet the understanding or expectation which has been breached may relate to something other than management participation. Thus, where a company was formed to undertake a particular project on the understanding that the profit of the venture would be distributed, a winding-up order was granted where the majority shareholder had used the money to support his other business ventures.[21]

It has also been held that a decision by directors to invest profits into a company's growth rather than make reasonable distributions by way of dividends in accordance with the legitimate expectations of members, could constitute grounds for a winding-up petition.[22]

There is ample authority that a company which has never been able, or which becomes unable, to achieve its main objects can be wound up on the just and equitable ground on the basis that its substratum has disappeared.[23] There are no reported examples in recent times, however, of petitions being presented on this basis and this is doubtless explained by the breadth of modern objects clauses, particularly with the inclusion of independent objects clauses. It has been observed, in a previous chapter, that a member of a quasi-partnership type company might, on the *Westbourne Galleries* principle, bring a winding-up petition on the ground that a company has altered its objects clause and this should be the case even though the member has lost the statutory right to object to the alteration itself.[24]

On a member's petition, the court will not order a just and equitable winding-up if it is of the opinion that another remedy is available to the petitioner and the petitioner is acting unreasonably in seeking to have the company wound up rather than pursuing that other remedy.[25] An alternative remedy might

---

[20] *Re Zinotty Properties Ltd.* [1984] 3 All E.R. 754.
[21] *ibid.* See also *Re Abbey Leisure Ltd.* [1990] BCC 60.
[22] *Re a Company (No. 00370 of 1987), ex p Glossop* [1988] BCLC 570.
[23] See, *e.g. Re German Date Coffee Co. Ltd.* (1882) 20 Ch.D. 169.
[24] Chap. 5, pp. 61–62, *ante*.
[25] s. 125(2) I.A. 1986.

be a judicial remedy[26] or an extra-judicial remedy. As has been seen, however, a petitioner is not necessarily unreasonable in refusing an offer by the other members to purchase his shares in accordance with the articles.[27]

D. Special provisions relating to contributories

1. *Liabilities and rights of contributories on winding-up of a company which has redeemed or purchased its own shares out of capital.*

Section 76 of the Insolvency Act 1986 provides that where a private company has under Chapter VII of Part V of the Companies Act 1985 redeemed or purchased its own shares out of capital, the former member from whom the shares were purchased and past directors of the company will, in certain circumstances, be liable to contribute to the assets of the company in a winding-up. The winding-up must have commenced within one year of the payment out of capital, and the company's assets, including contributions made otherwise than under section 76, must be insufficient to pay its debts and liabilities and the expenses of the winding-up. The former member is liable to contribute the amount of the payment out of capital made by the company in respect of his shares, and the former directors who had signed the declaration of solvency[28] (except a director who can show reasonable grounds for the opinion set out in the declaration) are jointly and severally liable with the former member for that amount. A person so liable to contribute to the company's assets may, under section 124(3) of the Insolvency Act 1986 petition for a winding-up by the court on the ground either that the company is unable to pay its debts or that it is just and equitable that the company be wound up. The usual shareholding requirements entitling a contributory to present a petition[29] do not apply in such cases, but unless the petitioner is a contributory otherwise than under

---

[26] *e.g.* a court order pursuant to a petition alleging unfairly prejudicial conduct under ss. 459–461 C.A. 1985.

[27] *Re Abbey Leisure Ltd.* [1990] BCC 60, see Chap. 12, pp. 197–198, *ante*.

[28] Required by s. 173(3) C.A. 1985.

[29] Normally, at least some of the contributory's shares must have been originally allotted to him, or must have been held by him and registered in his name for at least six of the 18 months prior to the commencement of the winding-up, or must have devolved to him on the death of a former holder: s. 124(2) I.A. 1986.

section 76, he may not petition as a contributory on any other ground.

2. *Liability of past members on winding-up of a limited company which was formerly unlimited*

The normal rule is that a past member is not liable to contribute to the assets of a company in a winding-up if he ceased to be a member one year or more before the commencement of the winding-up.[30] Where, however, a former unlimited company, which has, within the terms of section 51 of the Companies Act 1985, been re-registered as a private company limited by shares or guarantee, is being wound up, a person who was a member at the time of the re-registration is liable to contribute to the company's assets in respect of debts and liabilities contracted before re-registration if the winding-up commences within three years of the re-registration.[31]

If there are at the time of the winding-up, no longer any members left who were members at the time of re-registration, a person who was a present member (provided the winding-up commences within three years of re-registration) or a past member (provided the winding-up commences within a year of his ceasing to be a member) at the time of the re-registration is liable to contribute to the assets of the company as above notwithstanding that the exisiting members have satisfied their required contributions.[32] Liability of such past or present members to contribute to the company's assets by virtue of the foregoing provisions is unlimited.[33]

3. *Liability of past members on winding-up of an unlimited company which was formerly limited*

Where a company, formerly limited, but which has, by section 49 of the Companies Act 1985, been re-registered as unlimited, is being wound up, a past member at the time when the re-registration application was lodged, who did not subsequently become a member again, is not liable to contribute more to the company's assets than he would have been liable to contribute had the company not been re-registered.[34]

---

[30] s. 74(2)(a) I.A. 1986.
[31] s. 77(2) I.A. 1986.
[32] s. 77(3) I.A. 1986. The normal rule is that a past member is not liable to make a contribution unless it appears to the court that the present members are unable to satisfy the contributions required of them: s. 74(2)(c) I.A. 1986.
[33] s. 77(4) I.A. 1986.
[34] s. 78 I.A. 1986.

Chapter 22

EUROPEAN ECONOMIC INTEREST GROUPINGS

A. Introduction

1. *EEIGs and private companies*

The still relatively new[1] Community concept of the European Economic Interest Grouping (EEIG) is by no means limited in its application to private companies in that public companies, private companies, partnerships and, indeed, individuals[2] are equally entitled to avail themselves of this form of business vehicle for the purpose of cross-frontier co-operation. It does, however, seem reasonable to suppose that the "grouping" may prove to be a particularly useful device for those private companies which wish to enter into business relationships with organisations in other E.C. countries.[3]

In view, therefore, of the potential significance of EEIGs to private companies in particular and in line with the policy pursued throughout this work of focusing on issues which are of especial relevance to private companies,[4] it appears appropriate to include a short, final chapter explaining, albeit in outline only,[5] what EEIGs are and how they are operated.

---

[1] Introduced as from July 1, 1989; see *post.*

[2] *i.e.* natural persons.

[3] The position regarding EEIGs may be contrasted with the proposal for the "European Company" (Societas Europaea, SE), which will provide for the creation of organisations formed by companies from more than one Member State. An SE will require a minimum capital of 100,000 ECU. Although private companies as well as public companies will be entitled to form SEs it may be that this concept will prove less attractive to private companies than to public companies.

[4] Even when they are not exclusively so relevant.

[5] For complete details the reader should, of course, refer to the appropriate Statutory Instrument and E.C. Council Regulation, as mentioned *infra.* See Appendix 2, *post.* See also Severine Israel, "The EEIG—A major step forward for Community Law" in (1988) 9 Co. Lawyer 14, and Robert Drury and Martin Scheißl, "E.C. Competition Law Aspects of the European Economic Interest Grouping" [1994] J.B.L. 217, where, at 218, n. 4, the authors report that there had, by that time, been at least 447 registrations of EEIGs in the Community.

2. *EEIGs: the originating provisions*

European Economic Interest Groupings were created and made an integral part of the European Community legal order by Council Regulation 1985/2137. Although this item of community legislation, being a regulation, is directly applicable[6] in all Member States, it does, nevertheless, leave certain matters to be dealt with by the individual Member States.[7] So far as this country is concerned this has necessitated a statutory instrument,[8] which came into force on July 1, 1989. In fact, Council Regulation 1985/2137 is set out as Schedule 1 to this statutory instrument.

3. *The parameters of EEIG's*

Article 3(1) of Council Regulation 1985/2137 states:

> "The purpose of a grouping shall be to facilitate or develop the economic activites of its members and to improve or increase the results of those activities; its purpose is not to make profits for itself. Its activity shall be related to the economic activities of its members and must not be more than ancillary to those activities."

This provision, therefore, sets out the broad parameters for EEIGs, in particular indicating that they are intended to advance the activities of their members but not to participate in activities which fall outside the scope of operations of their members.

Article 3(2) of the Council Regulation[9] lists several specific limitations to which EEIGs are made subject. Thus, in particular, groupings may not directly or indirectly exercise a power of management or supervision over the activities of their members or of another undertaking; they may not, directly or indirectly in any way hold shares in their own members, the holding of shares in other undertakings being permissible only when necessary to achieve the grouping's objects and if done on members' behalf; they must not employ more than 500 persons; they must not, *inter alia*, make loans to directors, or to those

---

[6] As, indeed, it expressly stated itself to be.

[7] Some of these are mentioned, *post*.

[8] (S.I. 1989 No. 638): see Appendix 2, *post*.

[9] In the remainder of this chapter references to articles will be to articles of Regulation 1985/2137 and references to regulations will be to those of S.I. 1989 No. 638; see Appendix 2, *post*.

connected with directors when such lending is restricted or controlled by national company law; they must not be members of another EEIG.

It should also be noted that Article 23, set out in Appendix 2, *post*, provides that no grouping may invite the public to invest in it. In effect an EEIG amounts to a form of partnership entered into by its members for the limited purposes thus permitted by the E.C. Council Regulation.

B. Formalities for establishing EEIGs

1. *Formation and registration of EEIGs*

To create an EEIG two or more organisations or individuals from at least two Member States must enter into a contract as parties forming the grouping. In accordance with Article 5 the *minimum* requirements in respect of such a contract are: the name of the grouping preceded or followed either by the words "European Economic Interest Grouping" or by the initials "EEIG," unless the words or initials are already included in the name[10]; the grouping's *official address*[11]; a statement of the grouping's objects; the name and other specified details of each member of the grouping and the grouping's duration except where it is intended that the grouping shall continue indefinitely. As, in effect, provided by S.I. 1989 No. 638, regulation 9(10), any communication or notice may be addressed to an EEIG which has its official address in Great Britain, at that official address.

A contract, as above, is an essential requirement of a grouping.[12] The "partners" of the grouping must then decide where its "official address" shall be situated. This address determines in which national registry[13] registration of the EEIG

---

[10] Note also that S.I. 1989 No. 638, reg. 10, prohibits the registration, see *post*, of a grouping if its name contains any of the following, or any abbreviations thereof: "limited"; "unlimited"; "public limited company"; or the Welsh equivalents of these. Note also, *per* reg. 17 (S.I. 1989 No. 638), the application of the Business Names Act 1985 to EEIGs.

[11] See *post*. See Art. 12 for further details.

[12] Clearly such contract must be in writing since in order to form a grouping the formation contract must be filed at the appropriate registry: see Art. 7 and also *post*. If the contract is not in English a certified translation into English must also be provided to the Registrar: see S.I. 1989 No. 638, reg. 9(8).

[13] See Art. 6. In the case of the U.K. of course, there are separate registers at Cardiff, Edinburgh and Belfast.

shall be effected. With certain specified exceptions the law governing the contract for the formation of an EEIG and that EEIG's internal organisation shall be the national law of the state wherein the official address is registered.[14] When a grouping has been so registered[15] Article 1(2) provides that from the date of its registration it shall have the capacity, in its own name, to have rights and obligations, to make contracts or do other legal acts, and to sue and be sued. A certificate of registration in respect of an EEIG is conclusive evidence of compliance with the requirements regarding registration "and that the EEIG is an organisation authorised to be registered, and is duly registered".[16]

As permitted by Article 1(3), regulation 3 of S.I. 1989 No. 638 provides that from the date of its registration in Great Britain, as above, the grouping shall, subject to certain restrictions concerning its name[17] "be a body corporate by the name contained in the contract". For the benefit of those dealing with an EEIG, Article 25 provides that every grouping and every establishment[18] of a grouping must include, in a legible manner, certain prescribed details on its letters, order forms and similar documents.[19]

2. *The organs of EEIGs*

Article 16(1) provides that: "The organs of a grouping shall be the members acting collectively and the manager or managers." The article then goes on to allow the grouping

---

[14] See Art. 2(1).

[15] Where the official address is in Great Britain, filing will be at Companies House, Cardiff or Companies House, Edinburgh, as appropriate. Form EEIG 1 must be used. *N.B.* Although in some instances, as here, reference to the appropriate EEIG form is made, this has not been done comprehensively throughout this chapter. Reference should be made to the S.I., Art. 7 lists other documents and particulars which must be filed (where necessary with certified translation into English), *e.g.* amendments to the grouping formation contract. Some of the others are referred to *post*. For time limits for filing and fines for default see S.I. 1989 No. 638, reg. 13.

[16] See S.I. 1989 No. 638, reg. 9(7). Note that, *per* reg. 18, EEIGs and their establishments, see *post*, registered or in process of being registered under S.I. 1989 No. 638 will be subject to those provisions of the C.A. 1985 specified in Sched. 4 of that S.I., as if they were companies formed and registered or in process of being registered under the C.A. 1985, but subject as indicated; see reg. 18 and Sched. 4 for further details.

[17] See reg. 11. See also n. 10, *ante* regarding prohibition of registration of certain names.

[18] See *post*.

[19] See S.I. 1989 No. 638, reg. 16 for offences for failure to comply with these requirements.

formation contract to provide for other organs and, in so far as it does so provide, to determine what the powers of such additional organs shall be. Article 16(2) provides that the grouping's members, acting as a body, may take any decision in order to achieve the grouping's objects. In order that members may make decisions, on the initiative of a manager or at the request of a member, the manager(s) must arrange for the members to be consulted.[20]

3. *The manager(s) of EEIGs*

The role of the manager will be crucial to the operation of an EEIG. Article 19(1) points out, in the first place, that a grouping must be managed by one or more natural persons appointed by the formation contract or by the members' decision. However, Article 19(2) does permit legal persons[21] to be managers if this is allowed by the Member State in whose national registry the grouping has been entered for the purpose of Article 6,[22] above, and on condition that such legal person designates one or more natural persons to represent it.[23] Article 19(3) declares that the grouping formation contract, or, failing that, the members by unanimous decision, shall decide the conditions for the appointment and removal of managers as well as the powers of managers. Notice of appointment of managers and of termination of such appointment must be notified to the registry at which the official address has been notified.[24]

---

[20] See Art 17(4). Art. 17(1) provides, in effect, that prima facie each member shall have one vote but that the grouping formation contract may accord more than one vote to certain members so long as no single member has a voting majority. Art. 17(2) then specifies certain decisions which require the members to be unanimous, *e.g.* a decision to change the grouping's objects or to alter the contributions of every member or of some members to the grouping's financing. Art. 17(3) provides that except where, *per* Council Regulation 1985/2137, a decision must be made unanimously, the grouping formation contract may specify the conditions for a quorum and for a majority but that, unless otherwise permitted by the contract, decisions must be reached unanimously.

[21] Presumably meaning *artificial* legal persons, *viz.* corporations.

[22] This is permitted in Great Britain by S.I. 1989 No. 638, reg. 5(1). Such representative is subject to the same liability as if he were himself a manager, see reg. 5(2) of the S.I.; also Art. 19(2).

[23] Particulars of such representative must be filed, in accordance with Art. 7(d), see Art. 19(2).

[24] See Art. 7(d). For such notification in Great Britain, form EEIG 3 must be used. Where an *establishment* has been notified, see *post*, and the grouping's official address is outside the U.K., notification must be made, on form EEIG 4, to the registry at which the establishment has been notified.

Article 20 contains important provisions with regard to the dealings of groupings with third parties. First, Article 20(1) specifies that only managers can represent groupings in dealings with third parties. This provision then goes on to declare that a manager shall bind the grouping as regards third parties when acting for the grouping, even if his acts do not fall within the objects of the grouping, *unless the grouping can prove* that the third party was aware, or under the circumstances could not have been unaware, that the manager's act was outside the grouping's objects. This provision also points out that publication of the grouping's objects shall not, in itself, constitute such proof. Further, no limitation on a manager's powers may be relied on as against third parties even if there is publication. It is, however, possible, subject to compliance with prescribed conditions,[25] for the grouping's foundation contract to provide for the grouping only to be bound by two or more managers acting jointly.

C. Purposes of, liability for, and winding-up of EEIGs

1. *Registration of EEIG establishments*

As described earlier, the underlying purpose of the EEIG is to assist enterprises to co-operate within the EEC on a transnational footing. Accordingly, although a grouping must choose one national register in which to enrol its official address and other particulars,[26] any grouping establishment situated in an E.C. Member State other than the Member State in which its official address is registered must register and file copies of the documents and particulars, with certified translation if necessary, in that State's registry also.[27]

Article 7(b) requires that there shall be filed, at the registry at which its official address has been registered, notice of the

[25] See Art. 20(2). Note also Art. 25(d).

[26] See Art. 6, and also Art. 7 which lists the documents and particulars which require registration. S.I. 1989 No. 638, reg. 13 specifies the time limits for filing and fines in default.

[27] Art. 10. Registration of an establishment in Great Britain of an EEIG whose official address is outside the U.K. is covered by S.I. 1989 No. 638, reg. 12 which provides *inter alia* that registration, using form EEIG 2, is required within one month of the setting up of the establishment and imposes fines in default. Reg. 12 also specifies that any communication or notice may be addressed to an EEIG, the official address of which is outside the U.K., at any of its establishments in Great Britain.

setting-up and the closure of any establishment of the relevant grouping.

2. *Position of EEIG members*

Article 24(1) declares that the members of a grouping shall have unlimited joint and several liability for the grouping's debts and other liabilities of whatever nature. The article goes on to state that national law shall determine the consequences of such liability.

However, Article 24(2) then makes it clear that creditors may not proceed against a member in respect of the grouping's debts and other liabilities before the conclusion of the grouping's liquidation, unless they have first requested payment from the grouping and no such payment has been made "within an appropriate period".

A new member admitted to an existing grouping[28] will assume liability in accordance with Article 24, including liability for the grouping's activities before he joined. Such a new member may, however, be excused liability for grouping activities before his admission, on compliance with certain prescribed conditions.[29]

The liability of a member does not cease on termination of membership. Thus Article 34 provides that on ceasing to belong to a grouping a member remains answerable, under the conditions in Article 24,[30] "for the debts and other liabilities arising out of the grouping's activities before he ceased to be a member". However, the limitation period for bringing claims is five years[31] after publication, in the prescribed manner, of notice of the member's termination of membership.

With regard to any profits generated by the activities of an EEIG, Article 21(1) provides that these shall be deemed to be profits of the members and are divisible between the members in accordance with the grouping's formation contract or, if that contract is silent on the matter, profits are divisible equally. On the same principle Article 21(2) provides that a grouping's losses[32] shall be borne by the members in the proportions set

---

[28] Such admission requires the unanimous decision of the existing members: see Art. 26(1).

[29] See Art. 26(2).

[30] See *ante*.

[31] This is in substitution for any longer period prescribed by the relevant national law; see Art. 37(1); note also Art. 37(2).

[32] *i.e.* as stated in Art. 21(2), "... the amount by which expenditure exceeds income".

out in the formation contract or, where this matter is not covered by the contract, in equal shares. Article 40 states that the profits or losses resulting from the activities of a grouping shall be taxable only in the hands of its members.

Further provisions set out the conditions under which members may assign their membership[33] or use it for the purpose of granting security.[34] There are other provisions dealing with, *inter alia*, withdrawal from membership[35] and expulsion from membership.[36] Article 33 deals with valuation of the rights and obligations of a departing member, other than a member departing by reason of assignment of his rights in accordance with Article 22(1), *ante*.

3. *Winding-up of EEIGs*

Articles 31 and 32 provide for the winding-up of a grouping in certain specified situations, *e.g.* when a unanimous decision for winding-up is reached by the members or by court order after application by an individual member on the "just and proper ground." In effect, these articles cover grounds for both voluntary winding-up and compulsory winding-up.

Article 35(1) states that the winding-up of a grouping shall entail its liquidation. Article 35(2) then declares that a grouping's liquidation and the conclusion of its liquidation shall be governed by national law. Regulation 8(2) of S.I. 1989 No. 638 states that "[a]t the end of the period of three months beginning with the day of receipt by the registrar of a notice of the conclusion of the liquidation of an EEIG, the EEIG shall be dissolved".[37] As is pointed out in the Explanatory Note appended to (but not part of) S.I. 1989 No. 638, this applies whether or not the EEIG has been wound up by the court.

---

[33] Art. 22(1).

[34] Art. 22(2).

[35] Art. 27(1).

[36] Art. 27(2).

[37] See S.I. 1989 No. 638, regs. 8 and 20; note how under the latter provision many important provisions of the Company Directors' Disqualification Act 1986 are applied to managers and others involved in control or management, past or present, of the EEIG's business where an EEIG is wound up as an unregistered company under Pt. V of the Insolvency Act 1986. Note also in particular how S.I. 1989 No. 638, reg. 19 extends Pt. III of the Insolvency Act 1986 (Receivership) to EEIGs and their establishments.

APPENDICES

Appendix 1

THE COMPANIES (TABLES A TO F) REGULATIONS 1985

(S.I. 1985 No. 805)

Some preliminary comments

Sections 3 and 8 of the Companies Act 1985 refer respectively to standard forms of memorandum and articles of association for various types of registered companies. The statutory instrument, S.I. 1985 No. 805,[1] in which these model forms are to be found, is set out *in extenso* in the following pages of this appendix.

The statutory instrument contains the following:

Table A: Regulations for the management of a company limited by shares—applies both to private and public companies.

Table B: Memorandum of association of a private company limited by shares.

Table C: Memorandum and articles of association of a company limited by guarantee and not having a share capital.

Table D: Part I—Memorandum of association of a public company limited by guarantee and having a share capital.

Part II—Memorandum of association of a private company limited by guarantee and having a share capital.

Part III—Articles of association of a company (public or private) limited by guarantee and having a share capital.

Table E: Memorandum and articles of association of an unlimited company having a share capital.

Table F: Memorandum of association of a public company limited by shares.

It should be noted that this statutory instrument came into operation on July 1, 1985 (with certain amendments from August 1, 1985,

[1] The use of a statutory instrument in order to set out standard forms of memorandum and articles is a departure from the previous usual, but not invariable, practice of including these in schedules to Companies Acts.

under S.I. 1985 No. 1052). Thus, in particular, the set of articles contained in Table A of the statutory instrument will, by virtue of section 8 of the Companies Act 1985, automatically apply to both public and private companies limited by shares registered on or after that date in so far as other articles, inconsistent with the model form of articles, have not been filed in respect of such companies.

Companies limited by shares and incorporated before July 1, 1985, will still retain the articles with which they were registered, except in so far as they may have subsequently modified such articles. When, therefore, a company's articles consist of or contain regulations of a Table A from previous Companies Acts,[2] these regulations will continue to apply to that company until and unless the company changes them.[3]

Similarly, guarantee companies and unlimited companies registered before July 1, 1985, will retain any earlier standard forms of articles provided by statute which they may have adopted,[4] in so far as they have not, subsequent to registration, changed their articles.

The Companies (Tables A to F) Regulations 1985

(S.I. 1985 No. 805)

Made	*22nd May* 1985
Laid before Parliament	*3rd June* 1985
Coming into Operation	*1st July* 1985

The Secretary of State, in exercise of the powers conferred by section 454(2) of the Companies Act 1948, and now vested in him, of the powers conferred by sections 3 and 8 of the Companies Act 1985 and of all other powers enabling him in that behalf, hereby makes the following Regulations—

1. These Regulations may be cited as the Companies (Tables A to F) Regulations 1985 and shall come into operation on 1st July 1985.

2. The regulations in Table A and the forms in Tables B, C, D, E and F in the Schedule to these Regulations shall be the regulations and

---

[2] For more than a century these have been designated as "Table A".

[3] For details of such standard form of articles, where a company has simply incorporated them by implication or even by reference but has not set them out in full in its registered documents, it will be necessary to make reference to the appropriate companies legislation. Probably the majority of private companies currently on the register will, indeed, have articles which consist of or include regulations emanating from pre-1985 provisions.

[4] Although guarantee companies and unlimited companies are entitled, on registration, to adopt, in part or in whole, the appropriate standard set of articles, there is no question of automatic application where not expressly excluded, as with companies limited by shares: see s.8(2) of the Companies Act 1985.

forms of memorandum and articles of association for the purposes of sections 3 and 8 of the Companies Act 1985.

3. The Companies (Alteration of Table A etc) Regulations 1984 are hereby revoked.

Alexander Fletcher,
Parliamentary Under-Secretary of State,
Department of Trade and Industry.

22nd May 1985.

SCHEDULE

TABLE A

REGULATIONS FOR MANAGEMENT OF A COMPANY LIMITED BY SHARES*

INTERPRETATION

1. In these regulations—

"the Act" means the Companies Act 1985 including any statutory modification or re-enactment thereof for the time being in force.

"the articles" means the articles of the company.

"clear days" in relation to the period of a notice means that period excluding the day when the notice is given or deemed to be given and the day for which it is given or on which it is to take effect.

"executed" includes any mode of execution.

"office" means the registered office of the company.

"the holder" in relation to shares means the member whose name is entered in the register of members as the holder of the shares.

"the seal" means the common seal of the company.

"secretary" means the secretary of the company or any other person appointed to perform the duties of the secretary of the company, including a joint, assistant or deputy secretary.

"the United Kingdom" means Great Britain and Northern Ireland.

Unless the context otherwise requires, words or expressions contained in these regulations bear the same meaning as in the Act but excluding

---

* [Includes certain amendments, as indicated, introduced by S.I. 1985 No. 1052, from August 1, 1985].

any statutory modification thereof not in force when these regulations become binding on the company.

SHARE CAPITAL

2. Subject to the provisions of the Act and without prejudice to any rights attached to any existing shares, any share may be issued with such rights or restrictions as the company may by ordinary resolution determine.

3. Subject to the provisions of the Act, shares may be issued which are to be redeemed or are to be liable to be redeemed at the option of the company or the holder on such terms and in such manner as may be provided by the articles.

4. The company may exercise the powers of paying commissions conferred by the Act. Subject to the provisions of the Act, any such commission may be satisfied by the payment of cash or by the allotment of fully or partly paid shares or partly in one way and partly in the other.*

5. Except as required by law, no person shall be recognised by the company as holding any share upon any trust and (except as otherwise provided by the articles or by law) the company shall not be bound by or recognise any interest in any share except an absolute right to the entirety thereof in the holder.

SHARE CERTIFICATES

6. Every member, upon becoming the holder of any shares, shall be entitled without payment to one certificate for all the shares of each class held by him (and, upon transferring a part of his holding of shares of any class, to a certificate for the balance of such holding) or several certificates each for one or more of his shares upon payment for every certificate after the first of such reasonable sum as the directors may determine. Every certificate shall be sealed with the seal and shall specify the number, class and distinguishing numbers (if any) of the shares to which it relates and the amount or respective amounts paid up thereon. The company shall not be bound to issue more than one certificate for shares held jointly by several persons and delivery of a certificate to one joint holder shall be a sufficient delivery to all of them.

7. If a share certificate is defaced, worn-out, lost or destroyed, it may be renewed on such terms (if any) as to evidence and indemnity and payment of the expenses reasonably incurred by the company in investigating evidence as the directors may determine but otherwise free of charge, and (in the case of defacement or wearing-out) on delivery up of the old certificate.

---

* [Includes amendment introduced by S.I. 1985 No. 1052, from August 1, 1985].

LIEN

8. The company shall have a first and paramount lien on every share (not being a fully paid share) for all moneys (whether presently payable or not) payable at a fixed time or called in respect of that share. The directors may at any time declare any share to be wholly or in part exempt from the provisions of this regulation. The company's lien on a share shall extend to any amount payable in respect of it.

9. The company may sell in such manner as the directors determine any shares on which the company has a lien if a sum in respect of which the lien exists is presently payable and is not paid within fourteen clear days after notice has been given to the holder of the share or to the person entitled to it in consequence of the death or bankruptcy of the holder, demanding payment and stating that if the notice is not complied with the shares may be sold.

10. To give effect to a sale the directors may authorise some person to execute an instrument of transfer of the shares sold to, or in accordance with the directions of, the purchaser. The title of the transferee to the shares shall not be affected by any irregularity in or invalidity of the proceedings in reference to the sale.

11. The net proceeds of the sale, after payment of the costs, shall be applied in payment of so much of the sum for which the lien exists as is presently payable, and any residue shall (upon surrender to the company for cancellation of the certificate for the shares sold and subject to a like lien for any moneys not presently payable as existed upon the shares before the sale) be paid to the person entitled to the shares at the date of the sale.

CALLS ON SHARES AND FORFEITURE

12. Subject to the terms of allotment, the directors may make calls upon the members in respect of any moneys unpaid on their shares (whether in respect of nominal value or premium) and each member shall (subject to receiving at least fourteen clear days' notice specifying when and where payment is to be made) pay to the company as required by the notice the amount called on his shares. A call may be required to be paid by instalments. A call may, before receipt by the company of any sum due thereunder, be revoked in whole or part and payment of a call may be postponed in whole or part. A person upon whom a call is made shall remain liable for calls made upon him notwithstanding the subsequent transfer of the shares in respect whereof the call was made.

13. A call shall be deemed to have been made at the time when the resolution of the directors authorising the call was passed.

14. The joint holders of a share shall be jointly and severally liable to pay all calls in respect thereof.

15. If a call remains unpaid after it has become due and payable the person from whom it is due and payable shall pay interest on the amount unpaid from the day it became due and payable until it is paid at the rate fixed by the terms of allotment of the share or in the notice of the call or, if no rate is fixed, at the appropriate rate (as defined by the Act) but the directors may waive payment of the interest wholly or in part.

16. An amount payable in respect of a share on allotment or at any fixed date, whether in respect of nominal value or premium or as an instalment of a call, shall be deemed to be a call and if it is not paid the provisions of the articles shall apply as if that amount had become due and payable by virtue of a call.

17. Subject to the terms of allotment, the directors may make arrangements on the issue of shares for a difference between the holders in the amounts and times of payment of calls on their shares.

18. If a call remains unpaid after it has become due and payable the directors may give to the person from whom it is due not less than fourteen clear days' notice requiring payment of the amount unpaid together with any interest which may have accrued. The notice shall name the place where payment is to be made and shall state that if the notice is not complied with the shares in respect of which the call was made will be liable to be forfeited.

19. If the notice is not complied with any share in respect of which it was given may, before the payment required by the notice has been made, be forfeited by a resolution of the directors and the forfeiture shall include all dividends or other moneys payable in respect of the forfeited shares and not paid before the forfeiture.

20. Subject to the provisions of the Act, a forfeited share may be sold, re-allotted or otherwise disposed of on such terms and in such manner as the directors determine either to the person who was before the forfeiture the holder or to any other person and at any time before sale, re-allotment or other disposition, the forfeiture may be cancelled on such terms as the directors think fit. Where for the purposes of its disposal a forfeited share is to be transferred to any person the directors may authorise some person to execute an instrument of transfer of the share to that person.

21. A person any of whose shares have been forfeited shall cease to be a member in respect of them and shall surrender to the company for cancellation the certificate for the shares forfeited but shall remain liable to the company for all moneys which at the date of forfeiture were presently payable by him to the company in respect of those shares with interest at the rate at which interest was payable on those moneys before the forfeiture or, if no interest was so payable, at the appropriate rate (as defined in the Act) from the date of forfeiture until payment but the directors may waive payment wholly or in part or enforce payment without any allowance for the value of the shares at the time of forfeiture or for any consideration received on their disposal.

22. A statutory declaration by a director or the secretary that a share has been forfeited on a specified date shall be conclusive evidence of the facts stated in it as against all persons claiming to be entitled to the share and the declaration shall (subject to the execution of an instrument of transfer if necessary) constitute a good title to the share and the person to whom the share is disposed of shall not be bound to see to the application of the consideration, if any, nor shall his title to the share be affected by any irregularity in or invalidity of the proceedings in reference to the forfeiture or disposal of the share.

TRANSFER OF SHARES

23. The instrument of transfer of a share may be in any usual form or in any other form which the directors may approve and shall be executed by or on behalf of the transferor and, unless the share is fully paid, by or on behalf of the transferee.

24. The directors may refuse to register the transfer of a share which is not fully paid to a person of whom they do not approve and they may refuse to register the transfer of a share on which the company has a lien. They may also refuse to register a transfer unless—

(a) it is lodged at the office or at such other place as the directors may appoint and is accompanied by the certificate for the shares to which it relates and such other evidence as the directors may reasonably require to show the right of the transferor to make the transfer;
(b) it is in respect of only one class of shares; and
(c) it is in favour of not more than four transferees.

25. If the directors refuse to register a transfer of a share, they shall within two months after the date on which the transfer was lodged with the company send to the transferee notice of the refusal.

26. The registration of transfers of shares or of transfers of any class of shares may be suspended at such times and for such periods (not exceeding thirty days in any year) as the directors may determine.

27. No fee shall be charged for the registration of any instrument of transfer or other document relating to or affecting the title to any share.

28. The company shall be entitled to retain any instrument of transfer which is registered, but any instrument of transfer which the directors refuse to register shall be returned to the person lodging it when notice of the refusal is given.

TRANSMISSION OF SHARES

29. If a member dies the survivor or survivors where he was a joint holder, and his personal representatives where he was a sole holder or the only survivor of joint holders, shall be the only persons recognised by the company as having any title to his interest; but nothing herein contained shall release the estate of a deceased member from any liability in respect of any share which had been jointly held by him.

30. A person becoming entitled to a share in consequence of the death or bankruptcy of a member may, upon such evidence being produced as the directors may properly require, elect either to become the holder of the share or to have some person nominated by him registered as the transferee. If he elects to become the holder he shall give notice to the company to that effect. If he elects to have another person registered he shall execute an instrument of transfer of the share to that person. All the articles relating to the transfer of shares shall apply to the notice or instrument of transfer as if it were an instrument of transfer executed by the member and the death or bankruptcy of the member had not occurred.

31. A person becoming entitled to a share in consequence of the death or bankruptcy of a member shall have the rights to which he would be entitled if he were the holder of the share, except that he shall not, before being registered as the holder of the share, be entitled in respect of it to attend or vote at any meeting of the company or at any separate meeting of the holders of any class of shares in the company.

ALTERATION OF SHARE CAPITAL

32. The company may by ordinary resolution—

(a) increase its share capital by new shares of such amount as the resolution prescribes;
(b) consolidate and divide all or any of its share capital into shares of larger amount than its existing shares;
(c) subject to the provisions of the Act, sub-divide its shares, or any of them, into shares of smaller amount and the resolution may determine that, as between the shares resulting from the sub-division, any of them may have any preference or advantage as compared with the others; and
(d) cancel shares which, at the date of the passing of the resolution, have not been taken or agreed to be taken by any person and diminish the amount of its share capital by the amount of the shares so cancelled.

33. Whenever as a result of a consolidation of shares any members would become entitled to fractions of a share, the directors may, on behalf of those members, sell the shares representing the fractions for the best price reasonably obtainable to any person (including, subject to the provisions of the Act, the company) and distribute the net proceeds of sale in due proportion among those members, and the directors may authorise some person to execute an instrument of transfer of the shares to, or in accordance with the directions of, the purchaser. The transferee shall not be bound to see to the application of the purchase money nor shall his title to the shares be affected by any irregularity in or invalidity of the proceedings in reference to the sale.

34. Subject to the provisions of the Act, the company may by special resolution reduce its share capital, any capital redemption reserve and any share premium account in any way.

PURCHASE OF OWN SHARES

35. Subject to the provisions of the Act, the company may purchase its own shares (including any redeemable shares) and, if it is a private company, make a payment in respect of the redemption or purchase of its own shares otherwise than out of distributable profits of the company or the proceeds of a fresh issue of shares.

GENERAL MEETINGS

36. All general meetings other than annual general meetings shall be called extraordinary general meetings.

37. The directors may call general meetings and, on the requisition of members pursuant to the provisions of the Act, shall forthwith proceed to convene an extraordinary general meeting for a date not later than eight weeks after receipt of the requisition. If there are not within the United Kingdom sufficient directors to call a general meeting, any director or any member of the company may call a general meeting.

NOTICE OF GENERAL MEETINGS

38. An annual general meeting and an extraordinary general meeting called for the passing of a special resolution or a resolution appointing a person as a director shall be called by at least twenty-one clear days' notice. All other extraordinary general meetings shall be called by at least fourteen clear days' notice but a general meeting may be called by shorter notice if it is so agreed—

(a) in the case of an annual general meeting, by all the members entitled to attend and vote thereat; and

(b) in the case of any other meeting by a majority in number of the members having a right to attend and vote being a majority together holding not less than ninety-five per cent in nominal value of the shares giving that right.

The notice shall specify the time and place of the meeting and the general nature of the business to be transacted and, in the case of an annual general meeting, shall specify the meeting as such.

Subject to the provisions of the articles and to any restrictions imposed on any shares, the notice shall be given to all the members, to all persons entitled to a share in consequence of the death or bankruptcy of a member and to the directors and auditors.

39. The accidental omission to give notice of a meeting to, or the non-receipt of notice of a meeting by, any person entitled to receive notice shall not invalidate the proceedings at that meeting.

PROCEEDINGS AT GENERAL MEETINGS

40. No business shall be transacted at any meeting unless a quorum is present. Two persons entitled to vote upon the business to be transacted, each being a member or a proxy for a member or a duly authorised representative of a corporation, shall be a quorum.

41. If such a quorum is not present within half an hour from the time appointed for the meeting, or if during a meeting such a quorum ceases to be present, the meeting shall stand adjourned to the same day in the next week at the same time and place or to such time and place as the directors may determine.*

42. The chairman, if any, of the board of directors or in his absence some other director nominated by the directors shall preside as chairman of the meeting, but if neither the chairman nor such other director (if any) be present within fifteen minutes after the time appointed for holding the meeting and willing to act, the directors present shall elect one of their number to be chairman and, if there is only one director present and willing to act, he shall be chairman.

43. If no director is willing to act as chairman, or if no director is present within fifteen minutes after the time appointed for holding the meeting, the members present and entitled to vote shall choose one of their number to be chairman.

44. A director shall, notwithstanding that he is not a member, be entitled to attend and speak at any general meeting and at any separate meeting of the holders of any class of shares in the company.

45. The chairman may, with the consent of a meeting at which a quorum is present (and shall if so directed by the meeting), adjourn the meeting from time to time and from place to place, but no business shall be transacted at an adjourned meeting other than business which might properly have been transacted at the meeting had the adjournment not taken place. When a meeting is adjourned for fourteen days or more, at least seven clear days' notice shall be given specifying the time and place of the adjourned meeting and the general nature of the business to be transacted. Otherwise it shall not be necessary to give any such notice.

46. A resolution put to the vote of a meeting shall be decided on a show of hands unless before, or on the declaration of the result of, the show of hands a poll is duly demanded. Subject to the provisions of the Act, a poll may be demanded—

(a) by the chairman; or
(b) by at least two members having the right to vote at the meeting; or

(c) by a member or members representing not less than one-tenth of the total voting rights of all the members having the right to vote at the meeting; or

(d) by a member or members holding shares conferring a right to vote at the meeting being shares on which an aggregate sum has been paid up equal to not less than one-tenth of the total sum paid up on all the shares conferring that right;

and a demand by a person as proxy for a member shall be the same as a demand by the member.

47. Unless a poll is duly demanded a declaration by the chairman that a resolution has been carried or carried unanimously, or by a particular majority, or lost, or not carried by a particular majority and an entry to that effect in the minutes of the meeting shall be conclusive evidence of the fact without proof of the number or proportion of the votes recorded in favour of or against the resolution.

48. The demand for a poll may, before the poll is taken, be withdrawn but only with the consent of the chairman and a demand so withdrawn shall not be taken to have invalidated the result of a show of hands declared before the demand was made.

49. A poll shall be taken as the chairman directs and he may appoint scrutineers (who need not be members) and fix a time and place for declaring the result of the poll. The result of the poll shall be deemed to be the resolution of the meeting at which the poll was demanded.

50. In the case of an equality of votes, whether on a show of hands or on a poll, the chairman shall be entitled to a casting vote in addition to any other vote he may have.

51. A poll demanded on the election of a chairman or on a question of adjournment shall be taken forthwith. A poll demanded on any other question shall be taken either forthwith or at such time and place as the chairman directs not being more than thirty days after the poll is demanded. The demand for a poll shall not prevent the continuance of a meeting for the transaction of any business other than the question on which the poll was demanded. If a poll is demanded before the declaration of the result of a show of hands and the demand is duly withdrawn, the meeting shall continue as if the demand had not been made.

52. No notice need be given of a poll not taken forthwith if the time and place at which it is to be taken are announced at the meeting at which it is demanded. In any other case at least seven clear days' notice shall be given specifying the time and place at which the poll is to be taken.

53. A resolution in writing executed by or on behalf of each member who would have been entitled to vote upon it if it had been proposed at a general meeting at which he was present shall be as effectual as if it had been passed at a general meeting duly convened and held and may consist of several instruments in the like form each executed by or on behalf of one or more members.

VOTES OF MEMBERS

54. Subject to any rights or restrictions attached to any shares, on a show of hands every member who (being an individual) is present in person or (being a corporation) is present by a duly authorised representative, not being himself a member entitled to vote, shall have one vote and on a poll every member shall have one vote for every share of which he is the holder.

55. In the case of joint holders the vote of the senior who tenders a vote, whether in person or by proxy, shall be accepted to the exclusion of the votes of the other joint holders; and seniority shall be determined by the order in which the names of the holders stand in the register of members.

56. A member in respect of whom an order has been made by any court having jurisdiction (whether in the United Kingdom or elsewhere) in matters concerning mental disorder may vote, whether on a show of hands or on a poll, by his receiver, curator bonis or other person authorised in that behalf appointed by that court, and any such receiver, curator bonis or other person may, on a poll, vote by proxy. Evidence to the satisfaction of the directors of the authority of the person claiming to exercise the right to vote shall be deposited at the office, or at such other place as is specified in accordance with the articles for the deposit of instruments of proxy, not less than 48 hours before the time appointed for holding the meeting or adjourned meeting at which the right to vote is to be exercised and in default the right to vote shall not be exercisable.

57. No member shall vote at any general meeting or at any separate meeting of the holders of any class of shares in the company, either in person or by proxy, in respect of any share held by him unless all moneys presently payable by him in respect of that share have been paid.

58. No objection shall be raised to the qualification of any voter except at the meeting or adjourned meeting at which the vote objected to is tendered, and every vote not disallowed at the meeting shall be valid. Any objection made in due time shall be referred to the chairman whose decision shall be final and conclusive.

59. On a poll votes may be given either personally or by proxy. A member may appoint more than one proxy to attend on the same occasion.

60. An instrument appointing a proxy shall be in writing, executed by or on behalf of the appointor and shall be in the following form (or in a form as near thereto as circumstances allow or in any other form which is usual or which the directors may approve)—

"PLC/Limited

I/We , of

, being a member/members of the above-named company, hereby appoint

of

, or failing him,

of , as my/our proxy to vote in my/our name[s] and on my/our behalf at the annual/extraordinary general meeting of the company, to be held on 19 , and at any adjournment thereof.

Signed on 19 "

61. Where it is desired to afford members an opportunity of instructing the proxy how he shall act the instrument appointing a proxy shall be in the following form (or in a form as near thereto as circumstances allow or in any other form which is usual or which the directors may approve)—

"PLC/Limited

I/We , of

, being a member/members of the above-named company, hereby appoint

of

, or failing him,

of , as my/our proxy to vote in my/our name[s] and on my/our behalf at the annual/extraordinary general meeting of the company, to be held on 19 , and at any adjournment thereof.

This form is to be used in respect of the resolutions mentioned below as follows:

Resolution No. 1 *for *against
Resolution No. 2 *for *against.

*Strike out whichever is not desired.

Unless otherwise instructed, the proxy may vote as he thinks fits or abstain from voting.

Signed this day of 19 ."

62. The instrument appointing a proxy and any authority under which it is executed or a copy of such authority certified notarially or in some other way approved by the directors may—

(a) be deposited at the office or at such other place within the United Kingdom as is specified in the notice convening the meeting or in any instrument of proxy sent out by the company in relation to the meeting not less than 48 hours before the time for holding the meeting or adjourned meeting at which the person named in the instrument proposes to vote; or

(b) in the case of a poll taken more than 48 hours after it is demanded, be deposited as aforesaid after the poll has been demanded and not less than 24 hours before the time appointed for the taking of the poll; or

(c) where the poll is not taken forthwith but is taken not more than 48 hours after it was demanded, be delivered at the meeting at which the poll was demanded to the chairman or to the secretary or to any director;

and an instrument of proxy which is not deposited or delivered in a manner so permitted shall be invalid.

63. A vote given or poll demanded by proxy or by the duly authorised representative of a corporation shall be valid notwithstanding the previous determination of the authority of the person voting or demanding a poll unless notice of the determination was received by the company at the office or at such other place at which the instrument of proxy was duly deposited before the commencement of the meeting or adjourned meeting at which the vote is given or the poll demanded or (in the case of a poll taken otherwise than on the same day as the meeting or adjourned meeting) the time appointed for taking the poll.

NUMBER OF DIRECTORS

64. Unless otherwise determined by ordinary resolution, the number of directors (other than alternate directors) shall not be subject to any maximum but shall be not less than two.

ALTERNATE DIRECTORS

65. Any director (other than an alternate director) may appoint any other director, or any other person approved by resolution of the directors and willing to act, to be an alternate director and may remove from office an alternate director so appointed by him.

66. An alternate director shall be entitled to receive notice of all meetings of directors and of all meetings of committees of directors of which his appointor is a member, to attend and vote at any such meeting at which the director appointing him is not personally present, and generally to perform all the functions of his appointor as a director in his absence but shall not be entitled to receive any remuneration from the company for his services as an alternate director. But it shall not be necessary to give notice of such a meeting to an alternate director who is absent from the United Kingdom.

67. An alternate director shall cease to be an alternate director if his appointor ceases to be a director; but, if a director retires by rotation or otherwise but is reappointed or deemed to have been reappointed at the meeting at which he retires, any appointment of an alternate director made by him which was in force immediately prior to his retirement shall continue after his reappointment.

68. Any appointment or removal of an alternate director shall be by notice to the company signed by the director making or revoking the appointment or in any other manner approved by the directors.

69. Save as otherwise provided in the articles, an alternate director shall be deemed for all purposes to be a director and shall alone be responsible for his own acts and defaults and he shall not be deemed to be the agent of the director appointing him.

POWERS OF DIRECTORS

70. Subject to the provisions of the Act, the memorandum and the articles and to any directions given by special resolution, the business of the company shall be managed by the directors who may exercise all the powers of the company. No alteration of the memorandum or articles and no such direction shall invalidate any prior act of the directors which would have been valid if that alteration had not been made or that direction had not been given. The powers given by this regulation shall not be limited by any special power given to the directors by the articles and a meeting of directors at which a quorum is present may exercise all powers exercisable by the directors.

71. The directors may, by power of attorney or otherwise, appoint any person to be the agent of the company for such purposes and on such conditions as they determine, including authority for the agent to delegate all or any of his powers.

DELEGATION OF DIRECTORS' POWERS

72. The directors may delegate any of their powers to any committee consisting of one or more directors. They may also delegate to any managing director or any director holding any other executive office such of their powers as they consider desirable to be exercised by him. Any such delegation may be made subject to any conditions the directors may impose, and either collaterally with or to the exclusion of their own powers and may be revoked or altered. Subject to any such conditions, the proceedings of a committee with two or more members shall be governed by the articles regulating the proceedings of directors so far as they are capable of applying.

APPOINTMENT AND RETIREMENT OF DIRECTORS

73. At the first annual general meeting all the directors shall retire from office, and at every subsequent annual general meeting one-third of the directors who are subject to retirement by rotation or, if their number is not three or a multiple of three, the number nearest to one-third shall retire from office; but, if there is only one director who is subject to retirement by rotation, he shall retire.

74. Subject to the provisions of the Act, the directors to retire by rotation shall be those who have been longest in office since their last appointment or reappointment, but as between persons who became or were last reappointed directors on the same day those to retire shall (unless they otherwise agree among themselves) be determined by lot.

75. If the company, at the meeting at which a director retires by rotation, does not fill the vacancy the retiring director shall, if willing to act, be deemed to have been reappointed unless at the meeting it is resolved not to fill the vacancy or unless a resolution for the reappointment of the director is put to the meeting and lost.

76. No person other than a director retiring by rotation shall be appointed or reappointed a director at any general meeting unless—

(a) he is recommended by the directors; or
(b) not less than fourteen nor more than thirty-five clear days before the date appointed for the meeting, notice executed by a member qualified to vote at the meeting has been given to the company of the intention to propose that person for appointment or reappointment stating the particulars which would, if he were so appointed or reappointed, be required to be included in the company's register of directors together with notice executed by that person of his willingness to be appointed or reappointed.

77. Not less than seven nor more than twenty-eight clear days before the date appointed for holding a general meeting notice shall be given to all who are entitled to receive notice of the meeting of any person (other than a director retiring by rotation at the meeting) who is recommended by the directors for appointment or reappointment as a director at the meeting or in respect of whom notice has been duly given to the company of the intention to propose him at the meeting for appointment or reappointment as a director. The notice shall give the particulars of that person which would, if he were so appointed or reappointed, be required to be included in the company's register of directors.

78. Subject as aforesaid, the company may by ordinary resolution appoint a person who is willing to act to be a director either to fill a vacancy or as an additional director and may also determine the rotation in which any additional directors are to retire.

79. The directors may appoint a person who is willing to act to be a director, either to fill a vacancy or as an additional director, provided that the appointment does not cause the number of directors to exceed any number fixed by or in accordance with the articles as the maximum number of directors. A director so appointed shall hold office only until the next following annual general meeting and shall not be taken into account in determining the directors who are to retire by rotation at the meeting. If not reappointed at such annual general meeting, he shall vacate office at the conclusion thereof.

80. Subject as aforesaid, a director who retires at an annual general meeting may, if willing to act, be reappointed. If he is not reappointed, he shall retain office until the meeting appoints someone in his place, or if it does not do so, until the end of the meeting.

DISQUALIFICATION AND REMOVAL OF DIRECTORS

81. The office of a director shall be vacated if—

(a) he ceases to be a director by virtue of any provision of the Act or he becomes prohibited by law from being a director; or
(b) he becomes bankrupt or makes any arrangement or composition with his creditors generally; or
(c) he is, or may be, suffering from mental disorder and either—
  (i) he is admitted to hospital in pursuance of an application for admission for treatment under the Mental Health Act 1983 or, in Scotland, an application for admission under the Mental Health (Scotland) Act 1960, or
  (ii) an order is made by a court having jurisdiction (whether in the United Kingdom or elsewhere) in matters concerning mental disorder for his detention or for the appointment of a receiver, curator bonis or other person to exercise powers with respect to his property or affairs; or
(d) he resigns his office by notice to the company; or
(e) he shall for more than six consecutive months have been absent without permission of the directors from meetings of directors held during that period and the directors resolve that his office be vacated.

REMUNERATION OF DIRECTORS

82. The directors shall be entitled to such remuneration as the company may by ordinary resolution determine and, unless the resolution provides otherwise, the remuneration shall be deemed to accrue from day to day.

DIRECTORS' EXPENSES

83. The directors may be paid all travelling, hotel, and other expenses properly incurred by them in connection with their attendance at meetings of directors or committees of directors or general meetings or separate meetings of the holders of any class of shares or of debentures of the company or otherwise in connection with the discharge of their duties.

DIRECTORS' APPOINTMENTS AND INTERESTS

84. Subject to the provisions of the Act, the directors may appoint one or more of their number to the office of managing director or to any other executive office under the company and may enter into an agreement or arrangement with any director for his employment by the company or for the provision by him of any services outside the scope of the ordinary duties of a director. Any such appointment, agreement or arrangement may be made upon such terms as the directors determine and they may remunerate any such director for his services as they think fit. Any appointment of a director to an executive office shall terminate if he ceases to be a director but without prejudice to any claim to damages for breach of the contract of service between the director and the company. A managing director and a director holding any other executive office shall not be subject to retirement by rotation.

85. Subject to the provisions of the Act, and provided that he has disclosed to the directors the nature and extent of any material interest of his, a director notwithstanding his office—

(a) may be a party to, or otherwise interested in, any transaction or arrangement with the company or in which the company is otherwise interested;

(b) may be a director or other officer of, or employed by, or a party to any transaction or arrangement with, or otherwise interested in, any body corporate promoted by the company or in which the company is otherwise interested; and

(c) shall not, by reason of his office, be accountable to the company for any benefit which he derives from any such office or employment or from any such transaction or arrangement or from any interest in any such body corporate and no such transaction or arrangement shall be liable to be avoided on the ground of any such interest or benefit.

86. For the purposes of regulation 85—

(a) a general notice given to the directors that a director is to be regarded as having an interest of the nature and extent specified in the notice in any transaction or arrangement in which a specified person or class of persons is interested shall be deemed to be a disclosure that the director has an interest in any such transaction of the nature and extent so specified; and

(b) an interest of which a director has no knowledge and of which it is unreasonable to expect him to have knowledge shall not be treated as an interest of his.

DIRECTORS' GRATUITIES AND PENSIONS

87. The directors may provide benefits, whether by the payment of gratuities or pensions or by insurance or otherwise, for any director who has held but no longer holds any executive office or employment with the company or with any body corporate which is or has been a subsidiary of the company or a predecessor in business of the company or of any such subsidiary, and for any member of his family (including a spouse and a former spouse) or any person who is or was dependent on him, and may (as well before as after he ceases to hold such office or employment) contribute to any fund and pay premiums for the purchase or provision of any such benefit.

PROCEEDINGS OF DIRECTORS

88. Subject to the provisions of the articles, the directors may regulate their proceedings as they think fit. A director may, and the secretary at the request of a director shall, call a meeting of the directors. It shall not be necessary to give notice of a meeting to a director who is absent from the United Kingdom. Questions arising at a meeting shall be decided by a majority of votes. In the case of an equality of votes, the chairman shall have a second or casting vote. A director who is also an alternate director shall be entitled in the absence of his appointor to a separate vote on behalf of his appointor in addition to his own vote.

89. The quorum for the transaction of the business of the directors may be fixed by the directors and unless so fixed at any other number shall be two. A person who holds office only as an alternate director shall, if his appointor is not present, be counted in the quorum.

90. The continuing directors or a sole continuing director may act notwithstanding any vacancies in their number, but, if the number of directors is less than the number fixed as the quorum, the continuing directors or director may act only for the purpose of filling vacancies or of calling a general meeting.

91. The directors may appoint one of their number to be the chairman of the board of directors and may at any time remove him from that office. Unless he is unwilling to do so, the director so appointed shall preside at every meeting of directors at which he is present. But if there is no director holding that office, or if the director holding it is unwilling to preside or is not present within five minutes after the time appointed for the meeting, the directors present may appoint one of their number to be chairman of the meeting.

92. All acts done by a meeting of directors, or of a committee of directors, or by a person acting as a director shall, notwithstanding that it be afterwards discovered that there was a defect in the appointment of any director or that any of them were disqualified from holding office, or had vacated office, or were not entitled to vote, be as valid as if every such person had been duly appointed and was qualified and had continued to be a director and had been entitled to vote.

93. A resolution in writing signed by all the directors entitled to receive notice of a meeting of directors or of a committee of directors shall be as valid and effectual as if it had been passed at a meeting of directors or (as the case may be) a committee of directors duly convened and held and may consist of several documents in the like form each signed by one or more directors; but a resolution signed by an alternate director need not also be signed by his appointor and, if it is signed by a director who has appointed an alternate director, it need not be signed by the alternate director in that capacity.

94. Save as otherwise provided by the articles, a director shall not vote at a meeting of directors or of a committee of directors on any resolution concerning a matter in which he has, directly or indirectly, an interest or duty which is material and which conflicts or may conflict with the interests of the company unless his interest or duty arises only because the case falls within one or more of the following paragraphs—

(a) the resolution relates to the giving to him of a guarantee, security, or indemnity in respect of money lent to, or an obligation incurred by him for the benefit of, the company or any of its subsidiaries;

(b) the resolution relates to the giving to a third party of a guarantee, security, or indemnity in respect of an obligation of the company or any of its subsidiaries for which the director has assumed responsibility in whole or part and whether alone or jointly with others under a guarantee or indemnity or by the giving of security;

(c) his interest arises by virtue of his subscribing or agreeing to subscribe for any shares, debentures or other securities of the company or any of its subsidiaries, or by virtue of his being, or intending to become, a participant in the underwriting or sub-underwriting of an offer of any such shares, debentures, or other securities by the company or any of its subsidiaries for subscription, purchase or exchange;

(d) the resolution relates in any way to a retirement benefits scheme which has been approved, or is conditional upon approval, by the Board of Inland Revenue for taxation purposes.

For the purposes of this regulation, an interest of a person who is, for any purpose of the Act (excluding any statutory modification thereof not in force when this regulation becomes binding on the company), connected with a director shall be treated as an interest of the director and, in relation to an alternate director, an interest of his appointor shall be treated as an interest of the alternate director without prejudice to any interest which the alternate director has otherwise.

95. A director shall not be counted in the quorum present at a meeting in relation to a resolution on which he is not entitled to vote.

96. The company may by ordinary resolution suspend or relax to any extent, either generally or in respect of any particular matter, any provision of the articles prohibiting a director from voting at a meeting of directors or of a committee of directors.

97. Where proposals are under consideration concerning the appointment of two or more directors to offices or employments with the company or any body corporate in which the company is interested the proposals may be divided and considered in relation to each director separately and (provided he is not for another reason precluded from voting) each of the directors concerned shall be entitled to vote and be counted in the quorum in respect of each resolution except that concerning his own appointment.

98. If a question arises at a meeting of directors or of a committee of directors as to the right of a director to vote, the question may, before the conclusion of the meeting, be referred to the chairman of the meeting and his ruling in relation to any director other than himself shall be final and conclusive.

SECRETARY

99. Subject to the provisions of the Act, the secretary shall be appointed by the directors for such term, at such remuneration and upon such conditions as they may think fit; and any secretary so appointed may be removed by them.

MINUTES

100. The directors shall cause minutes to be made in books kept for the purpose—

(a) of all appointments of officers made by the directors; and
(b) of all proceedings at meetings of the company, of the holders of any class of shares in the company, and of the directors, and of committees of directors, including the names of the directors present at each such meeting.

THE SEAL

101. The seal shall only be used by the authority of the directors or of a committee of directors authorised by the directors. The directors may determine who shall sign any instrument to which the seal is affixed and unless otherwise so determined it shall be signed by a director and by the secretary or by a second director.

DIVIDENDS

102. Subject to the provisions of the Act, the company may by ordinary resolution declare dividends in accordance with the respective rights of the members, but no dividend shall exceed the amount recommended by the directors.

103. Subject to the provisions of the Act, the directors may pay interim dividends if it appears to them that they are justified by the profits of the company available for distribution. If the share capital is divided into different classes, the directors may pay interim dividends on shares which confer deferred or non-preferred rights with regard to dividend as well as on shares which confer preferential rights with regard to dividend, but no interim dividend shall be paid on shares carrying deferred or non-preferred rights if, at the time of payment, any preferential dividend is in arrear. The directors may also pay at intervals settled by them any dividend payable at a fixed rate if it appears to them that the profits available for distribution justify the payment. Provided the directors act in good faith they shall not incur any liability to the holders of shares conferring preferred rights for any loss they may suffer by the lawful payment of an interim dividend on any shares having deferred or non-preferred rights.

104. Except as otherwise provided by the rights attached to shares, all dividends shall be declared and paid according to the amounts paid up on the shares on which the dividend is paid. All dividends shall be apportioned and paid proportionately to the amounts paid up on the shares during any portion or portions of the period in respect of which the dividend is paid; but, if any share is issued on terms providing that it shall rank for dividend as from a particular date, that share shall rank for dividend accordingly.

105. A general meeting declaring a dividend may, upon the recommendation of the directors, direct that it shall be satisfied wholly or partly by the distribution of assets and, where any difficulty arises in regard to the distribution, the directors may settle the same and in particular may issue fractional certificates and fix the value for distribution of any assets and may determine that cash shall be paid to any member upon the footing of the value so fixed in order to adjust the rights of members and may vest any assets in trustees.

106. Any dividend or other moneys payable in respect of a share may be paid by cheque sent by post to the registered address of the person entitled or, if two or more persons are the holders of the share or are jointly entitled to it by reason of the death or bankruptcy of the holder, to the registered address of that one of those persons who is first named in the register of members or to such person and to such address as the person or persons entitled may in writing direct. Every cheque shall be made payable to the order of the person or persons entitled or to such other person as the person or persons entitled may in writing direct and payment of the cheque shall be a good discharge to the company. Any joint holder or other person jointly entitled to a share as aforesaid may give receipts for any dividend or other moneys payable in respect of the share.

107. No dividend or other moneys payable in respect of a share shall bear interest against the company unless otherwise provided by the rights attached to the share.

108. Any dividend which has remained unclaimed for twelve years from the date when it became due for payment shall, if the directors so resolve, be forfeited and cease to remain owing by the company.

ACCOUNTS

109. No member shall (as such) have any right of inspecting any accounting records or other book or document of the company except as conferred by statute or authorised by the directors or by ordinary resolution of the company.

CAPITALISATION OF PROFITS

110. The directors may with the authority of an ordinary resolution of the company—

(a) subject as hereinafter provided, resolve to capitalise any undivided profits of the company not required for paying any preferential dividend (whether or not they are available for distribution) or any sum standing to the credit of the company's share premium account or capital redemption reserve;

(b) appropriate the sum resolved to be capitalised to the members who would have been entitled to it if it were distributed by way of dividend and in the same proportions and apply such sum on their behalf either in or towards paying up the amounts, if any, for the time being unpaid on any shares held by them respectively, or in paying up in full unissued shares or debentures of the company of a nominal amount equal to that sum, and allot the shares or debentures credited as fully paid to those members, or as they may direct, in those proportions, or partly in one way and partly in the other: but the share premium account, the capital redemption reserve, and any profits which are not available for distribution may, for the purposes of this regulation, only be applied in paying up unissued shares to be allotted to members credited as fully paid;

(c) make such provision by the issue of fractional certificates or by payment in cash or otherwise as they determine in the case of shares or debentures becoming distributable under this regulation in fractions; and

(d) authorise any person to enter on behalf of all the members concerned into an agreement with the company providing for the allotment to them respectively, credited as fully paid, of any shares or debentures to which they are entitled upon such capitalisation, any agreement made under such authority being binding on all such members.

NOTICES

111. Any notice to be given to or by any person pursuant to the articles shall be in writing except that a notice calling a meeting of the directors need not be in writing.

112. The company may give any notice to a member either personally or by sending it by post in a prepaid envelope addressed to the member at his registered address or by leaving it at that address.

In the case of joint holders of a share, all notices shall be given to the joint holder whose name stands first in the register of members in respect of the joint holding and notice so given shall be sufficient notice to all the joint holders. A member whose registered address is not within the United Kingdom and who gives to the company an address within the United Kingdom at which notices may be given to him shall be entitled to have notices given to him at that address, but otherwise no such member shall be entitled to receive any notice from the company.

113. A member present, either in person or by proxy, at any meeting of the company or of the holders of any class of shares in the company shall be deemed to have received notice of the meeting and, where requisite, of the purposes for which it was called.

114. Every person who becomes entitled to a share shall be bound by any notice in respect of that share which, before his name is entered in the register of members, has been duly given to a person from whom he derives his title.

115. Proof that an envelope containing a notice was properly addressed, prepaid and posted shall be conclusive evidence that the notice was given. A notice shall be deemed to be given at the expiration of 48 hours after the envelope containing it was posted.*

116. A notice may be given by the company to the persons entitled to a share in consequence of the death or bankruptcy of a member by sending or delivering it, in any manner authorised by the articles for the giving of notice to a member, addressed to them by name, or by the title of representatives of the deceased, or trustee of the bankrupt or by any like description at the address, if any, within the United Kingdom supplied for that purpose by the persons claiming to be so entitled. Until such an address has been supplied, a notice may be given in any manner in which it might have been given if the death or bankruptcy had not occurred.

WINDING UP

117. If the company is wound up, the liquidator may, with the sanction of an extraordinary resolution of the company and any other sanction required by the Act, divide among the members in specie the whole or any part of the assets of the company and may, for that purpose, value any assets and determine how the division shall be carried out as between the members or different classes of members. The liquidator may, with the like sanction, vest the whole or any part of the assets in trustees upon such trusts for the benefit of the members as he with the like sanction determines, but no member shall be compelled to accept any assets upon which there is a liability.

---

* [Includes amendment introduced by S.I. 1985 No. 1052, from August 1, 1985].

INDEMNITY

118. Subject to the provisions of the Act but without prejudice to any indemnity to which a director may otherwise be entitled, every director or other officer or auditor of the company shall be indemnified out of the assets of the company against any liability incurred by him in defending any proceedings, whether civil or criminal, in which judgment is given in his favour or in which he is acquitted or in connection with any application in which relief is granted to him by the court from liability for negligence, default, breach of duty or breach of trust in relation to the affairs of the company.

TABLE B

A PRIVATE COMPANY LIMITED BY SHARES

Memorandum of Association

1. The company's name is "The South Wales Motor Transport Company cyfyngedig."
2. The company's registered office is to be situated in Wales.
3. The company's objects are the carriage of passengers and goods in motor vehicles between such places as the company may from time to time determine and the doing of all such other things as are incidental or conducive to the attainment of that object.
4. The liability of the members is limited.
5. The company's share capital is £50,000 divided into 50,000 shares of £1 each.

We, the subscribers to this memorandum of association, wish to be formed into a company pursuant to this memorandum; and we agree to take the number of shares shown opposite our respective names.

Name and Addresses of Subscribers	Number of shares taken by each Subscriber
1. Thomas Jones, 138 Mountfield Street, Tredegar.	1
2. Mary Evans, 19 Merthyr Road, Aberystwyth.	1
Total shares taken	2

Dated 19

Witness to the above signatures,
Anne Brown, "Woodlands", Fieldside Road, Bryn Mawr.

APPENDIX 1

TABLE C

A COMPANY LIMITED BY GUARANTEE AND NOT HAVING A SHARE CAPITAL

Memorandum of Association

1. The company's name is "The Dundee School Association Limited."

2. The company's registered office is to be situated in Scotland.

3. The company's objects are the carrying on of a school for boys and girls in Dundee and the doing of all such other things as are incidental or conducive to the attainment of that object.

4. The liability of the members is limited.

5. Every member of the company undertakes to contribute such amount as may be required (not exceeding £100) to the company's assets if it should be wound up while he is a member or within one year after he ceases to be a member, for payment of the company's debts and liabilities contracted before he ceases to be a member, and of the costs, charges and expenses of winding up, and for the adjustment of the rights of the contributories among themselves.

We, the subscribers to this memorandum of association, wish to be formed into a company pursuant to this memorandum.

Names and Addresses of
Subscribers.

1. Kenneth Brodie, 14 Bute Street,
   Dundee.
2. Ian Davis, 2 Burns Avenue,
   Dundee.

Dated   19

Witness to the above signatures.
Anne Brown, 149 Princes Street, Edinburgh.

Articles of Association

PRELIMINARY

1. Regulations 2 to 35 inclusive, 54, 55, 57, 59, 102 to 108 inclusive, 110, 114, 116 and 117 of Table A, shall not apply to the company but the articles hereinafter contained and, subject to the modifications hereinafter expressed, the remaining regulations of Table A shall constitute the articles of association of the company.

INTERPRETATION

2. In regulation 1 of Table A, the definition of "the holder" shall be omitted.

MEMBERS

3. The subscribers to the memorandum of association of the company and such other persons as are admitted to membership in accordance with the articles shall be members of the company. No person shall be admitted a member of the company unless he is approved by the directors. Every person who wishes to become a member shall deliver to the company an application for membership in such form as the directors require executed by him.

4. A member may at any time withdraw from the company by giving at least seven clear days' notice to the company. Membership shall not be transferable and shall cease on death.

NOTICE OF GENERAL MEETINGS

5. In regulation 38 of Table A—

(a) in paragraph (b) the words "of the total voting rights at the meeting of all the members" shall be substituted for "in nominal value of the shares giving that right" and

(b) the words "The notice shall be given to all the members and to the directors and auditors" shall be substituted for the last sentence.

PROCEEDINGS AT GENERAL MEETINGS

6. The words "and at any separate meeting of the holders of any class of shares in the company" shall be omitted from regulation 44 of Table A.

7. Paragraph (d) of regulation 46 of Table A shall be omitted.

VOTES OF MEMBERS

8. On a show of hands every member present in person shall have one vote. On a poll every member present in person or by proxy shall have one vote.

DIRECTORS' EXPENSES

9. The words "of any class of shares or" shall be omitted from regulation 83 of Table A.

PROCEEDINGS OF DIRECTORS

10. In paragraph (c) of regulation 94 of Table A the word "debentures" shall be substituted for the words "shares, debentures or other securities" in both places where they occur.

MINUTES

11. The words "of the holders of any class of shares in the company" shall be omitted from regulation 100 of Table A.

NOTICES

12. The second sentence of regulation 112 of Table A shall be omitted.

13. The words "or of the holders of any class of shares in the company" shall be omitted from regulation 113 of Table A.

TABLE D

PART I

A PUBLIC COMPANY LIMITED BY GUARANTEE AND HAVING A SHARE CAPITAL

Memorandum of Association

1. The company's name is "Gwestai Glyndwr, cwmni cyfyngedig cyhoeddus."

2. The company is to be a public company.

3. The company's registered office is to be situated in Wales.

4. The company's objects are facilitating travelling in Wales by providing hotels and conveyances by sea and by land for the accommodation of travellers and the doing of all such other things as are incidental or conducive to the attainment of those objects.

5. The liability of the members is limited.

6. Every member of the company undertakes to contribute such amount as may be required (not exceeding £100) to the company's assets if it should be wound up while he is a member or within one year after he ceases to be a member, for payment of the company's debts and liabilities contracted before he ceases to be a member, and of the costs, charges and expenses of winding up, and for the adjustment of the rights of the contributories among themselves.

7. The company's share capital is £50,000 divided into 50,000 shares of £1 each.

We, the subscribers to this memorandum of association, wish to be formed into a company pursuant to this memorandum; and we agree to take the number of shares shown opposite our respective names.

Name and Addresses of Subscribers	Number of shares taken by each Subscriber
1. Thomas Jones, 138 Mountfield Street, Tredegar.	1
2. Andrew Smith, 19 Merthyr Road, Aberystwyth.	1
Total shares taken	2

Dated 19

Witness to the above signatures,
Anne Brown, "Woodlands", Fieldside Road, Bryn Mawr.

PART II

A PRIVATE COMPANY LIMITED BY GUARANTEE AND HAVING A SHARE CAPITAL

Memorandum of Association

1. The company's name is "The Highland Hotel Company Limited."

2. The company's registered office is to be situated in Scotland.

3. The company's objects are facilitating travelling in the Highlands of Scotland by providing hotels and conveyances by sea and by land for the accommodation of travellers and the doing of all such other things as are incidental or conducive to the attainment of those objects.

4. The liability of the members is limited.

5. Every member of the company undertakes to contribute such amount as may be required (not exceeding £100) to the company's assets if it should be wound up while he is a member or within one year after he ceases to be a member, for payment of the company's debts and liabilities contracted before he ceases to be a member, and of the costs, charges and expenses of winding up, and for the adjustment of the rights of the contributories among themselves.

6. The company's share capital is £50,000 divided into 50,000 shares of £1 each.

We, the subscribers to this memorandum of association, wish to be formed into a company pursuant to this memorandum; and we agree to take the number of shares shown opposite our respective names.

Name and Addresses of Subscribers	Number of shares taken by each Subscriber
Kenneth Brodie, 14 Bute Street Dundee.	1
Ian Davis, 2 Burns Avenue, Dundee.	1
Total shares taken	2

Dated 19

Witness to the above signatures,
Anne Brown, 149 Princes Street, Edinburgh.

PART III

A COMPANY (PUBLIC OR PRIVATE) LIMITED BY GUARANTEE AND HAVING A SHARE CAPITAL

Articles of Association

The regulations of Table A shall constitute the articles of association of the company.

TABLE E

AN UNLIMITED COMPANY HAVING A SHARE CAPITAL

Memorandum of Association

1. The company's name is "The Woodford Engineering Company."
2. The company's registered office is to be situated in England and Wales.
3. The company's objects are the working of certain patented inventions relating to the application of microchip technology to the

improvement of food processing, and the doing of all such other things as are incidental or conducive to the attainment of that object.

We, the subscribers to this memorandum of association, wish to be formed into a company pursuant to this memorandum; and we agree to take the number of shares shown opposite our respective names.

Name and Addresses of Subscribers	Number of shares taken by each Subscriber
1. Brian Smith, 24 Nibley Road, Wotton-under-Edge, Gloucestershire.	3
2. William Green, 278 High Street Chipping Sodbury, Avon.	5
Total shares taken	8

Dated 19

Witness to the above signatures,

Anne Brown, 108 Park Way, Bristol 8.

Articles of Association

1. Regulations 3, 32, 34 and 35 of Table A shall not apply to the company, but the articles hereinafter contained and, subject to the modification hereinafter expressed, the remaining regulations of Table A shall constitute the articles of association of the company.

2. The words "at least seven clear days' notice" shall be substituted for the words "at least fourteen clear days' notice" in regulation 38 of Table A.

3. The share capital of the company is £20,000 divided into 20,000 shares of £1 each.

4. The company may by special resolution—

(a) increase the share capital by such sum to be divided into shares of such amount as the resolution may prescribe;
(b) consolidate and divide all or any of its share capital into shares of a larger amount than its existing shares;
(c) subdivide its shares, or any of them, into shares of a smaller amount than its existing shares;
(d) cancel any shares which at the date of the passing of the resolution have not been taken or agreed to be taken by any person;
(e) reduce its share capital and any share premium account in any way.

APPENDIX 1

TABLE F

A PUBLIC COMPANY LIMITED BY SHARES

Memorandum of Association

1. The company's name is "Western Electronics Public Limited Company."

2. The company is to be a public company.

3. The company's registered office is to be situated in England and Wales.

4. The company's objects are the manufacture and development of such descriptions of electronic equipment, instruments and appliances as the company may from time to time determine, and the doing of all such other things as are incidental or conducive to the attainment of that object.

5. The liability of the members is limited.

6. The company's share capital is £5,000,000 divided into 5,000,000 shares of £1 each.

We, the subscribers to this memorandum of association, wish to be formed into a company pursuant to this memorandum; and we agree to take the number of shares shown opposite our respective names.

Name and Addresses of Subscribers	Number of shares taken by each Subscriber
1. James White, 12 Broadmead, Birmingham.	1
2. Patrick Smith, 145A Huntley House, London Wall, London EC2.	1
Total shares taken	2

Dated   19 .

Witness to the above signatures,
Anne Brown, 13 Hute Street, London WC2.

EXPLANATORY NOTE

(This Note is not part of the Regulations.)

These Regulations replace the Companies (Alteration of Table A etc) Regulations 1984 which are revoked. They provide the regulations (Table A) and the forms of memorandum and articles of association

(Tables B, C, D, E and F) for the purposes of sections 3 and 8 of the Companies Act 1985.

Certain amendments have been made to Tables A and C. Table A has been amended as follows. The reference to "the Companies Acts 1948 to 1983" has been converted to "the Companies Act 1985" and the references to "the Acts" to "the Act." In regulation 33, the words "subject to the provisions of the Act" have been inserted after the word "including" in the words in parenthesis. In regulation 65, the words "resolution of" have been inserted after "approved by." In regulation 87, "directors" replaces "company" as the second word of this regulation. In regulation 90, the words "the continuing directors or director" are substituted for the word "they." In regulation 111, in the first sentence the words "to or by any person" have been inserted after "given" and the words "except that a notice calling a meeting of the directors need not be in writing" after the word "writing." The remainder of the first sentence (with the deletion of the words "and" and "such") and the second sentence of regulation 111 are removed and become the first and second sentences of regulation 112. In regulation 116, the words "by them" have been deleted.

The following amendments have been made to the Articles of Association in Table C. In regulation 1, the word "inclusive" has been deleted in the third place where it appeared. In regulation 10, the words "in both places where they occur" have been substituted for the words "where they twice occur." Regulation 12 has been amended to refer to regulation 112 of Table A.

The Regulations will come into operation simultaneously with the coming into force of the Companies Act 1985.

APPENDIX 2

EUROPEAN ECONOMIC INTEREST GROUPING REGULATIONS 1989

(S.I. 1989 No. 638)

Made	*10th April* 1989
Laid before Parliament	*19th April* 1989
Coming into force	*1st July* 1989

The Secretary of State, being a Minister designated for the purposes of section 2(2) of the European Communities Act 1972 in relation to measures relating to European Economic Interest Groupings and their members, in exercise of the powers conferred on him by that section and of all other powers enabling him in that behalf, hereby makes the following Regulations:—

PART I

GENERAL

Citation, commencement and extent

1. These Regulations, which extend to Great Britain, may be cited as the European Economic Interest Grouping Regulations 1989 and shall come into force on July 1, 1989.

Interpretation

2.—(1) In these Regulations—

"the 1985 Act" means the Companies Act 1985;

"the contract" means the contract for the formation of an EEIG;

"the EC Regulation" means Council Regulation (EEC) No. 2137/85 set out in Schedule 1 to these Regulations;

"EEIG"means a European Economic Interest Grouping being a grouping formed in pursuance of article 1 of the EC Regulation;

"officer", in relation to an EEIG, includes a manager, or any other person provided for in the contract as an organ of the EEIG; and

"the registrar" has the meaning given by regulations 9(1) and 12(1) below;

and other expressions used in these Regulations and defined by section 744 of the 1985 Act or in relation to insolvency and winding up by the Insolvency Act 1986 have the meanings assigned to them by those provisions as if any reference to a company in any such definition were a reference to an EEIG.

(2) A Form referred to in these Regulations by "EEIG" followed by a number means the Form so numbered in Schedule 2 to these Regulations.

(3) In these Regulations, "certified translation" means a translation certified to be a correct translation—

(a) if the translation was made in the United Kingdom, by
   (i) a notary public in any part of the United Kingdom;
   (ii) a solicitor (if the translation was made in Scotland), a solicitor of the Supreme Court of Judicature of England and Wales (if it was made in England or Wales), or a solicitor of the Supreme Court of Judicature of Northern Ireland (if it was made in Northern Ireland); or
   (iii) a person certified by a person mentioned above to be known to him to be competent to translate the document into English; or

(b) if the translation was made outside the United Kingdom, by—
   (i) a notary public;
   (ii) a person authorised in the place where the translation was made to administer an oath;
   (iii) any of the British officials mentioned in section 6 of the Commissioners for Oaths Act 1889;*
   (iv) a person certified by a person mentioned in sub-paragraph (i), (ii) or (iii) of this paragraph to be known to him to be competent to translate the document into English.

PART II

PROVISIONS RELATING TO ARTICLES 1–38 OF THE EC REGULATION

Legal personality (Article 1(3) of the EC Regulation)

3. From the date of registration of an EEIG in Great Britain mentioned in a certificate given under regulation 9(5) below the EEIG shall, subject to regulation 11 below, be a body corporate by the name contained in the contract.

---

* [as amended].

APPENDIX 2

Transfer of official address (Article 14 of the EC Regulation)

4.—(1) Notice of any proposal to transfer the official address of an EEIG registered in Great Britain to any other place shall, where such transfer would result in a change in the law applicable to the contract under article 2 of the EC Regulation, be filed at the registry where the EEIG was registered by delivery of a notice in Form EEIG 4 in pursuance of regulation 13(1) below.

(2) Where the registrar, being the competent authority within the meaning of article 14(4) of the EC Regulation, receives a notice under paragraph (1) above and within the period of two months beginning with its publication in the Gazette under regulation 15(1) below opposes that transfer on the grounds of public interest, that transfer shall not take effect.

Managers (Article 19(2) of the EC Regulation)

5.—(1) A manager of an EEIG registered in Great Britain may be a legal person other than a natural person, on condition that it designates one or more natural persons to represent it and notice of particulars of each such person is sent to the registrar in Form EEIG 3 as though he were a manager.

(2) Any natural person designated under paragraph (1) above shall be subject to the same liabilities as if he himself were a manager.

(3) There shall be delivered to the registrar in accordance with the provisions of regulation 13(1) below notice of appointment of any manager and the following particulars with respect to each manager—

(a) (i) his present Christian name and surname;
(ii) any former Christian name or surname;
(iii) his usual residential address;
(iv) his nationality;
(v) his business occupation (if any); and
(vi) the date of his birth; and

(b) in the case of a legal person other than a natural person, its name and registered or principal office.

(4) Section 289(2) of the 1985 Act applies as regards the meaning of "Christian name," "surname" and "former Christian name or surname."

Cessation of membership (Article 28(1) of the EC Regulation)

6. For the purposes of national law on liquidation, winding up, insolvency or cessation of payments, a member of an EEIG registered under these Regulations shall cease to be a member if—

(a) in the case of an individual—
(i) a bankruptcy order has been made against him in England and Wales; or

(i) a bankruptcy order has been made against him in England and Wales; or
(ii) sequestration of his estate has been awarded by the court in Scotland under the Bankruptcy (Scotland) Act 1985;

(b) in the case of a partnership—
(i) a winding up order has been made against the partnership in England and Wales;
(ii) a bankruptcy order has been made against its members in England and Wales on a bankruptcy petition presented under article 13(1) of the Insolvent Part-nerships Order 1986; or
(iii) sequestration of the estate of the partnership has been awarded by the court in Scotland under the Bank-ruptcy (Scotland) Act 1985;

(c) in the case of a company, the company goes into liquidation in Great Britain; or

(d) in the case of any legal person or partnership, it is otherwise wound up or otherwise ceases to exist after the conclusion of winding up or insolvency.

Competent authority (Articles 32(1) and (3) and 38 of the EC Regulation)

7.—(1) The Secretary of State shall be the competent authority for the purposes of making an application to the court under article 32(1) of the EC Regulation (winding up of EEIG in certain circumstances).

(2) The court may, on an application by the Secretary of State, order the winding up of an EEIG which has its official address in Great Britain, if the EEIG acts contrary to the public interest and it is expedient in the public interest that the EEIG should be wound up and the court is of the opinion that it is just and equitable for it to be so.

(3) The court, on an application by the Secretary of State, shall be the competent authority for the purposes of prohibiting under article 38 of the EC Regulation any activity carried on in Great Britain by an EEIG where such an activity is in contravention of the public interest there.

Winding up and conclusion of liquidation (Articles 35 and 36 of the EC Regulation)

8.—(1) Where an EEIG is wound up as an unregistered company under Part V of the Insolvency Act 1986, the provisions of Part V shall apply in relation to the EEIG as if any reference in that Act and the 1985 Act to a director or past director of a company included a reference to a manager of the EEIG and any other person who has or has had control or management of the EEIG's business and with the modification that in section 221(1) after the words "all the provisions" there shall be added the words "of Council Regulation (EEC) No. 2137/85 and."

(2) At the end of the period of three months beginning with the day of receipt by the registrar of a notice of the conclusion of the liquidation of an EEIG, the EEIG shall be dissolved.

PART III

REGISTRATION ETC (ARTICLE 39 OF THE EC REGULATION)

Registration of EEIG whose official address is in Great Britain

9.—(1) The registrar for the purposes of registration of an EEIG in Great Britain where its official address is in Great Britain shall be the registrar within the meaning of the 1985 Act and the contract shall be delivered—

(a) to the registrar or other officer performing under that Act the duty of registration of companies in England and Wales, if the contract states that the official address of the EEIG is to be situated in England and Wales, or that it is to be situated in Wales; and

(b) to the registrar or other officer performing under that Act the duty of registration of companies in Scotland, if the contract states that the official address of the EEIG is to be situated in Scotland.

(2) With the contract there shall be delivered a registration form in Form EEIG 1 containing a statement of the names and the particulars set out in article 5 of the EC Regulation.

(3) The registrar shall not register an EEIG under this regulation unless he is satisfied that all the requirements of these Regulations and of the EC Regulation in respect of registration and of matters precedent and incidental to it have been complied with but he may accept a declaration in Form EEIG 1 as sufficient evidence of compliance.

(4) Subject to paragraph (3) above, the registrar shall retain the contract, and any certified translation, delivered to him under this regulation and register the EEIG.

(5) On the registration of an EEIG the registrar shall give a certificate that the EEIG has been registered stating the date of registration.

(6) The certificate may be signed by the registrar, or authenticated by his official seal.

(7) A certificate of registration given in respect of an EEIG under this regulation is conclusive evidence that the requirements of these

Regulations and of the EC Regulation in respect of registration and of matters precedent and incidental to it have been complied with, and that the EEIG is an organisation authorised to be registered, and is duly registered, under these Regulations.

(8) Where an EEIG is to be registered with the contract written in any language other than English, the contract to be delivered under paragraph (1) above may be in the other language provided that it is accompanied by a certified translation into English.

(9) Where an EEIG has published a proposal to transfer its official address to a place in Great Britain under article 14(1) of the EC Regulation, the registrar responsible for the registration of the EEIG with the new official address shall, where the transfer of the official address has not been opposed under paragraph (4) of that article, register the EEIG with its new official address on receipt of a registration form in Form EEIG 1 containing—

(a) evidence of the publication of the transfer proposal; and
(b) a statement that no competent authority has opposed the transfer under article 14(4) of the EC Regulation.

(10) Any communication or notice may be addressed to an EEIG where its official address is in Great Britain at its official address stated on Form EEIG 1 or in the case of any change in the situation of that address at any new official address stated on Form EEIG 4.

Prohibition on registration of certain names

10.—(1) An EEIG shall not be registered in Great Britain under regulation 9 above by a name which includes any of the following words or expressions, or abbreviations thereof, that is to say, "limited," "unlimited" or "public limited company" or their Welsh equivalents.

(2) In determining for the purposes of section 26(1)(c) of the 1985 Act (as applied by regulation 18 of, and Schedule 4 to, these Regulations) whether one name is the same as another, there are to be disregarded the words "European Economic Interest Grouping" or the initials "EEIG" or their authorised equivalents in official languages of the Economic Community, other than English, the authorised equivalents being set out in Schedule 3 to these Regulations.

Change of name

11.—(1) Regulation 10(2) above applies in determining under section 28(2) of the 1985 Act as applied by regulation 18 of, and Schedule 4 to, these Regulations whether a name is the same as or too like another.

(2) Where an EEIG changes its name the registrar shall (subject to the provisions of section 26 of the 1985 Act which apply by virtue of

regulation 18 of, and Schedule 4 to, these Regulations and regulation 10 above) enter the new name on the register in place of the former name, and shall issue a certificate of registration altered to meet the circumstances of the case.

(3) A change of name has effect from the date on which the altered certificate is issued.

Registration of establishment of EEIG whose official address is outside the United Kingdom

12.—(1) The registrar for the purposes of registration under this regulation of an EEIG establishment situated in Great Britain where the EEIG's official address is outside the United Kingdom shall be the registrar within the meaning of the 1985 Act.

(2) For the purposes of registration under paragraph (1) above there shall be delivered, within one month of the establishment becoming so situated at any place in Great Britain, to the registrar at the registration office in England and Wales or Scotland, according to where the establishment is situated, a certified copy of the contract together with—

(a) a certified translation into English of the contract and other documents and particulars to be filed with it under article 10 of the EC Regulation if the contract and other documents and particulars, or any part thereof, are not in English; and

(b) a registration form in Form EEIG 2 containing a statement of the names and particulars set out in articles 5 and 10 of the EC Regulation.

(3) Paragraph (2) above shall not apply where an establishment is already registered in Great Britain under paragraph (1) above.

(4) The registrar shall not register an EEIG establishment under this regulation unless he is satisfied that all the requirements of these Regulations and of the EC Regulation in respect of registration and of matters precedent and incidental to it have been complied with but he may accept a declaration in Form EEIG 2 as sufficient evidence of compliance.

(5) Subject to paragraph (4) above, the registrar shall retain the copy of the contract and any certified translation, delivered to him under paragraph (2) above and register the EEIG establishment.

(6) Any communication or notice may be addressed to an EEIG where its official address is outside the United Kingdom at any of its establishments in Great Britain.

(7) Regulation 10 above shall apply to an EEIG establishment to be registered under this regulation as it applies to an EEIG to be registered under regulation 9.

(8) If an EEIG fails to comply with any provision of paragraph (2) above, the EEIG, and any officer of it who intentionally authorises or

permits the default, is guilty of an offence and liable on summary conviction to a fine not exceeding level 3 on the standard scale and if the failure to comply with any such provision continues after conviction, the EEIG and any such officer shall be guilty of a further offence of failure to comply with that provision and shall be liable to be proceeded against and punished accordingly.

Filing of documents

13.—(1) The documents and particulars referred to in paragraphs (a) to (j) of article 7 of the EC Regulation and required to be filed under that article in Great Britain shall be filed within 15 days (or, in the case of an EEIG whose official address is outside the United Kingdom, 30 days) of the event to which the document in question relates by delivery to the registrar for registration of a notice, together with a certified translation into English of any documents and particulars, or any part thereof, which are not in English—

(a) in the case of paragraph (d) where the official address of the EEIG is in Great Britain, in Form EEIG 3 of the names of the managers and the particulars referred to in regulation 5(3) above, of particulars of whether they may act alone or must act jointly and of the termination of any manager's appoint-ment;
(b) in the case of paragraphs (a), (c) and (e) to (j), and in the case of paragraph (d) where the official address of the EEIG is outside the United Kingdom, in Form EEIG 4 of the documents and particulars referred to in that Form; and
(c) in the case of paragraph (b), in Form EEIG 5 of the setting up or closure of an establishment of an EEIG in Great Britain, except where regulation 12(1) above applies.

(2) The registrar shall retain the documents and particulars and any certified translation delivered to him under this regulation.

(3) If an EEIG fails to comply with any provision of paragraph (1) above, the EEIG, and any officer of it who intentionally authorises or permits the default, is guilty of an offence and liable on summary conviction to a fine not exceeding level 3 on the standard scale and if the failure to comply with any such provision continues after conviction, the EEIG and any such officer shall be guilty of a further offence of failure to comply with that provision and shall be liable to be proceeded against and punished accordingly.

Inspection of documents

14. Any person may—

(a) inspect any document or particulars kept by the registrar under these Regulations or a copy thereof; and

(b) require the registrar to deliver or send by post to him a copy or extract of any such document or particulars or any part thereof.

Publication of documents in the Gazette and Official Journal of the Communities

15.—(1) The registrar shall cause to be published in the Gazette—

(a) the documents and particulars issued or received by him under these Regulations and referred to in article (8)(a) and (b) of the EC Regulation; and
(b) in the case of those documents and particulars referred to in article 7(b) to (j) of the EC Regulation a notice (stating in the notice the name of the EEIG, the description of the documents or particulars and the date of receipt).

(2) The registrar shall forward to the Office for Official Publications of the European Communities the information referred to in article 11 of the EC Regulation within one month of the publication of the relevant documents and particulars in the Gazette under paragraph (1) above.

EEIG identification

16.—(1) If an EEIG fails to comply with article 25 of the EC Regulation it is guilty of an offence and liable on summary conviction to a fine not exceeding level 3 on the standard scale.

(2) If an officer of an EEIG or a person on its behalf issues or authorises the issue of any letter, order form or similar document not complying with the requirements of article 25 of the EC Regulation, he is guilty of an offence and liable on summary conviction to a fine not exceeding level 3 on the standard scale.

PART IV

SUPPLEMENTAL PROVISIONS

Application of the Business Names Act 1985

17. The Business Names Act 1985 shall apply in relation to an EEIG which carries on business in Great Britain as if the EEIG were a company formed and registered under the 1985 Act.

Application of the Companies Act 1985

18. The provisions of the 1985 Act specified in Schedule 4 to these Regulations shall apply to EEIGs, and their establishments, registered or in the process of being registered under these Regulations, as if they were companies formed and registered or in the process of being registered under the 1985 Act and as if in those provisions any reference to the Companies Act included a reference to these Regulations and any reference to a registered office included a reference to an official address, but subject to any limitations mentioned in relation to those provisions in that Schedule and to the omission of any reference to a daily default fine.

Application of Insolvency Act 1986

19.—(1) Part III of the Insolvency Act 1986 shall apply to EEIGs, and their establishments, registered under these Regulations, as if they were companies registered under the 1985 Act.

(2) Section 120 of the Insolvency Act 1986 shall apply to an EEIG, and its establishments, registered under these Regulations in Scotland, as if it were a company registered in Scotland the paid-up or credited as paid-up share capital of which did not exceed £120,000 and as if in that section any reference to the Company's registered office were a reference to the official address of the EEIG.

Application of the Company Directors Disqualification Act 1986

20. Where an EEIG is wound up as an unregistered company under Part V of the Insolvency Act 1986, the provisions of sections 1, 2, 4 to 11, 12(2), 15 to 17, 20 and 22 of, and Schedule 1 to, the Company Directors Disqualification Act 1986 shall apply in relation to the EEIG as if any reference to a director or past director of a company included a reference to a manager of the EEIG and any other person who has or has had control or management of the EEIG's business and the EEIG were a company as defined by section 22(2)(b) of that Act.

Penalties

21. Nothing in these Regulations shall create any new criminal offence punishable to a greater extent than is permitted under paragraph 1(1)(d) of Schedule 2 to the European Communities Act 1972.

APPENDIX 2

SCHEDULE 1

Regulation 2(1)

COUNCIL REGULATION (EEC) NO. 2137/85 OF 25TH JULY 1985

on the European Economic Interest Grouping (EEIG)

THE COUNCIL OF THE EUROPEAN COMMUNITIES

Having regard to the Treaty establishing the European Economic Community, and in particular Article 235 thereof,

Having regard to the proposal from the Commission, (O.J. 1974, C14/30 and O.J. 1978, C103/4)

Having regard to the opinion of the European Parliament, (O.J. 1977, C163/17)

Having regard to the opinion of the Economic and Social Committee, (O.J. 1975, C108/46)

Whereas a harmonious development of economic activities and a continuous and balanced expansion throughout the Community depend on the establishment and smooth functioning of a common market offering conditions analogous to those of a national market; whereas to bring about this single market and to increase its unity a legal framework which facilities the adaptation of their activities to the economic conditions of the Community should be created for natural persons, companies, firms and other legal bodies in particular; whereas to that end it is necessary that those natural persons, companies, firms and other legal bodies should be able to co-operate effectively across frontiers;

Whereas co-operation of this nature can encounter legal, fiscal or psychological difficulties; whereas the creation of an appropriate Community legal instrument in the form of a European Economic Interest Grouping would contribute to the achievement of the abovementioned objectives and therefore proves necessary;

Whereas the Treaty does not provide the necessary powers for the creation of such a legal instrument;

Whereas a grouping's ability to adapt to economic conditions must be guaranteed by the considerable freedom for its members in their contractual relations and the internal organisation of the grouping;

Whereas a grouping differs from a firm or company principally in its purpose, which is only to facilitate or develop the economic activities of its members to enable them to improve their own results, whereas, by reason of that ancillary nature, a grouping's activities must be related to the economic activities of its members but not replace them so that, to that extent, for example, a grouping may not itself, with regard to third parties, practise a profession, the concept of economic activities being interpreted in the widest sense;

Whereas access to grouping form must be made as widely available as possible to natural persons, companies, firms and other legal bodies, in keeping with the aims of this Regulation; whereas this Regulation shall not, however, prejudice the application at national level of legal rules and/or ethical codes concerning the conditions for the pursuit of business and professional activities;

Whereas this Regulation does not itself confer on any person the right to participate in a grouping, even where the conditions it lays down are fulfilled;

Whereas the power provided by this Regulation to prohibit or restrict participation in a grouping on grounds of public interest is without prejudice to the laws of Member States which govern the pursuit of activities and which may provide further prohibitions or restrictions or otherwise control or supervise participation in a grouping by any natural person, company, firm or other legal body or any class of them;

Whereas, to enable a grouping to achieve its purpose, it should be endowed with legal capacity and provision should be made for it to be represented *vis-à-vis* third parties by an organ legally separate from its membership;

Whereas the protection of third parties requires widespread publicity; whereas the members of a grouping have unlimited joint and several liability for the grouping's debts and other liabilities, including those relating to tax or social security, without, however, that principle's affecting the freedom to exclude or restrict the liability of one or more of its members in respect of a particular debt or other liability by means of a specific contract between the grouping and a third party;

Whereas matters relating to the status or capacity of natural persons and to the capacity of legal persons are governed by national law;

Whereas the grounds for winding up which are peculiar to the grouping should be specific while referring to national law for its liquidation and the conclusion thereof;

Whereas groupings are subject to national laws relating to insolvency and cessation of payments; whereas such laws may provide other grounds for the winding up of groupings;

Whereas this Regulation provides that the profits or losses resulting from the activities of a grouping shall be taxable only in the hands of its members; whereas it is understood that otherwise national tax laws apply, particularly as regards the apportionment of profits, tax procedures and any obligations imposed by national tax law;

Whereas in matters not covered by this Regulation the laws of the Member States and Community law are applicable, for example with regard to:

(a) social and labour laws,
(b) competition law,
(c) intellectual property law;

Whereas the activities of groupings are subject to the provisions of Member States' laws on the pursuit and supervision of activities; whereas in the event of abuse or circumvention of the laws of a Member State by a grouping or its members that Member State may impose appropriate sanctions;

Whereas the Member States are free to apply or to adopt any laws, regulations or administrative measures which do not conflict with the scope or objectives of this Regulation;

Whereas this Regulation must enter into force immediately in its entirety; whereas the implementation of some provisions must nevertheless be deferred in order to allow the Member States first to set up the necessary machinery for the registration of groupings in their territories and the disclosure of certain matters relating to groupings; whereas, with effect from that date of implementation of this Regulation, groupings set up may operate without territorial restrictions,

HAS ADOPTED THIS REGULATION:

ARTICLE 1

1. European Economic Interest Groupings shall be formed upon the terms, in the manner and with the effects laid down in this Regulation.

Accordingly, parties intending to form a grouping must conclude a contract and have the registration provided for in Article 6 carried out.

2. A grouping so formed shall, from the date of its registration as provided for in Article 6, have the capacity, in its own name, to have rights and obligations of all kinds, to make contracts or accomplish other legal acts, and to sue and be sued.

3. The Member States shall determine whether or not groupings registered at their registries, pursuant to Article 6, have legal personality.

ARTICLE 2

1. Subject to the provisions of this Regulation, the law applicable, on the one hand, to the contract for the formation of a grouping, except as regards matters relating to the status or capacity of natural persons and to the capacity of legal persons and, on the other hand, to the internal organization of a grouping shall be the internal law of the State in which the official address is situated, as laid down in the contract for the formation of the grouping.

2. Where a State comprises several territorial units, each of which has its own rules of law applicable to the matters referred to in paragraph 1, each territorial unit shall be considered as a State for the purposes of identifying the law applicable under this Article.

ARTICLE 3

1. The purpose of a grouping shall be to facilitate or develop the economic activities of its members and to improve or increase the results of those activities; its purpose is not to make profits for itself.

Its activity shall be related to the economic activities of its members and must not be more than ancillary to those activities.

2. Consequently, a grouping may not:

(a) exercise, directly or indirectly, a power of management or supervision over its members' own activities or over the activities of another undertaking, in particular in the fields of personnel, finance and investment;
(b) directly or indirectly, on any basis whatsoever, hold shares of any kind in a member undertaking; the holding of shares in another undertaking shall be possible only in so far as it is necessary for the achievement of the grouping's objects and if it is done on its members' behalf;
(c) employ more than 500 persons;
(d) be used by a company to make a loan to a director of a company, or any person connected with him, when the making of such loans is restricted or controlled under the Member States' laws governing companies. Nor must a grouping be used for the transfer of any property between a company and a director, or any person connected with him, except to the extent allowed by the Member States' laws governing companies. For the purposes of this provision the making of a loan includes entering into any transaction or arrangement of similar effect, and property includes moveable and immovable property;
(e) be a member of another European Economic Interest Grouping.

ARTICLE 4

1. Only the following may be members of a grouping:

(a) companies or firms within the meaning of the second paragraph of Article 58 of the Treaty and other legal bodies governed by public or private law, which have been formed in accordance with the law of a Member State and which have their registered or statutory office and central administration in the Community; where, under the law of a Member State, a company, firm or other legal body is not obliged to have a registered or statutory office, it shall be sufficient for such a company, firm or other legal body to have its central administration in the Community;
(b) natural persons who carry on any industrial, commercial, craft or agricultural activity or who provide professional or other services in the Community.

2. A grouping must comprise at least:

(a) two companies, firms or other legal bodies, within the meaning of paragraph 1, which have their central administrations in different Member States, or
(b) two natural persons, within the meaning of paragraph 1, who carry on their principal activities in different Member States, or
(c) a company, firm or other legal body within the meaning of paragraph 1 and a natural person, of which the first has its central administration in one Member State and the second carries on his principal activity in another Member State.

3. A Member State may provide that groupings registered at its registries in accordance with Article 6 may have no more than 20 members. For this purpose, that Member State may provide that, in accordance with its laws, each member of a legal body formed under its laws, other than a registered company, shall be treated as a separate member of a grouping.

4. Any Member State may, on grounds of that State's public interest, prohibit or restrict participation in groupings by certain classes of natural persons, companies, firms, or other legal bodies.

ARTICLE 5

A contract for the formation of a grouping shall include at least:

(a) the name of the grouping preceded or followed either by the words "European Economic Interest Grouping" or by the initials "EEIG," unless those words or initials already form part of the name;
(b) the official address of the grouping;
(c) the objects for which the grouping is formed;
(d) the name, business name, legal form, permanent address or registered office, and the number and place of registration, if any, of each member of the grouping;
(e) the duration of the grouping, except where this is indefinite.

ARTICLE 6

A grouping shall be registered in the State in which it has its official address, at the registry designated pursuant to Article 39(1).

ARTICLE 7

A contract for the formation of a grouping shall be filed at the registry referred to in Article 6.

The following documents and particulars must also be filed at that registry:

(a) any amendment to the contract for the formation of a grouping, including any change in the composition of a grouping;
(b) notice of the setting up or closure of any establishment of the grouping;
(c) any judicial decision establishing or declaring the nullity of a grouping, in accordance with Article 15;
(d) notice of the appointment of the manager or managers of a grouping, their names and any other identification particulars required by the law of the Member State in which the register is kept, notification that they may act alone or must act jointly, and the termination of any manager's appointment;
(e) notice of a member's assignment of his participation in a grouping or a proportion thereof, in accordance with Article 22(1);
(f) any decision by members ordering or establishing the winding up of a grouping, in accordance with Article 31, or any judicial decision ordering such winding up, in accordance with Articles 31 or 32;
(g) notice of the appointment of the liquidator or liquidators of a grouping, as referred to in Article 35, their names and any other identification particulars required by the law of the Member State in which the register is kept, and the termination of any liquidator's appointment;
(h) notice of the conclusion of a grouping's liquidation, as referred to in Article 35(2);
(i) any proposal to transfer the official address, as referred to in Article 14(1);
(j) any clause exempting a new member from the payment of debts and other liabilities which originated prior to his admission, in accordance with Article 26(2).

ARTICLE 8

The following must be published, as laid down in Article 39, in the gazette refered to in paragraph 1 of that Article:

(a) the particulars which must be included in the contract for the formation of a grouping pursuant to Article 5, and any amendments thereto;
(b) the number, date and place of registration as well as notice of the termination of that registration;
(c) the documents and particulars referred to in Article 7(b) to (j).

The particulars referred to in (a) and (b) must be published in full. The documents and particulars referred to in (c) may be published either in full or in extract form or by means of a reference to their filing at the registry, in accordance with the national legislation applicable.

ARTICLE 9

1. The documents and particulars which must be published pursuant to this Regulation may be relied on by a grouping as against third parties under the conditions laid down by the national law applicable pursuant to Article 3(5) and (7) of Council Directive 68/151/EEC of 9 March 1968 on co-ordination of safeguards which, for the protection of the interests of members and others, are required by Member States of companies within the meaning of the second paragraph of Article 58 of the Treaty, with a view to making such safeguards equivalent throughout the Community. (O.J. 1968, L65/8).

2. If activities have been carried on on behalf of a grouping before its registration in accordance with Article 6 and if the grouping does not, after its registration, assume the obligations arising out of such activities, the natural persons, companies, firms or other legal bodies which carried on those activities shall bear unlimited joint and several liability for them.

ARTICLE 10

Any grouping establishment situated in a Member State other than that in which the official address is situated shall be registered in that State. For the purpose of such registration, a grouping shall file, at the appropriate registry in that Member State, copies of the documents which must be filed at the registry of the Member State in which the official address is situated, together, if necessary, with a translation which conforms with the practice of the registry where the establishment is registered.

ARTICLE 11

Notice that a grouping has been formed or that the liquidation of a grouping has been concluded stating the number, date and place of registration and the date, place and title of publication, shall be given in the *Official Journal of the European Communities* after it has been published in the gazette referred to in Article 39(1).

ARTICLE 12

The official address referred to in the contract for the formation of a grouping must be situated in the Community.

The official address must be fixed either:

(a) where the grouping has its central administration, or
(b) where one of the members of the grouping has its central administration or, in the case of a natural person, his principal activity, provided that the grouping carries on an activity there.

ARTICLE 13

The official address of a grouping may be transferred within the Community.

When such a transfer does not result in a change in the law applicable pursuant to Article 2, the decision to transfer shall be taken in accordance with the conditions laid down in the contract for the formation of the grouping.

ARTICLE 14

1. When the transfer of the official address results in a change in the law applicable pursuant to Article 2, a transfer proposal must be drawn up, filed and published in accordance with the conditions laid down in Articles 7 and 8.

No decision to transfer may be taken for two months after publication of the proposal. Any such decision must be taken by the members of the grouping unanimously. The transfer shall take effect on the date on which the grouping is registered, in accordance with Article 6, at the registry for the new official address. That registration may not be effected until evidence has been produced that the proposal to transfer the official address has been published.

2. The termination of a grouping's registration at the registry for its old official address may not be effected until evidence has been produced that the grouping has been registered at the registry for its new official address.

3. Upon publication of a grouping's new registration the new official address may be relied on as against third parties in accordance with the conditions referred to in Article 9(1); however, as long as the termination of the grouping's registration at the registry for the old official address has not been published, third parties may continue to rely on the old official address unless the grouping proves that such third parties were aware of the new official address.

4. The laws of a Member State may provide that, as regards groupings registered under Article 6 in that Member State, the transfer of an official address which would result in a change of the law applicable shall not take effect if, within the two-month period referred to in paragraph 1, a competent authority in that Member State opposes it. Such opposition may be based only on grounds of public interest. Review by a judicial authority must be possible.

ARTICLE 15

1. Where the law applicable to a grouping by virtue of Article 2 provides for the nullity of that grouping, such nullity must be established or declared by judicial decision. However, the court to which the matter is referred must, where it is possible for the affairs of the grouping to be put in order, allow time to permit that to be done.

2. The nullity of a grouping shall entail its liquidation in accordance with the conditions laid down in Article 35.

3. A decision establishing or declaring the nullity of a grouping may be relied on as against third parties in accordance with the conditions laid down in Article 9(1).

Such a decision shall not of itself affect the validity of liabilities, owed by or to a grouping, which originated before it could be relied on as against third parties in accordance with the conditions laid down in the previous subparagraph.

ARTICLE 16

1. The organs of a grouping shall be the members acting collectively and the manager or managers.

A contract for the formation of a grouping may provide for other organs; if it does it shall determine their powers.

2. The members of a grouping, acting as a body, may take any decision for the purpose of achieving the objects of the grouping.

ARTICLE 17

1. Each member shall have one vote. The contract for the formation of a grouping may, however, give more than one vote to certain members, provided that no one member holds a majority of the votes.

2. A unanimous decision by the members shall be required to:

(a) alter the objects of a grouping;
(b) alter the number of votes allotted to each member;
(c) alter the conditions for the taking of decisions;
(d) extend the duration of a grouping beyond any period fixed in the contract for the formation of the grouping;
(e) alter the contribution by every member or by some members to the grouping's financing;
(f) alter any other obligation of a member, unless otherwise provided by the contract for the formation of the grouping;
(g) make any alteration to the contract for the formation of the grouping not covered by this paragraph, unless otherwise provided by that contract.

3. Except where this Regulation provides that decisions must be taken unanimously, the contract for the formation of a grouping may prescribe the conditions for a quorum and for a majority, in accordance with which the decisions, or some of them, shall be taken. Unless otherwise provided for by the contract, decisions shall be taken unanimously.

4. On the initiative of a manager or at the request of a member, the manager or managers must arrange for the members to be consulted so that the latter can take a decision.

ARTICLE 18

Each member shall be entitled to obtain information from the manager or managers concerning the grouping's business and to inspect the grouping's books and business records.

ARTICLE 19

1. A grouping shall be managed by one or more natural persons appointed in the contract for the formation of the grouping or by decision of the members.

No person may be a manager of a grouping if:

(a) by virtue of the law applicable to him, or
(b) by virtue of the internal law of the State in which the grouping has its official address, or
(c) following a judicial or administrative decision made or recognized in a Member State

he may not belong to the administrative or management body of a company, may not manage an undertaking or may not act as manager of a European Economic Interest Grouping.

2. A Member State may, in the case of groupings registered at their registries pursuant to Article 6, provide that legal persons may be managers on condition that such legal persons designate one or more natural persons, whose particulars shall be the subject of the filing provisions of Article 7(d) to represent them.

If a Member State exercises this option, it must provide that the representative or representatives shall be liable as if they were themselves managers of the groupings concerned.

The restrictions imposed in paragraph 1 shall also apply to those representatives.

3. The contract for the formation of a grouping or, failing that, a unanimous decision by the members shall determine the conditions for the appointment and removal of the manager or managers and shall lay down their powers.

ARTICLE 20

1. Only the manager or, where there are two or more, each of the managers shall represent a grouping in respect of dealings with third parties.

Each of the managers shall bind the grouping as regards third parties when he acts on behalf of the grouping, even where his acts do not fall within the objects of the grouping, unless the grouping proves that the third party knew or could not, under the circumstances, have been unaware that the act fell outside the objects of the grouping;

publication of the particulars referred to in Article 5(c) shall not of itself be proof thereof.

No limitation on the powers of the manager or managers, whether deriving from the contract for the formation of the grouping or from a decision by the members, may be relied on as against third parties even if it is published.

2. The contract for the formation of the grouping may provide that the grouping shall be validly bound only by two or more managers acting jointly. Such a clause may be relied on as against third parties in accordance with the conditions referred to in Article 9(1) only if it is published in accordance with Article 8.

ARTICLE 21

1. The profits resulting from a grouping's activities shall be deemed to be the profits of the members and shall be apportioned among them in the proportions laid down in the contract for the formation of the grouping or, in the absence of any such provision, in equal shares.

2. The members of a grouping shall contribute to the payment of the amount by which expenditure exceeds income in the proportions laid down in the contract for the formation of the grouping or, in the absence of any such provision, in equal shares.

ARTICLE 22

1. Any member of a grouping may assign his participation in the grouping, or a proportion thereof, either to another member or to a third party; the assignment shall not take effect without the unanimous authorization of the other members.

2. A member of a grouping may use his participation in the grouping as security only after the other members have given their unanimous authorization, unless otherwise laid down in the contract for the formation of the grouping. The holder of the security may not at any time become a member of the grouping by virtue of that security.

ARTICLE 23

No grouping may invite investment by the public.

ARTICLE 24

1. The members of a grouping shall have unlimited joint and several liability for its debts and other liabilities of whatever nature. National law shall determine the consequences of such liability.

2. Creditors may not proceed against a member for payment in respect of debts and other liabilities, in accordance with the conditions

laid down in paragraph 1, before the liquidation of a grouping is concluded, unless they have first requested the grouping to pay and payment has not been made within an appropriate period.

ARTICLES 25

Letters, order forms and similar documents must indicate legibly:

(a) the name of the grouping preceded or followed either by the words "European Economic Interest Grouping" or by the initials "EEIG," unless those words or initials already occur in the name;
(b) the location of the registry referred to in Article 6, in which the grouping is registered, together with the number of the grouping's entry at the registry;
(c) the grouping's official address;
(d) where applicable, that the managers must act jointly;
(e) where applicable, that the grouping is in liquidation, pursuant to Article 15, 31, 32 or 36.

Every establishment of a grouping, when registered in accordance with Article 10, must give the above particulars, together with those relating to its own registration, on the documents referred to in the first paragraph of this Article uttered by it.

ARTICLE 26

1. A decision to admit new members shall be taken unanimously by the members of the grouping.

2. Every new member shall be liable, in accordance with the conditions laid down in Article 24, for the grouping's debts and other liabilities, including those arising out of the grouping's activities before his admission.

He may, however, be exempted by a clause in the contract for the formation of the grouping or in the instrument of admission from the payment of debts and other liabilities which originated before his admission. Such a clause may be relied on as against third parties, under the conditions referred to in Article 9(1), only if it is published in accordance with Article 8.

ARTICLE 27

1. A member of a grouping may withdraw in accordance with the conditions laid down in the contract for the formation of a grouping or, in the absence of such conditions, with the unanimous agreement of the other members.

Any member of a grouping may, in addition, withdraw on just and proper grounds.

2. Any member of a grouping may be expelled for the reasons listed in the contract for the formation of the grouping and, in any case, if he seriously fails in his obligations or if he causes or threatens to cause serious disruption in the operation of the grouping.

Such expulsion may occur only by the decision of a court to which joint application has been made by a majority of the other members, unless otherwise provided by the contract for the formation of a grouping.

ARTICLE 28

1. A member of a grouping shall cease to belong to it on death or when he no longer complies with the conditions laid down in Article 4(1).

In addition, a Member State may provide, for the purposes of its liquidation, winding up, insolvency or cessation of payments laws, that a member shall cease to be a member of any grouping at the moment determined by those laws.

2. In the event of the death of a natural person who is a member of a grouping, no person may become a member in his place except under the conditions laid down in the contract for the formation of the grouping or, failing that, with the unanimous agreement of the remaining members.

ARTICLE 29

As soon as a member ceases to belong to a grouping, the manager or managers must inform the other members of that fact; they must also take the steps required as listed in Articles 7 and 8. In addition, any person concerned may take those steps.

ARTICLE 30

Except where the contract for the formation of a grouping provides otherwise and without prejudice to the rights acquired by a person under Articles 22(1) or 28(2), a grouping shall continue to exist for the remaining members after a member has ceased to belong to it, in accordance with the conditions laid down in the contract for the formation of the grouping or determined by unanimous decision of the members in question.

ARTICLE 31

1. A grouping may be wound up by a decision of its members ordering its winding up. Such a decision shall be taken unanimously, unless otherwise laid down in the contract for the formation of the grouping.

2. A grouping must be wound up by a decision of its members:

(a) noting the expiry of the period fixed in the contract for the formation of the grouping or the existence of any other cause for winding up provided for in the contract, or
(b) noting the accomplishment of the grouping's purpose or the impossibility of pursuing it further.

Where, three months after one of the situations referred to in the first subparagraph has occurred, a members' decision establishing the winding up of the grouping has not been taken, any member may petition the court to order winding up.

3. A grouping must also be wound up by a decision of its members or of the remaining member when the conditions laid down in Article 4(2) are no longer fulfilled.

4. After a grouping has been wound up by decision of its members, the manager or managers must take the steps required as listed in Articles 7 and 8. In addition, any person concerned may take those steps.

ARTICLE 32

1. On application by any person concerned or by a competent authority, in the event of the infringement of Articles 3, 12 or 31(3), the court must order a grouping to be wound up, unless its affairs can be and are put in order before the court has delivered a substantive ruling.

2. On application by a member, the court may order a grouping to be wound up on just and proper grounds.

3. A Member State may provide that the court may, on application by a competent authority, order the winding up of a grouping which has its official address in the State to which that authority belongs, wherever the grouping acts in contravention of that State's public interest, if the law of that State provides for such a possibility in respect of registered companies or other legal bodies subject to it.

ARTICLE 33

When a member ceases to belong to a grouping for any reason other than the assignment of his rights in accordance with the conditions laid down in Article 22(1), the value of his rights and obligations shall be determined taking into account the assets and liabilities of the grouping as they stand when he ceases to belong to it.

The value of the rights and obligations of a departing member may not be fixed in advance.

ARTICLE 34

Without prejudice to Article 37(1), any member who ceases to belong to a grouping shall remain answerable, in accordance with the conditions laid down in Article 24, for the debts and other liabilities arising out of the grouping's activities before he ceased to be a member.

ARTICLE 35

1. The winding up of a grouping shall entail its liquidation.
2. The liquidation of a grouping and the conclusion of its liquidation shall be governed by national law.
3. A grouping shall retain its capacity, within the meaning of Article 1(2), until its liquidation is concluded.
4. The liquidator or liquidators shall take the steps required as listed in Articles 7 and 8.

ARTICLE 36

Groupings shall be subject to national laws governing insolvency and cessation of payments. The commencement of proceedings against a grouping on grounds of its insolvency or cessation of payments shall not by itself cause the commencement of such proceedings against its members.

ARTICLE 37

1. A period of limitation of five years after the publication, pursuant to Article 8, of notice of a member's ceasing to belong to a grouping shall be substituted for any longer period which may be laid down by the relevant national law for actions against that member in connection with debts and other liabilities arising out of the grouping's activities before he ceased to be a member.
2. A period of limitation of five years after the publication, pursuant to Article 8, of notice of the conclusion of the liquidation of a grouping shall be substituted for any longer period which may be laid down by the relevant national law for actions against a member of the grouping in connection with debts and other liabilities arising out of the grouping's activities.

ARTICLE 38

Where a grouping carries on any activity in a Member State in contravention of that State's public interest, a competent authority of that State may prohibit that activity. Review of that competent authority's decision by a judicial authority shall be possible.

ARTICLE 39

1. The Member States shall designate the registry or registries responsible for effecting the registration referred to in Articles 6 and 10 and shall lay down the rules governing registration. They shall

prescribe the conditions under which the documents referred to in Articles 7 and 10 shall be filed. They shall ensure that the documents and particulars referred to in Article 8 are published in the appropriate official gazette of the Member State in which the grouping has its official address, and may prescribe the manner of publication of the documents and particulars referred to in Article 8(c).

The Member States shall also ensure that anyone may, at the appropriate registry pursuant to Article 6 or, where appropriate, Article 10, inspect the documents referred to in Article 7 and obtain, even by post, full or partial copies thereof.

The Member States may provide for the payment of fees in connection with the operations referred to in the preceding sub-paragraphs; those fees may not, however, exceed the administrative cost thereof.

2. The Member States shall ensure that the information to be published in the *Official Journal of the European Communities* pursuant to Article 11 is forwarded to the Office for Official Publications of the European Communities within one month of its publication in the official gazette referred to in paragraph 1.

3. The Member States shall provide for appropriate penalties in the event of failure to comply with the provisions of Articles 7, 8 and 10 on disclosure and in the event of failure to comply with Article 25.

ARTICLE 40

The profits or losses resulting from the activities of a grouping shall be taxable only in the hands of its members.

ARTICLE 41

1. The Member States shall take the measures required by virtue of Article 39 before 1 July 1989. They shall immediately communicate them to the Commission.

2. For information purposes, the Member States shall inform the Commission of the classes of natural persons, companies, firms and other legal bodies which they prohibit from participating in groupings pursuant to Article 4(4). The Commission shall inform the other Member States.

ARTICLE 42

1. Upon the adoption of this Regulation, a Contact Committee shall be set up under the auspices of the Commission. Its function shall bc:

(a) to facilitate, without prejudice to Articles 169 and 170 of the Treaty, application of this Regulation through regular consultation dealing in particular with practical problems arising in connection with its application;

(b) to advise the Commission, if necessary, on additions or amendments to this Regulation.

2. The Contact Committee shall be composed of representatives of the Member States and representatives of the Commission. The chairman shall be a representative of the Commission. The Commission shall provide the secretariat.

3. The Contact Committee shall be convened by its chairman either on his own initiative or at the request of one of its members.

ARTICLE 43

This Regulation shall enter into force on the third day following its publication in the *Official Journal of the European Communities.*

It shall apply from 1 July 1989, with the exception of Articles 39, 41 and 42 which shall apply as from the entry into force of the Regulation.

This Regulation shall be binding in its entirety and directly applicable in all Member States.

Done at Brussels, 25 July 1985.

SCHEDULE 2

FORMS RELATING TO EEIGS

(These forms are not reproduced here)

SCHEDULE 3

Regulation 10(2)

AUTHORISED EQUIVALENTS IN OTHER COMMUNITY OFFICIAL LANGUAGES OF "EUROPEAN ECONOMIC INTEREST GROUPING" AND "EEIG"

DANISH:	Europæiske Økonomiske Firmagruppe (EØFG)
DUTCH:	Europese Economische Samenwerkingsverbanden (EESV)
FRENCH:	Groupement Européen d'intérêt économique (GEIE)
GERMAN:	Europäische Wirtschaftliche Interessenvereinigung (EWIV)

GREEK:	Ευρωπαϊκσς σμιλος οικουομικού σκοπού (ΕΟΟΣ) (written phonetically in letters of the Latin alphabet as "Evropaikos omilos economicou skopou (EOOS)")
IRISH:	Grupail Eorpach um Leas Eacnamaioch (GELE)
ITALIAN:	Gruppo Europeo d Interesse Economico (GEIE)
PORTUGUESE:	Agrupamento Europeu de Interesse Econômico (AEIE)
SPANISH:	Agrupación Europea de Interésse Económico (AEIE)

SCHEDULE 4

Regulation 18

PROVISIONS OF COMPANIES ACT 1985 APPLYING TO EEIGS AND THEIR ESTABLISHMENTS

1. section 26(1)(c) to (e), (2) and (3).
2. section 28(2) to (5) and (7) so far as it relates to a direction given under subsection (2).
3. section 29(1)(a).
4. Part XII for the purpose of the creation and registration of charges to which it applies.
5. section 432(1) and (2).
6. section 434 so far as it refers to inspectors appointed under section 432 as applied by regulation 18 above and this Schedule.
7. section 436 so far as it refers to inspectors appointed under section 432, and to section 434, as applied by regulation 18 above and this Schedule.
8. sections 437 to 439.
9. section 441 so far as it applies to inspectors appointed under section 432 as applied by regulation 18 above and this Schedule.
10. section 447, as if paragraph (1)(d) referred to any EEIG which is carrying on business in Great Britain or has at any time carried on business there, whether or not any such EEIG is a body corporate.
11. sections 448 to 452.
12. section 458.
13. Part XVIII relating to floating charges and receivers (Scotland).
14. section 694 as if it referred to—

(a) the registered name of an EEIG whose establishment is registered or is in the process of being registered under regulation 12 above with the necessary modifications;
(b) regulation 10 above as applied by regulation 12(7) in addition to section 26;

(c) in subsection (4)(a), a statement in Form EEIG 6; and
(d) in subsection (4)(b), a statement in Form EEIG 7.

15. section 697(2) as if it referred to an EEIG whose establishment is registered or is in the process of being registered under regulation 12 above.

16. section 704(5).

17. section 705(2).

18. sections 706, 707 and 710(1) to (3) and (5) as if they referred to documents and particulars delivered to or furnished by the registrar under these Regulations.

19. section 714(1) as if it referred to EEIGs or their establishments registered under these Regulations or in Northern Ireland.

20. section 718(2) as if it included a reference to an EEIG registered in Great Britain under these Regulations.

21. section 725.

22. section 730 and Schedule 24 so far as they refer to offences under sections applied by regulation 18 above and this Schedule.

23. section 731.

24. sections 732 and 733 so far as they refer to sections 447 to 451 as applied by regulation 18 above and this Schedule.

EXPLANATORY NOTE

(This note is not part of the Regulations)

These Regulations make provisions in respect of European Economic Interest Groupings formed under article 1 of the Council Regulation (EEC) No. 2137/85, which provides a legal framework for groupings of natural persons, companies, firms and other legal entities to enable them to co-operate effectively when carrying on business activities across national frontiers within the European Community. Such groupings, which have their official address in Great Britain, when registered there under these Regulations are bodies corporate and their members have unlimited joint and several liability for the debts and liabilities of such groupings.

The EC Regulation is directly applicable in U.K. law but these Regulations are necessary for implementation in part of the Community obligations and for other purposes mentioned in section 2(2) of the European Communities Act 1972. In particular certain provisions are left for national law by the EC Regulation. Articles 35 and 36 provide that groupings shall be subject to national laws governing their winding up and the conclusion of their liquidation and insolvency and cessation of payments. Regulation 8 of these Regulations provides for modifications to Part V of the Insolvency Act 1986, where a grouping is wound up as an unregistered company under Part V. Accordingly the Court has power to wind up a grouping in the circumstances set out in Articles 31 and 32 or the grouping may be wound up voluntarily in the circumstances set out in article 31; and a grouping is dissolved after 3 months of the receipt by the registrar of a notice of the conclusion of the liquidation, whether or not the grouping has been wound up by the Court.

INDEX

Abuses of company system,
  curbs on, generally, 18–19
  phoenix syndrome, 15–16
    combating, 16–18, 19, 318
  veil of incorporation, 15–16
  See also **Fraudulent trading; Wrongful trading.**
Accounts,
  auditors' report, 273
    revision of, 276
  basic requirements for all companies, 269–271
  content of, 271
  conventions of notation, 271–272
  defective, revision of, 276
  directors' liability, 269–271
  Directors' Report, 272–273
    revision of, 276
    small companies, 281–282, 283
  distribution of, 274
  dormant companies, 284–285
  duty to prepare, 269–273
  form of, 271
  general meeting, dispensed within, 88
  late submission, 274–276
  modified, small companies, 6, 276–285
  presentation of, 274
  publication of, 274–276
  regulations, 368–369
  revision of, 276
  small companies. *See* **Small companies.**
ACT. *See* **Corporation tax.**
Address of company,
  generally, 51–52
Administration,
  abuse of power by controllers to undermine creditors, 324
  floating charges, avoidance of, 328–329
  transactions at an undervalue, 324–326
  transactions entered into prior to, avoidance of, 324–329
Administration orders,
  effect of, 306–307
  efficacy of, 309–310
  generally, 304
  moratorium effect of, 306
  reasons for making, 305–306
Administrator,
  creditors and members, protection of, 309
  powers and duties of, 307–309
  preferences, setting aside, 326–328
Advance corporation tax (ACT). *See* **Corporation tax.**
Allotment,
  authority for, 144–145
  pre-emption rights on, 145–146
Annual accounts. *See* **Accounts.**
Annual general meetings. *See* **General meetings.**
Annual reports. *See* **Reports.**
Annual return,
  statement of business activities, in, 61
Arbitration,
  resolving disputes by, 75–76
Articles of association,
  arbitration clause, 75–76
  control and structure of companies by means of, 66–72
  directors' term of office. *See* **Directors.**
  effect on members, 64
  formalities, 64–65
  pre-emption provision. *See* **Transfer of shares.**
  purpose of, 64–65
  registration of, 64–65
  regulations, 372–374, 376, 377
  requirements of, 64–65
  share capital stated in, 64–65
  share transfer. *See* **Transfer of shares.**
  shareholders agreements outside, 74–75
  weighted voting to stop alteration, 72–74

Assets, improper disposition of,
directors and others as constructive trustees, 123–125
generally, 123
pre-emptive right of members to prevent, 127–128
ratification of, 126–127
statutory liability for, 125–126
Associates. *See* **Close companies.**
Audit,
dormant companies, 286
exempt private companies, of, 5
generally, 286–287
small companies exemption, 10, 290–293
audit subject to report, 291–292
right of members to require audit, 292
total exemption, 290–291
Auditors,
appointment of, 287–288
duties of, 289–290
general meetings, attendance at, 288
notice of resolutions, 83–84, 288
report, 273
rights of, 288–289

Balance sheet,
dispensation not to file, 3
small companies, 283
format, 277–281
statement, 282
"Benefiting a trade" test, 257–258. *See also* **Shares.**
Bills of exchange,
company name displayed on, 48
officers' liability, 27–28, 49. *See also* **Cheques.**
Board meetings, 97–99
formal meeting not required, 98–99
general meetings, relationship between, 99–100
division of powers of management and control, 100–102
notice of, 98
quorum, 98. *See also* **Meetings.**
Bonus Shares,
taxation of, 256–257
Business activities,
statement in annual return, 61
Business names,
rules relating to, 49–50
Buy-outs. *See* **Management buy-outs.**

Capital clause. *See* **Memorandum of association.**
Capital reduction for share purchase. *See* **Shares.**
Change of name. *See* **Names.**
Charitable companies,
alteration of objects, 62
liability of, 97
Cheques,
diversion of, single member companies, 185–186
See also **Bills of exchange.**
City Code on Takeovers and Mergers, 250
Close companies,
associates, 261
control test, 260–262
directors of, definition, 261–262
50 per cent net assets test, 260–262
generally, 259–260
participators, 261
tax implications of, 262–263
apportionment of income, 263–264
benefits and loans, 262–263
Commencement of business, 42–44
Companies Act 1907,
balance sheet, no requirement to file, 3
concessions under, 2–3
definition of private company, 1–2
members, minimum number, 1
statement in lieu of prospectus, 3
Companies (Single Member Private Limited Companies) Regulations, 1992. *See under* **Single member companies.**
Companies (Tables A to F) Regulations 1985, 347–379
Company law,
generally, 28–29
Company names. *See* **Names.**
Company rescue, 300–310
See also **Administration orders; Insolvency; Voluntary arrangements.**

Contracts,
directors' interests in. *See under* **Directors.**
pre-incorporation. *See* **Pre-incorporation contracts.**
with sole members who are directors, 179
Cork Committee, 300, 310, 311, 318, 321–322
Corporate personality, 21–22
avoidance of liability, 15–16
Corporate quasi-partnerships. *See* **Quasi-partnerships.**
Corporate restructuring,
financial assistance for, 171–172
Corporate veil. *See* **Veil of incorporation.**
Corporation tax,
advance corporation tax (ACT), 254–255
Franked Investment Income, 254–255
small companies rate, 252–254

De-regulation,
generally, 82–90
Definitions. *See* **Statutory definition.**
Directors,
accounts, preparation of. *See* **Accounts.**
agency status, 95–96
annual accounts and, 269–271
appointment of, 102–103
family companies, 212–216
board meetings. *See* **Board meetings.**
bona fide, duty to act, 108–109
Ebrahimi v. Westbourne Galleries Ltd., principle in, 111–112
meaning of "bona fide for the benefit of the company", 110–111
buy-outs, assistance for, 169–170
close companies, of, 261–262
constructive trustees, as, 123–125
contracts,
interests in,
disclosure of, 128–129
generally, 128
relief for liability, 134–135
waiver clauses,
effect of, 129–131

Directors—*cont.*
contracts—*cont.*
interests in—*cont.*
waiver clauses—*cont.*
validity of, 131
single member companies, 179
control by shareholders, 101
creditors, duties to, 114–117
dealings with third parties, 91–97
Directors' Report, 272–273
revision of, 276
small companies, 281–282, 283
disqualification of, 18–19, 35–36
insolvent companies, 311–318
unfitness, for, 311–318
determination of, 313–317
disqualification order, circumstances made in, 311–313
summary procedure, 317–318
dividend payments, liability for. *See* **Dividends.**
duties of,
balance of interests, 118
breach of,
ratification and assent for, 120–123, 126–127
relief from, by court and indemnity insurance, 134–135
See also improper disposition of corporate assets *below.*
care and skill, 118–120, 320–321
creditors, to, 114–117, 122
employees, to, 117–118
fiduciary, 113–114
takeover bids, in, 246–249
embargoed by liquidation, 19, 36, 331
employees, duties to, 117–118
entrenched. *See* **Family companies.**
exempt private companies, of, 5
family companies,
appointment, 212–216
veto rights, 218–221
fiduciary duties, 113–114
See also improper disposition of corporation assets *below.*
fraud on the minority, 112–113
fraudulent trading, 321–323
definition of, 322
sanctions and penalties for, 323
wrongful trading distinguished, 322–323

Directors—*cont.*
improper disposition of corporate assets,
directors and others as constructive trustees, 123–125
generally, 123
pre-emptive right of members to prevent, 127–128
ratification of, 126–127
statutory liability for, 125–126
indemnity, regulations, 371
independent objects clause and, 57
insolvent companies, of,
liabilities, 311–324
summary remedy against, 323–324
interests,
contracts, in. *See* contracts *above.*
shares, in. *See* shares *below.*
liabilities of,
annual accounts, 269–271
insolvent companies, in, 311–324
redemption or purchase of companies' own shares, 161, 163
voidable transactions, for, 96–97
winding-up, in, 331
wrongful trading, for, 331
loans to, 5, 137–141
management buy-outs, assistance for, 169–170
minimum number, 13
minority, fraud on, 112–113
misapplication of corporate property. *See* improper disposition of corporate assets *above.*
number of, 4, 13
objects clause and, 56–58
preparation of accounts. *See* **Accounts.**
regulations, 360–367
removal of, 102–103
remuneration of, 135–137
report, 272–273
secretary, sole director excluded as, 13
shadow, 17
share transfer, veto on, 66–68, 240
shareholders, control by, 101
shareholders, voting as, 107–113

Directors—*cont.*
shareholders, voting as—*cont.*
abuse of, as fraud on minority, 112–113
duty to act bona fide, 108–109
Ebrahimi v. Westbourne Galleries Ltd., principle in, 111–112
meaning of "bona fide", 110–111
takeover bids, 246–249
shares, dealings and interests in,
disclosure, 133–134
generally, 131–132
Percival v. Wright, rule in, 132–133
relief for liability, 134–135
single member companies. *See* **Single member companies.**
sole members, 179
subjective ancillary clause and, 57
takeovers,
duties in, 246–249
veto on, 249–250
family companies, 218–221
term of office in articles, 71–72
third parties, dealings with, 91–97
trustees, constructive, as, 123–125
unfitness of. *See under* disqualification of *above.*
veto powers,
share transfer, 66–68, 240
takeovers, 249–250
family companies, 218–221
voidable transactions, liability for, 96–97
voting powers. *See* shareholders, voting as *above.*
winding-up,
embargo on actions in, 19, 36, 331
liability in, 331
wrongful trading,
definition of, 319–320
fraudulent trading distinguished, 322–323
liability for, 17–18, 318–321
determination of, 320–321
"moment of truth", 319–320
requirement of application for, 318–319

Disclosure,
accounts. *See* **Accounts.**
distribution, 274

Disclosure—*cont.*
late submission, 274–276
modified requirements, small companies, 6, 276–285
presentation, 274
publication of, 274–276
reports. *See* **Reports.**
revision of defective accounts and reports, 276
share purchase or redemption, 159
Dissolution,
quasi-partnership. *See* **Quasi-partnerships.**
Distributions, 255–257
taxation of. *See* **Taxation.**
Dividends, 152–155
directors' liability for payments out of capital, 154–155
distribution,
definition of, 152–153
denial of, 154
regulations, 367–368
Domicile of company,
generally, 51
Donations. *See under* **Memorandum of association.**
Dormant companies,
accounts, 284–285
auditing requirements, 286

Economic significance of private companies, 14–15
Elective resolutions, 87–90
Enterprise Investment Scheme,
definitions and qualifications, 264–266
eligible shares, 265
generally, 264
qualifying companies, 264–265
qualifying individual, 265–266
qualifying trades, 265
relief provisions, 266–268
Entrenched directorships. *See* **Family companies.**
European Economic Interest Groupings (EEIGs),
formalities for establishing, 339–342
formation of, 339–340
generally, 337
managers of, 341–342
members, liability of, 343–344
organs of, 340–341
European Economic Interest Groupings (EEIGs)—*cont.*
originating provisions, 338
parameters of, 338–339
registration of, 339–340, 342–343
regulations, 380–409
winding-up of, 344
Exempt private companies,
abolition of, 5–6
auditing requirements, 5
Companies Acts 1947–48, 4–6
loans to directors, 5
meaning, 4
purpose of introduction of, 4
Extraordinary general meetings. *See* **General meetings.**

Family companies,
disputes in,
effects of, 207
matrimonial, 221–223
reluctance to relinquish control, 207–208
sibling dissension, 208–211
successors, disputes between, 211
types of, 207–212
entrenched directorships,
Bushell v. Faith principle, 214–216
establishment of, 212–214
purpose of creating, 212
matrimonial disputes in, 221–223
orders requiring sale of company assets, 226
meaning of, 206
negative control of, 216–218
siblings, disputes between, 208–211
successors, disputes between, 211
unfairly prejudicial conduct, 223–226
Floating charges,
avoidance of, 328–329
Formation of company,
procedure, 42–44
Franked investment income, 254–255
See also **Taxation.**
Fraudulent trading,
definition of, 322
generally, 321–322
sanctions and penalties for, 323
wrongful trading distinguished, 322–323

General meetings,
auditors,
appointment of, 287
attendance of, 288
board meetings, relationship between, 99–100
division of powers of management and control, 100–102
consent of all members, obtaining, 79
decisions requiring formal resolution of, 100
directors,
appointment and removal of, 102–103
relationship with, 97–113
dispensing with formalities, 78
extraordinary, calling of, 103–106
generally, 77–78
members' rights to requisition, 103–106
notice period for, varying, 80
powers of, 102–107
proxies, 78
residual powers of, 106–107
See also **Meetings.**
Gower Report, 157
Guarantee companies,
companies without share capital, 297–298
generally, 294
liability of members, 294–295
past members, 296
omission of "Ltd" from company names, 298–299
purpose and form of, 296–299

Incorporation,
certificate of, 33
See also **Pre-incorporation contracts.**
Independent objects clause. *See* **Memorandum of association.**
Insolvency,
abuse of powers by controllers to undermine creditors, 324
administration. *See* **Administration.**
administration orders. *See* **Administration orders.**
administrator. *See* **Administrator.**
avoidance of, 300–310
company rescue, 300–310

Insolvency—*cont.*
directors, embargo on actions of, 19, 36, 331
EEIGs. *See* **European Economic Interest Grouping.**
floating charges, avoidance of, 328–329
liquidation. *See* **Liquidation.**
remedies against officers, 323–324
replacement by new company, phoenix syndrome, 15–18, 19, 318
voluntary arrangements. *See* **Voluntary arrangements.**
winding-up. *See* **Winding-up.**

Lifting the veil. *See* **Veil of incorporation.**
"Limited,"
as essential element of name, 25–26
memorandum of association, in, 46–47
private companies, omission by, 298–299
use of, post-1980, 7
Limited liability,
change to unlimited, 62–63
memorandum of association, stated in, 62–63
Limited partnerships. *See* **Partnerships.**
Liquidation,
abuse of power by controllers to undermine creditors, 324
directors, embargo on actions of, 19, 36, 331
floating charges, avoidance of, 328–329
transactions at an undervalue, 324–326
transactions entered into prior to liquidation, avoidance of, 324–329
See also **Insolvency; Winding-up.**
Liquidator,
preferences, setting aside, 326–328
voluntary winding-up, 330–332

Majority shareholders. *See* **Shareholders.**
Management buy-outs,
company formed to undertake, 170–171

Management buy-outs—*cont.*
directors, disadvantages for, 169–170
financial assistance for, 169–171
Matrimonial disputes. *See* **Family companies.**
Medium-sized companies,
modified accounts, 6
See also **Small companies.**
Meetings,
annual general, dispensed with by resolution, 88
board. *See* **Board meetings.**
general. *See* **General meetings.**
notice of, 80, 98
one-member, 80–82
quorum, 80–82, 98
single member companies, 180
regulations, 355–358
resolution at. *See* **Resolutions.**
written resolutions,
adaptation of procedural requirements, 85
as alternatives to meetings, 82
auditors' notice of, 83–84
effect of, 83
procedure, 83
proposals for reform, 87
requirements, 83–84
See also **Written resolutions.**
Membership,
bound by articles, 64
consent of, obtaining, 79
liability in winding-up, 335–336
limit on, 2
removal of, 7–8
limited liability clause, 62
meetings. *See* **Meetings.**
minimum requirement, 2, 12–13
proxy, 78
quorate status, 80–82
relationship with directors. *See* **Directors.**
removal of limit, 7–8
single member companies. *See* **Single member companies.**
transfer of shares. *See* **Transfer of shares.**
unanimous consent of, 79
unrestricted, 7
voting. *See* **Voting rights.**
winding-up, liability in, 335–336
Memorandum of association,
capital clause, 63
Memorandum of association—*cont.*
charitable companies, 62
essential information to be included, 45–46
form of, 45–46
independent objects clause, 57
legal requirements, 45–46
liability clause, 62–63
"limited", 46–47
name clause, 46–50
objects clause,
alteration of, 61–62
donations and payments enabled, 55–56, 60
independent objects clause, 57
new short form of, 58–61
Companies Act 1985, 59
construction, 58–59
limitations of, 59–61
origin of, 52
specific clause, 56–58
subjective ancillary clause, 57
traditional, 52–53
ultra vires rule, 53–56
purpose of, 45
registered office clause, 51–52
regulations, 371–372, 374–377, 378
specific clauses, 56–58
subjective ancillary clause, 57
ultra vires actions. *See* ***Ultra vires.***
Minutes,
regulations, 367

Name clause. *See* **Memorandum of association.**
Names,
business. *See* **Business names.**
change of, 47–48
correct usage, 25–27
display and use, 48–49
passing-off actions, 38
Registrar's index of, 47
See also **"Limited".**
Notices,
meetings, of, 80, 98
regulations, 369–370

Objects clause. *See* **Memorandum of association.**
Officers,
indemnity, regulations, 371

Officers—*cont.*
personal liability of, 25–28, 49
bills of exchange, 27–28
See also **Directors; Secretary.**
veil of incorporation and, 25–28
One-man companies. *See* **Single member companies.**

Participators. *See* **Close companies.**
Partnership companies,
created by Companies Act 1989, 189
Partnerships,
limited, 3–4
quasi-partnerships. *See* **Quasi-partnerships.**
Passing-off actions,
change of name and, 48
Personality, corporate. *See* **Corporate personality.**
Phoenix syndrome,
combating, 16–18, 19, 318
generally, 15–16
veil of incorporation and, 15–16
Plc. *See* **Public limited company.**
Pre-emption rights, 68–69
on allotment, 145–146. *See also* **Transfer of shares.**
Pre-incorporation contracts,
non-binding nature of, 40–42
promoters' liability, 38–42
status of, 37–38
Preferences,
setting aside of, 326–328
Prentice Report, 54, 61, 92, 95
Private companies,
abuses of system,
curbs on, 16–19
phoenix syndrome, 15–18, 19, 318
accounts. *See* **Accounts.**
advantages of, 20–29
articles of association. *See* **Articles of association.**
business vehicles, as, 11–19
capital requirement, no minimum, 8–9, 14
commencement of business, 42–44
Companies Act 1907, 1–4
balance sheet, no requirement to file, 3
concessions under, 2–3
definition of private company, 2

Private companies—*cont.*
Companies Act 1907—*cont.*
members, minimum number, 2
statement in lieu of prospectus, 3
company law and, 28–29
contemporary status of, 6–10
de-regulation of, 82
definition, 11–12
Companies Act 1907, 1–2
Companies Act 1980, 6–7
deregulation, moves towards, 10
development of, 1–10
directors, minimum number, 13
disadvantages of, 20–29
disclosure requirements. *See* **Disclosure.**
economic significance of, 14–15
EEIGs and. *See* **European Economic Interest Groupings.**
exempt. *See* **Exempt private companies.**
formation of, 42–44
history of, 1–10
insolvency of. *See* **Insolvency.**
liquidation of. *See* **Liquidation.**
medium-sized. *See* **Medium-sized companies.**
meetings. *See* **Meetings.**
membership. *See* **Membership.**
memorandum of association. *See* **Memorandum of association.**
minimum requirements, 12–14
names of. *See* **Names.**
no minimum capital requirement, 8–9, 14
phoenix syndrome, 15–18, 19, 318
popularity of, 14–15
post-war developments, 4–6
pre-statutory, 1
promotion of, 30–37
See also **Promoters.**
reclassification of companies, 6–7
registration of, 42–44
role of, 11–15
secretaries of. *See* **Secretaries.**
single-member companies. *See* **Single member companies.**
small. *See* **Small companies.**
status of, 11–15
statutory definition,
post-1980, 6–7, 11–12
pre-1980, 1–2
subscription to shares, preclusion of public, 7–8

Private companies—*cont.*
taxation of. *See* **Taxation.**
winding-up of. *See* **Winding-up.**
Profits,
capitalisation of, regulations, 369
share valuation, in, 236–237
taxation of. *See* **Taxation.**
Promoters,
disqualification of, 35–36
duties of, 31–35
fraud by, 33–34
liabilities of, 31–35, 38–42
meaning of, 30–31
payment of, 36–37
See also **Pre-incorporation contracts.**
Prospectus,
statement in lieu (1907), 3
Proxy votes, 78
See also **Voting rights.**
Public limited company (plc),
identification of, 7
See also **"Limited".**
introduction of, 7
Public subscription. *See* **Subscription to shares.**
Purchase of own shares. *See under* **Shares.**

Quasi-partnerships,
dealings between quasi-partners, 197–205
legitimate expectations,
controlling interest, 203–204
generally, 201
management rights, 201–203
meaning of, 187
origins of, 187
receiver to hold the ring, 204–205
share transfer provisions,
obligatory, 197–201
types of, 187–189
valuation of shares, 231–234
Westbourne Galleries principle, 193–196
judicial explanation, 196–197
winding-up, 190–193
Yenidje principle, 189–191
delimiting, 191–193

Receivers,
appointment to quasi-partnerships, 204–205
Redemption of own shares. *See* **Shares.**
Registered office,
address of, 51–52
domicile of company, 51
Registration,
company not formed under Companies Legislation, of, 180
procedure, 42–44
Reports,
auditors', 273
purchase of own shares, 161–162
defective, revision of, 276
Directors' Report, 272–273
revision of, 276
small companies, 281–282, 283
dispensed with in general meeting, 88
distribution of, 274
late submission, 274–276
presentation of, 274
publication of, 274–276
revision of, 276
Resolutions,
elective, 87–90
written. *See* **Written resolutions.**
Restructuring. *See* **Corporate restructuring.**

Secretary,
appointment of, 9
duties of, 28–29
qualifications, 9
regulations, 367
sole director excluded as, 13
Shadow directors, 17
See also **Directors.**
Share capital,
articles of association, statement in, 64–65
Business Expansion Scheme. *See* **Business Expansion Scheme.**
class rights in, 69–71
EC law, 142–143
generally, 142
memorandum of association, statement in, 63
no minimum requirement, 8–9
regulations, 354–355
retention of control, 69–71
statement of,
articles of association, in, 64–65

Share capital—*cont.*
statement of—*cont.*
memorandum of association, in, 63
subscription to. *See* **Subscription to shares.**
taxation of, 257
Share certificates,
regulations, 350
Shareholders,
agreements outside articles of association, 74–75
directors, as. *See* **Directors.**
eviction protection for minority, 241–244
matrimonial disputes. *See* **Family companies; Membership.**
Shares,
acquisition of own shares. *See* purchase or redemption of own shares *below*.
advertisement of, restrictions on, 143–144
allottment of,
authority for, 144–145
pre-emption rights on, 145–146
"benefiting a trade" test, 257–258
bonus. *See* **Bonus shares.**
directors' interest. *See* **Directors.**
dividends. *See* **Dividends.**
Enterprise Investment Scheme. *See* **Enterprise Investment Scheme.**
lien on, 152
non-voting ordinary shares, 70
offer of, restrictions on, 143–144
payment for, 146–148
personal representatives, sale by, 244–246
pre-emption rights, 229–231
preference shares, 70
provision in articles, 229–231, 234–236
public offer and advertisement, restrictions on, 143–144
purchase or redemption of own shares, 69–71, 148–151
advertisement of, 162
"benefiting a trade" test, 257–258
directors' liability, 161, 163
disclosure requirements, 159
financial assistance for,
corporate restructure, 171–172
Shares—*cont.*
purchase or redemption of own shares—*cont.*
financial assistance for—*cont.*
declaration of solvency, 166–167
general exceptions, 163–165
management buy-outs,
disadvantages for directors, 169–170
formation of company to undertake, 170–171
generally, 169
proposals for reform, 174–175
"purpose" exemptions, 172
good faith requirement, 174
incidental purpose, 172–174
position of banks, 174
shareholders' special resolution, 167–169
special exception for private companies, 165–167
liability of past directors and shareholders, 163
objections to, 162–163
past directors and shareholders, liability of, 163
procedure for, 158–159
out of capital, 161–162
right to object to, 162–163
reduction of capital, 159–161
statutory provisions, 156–158
tax liability, 257–259
winding-up, liabilities and rights of contributories on, 335–336
quasi-partnerships, 231–234
redeemable, 70–71
redemption of own shares. *See* purchase or redemption of own shares *above*.
regulations, 349–355
restrictions on public offers and advertisements of, 143–144
sale by personal representatives, 244–246
transactions, 146–152
transfer of. *See* **Transfer of shares.**
valuation of,
in corporate quasi-partnerships, 231–234
criteria for, 227–229
date of, 238–239
generally, 227–229

Shares—*cont.*
valuation of—*cont.*
mechanism for evaluation, 229–238
projected profits basis, 236–237
Single member companies,
cheques, diversion of,
conversion by third parties, 185–186
protection of bank acting in good faith, 186
Companies (Single Member Private Limited Companies) Regulations 1992,
context of, 176–178
effect of, 178–180
generally, 176
company property,
damage to, 184–185
theft of, 181–184
contracts with sole members who are directors, 179
controller's criminal offences against, 180–185
damage to company property, 184–185
directors as sole members, 179
EC 12th Company Law Directive, 176
formation by one person, 178
generally, 9
meetings, 80–82
quorum at, 180
personal liability, 178–179
recording decisions, 180
registration of company not formed under Companies Legislation, 180
secretary, sole director excluded as, 13
sole member, liability of, 12–13
statement that company has only one member, 179
theft of company property, 181–184
trustee, liability of, 186
veil of incorporation, 177–178
winding-up, 180
Small companies,
accounts,
balance sheet, 283
format, 277–281
statement, 282
Directors' Report, 281–282, 283

Small companies—*cont.*
accounts—*cont.*
exemptions, 282–284
modified, 6, 276–285
notes to accounts, 283–284
profit and loss account, 283
audit exemption, 10
taxation, 251, 252–254
Statutory definition of private companies,
post-1980, 6–7, 11–12
pre-1980, 1–2
Statutory history of private companies, 1–10
Subjective ancillary clause. *See* **Memorandum of Association.**
Subscription to shares,
statutory preclusion of public, 7–8

Takeover bids,
City Code, 250
directors' duties in, 246–249
minority shareholdings, compulsory buy-out of, 242–243
veto on, 249–250
Taxation,
close companies. *See* **Close companies.**
company purchasing own shares, 257–259
corporation tax. *See* **Corporation tax.**
distributions, 255–257
Enterprise Investment Scheme. *See* **Enterprise Investment Scheme.**
franked investment income, 254–255
generally, 251
share purchase. *See* **Shares.**
small companies rate, 252–254
Third parties,
cheques, conversion of, 185–186
dealing in good faith, 92–93
Turquand rule, 95–96
directors and, 91–97
EEIGs, dealings with, 342
knowledge of company constitution, 93–95
protection for, 91–97
single member companies, dealings with, 185–186
Trading,
commencement of, 42–44

Trading—*cont.*
fraudulent. *See* **Fraudulent trading.**
wrongful. *See* **Wrongful trading.**
Transactions at an undervalue, 324–326
Transfer of shares,
articles of association, prohibited in, 66–68
directors' veto clause, 66–68, 240
family companies, 218–221
pre-emption rights, 68–69, 229–231
quasi-partners, 197–201
regulations, 353
Trustees,
directors and officers as. *See* **Directors.**

Ultra vires,
avoidance of object clause, 53
borrowing, 56
dividends, 155
misapplication of corporate property, 125–128
payments, 55–56
reform of rule, 53–54
Unlimited companies,
Companies Act 1967, 5–6
generally, 5–6
registration as, 5, 63

Valuation of shares. *See* **Shares.**
Veil of incorporation,
company officers and, 25–28
flexible, 22–25
lifting the veil, 22–25
personal liability and, 25–28
phoenix syndrome and, 15–16
Salomon principle, 20–22
single member companies, 177–178
Voluntary arrangements,
approval of, 302–304
generally, 301
modifications, 302–304
proposal for, 302
supervisor, appointment of, 304
Voluntary winding-up. *See* **Winding-up.**
Voting rights,
abuse of power, 112–113
proxy, 78
regulations, 358–360
Voting rights—*cont.*
weighted, 72–74, 215–216

Wilson Committee Report, 156
Winding-up,
company which has redeemed or purchased own shares, of, 335–336
compulsory,
generally, 332
inability to pay debts, 332
just and equitable grounds for, 332–335
liability of past members, 336
creditors, protection of, 330–332
directors, embargo on actions of, 19, 36, 331
EEIGs, of, 344
generally, 330
membership, liability in, 335–336
petition by contributories, 335–336
quasi-partnerships, 190–193
regulations, 370
single member companies, 180
voluntary, 330–332
liquidator, 330–332. *See also* **Administration orders; Voluntary arrangements.**
Written resolutions,
adaptations required, 85
as alternatives to meetings, 82
auditors' notice of, 83–84, 288
effect of, 83
general meeting not required, where, 10
procedure, 83
proposals for reform, 87
requirements, 83–84
unanimous agreement, passed by, 10
See also **Resolutions.**
Wrongful trading,
application for, requirement of, 318–319
civil remedy, 17–18
definition of, 319–320
determining liability for, 320–321
directors' liability for, 17–18, 318–321
fraudulent trading distinguished, 322–323
generally, 318
"moment of truth", 319–320